CW01263259

A PRACTITIONER'S GUIDE TO THE UNIFIED PATENT COURT AND UNITARY PATENT

A Practitioner's Guide to the Unified Patent Court and Unitary Patent provides practical and detailed advice on all aspects of the system for those using it.

The book explains how the UPC system works in the context of the wider European patent system, including the UK, and how parties can use it to enforce or revoke European patents and the Unitary Patent, in particular:

- The procedures of the UPC from initiating proceedings to appeal, damages and costs hearings;
- Rules on competence, substantive law, jurisdiction, language and judges;
- The operation of the system alongside the national courts of the contracting countries, the European Patent Office opposition and appeal procedure, and parallel English Patents Court proceedings.

The book is written for private practitioners and in-house counsel by a team of patent experts with many years of experience in patent litigation in France, Germany, the Netherlands, and the UK. It provides insights from national approaches to the features above and gives answers to common problems.

A Practitioner's Guide to the Unified Patent Court and Unitary Patent

Paul England

With contributions by:
Charlotte Garnitsch
Sir Christopher Floyd
Dr Christof Höhne
Dr Anja Lunze
Dr Wim Maas
Honorary Judge Alice Pezard

•HART•
OXFORD • LONDON • NEW YORK • NEW DELHI • SYDNEY

HART PUBLISHING

Bloomsbury Publishing Plc

Kemp House, Chawley Park, Cumnor Hill, Oxford, OX2 9PH, UK

1385 Broadway, New York, NY 10018, USA

29 Earlsfort Terrace, Dublin 2, Ireland

HART PUBLISHING, the Hart/Stag logo, BLOOMSBURY and the Diana logo are trademarks of Bloomsbury Publishing Plc

First published in Great Britain 2022

Copyright © Paul England, 2022

Paul England has asserted his right under the Copyright, Designs and Patents Act 1988 to be identified as Author of this work.

All rights reserved. No part of this publication may be reproduced or transmitted in any form or by any means, electronic or mechanical, including photocopying, recording, or any information storage or retrieval system, without prior permission in writing from the publishers.

While every care has been taken to ensure the accuracy of this work, no responsibility for loss or damage occasioned to any person acting or refraining from action as a result of any statement in it can be accepted by the authors, editors or publishers.

All UK Government legislation and other public sector information used in the work is Crown Copyright ©. All House of Lords and House of Commons information used in the work is Parliamentary Copyright ©. This information is reused under the terms of the Open Government Licence v3.0 (http://www.nationalarchives.gov.uk/doc/open-government-licence/version/3) except where otherwise stated.

All Eur-lex material used in the work is © European Union, http://eur-lex.europa.eu/, 1998–2022.

A catalogue record for this book is available from the British Library.

A catalogue record for this book is available from the Library of Congress.

Library of Congress Control Number: 2022933882

ISBN:	HB:	978-1-84946-782-7
	ePDF:	978-1-50990-421-1
	ePub:	978-1-50990-422-8

Typeset by Compuscript Ltd, Shannon
Printed and bound in Great Britain by CPI Group (UK) Ltd, Croydon CR0 4YY

MIX
Paper | Supporting responsible forestry
FSC® C013604

To find out more about our authors and books visit www.hartpublishing.co.uk. Here you will find extracts, author information, details of forthcoming events and the option to sign up for our newsletters.

PREFACE

As the Introduction to this book attests, the road to the Unified Patent Court (UPC) and the Unitary Patent has been long and winding. As a result, the preparations for this book have followed a similar path. Begun in 2013, it was shelved after the Brexit vote of July 2016, only to be revived (with references to the UK removed) and then shelved again for the considerable delays caused by complaints in the German BVerfG. The project had its full and (one hopes) final restoration in 2021. So I am particularly grateful to those contributors who have stayed with the project essentially throughout, Anja Lunze, Christof Höhne and Alice Pezard, but also more recent members of the contributor team, Sir Christopher Floyd, Charlotte Garnitsch and Wim Maas, all of whose names feature on the title page. I should also like to thank those who have given valued soundings and advice at points along this long journey, including Sir Colin Birss, Judge Peter Burgers and Matthias Hülsewig.

The UPC is a strange animal, put together from various limbs of civil and common law practice and procedure. The broad range of national practice from which these contributors come illustrates that, in its early years at least, it will have to be handled by teams of 'all the talents' able to understand and apply these various traditions, until a settled and characteristically UPC body of tradition emerges. And although they are not permitted to represent parties in UPC hearings, there is a role for English lawyers to play in that process. Who knows where it will lead?

Among the many knowns and unknowns about the UPC and the Unitary Patent that this book covers, there is, at the time of writing, one particularly big question mark: when will it open? This is particularly significant for deciding when to publish this book. Although preparations are advancing rapidly at the time of writing (including the publication of the final amendments to the Rules of Procedure, to be agreed on 1 September 2022, just in time to be covered), the new system is not expected to become operational until early 2023. This leaves plenty of time available for those wishing to get to grips with the new court and patent before the system comes into force.

Paul England
Taylor Wessing
July 2022

CONTENTS

Preface .... *v*
Abbreviations .... *xvii*
Figures and Tables .... *xix*
Table of Cases .... *xxiii*
Table of Legislation .... *xxxi*
Table of Other Materials .... *lxi*

Introduction 1
    I.   A Short History of the Unified Patent Court and the Unitary Patent 1
        A.   The Problem with Patents 1
        B.   The Proposed Solution 2
        C.   The Community Patent 3
        D.   The European Patent Litigation Agreement 4
        E.   The Unified Patent Litigation System 4
        F.   The Unified Patent Court and the Unitary Patent 6
    II. The UK Referendum on Leaving the EU and its Consequences 8
   III. Challenges in Germany 10
        A.   The First Decision (2020) 10
   IV. Current Participants in the UPC and the Unitary Patent System 12

PART I
THE STRUCTURE AND APPLICATION OF THE NEW SYSTEM

1. The Unitary Patent 17
    I.   The Unitary Patent in the Context of the European System 17
        A.   National Patents 17
    II. Features of the Unitary Patent 21
        A.   Uniformity of Protection 21
        B.   Uniformity of Revocation, Limitation and Transfer 21
        C.   Licensing Unitary Patents 22
        D.   Unitary Patent Licence Disputes 23
   III. Administration by the EPO 23
        A.   Administrative Tasks of the EPO 23
        B.   Obtaining and Maintaining a Unitary Patent 24
   IV. Supplementary Protection Certificates 27
        A.   SPCs and Unitary Patents 27
        B.   SPCs Based on European Patents 28
        C.   Opt-out of SPCs Based on a Unitary Patent 28
    V. Exhaustion of Rights and Licences 28

viii Contents

2. Structure, Context and Competence 30
   I. The UPC and Participating Member State Courts 30
   II. Non-contracting Member States 32
   III. Non-Member States Contracted to the EPC 32
   IV. The Structure of the UPC 33
   V. Subject Matter Jurisdiction of the Central Division Sections 34
      A. Subject Matter Classification 35
      B. Allocation Mechanism 36
   VI. Actions for which the UPC has Exclusive Competence 36
      A. Express Exclusive Competence 36
      B. Declaratory Powers 37
   VII. Non-exclusive Competence 37
      A. 'Objects of Property' under Article 7 UP Regulation 38
      B. Rights to an Employee's Invention and Compensation 38
      C. Patent Agreements 39
      D. Personal Possession as a Defence 40
   VIII. The Role of the CJEU 40
      A. The Obligation to Refer to the CJEU 40
      B. Questions Subject to Referral to the CJEU 41
   IX. Relationship with Proceedings in the EPO 43
      A. The European Patent Context 43
      B. Parallel UPC Proceedings and Stay 45
   X. Central Amendment Proceedings in the EPO 47
      A. Oversight of the EPO in Relation to Unitary Patents 47

3. Decision Making 48
   I. The Roles of the Judges 48
      A. Technical Judges and Legal Judges 48
      B. The Judge-Rapporteur, the Presiding Judge and the Standing Judge 49
   II. The Structure of the Panels 51
      A. The Court of First Instance 51
      B. Panels of the Court of Appeal 54
      C. The Full Court 54
   III. The Scope of Appeals 55
      A. Appeal and Referral Back 55
      B. Majority Decisions and Dissent 56
   IV. Case Management 56
      A. The Order of Actions 56
      B. Case Management Powers 56
   V. Ensuring Uniformity of Approach 57
      A. Achieving a Mix of Judges 57
      B. The Role of the Court of Appeal in Building Uniformity 58

Contents ix

4. Sources of Law...60
    I. Outline of Sources..60
    II. The Law of Infringement 61
        A. Acts of Infringement Applicable to European Patents 61
        B. Infringement of Unitary Patents and Article 5 UP Regulation 63
        C. The Scope of Protection of Unitary and European Patent Claims...............65
        D. Developing an Approach to Scope of Claim and Infringement...................66
        E. The Right Based on Prior Use of the Invention...67
    III. The Law of Validity...68
    IV. Unitary Patents as Objects of Property..68
        A. The Law Applicable to Objects of Property 68
        B. What are 'Objects of Property'?...69
        C. European Patents as Objects of Property 70
    V. Rights to Employees' Inventions and Compensation..71
    VI. Patent Licences and Other Agreements..71
        A. The Law Applicable to Patent Agreement Disputes......................................71
        B. Licences of Right..72
        C. Compulsory Licences..73
    VII. Application of Law During the Transitional Period...73
        A. Opted-out Patents 73
        B. Non-opted-out Patents Litigated in the National Courts During
           the Transitional Period 73

5. Language 74
    I. The Translation Regulation...74
        A. The Language of Grant of a Unitary Patent 74
        B. The Language of a Unitary Patent in a Dispute..75
        C. The Language of Amendments to a Patent in Infringement
           Proceedings 76
        D. The Language of a European Patent...77
    II. The Language of Proceedings at First Instance..77
        A. The Central Division..77
        B. The Regional and Local Divisions..78
        C. Timing when Raising Language Issues..81
    III. Language in the Court of Appeal..81
    IV. Translations of Documents in Proceedings..82
        A. Certification 82
        B. Costs of Interpreters and Translators...82
        C. Change of Language when Action is Transferred between Divisions.........82

6. The Opt-out and Transitional Regime 84
    I. The Opt-out and Transitional Period...84
        A. The Operation of the Transitional Period 84
        B. Extension of the Transitional Period 89

x   Contents

        C.   The Procedure for Opting-out and Withdrawal 89
        D.   Responsibility for Opting-out 90
        E.   Application of Law During the Transitional Period 92
   II. Issues Raised by Late Joiners to the UPC and the EPC 93
        A.   Late Ratification of the UPC Agreement 93
        B.   Late Joiners to the EPC 94

7. Parallel Proceedings in the Contracting Member State Courts and the UPC 95
   I.   Cross-border Actions under the Brussels Regulation 95
        A.   The Brussels Regulation 95
        B.   Cross-border Actions 97
   II. Parallel Proceedings between the UPC and National Courts 102
        A.   The Amendment of the Brussels I Regulation (Recast)
            to Include the UPC 102
        B.   Concurrent Proceedings During the Transitional Period
            (Non-opted-out Patents) 103
        C.   Parallel Actions between the UPC and Courts of Non-contracting
            Member States 107
        D.   'Cross-border' Actions 107

8. Parallel Proceedings: The Courts of England and Wales and the UPC 111
   I.   English National Actions 111
        A.   Extending General Persuasive Value 111
        B.   Expedition of English Proceedings 114
   II. English Cross-border Declarations of Non-infringement 116
        A.   Overview of Powers under English Law 116
        B.   Stay or Dismissal of a UPC Action 117
        C.   Accepting Cross-border Jurisdiction in the Context of the UPC 118
   III. Cross-border *Arrow* Declarations? 120

9. UPC Jurisdiction: Where to Bring the Claim 122
   I.   Forum by Agreement 122
   II. Forum by Operation of Article 33 123
        A.   'Domicile' 123
        B.   Bringing Infringement and Related Actions 123
        C.   Infringement where there is no Division and the Defendant
            is Domiciled in a Contracting Member State 125
        D.   Multiple Actions 126
        E.   Centralisation of Infringement Action Concerning Multiple
            Territories 128
        F.   Bringing Revocation Claims and Declarations of Non-infringement 128
        G.   Subsequent Infringement and Revocation Claims 129
        H.   Consolidation or Bifurcation of Actions (Article 33(3)) 132
        I.   Stay of Infringement Action Following an Article 33(3) Decision 135
        J.   Acceleration in the Central Division 136
        K.   The Effect of the Transfer of Revocation Counterclaim
            on Language 137

Contents xi

    L.   Actions Following a Declaration of Non-infringement
        in the Central Division 137
    M.   Actions for Compensation for Licences of Right..138
    N.   Actions Concerning Decisions of the EPO 140
III.   Formalities Relating to Choice of Forum 140
IV.   Preliminary Objections to Forum 141

PART II
PROCEEDINGS IN THE UNIFIED PATENT COURT

10. Written Procedure: Infringement Actions...145
    I.   Timeline of an Infringement Action 145
    II.   Initial Considerations...145
        A.   The Right to Bring an Action..145
        B.   Response to an Assertion of Infringement 146
        C.   Parties to the Action 146
        D.   Service..147
    III.   The Written Procedure..147
        A.   The Structure of Proceedings 147
        B.   Overview of the Infringement Procedure...147
        C.   Appointment of the Judge-Rapporteur 149
        D.   The Statement of Claim 149
        E.   Preliminary Objections 151
        F.   The Statement of Defence 151
        G.   The Counterclaim for Revocation..152
        H.   Reply to the Statement of Defence and Defence to the Counterclaim
            for Revocation 154
        I.   Rejoinder to a Reply to the Statement of Defence and a Reply
            to the Defence to the Counterclaim for Revocation.....................................154
        J.   Rejoinder to the Reply to the Defence to the Counterclaim
            for Revocation 154
        K.   Application by the Proprietor to Amend the Patent.....................................154
        L.   Closure of the Written Procedure..155
    IV.   Available Remedies...155
        A.   Preliminary Injunctions 155
        B.   Final Injunctions 155
        C.   Award of Damages 157
        D.   Recall, Removing from the Channels of Commerce and Destruction 158
        E.   Publication of the Judgment...159
        F.   An Order of the Communication of Information 160

11. Written Procedure: Revocation Actions 161
    I.   Timeline of a Revocation Action 161
    II.   Revocation Actions..161
        A.   Parties 161
        B.   Where to Start the Action 162

xii Contents

    C. Allocation in the Central Division According to Subject Matter 162
    D. Language of the Statement of Revocation 163
    E. Written Procedure in a Revocation Action 163
    F. Acceleration in the Central Division 169
    G. Stay of a Central Revocation Action Pending an Article 33(3)
       Decision 170
    H. The Revocation Decision 170

12. Written Procedure: Declarations of Non-infringement and Actions against the EPO 171
  I. Declaration of a Non-infringement Timeline 171
  II. Declaration of Non-infringement 172
    A. Parties 172
    B. Prior Assertion 172
    C. Where to Start the Action 172
    D. The Effect of Lodging a Later Infringement Action 173
    E. A Non-infringement Claim Following an Infringement Claim 173
    F. The Structure of Proceedings 173
    G. The Language of a Statement for a Declaration of Non-infringement 174
    H. The Contents of Pleadings 175
    I. Reply to the Defence to the Statement for a Declaration of
      Non-infringement and a Rejoinder to the Reply 177
    J. 'Torpedo' Non-infringement Actions 177
    K. Actions for the Revocation and Declaration of Non-infringement 177
  III. Actions against Decisions of the EPO 177
    A. Further to an Article 9 Decision (Article 9 Actions) 178
  IV. Actions against the EPO for a Refusal of Unitary Effect
     (Actions to Annul) 180

13. The Interim Procedure and Case Management 182
  I. The Interim Procedure 182
    A. Closure of the Written Procedure 182
    B. Transfer of Actions Further to Article 33(3) 182
    C. The Purpose of the Interim Procedure 184
    D. Preparation for the Interim Conference 184
    E. The Interim Conference 184
    F. Acceleration of Proceedings 186
    G. The Closure of the Interim Procedure 186
  II. Case Management Powers 186
    A. General Case Management Powers 186
    B. Leave to Change a Claim or Amend a Case 188
    C. Preliminary Reference to the CJEU 188

14. Oral Procedure, Final Decision and Early Termination 189
  I. Oral Procedure 189
    A. Timing of the Oral Hearing 189
    B. The Presence of the Parties and Representatives 190

		C.	Questioning	190
		D.	Simultaneous Interpretation	190
		E.	The Panel Sitting on an Oral Hearing	191
		F.	Video Conferencing	191
	II.	The Decision Following an Oral Hearing		192
		A.	The Timing of the Decision	192
		B.	Orders Resulting from the Decision	192
		C.	Subsequent Conditions	193
		D.	Enforcement and Security	193
		E.	Damages and Costs in the Decision on the Merits	194
	III.	The Early Termination of Actions		194
		A.	Withdrawal	194
		B.	Decision by Default	195
		C.	Actions Bound to Fail or Manifestly Inadmissible	195
		D.	Settlement	196

15. Preliminary Injunctions and Other Provisional Measures 197
    I. Obtaining a Provisional Measure 197
        A. Competence of the Court 197
        B. Proceedings for Obtaining a Provisional Measure 198
        C. Grant of Provisional Measures *Ex Parte* 201
        D. Substantive Requirements for Provisional Measures: Factors Relevant to the Court's Discretion 204
    II. Enforcement of a Provisional Measure 214
    III. Protective Letters 215
    IV. Appeal Proceedings 216
    V. Revocation of Provisional Measures 217
    VI. Preliminary Injunctions of Opted-out Patents in the UPC? 218

16. Obtaining and Using Evidence 220
    I. Sources of Evidence 220
    II. General Rules on Evidence 221
        A. The Burden of Proof 221
        B. The Obligation to Produce Documents 221
    III. Specific Procedures for Obtaining Evidence from Opponents 224
        A. Common Points of the Applications 224
    IV. Orders to Preserve Evidence and Order for Inspection 226
        A. Orders to Preserve Evidence 226
        B. Orders for Inspection 227
        C. Procedure 228
        D. *Inter Partes* and *Ex Parte* Preservation and Inspection Orders 231
        E. Safeguards for the Defendant 231
        F. The Parties Present 233
        G. The Timing of the Application 233
        H. Security 234
    V. Orders to Produce Evidence and Orders to Communicate Information 234
        A. General Considerations 234

			B.	Orders to Produce Evidence..235
			C.	Orders to Communicate Information...236
	VI.		Party Experts and Witnesses...236	
		A.	Overview of the Approach 236	
		B.	Duties of Experts and Witnesses 237	
		C.	Statements of Truth and Conflicts of Interest...238	
		D.	Application and Summons to an Oral Hearing.................................238	
		E.	Hearing Experts and Witnesses...239	
	VII.		Court-Appointed Experts 240	
		A.	The Role of the Court-Appointed Expert..240	
		B.	Duties 241	
		C.	Appointment 241	
	VIII.		Court-Appointed or Party-Appointed Experts? 242	
	IX.		The Relationship between the Advice of Technical Judges and Experts..........243	
	X.		The Expert and the Skilled Person..244	
	XI.		Court-Ordered Experiments 244	
		A.	The Procedure for Proving Facts by Experiment..244	
		B.	Experiments not Sanctioned by the Court..245	
	XII.		Judicial Cooperation in the Taking of Evidence 246	
	XIII.		Border Seizures under the Customs Regulation 246	
		A.	The Application for Customs Seizure...247	
		B.	Notification of Infringing Goods..247	
		C.	Matters Outside the Customs Regulation...247	
	XIV.		Confidentiality Protection 248	
		A.	General Considerations 248	
		B.	Public Access to the Register...248	
		C.	Restricting the Availability of Information to Other Parties 250	
	XV.		Privilege..253	
		A.	Attorney-Client Privilege...253	
		B.	Litigation Privilege 254	
		C.	Lawyers and Patent Attorneys...255	
		D.	The Relationship with Confidentiality...255	
		E.	Common Interest Privilege 256	
		F.	Without Prejudice Communications 256	

17. Appeal..258
I. The Scope and Effect of Appeal...258
A. Appealable Decisions and Time Periods 258
B. Leave to Appeal..259
C. Suspensive Effect...260
II. Written Procedure..261
A. The Statement of Appeal...261
B. The Statement of Grounds of Appeal...263
C. Challenge to the Decision to Reject an Appeal as Inadmissible...............264
D. The Statement of Response...264

		E. Reply to a Statement of Cross-appeal 266
		F. Decision to Refer 266
	III.	Interim Procedure 266
	IV.	Oral Procedure 267
	V.	The Decision of the Court of Appeal 267
		A. Referral Back 267
	VI.	Rehearing 268
		A. Overview 268
		B. Timeline and Content of the Application 268

18. Final Remedies and Costs 271
    I.   Damages 271
         A. Overview 271
         B. Procedure for the Determination of Damages and Compensation 273
         C. A Request to Lay Open Books 276
    II. Damages Following the Revocation of a Preliminary Measure 278
    III. Damage Caused Outside the EU 278
    IV. Other Corrective Measures 279
         A. Final Injunction 280
         B. Enforcement 282
    V.   Costs 282
         A. Costs of Provisional Measures 283
         B. Costs of a Decision on the Merits 283
         C. Security for Costs 286

19. Service and Miscellaneous Matters 287
    I.   Service 287
         A. Rules Applicable to Service by the Court 287
         B. Service within the Contracting Member States 287
         C. Service Outside the Contracting Member States 289
         D. Alternative Method or Place of Service of the Statement of Claim 290
         E. Service of Orders, Decisions and Written Pleadings 290
    II. Parties to Proceedings 291
         A. A Plurality of Parties 291
         B. Change in Party 291
    III. Intervention 292
         A. Intervention by Application 292
         B. Intervention by Invitation 293
         C. Forced Intervention 294
         D. Change of Patent Proprietor during Proceedings 294
    IV. Representatives 295
         A. Lawyers 295
         B. European Patent Attorneys 296
         C. Assisting Patent Attorneys 297
         D. Conduct of Representatives 297

		E.	Privileges and Immunities	298
		F.	Change of Representative	298
	V.	Time Periods		298
		A.	Calculating Time Periods	298
		B.	Failure to Observe Time Limits	299
	VI.	Legal Aid		300
		A.	The Scope of Legal Aid	300
		B.	Eligibility	301
		C.	The Application and Evidence	302
		D.	The Decision to Award Legal Aid	303
		E.	Withdrawal and Appeal	304

20. Court Fees 305
    I. Fixed and Value-Based Court Fees 305
   II. Reduction and Reimbursement of Court Fees 310
       A. Fee Reductions for Small Enterprises and Micro-enterprises 310
       B. Fee Reimbursements 310
       C. Threat to the Party's Economic Existence 311
  III. Calculating the Case Value 311

Annex A: Stay of Proceedings 313
Annex B: Applications and Hearings 316
Annex C: Regulation (EU) 1257/2012 of 17 December 2012: (UP Regulation) 322
Annex D: Regulation (EU) 1260/2012 of 17 December 2012: (Translation Regulation) 335
Annex E: Agreement on a Unified Patent Court of 19 February 2013: (UPC Agreement) 341

Index 389

ABBREVIATIONS

Brussels I Regulation (recast)	Regulation (EU) No 1215/2012 of the European Parliament and of the Council of 12 December 2012 on jurisdiction and the recognition and enforcement of judgments in civil and commercial matters (recast), and earlier iterations of this Regulation
CJEU	Court of Justice of the European Union
Contracting Member State	A Member State as defined in section III of the Introduction
CP	Community Patent
CPC 1973	Community Patent Convention 1973
CPC 1989	Community Patent Convention 1989
EEUPC	European and European Union Patents Court
Enforcement Directive	Directive 2004/48/EC of the European Parliament and of the Council of 29 April 2004 on the Enforcement of Intellectual Property Rights
EPA	European Patent Attorney
EPC	European Patent Convention
EPLA	European Patent Litigation Agreement
EPO	European Patent Office
Participating Member State	A Member State as defined in section III of the Introduction
Rules of Procedure	Rules of Procedure of the Unified Patent Court (as amended and agreed on 1 September 2022)
Service Regulation	Regulation (EU) 2020/1784 of the European Parliament and of the Council of 25 November 2020 on the service in the Member States of judicial and extrajudicial documents in civil or commercial matters (service of documents) (recast)
SPC	Supplementary protection certificate
SPC Regulation	Regulation (EC) 469/2009 of the European Parliament and of the Council of 6 May 2009 concerning the supplementary protection certificate for medicinal products

TEU	Treaty on European Union
TFEU	Treaty on the Functioning of the European Union
Translation Regulation	Regulation (EU) 1260/2012 of 17 December 2012 implementing enhanced cooperation in the area of the creation of unitary patent protection with regard to the applicable translation arrangements
TRIPS	Agreement on Trade-Related Aspects of Intellectual Property Rights
Unitary Patent	A European patent with unitary effect
UP Regulation	Regulation (EU) 1257/2012 of 17 December 2012 implementing enhanced cooperation in the area of the creation of unitary patent protection
UPC	Unified Patent Court
UPC Agreement	Agreement on a Unified Patent Court 19 February 2013

FIGURES AND TABLES

Figures

Figure 2.1	The UPC and national courts with mutually exclusive jurisdictions	31
Figure 2.2	The UPC jointly and severally present in the contracting Member States	31
Figure 2.3	The structure of the divisions of the Court of First Instance and the Court of Appeal. At the time of writing, the number and distribution of the local and regional divisions shown is incomplete	34
Figure 3.1	Judicial panels of the local and regional divisions	52
Figure 3.2	Judicial panels of the central divisions	53
Figure 3.3	Judicial panels of the Court of Appeal and the full court	54
Figure 5.1	Language of statement of claim and language of proceedings	83
Figure 6.1	The forum of national patent actions and unitary patent actions over time	86
Figure 6.2	The exclusive competence of the UPC for European patent disputes begins at the end of the transitional period (currently seven years). Prior to this, the UPC and the national courts both have competence	87
Figure 6.3	Opted-out European patent disputes are within the exclusive competence of the national courts, for the term of the patent and any SPC based on it (provided there has been no prior UPC action lodged concerning that patent)	87
Figure 6.4	The withdrawal of a European patent (providing there has been no prior national action lodged concerning that patent) brings disputes concerning the patent within the exclusive competence of the UPC	88
Figure 7.1	During the transitional period, a revocation action is lodged in a national court of a Member State by Party X against Party P. It is followed by an infringement action brought by P, relating to the same patent, A, in the UPC against X. An attempted infringement counterclaim then follows in the national court (where local rules permit)	104
Figure 7.2	During the transitional period, an infringement action is lodged in a national court against Party X. It is followed by a revocation action by X relating to the same patent, A, against the proprietor P, in the UPC. An attempted revocation counterclaim then follows in the national court (where local rules permit)	104

xx Figures and Tables

Figure 7.3	During the transitional period, a revocation action is lodged in the UPC by Party X. It is followed by an infringement action relating to the same patent, A, in the national court of a Member State, but against a different party, Y. An attempted revocation counterclaim is then lodged in the national court of the Member State by Y (where local rules permit)	106
Figure 7.4	During the transitional period, an infringement action is lodged in the UPC against Party X. It is followed by a revocation action brought by Y relating to the same patent (A) in the national court of a Member State, and an attempted infringement counterclaim against Y in the national court of the Member State (where local rules permit)	106
Figure 9.1	The claimant's choice of forum between Domicile and place of infringement	124
Figure 9.2	The claimant's choice when the defendant's Domicile is outside the contracting Member States	124
Figure 9.3	The claimant's choice when the defendant is domiciled outside the contracting Member States and the place of infringement has no local or regional division	125
Figure 9.4	Initiating revocation claims lodged in the central division	128
Figure 9.5	Lodging a revocation, revocation counterclaim or declaration of non-infringement when an infringement action has already been lodged	129
Figure 9.6	A subsequent infringement action lodged in the central division	130
Figure 9.7	A subsequent infringement action lodged in local or regional division	130
Figure 9.8	A revocation counterclaim in the local or regional division and the stay of a central division revocation action	132
Figure 9.9	The options under Article 33(3) to bifurcate or consolidate	135
Figure 9.10	Lodging a compensation action under a licence of right in the division of defendant's Domicile	139
Figure 9.11	Lodging a compensation action under a licence of right when the defendant's Domicile is outside the contracting Member States	139
Figure 9.12	Lodging a compensation action under a licence of right in the central division	140
Figure 10.1	An overview of the timeline of an infringement action on the merits	145
Figure 10.2	Order of pleadings in the written procedure of an infringement action	148
Figure 11.1	Overview of revocation and declaration of non-infringement actions	161
Figure 11.2	Written procedure: revocation action	164
Figure 12.1	Overview of revocation and declaration of non-infringement actions	171
Figure 12.2	Action for a declaration of non-infringement	174

Tables

Table I.1	Participating Member States: relation of EPC signatory states to the Regulations and UPC Agreement	13
Table 1.1	A comparison of EPC contracting states and EU Member States	19
Table 1.2	True Top 4 Unitary Patent renewal fees	26
Table 2.1	Subject matter competencies of the sections of the central division	35
Table 4.1	Hypothetical examples of the effect of Article 7	69
Table 7.1	The key provisions of the Brussels I Regulation (recast) relevant to patent actions	96
Table 9.1	Examples of how Article 33(1) might be applied	125
Table 18.1	Scale of recoverable 'costs of representation per instance and party'	285
Table 20.1	Court fees for actions: infringement, counterclaim for infringement, declaration of non-infringement, compensation for licence of right and application to determine damages	306
Table 20.2	Fixed fees	307
Table 20.3	Fees on appeal	308
Table 20.4	Fee reimbursements for withdrawal or settlement of an action	311
Table A	The circumstances in which a stay of proceedings may be ordered and the division concerned	313
Table B	Table of applications and hearings provided by the Rules of Procedure	316

TABLE OF CASES

Abbott Laboratories Ltd v Dexcom Incorporated [2021] EWHC 2246 (Pat)
   [2022] FSR 3, (6 August 2021) 115, 116
Abidin Daver, The [1984] AC 398, [1984] 2 WLR 196, [1984] 1 All ER 470
   (26 January 1984), HL 119
Actavis Group HF v Eli Lilly and Co; Medef EHF v Eli Lilly and Co
   [2012] EWHC 3316 (Pat), [2012] 11 WLUK 796 (27 November 2012) 116–7, 118–9
Actavis Group HF v Eli Lilly and Co; Medef EHF v Eli Lilly and Co
   [2013] EWCA Civ 517, [2013] RPC 37 (21 May 2013) 116, 119
Actavis UK Ltd v Eli Lilly & Co [2017] UKSC 48, [2017] RPC 21,
   [2017] Bus LR 1731 (12 July 2017) 2
Advanced Bionics AG and Another v MED-El Elektromedizinische Gerate
   GmbH [2021] EWHC 2415 (Pat), [2022] FSR 4 (31 August 2021) 115–6
Agilent / Waters, 97/20725 (14 January 2009), TGI Paris 273
AIB/Novisem, ECLI:NL:HR:2015:3304, ro 4.1.5 (13 November 2015), Dutch Sup Ct 228
Al Rawi v Security Service [2011] UKSC 34, [2012] 1 AC 531, [2012] 1 All ER 1
   (13 July 2011) 251
Alexander & Co v Henry & Co (1895) 12 RPC 360 (26 August 1895), ChD 273
American Cyanamid v Ethicon Ltd [1975] AC 396, [1975] 2 WLR 316,
   [1975] RPC 513, HL 212, 213
Anan Kasei Co Ltd v Neo Chemicals & Oxides (Europe) Ltd [2020]
   EWHC 2503 (Pat), [2020] 9 WLUK 357 (16 September 2020) 251
Apple v Samsung, Court of Appeal of The Hague, 20 May 2014,
   ECLI:NL:GHDHA:2014:1727 210
Applera v Stratagene, District Ct of The Hague (provisional measures judge),
   13 July 2003, ECLI:NL:RBSGR:2007:BB6737 210
Arrow Generics Ltd and Another v Merck & Co Inc [2007] EWHC 1900 (Pat),
   [2007] FSR 39 (31 July 2007) 120, 121
Ausgelagerte Rechtsabteulung – OLG Köln, GRUR -RR 2010, 493 206
B v Auckland District Law Society [2003] UKPC 38, [2003] 2 AC 736,
   [2003] 3 WLR 859, [2004] 4 All ER 269 (19 May 2003) (PC (NZ)) 256
Bayer Pharma AG v Richter Gedeon (Case C-688/17) EU:C:2019:722
   (12 September 2019) 211, 278
Belgische Vereniging van Auteurs, Componisten en Uitgevers CVBA (SABAM)
   v Netlog NV (Case C-360/10) EU:C:2012:85, [2012] 2 CMLR 18, [2012]
   ECR I-0000 (16 February 2012) 156, 281
BL Macchine Automatische v Windmoeller KG, 19 December 2003, n 19550,
   GRUR Int 2005, 264, Italian Sup Ct 102
British Coal Corp v Dennis Rye Ltd (No 2) [1988] 1 WLR 1113, [1988]
   3 All ER 816, CA (25 February 1988) 256

xxiv   Table of Cases

Bundesgerichtshof, 21 December 2005, GRUR 2006, 217 137
Buttes Gas & Oil Co v Hammer (No 3) [1981] 1 QB 223, [1980] 3 WLR 668,
    [1980] 3 All ER 475, CA (20 June 1980) 256
Celltech R&D Ltd v MedImmune Inc [2004] EWHC 1522 (Pat), (2004) 27(9)
    IPD 27096 (18 June 2004) 39
Centrafarm BV v Sterling Drug Inc (Case-15/74) EU:C:1974:114, [1974]
    ECR 1147, [1974] 2 CMLR 480 (31 October 1974) 29
Cephalon Inc v Orchid Europe Ltd [2010] EWHC 2945 (Pat), [2010]
    11 WLUK 518, (19 November 2010) 213
Chiron Corp v Organon Teknika Ltd (No 10) [1995] FSR 325
    (29 November 1994), ChD (Pat Ct) 282
Cinacalcet – OLG Düsseldorf, PharmR 2021, 270 .... 206, 207
Cinacalcet II – OLG Düsseldorf, GRUR -RR 2021, 249 209
Coflexip SA v Stolt Offshore MS Ltd (No 2) [2003] EWCA Civ 296,
    [2003] FSR 41, (2003) 147 SJLB 355 (13 March 2003) 273
Coloplast v Medical4you, Dist Ct of The Hague (provisional measures judge),
    14 August 2015 ECLI:NL:RBDHA:2015:9655 210
Decision of 13 February 2020 (published on 20 March 2020), German Federal
    Constitutional Court 10–12
    para 150 12
Decision of 23 July 2021, German Constitutional Court 12
DHL Express France SAS v Chronopost SA (Case C-235/09) EU:C:2011:238,
    [2011] ECR I-2801, [2011] FSR 38 (12 April 2011) 156, 281
Düsseldorf Court of Appeal, docket number I-15 U 135/14 2 February 2015 156
Düsseldorf Court of Appeal, docket number I-15 U 65/15 13 January 2016 156
Düsseldorf Court of Appeals (I-2 W 15/11, 10 May 2011) 312
Düsseldorf Appeals Court, Order of 21 July 2011, I-2 W 23/11 227
Düsseldorf Court of Appeals questions concerning the proper calculation
    of a reasonable royalty: I-15 U 21/14 (referral to CJEU) 16 October 2014 272
Eilbedürfnis in Patentsachen – OLG Frankfurt/ Main, GRUR 2002, 236, 237 206
Evalve v Edwards Lifesciences Ltd (unreported, 27 March 2019) 114
Evalve Inc v Edwards Lifesciences Ltd [2020] EWHC 513 (Pat), [2020] RPC 13
    (12 March 2020) 282
Fabio Perini SPA v LPC Group [2012] EWHC 1393 (Pat) (4 April 2012) 273
Faxkarte – BGH, GRUR 2002, 1046 228
FibroGen Inc v Akebia Therapeutics Inc [2020] EWHC 866 (Pat),
    [2020] RPC 15 (20 April 2020) 241
Fisher & Paykel Healthcare Ltd v Flexicare Medical Ltd [2020] EWHC 3282 (Pat),
    [2020] 12 WLUK 100, (8 December 2020) 241
Flupirtin-Maleat – LG Düsseldorf, GRUR-RR 2013, 236 .... 207, 209
Flupirtin Maleat – OLG Düsseldorf GRUR-RS 2018, 1291 209
Folien Fischer AG v Ritrama SpA (Case C-133/11), EU:C:2012:664,
    [2013] QB 523, [2014] 1 All ER (Comm) 569 (25 October 2012) 102
Formica Ltd v Export Credits Guarantee Department [1995] 1 Lloyd's
    Rep 692, QBD 256
Formstein – BGH, GRUR 1986, 803 277

Fujifilm Kyowa Biologics Co Ltd (FKB) v AbbVie Biotechnology Ltd
  [2016] EWHC 425 (Pat), [2017] RPC 6 (1 March 2016) 120–1
Fujifilm Kyowa Kirin Biologics Company Ltd v Abbvie Biotechnology Ltd (Rev 1)
  [2017] EWHC 395 (Pat), [2018] RPC 1 (3 March 2017) 120–1
Fujifilm Kyowa Kirin Biologics Co Ltd v Abbvie Biotechnology Ltd & Anor
  [2017] EWCA Civ 1, [2017] RPC 9 (12 January 2017) 120–1
German Federal Court of Justice X ZR 28/09, 12 April 2011 312
General Hospital Corp and Palomar Medical Technologies Inc v Asclepion Laser
  Technologies GmbH, 14508/13 IIC 2014, 822 (10 June 2013), Italian Sup Ct 102
Generics (UK) Ltd v Daiichi Pharmaceutical Co Ltd, Daiichi Sankyo Co Ltd [2008]
  EWHC 2413 (Pat), [2009] RPC 4 (15 October 2008) 244
Generics (UK) Ltd (t/a Mylan) v Yeda Research & Development Co Ltd
  [2012] EWHC 1848 (Pat), [2012] 7 WLUK 308 (11 July 2012) 244
Gerber Garment Technology Inc v Lectra Systems Ltd [1997] RPC 443,
  (1997) 20(5) IPD 20046, CA (18 December 1996) 273
German Graphics Graphische Maschinen (Case C-292/08) EU:C:2009:544,
  [2009] ECR I-8421, [2010] IL Pr 1 (10 September 2009) 96
Gesellschaft für Antriebstechnik mBH & Co KG (GAT) v Lamellen und
  Kupplungsbau Beteiligungs KG (LuK) (Case C-4/03), EU:C:2006:457,
  [2006] ECR I-6509, [2006] FSR 45 (13 July 2006) 97–8, 99, 101
Gillette Safety Razor Co Ltd v Anglo American Trading Co Ltd (1913)
  30 RPC 465 (3 September 1913), HL 120
Glaxo Group Ltd v Genentech Inc [2008] EWCA Civ 23, [2008] Bus LR 888,
  [2008] FSR 18 (31 January 2008) 45
Grimme Maschinenfabrik GmbH & Co KG v Derek Scott (t/a Scotts Potato Machinery)
  [2010] EWCA Civ 1110, [2011] FSR 7, [2011] Bus LR D129 (15 October 2010) 2
Harnkatheterset – InstGE 12, 114 209
Harnkatheterset – OLG Düsseldorf, GRUR -RS 2010, 15862 209
Helitune v Stewart Hughes [1991] RPC 78, [1991] FSR 171, Patents Ct
  (30 October 1990) 67
Henderson v All Around the World Recordings Ltd [2014] EWHC 3087 (IPEC),
  [2014] 10 WLUK 97 (3 October 2014) 273
HTC Corp v Nokia Corp [2013] EWHC 3778 (Pat), [2014] Bus LR 217,
  [2014] RPC 30 (3 December 2013) 281
HTC Europe Co Ltd v Apple Inc [2011] EWHC 2396 (Pat), [2011] 9 WLUK 375
  (19 September 2011) 115
Huawei Technologies Co Ltd v ZTE Corp (C-170/13) EU:C:2015:477
  (16 July 2015); GRUR 2015, 764 281
Inhalator – LG Düsseldorf, InstGE 10, 124 207
Inhalator – OLG Köln, GRUR -RR 2014, 127 206
IPCom GmbH & Co KG v HTC Europe Co Ltd [2013] EWHC 52 (Pat),
  [2013] 1 WLUK 436 (24 January 2013) 251
IPCom GmbH & Co KG v HTC Europe Co Ltd [2013] EWHC 2880 (Ch),
  [2013] 9 WLUK 588 (26 September 2013) 251
IPCom GmbH & Co KG v HTC Europe Co Ltd [2013] EWCA Civ 1496,
  [2014] RPC 12, [2014] Bus LR 187 (21 November 2013) 45

Jørn Hansson v Jungpflanzen Grunewald GmbH (Case C-481/14) EU:C:2016:419
(9 June 2016) 272
Karlsruhe Appeals Court, Beck RS 2011, 18386 234
Kleiderbügel – German Sup Ct GRUR 1995, 338 159
Koronarstent – LG Hamburg, GRUR -RR 2014, 137, 138 206
Laccio-Möbel – LG Hamburg, NJOZ 2009, 1456 207
Ladewagen – BGH, NJW 1974, 1710; BGH, GRUR 1975, 254, 256 225
Lancôme, ECLI:NL:HR:1998:ZC2553, Hoge Raad (Sup Ct of the Netherlands),
23 January 1998 207
LG München I, decision of 27 August 2003, AZ. 7 O 14788/03 206
L'Oréal SA v eBay International AG (Case C-324/09) EU:C:2011:474,
[2011] ECR I-6011, [2011] RPC 27 (12 July 2011) 156, 281
L'Oreal SA et al v eBay International AG, 12 July 2011 (docket number C-324/09)
EuZW 2011, 754 ff 157
Lucasfilm Ltd and Others v Ainsworth and Another [2011] UKSC 39,
[2012] 1 AC 208, [2011] FSR 41, [2011] ECDR 21 (27 July 2011) 119
MacShannon v Rockware Glass Ltd [1978] AC 795, [1978] 2 WLR 362,
[1978] 1 All ER 625 (26 January 1978) 119
Mannheim Regional Court NJOZ 2009, 1458 – Unterlassungsansprüche einer
Patentverwertungsgesellschaft 156
Matador v Bick, District Ct of The Hague (provisional measures judge),
22 April 2015, ECLI:NL:RBDHA:2015:8869 210
Medimmune Ltd v Novartis Pharmaceuticals UK Ltd [2011] EWHC 1669 (Pat),
[2011] 7 WLUK 92 (5 July 2011) 241
Merck & Co Inc v Primecrown Ltd (Joined Cases C-267/95 and C-268/95)
EU:C:1996:468, [1996] ECR 6285, [1997] FSR 237 (5 December 1996) 28
Merck & Co Inc v Stephar BV (Case 187/80) EU:C:1981:180, [1981] ECR 2063,
[1981] 3 CMLR 463 (14 July 1981) 29
Merck Canada Inc v Sigma Pharmaceuticals plc (No 2) [2013] EWPCC 21,
[2013] RPC 2 (3 May 2012), Pat Cty Ct 157, 281
Merck Sharp and Dohme Ltd v Wyeth LLC [2020] EWHC 2636 (Pat),
[2021] RPC 8 (15 October 2020) 241
Merrell Dow Pharmaceuticals Inc v HN Norton & Co Ltd [1995] UKHL 14,
[1996] RPC 76 (26 October 1995) 2
Monsanto Co v Stauffer Chemical Co (NZ) [1984] FSR 559 (6 June 1984), NZ HCt........207
Munich Regional Court, 24 November 2011, docket number 7 O 22100/10 159
Neurim Pharmaceuticals (1991) Ltd v Generics UK Ltd (t/a Mylan)
[2020] EWHC 1362 (Pat), [2020] 6 WLUK 23 (3 June 2020) 213
Neurim Pharmaceuticals (1991) Ltd v Generics UK Ltd (t/a Mylan)
[2020] EWHC 3270 (Pat), [2020] 12 WLUK 84 (4 December 2020) 241
Neurim Pharmaceuticals (1991) Ltd v Generics UK Ltd (t/a Mylan) and Another
[2020] EWCA Civ 793, [2021] RPC 7 (24 June 2020) 213–4
Neurim Pharmaceuticals (1991) Ltd v Teva UK Ltd [2022] EWHC 954 (Pat),
[2022] 4 WLUK 347 (26 April 2022) 213
Nokia v HMRC (Joined Cases C-446/09 and C-495/09) EU:C:2011:796
(1 December 2011), CJEU 247

Novartis AG v Hospira UK Ltd [2013] EWCA Civ 583, [2014] 1 WLR 1264,
[2014] RPC 3 (22 May 2013) 210
Oceanbulk Shipping & Trading SA v TMT Asia Ltd [2010] EWCA Civ 79,
[2010] 1 WLR 1803, [2010] 3 All ER 282 (15 February 2010) 256
Olanzapin – OLG Düsseldorf, GRUR 2008, 1077..208
Olanzapin – OLG Düsseldorf, InstGE 9, 140, 146 209
OLG Düsseldorf, GRUR -RS 2019, 33226..212
OnePlus Technology (Shenzhen) Co Ltd v Mitsubishi Electric Corp
[2020] EWCA Civ 1562, [2021] FSR 13 (19 November 2020) 251–2
Opinion 1/92, 10 April 1992 – Opinion pursuant to the second subparagraph
of Article 228 (1) of the EEC Treaty – Draft agreement between the Community,
on the one hand, and the countries of the European Free Trade Association,
on the other, relating to the creation of the European Economic Area.
(ECLI:EU:C:1992:189), [1992] ECR-I 2821, ECJ...9
Opinion 1/00, 18 April 2002 – Opinion pursuant to Article 300(6) EC – Proposed
agreement between the European Community and non-Member States on the
establishment of a European Common Aviation Area (ECLI:EU:C:2002:231),
[2002] ECR I-3493, ECJ 9
Opinion 1/09, 8 March 2011 – Request to the Court for an Opinion pursuant to
Article 218(11) TFEU, made on 6 July 2009 by the Council of the
European Union – Agreement on the Establishment of a Unified Patent
Litigation System ECLI:EU:C:2011:123, [2011] ECR I-01137, ECJ 6, 8, 9,
12, 40, 42
Owners of Cargo Lately Laden on Board the Ship Tatry v Owners of the Ship
Maciej Rataj (Case C-406/92) EU:C:1994:400, [1999] QB 515,
[1994] ECR I-5439 (6 December 1994)..118
Pfändung einer Domain – LG Frankfurt/Main, NJW 2000, 1961.......................................206
Pfizer Ltd v F Hoffmann-La Roche AG and Another [2019] EWHC 1520 (Pat),
[2019] RPC 14 (20 June 2019) 121
Phoenix Contact GmbH & Co KG v Harting Deutschland GmbH & Co KG,
Harting Electric GmbH & Co KG (Case C-44/21) EU:C:2022:309
(28 April 2022)..208
Procter & Gamble v Mölnlycke, Supreme Ct of the Netherlands, 15 December 1995,
ECLI:NL:HR:1995:ZC1919 212
Productores de Música de España (Promusicae) v Telefónica de España SAU
(Case C-275/06) EU:C:2008:54, [2008] ECR I-271, [2008] 2 CMLR 17
(29 January 2008) 156, 281
Qualitätssprung – OLG Köln, GRUR -RR 2014, 82...206
Raltegravir – BGH, GRUR 2017, 1017 281
RBS (Rights Issue Litigation), Re [2016] EWHC 3161 (Ch), [2017] 1 WLR 1991,
[2017] 1 BCLC 726, [2017] 1 Lloyd's Rep FC 83 (8 December 2016) 253, 254
Realchemie Nederland BV v Bayer CropScience AG (Case C-406/09)
EU:C:2011:668, [2011] ECR I-9773, [2012] Bus LR 1825 (18 October 2011) 96
Rechtsbestand im Verfügungsverfahren – LG München, GRUR 2021, 466 209
Research in Motion UK Ltd v Inpro Licensing SARL [2005] EWHC 1292 (Pat),
(2005) 28(7) IPD 28052, (2005) 102(40) LSG 27 (16 June 2005).................. 112, 114, 115

xxviii   Table of Cases

Research in Motion UK Ltd v Visto Corp [2008] EWHC 3025 (Pat), (2009)
    32(2) IPD 32012 (5 December 2008) 115
Roche Nederland and Others v Frederick Primus & Milton Goldenberg
    (Case C-539/03), EU:C:2005:749, 8 December 2005, A-G's Opinion 99
Roche Nederland BV v Frederick Primus & Milton Goldenberg
    (Case C-539/03), EU:C:2006:458, [2006] ECR I-6535, [2007] FSR 5,
    (13 July 2006), CJEU 98–9, 100, 101, 105
Routestone Ltd v Minories Finance Ltd [1997] BCC 180, [1997] 1 EGLR 123,
    [1996] NPC 83, ChD (16 May 1996) 244
Rush & Tompkins Ltd v Greater London Council [1989] AC 1280,
    [1988] 3 WLR 939, [1988] 3 All ER 737, HL (3 November 1988) 257
Samsung Electronics Ltd v Apple Retail UK Ltd [2014] EWCA Civ 376,
    [2014] 4 WLUK 1 (1 April 2014) 45
Samsung Electronics (UK) Ltd v Apple Inc [2012] EWHC 2049 (Pat),
    [2012] 7 WLUK 541 (18 July 2012) 159
Scarlet Extended SA v Société Belge des Auteurs, Composituers et Editeurs
    SCRL (SABAM) (Case C-70/10) EU:C:2011:771, [2011] ECR I-11959,
    [2012] ECDR 4 (24 November 2011) 156, 281
Schutz (UK) Ltd v Werit (UK) Ltd [2013] UKSC 16, [2013] RPC 16,
    [2013] 2 All ER 177, [2013] Bus LR 565 (13 March 2013) 2
Shevill v Presse Alliance (Case C-68/93) EU:C:1995:61, [1995] 2 AC 18,
    [1995] ECR I-415 (7 March 1995) 109
Simplify Your Production – LG Hamburg, GRUR -RR 2008, 366, 367 206
Smith & Nephew plc v ConvaTec Technologies Inc [2013] EWHC 3955 (Pat),
    [2014] RPC 22 (12 December 2013) 157, 281
Smithkline Beecham and Another v Apotex Europe Ltd and Others [2004]
    EWCA Civ 1568, [2005] FSR 23, (2005) 28(2) IPD 28003 (29 November 2004) 245
SmithKline Beecham Plc v Apotex Europe Ltd (No 2) [2004] EWCA Civ 1703 283
Solvay SA v Honeywell Fluorine Products Europe BV and Others
    (Case C-616/10), ECLI:EU:C:2012:445 (12 July 2012) 97, 99, 100, 101,
                                                                                    105, 107, 108, 109, 210
Sorafenib – GRUR-RS 2021, 37988 209
späte Besichtigung – Düsseldorf Appeals Ct, GRUR-RR 2011, 289 234
Spiliada Maritime Corp v Cansulex Ltd [1987] AC 460, [1986] 3 WLR 972,
    [1986] 3 All ER 843, HL (19 November 1986) 117, 118
Stowarzyszenie 'Olawska Telewizja Kablowa' v Stowarzyszenie Filmowców
    Polskich (Case C-367/15) EU:C:2017:36, [2017] ECDR 16 (25 January 2017) 272
Supreme Court of the Netherlands, decision of 29 November 2002,
    ECLI:NL:HR:2002:AE4553 207
Susan Yvonne Dore v Leicestershire County Council [2010] EWHC 34 (Ch),
    [2010] 1 WLUK 220 (15 January 2010) 256
Takeda UK Ltd v F Hoffmann-La Roche AG [2018] EWHC 2155 (Ch),
    [2018] 7 WLUK 526 (24 July 2018) 112
Three Rivers (No 5) [2003] EWCA Civ 474, [2003] QB 1556, [2003] 3 WLR 667
    (3 April 2003) 254

Three Rivers (No 6) [2004] UKHL 48, [2005] 1 AC 610, [2004] 3 WLR 1274 (HL)
(11 November 2004) 253, 254
TQ Delta LLC v Zyxel Communications UK Ltd [2018] EWHC 1515 (Ch),
[2018] Bus LR 1544, [2018] FSR 34 (13 June 2018) 251
Truvada – District Court Munich, PharmR 2017, 512 209
Unilin Beheer BV v Berry Floor NV [2007] EWCA Civ 364, [2008] 1 All ER 156,
[2007] Bus LR 1140 (25 April 2007) 44, 47
UPC Telekabel Wien GmbH v Constantin Film GmbH (Case C-314/12)
ECLI:EU:C:2014:192, [2014] Bus LR 541, [2014] ECDR 12 (27 March 2014) 156, 281
USA v Philip Morris Inc and British American Tobacco (Investments) Ltd
[2004] EWCA Civ 330, [2004] 1 CLC 811, (2004) 148 SJLB 388 (23 March 2004) 255
Vernichtungsanspruch – German Sup Ct GRUR 1997, 899 159
Virgin Atlantic Airways Ltd (Respondent) v Zodiac Seats UK Ltd (Formerly
Known as Contour Aerospace Ltd) [2013] UKSC 46, [2014] AC 160,
[2013] 3 WLR 299 (3 July 2013) 47
Wärmetauscher – BGH, GRUR 2016, 1031 281
Warner-Lambert Company LLC v Teva UK Ltd [2011] EWHC 1691 (Pat),
[2011] 6 WLUK 600 (27 June 2011) 203
Waugh v British Railways Board [1980] AC 521, [1979] 3 WLR 150,
[1979] 2 All ER 1169, HL (12 June 1979) 255
WL Gore & Associates GmbH v Geox SpA [2008] EWCA Civ 622,
[2008] 3 WLUK 467 (19 March 2008) 114
ZTE (UK) Ltd v Telefonaktiebolaget LM Ericsson [2011] EWHC 2709 (Pat),
[2011] 10 WLUK 476 (19 October 2011) 115
Zuid-Chemie BV v Philippo's Mineralenfabriek NV/SA (Case C-189/08)
EU:C:2009:475, [2009] ECR I-6917, [2010] Bus LR 1026 (16 July 2009) 96

TABLE OF LEGISLATION

DENMARK

Rules on Preservation of Evidence 236

FRANCE

Intellectual Property Code
    Art 129 228
    Art L332-4 227
    Art L521-6 §2 235
    Art L615-5 .... 226, 233
    Art L615-5-2 .... 234, 235

GERMANY

Act of Approval to the UPC Agreement 11, 12
    Art 1(1) 10
Basic Law (Constitution) (Grundgesetz) 11
    Art 20(1), (2) 10, 11
    Art 20(3) 12
    Art 23 11
    Art 38(1) 10, 11
    Art 79(3) 10, 11
Civil Procedure Code
    s 110 286
    s 142 .... 224, 225
    s 282 222
    s 296 222
    s 485 I 227
    ss 485ff 225
    s 538 II Nr 1 58
    s 926 para 1 214
    s 945 278
Civil Law
    ss 809, 810 228

Design Act
  s 43 158
IntPatÜbkG (Law on International Patent Treaties)
  Art II § 18 18
Geschäftsgeheimnisgesetz GeschGehG (Law of Business Secrets) 250
  s 16 224
  s 19 224
Patentgesetz (Patent Act) 18, 281
  s 139 281
  s 139 II 277
  s 140a) 158
  s 140b I 236
  s 140c 228
  s 142a 283
  s 145 .... 250, 265
Trademark Act
  s 18 158
Utility Model Act
  s 24a) 158

NETHERLANDS

Civil Code (DCC)
  Art 3:296(1) 212
Code of Civil Procedure (DCCP)
  Art 1019e(1) 202
  Art 1019e(3) 202
  Art 1019h 283
Patent Act
  Art 77 18

SPAIN

Patents Act
  Arts 129ff 227

UK

Civil Procedure Rules 1998, SI 1998/3132 223
  PD25B
    para 3.1 237
    para 4.1 237
    para 9.1 237

Pt 31
    r 31.22(2)......251
Pt 35
    r 35.3......241
    r 35.10(2)......241
    PD35......241
Pt 44
    r 44.3(5)......282
Pt 51
    PD51U, para 15......251
Patent Act 1977......45

EUROPE

Act Revising the Convention on the Grant of European Patents signed in Munich on November 29, 2000......44
Agreement between the European Union and the European Atomic Energy Community, of the one part, and the United Kingdom of Great Britain and Northern Ireland, of the other part [2021] OJ L149/10, 30 April......296
    Art 194(1)......296
    Art 194(2)(a), (b)......296
Agreement on a Unified Patent Court, signed on 19 February 2013 ('UPC Agreement') [2013] OJ C 175/1......8, 11, 12, 13, 19, 28, 30, 32, 33, 34, 36, 39, 43, 63, 64, 65, 70, 72, 73, 74, 75, 77, 86, 89, 91, 92, 93, 103, 104, 108, 112, 117, 145, 147, 156, 173, 193, 222, 242, 256, 296, 324, 341–387
    Preamble......32
    PART I – GENERAL AND INSTITUTIONAL PROVISIONS......343–357
    Ch I – General Provisions (Arts 1–5)......343–344
    Art 1......32, 33, 38, 375
    Art 1(2)......12, 117
    Art 2(b), (c)......12
    Art 2(c)......13
    Art 3......92, 93
    Art 3(a)–(d)......92
    Ch II – Institutional Provisions (Arts 6–14)......345–348
    Art 6......236
    Art 7......33
    Art 7(2)......181
    Art 8(1)......51
    Art 8(2)–(4)......52
    Art 8(5), (6)......53
    Art 8(7)......51, 150, 165, 175, 382

Art 9(1), (2)	54
Art 14(2)	377
Ch III – Judges of the Court (Arts 15–19)	348–350
Art 15	375
Art 15(1)	375
Art 15(2), (3)	48
Art 16	375
Art 17	269
Art 18	48, 383
Art 18(2)	49
Art 18(3)	48, 133
Art 19	379
Ch IV – The Primacy of Union Law, Liability and Responsibility of the Contracting Member States (Arts 20–23)	350–351
Art 20	11, 42, 61
Art 21	32, 41, 43
Arts 22, 23	32, 40
Ch V – Sources of Law And Substantive Law (Arts 24–30)	351–354
Art 24	61, 66
Art 24(1)	68
Art 24(1)(a)–(e)	61
Art 24(1)(c)	65, 68
Art 24(1)(e)	63
Art 24(2)	66
Art 24(2)(a)–(c)	66
Art 24(3)	66
Arts 25–27	42, 61, 65, 66
Arts 25–29	64
Art 25	62, 63
Art 25(a)–(c)	61
Art 26	63, 157
Art 26(1), (2)	62, 281
Art 26(3)	62
Art 27	63
Art 27(d)	63
Art 27(i)–(j)	62
Art 27(k), (l)	63
Art 28	38, 40, 65, 66, 67, 69, 152, 176
Art 29	29
Ch VI – International Jurisdiction and Competence (Arts 31–34)	354–357
Art 32	36, 37, 38, 39, 60, 128
Art 32(1)	38, 147, 287
Art 32(1)(a)	36, 37, 39, 72, 126
Art 32(1)(b)	36, 129, 146
Art 32(1)(c)	36, 37, 126, 197
Art 32(1)(d)	36, 72, 129

Art 32(1)(e)	36, 129
Art 32(1)(f)	36, 126, 194, 273
Art 32(1)(g)	36, 67, 126, 127
Art 32(1)(h)	36, 138
Art 32(1)(i)	36, 47, 53, 54, 122, 260, 295
Art 32(2)	37
Art 33	46, 76, 123, 129, 140
Art 33(1)–(6)	149
Art 33(1)	124, 125, 163
Art 33(1)(a)	83, 123, 127, 139, 141
Art 33(1)(b)	123, 127
Art 33(2)	127, 128, 131, 141, 151
Art 33(3)	53, 55, 82, 112, 113, 122, 129, 130, 131, 132, 133, 134, 135, 138, 152, 153, 155, 169, 170, 182, 314, 317
Art 33(3)(a)	50, 131, 133, 155, 183
Art 33(3)(b)	50, 133, 135, 183, 186, 313, 314, 315
Art 33(3)(c)	78, 113, 122, 183, 189
Art 33(4)	129, 131, 162, 170, 172
Art 33(5)	113, 130, 131
Art 33(6)	137, 173
Art 33(7)	78, 79, 122, 140, 149, 163, 165, 175
Art 33(8)	45
Art 33(9)	140
Art 33(10)	45
Art 34	85, 105, 157
Ch VII – Patent Mediation and Arbitration (Art 35)	357
PART II – FINANCIAL PROVISIONS (Arts 36–39)	357–358
Art 36(3)	305
Art 37	386
PART III – ORGANISATION AND PROCEDURAL PROVISIONS (Arts 40–82)	359–373
Ch I – General Provisions (Arts 40–48)	359–361
Art 41	8, 380
Art 44	185
Art 45	248, 253
Art 47	146, 204, 228, 301
Art 47(1)	145
Art 47(2), (3)	146
Art 47(5)	162, 164
Art 47(6)	146
Art 47(7)	178, 179
Art 48	90, 233, 295
Art 48(1)	295
Art 48(2)	295, 296
Art 48(3)	295, 296, 383

Art 48(4)–(7) 295
Ch II – Language of Proceedings (Arts 49–51) 361–362
Art 49 225
Art 49(1) 78, 79, 83, 163
Art 49(2) 78, 79, 80, 83, 163
Art 49(3) 80, 83, 163
Art 49(4) 83, 163
Art 49(5) 55, 80, 83, 163, 258, 260, 309
Art 49(6) 77, 83, 163, 179
Art 50(2), (3) 81, 262
Art 51(3) 77, 83
Ch III – Proceedings Before the Court (Arts 52–55) 363–364
Arts 52 ff 11
Art 52 147
Art 52(1) 147
Art 54 ....66, 221
Art 55 66
Art 55(1) 221
Art 55(3) 221
Ch IV – Powers of the Court (Arts 56–72) 364–370
Art 56(1) 46
Art 56(2) 200
Art 57(1) 240, 242
Art 57(2) 240, 383
Art 57(3) 237
Art 57(4) 242
Art 58 ....248, 250, 252, 276
Arts 59–62 .... 260, 282
Art 59 ....55, 234, 250, 258, 309
Art 59(1) 235
Art 60 ....225, 250, 258, 309, 318
Art 60(1) 226, 233
Art 60(2) 226
Art 60(4) 226, 233
Art 60(5) 201, 202, 231
Art 60(7) 198
Art 60(8) 214
Art 60(9) 217, 218
Art 61 .... 258, 309
Art 62 ....55, 160, 197, 219, 226, 258, 309
Art 62(1) 204
Art 62(2) 204, 205, 210, 319
Art 62(4) 319
Art 62(5) 198, 201, 214, 217
Art 63 ....155, 192, 280, 281

Art 63(1)	157, 280
Art 63(2)	280
Art 64	66, 158, 159, 192, 271, 279
Art 64(1)	158, 279
Art 64(2)	279
Art 64(2)(a)	279
Art 64(2)(b)	158, 279
Art 64(2)(c)	279
Art 64(2)(d), (e)	158, 279
Art 64(3)	279
Art 64(4)	159, 279
Art 65	192
Art 65(1)	170
Art 65(3), (4)	170
Art 67	55, 160, 192, 234, 236, 258, 260, 309, 318
Art 67(1)	160, 236
Art 67(2)(a)–(c)	160
Art 68	66, 147, 157, 194, 271, 272, 273
Art 68(1)	271
Art 68(2)(a)	271
Art 68(2)(b)	272
Art 68(3)	272
Art 68(3)(a), (b)	157
Art 68(4)	158
Art 69	11, 147, 194, 275, 276, 282, 283, 284
Art 69(1)–(3)	282, 286
Art 69(4)	282
Art 72	66
Ch V – Appeals (Arts 73–75)	370–371
Art 73	55, 58, 216, 258
Art 73(1), (2)	258
Art 73(2)(a)	217, 258, 259
Art 73(3)	33, 55, 58, 263
Art 73(4)	55, 263
Art 74	160, 319
Art 74(1)	260
Art 74(2)	55, 260
Art 74(3)	217, 260
Art 75(1), (2)	58, 267
Ch VI – Decisions (Arts 76–82)	371–373
Art 76	269
Art 77	270
Art 78	387
Art 78(1), (2)	56
Art 79	196

Art 80 .... 159, 192, 279
Art 81(1)–(4) 268
Art 82 196
Art 82(3) 282
PART IV – TRANSITIONAL PROVISIONS (Art 83) 373
Art 83 .... 30, 84, 85, 92, 383
Art 83(1) 84, 85, 86, 102, 103
Art 83(2) 84, 85
Art 83(3) 31, 84, 85, 86, 93
Art 83(4) 85, 88
Art 83(5) 85, 89, 380
PART V – FINAL PROVISIONS (Arts 84–89) 373–375
Art 89(1) 30
Annex I – Statute of the Unified Patent Court 375–387
    Art 7 .... 240, 269
    Art 7(4) 49, 315
    Art 15 55
    Art 19 51
    Art 19(1) 49
    Art 19(5) 49
    Art 21(1) 51
    Art 21(2) 54
    Art 21(4) 51
    Art 23(2)(d) 253
    Art 34 56
    Art 35 53
    Art 35(1), (2) 56
    Art 36 56
    Art 37(1) 195
    Art 38(1), (2) 41
Annex II – Distribution of cases within the central division 35, 181
Agreement on the Application of Article 65 EPC (London Agreement)
    OJ EPO 2001/549 .... 4, 20, 21
    Art 3(a), (b) 77
Agreement on Trade-Related Aspects of Intellectual Property Rights (TRIPS) 1
Agreement Relating to Community Patents 89/695/EEC [1989] OJ L401/1
    (Community Patent Convention 1989) 1, 2, 60, 63
    Arts 25–27 63
Brussels Convention 95
    Art 6(1) 98
Charter of Fundamental Rights of the European Union 342
Commission Recommendation of 6 May 2003 concerning the definition of micro,
    small and medium-sized enterprises (2003/361/EC) [2003] OJ L124/36
    Annex, Title I 310

Convention for the European Patent for the Common Market 76/76 EEC
 [1976] OJ L17/1 (Community Patent Convention 1973; in
 force 7 October 1977) 1, 2, 4, 7, 9, 12, 13, 19,
20, 21, 44, 60, 61, 65,
68, 74, 94, 99, 107, 109,
112, 323, 335, 341, 343, 351
 Art 6(1) 69, 329
 Art 14(2) 339
 Art 14(3) 24, 330, 338
 Art 14(6) 25, 74, 336, 338
 Art 30(3) 340
 Art 35(2) 325, 330
 Art 60 38
 Art 64 .... 170, 367
 Art 64(1) 323
 Art 67 .... 170, 367
 Art 69 .... 65, 119
 Art 69(1) 65
 Art 70(1) 74
 Pt II Ch IV (Arts 71–74) 69
 Art 71 69
 Art 73 69
 Art 74 70
 Art 76 28
 Art 84 168
 Art 105a 168, 264
 Art 105a(1) 44
 Art 105a(2) 45
 Art 123(2), (3) 168
 Art 127 327
 Art 129 327
 Art 134 .... 288, 289, 290, 295, 361
 Art 134(1) 255
 Art 138(1) 170, 367
 Art 138(3) 367
 Art 139(2) 170, 367
 Part IX (Arts 142–149) 323, 324
 Art 142 .... 323, 327
 Art 143 .... 329, 331, 339, 340
 Art 145 330
 Art 146 325
 Art 164 70
Convention on International Civil Aviation of 7 December 1944 62
 Art 27 .... 62, 353

xl   Table of Legislation

Council Decision 2011/167/EU – Council Decision of 10 March 2011
    authorising enhanced cooperation in the area of the creation
    of unitary patent protection [2011] OJ L76/53 .... 6, 322, 326, 327,
                                                                                       335, 336, 338
Council Regulation No 1 of 15 April 1958 determining the languages
    to be used by the European Economic Community O J 17, 6.10.1958,
    p. 385/58 338
Directive 98/5/EC of the European Parliament and of the Council of
    16 February 1998 to facilitate practice of the profession of lawyer on
    a permanent basis in a Member State other than that in which the
    qualification was obtained [1998] OJ L77/36 .... 295, 296
    Art 1 295
    Art 1(2)(a) 295
Directive 98/44/EC of 6 July 1998 of the European Parliament and of
    the Council of 6 July 1998 on the legal protection of biotechnological
    inventions – the Biotechnology Directive [1998] OJ L213/13 ....2, 42, 60
    Art 10 ....63, 353
Directive 2001/82/EC of the European Parliament and of the Council of
    6 November 2001 on the Community code relating to veterinary
    medicinal products [2001] OJ L311/1 62
    Art 13(6) 62, 63, 353
Directive 2001/83 of 6 November 2001 on the Community code relating
    to medicinal products for human use [2001] OJ L311/67 62
    Art 10 60
    Art 10(6) 2, 42, 62, 63, 353
Directive 2004/48/EC of the European Parliament and of the Council of
    29 April 2004 on the enforcement of intellectual property rights
    [2004] OJ L157/45; corrigendum [2004] OJ L195/16 .... 42, 60, 156, 159, 160,
                                                                                    209, 220, 225, 271, 272,
                                                                                         279, 281, 282
    Recital (22) 211
    Recital (26) 272
    Art 3(1) 156, 280
    Art 3(2) 156, 280, 281
    Art 6 235
    Art 8 160
    Art 9(1) 209
    Art 10 ....158, 279
    Art 11 ....155, 156, 280
    Art 11(1), (2) 156
    Art 11(3) 157
    Art 12 ....156, 280
    Art 13 ....272, 324
    Art 13(1)(a), (b) 157
    Art 13(2) 158, 211

Table of Legislation   xli

Art 14 282
Art 15 .... 159, 279
Art 27 160
Directive 2008/52/EC of the European Parliament and of the Council of
   21 May 2008 on certain aspects of mediation in civil and commercial
   matters [2008] OJ L136/3 196
Directive 2009/24/EC of the European Parliament and of the Council of
   23 April 2009 on the legal protection of computer programs [2009] OJ L111/16
   Arts 5, 6 .... 63, 353
Directive (EU) 2016/943 of the European Parliament and of the Council of
   8 June 2016 on the protection of undisclosed know-how and business
   information (trade secrets) against their unlawful acquisition, use and
   disclosure (Text with EEA relevance) [2016] OJ L157/1 251
   Art 9(2) 251
EC Treaty
   Arts 28, 29 29
EPC 2000 44
   Art 105a 168
Hague Convention of 18 March 1970 on the Taking of Evidence Abroad
   in Civil or Commercial Matters 246, 290
Lugano Convention – Convention on Jurisdiction and the Recognition
   and Enforcement of Judgments in Civil and Commercial Matters
   [2007] OJ L147/5 .... 109, 117, 315, 354
Maastricht Treaty 1 November 1993 3
New York Arbitration Convention 1958 196
Paris Convention for the Protection of Industrial Property Signed
   in Paris on 20 March 1883 and most recently amended on
   28 September 1979 .... 17, 18, 323
Patent Cooperation Treaty (Signed in Washington DC on 19 June 1970
   and most recently amended on 3 October 2001) 17, 18, 323
Protocol to the Agreement on a Unified Patent Court on provisional
   application, 1 October 2015 90
Protocol to the Interpretation of Article 69 of 5 October 1973, as revised
   by the Act Revising the EPC of 29 November 2000 65
   Arts 1, 2 65
Protocol on Jurisdiction and the Recognition of Decisions in Respect
   of the Right to the Grant of a European Patent (Protocol on Recognition)
   of 5 October 1973 .... 70, 71
   Arts 2–6 70
Regulation (EC) No 2100/94 – Council Regulation (EC) No 2100/94 of
   27 July 1994 on Community plant variety rights [1994] OJ L227/1
   Art 14 .... 62, 353
Regulation (EU) 1610/96 of 23 July 1996 concerning the creation of a
   supplementary protection certificate for plant protection products
   ('Plant Products SPC Regulation') [1996] OJ L198/30 .... 2, 42, 343

xlii *Table of Legislation*

Regulation (EC) 44/2001 on jurisdiction and the recognition and enforcement
 of judgments in civil and commercial matters [2001] OJ L12/1
 (Brussels I Regulation) 95
 Art 6(1) 105, 107
 Art 24(4) 119
Regulation (EC) 1206/2001 of 28 May 2001 on cooperation between the
 courts of the Member States in the taking of evidence in civil or commercial
 matters [2001] OJ L174/1 246
Regulation (EC) No 593/2008 of the European Parliament and of the Council
 of 17 June 2008 on the law applicable to contractual obligations
 (Rome I Regulation) [2008] OJ L 177/6 ....23, 344
 Art 3 ....71, 72
Regulation (EC) 864/2007 of the European Parliament and of the Council
 of 11 July 2007 on the law applicable to non-contractual obligations
 (Rome II Regulation) [2007] OJ L199/40 ....66, 119, 344
 Art 8 66
 Art 8(1), (2) 66
Regulation (EC) 1393/2007 of the European Parliament and of the Council
 of 13 November 2007 on the service in the Member States of judicial
 and extrajudicial documents in civil or commercial matters
 (the 'Service Regulation') [2007] OJ L324/79 ....147, 287
Regulation (EC) 469/2009 of 6 May 2009 concerning the supplementary
 protection certificate for medicinal products ('SPC Regulation') [2009]
 OJ L152/1 ....2, 28, 41–2, 60, 343
Regulation (EU) 1215/2012 of the European Parliament and of the
 Council of 12 December 2012 on jurisdiction and the recognition
 and enforcement of judgments in civil and commercial matters
 (recast) [2012] OJ L 351/1 'Brussels I Regulation (recast)' 9, 30, 31, 32, 72, 95,
  96, 97, 98, 102, 103, 107,
  109, 117, 122, 219, 278,
  342, 354, 375
  Recitals 96
  Recital (15) 96
  Ch II – Jurisdiction (Arts 4–35) 108
  Art 4 117
  Art 4(1) 96, 101, 116
  Art 7 117
  Art 7(2) 96, 101, 102, 116
  Art 8 117
  Art 8(1) 96, 98, 99, 100, 101, 105, 107
  Art 9 117
  Art 24(4) 31, 96, 97, 99, 100, 101
  Art 25(4) 39
  Art 27 96
  Art 29 .... 101, 103, 104, 107, 108, 177
  Art 30 ....101, 103, 105, 107, 108

Art 30(3)	103
Art 32	103
Art 33	117, 118
Art 33(1)(a), (b)	117
Art 33(2)(a)–(c)	118
Art 33(3), (4)	118
Art 35	96, 100, 109, 218
Art 71a(1)	32, 218
Art 71a(2)	218
Art 71b(1)	108, 109
Art 71b(2)	103, 108, 109
Art 71b(3)	108, 109
Art 71c	103, 117
Art 71c(1)	107
Regulation (EU) 1257/2012 of the European Parliament and of the Council of 17 December 2012 implementing enhanced cooperation in the area of the creation of unitary patent protection 'UP Regulation [2012] OJ L361/1	7, 8, 13, 17, 21, 22, 24, 25, 28–9, 30, 42, 61, 63, 64, 65, 69, 70, 74, 178, 315, 322–334, 335, 338, 341, 343, 351
Recital (1)	17
Recital (7)	21, 23, 73
Recital (10)	23, 40, 73
Recital (17)	23
Recital (18)	24
Recital (26)	84
Art 1	21
Art 2	22
Art 2(e)	21, 288, 289, 290
Art 3	25, 64
Art 3(1)	21, 93, 94
Art 3(2)	21, 22
Art 4(1), (2)	25
Art 5	42, 43, 63, 64, 65
Art 5(1)	42, 43, 63, 64
Art 5(2)	21, 42, 63, 64
Art 5(3)	43, 64
Art 5(4)	43
[Art 5a	65]
Art 6	7, 28
Art 7	7, 38, 39, 43, 64, 67, 68, 69, 70, 71, 72
Art 7(1), (2)	38, 68, 69
Art 7(3)	38, 69
Art 7(4)	69
Art 8	7, 23, 36, 60, 126, 138, 355

Art 8(1) 22
Art 8(2) 22, 40, 72
Art 9 ....21, 23, 36, 37, 47, 53, 55, 140, 178, 179, 180, 260, 337, 338, 339, 340, 355, 360, 368
Art 9(1) 23, 24, 178
Art 9(1)(i)–(iii) 23
Art 9(1)(iv)–(viii) 24
Art 9(3) 24
Art 11 339
Art 11(1) 25
Art 11(3) 22
[Arts 14f–14i ....65]
Art 16(1) 43, 64
Art 18(2) 32, 93
Art 18(3) 374
Art 143 23
Regulation (EU) 1260/2012 of 17 December 2012 implementing enhanced cooperation in the area of the creation of unitary patent protection with regard to the applicable translation arrangements Translation Regulation [2012] OJ L361/89 ....7, 8, 25, 42, 61, 64, 74, 77, 178, 324, 325, 326, 335–340, 351
Art 3 74
Art 3(2) 25, 75
Art 4 ....75, 76
Art 4(1) 75, 76
Art 4(2) 75
Art 4(4) 76
Art 5 ....24, 330
Art 6 ....24, 25, 75, 330
Regulation (EU) 608/2013 of the European Parliament and of the Council of 12 June 2013 concerning customs enforcement of intellectual property rights and repealing Council Regulation (EC) No 1383/2003 (the 'Customs Regulation') [2013] OJ L181/15 ....246, 247
Regulation (EU) 542/2014 of the European Parliament and of the Council of 15 May 2014 amending Regulation (EU) 1215/2012 as regards the rules to be applied with respect to the Unified Patent Court and the Benelux Court of Justice [2014] OJ L163/1 ....30, 32, 103, 108, 117, 218
Art 71(b)(3) 278
Regulation (EU) 2016/679 of the European Parliament and of the Council of 27 April 2016 on the protection of natural persons with regard to the processing of personal data and on the free movement of such data, and repealing Directive 95/46/EC (General Data Protection Regulation) [2016] OJ L119/1 249

Regulation (EU) 2020/1783 of the European Parliament and of the Council
  of 25 November 2020 on cooperation between the courts of the Member
  States in the taking of evidence in civil or commercial matters (taking
  of evidence) (recast) [2020] OJ L405/1 246
  Arts 5–22 246
Regulation (EU) 2020/1784 of the European Parliament and of the
  Council of 25 November 2020 on the service in the Member States of
  judicial and extrajudicial documents in civil or commercial matters
  (service of documents) (recast) [2020] OJ L405/40... 287, 290
  Art 16–18...288
  Art 19 287
  Annex I form L..288
Rules of the Procedure of the Court of Justice [2012] OJ L265/1 41
Rules of Procedure of the Unified Patent Court (as amended
  and agreed on 1 September 2022).. 13, 39, 49, 56, 74, 75, 89, 90,
                                                                91, 114, 138, 147, 173, 186, 193,
                                                                201, 205, 208, 222, 232, 240, 243,
                                                                256, 264, 286, 287, 290, 295, 299,
                                                                343, 346, 359, 360, 361, 363,
                                                                368, 369, 371, 380, 382, 384, 387
  Preamble, para (2)...57, 188
  Preamble, para (4)..57
  Preamble, para (7)..145
  r 1.2(a), (b) 49
  r 1.2(c)...50
  r 3...162
  r 4...215
  r 4.1 162
  r 5.. 84, 85, 90, 316
  r 5.1 ....28, 88
  r 5.1(a) 88, 89, 90
  r 5.1(b) 86, 91
  r 5.2 88
  r 5.2(a)..28, 91
  r 5.2(d) 28, 88
  r 5.3(a)...91
  r 5.3(e)...90
  r 5.5 90
  r 5.6 86
  r 5.7 ....85, 86, 88, 89, 90
  r 5.8 89
  r 5.9 ....85, 89
  [former r 5.13 (17th draft Rules)] 90

r 5A	85
r 5A.1–5A.3	92
r 7.1	77, 78, 79, 82, 163
r 7.2	82, 193
r 8.1	288, 295
r 8.2	295
r 8.3	298
r 8.4	316
r 8.5	90, 91, 288, 290
r 8.5(a)	91, 161, 172
r 8.5(b)	161, 172
r 8.6	161, 172
r 9	147, 184, 186
r 9.1	186
r 9.2	187, 299
r 9.3	187, 300
r 9.3(b)	261
r 9.4	187

Pt 1 – Procedures Before the Court of First Instance

r 10	147
r 11.1, 11.2	196
r 11.3	257
r 12.1	147
r 12.2	148
r 12.3(a)	316
r 12.4	148
r 13	148, 149, 224
r 13.1	149
r 13.1(a)	150, 165, 175, 198, 228, 274, 276, 285
r 13.1(b)	150, 153, 165, 175, 198, 228, 274, 276, 285
r 13.1(c)	165, 175, 198, 228, 274, 276, 285
r 13.1(d)	153, 165, 175, 183, 198, 228, 274, 276, 285
r 13.1(e)	153, 175, 198, 228
r 13.1(f)	175, 198, 228
r 13.1(g)	165, 175, 198, 228
r 13.1(h)	140, 150, 165, 175, 198, 216, 228
r 13.1(i)	140, 198, 228
r 13.1(k)	159, 167, 279
r 13.1(l)	167
r 13.1(l)(i), (ii)	224
r 13.1(m)	167, 223, 224
r 13.1(n)	167, 224
r 13.1(o), (p)	167
r 13.1(q)	50, 167
r 13.2	150, 152, 153, 165, 167, 169
r 13.3	50, 153, 165, 167

Table of Legislation xlvii

r 14	79, 81, 166, 200
r 14.1	79, 225
r 14.2	225
r 14.2(a), (b)	79, 83
r 14.2(c)	80, 82, 83
r 15	199, 308
r 16	137, 200, 229, 310
r 16.2	140
r 16.4	274
r 16.5	274, 316, 318
r 17	137, 200
r 17.1(a)	162, 229
r 17.1(b), (c)	229
r 17.2	141, 183, 229
r 17.3	141, 183, 184
r 17.3(a), (b)	162
r 17.3(c)	163
r 17.4	141, 162
r 18	49, 149, 200, 229
r 19	81, 148, 151, 164, 174, 176, 316
r 19.1	317
r 19.1(b)	141, 165, 174
r 19.2	166
r 19.4	141
r 19.6	165
r 19.7	141, 151, 166
r 20.1	141, 166, 316, 317
r 20.2	166
r 21.2	166
r 22	70
rr 23, 24	148, 151
r 24(a)–(c)	166, 176
r 24(d)	176
r 24(e), (f)	168, 176
r 24(g), (h)	168, 169, 176
r 24(i)	176
r 24(j)	168, 169, 176
r 25	148
r 25.1	152
r 25.1(a)	152
r 25.1(f), (g)	153
r 26	308
r 27	316
r 28	50, 189
r 29(a)–(e)	148, 154
r 29A(a)–(d)	167

r 29A(f)	167
r 30	148, 316
r 30.1	154
r 30.1(a)	76, 154, 167, 168
r 30.1(c)	167, 168
r 30.2	154, 168, 316
r 32	80, 155, 164, 169
r 32.1	148
r 32.3	148, 155
r 33	191, 317
r 33.2	317
r 33.3	50
r 34	50, 191
r 35	155
r 35(a)	50, 155, 182
r 35(b)	50, 182
r 36	155, 173, 182
r 37	153, 317
r 37.1	134, 153, 182
r 37.2	182
r 37.3	50, 155, 183
r 37.4	113, 135, 152, 183, 313, 314, 315
r 37.5	136, 183
r 38(a)	183, 184
r 38(b)	49, 183
r 38(c)	183
r 39	50
r 39.1	82, 137, 183, 184
r 39.2	82, 183, 184
r 40	50
r 40(a)	136, 169, 183
r 40(b)	113, 135, 136, 169, 183, 186
r 41(b), (c)	184
r 41(d)	78, 184
r 41(e)	184
r 42	161
r 42.1	153, 161
r 44	164, 165, 288
r 45	163
r 45.1	175
r 45.2	78, 79, 175
r 46	308
r 49	164, 299
r 49.2(a), (b)	167
r 50	164
r 50.1	166

r 50.2	164, 167
r 50.3	164
r 51	164, 168
r 52	164, 168, 169
r 53	308
r 55	164, 169
r 56.2	164, 168, 169
r 56.3, 56.4	164, 169
r 61	146, 175
r 61.1	146, 172
r 61.2	172, 174
r 62	317
r 63	174, 175, 288
r 63(a)–(j)	175
r 64	175
r 66	317
rr 67, 68	174, 176
r 69.1, 69.2	174, 177
r 70	308
r 75.2	131
r 75.3	112, 131, 170, 314
r 75.4	134
r 76	137, 173
r 76.3	138, 173, 314
r 77	138, 177
r 80	317
r 80.2	308
Pt 1 Ch 1 Section 6 (rr 85–98)	178
r 85	70, 178
r 85.1	178
rr 86, 87	178
r 88	317
r 88.1, 88.2	178
r 88.3	309
r 88.4	295
r 89	318
r 89.3, 89.4	179
r 90	179, 181
r 91	317
r 91.1, 91.2	179
r 92	180
r 93	317
r 93.1, 93.2	180
r 94	180, 317
r 95	180
r 96.2	180

l *Table of Legislation*

r 97	318
r 97.1	180
r 97.2	181, 309
r 97.4	51, 318
r 97.5	181, 258, 263
r 97.6	181
r 98	180, 181
rr 101–110	266
r 101.1	50, 184
r 101.3	184
rr 103–109	187
r 102	187
r 102.2	260
r 103	184
r 103.1	184
r 103.1(c)	223
r 103.2	186
r 104	81, 184
r 104(c)	136, 169
r 104(e)	150, 152, 165, 167, 176, 236, 239
r 104(f)	236, 239
r 104(g)	236
r 104(h)	136, 169, 189
r 104(i)	50
r 104(j)	185, 194
r 105	249
r 105.1–105.3	185
r 105.4	50
r 105.5	186
r 108	56, 189
rr 108–111	50
r 109	238
r 109.1–109.5	191
r 110.1, 110.2	186
r 110.3	180, 186
rr 111–116	201, 230
r 111	180, 267
r 112	267
r 112.2(b)	318
r 112.3	185, 191
r 112.4	50, 190
r 112.5	190
r 112.6	189, 190
r 113.1	50, 189
r 113.2	50, 190
r 113.3	189

r 114	190
r 115	180, 189, 249, 267
r 116	190, 195, 267
r 116.1–116.5	190
r 117	180, 190, 195, 267
r 118.1	194, 273
r 118.2	45, 313
r 118.2(a)	46, 82, 313, 314
r 118.2(b)	46, 183, 193
r 118.3	192
r 118.3(a)	82
r 118.4	46, 193, 318
r 118.5	194, 283
r 118.6	180, 185, 192
r 118.7	192
r 118.8	80, 82, 193
r 119	194, 273
r 125	273
r 126	274, 277
r 131	318
r 131.1	274
r 131.2	274, 275
r 131.2(d), (e)	274
r 132	274, 308
r 134	276
r 134.1, 134.2	274
r 134.4	318
r 135	276
r 135.1	274
r 135.2	275
r 136	275, 276, 315
r 137.2	275
rr 138, 139	275
r 140.1	275, 276
r 141	276
r 142.1–142.3	276
r 144.1(b)	277
r 144.2	277
r 150.1	82, 284
r 150.2	283
r 151	285, 318
r 152.1	301
r 152.2	284
r 155	82
r 156.1	286, 318
r 156.2, 156.3	286

r 157	260
r 158.1–158.4	286
r 159	286
Pt 2 – Evidence	204
r 170.1	150, 152, 167, 176, 205, 216, 220
r 170.2	205, 220
r 170.3	221
r 171.1, 171.2	221
r 172.1	222
r 172.2	223
r 173	246
r 175.1–175.3	238
r 176	237, 238
r 176.1	318
r 177	238
r 177.2	238
r 177.2(f)	238
r 178.1	239
r 178.5, 178.6	239
r 179	248
r 179.1, 179.2	237
r 179.3	250
r 179.4	237, 238
r 180.1	284
r 180.2	286
r 181.2(a), (b)	237
r 181 II(a), (b)	240
r 185.1	240
r 185.2, 185.3	241
r 185.4	242
r 185.4(c)	240
r 185.5, 185.6	242
r 185.7	242, 284
r 185.8	241
rr 186.1–186.5	241
r 186.6	240
r 186.7	241
r 190	234, 250, 318
r 190.1	226, 235, 248, 277
r 190.4	276
r 190.4(b)	248
r 190.5, 190.6	248
r 191	160, 234, 236, 248, 318
r 192	318
rr 192–198	228
rr 192–199	225, 227

r 192.1	233
r 192.2	229
r 192.2(b)	228
r 192.3	231, 232
r 193.1, 193.2	229
r 194	231
r 194.1	229, 232
r 194.1(a)(i)–(iii)	230
r 194.2(a)	230, 233
r 194.2(b), (c)	230
r 194.3	229
r 194.4	51, 229
r 194.5	230, 232, 250
r 195	203
r 195.2	230
r 195.3	203, 230
r 196.1	226, 228, 250
r 196.2, 196.3	226, 227
r 196.3(a)	233
r 196.3(b)	232
r 196.4, 196.5	233
r 196.6	234
r 197	318
r 197.1	199, 201, 202, 229, 230, 231
r 197.2	229, 231, 232
r 197.3	203, 229, 230, 232
r 197.4	203, 231, 232, 250
r 198	224, 234
r 198.1	187, 300
r 198.2	232, 274
r 199.1	250
r 199.2	228, 231
r 201	284
r 201.1	244
rr 201.2–201.7	245
Pt 3 – Provisional Measures	
r 205	198
r 205(b)	201
r 206	319
r 206.1	198, 214
r 206.2	198
r 206.2(d)	205
r 206.2(e)	204, 205
r 206.3	199, 200
r 206.4	199
r 206.5	199, 309

r 207	230
r 207.2	215
r 207.3	216
r 207.7	250
r 207.8	215, 216
r 208.1	200
r 208.2	198, 200
r 208.3	126, 198, 200
r 208.4	200
r 209	201
r 209.1	201
r 209.1(a)–(c)	200
r 209.2	114, 201, 202, 208
r 209.2(a)–(d)	201, 206
r 209.3	51, 201
r 209.4	201, 203, 250
r 209.5	201
r 210	201
r 210.1	201
r 210.2	201, 204
r 210.3, 210.4	201
r 211	206, 226
r 211.1	197, 198
r 211.1(d)	283
r 211.2	113, 199, 204, 205, 208
r 211.3	199, 204, 205, 206, 210
r 211.4	199, 204, 205
r 211.5	198
r 211.6	216
r 212	319
r 212.1, 212.2	201, 202
r 212.3	203
r 213.1	187, 214, 217, 300
r 213.2	217, 218, 274, 278

Pt 4 – Procedures Before the Court of Appeal

r 220	180, 196, 259, 311, 319
r 220.1	216, 226, 227, 308
r 220.1(a), (b)	258
r 220.1(c)	216, 258, 309
r 220.2	55, 141, 166, 188, 259, 260, 286, 310
r 220.3	259, 260, 319
r 220.4	51, 55, 259, 319
r 220.5	56, 267
r 221	309, 319
r 221.1	260
r 221.2	259

r 221.3	260
r 222	265, 267
r 222.2	55, 223, 263
r 223	51, 56, 260, 319
r 223.2–232.4	261
r 223.5	260
r 224.1	187, 262, 265, 266, 300
r 224.1(b)	217, 258
r 224.2	264
r 224.2(a), (b)	263, 265
r 225	261, 262
r 225(e)	263
r 226	263, 264
r 227	81, 262
r 227.1(a)	81, 262
r 228	262, 307, 309
r 229.1–229.3	262
r 230.1	262, 263
r 230.2	263
r 231	263
r 232	51
rr 232.1, 232.2	81
r 233	51, 264
r 233.2	51, 264
r 233.3	264
r 234.1–234.3	264
r 235.1	266
r 235.3	265
r 236.1, 236.2	265
r 237	266
r 237.1, 237.2	265
r 237.4	266
r 237.5	265
r 238	266
r 238A	266
r 238A.1	59
r 238A.2	55
r 239	51
r 239.1	266
r 239.2	51, 267
r 240	51, 267
r 241	267
r 242.1	58, 267
r 242.2(a)	58, 267
r 242.2(b)	59, 192, 267
r 243.1, 243.2	267

rr 245ff	268
r 245	269, 319
r 245.1	268
r 245.2(1)	268
rr 246–249	269
r 250	268, 269, 309
r 251	268
r 252	269
r 253.1	270
r 253.2	270, 319
r 255	319
r 255(a)	270
Pt 5 – General Provisions (rr 260–267)	
r 260.1	90
r 260.2	127
r 262	250, 319
r 262.1	50, 319
r 262.1(b)	249
r 262.2	150, 152, 153, 165, 167, 169, 176, 179, 249
r 262.3	249
r 262.4	319
r 262.5	250
r 262.6	249, 250
r 262.7	250
r 262A	150, 152, 153, 165, 167, 169, 176, 179, 250, 252
r 262A.1	250
r 262A.2–262A.5	252
r 263	319
r 263.1, 263.2	188
r 263.4, 263.5	188
r 264	193, 316
r 265	319
r 265.1	194
r 265.2(a)–(c)	194
r 266	7, 11, 41, 315
r 266.1–266.4	188
r 266.5	41, 188
Pt 5, Ch 2 – Service (rr 270–279)	147, 287
r 270.1	147, 287
r 271	153
r 271.1(a)	287
r 271.1(b), (c)	288
r 271.3	288
r 271.4(a), (b)	288
r 271.4(c)	289
r 271.5	288

r 271.6(a)	289
r 271.6(b)	288, 289
r 271.7, 271.8	288
r 272.1–272.3	289
r 274.1	289
r 274.1(a)	290
r 274.1(a)(i)	289
r 274.1(a)(ii)	290
r 274.1(a)(iii)	289
r 274.1(b)	290
r 274.2	290
r 275	289, 319
r 275.2–275.4	290
r 276.1	290
r 278.1	291
r 278.3(a), (b)	291
r 279	288
r 284	297
r 286	255
r 286.1	255, 295, 296
rr 287–289	248
r 287	255
r 287.1, 287.2	253
r 287.3	254
r 287.4	253
r 287.5	253, 256
r 287.6	297
r 287.6(a), (b)	255
r 289.1	298
r 289.3	299
r 289.5	299
r 290.2	297
r 291.1–291.2	298
r 292.1–292.2	297
r 293	298
r 294	295
r 295	314
r 295(a)	313, 314
r 295(b)	314
r 295(c)(i)	314
r 295(c)(ii)	315
r 295(d)	315
r 295(e)	313, 314, 315
r 295(f)	314
r 295(g)	313, 314, 315
r 295(h)–(m)	315

r 296.1–296.3	313
rr 297, 298	313
r 300(a)	298
r 300(b)–(g)	299
r 302.1	127, 146, 291
r 302.3	127, 146, 291
r 303.1, 303.2	146, 291
r 303.3	291
r 305	294, 320
r 305.1	291
r 305.1(c)	161, 172, 316
r 305.3	292
r 306	292
r 310	315, 320
r 310.1–310.3	292
r 311.1, 311.2	292, 315
r 311.3, 311.4	292
r 312.1–312.3	294
rr 313–317	146
r 313	320
r 313.1	146, 293
r 313.2	293
r 313.4	293
r 314	293
r 315.2	250
r 315.3–315.4	293
r 316	147
r 316.1	293
r 316.3	147, 292
r 316A	147
r 316A.1–316A.2	294
r 317	293
r 320	320
r 320.1	300
r 320.2	300, 309
r 320.3	300
r 320.7	300
r 321	80, 83, 320
r 322	81, 83, 320
r 323	83, 320
rr 331–40	147
r 332	57
r 332(h)	134
r 332(l)	134
r 333	320
r 333.1	57, 187, 260

r 333.2	188
r 333.3	309
r 333.4	188
r 334	187
r 335	188
rr 336, 337	187, 320
r 340	127, 187
r 340.1	173
r 343.1, 343.2	56
r 344.1–344.3	56
r 345.3	263
r 345.4	49
r 345.5	50, 51, 229
r 345.6	310
r 345.8	51, 263
r 346	49, 315
r 352	193, 275, 320
r 352.2	194
r 353	193, 321
r 354	282
r 354.2	193, 194, 218, 278
r 354.3, 354.4	193
r 355	286, 310
r 355.1	195
r 355.1(a)	195
r 355.1(b)	190, 195
r 355.2, 355.3	195
r 356	179, 195, 321
r 356.1	195
r 356.2	309
r 356.3	195
r 357	81, 262
r 360	195, 321
r 361	195
r 362	195, 321
r 363	196
r 365.1	196
r 365.2	196, 250
r 365.3, 365.4	196
Pt 6 – Fees and Legal Aid	307
r 370	274, 300
r 370.4	300
r 370.5	300, 311, 312
r 375	300
r 375(a)	300
r 375(b)(i)–(v)	300

r 376.1 300
r 376.1(c) 301
r 376.2 301
r 377 321
r 377.2–377.3...301
r 377A.1–377A.3..302
r 378 295
r 378.2 302
r 378.3(a), (b) 302
r 378A.2 303
r 379.2–379.5...303
r 379.6 301
r 379.7–379.10 303
r 379A 303
r 380 304
r 380.1 321
r 380.3 304
r 381.1–381.2...304
r 382 301
r 382.2 304
Rules on Court Fees and Recoverable Costs of the Preparatory
  Committee, 25 February 2016 ....283, 284, 285, 310, 311
  s A.6..311
  s A.7..305
  s A.8..310
  s A.9(d) 310
  s A.9(e)...311
  Art 1(3) 284
  Art 2(1), (2) 284
  Art 2(3), (4)...285
Treaty of Lisbon 1 December 2009 3
Treaty on European Union (TEU) 41, 342, 387
  Art 3(3)...322
  Art 4(3) 342
  Art 5 338
  Art 20 12
Treaty on the Functioning of the European Union (TFEU).......... 41, 342, 387
  Art 118.. 322, 335, 336
  Art 118(2)...5, 326
  Arts 258–260... 342, 351
  Art 267 .... 41, 342, 350
  Arts 326 ff..12
  Art 333(1)..327
  Art 342...338
  Protocol 7 – Protocol on the privileges and immunities of the
    European Union 378

TABLE OF OTHER MATERIALS

Administrative Committee Table of Court Fees AC /05/08072022_E – section 1.II 150
EPLC draft Decision of the Administrative Committee, Rules of the European
    Patent Litigation Certificate and Other Appropriate Qualifications Pursuant
    to Article 48(2) of the Agreement on a Unified Patent Court, agreed
    3 September 2015 296
    rr 11, 12 297
    Explanatory Memorandum to the Draft Decision of the Administrative
        Committee, Rules of the European Patent Litigation Certificate and
        Other Appropriate Qualifications 297
Guidelines for Examination in the EPO 43

Introduction

I. A Short History of the Unified Patent Court and the Unitary Patent

A. The Problem with Patents

Patent rights are national in scope – their protection ends at the borders of the country in which they are registered. Even if patents are registered in every country necessary to cover the commercially important markets in which a product is sold or a process is used, differences in national patent laws or their interpretation by national courts may be encountered. These can prove significant: the difference between an infringement in one country and not in another; or the invalidity of a patent in one country and not in another. Preparing to contend with the differences in national patent regimes, either as a patent owner or a competing third party, can require the services of patent attorneys and patent lawyers in every country of commercial significance, which can incur a large cost in terms of time and money.

    How then can these differences be mitigated so as to allow businesses to operate more smoothly and cost-effectively across borders?

    At a substantive level, even before the Agreement on Trade-Related Aspects of Intellectual Property Rights (TRIPS) was negotiated, the issue had been a decades-long concern for the European countries (including, but not limited to, the European Union (EU) Member States). Although the European countries maintain their own national courts and legislatures, pan-European treaty instruments have provided a basis for the harmonisation of national patent validity and infringement law rules. These first took shape with the introduction of the European Patent Convention (EPC), which came into force on 7 October 1977.[1] The EPC provided, amongst other things, for the central grant by the European Patent Office (EPO) of European patents protecting national territories. The latter rules were provided by the Convention for the European Patent for the Common Market,[2] often referred to as the Community Patent Convention 1973 (CPC 1973), which was signed on 15 December 1975 by the nine Member States at that time. The CPC 1973 was never fully ratified and it was not until 14 years later that another attempt to revive it was made in the form of the Agreement Relating to Community Patents,[3] more commonly referred to as the Community Patent Convention 1989 (CPC 1989). Much like its predecessor, although

---

[1] For the first participating countries, Belgium, France, Luxembourg, the Netherlands, Switzerland, the UK and (the former) West Germany.
[2] 76/76 EEC OJ L17/1, 26 January 1976.
[3] 89/695/EEC OJ L401, 15 December 1989.

2   Introduction

this Agreement was signed, it was never fully ratified and did not come into force,[4] but it remains the model for the statutory acts of infringement in many European countries.

The EU itself has also provided harmonising and directly effective legislation of a narrower scope. The experience of national courts is that out of this legislation, the most likely to give rise to referrals is Regulation 469/2009 of 6 May 2009 concerning the supplementary protection certificate for medicinal products (hereinafter the 'SPC Regulation'). However, other EU instruments relevant to patent matters include: Article 10(6) of Directive 2001/83 of 6 November 2001 on the Community code relating to medicinal products for human use (the 'Bolar Exemption' is the name commonly given to Article 10(6), which is also known as the regulatory review defence); Regulation (EU) 1610/96 of 23 July 1996 concerning the creation of a supplementary protection certificate for plant protection products (hereinafter the 'Plant Products SPC Regulation'); and Directive 98/44/EC of 6 July 1998 on the legal protection of biotechnological inventions (hereinafter the 'Biotechnology Directive').

The EPO has also had some centralising role, of course, allowing central amendment or revocation. The EPO thus has a direct impact on the national registers. Moreover, in the process of their decision making, the Technical Board of Appeal (TBA) and Enlarged Board of Appeal (EBA) have built up a significant body of case law, which has varying degrees of influence in the national courts.[5]

However, the EPO is essentially an administrative body for granting patents, with associated and quasi-judicial functions of opposition and appeal. Its role is therefore limited and, most significantly, it is not a forum for enforcement. Therefore, whilst the signatories of the EPC (and, within that group, the EU Member States) share very similar substantive laws at the statutory level, it is still not unusual for different national courts to come to different decisions when presented with cases arising from the same or similar facts. This is despite the fact that although they are not obliged to do so,[6] European judges of the higher instance courts frequently take notice of each other's judgments. And, where it is possible to do so, they will be consistent with the decisions of each other.[7]

B. The Proposed Solution

The reason why national decisions in parallel cases – that is, concerning the equivalent European patent – continue to differ are complex. However, there are three particular difficulties faced when trying to achieve consistency of decision making between national courts: first, procedural differences in the national European systems can present foreign judges with different evidence by which to assess the facts; second, there are differences in the implementation of international instruments in national law; and, third, there are differences in the way in which the national courts interpret those laws. The proposed

---

[4] The Agreement was signed by 12 states, but only seven ratified it.
[5] See, for instance, Lord Hoffmann in *Merrell Dow Pharmaceuticals Inc v HN Norton & Co Ltd* [1995] UKHL 14 (26 October 1995).
[6] The Supreme Court in *Schutz (UK) Ltd v Werit (UK) Ltd* [2013] UKSC 16, para 40.
[7] See, for instance, *Grimme Maschinenfabrik GmbH & Co KG v Derek Scott (t/a Scotts Potato Machinery)* [2010] EWCA Civ 1110; and *Actavis UK Ltd v Eli Lilly & Co* [2017] UKSC 48 (12 July 2017).

answer to resolving these sources of inconsistency is the Unified Patent Court (UPC) and the European patent having unitary effect (Unitary Patent) system.

The rules governing the constitution of judicial panels in the UPC are designed to achieve convergence in the approach to procedural rules, convergence of the substantive law applied and, as a result, consistency in judicial decision making. The rules by which judges are assigned to the panels of the local, regional and central divisions of the UPC Court of First Instance and the Court of Appeal are designed to achieve consistency of quality in decision making and in the application of substantive and procedural law. They do so by providing for a mix of national legal experience. The expertise of existing national patent judges is particularly important to the UPC. Those contracting Member States that have an average number of fewer than 50 patent cases per year over a consecutive period of three years will have only one local judge per panel of three in a local division. The remaining seats on the panel will be occupied by judges foreign to the division but allocated from the international pool of judges, recruited from across the contracting states to the UPC. This allows more experienced judges to be in the majority where they are most needed. These judges can be expected to share their expertise with judges from countries where patent cases are rare or who have had no experience of patent matters prior to sitting in the UPC. In reviewing the law applied in first instance decisions, the Court of Appeal and, exceptionally, the Full Court are thus expected to establish a body of case law that provides an increasingly uniform approach to patent law for a large part of Europe over time. To maximise harmonisation, there is only one Court of Appeal.

The idea of a single, *pan*-European patent protecting all territories in what was then the European Economic Community dates back to the CPC 1973. So why has it taken so long? A flavour of the difficulties that have been encountered can be had by picking up the story from 20 years ago.

C. The Community Patent

In March 2000, the Lisbon Summit of the European Council proclaimed that the EU[8] would be the largest knowledge-based economy by 2010. A new EU-wide system was therefore proposed as a means to ensure that this economy would be adequately served in Europe by the use of patents. To this end, in August 2000, the European Commission published a fresh proposal for the creation of a Community Patent (CP).[9] The CP would have cost-effective translation arrangements and would be effective across all 15 Member States (as they were at the time) as a single, pan-European right. In addition, a Community Patent Court (CPC) was proposed, which would be granted powers to revoke or enforce CPs across the EU. This court would be attached to the European Court of Justice and the Court of First Instance (as they were known at the time).[10] This proposal failed to gain unanimity of support,[11] but was followed in 2003 by further discussions that culminated in a 'common political approach'

---

[8] Brought into effect by the Maastricht Treaty on 1 November 1993.
[9] Proposal for a Council Regulation on the Community patent, COM (2000) 412, 1 August 2000.
[10] These were renamed the Court of Justice and the General Court (collectively the Court of Justice of the European Union) following the entry into force of the Treaty of Lisbon on 1 December 2009.
[11] See the press release of the 2389th Council meeting, 14400/01, 26 November 2001.

4   Introduction

agreed by the Council of Ministers.[12] The common political approach had settled on a proposal to translate the claims of the Unitary Patent, but not the body of the specification, into all official EU languages.[13] However, following the EU enlargement on 1 May 2004, nine new official EU languages were added.[14] As a result, concern arose that this was an unworkable and costly procedure that would not be used. There were also concerns about the detail of how the CPC would operate. Consequently, the project lost momentum and talks stalled in 2004.[15]

D. The European Patent Litigation Agreement

In parallel to the discussions about the Commission's proposal of 2000, another attempt was being made to establish a single, European patent system. At an Intergovernmental Conference in Paris in 25 June 1999, the contracting states of the EPO set up a Working Party on Litigation to draft an optional protocol to the EPC. This protocol would commit its signatory states to an integrated judicial system to deal with infringement and revocation actions concerning European patents. The system envisaged that contracting states would cede their own national jurisdictions to deal with patent enforcement and validity matters to a centralised European Patent Court, which would have a pan-European jurisdiction, subject to certain limitations. Beginning with discussions in 2003, the Working Party produced a final draft European Patent Litigation Agreement (EPLA) in September 2005. In broad terms, the EPLA proposed a specialised pool of judges, panels of whom would sit in Courts of First Instance and Appeal, with a central division and regional divisions. For translation issues, the EPLA adopted the Agreement on the Application of Article 65 EPC (London Agreement).[16] Parties would be able to agree to hold the proceedings before the European Patent Court regional divisions in a language of their choosing, although the central division would hold proceedings in the EPO languages.

However, the EPLA project was shelved after the EU made it clear in 2007 that EU Member States could not contract together to form the EPLA outside of EU governance.

E. The Unified Patent Litigation System

i. The Proposal

In January 2006 the European Commission again sought to revive the single European patent project, described by Charlie McCreevy, the EU internal market commissioner, as 'one final effort' – by launching a public consultation on the CP, and improvements to the European patent system in general. A White Paper entitled *Enhancing the Patent System*

---

[12] Council Document 6874/03.
[13] The official EU languages at the time were: Danish, Dutch, English, Finnish, French, German, modern Greek, Italian, Portuguese, Spanish and Swedish.
[14] Czech, Estonian, Hungarian, Latvian, Lithuanian, Maltese, Polish, Slovak and Slovenian.
[15] See the press release of the 2570th Council meeting, 6648/04, 11 March 2004.
[16] Concluded at the Intergovernmental Conference held in London on 17 October 2000 (see OJ EPO 2001, 549).

in Europe followed in April of the following year.[17] This outlined a unified patent litigation system (UPLS), with a court called the European and European Union Patents Court (EEUPC) at its centre. The first draft Agreement for this court, which included the EU as a party, was produced in 2008. Furthermore, a revised proposal was made for a Community Patent Regulation.[18] By December 2009, the EU Council had unanimously agreed on the key elements of the UPLS and (by then) the EU patent,[19] which would be integrated into the existing EPC system of prosecution and granting of European patents. In essence, the proposal provided that the EU accede to the EPC, allowing the EPO to grant EU patents as well as European patents, and to set up an EU patent court to hear disputes relating to both forms of patent.

The UPLS proposals provided for the language of the proceedings to be that in which the patent was granted or one of the three official languages of the EPO. Any cases heard before the central division would be heard in the language in which the patent was granted. However, contracting states might designate one or more of the official languages of the EPO to be the language(s) of proceedings in their local courts or the official language of that state. However, the Council agreement on the outline of the UPLS did not cover the translation arrangements for the Unitary Patent, which would require separate legislation.[20]

ii. Languages

As a result, in parallel to the EU Patent and EEUPC proposals, in June 2010 the European Commission proposed a Council Regulation on the translation arrangements for the Unitary Patent.[21] The aim of the Regulation was to set up translation arrangements that are cost-effective, simplified and ensure legal certainty. According to this proposal, which kept to the arrangements in the 2008 proposal for a Community Patent Regulation, the EU patent would be examined and granted in one of the official languages of the EPO. In addition, the granted patent would be published in the language of the proceedings – forming the authentic, legally binding text – and the publication would include translations of the claims into the other two EPO official languages. No validations in the Member States would be required to enforce the patent throughout the EU and no further translations would be required by the patent proprietor, the exception being in the case of a legal dispute concerning the EU patent. In these circumstances, the patent proprietor might be required to provide a full translation into the language of the litigation at its own expense.

This proposal required the unanimous support of all 27 Member States to come into effect, but not all 27 could agree on the proposed language regime; in particular, there was vociferous opposition by Italy and Spain to the EU patent and its proposed trilingual system. Consequently, 12 Member States made formal requests to the European Commission expressing the wish to use enhanced cooperation for the purpose of establishing the creation of EU patent protection and its associated translation arrangements. Use of this procedure

---

[17] Communication from the Commission to the European Parliament and the Council, COM (2007) 165.
[18] Council Document 9465/08.
[19] Council Documents 17229/09 and 16113/09.
[20] Pursuant to Article 118(2) of the Treaty on the Functioning of the European Union.
[21] COM (2010) 350, 30 June 2010.

would enable the Regulations for the proposed patent and its language regime to proceed without the support of the dissenting nations.

iii. *The Court of Justice Says 'No' to UPLS*

On 6 July 2009, in parallel to discussions concerning the UPLS, the Council of the European Union made a request to the Court of Justice of the European Union (CJEU), as it was known by this time, for an opinion on whether the envisaged system would be compatible with EU law. Dealing a blow to the project, the CJEU stated in *Opinion 1/09*[22] that the UPLS proposals were not compatible with EU law. The reasoning for the decision was summarised as follows:

> Consequently, the envisaged agreement, by conferring on an international court which is outside the institutional and judicial framework of the European Union an exclusive jurisdiction to hear a significant number of actions brought by individuals in the field of the Community patent and to interpret and apply European Union law in that field, would deprive courts of the Member States of their powers in relation to the interpretation and application of European Union law and the Court of its powers to reply, by preliminary ruling, to questions referred by those courts and, consequently, would alter the essential character of the powers which the Treaties confer on the institutions of the European Union and on the Member States and which are indispensable to the preservation of the very nature of European Union law.[23]

In other words, the Member States could not, as part of the EU order, divest to the UPLS, an international body, their powers to apply EU law and, if necessary, to refer questions to the CJEU.

F. The Unified Patent Court and the Unitary Patent

Two days after the CJEU's decision ruling the UPLS incompatible with EU law, the European Council authorised the use of the enhanced cooperation procedure to adopt, as it was being referred to by this stage, the Unitary Patent.[24] This was followed in April 2011 by the European Commission's publication of a 'Proposal for a Regulation implementing enhanced cooperation in the area of the creation of unitary patent protection'[25] and a 'Proposal for a Regulation implementing enhanced cooperation in the area of the creation of unitary patent protection with regard to the applicable translation arrangements'.[26] Shortly afterwards in October 2011, a draft Agreement on a UPC was published by the European Commission, which sought to avoid the problems identified by CJEU Opinion 1/09. In particular, the draft Agreement had been amended to state that the UPC is 'a court common to the Contracting Member States', as well as being an international court, such that Member States are deemed responsible for the application of EU law. The obligation to make a preliminary reference

---

[22] *Opinion 1/09 – Agreement on the Establishment of a Unified Patent Litigation System* [2011] ECR I-01137 (8 March 2011).
[23] ibid para 109.
[24] Council Decision 2011/167.
[25] COM (2011) 215 final, 13 April 2011.
[26] ibid.

to the CJEU on the interpretation of all sources of EU law, where it is considered necessary, was also imposed on the Court of Appeal of the UPC.[27]

By 1 December 2011, the draft text of the Regulations for the Unitary Patent and its translation arrangements had been agreed at a political level by the Legal Affairs Committee of the European Parliament. On 5 and 6 December 2011, the Competitiveness Council of the European Union met to agree the key points of the Unitary Patent, the translation arrangements and the draft Agreement for the UPC. However, the issue of the location of the Central Division remained a major outstanding matter following the agreement of December 2011.

The solution to this problem came in the form of the surprising news that emerged from a meeting of the European Council of 29 June 2012: the UPC would have the seat of its central division in Paris, but with further sections in London and Munich. The London section of the central division would take jurisdiction for patents with 'life sciences, chemistry and human necessities' subject matter, while Munich would be responsible for advanced mechanical engineering, with Paris responsible for all other subject matter, including computer electronics and telecommunications. The Court of Appeal would be in Luxembourg. Perhaps more significantly, the official summary of the Conclusions of the European Council Meeting on 28 and 29 June contained this statement:

> We suggest that Articles 6 to 8 of the Regulation implementing enhanced cooperation in the area of the creation of unitary patent protection to be adopted by the Council and the European Parliament be deleted.

Article 6 had defined a direct infringement of a Unitary Patent, Article 7 an indirect infringement and Article 8 the limits on rights conferred by the Unitary Patent. The 'suggestion' being proposed was therefore that the draft Unitary Patent Regulation should be amended to remove the jurisdiction of the CJEU for matters of patent infringement.

Within a few days of the European Council's decision that these Articles should be deleted, the European Parliament responded that the removal of Articles 6–8 to reduce the CJEU's power to enforce Unitary Patents 'infringes EU law' and would result in a further reference to the CJEU about the validity of the patent package. This never happened and negotiations for a compromise continued in private in the following months. Finally, on 11 December 2012, the European Parliament issued the following statement:

> After over 30 years of talks, a new regime will cut the cost of an EU patent by up to 80%, making it more competitive vis-à-vis the US and Japan. MEPs cut costs for small firms and tailored the regime to their needs, in a compromise deal with the Council endorsed by Parliament on Tuesday.

Regulation 1257/2012 of the European Parliament and of the Council of 17 December 2012 implementing enhanced cooperation in the area of the creation of unitary patent protection and Regulation 1260/2012 of 17 December 2012 implementing enhanced cooperation in the area of the creation of unitary patent protection with regard to the applicable translation arrangements had been agreed. Then, on 19 February 2013, the representatives of 24 EU Member State governments met in Brussels to sign the Agreement on a Unified Patent Court, setting up the most radical change to the European patent system since the European Patent Convention (EPC) was introduced in 1977.

---

[27] Rule 266 of the Rules of Procedure. This remains discretionary at the level of first instance.

8 Introduction

Finally, at its 11th meeting in Brussels on 1 October 2015, the UPC Preparatory Committee agreed the Provisional Application Protocol, allowing a 'provisional operation' period for the UPC, allowing the appointment of judges, a Registrar and other key roles, the recording of opt-outs of European patents and further ratifications of the UPC Agreement by Contracting Member States, ahead of the formal opening of the court.

The legislative foundations for the new UPC and the Unitary Patent system thus consist of three principal instruments:[28]

1. Council Regulation (EU) No 1257/2012 of the European Parliament and of the Council of 17 December 2012, implementing enhanced cooperation in the area of the creation of unitary patent protection (hereinafter the 'UP Regulation').
2. Council Regulation (EU) No 1260/2012 of the European Parliament and of the Council of 17 December 2012 implementing enhanced cooperation in the area of the creation of unitary patent protection with regard to the applicable translation arrangements (hereinafter the 'Translation Regulation').
3. The Agreement on a Unified Patent Court, signed on 19 February 2013 (hereinafter the 'UPC Agreement').

II. The UK Referendum on Leaving the EU and its Consequences

In the wake of the UK referendum decision to leave the EU (Brexit) announced on 24 June 2016, a number of questions were immediately raised about the future of the UPC and the Unitary Patent. In particular, there were doubts that the UK would ratify the UPC Agreement, given that it is subject to rulings of the CJEU and that it would bind the UK to further EU law in the form of the Unitary Patent. It was therefore a surprise that Baroness Neville-Rolfe, UK Minister of State for Energy and Intellectual Property, stated at a meeting of the EU Competitive Council on 28 November that the UK would ratify the UPC Agreement.

Questions remained about the details of how the UK could continue to participate in the UPC and the Unitary Patent after Brexit. A particular issue was whether *Opinion 1/09* of the CJEU (see above) precluded the participation of non-EU Member States, as thought by the European Commission when the UPC Agreement in its current form was drafted.[29] The alternative view was that the UK might participate, provided it agreed safeguards to ensure the supremacy and uniformity of EU law. In particular, it had been observed[30] that *Opinion 1/09* does not expressly say that non-EU Member States are excluded from participation. Moreover, an interpretation that this was the implicit effect of the Opinion would

---

[28] The details of the procedure of the UPC cannot be encompassed by the Agreement. Article 41 of the Agreement therefore provides that the Rules of Procedure will lay down the details of the proceedings of the UPC.

[29] See 'Non-paper of the Commission Services' attached to Note from the Presidency to the Council (Doc 10630/11).

[30] Re the Effect of 'Brexit' on the Unitary Patent Regulation and the UPC Agreement, Opinion, Richard Gordon QC and Tom Pascoe, Brick Court Chambers, 12 September 2016, paras 50–71.

have the effect that the UPC itself, in its present form, would be unlawful. This was thought to be because the UPC, as an international court, is itself outside the EU legal order.[31] There is also CJEU authority to the effect that there is no objection to the application of EU law outside the Member State territories.[32]

As regards the Unitary Patent, a number of commentators argued that the UK would be permitted to participate after Brexit, provided that an international agreement for that purpose could be concluded, further to Article 142 EPC:

> Any group of Contracting States [of the EPC], which has provided by a special agreement that a European patent granted for those States has a unitary character throughout their territories, may provide that a European patent may only be granted jointly in respect of all those States.

However, an agreement that incorporates EU law in this way would also have to contain safeguards sufficient to ensure the uniform application of its provision throughout the Member States.[33] This would appear to require the exact replication of the wording of the UP Regulation, including such provisions as the exhaustion of rights, in order to ensure the consistent scope and effect of the Unitary Patent across the territories. According to this view, obligations to make preliminary references to the CJEU, to respect the primacy of EU law and to comply with CJEU judgments would also be required.

Therefore, it has been argued[34] that in order to participate in the UPC and the Unitary Patent, in addition to amendments being made to the UPC Agreement itself, it would be necessary for the UK to agree to comply with three elements of EU constitutional law arising from *Opinion 1/09*: respect for the supremacy of EU law (as regards disputes before the UPC); the possibility of claiming damages and/or instituting infringement proceedings for breach of EU law; and uniformity through the making of preliminary references. Yet this need for such an agreement was not universally accepted. This is because participation in the UPC Agreement arguably already required the contracting parties to submit to EU law in its entirety as regards disputes in the UPC.[35] It was also remarked that the UK would need to participate in an arrangement for the UK recognition and enforcement of judgments made by the UPC.[36]

All of the above arguments became academic when on 28 February 2020, it was made known by the UK government that the UK would not participate in the UPC after all; post-Brexit, it simply did not want to sign up to an agreement that would allow the referral of cases affecting UK rights to the CJEU. The result is that the UK sits outside the UPC jurisdictionally, but remains connected to it as a strategic forum in Europe.

---

[31] The example is given of the European Free Trade Agreement (EFTA) Court. According to Opinion 1/92, European Court of Justice, 10 April 1992 (ECLI:EU:C:1992:189), the EFTA Court is lawful, in particular because it provides sufficient safeguards to protect the supremacy and uniformity of EU law.
[32] Opinion 1/00, 18 April 2002 (ECLI:EU:C:2002:231).
[33] Richard Gordon QC and Tom Pascoe (n 29) para 46.
[34] ibid paras 72–91.
[35] Professor Dr Ansgar Ohly, lecture at the European Judges' Forum, San Servolo, Venice, 28 November 2016; Professor Dr Winfried Tilmann, 'Unitary Patent and UPC: The Way Forward', EPLAW Congress and General Assembly, 25 November 2016.
[36] Gordon and Pascoe (n 29) para 122. This is on the basis that by leaving the EU, the UK also leaves the amended Regulation (EU) 1215/2012 of the European Parliament and of the Council of 12 December 2012 on jurisdiction and the recognition and enforcement of judgments in civil and commercial matters (recast).

III. Challenges in Germany

A. The First Decision (2020)

Following the filing of a constitutional action by a private individual that put the UPC project as a whole at a standstill for many months, the German Federal Constitutional Court in its decision of 13 February 2020 (and published on 20 March 2020) decided that Article 1(1) of the Act of Approval to the UPC Agreement (hereinafter the 'Act of Approval') was unconstitutional and thus void because of lack of the necessary majority. Otherwise, the Court dismissed the constitutional complaint as inadmissible. In its decision, the Federal Constitutional Court also stated that the Convention is open exclusively to EU Member States.

i. *Necessary Majority*

The German Federal Constitutional Court held that the constitutional complaint in question was inadmissible in its major parts. However, the complainant had the right to sovereign powers being conferred only in the forms provided for by the Basic Law (so-called review of the formal aspects of conferral). In particular, a two-thirds majority in parliament had to be achieved for a conferral of sovereign powers. Since these formal requirements were not adhered to in the legislative process for the Act of Approval, the complainant's right equivalent to a fundamental right to democratic self-determination under Articles 38(1), 20(1) and (2) and 79(3) of the Basic Law had been violated and the Act was therefore null and void.

Although the draft of the Act of Approval was unanimously adopted in its third reading on 10 March 2017, only 35 Members of Parliament were present at that time. Therefore, the required qualified majority was not achieved. An act of approval to an international treaty that has been adopted in violation of the constitutionally prescribed procedures violates the citizens' right equivalent to a fundamental right to democratic self-determination derived from Articles 38(1), 20(1) and (2), and 79(3) of the Basic Law. If sovereign rights are not conferred in the procedures provided by the Basic Law, they are not transferred at all. However, without an effective conferral of sovereign powers, each subsequent measure issued by the EU or a supranational organisation would lack democratic legitimation. Therefore, citizens can demand that sovereign powers be conferred only in the forms provided for by the Basic Law. This 'review of the formal aspects of conferral' is derived from the principle of democracy and serves to secure democratic influence in the process of European integration.

Judges König, Langenfeld and Maidowski did not agree with this view and stated in a dissenting opinion that the 'right to democracy' does not give rise to a right to review the formal aspects of conferral. Such a right would lead to a fundamental extension of the rights derived from Article 38(1) of the Basic Law that fails to recognise its substance and limits.

However, the creation of this 'review of the formal aspects of conferral' has met with considerable resistance even within the senate of the Federal Constitutional Court. This review did not serve to protect the right to democracy from a disempowerment of the Parliament, but was a general control of legality. However, the substance of the right to democracy was not encroached upon by a mere formal error.

ii. A Question on the Unconditional Primacy of EU Law

The German Federal Constitutional Court did not decide whether the determination of the unconditional primacy of EU law in Article 20 UPC Agreement violates Article 20(1) and (2) in conjunction with Article 79(3) of the German Basic Law (the German Constitution). This question has been left open by the Federal Constitutional Court, since the unconstitutionality and nullity of the law already result from the formal constitutional requirements.

In particular, it rejected the complaint as inadmissible on the grounds of lack of authority to file a complaint, insofar as the complainant alleged a possible violation of his right under Article 38(1) in conjunction with Article 20(1) and (2) and Article 79(3) of the Basic Law. The claimant alleged that the legal status of judges of the UPC would have been insufficiently regulated under the rule of law, that encroachments on fundamental rights by the UPC would not be sufficiently legitimised by law and finally that the UPC Agreement would violate EU law. Regardless of the inadmissibility, the German Federal Constitutional Court commented on these three issues in its decision:

i) The complainant stated that there is a lack of a sufficiently specific legal basis for the appointment and selection of the judges of the UPC. Moreover, the encroachments on fundamental rights entailed by the jurisdiction of the UPC could not be legitimised for lack of parliamentary involvement. The complainant claimed that this also violated his right to democratic self-determination derived from Article 38(1) of the Basic Law.

ii) On the second point raised by the complainant, the German Federal Constitutional Court considered the democratic legitimacy to be ensured by the fact that Germany has an equal say in the decisions of the administrative committee and that these decisions require a three-quarters majority. In addition, Germany is granted the right of veto on revisions of the UPC Agreement. Moreover, the activity of the Administrative Committee is always tied back to Parliament in accordance with Article 23 of the Constitution. Furthermore, neither the competences nor the regulations concerning the procedure of the UPC (Articles 52 ff UPC Agreement) and its authority to decide can be changed or extended by the Administrative Committee. Starting points for a concretisation of the maximum amount for the reimbursement of costs can be derived from the fact that the costs to be reimbursed must be 'reasonable and appropriate' according to Article 69 UPC Agreement and a fair balance between the interests of the parties must be guaranteed. Therefore, the appellant's right of appeal is also lacking in this respect.

iii) Third, an infringement of the complainant's right under Article 38 I 1 of the Basic Law on account of infringements of EU law by the UPC Agreement is precluded from the outset. EU law does not provide formal or substantive requirements for national laws, the infringement of which necessarily results in their invalidity. Moreover, according to the established case law of the Federal Constitutional Court, EU law does not have any priority of validity over German law, but only a priority of application. This means that a violation of EU law does not lead to the invalidity of the national provision and does not automatically entail a violation of the Constitution. Nor does the principle that the Basic Law should be interpreted in an EU-law friendly way mean that EU law itself becomes a constitutional yardstick.

12 Introduction

iii. The UPC Only for EU Member States

Paragraph 150 of the Decision contains the interesting observation that the UPC Agreement is open only to EU Member States. The Federal Constitutional Court refers to Article 1(2) UPC Agreement, which defines the UPC in this respect as a 'common court of the contracting member states'. In this respect, the term 'contracting member state' pursuant to Article 2(b) and (c) UPC Agreement refers to an EU Member State which is a contracting party to this agreement.

The fact that, on the other hand, not all EU Member States are also contracting Member States of the UPC Agreement is confirmed by the Institute of Enhanced Cooperation pursuant to Article 20 of the Treaty in European Union (TEU) and Articles 326 ff of the Treaty on the Functioning of the European Union (TFEU) and does not, in the opinion of the Federal Constitutional Court, call into question that the UPC Agreement is supplementary to or otherwise closely tied to the EU's integration agenda. Rather, this underlines the close interlocking with the institutional structure of the EU.

iv. The Second Decision (2021)

There has been great political support from the German government, in particular the Ministry of Justice, which immediately after the first decision of the German Federal Constitutional Court prepared the second vote on the Act of Approval. On 26 November 2020, the German Parliament again approved the Federal Government's draft law on the UPC Agreement. In a roll-call vote, 571 Members of Parliament voted in favour of the bill, 73 voted against, with three abstentions. A two-thirds majority of 473 votes was required. Subsequently, and according to German legislative procedure, the law then still had to be executed by the Federal President.

Against this second ratification bill, two further constitutional complaints, combined with requests for provisional orders, were filed.[37] The German Constitutional Court dismissed the requests for provisional orders on 23 June 2021 for inadmissibility because the claimants had not sufficiently substantiated a possible violation of their fundamental rights. In particular, they failed to demonstrate why and how the UPC Agreement, in its organisational structuring of the UPC and in the legal status afforded to judges, could violate the principle of the rule of law enshrined in Article 20, para 3 of the German Constitution (Grundgesetz) in a manner that would also encroach upon the principle of democracy.[38]

With this decision, the UPC was finally placed on the final stretch to opening.

IV. Current Participants in the UPC and the Unitary Patent System

As explained above, due to the interpretation of Opinion 1/09 by the European Commission, all contracting Member States to the EPC which are not also EU Member States were

---

[37] See https://www.bundesverfassungsgericht.de/SharedDocs/Entscheidungen/DE/2021/06/rs20210623_2bvr221620.html;jsessionid=0B3AD4C1F161694151DE93BC3D885FB0.2_cid344.
[38] The decision in English translation can be found at: https://www.bundesverfassungsgericht.de/SharedDocs/Entscheidungen/EN/2021/06/rs20210623_2bvr221620en.html.

Current Participants in the UPC and the Unitary Patent System

excluded from contracting to the UPC Agreement. Of the 27 EU Member States, Spain, Poland, Hungary and the Czech Republic have declined either to sign or ratify the UPC Agreement, meaning that they cannot participate in the UPC or the Unitary Patent. Croatia has yet to sign either the UPC Agreement or the Regulations. The result is that there are several groupings of states who are members of the EPC and have to some degree engaged with the legislation for the UPC and the Unitary Patent, but only one group of which have either ratified the UPC already or are expected to do so, of which there are 22 countries. It is only the countries in this latter group that will take part in the UPC and the Unitary Patent. These are shown in Table I.1.

Table I.1 Participating Member States: relation of EPC signatory states to the Regulations and UPC Agreement

EPC members	Signatory to the UP Regulation	Signatory to the UPC Agreement (Contracting Member State)**	Ratified or expected to ratify the UPC Agreement
EU Member States Spain (ES), Croatia (HR),	No	No	No
EU Member States Poland (PL)*	Yes	No	No
EU Member States Czech Republic (CZ) *, Hungary (HU) *.	Yes	Yes	No
EU Member States Austria (AT), Belgium (BE), Bulgaria (BG), Cyprus (CY), Germany (DE), Denmark (DK), Estonia (EE), Greece (GR), Finland (FI), France (FR), Ireland (IE), Italy (IT), Latvia (LV), Lithuania (LT), Luxembourg (LU), Malta (MT), the Netherlands (NL), Portugal (PT), Romania (RO), Slovakia (SK), Slovenia (SL), Sweden (SE).	Yes	Yes	Yes
Non-EU EPC signatories United Kingdom (UK)	Yes	Yes	No*
Non-EU EPC signatories Albania (AL), Switzerland (CH), Iceland (IS), Lichtenstein (LI), Monaco (MC), Former Yugoslav Republic of Macedonia (MC), Norway (NO), Serbia (RS), San Marino SM), Turkey (TR)	No	No	No

* Because these countries will not ratify the UPC, they will not participate in the Unitary Patent. Participating Member States are referred to accordingly.

** Defined by Article 2(c) of the UPC Agreement. The term 'Contracting Member States' is used in this book where it is found in the relevant article of the UPC Agreement, although it is not clear in all instances (for example, the recruitment of judges) whether the term should be understood to mean Contracting Member States that have ratified the UPC Agreement.

PART I

The Structure and Application of the New System

1

The Unitary Patent

The 'European patent with unitary effect'[1] (hereinafter 'Unitary Patent') is an alternative form of European patent created by Regulation (EU) 1257/2012 of 17 December 2012 implementing enhanced cooperation in the area of the creation of unitary patent protection (hereinafter 'UP Regulation'). Whereas the protection of European patents is limited to national territories, the Unitary Patent is a single means of protection covering most of the Member States of the European Union (see Table I.1 in the Introduction). The purpose of the Unitary Patent is to bring uniform protection in the EU internal market, as stated in the first recital of the UP Regulation:

> The creation of the legal conditions enabling undertakings to adapt their activities in manufacturing and distributing products across national borders and providing them with greater choice and more opportunities contributes to the attainment of the objectives of the Union. Uniform patent protection within the internal market, or at least a significant part thereof, should feature amongst the legal instruments which undertakings have at their disposal.

This chapter examines the features and effects of the Unitary Patent, which are designed to achieve the above purpose, as well as its licensing, administration, translation requirements and renewal fees. The relationship between the Unitary Patent and supplementary protection certificates (SPCs) is also discussed.

I. The Unitary Patent in the Context of the European System

A. National Patents

i. Outside the UPC System

National patents are applied for in the national patent office of the particular country to be protected, either by filing directly or through an international application under the Patent Cooperation Treaty.[2] Under the PCT, it is possible to seek patent protection simultaneously in up to 153 contracting countries[3] using a single 'international' patent application. If the first patent application is filed in a country[4] that is a member of the Paris Convention for the

---

[1] Article 3(1) UP Regulation.
[2] Signed in Washington DC on 19 June 1970 and most recently amended on 3 October 2001.
[3] A list of the contracting Member States of the PCT is available at: www.wipo.int/pct/en/pct_contracting_states.html.
[4] Currently 177. A full list of contracting parties is available at: https://wipolex.wipo.int/en/treaties/ShowResults?search_what=C&treaty_id=2.

18 The Unitary Patent

Protection of Industrial Property[5] (hereinafter the 'Paris Convention'), patents subsequently filed in a Paris Convention country within 12 months of that application (including those made through the PCT) may claim the same filing date. National patents are subject to revocation and amendment by the national courts of the country of grant. The protection of a national patent is limited to acts of infringement taking place in the jurisdiction of the country concerned, although such acts may require certain steps to have been performed outside the jurisdiction.[6] In the new system, unlike European patents, national patents cannot be converted into a Unitary Patent. Furthermore, national patents cannot be litigated in the UPC (see Chapter 6).

ii. Double Patenting

In some countries it will be possible to obtain national patents at the same time as a Unitary Patent, reflecting national practice in respect of European patents. This will be the case, for example, in France. By contrast, in the Netherlands, once a European patent is granted, there will be a loss of right regarding the national equivalent or priority document[7] and it is expected that the same will apply to a Unitary Patent.

In Germany, an objection[8] can be raised before a national German court in the event of a parallel action (same party and same embodiment) before the UPC, subject to the following conditions:

(1) An action for infringement or threatened infringement of a patent granted in proceedings under the Patent Act shall be inadmissible,
   1. insofar as the subject-matter of the patent is an invention for which the same inventor or his successor in title has been granted a patent with effect in the Federal Republic of Germany has been granted a European patent or a European patent with unitary effect with the same priority, and
   2. if proceedings are pending before the Unified Patent Court against the same party for infringement or threatened infringement of the European patent or the European patent with unitary effect referred to in point 1 by the same embodiment or if the Unified Patent Court has given a final decision on such a request, and
   3. provided that the defendant raises it at the first hearing after the plea has arisen, before the commencement of the hearing on the substance of the case.

(2) If the defendant raises a plea under paragraph 1, the Court may order that the proceedings be stayed pending the outcome of the proceedings before the Unified Patent Court.
(3) Paragraphs 1 and 2 shall apply mutatis mutandis to supplementary protection certificates.
(4) Paragraphs 1 and 2 shall not apply to provisional or protective measures.

As can be noted by paragraph 4, the objection does not apply to provisional or protective measures.

Regarding validity, the UPC can – upon a respective request of the defendant – decide on the validity of the patent at issue. A decision would then cover the UPC territory

---

[5] Signed in Paris on 20 March 1883 and most recently amended on 28 September 1979.
[6] For example, the importation of a product made abroad using a process not patented in the country of manufacture, but patented in the country of import.
[7] Article 77 of the Dutch Patent Act.
[8] Under Article II § 18 IntPatÜbkG (German Law on International Patent Treaties).

(in the case of a unitary patent) or the UPC countries covered by a European bundle patent. As the German national patent is formally a protective right separate of the Unitary Patent or non-opted out European Patent bundle patent, invalidation before the UPC would not directly affect the validity of the national patent. However, it may be assumed that a decision of the UPC would, in terms of substance, also carry weight within the German bifurcated system.

iii. European Patents

Once granted, a European patent is also a nationally registered right, limited to the protection of the national territory of registration. However, it differs from a national patent in terms of the process of prosecution and the continuing competence of the EPO. Specifically, European patents may be opposed (subject to a nine-month time limit) or amended in the EPO, in addition to the national court of the country of registration.

The EPO was created and is governed by the EPC for the purpose of establishing a central body able to receive and prosecute applications to grant, and to provide harmonising pan-European patent laws broadly concerned with validity (see the Introduction). The EPC also provides a tribunal system within the EPO by which European patents may be opposed post-grant. Like the UPC, the EPC is an inter-governmental treaty, not an EU legal instrument. It is now signed and ratified by 38 countries, including all 27 EU Member States (see Table 1.1).

Table 1.1 A comparison of EPC contracting states and EU Member States

	EPC contracting state	EU Member State
Albania	Yes	No
Austria	Yes	Yes
Belgium	Yes	Yes
Bulgaria	Yes	Yes
Croatia	Yes	Yes
Cyprus	Yes	Yes
Czech Republic	Yes	Yes
Denmark	Yes	Yes
Estonia	Yes	Yes
Finland	Yes	Yes
France	Yes	Yes
Germany	Yes	Yes
Greece	Yes	Yes
Hungary	Yes	Yes
Iceland	Yes	No
Ireland	Yes	Yes
Italy	Yes	Yes

(continued)

Table 1.1 *(Continued)*

	EPC contracting state	EU Member State
Latvia	Yes	Yes
Liechtenstein	Yes	No
Lithuania	Yes	Yes
Luxembourg	Yes	Yes
Malta	Yes	Yes
Monaco	Yes	No
The Netherlands	Yes	Yes
Norway	Yes	No
Poland	Yes	Yes
Portugal	Yes	Yes
Romania	Yes	Yes
San Marino	Yes	No
Serbia	Yes	No
Slovakia	Yes	Yes
Slovenia	Yes	Yes
Spain	Yes	Yes
Sweden	Yes	Yes
Switzerland	Yes	No
Turkey	Yes	No
UK	Yes	No
Former Yugoslav Republic	Yes	No

The applicant for a European patent can designate those EPC countries in which it would like the patent to take effect. However, the filing of a single application in the EPO for protection in more than one EPC country does not imply that the patent is a single pan-European right. Instead, after the European patent application has been examined by the EPO, and upon grant, a 'bundle' of national counterparts of the patent is formed: one patent for each of the designated countries. As stated above, each of these is registered at the respective national patent office.

Prior to ratification of the Agreement on the application of Article 65 EPC[9] (hereinafter the 'London Agreement'), first adopted in London on 17 October 2000 (see also Chapter 5), all EPC contracting states required European patents to be translated into their own language as a pre-condition of national registration. This could be expensive in cases of patents granted in multiple jurisdictions and could result in inconsistencies being introduced in the meaning of otherwise identical claims. To reduce costs and inconsistencies,

---

[9] Official Journal of the EPO 2001, 549.

the London Agreement introduced a reciprocal arrangement to waive the national right to require a translation.[10] As a result, contracting countries that have an official language in common with one of the three official languages of the EPC – English, French and German – waive their right to require a translation of the patent specification (although the claims must still be translated into all of the official languages). Countries that do not have an official language in common with the EPO waive their right to a translation, provided the patent is granted or translated into one of the EPO languages of their choice. However, they may still require that the *claims* of the patent are translated into one of their official languages.

II. Features of the Unitary Patent

A. Uniformity of Protection

The UP Regulation establishes the Unitary Patent: a European patent that has been registered as having unitary effect.[11] The Unitary Patent is a single right conferring on its proprietor and licensees the right to prevent a third party from committing infringing acts in all the participating Member States (for which, see Table I.1 in the Introduction):

1. A European patent granted with the same set of claims in respect of all the participating Member States shall benefit from unitary effect in the participating Member States provided that its unitary effect has been registered in the Register for unitary patent protection.[12]

The protection provided by a Unitary Patent across the participating Member States is uniform:[13] only European patents granted for *all* these Member States[14] and with the *same* set of claims can benefit from unitary status. The UP Regulation recitals state that this ensures the fundamental purpose of the Unitary Patent as a patent of uniform scope of protection across Europe.[15]

B. Uniformity of Revocation, Limitation and Transfer

Uniformity of protection means that any change to the status of the patent must also take effect uniformly. This is a risk for a patentee who has registered for unitary effect (and for those holding rights in European patents that have not been opted-out of the UPC;

---

[10] The status of accession and ratification of the London Agreement in the EPC states is available at: https://documents.epo.org/projects/babylon/eponet.nsf/0/7FD20618D28E9FBFC125743900678657/$File/London_Agreement.pdf.
[11] Article 3(2) UP Regulation.
[12] This is the part of the European Patent Register in which the unitary effect and any limitation, licence, transfer, revocation or lapse of a European patent with unitary effect are registered (ibid Article 2(e)).
[13] ibid Article 5(2).
[14] That is, all those participating Member States that have ratified the UPC Agreement by the time the request for unitary effect is made under ibid Article 9.
[15] See ibid Recital 7 and Article 3(1).

see Chapter 6): a successful revocation of a Unitary Patent has effect across all the participating Member States, per Article 2 UP Regulation:

> 2. It may only be limited, transferred or revoked, or lapse, in respect of all the participating Member States.

The effect of Article 2 is also that limitations on a Unitary Patent by post-grant amendment will have equal effect across the participating Member States. Equally, the lapse of a Unitary Patent is effective across all the participating Member States. A Unitary Patent must also be assigned as a whole. This is in contrast to European patents, for which different national designations may be assigned to different parties. The requirement for Unitary Patents to be assigned as a whole also contrasts with the right provided by the UP Regulation to license in part (see section II.B.i below).

C. Licensing Unitary Patents

i. Licensing in Part

The UP Regulation provides that a Unitary Patent may be licensed in part:

> [The Unitary Patent] may be licensed in respect of the whole or part of the territories of the participating Member States.[16]

The effect of this provision is that a Unitary Patent may be licensed on a geographical basis. The Unitary Patent owner or its licensee may grant the right to a licensee or sub-licensee to develop and/or commercialise a product protected by the patent in a specific participating Member State or a number of Member States. The licensor may grant a separate licence to several different licensees, each in a different participating Member State. The licensor may, or may not, also reserve for itself the right to work within the patent in a particular participating Member State or Member States. The right to license in the whole or part of the territories of the participating Member States implies that dealings based on licensing will also be possible in respect of particular participating Member State.

ii. Licences of Right

The proprietor of a Unitary Patent may file a statement with the EPO stating that it is prepared to grant a licence in return for appropriate consideration.[17] Such a statement will allow a reduction in the renewal fee for the Unitary Patent in question.[18] In the 'True Top 4' fee proposal, this would be a reduction of 15 per cent in the renewal fees payable throughout a Unitary Patent's term.[19] Licences of right are treated as contractual licences[20] (see Chapter 2).

---

[16] ibid Article 3(2).
[17] ibid Article 8(1).
[18] ibid Article 11(3).
[19] Adjusted proposals for the level of renewal fees for European patents with unitary effect, SC/18/15, dated 17 May 2015 and adopted by the Select Committee of the Administrative Council of the EPO on 24 June 2015.
[20] Article 8(2) UP Regulation.

iii. Compulsory Licences

Compulsory licences for Unitary Patents should be obtained in respect of each national territory of a participating Member State according to the respective laws of the Member State concerned.[21] Although this system deviates from a strict unitary scheme, it is consistent with the ability to voluntarily licence in particular Member State territories.[22] Although the right to a compulsory licence is to be determined by the national law of the participating Member State concerned, it is arguable that the decision to grant such a licence can be determined by the UPC (see Chapter 2).

D. Unitary Patent Licence Disputes

Disputes concerning the terms of Unitary Patent licences and assignments must be dealt with under the law agreed in the licence or, in the absence of such agreement, the provisions of Regulation (EC) No 593/2008 (hereinafter the 'Rome I Regulation'). The jurisdiction for such disputes will be that agreed in the licence, subject to the hearing of substantive matters of patent law in the UPC (see Chapter 2).

III. Administration by the EPO

A. Administrative Tasks of the EPO

The Member States participating in the Unitary Patent assign a number of administrative tasks relating to the Patent to the EPO.[23] These are provided in Article 9 UP Regulation and, in particular, include the administration of requests for unitary effect, the registration of unitary effect and of any limitation, licence, transfer, revocation or lapse of the Unitary Patent. The EPO is also responsible for: the collection and distribution of renewal fees; the publication of translations for information purposes during the transitional period in which a machine translation system is set up; and the administration of a compensation scheme for the reimbursement of translation costs incurred by applicants filing European patent applications in a language other than one of the official languages of the EPO.

Article 9(1) UP Regulation sets out the administrative tasks of the EPO with regard to the Unitary Patent regime:

> The participating Member States shall, within the meaning of Article 143 of the EPC, give the EPO the following tasks, to be carried out in accordance with the internal rules of the EPO:
>
> (i) to administer requests for unitary effect by proprietors of European patents;
> (ii) to include the Register for unitary patent protection within the European Patent Register and to administer the Register for unitary patent protection;
> (iii) to receive and register statements on licensing referred to in Article 8, their withdrawal and licensing commitments undertaken by the proprietor of the European patent with unitary effect in international standardisation bodies;

---

[21] ibid Recital 10; there is no article reflecting this in the UP Regulation.
[22] ibid Recital 7.
[23] Further to ibid Recital 17.

(iv) to publish the translations referred to in Article 6 of Regulation (EU) No 1260/2012 during the transitional period referred to in that Article;
(v) to collect and administer renewal fees for European patents with unitary effect, in respect of the years following the year in which the mention of the grant is published in the European Patent Bulletin; to collect and administer additional fees for late payment of renewal fees where such late payment is made within six months of the due date, as well as to distribute part of the collected renewal fees to the participating Member States;
(vi) to administer the compensation scheme for the reimbursement of translation costs referred to in Article 5 of Regulation (EU) No 1260/2012;
(vii) to ensure that a request for unitary effect by a proprietor of a European patent is submitted in the language of the proceedings as defined in Article 14(3) of the EPC no later than one month after the mention of the grant is published in the European Patent Bulletin; and
(viii) to ensure that the unitary effect is indicated in the Register for unitary patent protection, where a request for unitary effect has been filed and, during the transitional period provided for in Article 6 of Regulation (EU) No 1260/2012, has been submitted together with the translations referred to in that Article, and that the EPO is informed of any limitations, licences, transfers or revocations of European patents with unitary effect.

Article 9(3) UP Regulation requires that the participating Member States ensure effective legal protection before a competent court of one or several participating Member States against the decisions of the EPO in carrying out the tasks referred to in Article 9(1). This legal protection is provided by the UPC, in which a party may bring an action *ex parte* to annul or alter decisions made by the EPO when carrying out its tasks under Article 9(1) UP Regulation and, in particular, decisions not to grant unitary effect (see Chapter 12).

B. Obtaining and Maintaining a Unitary Patent

i. Requesting Unitary Effect

There is no application and prosecution procedure, as such, for a Unitary Patent. Instead, the application and prosecution is that for a European patent, in the EPO, followed by a request for unitary effect. The request for unitary effect must be filed with the EPO within one month of the date of publication of the mention of grant of the European patent in the European Patent Bulletin.[24] If unitary effect is not applied for by the end of this one-month window, the opportunity to obtain Unitary Patent status for the European patent is lost. The details of this procedure remain to be established, but there are two particular features that the EPO has introduced to facilitate applications for unitary effect: (i) filing of applications at the EPO requesting unitary status will be possible from the date of deposit of the German ratification, before the UP Regulation comes into force; and (ii) the possibility for applicants to request a delay in issuing the decision to grant a European patent until after the UP Regulation comes into force (that is, until after the UPC has opened).[25]

There will inevitably be a gap between the date of publication by the EPO of the mention of the grant of the European patent and the date at which a request for unitary effect is

---

[24] ibid Recital 18.
[25] https://www.epo.org/law-practice/unitary/unitary-patent/transitional-arrangements-for-early-uptake.html.

filed. However, the Unitary Patent nonetheless takes effect retrospectively in the participating Member States, on the date of publication by the EPO of the mention of the grant of the European patent.[26] Apparently, to address the gap, the UP Regulation provides that the participating Member States must 'take the necessary measures' to ensure that, after unitary effect has been registered, the underlying European patent is 'deemed not to have taken effect' as a national patent in that Member State on the date of publication of the mention of the grant.[27]

ii. Filing a Translation

The language regime applicable to Unitary Patents is provided in the Translation Regulation (see Chapter 5). The *specification* of a unitary patent must be published in the language of prosecution – English, French *or* German – and must also include a translation of the claims in the other two official languages of the EPO.[28] In other words, the *claims* must be published in all three: English, French *and* German.

The EPO states that after the granting of the underlying European patent, no further human translations will be required if the patent holder registers the patent with unitary effect. If it is necessary to communicate the contents of the patent in other languages, high-quality machine translations will be available. There will be a transitional period (currently 12 years) whilst the machine translation system is set up.[29] During this period, if the language of the proceedings before the EPO is French or German, a full translation of the European patent specification must be provided in English; if the language of the proceedings is English, a full translation into an official language of another EU Member State must be provided. Such a translation must be filed at the EPO together with the request for unitary effect. If a Unitary Patent is obtained by a proprietor who has a residence or principal place of business in an EU Member State with an official language other than the three EPO languages, a system of additional reimbursement will be introduced for the costs of translating their application into the EPO language of proceedings[30] (see also Chapter 5).

The request for unitary effect must be submitted in the language of proceedings.[31]

iii. Renewal Fees

Upon grant, the Unitary Patent is subject to a renewal fee regime that is separate from that of the European patent. Unlike European patents, the EPO is responsible for collecting, administering and remitting renewal fees for Unitary Patents. Renewal fees must be paid by the proprietor to the EPO.[32] They must be paid for the years following the year of publication of grant of the patent rather than the date at which unitary effect is entered in the

---

[26] Article 4(1) UP Regulation.
[27] ibid Article 4(2).
[28] Article 3, by reference to Article 14(6) EPC.
[29] Article 6 Translation Regulation. The 12-year period is intended to allow for the available machine translation technology to be sufficiently advanced for this purpose.
[30] See www.epo.org/law-practice/unitary/unitary-patent.html.
[31] Article 3(2) Translation Regulation.
[32] Article 11(1) UP Regulation.

Register. Further fees are payable for late payment of the renewal fee. Failure to pay a fee will result in the lapse of the Unitary Patent. The most recent renewal fees for a Unitary Patent are those in the 'True Top 4' proposal[33] and although set in 2015, it is expected that these will remain in place at the time that the first patents are granted.

According to this fee model, the annual renewal fee for the Unitary Patent was intended to correspond to the combined renewal fees of the four EU countries in which, under the EPO system, European patents are most frequently validated by patent applicants: Germany, the UK, France and the Netherlands. The Unitary Patent renewal fees will be less than €5,000 in the first 10 years and the total fees for maintaining the patent over the full 20-year term will amount to just over €35,000. A full table of the True Top 4 renewal fees is given in Table 1.2.

Table 1.2 True Top 4 Unitary Patent renewal fees

Year	'True Top 4' renewal fee (€)
2	35
3	105
4	145
5	315
6	475
7	630
8	815
9	990
10	1,175
11	1,460
12	1,775
13	2,105
14	2,455
15	2,830
16	3,240
17	3,640
18	4,055
19	4,455
20	4,855
Total	35,555

If the proprietor of a Unitary Patent has filed a statement with the EPO to say the patent is available for licences of right, renewal fees will be reduced by 15%.

---

[33] SC/18/15, dated 17 May 2015 and adopted by the Select Committee of the Administrative Council of the EPO on 24 June 2015.

IV. Supplementary Protection Certificates

A. SPCs and Unitary Patents

SPCs are currently examined and granted by national patent offices, even when based on centrally granted European patents. However, with the advent of the UPC and the pan-European Unitary Patent, the need for unitary SPC protection (a Unitary SPC) has now arisen.

If a Unitary SPC is to be established, this brings with it issues of legal certainty and transparency in the granting procedure that will need to be ensured. An example of some of the issues that are currently under discussion are as follows:

- Who should be the Unitary SPC granting body as the unitary character of the right would require that it is controlled by EU bodies? Options discussed include the EPO, the European Union Intellectual Property Office or another EU institution like the European Medicines Agency or even a virtual office with examiners from national patent offices. There also need to be clear timings and final deadlines for filing the application for an SPC.
- The forum for legal recourse under the right must be clarified: should remedies for revocation be brought before national courts with the decision having effect for the whole territory of the Unitary SPC or rather before the UPC itself? In addition, the fee system must be affordable, in particular for SMEs.
- Territorial scope is another point of discussion. The Unitary SPC would logically require that the patentee obtain marketing authorisations in all participating Member States. In this regard, it needs to be decided whether only a centralised marketing authorisation would allow for the grant of the Unitary SPC, or whether national/decentralised marketing authorisations would also be sufficient, provided that it is ensured that the Unitary SPC will not then cover countries where no marketing authorisation was obtained.

In addition to the Unitary SPC, there is also the issue of the shortcomings of the current SPC system due to its national character, in particular with regard to divergent outcomes of national grant and revocation procedures, sub-optimal transparency of SPC-related information, and high costs and administrative burdens with regard to the enforcement and litigation of SPCs.

To address all of these issues, the European Commission opened a 'call for evidence' to receive views from stakeholders, with the purpose of preparing an impact assessment and any necessary legislation.[34]

---

[34] See https://ec.europa.eu/info/law/better-regulation/have-your-say/initiatives/13353-Medicinal-&-plant-protection-products-single-procedure-for-the-granting-of-SPCs_en. This follows an earlier European Commission Communication titled 'Upgrading the Single Market: more opportunities for people and business', published on 28 October 2015, which suggests for now that the Commission may be moving in the direction of the unitary SPC option. The Communication states: 'The Unitary Patent system will play an essential role in enabling innovation in the participating Member States. Europe is now on the cusp of making this patent a reality and establishing the European patent specialised court for which the industry has been calling for decades. However, the key challenge now is to get the endgame right, including addressing uncertainties over how the Unitary Patent will work together with national patents and national supplementary protection certificates (SPC) granted under the SPC regime and the possible creation of a unitary SPC title.' On 25 November 2020, the EU Commission published the latest iteration of its IP strategy in 'Making the most of the

B. SPCs Based on European Patents

At present, the system by which SPCs are granted on European patents by national patent offices[35] remains unchanged by the introduction of the Unitary Patent and the UPC. SPCs automatically follow the European patent on which they are based for the purposes of opt-out. If a dispute concerning the underlying patent is lodged in the relevant national court during the transitional period (see Chapter 6), it is doubted that the SPC can be litigated separately in the UPC, even if the cause of action is the invalidity of the SPC for reasons other than the invalidity of the underlying patent.

C. Opt-out of SPCs Based on a Unitary Patent

Opt-out automatically extends to an SPC based on an opted-out European patent.[36] A European patent can also be opted-out post-expiry, such that an SPC that is based on it and still in force is also opted-out.[37] If an assignment results in an SPC having a different owner from the European patent on which it is based, the SPC owner must lodge the opt-out application together with the patent proprietor[38] (see Chapter 6).

As the discussion above explains, there is currently no basis for an SPC to be granted on a Unitary Patent. Nonetheless, the Rules of Procedure stipulate, for the avoidance of doubt, that an SPC granted on the basis of a Unitary Patent cannot be opted-out.[39]

V. Exhaustion of Rights and Licences

Both the UP Regulation and the UPC Agreement contain provisions on the exhaustion of rights. The exhaustion of rights to patent protection attach to a particular product, protected by that patent, once that product has been put on the market in the EU by the patent proprietor or with the patent proprietor's consent. These provisions are framed in similar terms and applicable to Unitary Patents and European patents, respectively:[40]

> Article 6 [UP Regulation]
>
> Exhaustion of rights conferred by a European patent with unitary effect
>
> The rights conferred by a European patent with unitary effect shall not extend to acts concerning a product covered by that patent which are carried out within the participating Member States in

---

EU's innovative potential – An intellectual property action plan to support the EU's recovery and resilience' COM (2020) 760 final. The paper repeats the need for a unified SPC grant mechanism and a unified SPC title.

[35] Further to Regulation (EC) 469/2009 of the European Parliament and of the Council of 6 May 2009 concerning the supplementary protection certificate for medicinal products.
[36] Rule 5.2 Rules of Procedure.
[37] ibid Rule 5.1.
[38] ibid Rule 5.2(a).
[39] ibid Rule 5.2(d).
[40] Both provisions closely follow the wording in Article 76 of the Community Patent Convention. See also, for example, *Merck & Co v Primecrown Ltd* (Joined Cases C-267/95 and C-268/95) [1996] ECR 6285 for the principle of EU patent exhaustion in CJEU case law.

which that patent has unitary effect after that product has been placed on the market in the Union by, or with the consent of, the patent proprietor, unless there are legitimate grounds for the patent proprietor to oppose further commercialisation of the product.

Article 29 [Agreement]
Exhaustion of rights conferred by a European patent

The rights conferred by a European patent shall not extend to acts concerning a product covered by that patent after than product has been placed on the market in the European Union by, or with the consent of, the patent proprietor, unless there are legitimate grounds for the patent proprietor to oppose further commercialisation of the product.

In keeping with the free movement rules of Articles 28 and 30 of the EC Treaty, patent exhaustion is not limited to individual territories in which a patent is granted, but extends to all such territories in the EU.[41] The rules of exhaustion apply to European patent-protected territories in the EU regardless of whether the Member State in which the product was first placed on the market is a Member State of the UPC Agreement that will not ratify (Spain, Poland, Croatia, Hungary and the Czech Republic) or if it is a Member State that has contracted but has not yet ratified. Furthermore, it is submitted that the marketing of a product protected by a Unitary Patent in an EU Member State that is not a participating Member State of the UP Regulation, or that has not ratified the UPC Agreement, exhausts the rights in the Unitary Patent for that product, whether or not the Member State of marketing is protected by an equivalent patent.[42]

---

[41] See *Centrafarm v Sterling Drug* (Case-15/74) [1974] ECR 1147.
[42] *Merck v Stephar* [1981] ECR 2063.

2
Structure, Context and Competence

Together with the UP Regulation, the UPC Agreement lays the other key legislative foundation for the new European patent litigation system: a pan-European court in which disputes concerning Unitary Patents and European patents can be decided for all participating courts. Importantly, however, the national courts will continue to operate alongside this new system: those European patents that have been 'opted-out' of the UPC must be litigated in the national courts for the duration of their term and that of any SPC based on them. Furthermore, during the transitional period set out in Article 83 UPC Agreement, the national courts will remain an alternative choice of forum for litigating European patents that have not opted out (see Chapter 6). Patents granted by national offices will continue within the exclusive jurisdiction of the national courts. The UPC is thus in part a replacement of the existing system and in part an addition to it. Therefore, as well as understanding how the UPC is structured – a court of first instance divisions and a court of appeal, the subject matter of the patents for which the branches of the central division will be responsible and the actions for which the UPC will have competence – it is necessary to examine how it fits into the existing system of EU Member State courts and the national courts of the non-EU EPC contracting countries. The relationship between the UPC, the CJEU and the EPO is also important. This chapter discusses these aspects of the UPC.

I. The UPC and Participating Member State Courts

In order for the UPC Agreement to enter into force, amendments to Regulation (EU) No 1215/2012 on Jurisdiction and the Recognition and Enforcement of Judgments in Civil and Commercial Matters (recast) (hereinafter 'Brussels I Regulation (recast)') were necessary.[1] The Explanatory Memorandum in the Proposal[2] for the amended Regulation explains that the amendments introduce the UPC as a jurisdiction within the Brussels I Regulation (recast) framework. To appreciate the connection between the UPC and the participating Member States' national courts under the amended Brussels I Regulation (recast), the nature and status of the UPC must be understood.

---

[1] Article 89(1) UPC Agreement. The amendments to the Brussels I Regulation (recast) came into force on 30 May by virtue of Regulation (EU) 542/2014 amending Regulation (EU) 1215/2012 as regards the rules to be applied with respect to the UPC and the Benelux Court of Justice. The amendments apply from 10 January 2015.

[2] Proposal for a Regulation of the European Parliament and of the Council amending Regulation (EU) No 1215/2012 on jurisdiction and the recognition and enforcement of judgments in civil and commercial matters.

The UPC and Participating Member State Courts 31

There are two alternatives in theory. The first is that the UPC is governed by the Brussels I Regulation (recast) as a discrete court, separate and distinct as a jurisdiction from the national courts of the participating Member States. According to this interpretation, the UPC and the national courts would have mutually exclusive jurisdictions, as shown in Figure 2.1.

Figure 2.1 The UPC and national courts with mutually exclusive jurisdictions

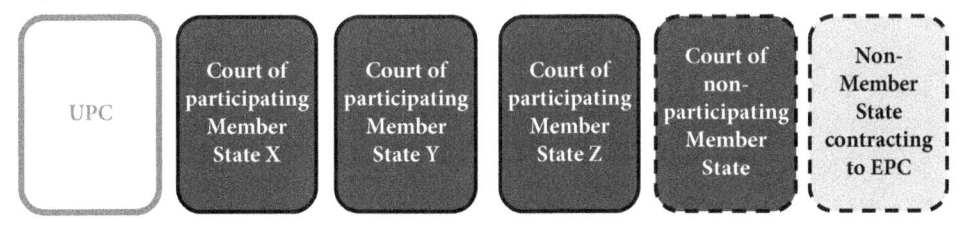

This interpretation gives rise to a number of difficulties, in particular under Article 24(4) of the Brussels I Regulation (recast).[3] The UPC is a forum in which European patents (provided they are not opted-out) can be revoked.[4] However, the Member States have exclusive competence under the Brussels I Regulation (recast) for actions concerning the revocation of those designations of a European patent registered in their respective jurisdictions.[5] Therefore, if the UPC is to share competence for revocation with the Member States the Regulation would need to be amended accordingly. No such amendment has been made.

The alternative interpretation is that the UPC is not a jurisdiction separate to those of the Member States. Instead, it is a court simultaneously present, jointly and severally in the jurisdictions of the contracting Member States (see Figure 2.2). During the transitional period, a revocation action concerning a European patent can therefore be lodged in either the national court of the Member State in which it is validated or the UPC – the lodging of a revocation action in the UPC is simultaneously a lodging within the Member State of validation. Any conflict with Article 24(4) of the Brussels I Regulation (recast) is therefore avoided.

Figure 2.2 The UPC jointly and severally present in the contracting Member States

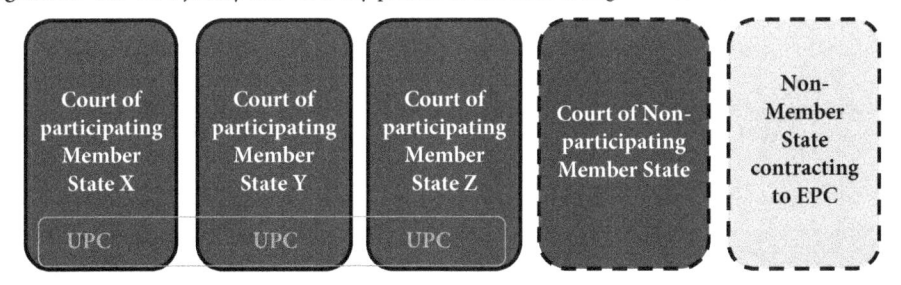

---

[3] A conflict with EU law rules on the application of national law under 'Rome II' would also arise (see the discussion in ch 4).
[4] Article 83(3) UPC Agreement.
[5] Article 24(4) Brussels I Regulation (recast).

There is also support in the UPC Agreement and the Brussels I Regulation (recast) for this view: the preamble to the UPC Agreement states that 'the Unified Patent Court should be a court common to the contracting Member States and thus part of their judicial system'[6] and the Brussels I Regulation (recast) also provides that the UPC is a court of a Member State.[7] In order to emphasise the status of the UPC as a national body, the UPC Agreement states that 'the Court shall cooperate with the Court of Justice of the European Union to ensure the correct application and uniform interpretation of Union law, as any national court'.[8] Similarly, the UPC Agreement stipulates the liability of Member States for breaches of EU law by the UPC[9] and attributes actions of the UPC to each contracting Member State.[10]

II. Non-contracting Member States

Spain, Croatia, the Czech Republic, Hungary and Poland have either not signed the UPC Agreement or have said they will not ratify it and, as a result, they are not subject to the jurisdiction of the UPC (see Figure 2.3). This also has the consequence that the Unitary Patent cannot apply in their territories.[11] In these countries, the present system of European patents and national patents continues unchanged – disputes concerning European rights designated in these countries remain within the jurisdiction of their respective national courts. However, as EU Member States, they continue to be subject to the jurisdiction of the CJEU. They are also bound by the Brussels I Regulation (recast). Furthermore, the *lis pendens* provisions introduced by amendment to the Brussels I Regulation (recast)[12] provide rules for dealing with duplicative actions lodged in the UPC and the non-contracting Member States (see Chapter 7).

III. Non-Member States Contracted to the EPC

There is also a large group of countries which are contracted to the EPC, but which are not EU Member States. They include the European Free Trade Agreement (EFTA) signatories: members of the European Economic Area (EEA) – Iceland, Norway and Liechtenstein, and the non-EEA EFTA state Switzerland. After exiting the EU, the UK is also in this group.

---

[6] Similar wording is found in Articles 1 and 21 UPC Agreement.
[7] Article 71a(1) of the Brussels I Regulation (recast).
[8] ibid Article 21.
[9] ibid Article 22.
[10] ibid Article 23.
[11] Article 18(2) UP Regulation.
[12] By Regulation (EU) 542/2014.

As non-Member States, they are arguably not entitled to contract to the UPC Agreement[13] (for which see the Introduction). Consequently, the system of European patents and national patents continues unchanged by the UPC Agreement in these countries. Disputes concerning European patents designated in these countries are decided by the respective national courts.

IV. The Structure of the UPC

The UPC comprises a Court of First Instance and a Court of Appeal. The divisions of first instance consist of a central division in three sections, and several local and regional divisions. Local divisions are hosted by a single Member State. Regional divisions are hosted by two or more Member States, but are based in only one of those Member States. The significance of these different divisions is essentially jurisdictional, both in terms of the territory covered and the nature of the action at issue, and rules apply (see Chapter 9).

Each Member State is entitled to at least one local division. The maximum number of local divisions that a contracting Member State is entitled to host is determined by the number of patent cases that have been heard in the courts of that Member State over a period of three successive years prior to or subsequent to the coming into force of the UPC Agreement. An additional local division may be requested for each 100 patent cases heard every year over the three-year period. This is subject to a total limit of four local divisions per Member State. The only country to have four local divisions is Germany.

Regional divisions serve two or more Member States.[14] The purpose of regional divisions is to avoid the cost and complexity of establishing local divisions in Member States where fewer cases are expected. There is likely to be only one regional division and this is the 'Nordic-Baltic' region representing Sweden, Latvia, Lithuania and Estonia. This regional division will be situated in Stockholm and will use the English language.

The central division will have its seat in Paris together with two sections: one currently designated to London, which now the UK has exited the EU and declined to ratify the UPC Agreement, must be relocated;[15] and one in Munich (see section V below). The Court of Appeal has its seat in Luxembourg and hears appeals from the Court of First Instance (see Chapters 3 and 17).[16] A UPC Registry, which is responsible for keeping records of the cases before the UPC, also has its seat in Luxembourg. In addition, sub-registries are situated with all the divisional courts of first instance and are responsible for reporting the filing of new cases in those divisions to the Registry.

---

[13] Article 1 UPC Agreement states that: 'The Unified Patent Court shall be a court common to the Contracting *Member States*' (emphasis added).
[14] Article 7 UPC Agreement.
[15] At the time of writing, Italy and the Netherlands are the leading contenders to host this section.
[16] Article 73(3) UPC Agreement.

34 *Structure, Context and Competence*

Figure 2.3 The structure of the divisions of the Court of First Instance and the Court of Appeal. At the time of writing, the number and distribution of the local and regional divisions shown is incomplete

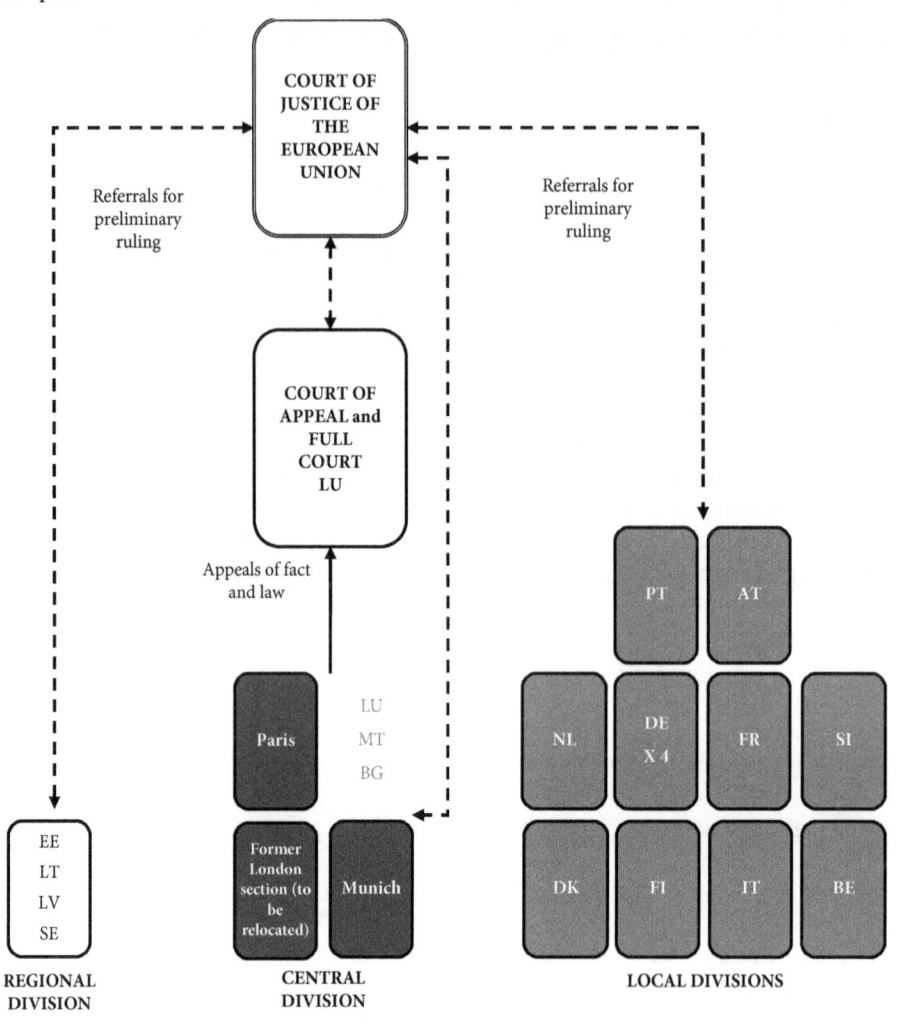

V. Subject Matter Jurisdiction of the Central Division Sections

The central division is largely concerned with revocation proceedings and declarations of non-infringement. However, there are circumstances in which an infringement action can proceed in the central division, either from commencement or by transfer (see Chapter 9).

A largely unexpected outcome of the negotiations preceding the signing of the UPC Agreement in February 2013 was an agreement at the national political level to split the central division between, at that time, France, Germany and the UK. As a result, the central division has its seat in Paris, but there are further sections in Munich and what was originally

Subject Matter Jurisdiction of the Central Division Sections

to have been London. These sections hear patent disputes according to the subject matter competences assigned to them.

A. Subject Matter Classification

The focus of what was to have been the London section is 'human necessities', which includes chemicals and life sciences. Munich is responsible for largely mechanical engineering-related subject matter. Paris is responsible for all other subject matter, including computer electronics and telecommunications. The full subject matter competences are shown in Table 2.1.[17]

Table 2.1 Subject matter competencies of the sections of the central division

FORMER LONDON SECTION	PARIS SEAT	MUNICH SECTION
(A) Human necessities Agriculture Foodstuffs; Tobacco Personal or domestic articles Health; Life-saving; Amusement	**(B) Performing operations, transporting.** Separating; Mixing Shaping Printing Transporting Micro-structural technology; Nano-technology	**(F) Mechanical engineering, lighting, heating, weapons, blasting.** Engines or pumps; Engineering in general Lighting; Heating; Weapons; Blasting
(C) Chemistry, metallurgy Chemistry Metallurgy Combinatorial technology	**(D) Textiles, paper** Textiles or flexible materials not otherwise provided for Paper	
	(E) Fixed constructions Building Earth or rock drilling; mining	
	(G) Physics Instruments Nucleonics	
	(H) Electricity.	

In broad terms, these subject areas correspond to the three categories of technology into which most patent litigation in the national courts falls: life sciences; electronics and telecommunications; and mechanical engineering. In particular:

(a) the former London section: diagnostics, medical devices and delivery apparatus, wound dressings, small-molecule and biological medicinal preparations, and the formulation of such preparations;

---

[17] Classifications A–H are based on the International Patent Classification of the World Intellectual Property Organization (www.wipo.int/classifications/ipc/en); see Annex II to the UPC Agreement.

(b) the Paris section: electronic circuits, radio and electric communications, including telephones and wireless networks, calculating, computation and digital information storage; and
(c) the Munich section: machines, including engines and related equipment and systems, lighting, combustion apparatus, heating and ventilating equipment, heat-pumps and refrigeration, and weapons equipment.

B. Allocation Mechanism

The central division requires a mechanism by which cases can be distributed without splitting up an action concerning two or more patents with different subject matter classifications (see Chapter 11).

VI. Actions for which the UPC has Exclusive Competence

A. Express Exclusive Competence

The UPC Agreement lists those actions for which the court has exclusive competence.[18] These are actions that may not be heard in the national courts in relation to a Unitary Patent or in relation to a European patent after the expiry of the transitional period unless that European patent has been opted-out (see Chapter 6). This is an exhaustive list, which is given below:

ARTICLE 32

Competence of the Court

(1) The Court shall have exclusive competence in respect of:
   (a) actions for actual or threatened infringements of patents and supplementary protection certificates and related defences, including counterclaims concerning licences;
   (b) actions for declarations of non-infringement of patents and supplementary protection certificates;
   (c) actions for provisional and protective measures and injunctions;
   (d) actions for revocation of patents and for declaration of invalidity of supplementary protection certificates;
   (e) counterclaims for revocation of patents and for declaration of invalidity of supplementary protection certificates;
   (f) actions for damages or compensation derived from the provisional protection conferred by a published European patent application;
   (g) actions relating to the use of the invention prior to the granting of the patent or to the right based on prior use of the invention;
   (h) actions for compensation for licences on the basis of Article 8 of Regulation (EU) No 1257/2012; and
   (i) actions concerning decisions of the European Patent Office in carrying out the tasks referred to in Article 9 of Regulation (EU) No 1257/2012.

---

[18] Article 32 UPC Agreement.

The UPC thus has exclusive competence for proceedings concerned with the principal causes of action: infringement of patents and SPCs (including the recovery of damages) and related defences; declarations of non-infringement of patents and SPCs; provisional and protective measures, including preliminary injunctions; and patent revocation and declaration of invalidity of SPCs. In addition, the UPC has exclusive jurisdiction for matters of prior use, and actions for compensation in respect of compulsory licences granted on Unitary Patents may also be heard.[19] The UPC also has the power to decide disputes concerning decisions made by the EPO when carrying out the tasks assigned to it for the administration of the Unitary Patent system[20] (see Chapter 12).

B. Declaratory Powers

It should be noted that Article 32 is concerned with causes of action over which the UPC has exclusive competence, but not specifically with the type of order a court may make. If the action is of a type which falls within Article 32, then the court may conclude that it has a power to make a declaration of matters which fall for decision within that action.

Different considerations apply to FRAND declarations and Arrow declarations. A party who contended that it was entitled to a FRAND licence could say that this was a defence to an infringement action so that its claim to be entitled to such a licence fell within 'related defences' in Article 32(1)(a). The court would inevitably have to reach a decision on that defence, and in so doing it would have to decide whether the defendant was entitled to a licence on fair, reasonable and non-discriminatory (FRAND) terms. Such a decision would, to all intents and purposes, be the equivalent of a declaration. More controversially, perhaps, the defendant could raise a 'counterclaim concerning a licence' under the closing words of Article 32(1)(a) and seek a declaration, but it is difficult to see that this would be of additional value.

This is fine if the court decides that the set of terms put forward by the defendant is FRAND. What happens when the court decides they are not FRAND, but the claimant or the parties wish the court to decide on what terms would be FRAND? There is reason to think that the court will try to find a way to do this because the FRAND defence could be formulated on the basis that the defendant is entitled to a licence on the terms they put forward, or alternatively on such terms as the court decides are FRAND. The absence of an express declaratory power should not prevent the court from deciding the case in that way.

Arrow declarations are likely to be more difficult. This is a declaration that no valid patent could be granted for particular subject matter. Whilst this might arguably be regarded as a 'protective measure' within Article 32(1)(c), it is doubtful that this was within the contemplation of the drafters of the UPC when they used that term.

VII. Non-exclusive Competence

The list of actions under Article 32(1) UPC Agreement is exhaustive. As regards actions that are not on this list, Article 32(2) UPC Agreement states that: 'The national courts of the Contracting Member States shall remain competent for actions relating to patents and

---

[19] Further to Article 9 UP Regulation.
[20] Article 9 of Regulation (EU) 1257/2012.

supplementary protection certificates which do not come within the exclusive competence of the [UPC].' It is not said that the national courts retain *exclusive* competence in respect of these matters and it is submitted that if such exclusivity were intended, it would be expected that this provision say so (in the same way that exclusivity is expressly granted to the UPC in Article 32(1)). As a result, it is arguable that the UPC may hear certain actions in addition to those listed in Article 32(1).

This begs the question as to how much larger, if at all, the court's overall or non-exclusive jurisdiction is. A court such as the UPC has no pre-existing or inherent jurisdiction. Therefore, the court's overall jurisdiction, if wider than Article 32, has to be found elsewhere in the Agreement. Reading the UPC Agreement as a whole, and in particular Article 1, the Court's overall jurisdiction is arguably the 'settlement of disputes relating to European patents and European patents with unitary effect'. This jurisdiction is to be interpreted broadly because, without such a broad jurisdiction, the objectives of the UPC as revealed in the recitals are likely to be frustrated. For example, if an ownership dispute arose in the context of an infringement action, it would be nonsensical if the court lacked jurisdiction (as opposed to exclusive jurisdiction) to settle that aspect of the dispute because it is not a matter specifically listed in Article 32.

Examples in which such non-exclusive jurisdiction of the UPC may apply are considered below.

A. 'Objects of Property' under Article 7 UP Regulation

Under Article 7 UP Regulation, in matters concerning Unitary Patents as an 'object of property', the patent is to be 'treated as a national patent' of a participating Member State.[21] The particular Member State in question is determined using the formula provided in Article 7 (see Chapter 4). It is not clear from this whether treatment as a national patent refers only to the applicable law or also to the forum of the dispute. If the Member State whose law applies to a Unitary Patent dispute under Article 7 must also provide the exclusive forum, defences based on the Unitary Patent as an object of property (for example, a defence of personal possession)[22] must be decided in a separate national action, either prior to or in parallel with the UPC proceedings. By contrast, a non-exclusive jurisdiction of the UPC for such matters would allow such actions to proceed together with infringement, subject to the application of the appropriate national law, as determined by Article 7 UP Regulation. The latter would provide the more efficient way to dispose of a dispute.

B. Rights to an Employee's Invention and Compensation

In respect of a granted European patent,[23] the right to the invention of an employee and compensation for employee inventors are matters of national law, which are linked to national territories (see Chapter 4). However, again there is no apparent bar on the UPC

---

[21] Article 7(1)–(3) UP Regulation.
[22] Article 28 UPC Agreement.
[23] In contrast to granted patents, the law applicable to the right to a European patent application is provided by Article 60 EPC.

providing the forum for a dispute on these issues, subject to the application of the appropriate national law, as determined by Article 7 UP Regulation.[24]

C. Patent Agreements

i. General Considerations

Disputes concerning the existence and terms of patent-related agreements, such as patent licences, are not included within the list of matters for which the UPC has exclusive competence under Article 32 UPC Agreement, except as a counterclaim to an action for infringement.[25]

Patent agreements are based on contract law. The applicable contract law as well as the forum for disputes concerning the agreement are usually determined by a governing law and jurisdiction clause. A claim for a breach of a patent agreement (whether concerning a Unitary Patent or a European patent) must be brought in the country contractually agreed upon in that agreement. It would appear open to the parties to agree that the UPC will be the forum in which disputes concerning that agreement are determined,[26] albeit under an agreed national law of contract, even though they may be reluctant to do so given the uncertainty on the issue and whether the UPC would be adequately equipped to handle such disputes, regardless of jurisdiction.[27]

However, the UPC does have exclusive jurisdiction for disputes relating to the validity and infringement of non-opted-out European patents (and all new European patents after the transitional period has expired) and Unitary Patents. Hence, even if an agreement stipulates that the governing jurisdiction for disputes is a national court, these substantive matters must be determined in the UPC.[28] This raises, as a practical step, a point in favour of bringing disputes concerning an agreement on Unitary Patents or European patents within the UPC as the exclusive jurisdiction, if possible, because it is a single forum for the dispute. If a non-UPC forum is stipulated in the patent agreement under a jurisdiction clause, disputed contractual matters must be determined in that forum according to the national law agreed, but the UPC has exclusive jurisdiction in respect of validity and infringement.[29]

ii. Compulsory Licences

Compulsory licences are not amongst the actions for which the UPC has exclusive competence under the UPC Agreement. Compulsory licences for Unitary Patents are governed

---

[24] In contrast to granted patents, the forum of a dispute concerning the right to the grant of a European patent application for an employee's invention is governed by Article 4 of the Protocol on Jurisdiction and the Recognition of Decisions in Respect of the Right to the Grant of a European Patent (Protocol on Recognition), 5 October 1973.

[25] Article 32(1)(a) UPC Agreement.

[26] As a court of each and all of the contracting Member States, an agreement to use the UPC as the forum is equivalent to an agreement to use a national court of a contracting Member State.

[27] The procedures of the UPC Agreement and the Rules of Procedure do not envisage such disputes.

[28] See Article 25(4) Brussels I Regulation and compare with disputes concerning patent licences in the national courts, in which the validity of European patents must be determined in the country of validation, regardless of the forum of the licence dispute. See, for example, Laddie J in *Celltech R&D Ltd v MedImmune Inc* [2004] EWHC 1522 (Pat).

[29] It seems that the agreement could nonetheless provide that those patent issues are determined according to a particular national patent law.

40 *Structure, Context and Competence*

by the laws of the Contracting Member State territory for which the licence is sought.[30] However, as with the other matters discussed in this section, it would seem possible to hear such actions in the UPC under the non-exclusive jurisdiction.

iii. Licences of Right

Unitary Patents may be made available for licences of right by filing a statement with the EPO to this effect. A licence obtained under this provision is to be treated as a contractual licence.[31] The same considerations should apply in respect of the competence of the UPC as a forum for disputes concerning licences of right as for patent agreements in general (see section VII.C.i above).

D. Personal Possession as a Defence

Prior use and rights of personal possession are a defence to an infringement action concerning a Unitary Patent or European patent.[32] These defences apply if they would have been available as a defence in a patent dispute in a contracting Member State court.[33] The defence extends to acts alleged to infringe in the contracting Member State in question.

While actions relating to the use of an invention prior to the grant of a patent are within the exclusive competence of the UPC, it is submitted that actions based on the right of personal possession (entitlement, co-ownership and contractual rights) ought to be considered matters of non-exclusive competence. Such an approach would allow both matters to be heard in the UPC, subject to the application of the appropriate national law (see Chapter 4).

VIII. The Role of the CJEU

A. The Obligation to Refer to the CJEU

As Figure 2.3 above illustrates, the European patent system comprising the UPC also includes the CJEU. The CJEU in *Opinion 1/09* of 8 March 2011[34] has held that Member States cannot, as part of the EU order, divest to an international body their powers over matters that should be subject to EU law. The system was amended to make it clear that Member States are jointly and severally liable for breaches of EU law[35] and that actions of the UPC are directly attributable to the contracting Member States.[36] Just as matters of EU

---

[30] See Recital 10 UP Regulation.
[31] ibid Article 8(2).
[32] Article 28 UPC Agreement.
[33] ibid.
[34] *Opinion 1/09*, Request to the Court for an Opinion pursuant to Article 218(11) TFEU, made on 6 July 2009 by the Council of the European Union (see the Introduction).
[35] Article 22 UPC Agreement.
[36] ibid Article 23. This is consistent with the UPC as a court of the Member States, rather than a discrete court sitting apart from the jurisdictions of the Member States.

law must be referred to the CJEU by national courts in appropriate cases, they must also be referred by the UPC:

ARTICLE 21
Requests for preliminary rulings

As a court common to the Contracting Member States and as part of their judicial system, the Court shall cooperate with the Court of Justice of the European Union to ensure the correct application and uniform interpretation of Union law, as any national court, in accordance with Article 267 TFEU in particular. Decisions of the Court of Justice of the European Union shall be binding on the Court.

Article 38 of Annex I to the UPC Agreement provides that such referrals are to be made according to the established procedures operating for national referrals:

Questions referred to the Court of Justice of the European Union:
(1) The procedures established by the Court of Justice of the European Union for referrals for preliminary rulings within the European Union shall apply.
(2) Whenever the Court of First Instance or the Court of Appeal has decided to refer to the Court of Justice of the European Union a question of interpretation of the Treaty on European Union or of the Treaty on the Functioning of the European Union or a question on the validity or interpretation of acts of the institutions of the European Union, it shall stay its proceedings.

Referrals to the CJEU can be made either by the divisions of the Court of First Instance or by the Court of Appeal (as represented in Figure 2.3).[37] The proceedings giving rise to the referral may be stayed pending the ruling of the CJEU on the matter referred, but where proceedings are not stayed, a judgment must not be given until the CJEU has given a ruling on the matter.[38]

B. Questions Subject to Referral to the CJEU

i. Instruments of EU Law

Questions on the 'interpretation of the Treaty on European Union [TEU] or of the Treaty on the Functioning of the European Union [TFEU] or a question on the validity or interpretation of acts of the institutions of the European Union' are referable to the CJEU.[39] In practice, matters arising directly under the TEU and the TFEU in a case before the UPC are likely to be limited to competition law.[40] The experience of national courts is that the instrument most likely to give rise to referrals is Regulation 469/2009 of 6 May 2009 concerning

---

[37] See Rule 266 of the Rules of Procedure and the Rules of the CJEU. If the court asks the CJEU to apply its expedited procedure, it must both explain the matters of fact and law which establish urgency and the reasons why expedition is appropriate.
[38] Rule 266.5 of the Rules of Procedure. Under Article 267 TFEU, a stay of the entire proceedings is not compulsory and so Rule 266.5 clarifies that the UPC cannot give its judgment before the CJEU has ruled on the request, but that it is not forced to automatically cease activities and stay its proceedings as soon as a request is sent to the CJEU.
[39] Article 38(2) of Annex I to the UPC Agreement.
[40] For example, regarding whether the terms and conduct behind an offer to license SEPs is FRAND.

the supplementary protection certificate for medicinal products (hereinafter the 'SPC Regulation'). However, other EU instruments are relevant to the matters for which the UPC has competence. In particular:

- Regulation (EU) 1257/2012 – the UP Regulation;
- Regulation (EU) 1260/2012 – the Translation Regulation;
- Article 10(6) of Directive 2001/83 of 6 November 2001 on the Community code relating to medicinal products for human use (the Bolar Exemption);
- Directive 98/44/EC of 6 July 1998 on the legal protection of biotechnological inventions – the Biotechnology Directive;
- Directive 2004/48/EC[41] – the Enforcement Directive; and
- Regulation (EU) 1610/96 of 23 July 1996 concerning the creation of a supplementary protection certificate for plant protection products – the 'Plant Products SPC Regulation'.

The obligation on the UPC to apply EU law[42] means that referrals of matters of interpretation under these instruments, and the body of existing rulings of the CJEU that apply to them, continue to be a feature of decision making in the UPC.

ii. Referring Matters of Infringement to the CJEU?

The penultimate draft of the UP Regulation contained three provisions – Articles 6–8 – mirroring those presently in the UPC Agreement in Articles 25–27. Articles 6–8 provided the substantive rules on infringement: respectively, the right to prevent the direct use of the invention; the right to prevent the indirect use of the invention; and limitations of the effects of a patent. The inclusion of these provisions in the UP Regulation signed on December 2012 would have meant that matters of substantive infringement law were referable to the CJEU. However, as a result of late negotiations, Articles 6–8 were removed (see the Introduction).

The present Article 5 which replaced these provisions was designed to steer a course around political objections to this late change (the European Parliament had already approved the previous drafting) – Opinion 1/09 of the CJEU and the desire to remove questions of infringement from the possibility of referral to the CJEU. Article 5 attempts to do this by retaining the substantive laws of infringement in a European instrument, but only by reference to national law:

ARTICLE 5
Uniform protection

1. The European patent with unitary effect shall confer on its proprietor the right to prevent any third party from committing acts against which that patent provides protection throughout the territories of the participating Member States in which it has unitary effect, subject to applicable limitations.
2. The scope of that right and its limitations shall be uniform in all participating Member States in which the patent has unitary effect.

---

[41] Directive 2004/48/EC of the European Parliament and of the Council of 29 April 2004 on the enforcement of intellectual property rights.
[42] Article 20 UPC Agreement.

3. The acts against which the patent provides protection referred to in paragraph 1 and the applicable limitations shall be those defined by the law applied to European patents with unitary effect in the participating Member State whose national law is applicable to the European patent with unitary effect as an object of property in accordance with Article 7.
4. In its report referred to in Article 16(1), the Commission shall evaluate the functioning of the applicable limitations and shall, where necessary, make appropriate proposals.

The national law in question is the UPC Agreement as implemented in national law. The UPC is itself not an EU instrument – it is a treaty of the contracting states. In theory, therefore, it should not trigger a referral under Article 21 UPC Agreement. However, this understanding of Article 5 has not been without controversy.[43]

IX. Relationship with Proceedings in the EPO

A. The European Patent Context

i. The Relationship between the EPO and National Proceedings

European patents take effect as a bundle of national rights upon grant, but it is still possible for them to be revoked centrally at the EPO, using the opposition procedure. An opposition must be initiated within nine months of grant of the patent or the right to oppose the patent in the EPO is permanently lost. The opposition will typically end with an oral hearing, followed by a decision of the Opposition Division that the patent in issue is invalid, is valid or is partially valid and must be amended. It is not unusual for the decision of the Opposition Division to take two to three years from the date of grant of the patent in question. The Opposition Division decision may then be appealed to the TBA, which may uphold or overturn it. A final decision of the TBA that a patent is invalid will result in the patent being revoked in all the national offices in which it is registered. The decision of the TBA may take a further two years or more after the decision of the Opposition Division.[44]

ii. Outcomes of Parallel National and EPO Proceedings

A decision that a European patent is invalid in the EPO results in the revocation of all patents in the granted European patent bundle in their national offices of registration. If the nine-month opposition period passes without an opposition being filed, a party can only seek to invalidate a European patent in the respective courts of the countries in which its national counterparts are registered.

---

[43] The counterview is that Article 5 UP Regulation, as a provision of EU law that provides for uniform protection against certain acts, is sufficient to import substantive rules into EU law, bringing them within the competence of the CJEU.

[44] More complex proceedings may involve remittal to the Opposition Division. Acceleration of EPO proceedings is also possible under certain circumstances. A review of EPO procedure is beyond the scope of this book and reference should be made to the Guidelines for Examination in the EPO, https://www.epo.org/law-practice/legal-texts/guidelines.html.

In the courts of some European countries, a party can seek to invalidate the national counterpart of the European patent at the same time that an opposition is already under way in the EPO. Other national courts retain a discretion to decide whether the national proceedings should be stayed whilst the opposition and appeal proceedings continue. If there is no stay, and parallel proceedings continue, then the following combination of outcomes is possible, depending on whether the patent is held invalid or upheld in each proceeding:

- the TBA holds the patent invalid for all EPC countries first, in which case, it is revoked and cannot be reinstated in any EPC country later on, regardless of the outcome of the national proceedings;
- the patent is upheld first in the national proceedings of an EPC country, in which case, it may later be later invalidated in the TBA and revoked in all EPC countries;
- the patent is upheld in the TBA for all EPC countries, in which case, it may later be held invalid and revoked by a national court of an EPC country in the respective national jurisdiction; or
- the patent is held invalid by a national court of an EPC country and revoked, in which case, it may not be reinstated in that EPC country by a later decision of the TBA to uphold it centrally.

If a patent is successfully defended in the national court only to be invalidated later on in the TBA, the reasons for requesting a stay of the national proceedings may include the desire to avoid wasted costs. Against a stay may be the fact that proceedings in the EPO will conclude much later than those in the national proceedings. In particular, if a national appeal court can decide in just two years that a patent is invalid, the parties are provided with the commercial certainty that comes from knowing that the patent cannot then be reinstated by the TBA. The alternative may be to wait several years longer for a final decision of the TBA.

However, a decision of a national court to proceed can create problems. One particular example of this is where national proceedings result in a successful patent infringement claim and damages are awarded. If that patent is later invalidated in the EPO, questions may arise as to the status of the damages and costs awarded.[45]

iii. EPO Central Amendment and National Actions

Further questions may arise from the parallel operation of the EPO as a forum for claim amendment. In particular, if a patent is held invalid at first instance in a national court, the appeal court may need to respond to an application to amend the patent in the EPO under Article 105a:[46]

<blockquote>

Article 105a

(1) At the request of the proprietor, the European patent may be revoked or be limited by an amendment of the claims. The request shall be filed with the European Patent Office in

</blockquote>

---

[45] See, for comparison, the English approach in *Unilin Beheer BV v Berry Floor NV* [2007] EWCA Civ 364 in respect of the English courts. For a full discussion, see Paul England et al, *A Practitioner's Guide to European Patent Law*, 2nd edn (Hart Publishing, 2022).
[46] Under Article 105a, introduced by the EPC 2000.

accordance with the Implementing Regulations. It shall not be deemed to have been filed until the limitation or revocation fee has been paid.

(2) The request may not be filed while opposition proceedings in respect of the European patent are pending.

One answer is for the national court to adjourn the substantive appeal proceedings pending such amendments.[47]

B. Parallel UPC Proceedings and Stay

There is no requirement to file opposition proceedings against a European patent or a Unitary Patent in the EPO before bringing a revocation action or revocation counterclaim in respect of that patent in the UPC[48] – an opposition or appeal can proceed in the EPO simultaneously with an action in a UPC division. Third parties thus have a choice as to whether to bring revocation proceedings in one forum or the other, or both. However, the jurisdiction of the UPC is connected to and affected by concurrent opposition and appeal proceedings in certain respects.

i. Stay of Proceedings Generally

If 'revocation, limitation or opposition proceedings' are in progress in the EPO, a party to UPC litigation is required to inform the court that there are opposition proceedings pending in the EPO concerning the patent in suit in the UPC. It is not specified whether this party must be the patentee or the party bringing the revocation action. The court must also be informed if the EPO proceedings have been accelerated.[49] The panel of the UPC dealing with the action then has the discretion to stay its proceedings in circumstances where a final 'rapid decision' may be expected from the EPO.[50] There is no guidance on the meaning of 'rapid decision', but the wording reflects that found in the Rules (see section IX.B.ii below).[51]

The discretion of the UPC to stay parallel proceedings invites comparison with, for example, the Dutch and English courts. If a final decision of the EPO is still many years away at the time the stay is sought, some national proceedings permit proceedings to continue, despite the risk of wasted costs or inconsistent decisions.[52]

---

[47] For comparison, in *Samsung Electronics* [2014] EWCA Civ 376, the English Court of Appeal noted that, in marked contrast to opposition proceedings, the EPO amendment procedure is intended to be simple and quick and, in that case, amendment was likely to be determined before the UK proceedings themselves concluded. The Court also stated that the UK Patent Act 1977 specifically contemplated the possibility of concurrent proceedings between the UK and the EPO, and that there is no prohibition on central amendment while proceedings are pending in a national court. The Court's judgment was reinforced by its concern that it might otherwise come to a decision on patent claims that were deemed, post-amendment, never to have existed.
[48] Article 33(8) UPC Agreement.
[49] ibid Article 33(10).
[50] ibid.
[51] Rule 118.2 of the Rules of Procedure.
[52] For comparison, this approach is summarised in *Glaxo Group Ltd v Genentech Inc* [2008] Bus LR 888, in which the English Court of Appeal established a number of guidelines on the stay of an action pending EPO proceedings. In *IPCom GmbH & Co KG v HTC Europe Co Ltd and Others* [2013] EWCA Civ 1496, the Court of Appeal updated the guidelines in *Glaxo v Genentech*, but maintained the view that the considerable duration of EPO proceedings beyond the anticipated date of a decision in the UK court would point in favour of refusing to stay the UK action in most cases.

ii. Stay of Infringement Proceedings Specifically

The internal jurisdictional rules governing the divisions of the UPC may result in the bifurcation of infringement and revocation actions concerning the same parties and the same patent (see Chapter 9).[53] In order to prevent the possibility in such circumstances that a final injunction is obtained before the validity of the relevant patent is tested – an 'injunction gap' – infringement proceedings may be stayed if a revocation action is pending in the central division as well as if an EPO opposition is pending:[54]

> 2. If, while there are infringement proceedings before a local or regional division, a revocation action is pending between the same parties before the central division or an opposition is pending before the European Patent Office, the local or regional division:
>
> ...
>
> (b) may stay the infringement proceedings pending a decision in the revocation procedure or a decision of the European Patent Office and shall stay the infringement proceedings if it is of the view that there is a high likelihood that the relevant claims of the patent will be held to be invalid on any ground by the final decision in the revocation proceedings or of the European Patent Office where such decision of the European Patent Office may be expected to be given rapidly.

The panel hearing a UPC infringement action (whether a local or regional division) may stay the UPC infringement action at its discretion if there is a pending EPO opposition, or a pending revocation action in the central division, and the decision is expected rapidly. Furthermore, the panel has an obligation to stay an infringement action if there is a high likelihood of the patent being held invalid in the revocation action or the EPO, and the decision is expectedly rapidly.

iii. Conditions Subsequent to Stay

A local or regional division may make its order on infringement conditional upon a final decision of the UPC or the EPO on validity:[55]

> (a) [the local or regional division] may render its decision on the merits of the infringement claim, including its orders, under the condition subsequent to Article 56(1) of the Agreement that the patent is not held to be wholly or partially invalid by the final decision in the revocation proceedings or a final decision of the European Patent Office or under any other term or conditions; or
>
> ...

Any party to the proceedings may apply to the local or regional division concerned with the infringement action within two months of a final decision of the EPO on the validity of the patent in the litigation for the appropriate consequential order.[56] Invalidation of a European patent in the EPO has the effect of revoking all national validations of the patent in their national registers, which is effective *ab initio*. Subsequent conditions can therefore prevent

---

[53] Article 33 UPC Agreement.
[54] Rule 118.2(b) of the Rules of Procedure.
[55] ibid Rule 118.2(a).
[56] ibid Rule 118.4.

a party held liable for infringement in a local or regional court remaining responsible for damages or other relief on a patent that the EPO later holds never to have existed.[57]

X. Central Amendment Proceedings in the EPO

Any division of the EPO may stay an action (including revocation and infringement) if a rapid decision can be expected from the EPO in respect of 'any pending revocation, limitation or opposition proceedings before the EPO'. The word 'limitation' in this context is broad enough to refer to the central amendment procedure (see section IX.A.iii above), indicating that the UPC may stay proceedings pending a final decision of this procedure if it is expected rapidly.

A. Oversight of the EPO in Relation to Unitary Patents

The EPO has a number of tasks related to requests, registration requirements and administration of Unitary Patents (see Chapter 1).[58] Actions against the EPO for decisions made when carrying out these tasks are within the exclusive competence of the UPC.[59]

---

[57] For comparison, this problem has arisen in the UK, where a damages award stands even if the patent is later revoked in the EPO – for example, see *Unilin Beheer BV v Berry Floor NV* [2007] EWCA Civ 364. More recently, the question has arisen as to whether a party that has been held to infringe a valid patent in the UK can use the later revocation of the patent in the EPO as a defence in the enquiry as to damages. This question arose most recently before the UK Supreme Court in *Virgin Atlantic Airways Ltd (Respondent) v Zodiac Seats UK Ltd (Formerly Known as Contour Aerospace Ltd)* [2013] UKSC 46, in which the Supreme Court concluded that where judgment is given in a UK court that a patent (whether UK or European) is valid and infringed, and the patent is subsequently revoked or amended (whether in the UK or at the EPO), the defendant is entitled to rely on the retrospective effect of revocation or amendment on the enquiry as to damages.
[58] Article 9 UP Regulation.
[59] Article 32(1)(i) UPC Agreement.

3
Decision Making

The rules governing the constitution of judicial panels in the UPC are designed to achieve three primary aims: convergence in the approach to procedural rules; convergence of the substantive law applied; and, as a result, consistency in judicial decision making. In part as a logistical measure and in part to achieve the above aims, the judiciary of the UPC is organised around a 'Pool of Judges'.[1] The judges in the Pool are drawn from all the contracting Member States and thus bring a mixture of skills and expertise to the Court, as well as a range of approaches to substantive and procedural patent matters. The Pool of Judges is composed of both legally qualified and technically qualified judges, and the panels of the divisions of the Court of First Instance are allocated from it[2] (but not the judges of the Court of Appeal). The roles of the judges, the structures of the panels in which they sit and the relationship between the Court of First Instance and the Court of Appeal are all addressed in this chapter.

I. The Roles of the Judges

A. Technical Judges and Legal Judges

Legally qualified judges are required to 'possess the qualifications required for appointment to judicial offices in a Contracting Member State'.[3] This does not require that they already hold judicial office in their respective home states.[4] A small minority of legally qualified judges from the contracting Member States have technical backgrounds, leaving a majority that do not. The presence of one or more technical judges on panels of the Court of First Instance and the Court of Appeal therefore solves the problem that would otherwise encumber many divisions of the UPC: a lack of understanding of the technical subject matter that typifies patent actions. The role of the technical judges is therefore to assist in the evaluation of technical evidence and other material for the legally qualified judges. Technically qualified judges are required to have a university degree and proven expertise in a field of technology, in addition to proven knowledge of civil law and procedure relevant to patent litigation.[5] However, technical judges are not intended to substitute for the role of experts. A panel has the option to appoint a Court expert for the purpose of providing an impartial

---

[1] Article 18 UPC Agreement.
[2] ibid Article 18(3).
[3] ibid Article 15(2).
[4] The candidate must only be eligible for such appointment.
[5] Article 15(3) UPC Agreement.

and detailed account of a particular technology if it considers it necessary. Each party may also instruct one or more experts unilaterally (see Chapter 16). The result is that a panel may have available to it as many as three sources of input on technical matters.

The Pool of Judges is intended to include at least one technical judge with the relevant qualifications and experience per 'field of technology'.[6] How the fields of technology are to be identified and how many there will be is unclear: it would be unrealistic to provide a technical judge for each and every classification and sub-classification of patentable subject matter in the International Patent Classification (IPC) of the World Intellectual Property Organization; at the other extreme, it would seem unsatisfactory for technical judges to be appointed merely according to the broadest classifications in that scheme, such as 'Agriculture' and 'Tobacco'. Furthermore, whilst knowledge and expertise relating to a diverse range of subject matters may occasionally be necessary, most expertise will be needed on the more commonly disputed subject areas: life sciences, electronics and mechanical engineering.

B. The Judge-Rapporteur, the Presiding Judge and the Standing Judge

i. The Court of First Instance

Unless the Rules of Procedure specify that an action is exclusively reserved for a panel of the Court, the President of the Court of First Instance or the President of the Court of Appeal, the action may be performed by the presiding judge or the judge-rapporteur of the panel to which the action was assigned[7] or the standing judge.[8] A party who believes they have reason to object to a judge taking part in proceedings[9] must as soon as is reasonably practicable in the circumstances notify the President of the Court of First Instance or the President of the Court of Appeal, as appropriate.[10] A single legally qualified judge may perform the action if it has been assigned to them.[11] The judge-rapporteur is responsible for most of the management of an action on the merits up until the beginning of the oral procedure. At the beginning of the oral procedure, the presiding judge takes over general responsibility for case management. There is a similar division of responsibility between the judge-rapporteur and the presiding judge in the procedure for the determination of damages. Proceedings for costs are the primary responsibility of the judge-rapporteur alone.

After an action is assigned to a panel of a division, one judge of the panel is appointed as the presiding judge.[12] The presiding judge then appoints a judge of the panel as the judge-rapporteur[13] and the parties are informed of the appointment. The judge-rapporteur may be the presiding judge.[14]

---

[6] ibid Article 18(2).
[7] Rule 1.2(a) of the Rules of Procedure.
[8] Designated according to ibid Rule 345.4.
[9] Under Article 7(4) of the Statute of the UPC Agreement.
[10] Rule 346 of the Rules of Procedure.
[11] ibid Rule 1.2(b).
[12] Article 19(1) of the Statute of the UPC Agreement.
[13] Rules 18 and 38(b) of the Rules of Procedure; Article 19(5) of the Statute of the UPC Agreement.
[14] Rule 18 of the Rules of Procedure.

50 Decision Making

a. The Judge-Rapporteur

The judge-rapporteur's role includes the following:

(a) *During the written procedure* – following appointment, the judge-rapporteur may be required to: decide, and make any necessary order, arising from a preliminary objection; following service of the statement of defence, consult with the parties and set a date and time for an interim conference, and set a date for the oral hearing;[15] request the allocation of a technically qualified judge[16] or, further to an application by a party, consult with the President of the Court of First Instance on the appointment of a technically qualified judge;[17] order the lodging of translations of pleadings and other documents;[18] make orders about the translation and confidentiality of documents;[19] accelerate proceedings when a revocation action is assigned to the central division;[20] close the written procedure and notify the parties;[21] and inform the central division of the dates of the interim conference and the oral hearing.[22]

(b) *During the interim procedure*: the judge-rapporteur will: make all necessary preparations for the oral hearing, including one or more interim conferences;[23] make orders further to decisions made at the interim conference;[24] determine the value of the dispute;[25] summon the parties to an oral hearing;[26] make decisions about the need for simultaneous interpretation at the oral hearing;[27] and inform the parties and the presiding judge that the interim procedure is closed.[28]

b. The Presiding Judge

The presiding judge manages and conducts the oral hearing,[29] including controlling the questions to witnesses and experts,[30] and setting time limits on oral submissions and testimony.[31]

c. The Standing Judge

A standing judge is appointed by the presiding judge of each division to hear urgent actions.[32] In particular, the standing judge will decide applications by a proprietor of a patent whose

---

[15] ibid Rule 28.
[16] By its own initiative (having consulted with the parties and the presiding judge) further to ibid Rule 34; or further to the panel of a regional or local division deciding to hear both infringement and revocation actions under Article 33(3)(a) UPC Agreement (Rule 37.3 of the Rules of Procedure).
[17] Rule 33.3 of the Rules of Procedure.
[18] Where proceedings have been transferred: ibid Rule 39.
[19] ibid Rules 13.3, 13.1(q) and 262.1.
[20] Further to Article 33(3)(b) UPC Agreement and Rule 40 of the Rules of Procedure.
[21] Rule 35(a) of the Rules of Procedure.
[22] ibid Rule 35(b).
[23] ibid Rule 101.1.
[24] ibid Rule 105.4.
[25] ibid Rule 104(i).
[26] ibid Rule 108.
[27] ibid Rule 109.
[28] ibid Rule 110.
[29] ibid Rule 111.
[30] ibid Rule 112.4.
[31] ibid Rule 113.1 and 113.2.
[32] ibid Rule 345.5; see also Rule 1.2(c).

request for unitary effect has been rejected by the EPO.[33] In cases of 'extreme urgency', the standing judge may immediately decide applications for preserving evidence[34] or provisional measures[35] *ex parte*.

ii. The Court of Appeal

Similar to the Court of First Instance, in the Court of Appeal one judge of the panel is appointed as the presiding judge.[36] A further judge, or the same judge, of the panel of the Court of Appeal is appointed the rapporteur[37] and a standing judge is also appointed.[38]

The judge-rapporteur of the Court of Appeal is responsible for the preparation of the action for the oral hearing.[39] Issues that will be dealt with by the judge-rapporteur will include: translations of the file;[40] preliminary examination of the statement of grounds of appeal,[41] including the power to rule an appeal inadmissible;[42] and deciding when the appeal is ready for the oral hearing and summoning the parties to the hearing. At this point, the interim procedure is deemed closed and the presiding judge of the Court of Appeal takes over conduct of the oral hearing.[43]

The standing judge of the Court of Appeal will hear appeals of a decision of the standing judge of the Court of First Instance regarding annulling a decision of the EPO to reject a request for unitary effect.[44] The standing judge will also decide on a discretionary review in the event of a refusal of the Court of First Instance to grant leave to appeal.[45]

II. The Structure of the Panels

A. The Court of First Instance

Oral proceedings in the divisions of the Court of First Instance of the UPC are heard by panels of judges, except in the circumstances where the parties have agreed that a single judge can sit.[46] One judge of each panel will be designated as the presiding judge, but certain other functions may be delegated to one or more of the judges.[47] First instance panels comprise three legally qualified judges drawn from different contracting Member States.[48] The rules governing the mix between local and foreign judges on a panel are as follows.

---

[33] ibid Rule 97.4.
[34] ibid Rule 194.4.
[35] ibid Rule 209.3. See also applications for suspensive effect (ibid Rule 223).
[36] Article 21(1) of the Statute of the UPC Agreement.
[37] ibid Article 21(4).
[38] Rule 345.8 and 345.5 of the Rules of Procedure.
[39] ibid Rule 239.
[40] ibid Rule 232.
[41] ibid Rule 233.
[42] ibid Rule 233.2.
[43] ibid Rules 239.2 and 240.
[44] ibid Rule 97.4.
[45] ibid Rule 220.4.
[46] Article 8(7) UPC Agreement.
[47] ibid Article 19 Annex I.
[48] ibid Article 8(1).

52 Decision Making

i. Regional and Local Divisions

a. Local and Foreign Judges

A panel comprises a mixture of judges who are local and foreign to the country where the division is located. Local judges are those from the contracting Member State (or States) hosting the division in question, and foreign judges are from other contracting Member States.

A local division that has a record of dealing with an average of 50 or more cases per year over three successive years[49] has a panel consisting of two legally qualified local judges and one legally qualified foreign judge.[50] Those local divisions that have an average of fewer than 50 cases over three successive years have panels consisting of one legally qualified local judge and two legally qualified foreign judges, allocated from the Pool of Judges.[51] The panels of the regional divisions will be occupied by two legally qualified judges from the contracting Member States hosting that division and one foreign judge[52] (see Figure 3.1).

Figure 3.1 Judicial panels of the local and regional divisions

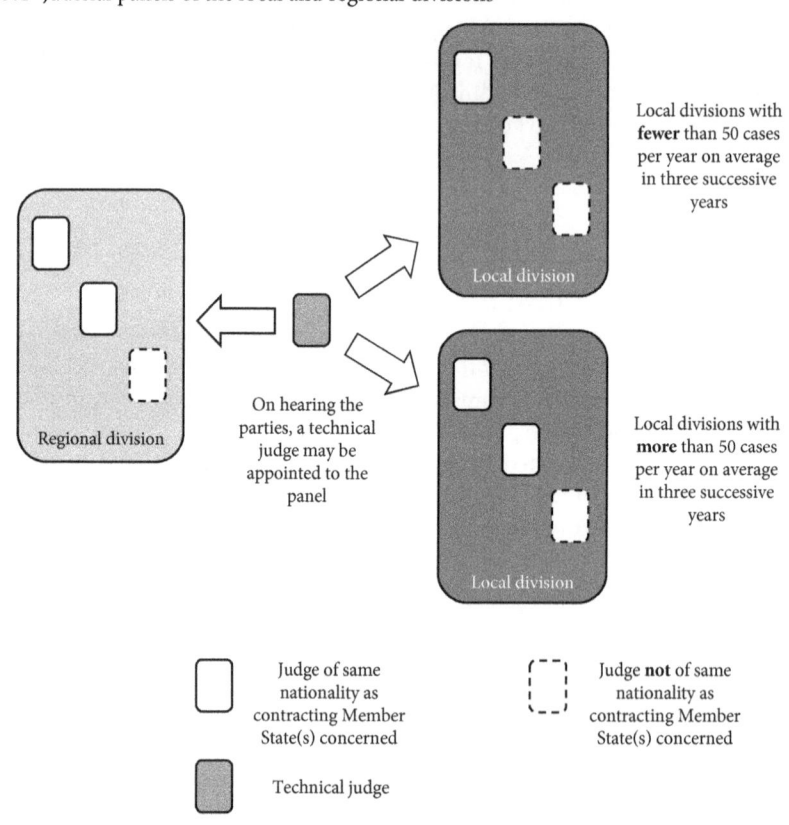

---

[49] In the first three years of the UPC's operation, this will be the record of cases in the national court of the same contracting Member State,
[50] Allocated from the Pool of Judges, further to Article 8(3) UPC Agreement.
[51] ibid Article 8(2).
[52] ibid Article 8(4).

b. Appointing a Technical Judge

A technical judge with qualifications and expertise in the field of technology at issue in an action may be appointed to a regional or local division by request of either one of the parties to the President of the Court of First Instance. The panel itself may make this request of its own initiative if it deems it appropriate, having first heard the parties.[53] Alternatively, the UPC Agreement allows the appointment of a technical judge if a local or regional division decides to hear an action for patent revocation.[54]

The addition of a technical judge to a panel of a division of the Court of First Instance has the consequence that there are four judges sitting and the possibility of a split decision. In this situation, the decision of the presiding judge will prevail.[55]

ii. The Central Division

Central division panels are composed differently from the regional and local divisions. The central division has panels, each comprising two legally qualified judges from different contracting Member States. There are no rules governing how many of the legally qualified judges, if any, must come from the contracting Member State hosting the section of the central division in question. There is also a technically qualified judge who sits in all cases[56] (Figure 3.2).

Panels hearing actions concerning decisions of the EPO made when carrying out its administrative tasks[57] are dealt with differently. Panels on these cases comprise three legally qualified judges who are nationals of different contracting Member States (see Chapter 12).

Figure 3.2 Judicial panels of the central divisions

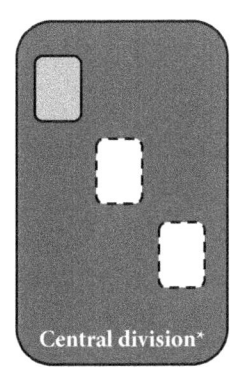

*Except for cases under Article 31(1)(i), which have three legally qualified judges

---

[53] ibid Article 8(5).
[54] Further to a decision under Article 33(3) UPC Agreement.
[55] ibid Article 35, Annex I.
[56] ibid Article 8(6).
[57] Referred to in Article 9 UP Regulation and Article 32(1)(i) UPC Agreement.

B. Panels of the Court of Appeal

The Court of Appeal sits in panels of five judges: three legally qualified judges who are drawn from different contracting Member States; and two technically qualified judges[58] (Figure 3.3). In common with the Court of First Instance, technically qualified judges do not sit on cases concerning the administrative tasks of the EPO.[59]

C. The Full Court

When the case is of 'exceptional importance, and in particular when the decision may affect the unity and consistency of the case law of the Court', and if the presiding judge proposes it, the Court of Appeal has the discretion to refer the case to the 'full court'.[60] When a referral to the full court is made, the presiding judge of the panel requests that the President of

Figure 3.3 Judicial panels of the Court of Appeal and the full court

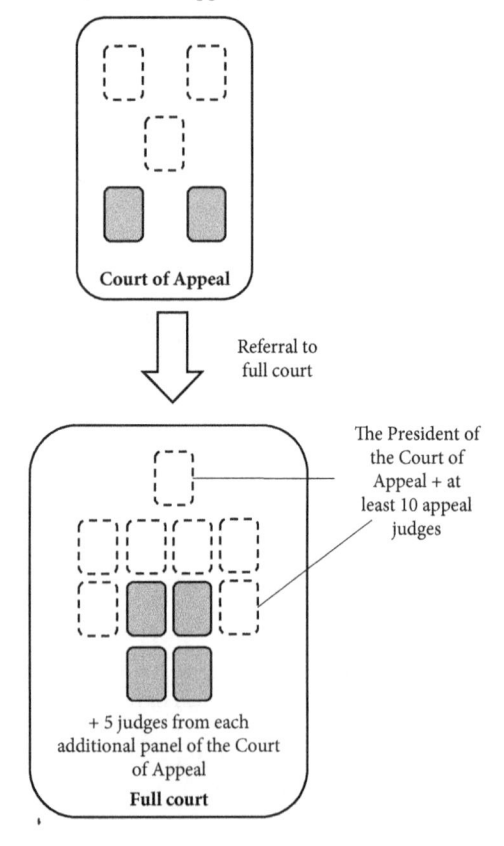

---

[58] Article 9(1) UPC Agreement.
[59] See ibid Article 32(1)(i) and (9)(2).
[60] Article 21(2) Annex 1 UPC Agreement, Statute of the Unified Patent Court.

the Court of Appeal and the two judges of the Court of Appeal who are members of the 'Presidium'[61] appoint the President and no fewer than 10 (legal and technical) judges of the Court of Appeal to represent the current two panels of the Court of Appeal. In the event that the Court of Appeal has more than two panels, the appointees to the full Court must increase by five judges (legal and technical) for each additional panel.[62]

III. The Scope of Appeals

A. Appeal and Referral Back

Decisions of the Court of Appeal may be based on issues of fact as well as law.[63] However, new requests, facts and evidence may only be introduced on appeal having taken account of: whether they could not reasonably have been expected to be submitted during proceedings at first instance;[64] they are relevant; and the position of the other party to the appeal.[65] The power of the Court of Appeal to revisit the finding of facts based on evidence heard at first instance is unclear in the absence of new evidence being submitted at the appeal stage. The limitation of the appeal to 'requests' made at first instance appears to refer to the issues raised and relief sought at that stage.

There is an automatic right to appeal to the Court of Appeal[66] of final decisions of the Court of Instance, decisions terminating proceedings as regards one of the parties, and certain orders: that the language of proceedings should be the language in which the patent was granted;[67] the production of evidence;[68] provisional and protective measures;[69] and communication of information[70] (sometimes referred to as 'privileged orders'). All other orders, including orders following a decision under Article 33(3),[71] are subject to leave to appeal from the Court of First Instance.[72] If the Court of First Instance refuses leave to appeal, a discretionary review of that decision may be requested (see Chapter 17).[73]

Except in appeals against decisions on revocation and decisions of the EPO concerning its administrative tasks under Article 9 UP Regulation,[74] appeals do not generally have a suspensive effect. However, this is subject to a decision of the Court of Appeal to the

---

[61] See ibid Article 15 Annex 1. Chaired by the President of the Court of Appeal, the Presidium comprises two judges elected from the Court of Appeal, three full-time judges elected from the Court of First Instance and the Registrar (as a non-voting member).
[62] Rule 238A(2) of the Rules of Procedure.
[63] Article 73(3) UPC Agreement.
[64] ibid Article 73(4).
[65] Rule 222.2 of the Rules of Procedure.
[66] Article 73 UPC Agreement.
[67] ibid Article 49(5).
[68] ibid Article 59.
[69] ibid Article 62.
[70] ibid Article 67.
[71] Arising from decisions made under ibid Article 33(3) (see ch 15).
[72] Rule 220.2 of the Rules of Procedure.
[73] ibid Rule 220.4.
[74] Article 74(2) UPC Agreement.

contrary at the request of one of the parties (see Chapter 17).[75] The Court of Appeal may hear appeals of decisions from separate courts on validity and infringement together.[76]

B. Majority Decisions and Dissent

In circumstances where a technical judge is appointed to a local or regional panel of the Court of First Instance, the number of judges on the panel increases to four. This even number of judges could result in a split decision of two judges against two. In these circumstances, the presiding judge's decision prevails.[77] The deliberations of the judges of the Court of First Instance and the Court of Appeal are made as soon as possible after the closure of the oral hearing, in private.[78] Only judges who were present at the oral hearing may take part in the deliberations on the decision.[79] A judge who dissents from the decision of the majority will be required to provide a reasoned, written opinion signed by the judge in question.[80]

Decisions of the full court must be made by three-quarters of the judges on the panel of that court.[81] This would require 9 out of the 11 judges who currently make up the full court to concur.

IV. Case Management

A. The Order of Actions

The general rule is that the Court must deal with actions in the order for which they become ready for hearing according to the date set for the oral hearing.[82] However, after hearing the parties, the presiding judge of a panel may direct that a particular action is given priority and that the relevant time limits in the Rules of Procedure are shortened accordingly, or that the action is deferred to be dealt with later, in particular if it is for the purpose of facilitating a settlement[83] (see Chapter 14).

B. Case Management Powers

Considerable emphasis is placed on the judges of the UPC to actively manage cases. Subject to ensuring consistency in the application and the interpretation of the Rules, the principles

---

[75] Rule 223 of the Rules of Procedure.
[76] ibid Rule 220.5.
[77] Article 78(1) UPC Agreement and Article 35(1), Annex 1 UPC Agreement, Statute of the Unified Patent Court.
[78] Rules 344.3 and 344.1 of the Rules of Procedure; Article 34 Annex 1 UPC Agreement, Statute of the Unified Patent Court.
[79] Rule 344.2 of the Rules of Procedure.
[80] Article 78(2) UPC Agreement; and Article 36 Annex 1 UPC Agreement, Statute of the Unified Patent Court.
[81] Article 35(2) Annex 1 UPC Agreement, Statute of the Unified Patent Court.
[82] Rule 343.1 of the Rules of Procedure; see also Rule 108.
[83] ibid Rule 343.2.

to be applied are those of proportionality, flexibility, fairness and equity[84] rather than rigid adherence to formality. This is stated in the Preamble to the Rules of Procedure:

> 4. Flexibility shall be ensured by applying all procedural rules in a flexible and balanced manner with the required level of discretion for the judges to organise the proceedings in the most efficient and costs effective manner.

Ensuring this flexibility requires that the UPC system provides its judges with a wide range of powers to actively manage cases. Matters encompassed by active case management include:[85]

(a) encouraging the parties to cooperate with each other during the proceedings;
(b) identifying the issues at an early stage;
(c) deciding promptly which issues need to full investigation and disposing summarily of other issues;
(d) deciding the order in which issues are to be resolved;
(e) encouraging parties to make use of the patent medication and arbitration centre and facilitating this use;
(f) helping the parties to settle the whole or part of the action;
(g) fixing a timetable or otherwise controlling the progress of the action;
(h) considering whether the likely benefits of taking a particular step justify the cost of taking it;
(i) dealing with as many aspects of the action as the UPC can on the same occasion;
(j) dealing with the action without the parties needing to attend in person;
(k) making use of available technical means; and
(l) giving directions to ensure that the hearing of the action proceeds quickly and efficiently.

In the written and interim procedures, implementing these principles is the responsibility of the judge-rapporteur[86] and, after closure of the interim procedure, it is the responsibility of the presiding judge in consultation with the judge-rapporteur. The judge-rapporteur may refer their proposed decisions on these matters to the panel. Furthermore, decisions and orders of the judge-rapporteur may be reviewed by the panel on a reasoned application by a party[87] (see Chapter 13).

V. Ensuring Uniformity of Approach

A. Achieving a Mix of Judges

The rules by which judges are assigned to the panels of the local, regional and central divisions of the Court of First Instance and the Court of Appeal are designed to achieve

---

[84] Paragraph 2 of the Preamble to the Rules of Procedure.
[85] ibid Rule 332.
[86] ibid Rule 331.1.
[87] ibid Rule 333.1.

consistency of quality in decision making and in the application of substantive and procedural law. They do so by providing for a mix of national legal experience. The expertise of existing national patent judges is particularly important to the UPC. Those contracting Member States that have an average number of fewer than 50 patent cases per year over a consecutive period of three years will have only one local judge per panel of three in a local division. The remaining seats on the panel will be occupied by judges foreign to the division, but allocated from the international pool of judges recruited from across the contracting states to the UPC. This allows more experienced judges to be in the majority where they are most needed. For example, there are judges from Germany, the Netherlands and France, amongst other countries, who have patent experience. These judges can be expected to share their expertise with judges from countries where patent cases are rare or who have had no experience of patent matters prior to sitting in the UPC.

B. The Role of the Court of Appeal in Building Uniformity

In most national jurisdictions, the role of the Court of Appeal is to review the decisions of the lower courts, both as a guard against manifest errors and also to provide authority for interpretation of the law to the lower courts. However, Courts of Appeal in different countries in Europe have different approaches to findings of fact. Courts such as the Dutch Court of Appeal conduct a complete review of findings of both fact and law from first instance. German appeal courts review only findings of law; submission of new evidence is generally not allowed. If the legal review of the appeals court should require that comprehensive new evidence would need to be taken, the case is remitted to first instance.[88]

The Court of Appeal of the UPC has all the powers of the Court of First Instance and can either reject an appeal or set the decision or order aside, totally or in part substituting its own decision or order, including an order for costs of the proceedings at first instance and on appeal.[89] Although the Court of Appeal of the UPC can review decisions on facts and legal issues,[90] the extent to which it will revisit first instance findings of fact, in the absence of new evidence is unclear. Furthermore, the Court of Appeal does not generally determine issues of law and then refer its decision back for application to the facts, per Article 75:

> Decision on appeal and referral back
> (1) If an appeal pursuant to Article 73 is well-founded, the Court of Appeal shall revoke the decision of the Court of First Instance and give a final decision. The Court of Appeal may in exceptional cases and in accordance with the Rules of Procedure refer the case back to the Court of First Instance for decision.
> (2) Where a case is referred back to the Court of First Instance pursuant to paragraph 1, the Court of First Instance shall be bound by the decision of the Court of Appeal on points of law.

Referrals back to the Court of First Instance may happen only in 'exceptional cases'. For this purpose, an exceptional case does not include one in which the Court of First Instance

---

[88] Section 538 II Nr 1 of the German Civil Procedure Code.
[89] Rule 242(1) and (2)(a) of the Rules of Procedure.
[90] Article 73(3) UPC Agreement.

failed to decide an issue which it is necessary for the Court of Appeal to decide on appeal.[91] This function should be compared with that of the Full Court, which is intended to decide matters of law for the purpose of establishing consistency and uniformity.[92]

In reviewing the law applied in first instance decisions, the Court of Appeal and, exceptionally, the Full Court, are thus expected to establish a body of case law that provides an increasingly uniform approach to patent law in the UPC over time.

---

[91] Rule 242(2)(b) of the Rules of Procedure.
[92] ibid Rule 238A.1.

4

Sources of Law

The most common matters of substantive law that will arise before the UPC are those listed within the exclusive competence of the UPC:[1] infringement (including non-infringement) and validity of patents and SPCs; associated damages and relief; rights based on prior use; and compensation for licences of right.[2] Furthermore, as Chapter 2 explains, there may be matters for which the UPC has non-exclusive jurisdiction: disputes concerning the terms of patent agreements; employee inventor rights and compensation; and issues of patents as objects of property. This chapter outlines the sources of law that will be applicable to these matters and associated issues.[3]

I. Outline of Sources

The sources of law from which national courts draw when making decisions in national patent disputes are already multi-layered. They include the EPC, the Community Patent Convention 1989 (CPC 1989)[4] and respective domestic laws. EU laws are also relevant: Article 10 of Directive 2001/83/EC,[5] the Bolar Exemption; Directive 2004/48/EC,[6] the Enforcement Directive; Regulation 469/2009,[7] the SPC Regulation; and Directive 98/44/EC,[8] the Biotechnology Directive. However, these instruments are merely the statutory lining to a much larger fabric of case law: first, national courts must interpret the provisions of these instruments case by case, providing a mixture of persuasive opinion and binding

---

[1] Article 32 UPC Agreement.
[2] Further to Article 8 UP Regulation.
[3] For national, substantive law, see Paul England et al, *A Practitioner's Guide to European Patent Law*, 2nd edn (Hart Publishing, 2022).
[4] The Agreement relating to Community Patents signed in Luxembourg on 15 December 1989, which attempted, for a second time, to establish the Community Patent Convention instrument was itself never actually ratified. However, the harmonisation of the infringement laws of several Member States in anticipation that the Convention would come into force means that the CPC is an important guide to the interpretation on national laws on acts of infringement.
[5] Directive 2001/83/EC of the European Parliament and of the Council of 6 November 2001 on the Community Code relating to medicinal products for human use.
[6] Directive 2004/48/EC of the European Parliament and of the Council of 29 April 2004 on the enforcement of intellectual property rights.
[7] Regulation 469/2009 of the European Parliament and of the Council of 6 May 2009 concerning the supplementary protection certificate for medicinal products.
[8] Directive 98/44/EC of the European Parliament and of the Council of 6 July 1998 on the legal protection of biotechnological inventions.

authority; second, the decisions of the Boards of Appeal of the EPO add case law to the interpretation and application of the EPC; and, third, decisions are being made by the CJEU, interpreting those EU instruments listed above.

Article 24(1) of the UPC Agreement makes all of these sources of law available to the panels of the UPC divisions on which to base their decisions:

Article 24

Sources of law

(1) In full compliance with Article 20, when hearing a case brought before it under this Agreement, the Court shall base its decisions on:
   (a) Union law, including [the UP Regulation and the Translation Regulation];
   (b) this Agreement;
   (c) the EPC;
   (d) other international agreements applicable to patents and binding on all the Contracting Member States; and
   (e) national law.

One of the principal objectives of the UPC is to establish a common and consistent approach to the application of patent law. In order to do so, it is necessary to examine how the legal instruments of these various sources can be applied in a structured way. The way in which these provisions apply to infringement and validity are discussed further below.

II. The Law of Infringement

A. Acts of Infringement Applicable to European Patents

The substantive law provisions on infringing acts and their exceptions were removed from the UP Regulation shortly before it was signed (see section II.B below). As a result, there is no EU law available under Article 24(1)(a) UPC Agreement that directly determines matters of infringement. Instead, the UPC Agreement is a direct source of substantive law on the acts of infringement and their exceptions. These are found in Articles 25–27:

Article 25

Right to prevent the direct use of the invention

A patent shall confer on its proprietor the right to prevent any third party not having the proprietor's consent from the following:

(a) making, offering, placing on the market or using a product which is the subject matter of the patent, or importing or storing the product for those purposes;
(b) using a process which is the subject matter of the patent or, where the third party knows, or should have known, that the use of the process is prohibited without the consent of the patent proprietor, offering the process for use within the territory of the Contracting Member States in which that patent has effect;
(c) offering, placing on the market, using, or importing or storing for those purposes a product obtained directly by a process which is the subject matter of the patent.

Article 26
Right to prevent the indirect use of the invention

(1) A patent shall confer on its proprietor the right to prevent any third party not having the proprietor's consent from supplying or offering to supply, within the territory of the Contracting Member States in which that patent has effect, any person other than a party entitled to exploit the patented invention, with means, relating to an essential element of that invention, for putting it into effect therein, when the third party knows, or should have known, that those means are suitable and intended for putting that invention into effect.

(2) Paragraph 1 shall not apply when the means are staple commercial products, except where the third party induces the person supplied to perform any of the acts prohibited by Article 25.

(3) Persons performing the acts referred to in Article 27(a) to (e) shall not be considered to be parties entitled to exploit the invention within the meaning of paragraph 1.

Article 27
Limitations of the effects of a patent

The rights conferred by a patent shall not extend to any of the following:

(a) acts done privately and for non-commercial purposes;

(b) acts done for experimental purposes relating to the subject matter of the patented invention;

(c) the use of biological material for the purpose of breeding, or discovering and developing other plant varieties;

(d) the acts allowed pursuant to Article 13(6) of Directive 2001/82/EC or Article 10(6) of Directive 2001/83/EC in respect of any patent covering the product within the meaning of either of those Directives;

(e) the extemporaneous preparation by a pharmacy, for individual cases, of a medicine in accordance with a medical prescription or acts concerning the medicine so prepared;

(f) the use of the patented invention on board vessels of countries of the International Union for the Protection of Industrial Property (Paris Union) or members of the World Trade Organisation, other than those Contracting Member States in which that patent has effect, in the body of such vessel, in the machinery, tackle, gear and other accessories, when such vessels temporarily or accidentally enter the waters of a Contracting Member State in which that patent has effect, provided that the invention is used there exclusively for the needs of the vessel;

(g) the use of the patented invention in the construction or operation of aircraft or land vehicles or other means of transport of countries of the International Union for the Protection of Industrial Property (Paris Union) or members of the World Trade Organization, other than those Contracting Member States in which that patent has effect, or of accessories to such aircraft or land vehicles, when these temporarily or accidentally enter the territory of a Contracting Member State in which that patent has effect;

(h) the acts specified in Article 27 of the Convention on International Civil Aviation of 7 December 1944, where these acts concern the aircraft of a country party to that Convention other than a Contracting Member State in which that patent has effect;

(i) the use by a farmer of the product of his harvest for propagation or multiplication by him on his own holding, provided that the plant propagating material was sold or otherwise commercialised to the farmer by or with the consent of the patent proprietor for agricultural use. The extent and the conditions for this use correspond to those under Article 14 of Regulation (EC) No. 2100/94;

(j) the use by a farmer of protected livestock for an agricultural purpose, provided that the breeding stock or other animal reproductive material were sold or otherwise commercialised to the farmer by or with the consent of the patent proprietor. Such use includes making the animal or other animal reproductive material available for the purposes of pursuing the farmer's agricultural activity, but not the sale thereof within the framework of, or for the purpose of, a commercial reproductive activity;

(k) the acts and the use of the obtained information as allowed under Articles 5 and 6 of Directive 2009/24/EC, in particular, by its provisions on decompilation and interoperability; and

(l) the acts allowed pursuant to Article 10 of Directive 98/44/EC.

The wording of Articles 25 and 26 UPC Agreement is closely based on the equivalent Articles in the CPC 1989.[9] The exceptions to infringement found in the CPC 1989[10] are also incorporated into Article 27 UPC Agreement, together with a number of additional exceptions that have been introduced by EU law since CPC 1989 was drafted.[11]

Aside from setting out the acts of infringement and their exceptions in Articles 25–27, the UPC Agreement provides no further detail on how these rules are to be applied. The UPC will develop its own approach to this, but in doing so its attention must ('shall') be drawn to the national law approaches, as expressly envisaged by Article 24(e) UPC Agreement.[12]

B. Infringement of Unitary Patents and Article 5 UP Regulation

Until shortly before the present text of the UP Regulation was signed, it had contained substantive provisions on the acts of infringement and the exceptions to infringement that were to apply to unitary patents in the UPC. These provisions reproduced those found in the UPC Agreement (see section II.A above). The inclusion of these provisions in an EU law instrument implied that referral to the CJEU on points of interpretation would be necessary – the CJEU would make rulings on infringement law. In order to remove this possibility but retain the formal primacy of EU law, the UP Regulation was amended to replace these provisions with Article 5, which in its entirety states as follows:

Article 5

Uniform protection

1. The European patent with unitary effect shall confer on its proprietor the right to prevent any third party from committing acts against which that patent provides protection throughout the territories of the participating Member States in which it has unitary effect, subject to applicable limitations.
2. The scope of that right and its limitations shall be uniform in all participating Member States in which the patent has unitary effect.

---

[9] Itself never ratified. See n 4.
[10] Article 27.
[11] In particular, Article 27(d) UPC Agreement, which incorporates the exemption under Article 13(6) of Directive 2001/82/EC and Article 10(6) of Directive 2001/83/EC; Article 27(k) UPC Agreement, which incorporates Articles 5 and 6 of Directive 2009/24/EC relating to the legal protection of computer programs; and Article 27(l) UPC Agreement, which incorporates Article 10 of Directive 98/44/EC relating to the legal protection of biological inventions.
[12] See England et al (n 3).

3. The acts against which the patent provides protection referred to in paragraph 1 and the applicable limitations shall be those defined by the law applied to European patents with unitary effect in the participating Member State whose national law is applicable to the European patent with unitary effect as an object of property in accordance with Article 7.
4. In its report referred to in Article 16(1), the Commission shall evaluate the functioning of the applicable limitations and shall, where necessary, make appropriate proposals.

Articles 5(1) and 5(2) UP Regulation reflect the unitary protection and uniformity of scope conferred on the participating Member States by a Unitary Patent.[13] To guarantee this uniform scope of protection, claim construction, and the acts of infringement and their exceptions, must be approached in the same way in the participating Member States. How is this achieved?

Article 5(3) chooses very specific words to direct that the applicable law should be:

[T]he law applied to [Unitary Patents] in the participating Member State whose national law is applicable to the [Unitary Patent] as an object of property in accordance with Article 7.

There are two principal ways of interpreting Article 5(3):

- Interpretation (1): Article 5(3) applies Article 7 UP Regulation, meaning the same national laws apply to infringement as would apply to the Unitary Patent as an object of property – they are determined by the place of business of the applicant (see section IV.A below).

- Interpretation (2): the words 'the law applied to European patents with unitary effect in the participating Member State' in Article 5(3) refer to the laws that have been enacted by the participating Member States to apply to Unitary Patents. The only such laws (statute or case law) that currently exist are the UPC Agreement, the UP Regulation and the Translation Regulation. Specifically, as regards infringement, they are Articles 25–29 UPC Agreement.

It is submitted that there are three reasons why interpretation (2) should be preferred. First, if interpretation (1) were correct, different Unitary Patents would be subject to wide-ranging approaches to infringement and claim construction, according to the place of business of the patent applicant. This result would conflict with the consistency and uniformity of decision making that the Unitary Patent and the UPC are intended to promote. In contrast, interpretation (2) enables a single and uniform approach to be developed by the UPC over time.

Second, there is a significant difference in wording between Article 5 and Article 7. In the latter, the Unitary Patent must be treated as if it is a 'national patent', meaning it is subject to the laws of one Member State. This requirement is not in Article 5. It is fair to presume that this omission is deliberate, and that for matters of infringement Unitary Patents were not intended to be treated as national patents subject to the national laws of one Member State.

---

[13] See Article 3 UP Regulation.

Third, an explanatory note accompanying the new Article 5[14] states that the reference to national law regarding acts of direct and indirect infringement of a Unitary Patent, as well as the limitations on these, implicitly refers to Articles 25–28[15] UPC Agreement.[16]

As regards the application of infringement law, Unitary Patents are thus treated in the same way as European patents. For both, the UPC must establish its own approach to the application of Articles 25–27, based on existing national approaches.

C. The Scope of Protection of Unitary and European Patent Claims

Neither the UPC Agreement nor the UP Regulation provides substantive approaches to determining the claim scope of Unitary Patents and European patents. The starting point for determining scope of claims is instead the EPC – as a source of law, the EPC is listed in the UPC Agreement.[17] The EPC provides the correct approach to the interpretation of claims in Article 69(1):

> The extent of the protection conferred by a European patent or a European patent application shall be determined by the claims. Nevertheless, the description and drawings shall be used to interpret the claims.

Article 69 is itself to be understood according to the Protocol to the Interpretation of Article 69:[18]

Article 1 General principles

Article 69 should not be interpreted as meaning that the extent of the protection conferred by a European patent is to be understood as that defined by the strict, literal meaning of the wording used in the claims, the description and drawings being employed only for the purpose of resolving an ambiguity found in the claims. Nor should it be taken to mean that the claims serve only as a guideline and that the actual protection conferred may extend to what, from a consideration of the description and drawings by a person skilled in the art, the patent proprietor has contemplated. On the contrary, it is to be interpreted as defining a position between these extremes which combines a fair protection for the patent proprietor with a reasonable degree of legal certainty for third parties.

Article 2 Equivalents

For the purpose of determining the extent of protection conferred by a European patent, due account shall be taken of any element which is equivalent to an element specified in the claims.

There is no single, model approach to these provisions available from the national courts on which the UPC judges can rely. The approach to the application of Article 69 and the Protocol, like the application of the acts of infringement and their limitations, requires the UPC to develop its own approach in its own case law. The role of existing national law approaches in this process is discussed below.

---

[14] Explanation 3, 20 November 2012. The note was drafted to refer to Article 5a at the time.
[15] At the time the note was drafted, these were Articles 14f–14i.
[16] Earlier drafts of the infringement provisions of UPC Agreement had referred to European patents alone. The signed UPC Agreement refers to 'patents', which includes Unitary Patents.
[17] Article 24(1)(c).
[18] Protocol to the Interpretation of Article 69 of 5 October 1973, as revised by the Act Revising the EPC of 29 November 2000.

D. Developing an Approach to Scope of Claim and Infringement

The panels of the UPC must look to national law for guidance on how to construe patent claims. They are assisted in this task by Article 24(2), which provides a hierarchy of rules to be followed when deciding which national law to apply:

Article 24
Sources of law

(2) To the extent that the Court shall base its decisions on national law, including where relevant the law of non-contracting States, the applicable law shall be determined:

(a) by directly applicable provisions of Union law containing private international law rules; or

(b) in the absence of directly applicable provisions of Union law or where the latter do not apply, by international instruments containing private international law rules; or

(c) in the absence of provisions referred to in (a) and (b), by national provisions on private international law as determined by the Court.

The hierarchy begins with 'directly applicable provisions of Union law containing private international law rules'. EU law on private international law rules for non-contractual matters is provided by Regulation (EC) 864/2007.[19] Article 8 of Rome II expressly provides for the infringement of intellectual property rights:

Article 8
Infringement of intellectual property rights

1. The law applicable to a non-contractual obligation arising from an infringement of an intellectual property right shall be the law of the country for which protection is claimed.

2. In the case of a non-contractual obligation arising from an infringement of a unitary Community intellectual property right, the law applicable shall, for any question that is not governed by the relevant Community instrument, be the law of the country in which the act of infringement was committed.

Article 8 poses its own problem. Following Article 8(2) would require the law of the country in which the infringement was committed to apply to a Unitary Patent. Furthermore, following Article 8(1) would require the law of the country for which protection is claimed – the *lex loci protectionis* – to be applicable to nationally validated European patents. Both would have the unworkable result that more than one national law applies if an infringement takes place in more than one Member State. This would also be inconsistent with unity of protection that the UPC is intended to promote.

The UPC panels of the Court of First Instance and the Court of Appeal are therefore clearly not bound to any one national approach to infringement and scope of claim, but are instead to 'base' their decisions on national law, as Article 24(2) says, drawing on them to develop their own case law.[20] It should be noted that national law for this purpose includes where relevant the law of non-contracting Member States.[21]

---

[19] Regulation (EC) 864/2007 of the European Parliament and of the Council of 11 July 2007 on the law applicable to non-contractual obligations (hereinafter 'Rome II').

[20] As discussed in ch 13, as a court common to all the participating Member States, the law applied by the UPC is the law of all the contracting Member States on these issues. Hence, there is arguably no conflict with the application of Rome II.

[21] In particular in relation to Articles 25–28, 54, 55, 64, 68 and 72 (Article 24(3)).

E. The Right Based on Prior Use of the Invention

The UPC has exclusive competence (see Chapter 2) for matters 'relating to the use of the invention prior to the granting of the patent or to the right based on prior use of the invention'.[22] The substantive law defence of prior use is found in Article 28 UPC Agreement:

Article 28

Any person, who, if a national patent had been granted in respect of an invention, would have had, in a Contracting Member State, a right based on prior use of that invention or a right of personal possession of that invention, shall enjoy, in that Contracting Member State, the same rights in respect of a patent for the same invention.

There are two related but distinct elements to the defence in Article 28: prior use and the right of personal possession.

i. Prior Use

The prior use defence has been characterised as a 'statutory licence',[23] which permits the post-grant continuation of acts performed before the priority date of the patent; acts which, had that patent been granted, would constitute infringement. Such matters, Article 28 implies, are determined by national law. However, this gives rise to two effects: first, the UPC, as the forum for deciding whether the defence applies, is required to decide the issue for each designation of the European patent in dispute, applying the law of the relevant Member State; and, second, the application of different national laws may result in the defence being successful in respect of some Member States and not others.

ii. Personal Possession

A distinction is made between the right of personal possession of an invention for the purpose of a European patent on the one hand and a Unitary Patent on the other hand.

a. Unitary Patents

The right to personal possession of an invention – entitlement – defence is an issue of the Unitary Patent as an 'object of property'. As an object of property, a Unitary Patent is to be dealt with according to the law of the particular Member State assigned by Article 7 UP Regulation (see section IV.A below).

b. European Patents

Article 7 UP Regulation has no application to European patents. Like prior use, matters of entitlement are instead dealt with according to the national law of the Member State in which the patent is registered. As with prior use, the application of the defence must

---

[22] Article 32(1)(g) UPC Agreement.
[23] English Patents Court, *Helitune v Stewart Hughes* [1991] FSR 171, 206.

therefore be determined for every national counterpart of the European patent in dispute, giving rise to the potential for different results in different contracting Member States.

III. The Law of Validity

Article 24(1) of the UPC Agreement provides the sources of law applicable to issues of the validity of Unitary Patents and European patents in the UPC. The EPC, which is the principal source of law on matters of validity in Europe, is specifically listed under Article 24(1)(c). As with infringement matters, the difficulty faced by the UPC judges is that there is variation in terms of how the national courts interpret the EPC. Which approach should the UPC take? The answer is again that the judges of the UPC must develop a single, consistent approach guided as appropriate 'based on' the existing national approaches. Unlike matters of infringement, the judges are also able to take notice of the case law of the Boards of Appeal of the EPO on validity matters. The decisions of the Boards of Appeal of the EPO are not expressly included as a source of law in Article 24(1) UPC Agreement. However, as the largest single body of European-wide law interpreting the provisions of the EPC on patent validity, they are influential. Furthermore, the courts of a number of jurisdictions in Europe already regard Boards of Appeal case law as important for the purpose of assisting in national decisions.

IV. Unitary Patents as Objects of Property

A. The Law Applicable to Objects of Property

When framing the law that should apply to patents as 'objects of property' in the UP Regulation, the approach settled on was Article 7 UP Regulation. This states that the law applicable to patents as objects of property is to be determined according to the domicile of the applicant:

Article 7

Treating a European patent with unitary effect as a national patent

1. A European patent with unitary effect as an object of property shall be treated in its entirety and in all the participating Member States as a national patent of the participating Member State in which that patent has unitary effect and in which, according to the European patent Register:
    (a) the applicant had his residence or principal place of business on the date of filing of the application for the European patent; or
    (b) where point (a) does not apply, the applicant had a place of business on the date of filing of the application for the European patent.
2. Where two or more persons are entered in the European patent Register as joint applicants, point (a) of paragraph 1 shall apply to the joint applicant indicated first. Where this is not possible, point (a) of paragraph 1 shall apply to the next joint applicant indicated in the order of entry. Where point (a) of paragraph 1 does not apply to any of the joint applicants, point (b) of paragraph 1 shall apply accordingly.

3. Where no applicant had his residence, principal place of business or place of business in a participating Member State in which that patent has unitary effect for the purposes of paragraphs 1 or 2, the European patent with unitary effect as an object of property shall be treated in its entirety and in all the participating Member States as a national patent of the State where the European Patent Organisation has its headquarters in accordance with Article 6(1) of the EPC.
4. The acquisition of a right may not be dependent on any entry in a national patent register.

Article 7 states that disputes concerning Unitary Patents as objects of property must be heard as if the patent at issue were a national patent – meaning, it is submitted, according to national law rather than in the national courts.[24] The national law in question is determined according to the participating Member State of residence or place of business of the applicant at the time of filing the patent application. If the country is not a signatory to the UP Regulation, the matter will be determined according to German law.

Table 4.1 illustrates five hypothetical examples of the practical effect of Article 7 for corporate patent applicants with offices in locations inside and outside the participating Member States. In examples 3-5, there is no headquarters or other place of business in a participating Member State and the default law, of Germany, applies.

Table 4.1 Hypothetical examples of the effect of Article 7

	Place of business or residence of applicant	Applicable law
1.	Paris HQ	French
2.	New Jersey HQ, Amsterdam office	Dutch
3.	Swiss HQ, German office	German
4.	Swiss HQ, no other European office	German
5.	Spanish HQ	German

B. What are 'Objects of Property'?

i. Recordal of Assignments, Licences and Other Encumbrances

The scope of the meaning of the words 'objects of property' in Article 7 UP Regulation is unclear. These words have been used in a number of previous European intellectual property instruments, including EPC Chapter IV, which is entitled: 'The European patent application as an object of property.' This is concerned with the transfer[25] and licensing[26] of patent applications. Related rules deal with the recordal of assignments and licences of European patent applications in the European patent register. Chapter IV also explains that

---

[24] This is consistent with the UPC as a forum in which matters concerning patents as registrable rights, most notably validity, can be heard by the UPC as a court of each of the contracting Member States. The contrary conclusion would also give rise to odd results. For example, a national court would be required to determine a defence of personal possession of a Unitary Patent (Article 28 UPC Agreement) separately to the infringement action, whereas the same defence for a European patent can be heard in the UPC together with the infringement action.
[25] Article 71 EPC.
[26] ibid Article 73.

post-grant recordals of licences must be made with the national authorities of the designated contracting states, where local laws apply.[27] Recordals of assignments may still be made centrally during a pending opposition or appeal, but thereafter they must also be made in the contracting states of validation.[28] However, unlike European patents, a Unitary Patent is created upon registration in the Register for unitary patent protection – part of the European patent register – and not with national authorities. Hence, Article 7 cannot be intended to apply to these matters.

ii. Entitlement and Co-ownership

The Protocol on Recognition[29] of the EPC[30] mirrors the terms of Article 7. The Protocol provides that the courts of the EPC contracting states have jurisdiction to decide claims for the right to the grant of a European patent in one or more of the countries of designation.[31] The rules in the Protocol for deciding which national court has jurisdiction are determined by reference to the residence or principal place of business of the applicant.[32] Although Article 7 UP Regulation is not drafted in identical terms to the Protocol on Recognition, its similarity suggests that matters of a Unitary Patent as an 'object of property' are intended to include entitlement and co-ownership.

iii. Patent Agreements

In the absence of any explicit indication to the contrary, it is submitted that the framers of the UP Regulation did not intend Article 7 to overrule the choice of law and forum expressly agreed by the parties to a patent agreement, such as a licence (see section VI below).

iv. Rights to Employees' Inventions and Compensation

The rights available to an employee inventor are generally dictated by the location of their place of work. It would therefore be unworkable to apply the formula in Article 7 to these matters and unlikely that this was intended.

C. European Patents as Objects of Property

The UP Regulation is not concerned with European patents and the UPC Agreement is silent on the subject of European patents as objects of property. These matters are therefore left to be determined in accordance with the national law of the country of validation

---

[27] ibid Article 74.
[28] ibid Rules 22 and 85.
[29] Protocol on Jurisdiction and the Recognition of Decisions in Respect of the Right to the Grant of a European Patent (Protocol on Recognition) of 5 October 1973.
[30] Article 164 EPC.
[31] The claim is made against the patent applicant.
[32] Articles 2–6 of the Protocol on Recognition.

(as regards granted patents) and the national law determined according to the Protocol on Recognition (as regards applications).

V. Rights to Employees' Inventions and Compensation

The laws applicable to an employer's right to the invention of an employee and compensation for employee inventors are provided by national legislators and vary from one Member State to another. Unlike matters of entitlement, the right to a European patent is normally determined in accordance with the law of the state in which the employee is mainly employed or, if the former cannot be determined, the law of the state in which the employer has the place of business to which the employee is attached. The effect of this territorial link is that a claim to ownership would be prejudiced if, by the application of Article 7 UP Regulation, the applicable law were that of a country to which the employee or employer is not attached by their place of employment. For example, an inventor employee working in the UK cannot claim the right if it so happens that the applicable law is that of Germany, as a result of the patent applicant being based in Switzerland. It cannot have been the intention of Article 7 UP Regulation that the application of such rights in a Unitary Patent should fall to be determined on this chance basis or that an employer should be provided with this simple means of avoidance.

VI. Patent Licences and Other Agreements

A. The Law Applicable to Patent Agreement Disputes

i. Choice of Contract Law

It is submitted that matters which are based on the law of contract are not intended to fall within the scope of Article 7 UP Regulation as 'objects of property'. Patent agreements such as assignments and licences, like any other contract, depend on the free negotiation and conclusion of terms, including those relating to law and jurisdiction. This freedom is codified in Article 3 of Regulation (EC) No 593/2008 of the European Parliament and of the Council of 17 June 2008 on the law applicable to contractual obligations (hereinafter 'Rome I'), which the application of Article 7 would otherwise override. There is no basis in the founding instruments of the Unitary Patent or the UPC to suggest that such a result is intended. This view is also supported by comparison to the Protocol on Recognition. The Protocol, which provides for the law and jurisdiction of entitlement disputes concerning European patent applications, provides that where parties to a dispute have agreed that the courts of a particular contracting state shall decide on a dispute, the court or courts of that state have exclusive jurisdiction. Article 7 UP Regulation largely reflects the Protocol and, in the absence of express terms to the contrary, it is reasonable to presume that Article 7 does not override freely agreed contract terms in circumstances where the Protocol does not.

In keeping with the ability of parties to agree their own terms on law and jurisdiction, there would seem to be no bar on an agreement that the UPC is the forum for hearing a patent licence dispute in, for example, Dutch law. In view of the following discussion, this may be advantageous.

ii. Choice of Law Applicable to Patent Issues

If a patent agreement is in dispute, then issues of patent validity and scope of claims may also be in issue; typically, the claim scope or validity of one or more licensed patents is raised in order to challenge the payment of a royalty on a patent or patents in a licence. This raises the question of which substantive patent law should apply to validity and infringement when the agreement itself has stipulated a particular law. In accordance with the exclusive competence granted by the UPC Agreement,[33] it is only the UPC that has the jurisdiction to revoke a Unitary Patent or a non-opted-out European patent (after the transitional period) (see also Chapter 6). Exclusive jurisdiction for matters of infringement, and therefore matters of determination of claim scope, is also granted to the UPC in respect of these patents.[34] However, the UPC Agreement stipulates that the law to be applied is private international law, which includes Article 3 of Rome I on choice of law. It follows that the UPC is free to apply the national law that is stipulated in the patent agreement.[35]

iii. Patent Licences Raised in Defence

The UPC Agreement[36] envisages that defences and counterclaims concerning licences can be brought in infringement proceedings in the UPC. As explained above, in the absence of any explicit indication to the contrary, it is unlikely that the framers of the UP Regulation intended Article 7 on objects of property to overrule the choice of law agreed by the parties in a patent licence or other agreement. As a consequence, if a patent licence is to form the basis of a counterclaim (or defence), the existence and terms of that licence would have to first be determined according to the law agreed, which may be applied by the UPC itself (see Chapter 2).

B. Licences of Right

Unitary Patents may be made available for licences of right by the filing of a statement with the EPO to this effect. A licence obtained under this provision is to be treated as a contractual licence.[37] Hence, the same considerations as those discussed above in relation to patent agreements in general apply to the terms of a licence of right and the patent licensed.

---

[33] Article 32(1)(d) UPC Agreement.
[34] ibid Article 32(1)(d).
[35] Hence, it is possible for the UPC to determine a dispute concerning Unitary Patents licensed in an agreement that stipulates, for example, the law of New Jersey or California. This is consistent with the freedom of choice of contract law permitted by Article 3 of Rome I. Under the amended Brussels I Regulation (recast), matters of substantive validity and infringement, respectively, must be litigated under the courts as well as the law of the Member State of registration of the patent in question. However, as a court common to all the participating Member States, a revocation or infringement action in one division of the UPC is simultaneously an action in all contracting Member States.
[36] Article 32(1)(a).
[37] Article 8(2) UP Regulation.

C. Compulsory Licences

Recital 10 of the UP Regulation states that:

> Compulsory licences for European patents with unitary effect should be governed by the laws of the participating Member State as regards their respective territories.

The effect of this provision is that a compulsory licence sought for a Unitary Patent for the territory of, for example, France is governed by French compulsory law provisions, while a licence for Sweden is governed by Swedish law provisions. This is consistent with the Unitary Patent, as a right that may be licensed in respect of the whole or part of the territories of the participating Member States.[38]

VII. Application of Law During the Transitional Period

A. Opted-out Patents

The issue of which law applies to opted-out European patents has been expressly identified by the Preparatory Committee,[39] which recognises that national courts must know which law to apply when ruling on European patents from the first day that the UPC comes into force, and, for patentees who are considering which of the European patents in their portfolios, they may wish to opt out.

The view of the Preparatory Committee is that if a European patent or a patent application is opted-out, the UPC Agreement no longer applies. Hence, the law that applies to a dispute in a national court concerning any one of these is national law.

However, the view of the Preparatory Committee is not binding and the contrary view has been expressed that, at all times, a European patent remains subject to the UPC Agreement, whether it is opted-out or not.[40] As such, the law of the UPC would apply to opted-out patents. At present, this issue remains to be resolved.

B. Non-opted-out Patents Litigated in the National Courts During the Transitional Period

The interpretation of the law applicable to opted-out patents put forward by the Preparatory Committee, and discussed above, implies that non-opted out patents remain under the full jurisdiction of the UPC Agreement, including its substantive patent law, whether litigated in the UPC or, during the transitional period, in the national courts.

---

[38] Recital 7 UP Regulation.
[39] In an opinion published on 29 January 2014.
[40] Winfried Tillmann, 'The Transitional Period of the Agreement on a Unified Patent Court' (2014) 9(7) *Journal of Intellectual Property Law & Practice* 575.

5

Language

The UPC will make decisions applicable in up to 22 participating Member States in the near future (see Table I.1 in the Introduction). In a continent where most countries have their own language and may have additional regional languages, a regime is required to govern the language to be used in the UPC and for the Unitary Patent. The language of the proceedings is important not just as a matter of convenience between the parties, who will be from inside and outside Europe, but also because of the costs that may potentially be incurred in translating pleadings, evidence and other documents. Regulation 1260/2012[1] (hereinafter the 'Translation Regulation'), the UPC Agreement and the Rules of Procedure all contain provisions relating to language for this purpose. This chapter examines how the Translation Regulation determines the language in which the Unitary Patent specification and claims are written, and the translations that are necessary in the event of a dispute about that patent. It also explains how the UPC Agreement and the Rules of Procedure determine the language to be used when drafting a statement of claim and in proceedings.

I. The Translation Regulation

The Translation Regulation complements the UP Regulation by providing the translation requirements for the Unitary Patent. It deals with essentially two issues of language:

(a) the language of grant of Unitary Patents; and
(b) the language of translation in cases where a Unitary Patent is disputed in the UPC.

However, the Translation Regulation does not affect the authentic text of the Unitary Patent as that of grant.[2]

A. The Language of Grant of a Unitary Patent

The language of grant of a Unitary Patent is provided in Article 3 of the Translation Regulation by reference to the EPC.[3] This means that the *specification* of a unitary patent must be published in the language of prosecution – English, French *or* German – and must

---

[1] Council Regulation (EU) No 1260/2012 of 17 December 2012 implementing enhanced cooperation in the area of the creation of unitary patent protection with regard to the applicable translation arrangements.
[2] Article 70(1) EPC.
[3] ibid Article 14(6).

also include a translation of the *claims* in the other two official languages of the EPO. In other words, the claims must be present in all three of English, French *and* German.

If the patent holder opts for a Unitary Patent after the grant of the European patent, no further translations will be required. Where it is necessary to communicate the content of the patent in other languages, high-quality machine translations will be available. However, further to Article 6 of the Translation Regulation, there will be a transitional period while the machine translation system is set up. This is currently 12 years. During this period, where the language of the proceedings before the EPO is French or German, a full translation of the European patent specification must be provided in English or, when the language of the proceedings is English, a full translation into another official language of an EU Member State must be provided. This translation must be filed by the patentee together with the request for unitary effect. Furthermore, for those who obtain a Unitary Patent whose residence or principal place of business is in an EU Member State with an official language that is not one of the three EPO languages, a system of additional reimbursement will be introduced for the costs of translating the application into the EPO language of proceedings.[4]

A request for unitary effect must also be submitted in the language of proceedings in the EPO.[5]

B. The Language of a Unitary Patent in a Dispute

i. General Rules

Article 4 of the Translation Regulation provides for the translation requirements in the event of a dispute concerning a Unitary Patent, the cost of which is to be borne by the patent proprietor. The Article provides two scenarios in which translation is required:

(a) Article 4(2) states that in the event of a dispute, the patent proprietor must provide at the request of the court a translation into the language used in the proceedings of that court. The language used in the proceedings of the court is itself determined by rules contained in the UPC Agreement and the Rules of Procedure.

(b) Article 4(1) provides that in cases where issues of alleged infringement of a unitary patent are in dispute, the alleged infringer can require the patent proprietor to provide a full translation of the Unitary Patent into an official language of the participating Member State in which the infringement took place, or the Member State of the alleged infringer's domicile.

Article 4(2) appears to be an underlying requirement applying to any dispute concerning a Unitary Patent, whereas Article 4(1) applies only to those disputes concerning infringement. As such, the requirements of Article 4(1) are additional to those in Article 4(2).

The choice of the alleged infringer provided by Article 4(1), between translating into the language of the Member State in which the infringement took place and the Member State of the alleged infringer's domicile, reflects the choice that the patentee has of where to

---
[4] See www.epo.org/law-practice/unitary/unitary-patent.html.
[5] Article 3(2) of the Translation Regulation.

file when bringing an infringement claim[6,7] (see Chapter 9), but it is not dictated by it – an alleged infringer may opt for a translation into its language of domicile even if the claim is lodged in the territory of the infringement.[8]

ii. The Effect of Knowledge of Infringement

The translation requirements in Article 4(1) have further significance. Article 4(4) of the Translation Regulation provides that in a dispute concerning a claim for damages, the court will take into consideration whether the alleged infringer acted without knowing or without reasonable grounds for knowing that they were infringing the Unitary Patent before having been provided with the translation. When considering knowledge, the provision takes particular account of knowledge of the infringement by an 'SME, a natural person or a non-profit organisation, a university or a public research organisation'. It is unclear from Article 4(4) whether the provision of a translation to the alleged infringer is intended to put them on notice, such as to automatically satisfy the knowledge requirement of the Article, or whether it is a factor amongst others. In any case, proprietors should provide a translation to the alleged infringer as soon as they become aware that an infringement may be taking place or about to take place if they wish to protect their position on damages as much as possible.

Article 4(4) of the Translation Regulation raises an unresolved question regarding the proprietor who wishes to provide a translation at a time before a dispute commences in order to protect their position on damages, but the alleged infringer has not had the opportunity to elect the language further to Article 4(1): must the translation be provided in the language of the domicile of the alleged infringer or the language of the participating Member State in which the alleged infringement took place?

C. The Language of Amendments to a Patent in Infringement Proceedings

An application by the proprietor of a patent to amend the patent included in a defence to a counterclaim for revocation must contain: the proposed amendments (and, if applicable, auxiliary requests) in the language in which the patent was granted; and, where it is different, translated into the language of the proceedings. If the patent is a Unitary Patent, it must be translated into the language of the EU Member State in which the defendant is domiciled or the language of the contracting Member State in which the infringement occurred or was threatened, if so requested by the defendant.[9]

---

[6] Article 33 UPC Agreement.
[7] Assuming that a local or regional division is available, that the infringer is domiciled in a contracting Member State of the UPC and that it is also a participating Member State of the Translation Regulation.
[8] As a result, Article 4 may offset to some extent the potential disadvantage to the defendant of an action being brought in a local or regional division of a Member State in which the official language is unfamiliar.
[9] Rule 30.1(a) of the Rules of Procedure. An explanatory note to the changes made by the Legal Group of the Preparatory Committee in the 17th draft of the Rules of Procedure explains that Rule 30.1(a) ensures compliance with Article 4 of the Translation Regulation: where amendment to a patent is sought in an infringement action, the defendant may request that a translation of the amendments in the language of the defendant's domicile (that is, any EU Member State and not merely a participating Member State) is lodged, or of the language of the place of the infringement or threat of infringement.

D. The Language of a European Patent

The Translation Regulation only applies to Unitary Patents and not European patents for which unitary effect has not been requested. European patents remain governed by the provisions of the Agreement on the application of Article 65 of the Convention on the Grant of European Patents (hereinafter the 'London Agreement') in Article 3 (see also Chapter 1):

> [I]n the case of a dispute relating to a European patent, the patent proprietor, at his own expense,
> (a) shall supply, at the request of an alleged infringer, a full translation into an official language of the State in which the alleged infringement took place,
> (b) shall supply, at the request of the competent court or quasi judicial authority in the course of legal proceedings, a full translation into an official language of the State concerned.

Article 3(b) ensures that in the event that a European patent is litigated in the UPC, the language into which it must be translated is that of the language of proceedings.

II. The Language of Proceedings at First Instance

A. The Central Division

i. The General Rule

At first instance, the language of proceedings in the central division is the language of grant of the patent.[10] This is the language in which the pleadings, written evidence and other documents are to be lodged.[11]

ii. Exception to the General Rule

The UPC Agreement provides that when an infringement action is brought before the central division, the defendant has the right, upon request and in certain circumstances, to translations of relevant documents.[12] The circumstances are as follows:

(a) the defendant has its residence, principal place of business or, in the absence of residence or principal place of business, place of business (together referred to for the purposes of this chapter as 'Domicile') in a Member State;
(b) the infringement action must have been lodged in the central division because either the defendant has its Domicile outside the territory of the contracting Member States or the contracting Member State of Domicile does not host a regional or local division (see Chapter 9);
(c) the language of grant of the patent is not an official language of the Member State where the defendant has its Domicile; and
(d) the defendant does not have a proper knowledge of the language of proceedings.

---

[10] Article 49(6) UPC Agreement.
[11] Rule 7.1 of the Rules of Procedure.
[12] Article 51(3) UPC Agreement.

78 *Language*

If all these circumstances are met, the language of the translation will be the language of Domicile. The effect of the difference in wording between 'Member State' and 'contracting Member State', in (a) and (b), respectively, is that the defendant does not need to be Domiciled in a Member State that is contracted to the UPC. It follows that the language to which the defendant is entitled is not necessarily a contracting Member State language.

The effect of (b) is that a defendant in an infringement action that has been transferred to the central division as a result of a decision under Article 33(3)(c) does not have the right to such a translation. Instead, in these cases, it is at the discretion of the judge-rapporteur to order that the parties lodge translations of pleadings in the language of grant.[13] The meaning of a 'proper knowledge' in (d) of the language of proceedings is not explained in the Agreement or the Rules of Procedure and will be a matter for the judges to determine in case law.

In practice, these circumstances are limited to defendants domiciled in Spain, Poland, Croatia and the minority of Member States that will not host a local or regional division, and are further restricted by condition (d), suggesting that the rule will apply in only a small number of cases.

B. The Regional and Local Divisions

Contracting Member States hosting a local or regional division have two sources from which they can choose the language of proceedings:

(a) the official European language or one of the official European languages of the contracting Member State hosting the local division or designated by a contracting Member State sharing a regional division;[14] and/or
(b) one or more of the official languages of the EPO.[15]

The result is that a contracting Member State can designate one or more languages of proceedings for use in the local or regional division for which it is responsible. The consequences of one or more languages being chosen are different and these are discussed below.

i. One Language Designated

If one language is designated by the contracting Member State of a local or regional division, that language becomes the language of proceedings, subject to a change to using the language of grant of the patent (see section II.B.iii below). The language of proceedings is the language in which the pleadings, written evidence and other documents must be lodged.[16] This includes statements of revocation, which, by virtue of Article 33(7) UPC Agreement, are lodged in a local or regional court.[17]

---

[13] Rule 41(d) of the Rules of Procedure. The judge-rapporteur may consider it appropriate only for excerpts of pleadings and other documents to be translated.
[14] Article 49(1) UPC Agreement.
[15] ibid Article 49(2).
[16] Rule 7.1 of the Rules of Procedure.
[17] ibid Rule 45.2.

ii. More Than One Language Designated

If the local or regional division has designated more than one language, Rule 14 of the Rules of Procedure determines which single language is selected as the language of proceedings.[18] This depends on whether or not proceedings take place in a division in which the defendant is domiciled or has a principal place of business. The language of proceedings chosen must again be adopted in the pleadings, written evidence and other documents lodged.[19] This includes statements of revocation, which by virtue of Article 33(7) are lodged in a local or regional court.[20]

a. Language Chosen by the Claimant

Where there is more than one language designated by the contracting Member State or States hosting the local or regional division in which the action is proceeding, the claimant may choose the language of proceedings,[21] subject to the language rule for infringement proceedings local to the defendant (see section II.B.ii.b below).

b. Infringement Action in the Member State of the Defendant's Domicile

Particular considerations apply to proceedings that take place in a local or regional division in a contracting Member State against a defendant domiciled in or having a principal place of business in that Member State (but not any place of business).[22] In these circumstances, if there was no alternative other than to bring the action in that division, because it is the only division available under Article 33(3)(1)(a) of the UPC Agreement,[23] the language of proceedings must be the 'official language', or one of the official languages, designated by the contracting Member State in question.

If the contracting Member State in question designates several official regional languages, the language of proceedings must be the official regional language of the place of domicile or principal business of the defendant. If there are two or more defendants with different official regional languages of domicile or principal places of business, the right to choose the language of proceedings returns to the claimant.

---

[18] An explanatory note to the changes made by the Legal Group of the Preparatory Committee in the 17th draft of the Rules of Procedure states that Rule 14 is specifically addressed to the situation in which a contracting Member State has designated one or more EPO languages under Article 49(2) UPC Agreement, in addition to the language of proceedings under Article 49(1) UPC Agreement. Rule 14 determines under what conditions the additional language can be used in proceedings. As such, it attempts to reconcile a number of competing considerations: the interest of the claimant in using the additional language; the interest of individuals and SMEs to have proceedings heard in their language of domicile; and the interests of the judges in having the proceedings heard in the additional language. Rule 14.1 distinguishes between the 'official language', being that under Article 49(1) UPC Agreement, and the 'additional language', being that under Article 49(2) UPC Agreement.

[19] Rule 7.1 of the Rules of Procedure.

[20] ibid Rule 45.2.

[21] ibid Rule 14.2(a).

[22] ibid Rule 14.2(b). The 'small local operator' clause, designed to ensure that locally operating defendants will only be sued in their home language. It is not clear from the Rule whether the Regional Division must be geographically located in the Member State of the defendant's domicile or that it is merely hosted by it. Logically, it should be the latter. The place of business must be the principal place of business, not any place of business.

[23] In other words, there is no other contracting Member State hosting a local or regional division in which the act of infringement occurs. The wording of Rule 14.2(b) does not appear to rule out the possibility that an infringement may additionally occur in a contracting Member State or States that do not host a local or regional division.

c. Use of Official Language by the Panel in Oral Proceedings

If an EPO language is designated by a contracting Member State,[24] the designation may also indicate that the judge-rapporteur has the discretion to order, in the interests of the panel, that the official language designated by the contracting Member State is:

(a) used for the oral proceedings;[25] and/or
(b) to make any order or decision that a certified translation into the designated EPO language is provided for the purpose of enforcement on the defendant.[26]

iii. Changing the Language of Proceedings to the Language of Grant

Regardless of the language designated, chosen by the claimant or determined by the domicile of the defendant in local proceedings, as described in the previous section, there are options for one or more parties to an action to have the language of proceedings changed to those of the language of grant of the patent.

a. Application by Both Parties

During the written procedure, an Application can be lodged to use the language in which the patent was granted as the language of the proceedings. The Application must be on behalf of all the parties, but can be lodged by any of them. The Registry will then forward the Application to the panel as soon as practicable. As soon as practicable, the panel will decide whether it approves the Application. If the Application is not approved, the Registry informs the parties. The parties then have within 10 days to request that the action is referred to the central division, following which it will be transferred (see section marked * in Figure 5.1).[27]

b. Application by One Party

If a particular party wants to use the language of grant of the patent as the language of the proceedings, this must be included in that party's Statement of Claim or Statement of Defence, as applicable. This application is then forwarded by the Judge-Rapporteur to the President of the Court of First Instance, who invites the other party to within 10 days give its own position on the use of this language. After having consulted with the panel of the division, the President may order that the language of grant be used as the language of proceedings. Such an order may be on condition of specific translation or interpretation arrangements (see section marked † in Figure 5.1).[28]

c. The Proposal of the Judge-Rapporteur

During the written procedure or the interim procedure, the judge-rapporteur may propose to the parties that the language of grant of the patent be used as the language of proceedings. Such

---

[24] Further to Article 49(2) UPC Agreement.
[25] Rule 14.2(c) of the Rules of Procedure. The Rule was added in response to concerns from German judges that they should have the possibility to conduct the oral procedure and deliver decisions in their home language in German local divisions. Note that the Member State in question must indicate this option when designating the languages to be used by its local division/s and it is at the discretion of the judge-rapporteur.
[26] Rule 118.8 of the Rules of Procedure.
[27] Rule 321 of the Rules of Procedure and Article 49(3) UPC Agreement.
[28] Rule 32 of the Rules of Procedure and Article 49(5) UPC Agreement.

a proposal may either be of the judge-rapporteur's own motion or on a request by a party, and in either case must follow consultation with the panel. If the parties and the panel agree, the language of the proceedings must be changed accordingly (see section marked ‡ in Figure 5.1).[29]

C. Timing when Raising Language Issues

A party which has reasons to object to the language of proceedings for non-compliance with the language designated by the contracting Member State needs to be able to do so promptly, before potential translation costs increase with the number of documents lodged. The first opportunity to object to the language of the statement of claim is with a preliminary objection lodged within one month of the service of the statement of claim.[30] The preliminary objection must itself be drawn up according to the language determined according to Rule 14.

Applications by one or both parties to change the language of proceedings to that of grant must be made during the written procedure. The interim procedure does not include language matters amongst those listed as subject to review by the judge-rapporteur.[31] However, the judge-rapporteur may propose a change to the language of grant of the patent during the interim procedure on their own motion (see section II.B.iii.c above).

III. Language in the Court of Appeal

The statement of appeal and the statement of grounds of appeal must be drawn up either in the language of the proceedings before the court of first instance or, where the parties have agreed, in the language in which the patent was granted.[32] In the latter case, the evidence of the respondent's agreement to the choice of language must be lodged by the appellant together with the statement of appeal. In exceptional cases and to the extent deemed appropriate, the Court of Appeal may nevertheless decide on another official language of a contracting Member State as the language of proceedings for the whole or part of the proceedings, subject to agreement by the parties.[33]

If the language of the proceedings in the first instance should be different from the language in the appeal proceedings, the judge-rapporteur may order the appellant to lodge translations into the language of the proceedings before the Court of Appeal and may set a time period for the submission of the translations.[34] The documents to be translated may comprise written pleadings and other documents lodged by the parties before the court of first instance, as specified by the judge-rapporteur and decisions or orders of the court of first instance. Should the appellant fail to lodge the translation within the time period specified, a decision by default may be given,[35] provided that the judge-rapporteur has informed the appellant about this consequence beforehand.[36]

---

[29] Rule 322 of the Rules of Procedure.
[30] ibid Rule 19.
[31] ibid Rule 104.
[32] See Article 50(2) UPC Agreement and Rule 227 of the Rules of Procedure.
[33] Article 50(3) UPC Agreement and Rule 227(1)(a) of the Rules of Procedure.
[34] Rule 232.1 of the Rules of Procedure.
[35] ibid Rule 357.
[36] ibid Rule 232.2.

IV. Translations of Documents in Proceedings

A. Certification

Where a pleading or other document must be translated, it is not necessary for a formal certificate of the translator to be provided regarding the accuracy of that statement, unless the statement is challenged by a party, or required by the court or the Rules of Procedure.[37]

Orders of the court on the merits, for infringement or revocation (or partial invalidity) as well as orders for damages or compensation[38] can only be enforced on the defendant: after the claimant has notified the court which part of the orders they intend to enforce; and provided a certified translation of the orders[39] in the official language of the contracting Member State in which the enforcement is to take place. In particular, certification is required for orders or decisions translated into an EPO language for the purpose of enforcement on the defendant when an EPO language has been designated in addition to an official language.[40]

B. Costs of Interpreters and Translators

A cost decision following a decision on the merits (see Chapter 18) must cover costs incurred by the successful party, including translation costs, and costs incurred by the court, including simultaneous interpretation. However, costs for interpretation and translation which are necessary for the judges of the court to conduct the case in the language of proceedings are borne solely by the court.[41] The Rules of Procedure provide that compensation for the costs of translators are the rates that are customary in the country of the division in question, depending on the translator's or interpreter's training and professional experience.[42]

C. Change of Language when Action is Transferred between Divisions

The circumstances under which an action may be transferred from a local or regional court to the central division will be explained in Chapter 9. A decision to refer a case to an alternative division under Article 33(3) may affect the language of proceedings. If the language of the proceedings before the regional or local division that has referred a counterclaim for revocation to the central division is not that in which the patent was granted, the judge-rapporteur may order that the parties translate the written pleadings and other documents lodged during the written procedure (or excerpts of those documents)[43] into the language of grant of the patent, within a period of one month.[44]

---

[37] ibid Rule 7.1.
[38] See ibid Rule 118.8. There is an error in the Rule, which refers to Rule 118.3(a) rather than 118.2(a).
[39] In accordance with ibid Rule 7.2.
[40] Under ibid Rule 14.2(c).
[41] ibid Rule 150.1.
[42] ibid Rule 155.
[43] ibid Rule 39.2.
[44] ibid Rule 39.1.

Translations of Documents in Proceedings 83

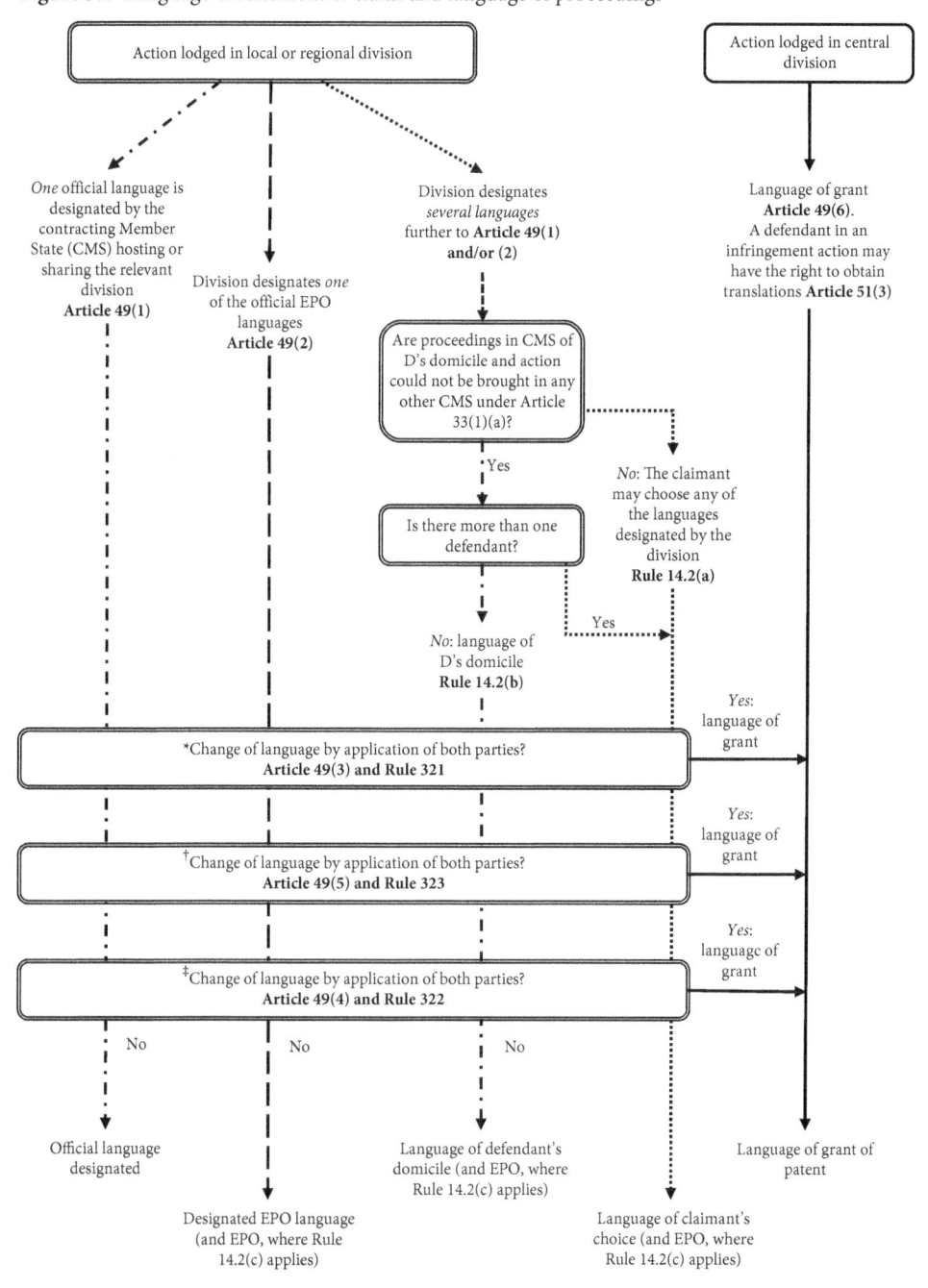

Figure 5.1 Language of statement of claim and language of proceedings

6

The Opt-out and Transitional Regime

An important characteristic of the new European patent system is the co-existence of national patents, European patents and Unitary Patents, and also the co-existence of the UPC and the national courts. The litigation of national patents remains within the exclusive competence of the national courts.[1] Disputes concerning the Unitary Patent are for the most part within the competence of the UPC. European patents are treated differently: Article 83 UPC Agreement provides a transitional period during which a party owning a European patent can 'opt out' of the jurisdiction of the UPC. The transitional period also provides the party initiating litigation with the choice as to whether they pursue their action in the UPC or the national courts. This chapter examines the meaning and effect of the opt-out and the transitional period and the procedures that apply.

I. The Opt-out and Transitional Period

A. The Operation of the Transitional Period

i. Article 83 UPC Agreement

The competence of the UPC to hear disputes concerning European patents is shared with the national courts of the contracting Member States for the first seven years of the UPC's operation – the 'transitional period'. Furthermore, during this seven-year period, proprietors of European patents and European patent applications may opt those patents out of the competence of the UPC entirely.[2] The transitional regime is set out in Article 83 UPC Agreement:

(1) During a transitional period of seven years after the date of entry into force of this Agreement, an action for infringement or for revocation of a European patent or an action for infringement or for declaration of invalidity of a supplementary protection certificate issued for a product protected by a European patent may still be brought before national courts or other competent national authorities.

(2) An action pending before a national court at the end of the transitional period shall not be affected by the expiry of this period.

(3) Unless an action has already been brought before the Court, a proprietor of or an applicant for a European patent granted or applied for prior to the end of the transitional period

---

[1] The parallel existence of the national patent and European patent systems alongside the Unitary Patent is expressly envisaged by Recital 26 UP Regulation.
[2] Note that in discussions following the drafting committee meeting of 14 December 2014, it was decided that the opt-out of a parent patent or patent application does not include any divisional patent. Divisional patents must therefore be opted out separately under Rule 5 of the Rules of Procedure.

under paragraph 1 and, where applicable, paragraph 5, as well as a holder of a supplementary protection certificate issued for a product protected by a European patent, shall have the possibility to opt out from the exclusive competence of the Court. To this end they shall notify their opt-out to the Registry by the latest one month before expiry of the transitional period. The opt-out shall take effect upon its entry into the register.

(4) Unless an action has already been brought before a national court, proprietors of or applicants for European patents or holders of supplementary protection certificates issued for a product protected by a European patent who made use of the opt-out in accordance with paragraph 3 shall be entitled to withdraw their opt-out at any moment. In this event they shall notify the Registry accordingly. The withdrawal of the opt-out shall take effect upon its entry into the register.

Article 83 is supplemented by a number of provisions in the Rules of Procedure, which govern opt-outs and the withdrawal of an opt-out.[3]

The transitional period runs from the date of entry into force of the UPC Agreement.[4] During this time, European patents and SPCs may be litigated in either the UPC, as a bundle,[5] or in the national court of the respective contracting Member State of the patent's designation.[6] However, the right to opt out a patent is *permanently* barred if the UPC has already been seised with an action concerning that patent or an SPC based on it.[7] Such an action and any further actions concerning the patent must be heard in the UPC.[8]

An ambiguity has been identified concerning the effect of the opt-out after the expiry of the seven-year transitional period. This arises from the word 'exclusive' in Article 83(3): 'opt out from the exclusive competence of the Court'. This could be understood to imply that the patent holder remains subject to a continuing non-exclusive jurisdiction of the court – a parallel competence of the UPC and the national courts. However, it is difficult to reconcile such a continuing shared competence between the UPC and national courts after the end of the transitional period: it would effectively mean that the transitional period extends for the lifetime of the opted-out patent. It is also inconsistent with the idea of opting out from the UPC. Instead, the word 'exclusive'[9] in Article 83(3) merely refers to the exclusive competence of the UPC that would have applied if the European patent were not opted out; the opt-out takes the European patent in question out of the jurisdiction of the UPC entirely.[10]

---

[3] Rules 5 and 5A of the Rules of Procedure.
[4] There is the possibility that the seven-year period will be extended by a further seven years (Article 83(5) UPC Agreement).
[5] ibid Article 34.
[6] ibid Article 83(1).
[7] ibid Article 83(3) and Rule 5.9 of the Rules of Procedure. This absolute bar is emphasised by the explanatory notes to the changes made by the Legal Group of the Preparatory Committee in the 17th draft of the Rules of Procedure. The purpose of the bar is to reduce the risk of national courts making later decision about a patent that diverge from the decision of the UPC.
[8] Article 83(2) UPC Agreement and Rule 5.7 of the Rules of Procedure.
[9] Article 83(3) UPC Agreement.
[10] This interpretation had been supported by the note to Rule 5 of the 16th draft Rules of Procedure, which stated that the provisions of Article 83(3) UPC Agreement provide for a complete ousting of the jurisdiction of the UPC: https://www.unified-patent-court.org/sites/default/files/revised-draft-rules-of-procedure.pdf. This note was intended to be explanatory and was deleted in the 17th draft Rules. Support for this view is also provided by the Preparatory Committee at https://www.unified-patent-court.org/faq/opt-out: 'If the effect of an opt-out was limited to removing the exclusivity of the UPC's jurisdiction, Article 83(3) UPCA would, at least during the transitional period, have exactly the same effect as Article 83(1) UPCA, i.e. result in shared jurisdiction of the UPC and

86   The Opt-out and Transitional Regime

Unless they are opted out, designations of a European patent,[11] become subject to the exclusive competence of the UPC, as a bundle, after seven years from entry into force of the UPC Agreement. By contrast, an opted-out European patent can only be litigated in the national court for which it is designated (subject to a later withdrawal of the opt-out; see section I.A.iii below). European patent applications filed after the expiry of the transitional period are automatically subject to the exclusive competence of the UPC.

An opt-out is not possible if an action concerning the European patent has already been lodged in the UPC, regardless of whether that action has concluded.[12]

Figures 6.1–6.4 show schematic illustrations of the forum in which European patent actions must be lodged during and after the transitional regime, in circumstances of opt-out, no opt-out and withdrawal of an opt-out.

Figure 6.1 The forum of national patent actions and unitary patent actions over time

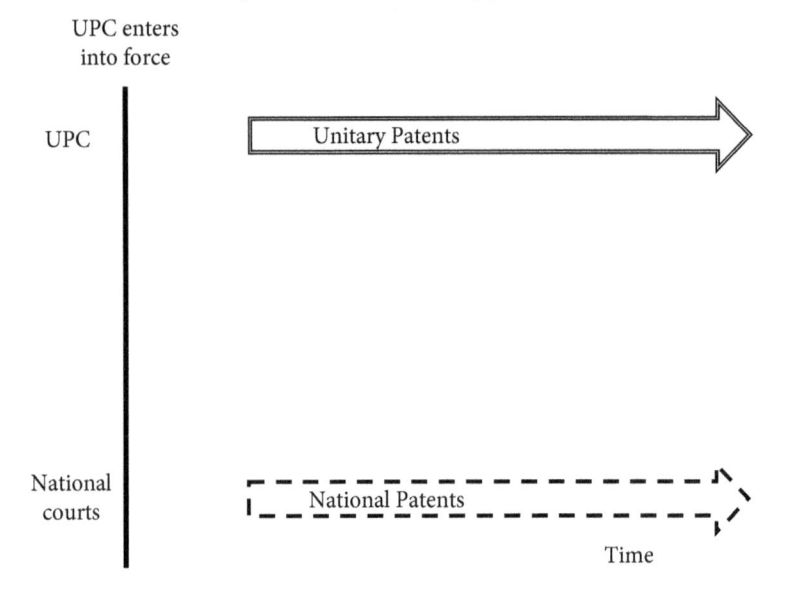

national courts and a choice of forum for the parties. Thus there would be no need for two different provisions in Article 83 (1) and (3). Therefore it was the legislator's intent with the opt-out to give an alternative to patent holders, allowing them to remove their patents entirely from any jurisdiction of the UPC.'

[11] Note that a prior reference to 'Contracting Member States' in Rule 5(b) of the Rules of Procedure was deleted in order to require all designations of the European patent to be opted out. An explanatory note in the Amendments to the text of the UPC draft Rules of Procedure approved by the Preparatory Committee on 15 March 2017 AC/04/08072022_E – ANNEX 1 explains that the previous wording provided that 'the Application to opt out shall be made in respect of all of the Contracting Member States for which the European patent has been granted or which have been designated in the application'. This wording is inconsistent with the indivisibility of the application to opt out. It implies that the UPC solely has jurisdiction over the UPC Agreement contracting Member States, which is not the case. Therefore, the words 'Contracting Member' have to be deleted in Rule 5.1(b). The same amendment has to be made in the context of Rule 5.7 as the withdrawal simply mirrors the opt-out. The reference to the UPC's jurisdiction beyond the contracting states is unclear, but may be a reference to the 'long-arm' jurisdiction described in ch 7.

[12] Article 83(3) UPC Agreement and Rule 5.6 of the Rules of Procedure.

The Opt-out and Transitional Period 87

Figure 6.2 The exclusive competence of the UPC for European patent disputes begins at the end of the transitional period (currently seven years). Prior to this, the UPC and the national courts both have competence

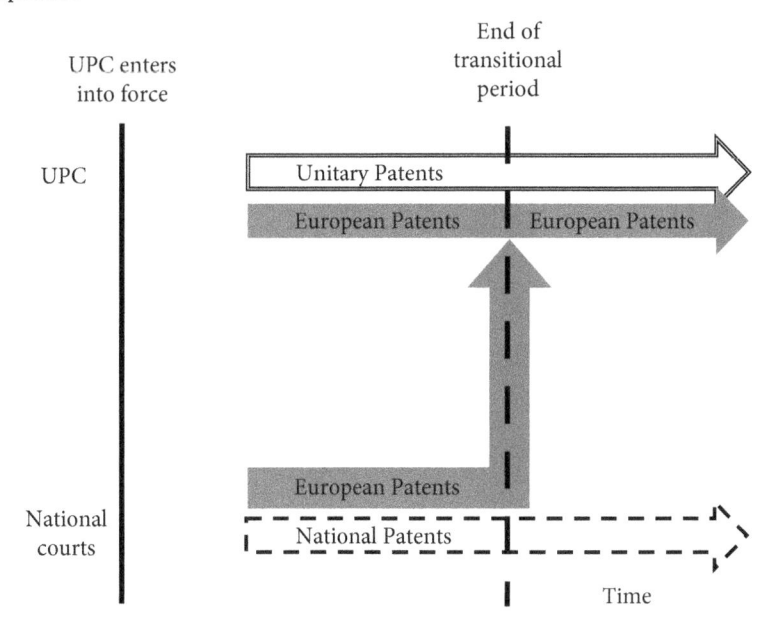

Figure 6.3 Opted-out European patent disputes are within the exclusive competence of the national courts, for the term of the patent and any SPC based on it (provided there has been no prior UPC action lodged concerning that patent)

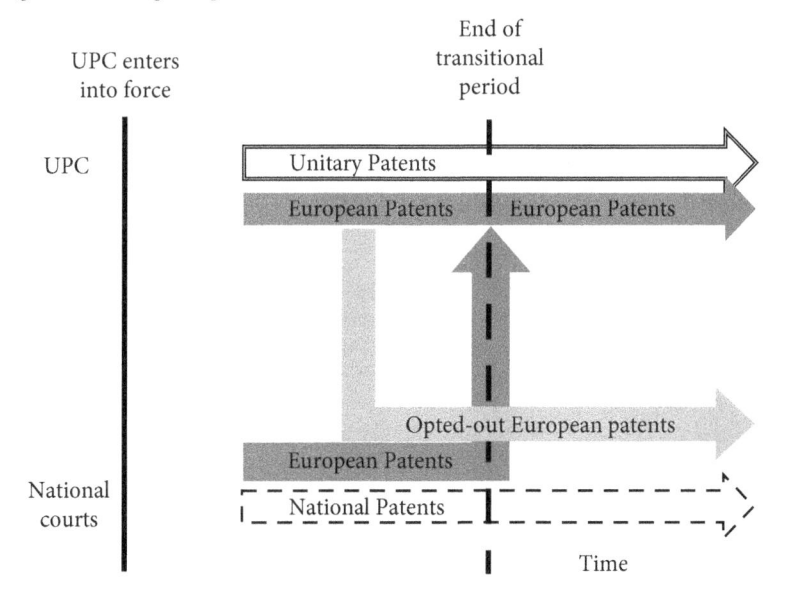

88 *The Opt-out and Transitional Regime*

Figure 6.4 The withdrawal of a European patent (providing there has been no prior national action lodged concerning that patent) brings disputes concerning the patent within the exclusive competence of the UPC

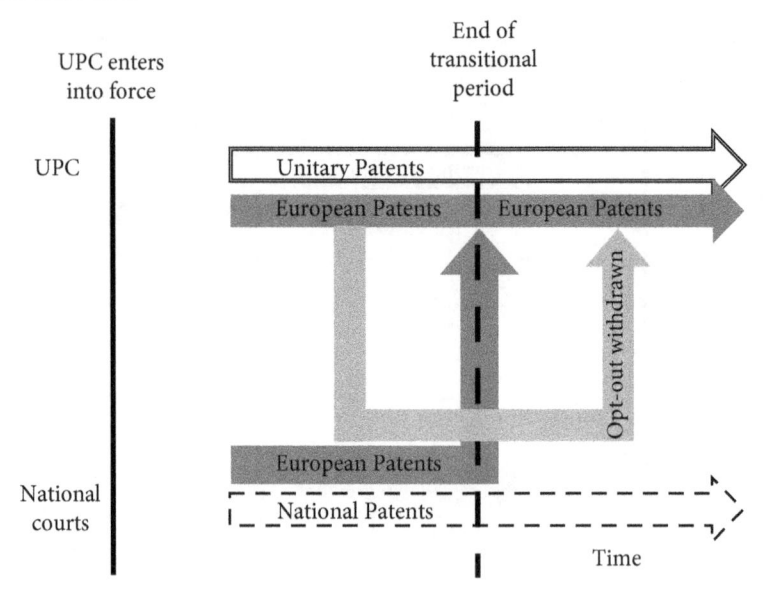

ii. *The Effect on SPCs*

The opt-out of a European patent automatically extends to an SPC that is based on it or later granted based on it.[13] An expired European patent may also be opted out, with the effect that any SPC is automatically opted out.[14] The owner of the SPC, if different from the proprietor of the patent on which it is based, must lodge the application together with the patent proprietor (see section I.D.i below).[15]

An SPC granted on the basis of a Unitary Patent cannot be opted out[16] (see Chapter 1).

iii. *The Withdrawal of an Opt-out*

The opt-out of European patents, and SPCs based on them, may be withdrawn. The withdrawal of an opt-out places all the designations of the European patent[17] back within the exclusive competence of the UPC, 'unless an action has already been brought before a national court' concerning the patent or SPC in question.[18] Such a national action in a

---

[13] Rule 5.2 of the Rules of Procedure. The explanatory notes to the changes made by the Legal Group of the Preparatory Committee in the 17th draft of the Rules of Procedure explain that in view of the principle that an application to opt out a European patent must extent to any SPC based on it, it was considered superfluous to require the holder of the SPC to notify the Registry of details already received when the opt-out of the European patent or European application was lodged.
[14] Rule 5.1 of the Rules of Procedure.
[15] ibid Rule 5.1(a).
[16] ibid Rule 5.2(d).
[17] This is not limited to the designations in the contracting Member States (see ibid Rule 5.7).
[18] Article 83(4) UPC Agreement.

contracting Member State permanently deprives the patentee or SPC holder of the right to withdraw the opt-out.[19]

It is not possible to opt out or withdraw the opt-out of some, but not all, of the designations of a European patent[20] (see section I.A.iv below). It follows that each SPC based on the national designation of a European patent in a contracting Member State will be opted out or withdrawn from the opt-out together.

iv. *The Deemed Withdrawal of an Opt-out by Unitary Effect*

If unitary effect is sought after the grant of an opted-out European patent application, it is deemed to withdraw the opt-out.[21]

B. Extension of the Transitional Period

The UPC Administrative Committee will carry out a consultation with users of the patent system after five years of the entry into force of the UPC Agreement and a survey of the numbers of patents still being litigated in the national courts. Depending on the findings of this exercise, the transitional regime may be extended for a further period of up to seven years.[22]

C. The Procedure for Opting-out and Withdrawal

i. *Opting Out after the UPC Comes into Force*

To opt a European patent or application out from the exclusive competence of the UPC, together with any SPC based on it, an 'Application to opt-out' must be lodged with the Registry.[23] The application to opt-out must contain the details of the European patent, including the EP publication number, any SPC granted on the basis of the patent, and any

---

[19] Rule 5.8 of the Rules of Procedure. It has been doubted by some commentators that the bar on withdrawal applies to infringement actions. However, no distinction is made in the UPC Agreement or the Rules of Procedure. The explanatory notes to the changes made by the Legal Group of the Preparatory Committee in the 17th draft of the Rules of Procedure make it clear that this bar is absolute – any future actions concerning the European patent must be brought in the national court in order to reduce the risk that the UPC comes to a later decision that diverges from a decision of the national court.

[20] Rule 5.7 of the Rules of Procedure. Further to the amendment to Rule 5.7 to extend the withdrawal of opt-out to all designations of a European patent, regardless of whether they are contracting Member States, it is unclear whether an action relating to an opted-out European patent in a country such as the UK would prevent withdrawal of the opt-out for all patents in the bundle under Rule 5.8. The unamended use of 'Contracting Member State' in that provision suggests otherwise.

[21] ibid Rule 5.9. The explanatory notes to the changes made by the Legal Group of the Preparatory Committee in the 17th draft of the Rules of Procedure explained that Rule 5.9 allowed for the fact that the territorial scope of the first Unitary Patents is unlikely to cover all contracting Member States. Therefore, as conceived at that time, for those contracting Member States that had not ratified the UPC Agreement, it would still be possible to obtain a European patent. A deemed withdrawal of an opt-out by application for unitary effect would not affect European patents in the Member States that had not ratified. However, this appears to have changed with revisions made to Rule 5.9 in the 18th draft Rules on 15 March 2017, which now encompass all possible contracting Member State designations within the withdrawal of the opt-out.

[22] Article 83(5) UPC Agreement.

[23] Rule 5.1(a) of the Rules of Procedure.

application filed, including numbers and designated states of the application. The application must also contain the name of each proprietor or applicant, as well as the name of the holder of any SPC based on it, together with the postal and (where applicable) electronic addresses of: (i) the representative appointed by the applicant or the proprietor;[24] or (ii) any other person lodging the application to opt out on behalf of the proprietor or the applicant and the mandate for lodging the application to opt-out.[25] The application to opt-out must also contain a declaration by or on behalf of each proprietor or applicant that they are entitled to be registered in the national patent register (see section I.D below).[26] There is no fee payable for opting-out. The opt-out is effective from the date of entry in the register.[27]

ii. Opting-out before the UPC Comes into Force

During the drafting of the Rules of Procedure, the concern was raised that an action concerning a European patent could be pre-emptively lodged in the central division of the UPC before there is time for the proprietor to register an opt-out of the patent. The Rules of Procedure initially addressed this concern using a 'sunrise' provision,[28] which would enable applications to be lodged with the EPO before the UPC Agreement comes into force. Subsequently, the UPC Preparatory Committee agreed the Provisional Application Protocol,[29] which allows a 'provisional operation' period for the UPC. In addition to allowing other steps to be taken in preparation for the full entry of the UPC into force, the recording of opt-outs of European patents in the Registry is permitted during this period.[30]

iii. The Procedure for Withdrawing an Opt-out

The withdrawal of an existing opt-out must be made by the proprietor by lodging an application to withdraw the opt-out with the Registry.[31] No fee is payable. The application will be entered as soon as possible and will be regarded as effective from the date of entry in the register. It is the responsibility of the Registrar to notify the EPO of entries in the register of both opt-outs and withdrawals.

D. Responsibility for Opting-out

i. Co-proprietors of a Patent

The Rules state that where there is more than one proprietor or applicant of a granted patent or application, respectively, all of them must lodge the application to opt out.[32] The practical

---

[24] In accordance with Article 48 UPC Agreement.
[25] Rule 5. of the, Rules of Procedure.
[26] ibid Rules 5.3(e) and 8.5.
[27] ibid Rule 5.5. In any proceedings before the court, the Registry will of its own motion, as soon as practicable, examine whether an opt-out has effect for the patent concerned (ibid Rule 260.1).
[28] Formerly Rule 5.13 in the 17th draft Rules of Procedure.
[29] Protocol to the Agreement on a Unified Patent Court on provisional application, 1 October 2015.
[30] As a result, the sunrise period, as conceived in draft Rule 5.13, has been removed from the Rules of Procedure.
[31] ibid Rule 5.7.
[32] ibid Rule 5.1(a).

effect of this provision is that co-owners of a patent must agree whether they wish that patent to be opted out. A declaration of proprietorship is necessary in the absence of a record of the proprietor in the relevant national register or, in respect of applicants, the European patent register (see section I.C.i above).[33]

ii. Designations with Different Proprietors

An application to opt-out must be made in respect of all of the contracting Member States for which the European patent is designated.[34] As a consequence, agreement must be reached between different proprietors in circumstances where one or more designations of a European patent have been assigned to them. This includes the proprietors of designations of the patent in contracting Member States that have not ratified the UPC Agreement at the time of the opt-out (see section I.D.iii below).

iii. The Relevance of a Ratification to Opt Out

An opt-out has effect for designations of the European patent in all contracting Member States, without reference to whether those Member States have ratified the UPC Agreement.[35] Detaching an opt-out from ratification in this way has the advantage that it is unnecessary to make subsequent opt-out applications for each new contracting Member State that ratifies after the beginning of the provisional operation period.

iv. Status of an Exclusive Licensee

There is no apparent intention in the Rules of Procedure that an exclusive licensee is to be included within the meaning of 'proprietor' for the purpose of an opt-out. Therefore, an exclusive licensee is not required to provide consent to the opt-out of the European patent licensed.[36] An exclusive licensee that wants the right to consent to the opt-out of a European patent to which they are licensed must therefore negotiate this right in the terms of the licence.

v. The Responsibility of the SPC Holder

If the holder of the SPC is different from the proprietor of the patent on which it is based, both the holder and the patent proprietor must lodge the application to opt out.[37] If an SPC is granted after an application has been lodged, the holder of the SPC must notify the Registry of the same details that would be required of the patent proprietor.[38]

---

[33] ibid Rule 8.5.
[34] ibid Rule 5.1(b).
[35] ibid.
[36] Rule 8.5(a) provides that the proprietor of a European patent is the person entitled to be registered as a proprietor under the law of each contracting Member State, implying that an exclusive licensee is not included.
[37] ibid Rule 5.2(a).
[38] ibid Rule 5.3(a).

92 The Opt-out and Transitional Regime

vi. Removal of an Unauthorised Application

The proprietor of a European patent or the applicant for a published application for a European patent or holder of an SPC in relation to which an application to opt out or withdraw an opt-out is entered in the register may remove the entry of such an unauthorised application.[39] The request to remove the opt-out or withdrawal of the opt-out must be made by application to the Registry setting out the reasons for doing so. The Registrar must decide on the application for removal as soon as practicable.[40] which may be subject to an application for review to the President of the Court of Appeal.[41]

E. Application of Law During the Transitional Period

The question has been raised concerning which substantive law applies to disputes concerning European patents in the national courts during the transitional period. This question was addressed by the Preparatory Committee,[42] on the basis that national courts should know which law to apply when ruling on classical European patents from the first day that the UPC comes into force. It is also important to know for patentees who are considering which of the classical European patents in their portfolios they may wish to opt out.

i. Opted-out Patents

The application of the UPC Agreement to European patents and patent applications is provided for in Article 3 UPC Agreement, which states that it applies to any:

(a) European patents with unitary effect;
(b) supplementary protection certificate issued for a product protected by a patent;[43]
(c) European patent which has not yet lapsed at the date of entry into force of this Agreement or was granted after that date, without prejudice to Article 83; and
(d) European patent application which is pending at the date of entry into force of this Agreement or which is filed after that date, without prejudice to Article 83.

The UPC Agreement thus states that it applies without prejudice to the transitional provisions, which allows disputes in respect of European patents and applications to be brought in the national courts of the respective contracting Member States, as well as the right to opt-out from the exclusive jurisdiction of the UPC. The Preparatory Committee has noted that the transitional provisions are silent about the law that applies to opted-out European patents. In the absence of guidance, the Preparatory Committee concluded that the UPC Agreement no longer applies to an opted-out European patent or European patent application – the law that applies is national law. In coming to this conclusion, the Committee was concerned that there is no possibility for national judges to refer interpretative questions to

---

[39] ibid Rule 5A.1.
[40] ibid Rule 5A.2.
[41] ibid Rule 5A.3.
[42] In an opinion published on 29 January 2014.
[43] The Agreement does not apply to applications for SPCs.

the UPC, and therefore interpretation by national courts of UPC law would risk inconsistent approaches developing.[44]

ii. Non-opted-out European Patents Litigated in the National Courts

European patents that have not been opted-out remain under the full jurisdiction of the UPC Agreement, including its substantive patent law, whether litigated in the UPC or the national courts.

II. Issues Raised by Late Joiners to the UPC and the EPC

A. Late Ratification of the UPC Agreement

A Unitary Patent does not protect the territories of those participating Member States that have not ratified the UPC Agreement at the date on which unitary effect is registered in the EPO Register.[45] The territories covered are fixed at this date and do not increase to include participating Member States that ratify the UPC Agreement after unitary effect has been recorded. Patents for which unitary effect is registered subsequently will cover a broader territorial scope according to the Member States that have ratified in the interim period. This is an express derogation from the uniform protection afforded to Unitary Patents.[46] This has the important practical consequence for those using the new system that, as the new system proceeds, all Unitary Patents will not have the same territorial scope.

In order to fill the potential gap in patent protection that is a consequence of continuing ratifications of Member States in the Unitary Patent, equivalent European patents must continue in Member States that have not ratified the UPC Agreement at the time that unitary effect is requested. These patents must be litigated in the national courts. Ratification of the UPC Agreement by a Member State cannot later confer Unitary Patent status upon such a European patent.[47]

---

[44] However, the opinion of the Preparatory Committee is not binding and there is a contrary view, which is that the transition provisions only contain a choice of forum rule and not a choice of law rule. Accordingly, a European patent is subject to the law of the UPC Agreement, whether it is opted out or not and whether the action commences in the UPC or a national court. See Winfried Tilmann, 'The Transitional Period of the UPCA' (2014) 9(7) *Journal of Intellectual Property Law & Practice* 575. This approach has the attraction of treating Article 3 UPC Agreement as meaning what it says: the UPC Agreement applies to European patents, without prejudice to the transitional provisions. Furthermore, if the UPC Agreement were not applicable to opted-out patents, it would not be possible to withdraw the opt-out. From a practical perspective, treating opted-out patents and non-opted-out patents with conformity will speed up the process of converging the approaches to patent law taken by the contracting Member States.

[45] Article 18(2) UP Regulation.

[46] As provided by ibid Article 3(1).

[47] With ratification of the UPC Agreement, European patents equivalent to a Unitary Patent become subject to Article 83(3). In theory, this appears to mean that these European equivalents of a Unitary Patent can be opted out from the UPC, although this cannot be the intention.

B. Late Joiners to the EPC

As regards patent applications that were filed before the two most recent signatories, Malta and Croatia, joined the EPC (Malta joined the EPC on 1 March 2007 and Croatia on 1 January 2008), the question has been raised as to whether a European patent filed before Malta and Croatia joined the EPC can be granted unitary effect. This is on the basis that if there is no Maltese or Croatian designation, the European patent bundle has 'different sets of claims for different participating Member States'.[48] However, the natural interpretation of 'different sets of claims for different participating Member States' is that it applies to inconsistent claim protection across the participating Member States and not the absence of claims. It follows that there is no bar to unitary effect on this basis.

---

[48] ibid Article 3(1).

7

Parallel Proceedings in the Contracting Member State Courts and the UPC

The existence of the UPC as a court system running in parallel to the continued litigation of patents in the national courts raises the issue of the UPC's jurisdictional relationship with those courts. This relationship is governed by Regulation (EU) 1215/2012 of the European Parliament and of the Council of 12 December 2012 on jurisdiction and the recognition and enforcement of judgments in civil and commercial matters (recast), as amended for the setting of the UPC as a court of the Member States. The amended Regulation allows, in certain circumstances, the continuance of cross-border issues seen in the European patent system prior to the introduction of the UPC and the Unitary Patent, both between national courts and between the national courts and the UPC itself, depending on whether Member States are contracting to the UPC and, in the matter of European patents, whether an opt-out has been exercised. In particular, the *lis pendens* provisions of the Regulation play a significant role in preventing the duplication of actions between the UPC and national courts during the transitional period, and between the UPC and non-contracting Member States. This chapter examines these issues.

I. Cross-border Actions under the Brussels Regulation

A. The Brussels Regulation

Cross-border patent actions in the EU are presently governed by the rules of Regulation (EU) 1215/2012 of the European Parliament and of the Council of 12 December 2012 on jurisdiction and the recognition and enforcement of judgments in civil and commercial matters (recast).[1] There have been successive versions of this legislation: Regulation 1215/2012 replaces Regulation 44/2001, which itself replaced the Brussels Convention. The article numbering of the relevant provisions in these instruments for patent matters has, accordingly, changed a number of times. However, for the purposes of patent matters, their substance has not changed significantly, and the interpretation provided by the Court of Justice of the European Union (CJEU) of the provisions under their earlier numbering is also

---

[1] Regulation (EU) 1215/2012 of the European Parliament and of the Council of 12 December 2012 on jurisdiction and the recognition and enforcement of judgments in civil and commercial matters (recast) [2012] OJ L351/1, 20 December.

valid for Regulation 1215/2012 (recast).[2] This chapter refers throughout to the 'Brussels I Regulation (recast)' and the most recent numbering scheme (employed in 1215/2012) is used, as shown in Table 7.1 below.[3]

Table 7.1 The key provisions of the Brussels I Regulation (recast) relevant to patent actions

Article number	Provision
4(1)	The rules of jurisdiction should be highly predictable and founded on the principle that jurisdiction is generally based on the defendant's domicile.
7(2)	A person domiciled in a Member State may be sued in another Member State:
	(2) in matters relating to tort, delict or quasi-delict, in the courts for the place where the harmful event occurred or may occur.
8(1)	A person domiciled in a Member State may also be sued:
	(1) where he is one of a number of defendants, in the courts for the place where any one of them is domiciled, provided the claims are so closely connected that it is expedient to hear and determine them together to avoid the risk of irreconcilable judgments resulting from separate proceedings.
24(4)	The following courts of a Member State shall have exclusive jurisdiction, regardless of the domicile of the parties:
	(4) in proceedings concerned with the registration or validity of patents, trade marks, designs, or other similar rights required to be deposited or registered, irrespective of whether the issue is raised by way of an action or as a defence, the courts of the Member State in which the deposit or registration has been applied for, has taken place or is under the terms of an instrument of the Union or an international convention deemed to have taken place.
27	Where a court of a Member State is seised of a claim which is principally concerned with a matter over which the courts of another Member State have exclusive jurisdiction by virtue of Article 24, it shall declare of its own motion that it has no jurisdiction.
35	Application may be made to the courts of a Member State for such provisional, including protective, measures as may be available under the law of that Member State, even if the courts of another Member State have jurisdiction as to the substance of the matter.

As the Recitals[4] of the Brussels I Regulation (recast) explain, the rules of jurisdiction are founded on the Article 4(1) principle – jurisdiction is generally based on the defendant's domicile. Articles 7(2), 8(1) and 24(4) are exceptions to this general rule.

---

[2] *Zuid-Chemie* (Case C-189/08) [2009] ECR I-6917, paragraph 18; *German Graphics Graphische Maschinen* (Case C-292/08) [2009] ECR I-8421, paragraph 27; and *Realchemie Nederland* (Case C-406/09) [2011] ECR I-9773, paragraph 38.
[3] 'Brussels I Regulation (recast)' is substituted for the titles of previous instruments and the most recent numbering is substituted in case discussions and quotes from the courts.
[4] See Recital 15 of Regulation 1215/2012.

The Brussels I Regulation (recast) serves another purpose: it provides simplified rules for the recognition and enforcement of judgments in the courts of the EU Member States, which avoids the need for special procedures in individual jurisdictions.

B. Cross-border Actions

i. *Invalidity*: GAT v LuK

Is it possible, under the Brussels I Regulation (recast), to claim in the courts of one Member State that the European patent registered in that State and one or more of its national counterparts,[5] registered in other Member States, are invalid?

The answer to this question is a decisive 'no': courts of a Member State have exclusive jurisdiction concerning the registration or validity of patents granted in their own country. This is guaranteed by Article 24(4) of the Brussels I Regulation (recast). As a general matter, the purpose of Article 24(4) is to ensure that in certain matters, jurisdiction rests with the courts most closely linked to the proceedings in fact and law. This is all the more important in the field of patents in order to ensure that these types of cases are dealt with by specialised courts – patent law is a specialised area and a number of countries have systems of specific judicial protection. Exclusive jurisdiction is also necessary because the grant of patents involves the national administrative authorities.

The case in which the CJEU explained this, *GAT v LuK*,[6] also dealt with a further question concerning validity. In a reference for a preliminary ruling, the court was asked whether Article 24(4) should be interpreted as applying where, in addition to a claim to invalidity which initiates the action:

> [T]he defendant in a patent infringement action or the claimant in a declaratory action to establish that a patent is not infringed pleads that the patent is invalid or void and that there is also no patent infringement for that reason.

The question is important, as the CJEU acknowledges, because the invalidity of a patent is often raised as a defence to an infringement action. A claim to invalidity can also be brought in support of a declaratory action when seeking to establish that there has been no infringement. Indeed, this was the case in *GAT v LuK*. There, GAT had sought to establish in the Landgericht (Regional Court) Düsseldorf that two of LuK's French designated European patents were invalid, as well as a declaration that it did not infringe them.

On the face of it, *GAT v LuK* rules that the exclusive jurisdiction provided for by Article 24(4) should apply whatever the form of the proceedings in which the issue of a patent's validity is raised: by way of an action or a defence, or at whatever stage in the proceedings (although the *Solvay v Honeywell* case discussed below provides an exception to this). The principal reasons for this ruling are that otherwise:

(1) the parties would be able, simply by the way they formulate their claims to circumvent the mandatory nature of Article 24(4);

---

[5] Other national parts of the same patent bundle granted by the EPO.
[6] *Gesellschaft für Antriebstechnik mBH & Co KG (GAT) v Lamellen und Kupplungsbau Beteiligungs KG (LuK)* (Case C-4/03), ECLI:EU:C:2006:457.

(2) such circumvention would also multiply the heads of jurisdiction under the Regulation, undermining the predictability of the rules and consequently undermining the principle of legal certainty;
(3) allowing decisions in which foreign courts rule indirectly on the validity of a patent would multiply the risk of conflicting decisions, which the Brussels Regulation seeks specifically to avoid.

The role of *GAT v LuK* when validity is raised in infringement cases is key to the use of cross-border relief in a number of scenarios, as will be discussed further in section B.ii.a.

ii. Infringement

There are principally two ways that the Brussels Regulation has been applied to permit cross-border infringement actions in the past:

- 'Spider-in-the-web' – in this form of cross-border action, which has been favoured by the Dutch courts, an injunction is granted in one court against defendants who are both based and infringing in Member States other than those of the granting court. The infringing activities must be coordinated from an office domiciled in the country of the granting court. This is so that the connection between them warrants a single action in order to avoid the irreconcilable judgments that might otherwise arise from parallel proceedings.
- Single defendant actions – this kind of action is taken against a single defendant in their country of domicile and concerns their alleged infringing activity at home and of equivalent parts of a European patent abroad.

There have been two key decisions of the CJEU in the last 10 years that have considered spider-in-the-web actions. As discussed below, one of these may have implications for single defendant type cross-border actions, although these actions have not been considered by the CJEU directly.

a. Roche v Primus

On the same day as *GAT v LuK*, the CJEU published its decision in *Roche v Primus*.[7] In this case, proceedings for infringement of a European patent had been brought before the Rechtsbank-Gravenhage (District Court of The Hague). The defendants were Roche Nederland BV, a Dutch domiciled company, and companies in the Roche group, which included several companies based in different European Member States. It was alleged that each of these companies infringed the *respective national part* of the European patent *for its country of domicile* only by placing on the market in those countries certain immunoassay kits. On appeal, the Hoge Raad (Dutch Supreme Court) referred for a preliminary ruling the question of whether the defendants were sufficiently closely connected for the purpose of the application of Article 8(1) of the Brussels I Regulation (recast),[8] such that the Dutch court could deal with all defendants in one action.

---

[7] *Roche Nederland and Others v Frederick Primus & Milton Goldenberg* (Case C-539/03), ECLI:EU:C:2006:458.
[8] Article 6(1) of the Brussels Convention at the time.

The CJEU ruled that there was not a sufficient connection for the purpose of the application of Article 8(1) – the infringement of each national part of the European patent should be heard in the court of its country of registration. Adopting the assumption that 'irreconcilable' judgments in Article 8(1) means contradictory decisions, the Court reasoned as follows (partially paraphrased for simplicity):

(1) When defendants commit infringements only in the territory in which they are domiciled, there is no risk of contradictory decisions being given if infringement proceedings are brought in their Member States of domicile separately – the existence of the same facts cannot be inferred because the defendants are different and the infringements they are accused of, committed in different Member States, are not the same.
(2) Despite the common rules laid down by the European Patent Convention, European patents continue to be governed by the national law of the Member States for which the patent is granted. Therefore, when infringement proceedings are brought before a number of courts in different Member States against defendants domiciled and allegedly infringing in their respective States alone, any divergences between the decisions given by the courts concerned do not arise from the same legal situation.
(3) Founding jurisdiction solely on the factual criteria set out by a national court would lead to a multiplication of the potential heads of jurisdiction laid down by the Brussels Regulation and consequently would undermine the principle of legal certainty.

There is then a further point (*Roche* Point 4):

(4) Even assuming that the court seised were able to accept jurisdiction, the consolidation of the patent infringement actions could not prevent 'at least a partial fragmentation' of the patent proceedings. This is because it is often the case in practice that the validity of the patent is raised indirectly, which would be a matter of the exclusive jurisdiction laid down in Article 24(4) of the Brussels I Regulation (recast) (see *GAT v LuK*).

In *Roche v Primus*, because the alleged infringements by several defendants were in their own territories only, national infringement actions concerned their own facts and law, and therefore could not give rise to irreconcilable decisions. Furthermore, the CJEU seems to say that if a different rule of jurisdiction were to arise each time the facts of a case differed, the certainty intended by the general rule that the action should be brought in the court of the defendant's domicile would be undermined.

Lastly, in *Roche* Point 4, the CJEU seems to reason that even when validity is not at issue, there is a risk that it could be raised at a later stage. This means it is appropriate for the proceedings to be heard separately, in the courts of the Member State in which the patent is registered, to pre-empt a later splitting of the actions under Article 24(4).[9] *Roche* Point 4 is discussed further below in the context of single defendant cross-border infringement actions.

Roche v Primus cast doubt on whether it would ever be appropriate to seek a 'spider-in-the-web' cross border infringement action. However, the extent of its application was limited almost exactly six years later in *Solvay v Honeywell*.

---

[9] Note that AG Legér's Opinion had suggested that Article 8(1) should not apply to scenarios of the spider-in-the-web type per se: *Roche v Primus* (n 7) ECLI:EU:C:2005:749, 8 December 2005.

b. Preliminary Injunctions: *Solvay v Honeywell*

It was again the Dutch courts that referred questions to the CJEU on Article 8(1) of the Brussels Regulation in *Solvay SA v Honeywell Fluorine Products Europe BV and Others*.[10]

The facts of this case differed from those of *Roche v Primus* in important ways. The European patent at issue in *Solvay v Honeywell* was allegedly infringed by each of the Honeywell companies, one Dutch and two Belgian, in their own country of domicile *as well as* in the countries of domicile of their co-defendants. Furthermore, the case concerned a claim for a preliminary injunction rather than a claim on the merits. The Honeywell companies raised a defence of invalidity in response to the preliminary injunction.

The Rechtsbank-Gravenhage referred a series of questions, the key parts of which concerned Articles 8(1) and 24(4):

(1) Under Article 8(1), where two or more companies from different Member States are each separately alleged to infringe, with the same product, the same national part of a European patent which is in force in another Member State, does the possibility of 'irreconcilable judgments' arise from separate proceedings?
(2) Is Article 24(4) applicable in proceedings seeking provisional relief on the basis of a foreign patent if a defence is raised that the patent invoked is invalid, but the court does not make a final decision on the validity of the patent?

Referring to *Roche v Primus*, the CJEU repeated that in order for Article 8(1) to apply, it is not sufficient that there is a divergence in the outcome of the dispute, but that this divergence must arise from the same situation of fact and law. In this case, the situation of fact and law determined by different courts would be the same and potential divergences would therefore be likely to arise. Article 8(1) applies in these circumstances, the Court held, because the defendants in the main proceedings are each separately accused of committing the same infringements with respect to the same products and, furthermore, such infringements were committed in the same Member States, so that they adversely affect the same national parts of the European patent at issue. The CJEU gave the example of two or more courts (being the courts of domicile of two or more defendants) being called on to assess, according to the same Finnish law (the same legal situation), the infringement of the Finnish part of the European patent as a result of the marketing of an identical infringing product by all those defendants in Finland (the same factual situation).

As regards the invalidity defence, the CJEU views this as a matter of whether Article 35 of the Brussels I Regulation (recast) concerning provisional measures applies. This states that the court of a Member State is authorised to rule on a claim for provisional measures even if, under the Brussels I Regulation (recast), the courts of another Member State have jurisdiction over the matter. The Court concluded that in circumstances where the court hearing the preliminary injunction does not make a final decision on the validity of the patent invoked in defence, it does not risk making a conflicting decision of the kind Article 24(4) is designed to avoid – Article 35 applies. In other words, Article 24(4) applies only when there will be a final decision on validity requiring revocation from the register. This is not the case at the preliminary stage.

---

[10] *Solvay SA v Honeywell Fluorine Products Europe BV and Others* (Case C-616/10), ECLI:EU:C:2012:445.

c. Single Defendant Cross-border Infringement Actions

Both *Roche v Primus* and *Solvay v Honeywell* have in common that they are broadly cases of the 'spider-in-the-web' type, in which an action is taken in one national court against foreign-domiciled defendants who are infringing one or more national counterparts of a European patent, under the coordination of the defendant in the granting court. The actions are brought under Article 8(1), but, as the above case illustrates, whether they are permissible depends on the pattern of the infringement. The principal, alternative form of cross-border infringement action is based on a different approach. In these cases, there is one defendant and they are sued in respect of alleged infringements of foreign and domestic parts of a European patent. These actions are based on Article 4(1) of the Brussels Regulation and so the defendant is sued in its country of domicile. These actions are not permitted as soon as validity is raised, due to the application of Article 24(4), as ruled by the CJEU in *GAT v LuK*.

There is a question of what the CJEU meant by *Roche* Point 4 and how this applies to such cases. As discussed above, *Roche* Point 4 appears to say that the mere *potential* for a validity defence to be raised, and the consequent fragmentation of the action further to Article 24(4), is a reason why actions concerning patents should proceed in the national courts. Why should the reasoning behind *Roche* Point 4 not be applied to single defendant cross-border actions?

'Torpedo' actions follow a similar pattern in which a claim is made in a single jurisdiction in respect of more than one equivalent part of a European patent. These are considered next.

iii. Cross-border Declarations of Non-infringement

Cross-border declarations of non-infringement have typically been filed in one jurisdiction by a party, with the intention of preventing, or at least slowing down, anticipated national infringement actions in other jurisdictions – hence the nickname 'torpedo'. For this reason, jurisdictions have been favoured that are slow and will take a long time to determine whether there is jurisdiction to hear the matter. This has allowed the torpedo to exploit the *lis pendens* provisions of the Brussels I Regulation (recast), even in cases where the jurisdiction for the action is later discovered to be unfounded. In particular, *lis pendens* Article 29 stays an action in a country for which jurisdiction has already been seised by the cross-border action:

> [W]here proceedings involving the same cause of action and between the same parties are brought in the courts of different Member States, any court other than the court first seised shall of its own motion stay its proceedings until such time as the jurisdiction of the court first seised is established.

This is supplemented by Article 30:

> Where related actions are pending in the courts of different Member States, any court other than the court first seised may stay its proceedings.

The legal basis used for filing a cross-border torpedo action in one particular country, such as Italy, under the Brussels I Regulation (recast) is Article 7(2) 'as a place where the harmful event occurred or may occur' or, in the event that the patentee or their licensee is domiciled in the desired jurisdiction, Article 4(1).

The wording of Article 7(2) has led the Italian courts to ask whether seeking a declaration that certain activities do not infringe a patent in Italy can actually concern a 'harmful event'. This question was initially addressed by the Italian Supreme Court in *BL Macchine Automatische v Windmoeller KG*.[11] In that case, the Court ruled that it could not be seised with a declaratory action under Article 7(2) because it was inherent in bringing such an action that the claimant *denies* that any harmful event has occurred. As such, according to *Windmoeller*, the Article 7(2) basis for the Italian Torpedo was unfounded.

However, subsequent to *Windmoeller*, the CJEU was asked to decide, in *Folien Fischer AG and Another v Ritrama SpA*,[12] whether Article 7(2) must be interpreted 'as meaning that an action for a negative declaration seeking to establish the absence of liability in tort, delict, or quasi-delict, falls within the scope of that provision'. The CJEU ruled that it did, leaving the *Windmoeller* decision in doubt. In its second opportunity to rule on the issue, the Italian Supreme Court, referring to *Folien Fischer*, ruled in *Asclepion* on 10 June 2013[13] that the Italian courts not only had jurisdiction to order a declaration of non-infringement for the Italian designation under Article 7(2), but also for its German counterpart.

II. Parallel Proceedings between the UPC and National Courts

During the seven-year transitional period (see Chapter 6), Article 83(1) provides a choice of forum between the UPC and the national courts for actions concerning European patents that have not been opted out. The choice is limited to the action and not the patent concerned. As a result, Article 83(1) provides the freedom for different actions concerning the same non-opted-out European patent and the same parties to be filed in a national court and the UPC concurrently. For example, an action for revocation of a bundle of European patents can proceed in the UPC concurrently with a national infringement action concerning one national designation of the same European patent, or a national revocation action against a designation of a European patent can proceed concurrently with an action to enforce the whole European patent bundle in the UPC. However, if revocation or infringement counterclaims were to follow these examples, the result is that the UPC and national court would be seised simultaneously with the same cause of action, in respect of the same patent and the same parties. The *lis pendens* rules in the Brussels I Regulation (recast) are intended to avoid such duplicative actions and the risk of conflicting decisions that may result.

A. The Amendment of the Brussels I Regulation (Recast) to Include the UPC

The Brussels I Regulation (recast) (see Chapter 2) provides for the introduction of the UPC within the wider framework of European jurisdictional rules.[14] The risk of duplicative

---

[11] *BL Macchine Automatische v Windmoeller KG*, 19 December 2003, n 19550, GRUR Int 2005, 264.
[12] *Folien Fischer AG and Another v Ritrama SpA* (Case C-133/11), ECLI:EU:C:2012:664.
[13] *General Hospital Corporation and Palomar Medical Technologies Inc v Asclepion Laser Technologies GmbH*, 14508/13 IIC 2014, 822 (10 June 2013).
[14] See Explanatory Memorandum in Proposal for a Regulation of the European Parliament and of the Council amending Regulation (EU) 1215/2012 on jurisdiction and the recognition and enforcement of judgments in civil and commercial matters.

actions between the UPC and the national courts, is addressed in amendments to the Brussels I Regulation (recast) by the extension of its *lis pendens* measures to actions concerning non-opted-out European patents lodged in the UPC simultaneously with:

(a) a national court of the contracting Member States during the transitional period; or
(b) a national court of a non-contracting Member State.[15]

The relevant *lis pendens* provisions are Article 29s and 30.[16]

Article 29 states that if proceedings involving the *same cause of action and between the same parties* are brought in the UPC and a court of a Member State,[17] the court other than the court first seised must of its own motion stay its proceedings until such time as the jurisdiction of the court first seised is established. Upon the request of one of the courts seised, the other court must without delay inform it of the date when it was seised and once the court first seised has been established, the other must decline jurisdiction.

Article 30 states that when *related* actions are pending in both the UPC and the courts of a Member State, the court that is not first seised may stay its proceedings. The court not first seised may also, on the application of one of the parties, decline jurisdiction if the court first seised has jurisdiction over the actions in question and consolidation of the cases is permitted under its laws. Actions are deemed to be related where they are 'so closely connected that it is expedient to hear and determine them together to avoid the risk of irreconcilable judgments resulting from separate proceedings'.[18]

The following sections consider how Articles 29 and 30 apply to non-opted-out European patents during the transitional period.

B. Concurrent Proceedings During the Transitional Period (Non-opted-out Patents)

i. Actions in the UPC and National Courts Concerning the 'Same Cause of Action' and the Same Parties

Article 83(1) UPC Agreement provides the possibility for a national revocation action of a not opted-out European patent to be lodged concurrently with an enforcement action between the same parties concerning the same patent in the UPC during the transitional period. Similarly, during the transitional period, a party may enforce a European patent in a national court concurrently with a revocation action between the same parties concerning the same patent in the UPC. In each case, the national action concerns the national

---

[15] Article 71c of the Brussels I Regulation (recast), as amended by Regulation (EU) 542/2014. This entails removing the requirement that the defendant is domiciled within an EU Member State (see Article 71b(2)).

[16] Article 32 stipulates how a court is seised: (a) at the time a document starting proceedings or an equivalent document is lodged with a court, provided that the document has subsequently been served on the defendant; or (b) if service of the document starting proceedings is required before lodging with the court, then the court is seised when the document is received by the authority responsible for service, provided that the document is subsequently lodged with the court. The authority responsible for service, in accordance with Article 32, is the first authority to receive the documents to be served. The court, or the authority responsible for service, is required to note the date on which the document starting proceedings is lodged or the date of receipt of the documents to be served, respectively.

[17] Note that 'Member State' is intended to encompasses both contracting and non-contracting Member States to the UPC Agreement.

[18] Article 30(3) of the amended Brussels Regulation I (recast).

designation of the European patent only, and the UPC action concerns all patents in the European patent bundle that are designated to a contracting Member State that has ratified the UPC Agreement.

Figures 7.1 and 7.2 schematically illustrate these two alternatives. However, in each case a counterclaim then follows in the national court, for revocation and infringement, respectively.[19] In both Figures 7.1 and 7.2, Article 29 is not triggered until the counterclaim is filed. Until this point, the UPC and the national court of the contracting Member State are not seised with the same cause of action, between the same parties and concerning the same patent. When the validity and infringement counterclaims ensue, as shown in the third step of both Figures 7.1 and 7.2, the UPC is then seised with the same cause of action as the national court, between the same parties and concerning the same patent. At this point, the court not first seised must stay, pending a decision of the first court seised regarding its jurisdiction.

Figure 7.1 During the transitional period, a revocation action is lodged in a national court of a Member State by Party X against Party P. It is followed by an infringement action brought by P, relating to the same patent, A, in the UPC against X. An attempted infringement counterclaim then follows in the national court (where local rules permit)[20]

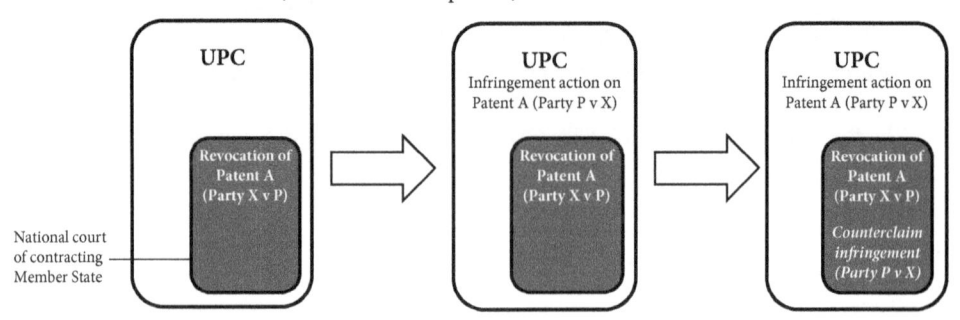

Figure 7.2 During the transitional period, an infringement action is lodged in a national court against Party X. It is followed by a revocation action by X relating to the same patent, A, against the proprietor P, in the UPC. An attempted revocation counterclaim then follows in the national court (where local rules permit)

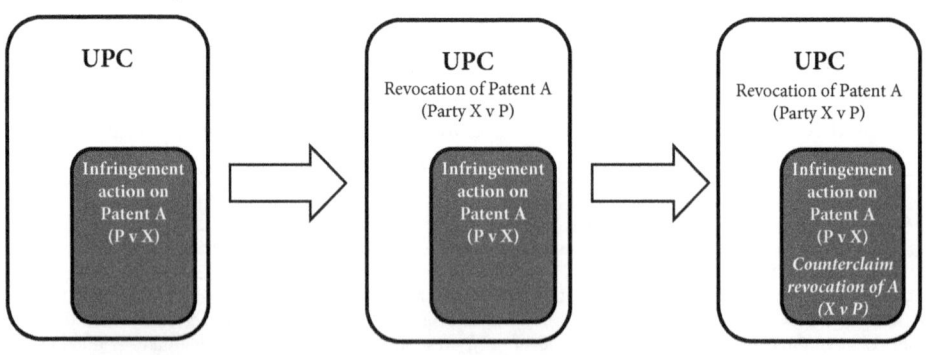

---

[19] The figures do not consider a counterclaim that is filed in the UPC (the UPC is regulated by its own internal jurisdictional rules, for which see ch 9).

[20] The figure assumes that infringement and revocation actions are not bifurcated under national procedures.

ii. Actions in the UPC and National Courts that are 'Related'

Article 30 of the Brussels I Regulation (recast) addresses cases where the action lodged in the UPC and the action lodged in the national court are 'related'. If they are related, and a party requests it, a court may decline jurisdiction in favour of the court first seised if the actions can be consolidated in that court. Related actions are those 'so closely connected that it is expedient to hear and determine them together to avoid the risk of irreconcilable judgments resulting from separate proceedings'. The question is then how this language is to be interpreted. It is clear that the same parties do not need to be involved in each action (see Figures 7.3 and 7.4 for two schematic illustrations of this). One interpretation is suggested by comparison with Article 8(1) of the Brussels I Regulation (recast). This permits a number of defendants to be sued in one court 'to avoid the risk of irreconcilable judgments':

> A person domiciled in a Member State may also be sued:
>
> (1) where he is one of a number of defendants, in the courts for the place where any one of them is domiciled, provided the claims are so closely connected that it is expedient to hear and determine them together to avoid the risk of irreconcilable judgments resulting from separate proceedings.

The CJEU has ruled on the application of this provision in *Solvay SA v Honeywell Fluorine Products Europe BV and Others*[21] and *Roche Nederland BV and Others v Frederick Primus and Milton Goldenberg*.[22] In *Solvay*, the CJEU ruled that 'irreconcilable judgments' may result from separate proceedings if the defendants are infringing the same European patent with the same product in their own countries of domicile, as well as those of their co-defendants. *Solvay* is to be contrasted with the facts of *Roche Nederland*, in which irreconcilable judgments were held by the CJEU not to be at risk. The infringements at issue in *Roche Nederland* were confined to the marketing of products by defendants in their respective countries of domicile only. Application of these rulings to Article 30 would suggest that a '*risk of irreconcilable judgments*' arises when there is an infringement of the same national designation of a European patent by the same product. All contracting Member State designations of a European patent[23] must be litigated as a bundle in the UPC[24] and so, on the *Solvay* interpretation, there will be a risk of conflicting judgments between the UPC and a contracting Member State court dealing with the same patent if the facts if the infringement are the same (as is likely to be the case with alleged infringers belonging to the same group), unless the UPC can 'carve-out' the national designation being litigated in the national court (see section II.B.iii below).

---

[21] *Solvay SA v Honeywell* (n 10). The decision was made under Article 6(1) of Council Regulation (EC) 44/2001 of 22 December 2000 (Brussels I Regulation), which is the predecessor to Article 8(1).

[22] *Roche Nederland BV and Others v Frederick Primus and Milton Goldenberg* (Case C-539/03) [2006] ECR I-06535.

[23] Those for contracting Member States that have ratified.

[24] Article 34 UPC Agreement.

Figure 7.3 During the transitional period, a revocation action is lodged in the UPC by Party X. It is followed by an infringement action relating to the same patent, A, in the national court of a Member State, but against a different party, Y. An attempted revocation counterclaim is then lodged in the national court of the Member State by Y (where local rules permit)

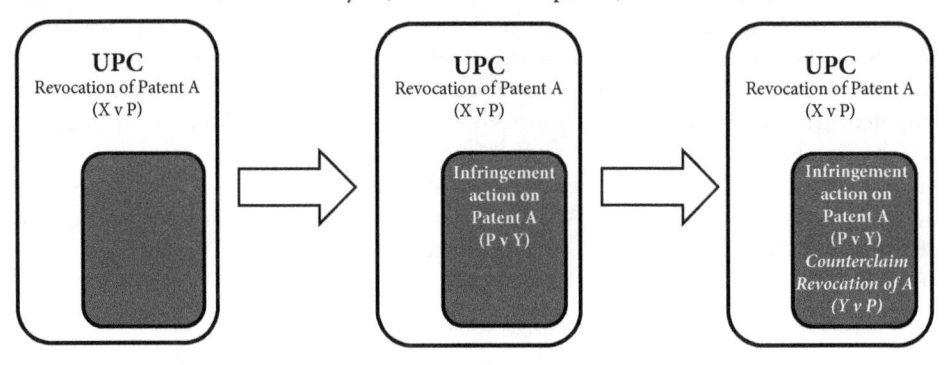

Figure 7.4 During the transitional period, an infringement action is lodged in the UPC against Party X. It is followed by a revocation action brought by Y relating to the same patent (A) in the national court of a Member State, and an attempted infringement counterclaim against Y in the national court of the Member State (where local rules permit)

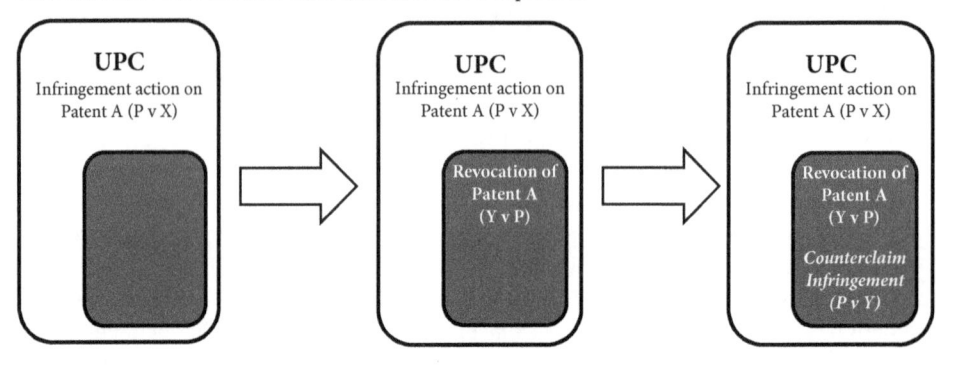

iii. Must the UPC Stay an Action in Respect of All Patent Validations?

The question also arises as to whether the UPC is barred by the *lis pendens* provisions from proceeding with a revocation action or an infringement action in respect of all European patents in the bundle, when a national court has already been seised with an action concerning a designation of the patent and between the same parties. Must the UPC: (i) stay the action with which it is seised in respect of all designations in the European bundle; or (ii) merely decline to make a decision regarding the national designation at issue in the national action, but proceed with the others?[25] Interpretation (ii) appears to be inconsistent with the requirement that all European patent designations are dealt with by the UPC together and at

---

[25] This issue remained outstanding following the Consultation on the 17th draft Rules of Procedure at Trier on 26 November 2014.

the same time. However, it has the advantage of avoiding the risk of an irreconcilable judgment while allowing the action concerning the other designations to progress. But there is yet another interpretation, which is that the action – the *lis* – is only identical if one focuses on the national designation which is already in issue. If one defines the *lis* as the entire bundle of European national designations, then the *lis* is different in the two jurisdictions. If the UPC and the national court come to different conclusions, the two judgments are no more irreconcilable than is the case now when a patent is held valid in one EPC state and invalid in another. However, this interpretation has the disadvantage that one might argue that it defeats the point of having amending the Brussels I Regulation (recast) to include *lis pendens* designed to cover the UPC.

C. Parallel Actions between the UPC and Courts of Non-contracting Member States

Articles 29 and 30 of the Brussels I Regulation (recast) also apply to parallel proceedings between a common court (which includes the UPC) and a court of a Member State that is not a party to the UPC Agreement.[26] Analogous scenarios to those illustrated by Figures 7.1–7.4 apply to parallel proceedings between non-contracting Member States and the UPC, as they do between contracting Member States and the UPC during the transitional period. As between the UPC and non-contracting Member States, Articles 29 and 30 apply indefinitely, or until such time as those Member States join the UPC[27] (see also Chapter 8 in respect of UK cross-border declarations of non-infringement).

D. 'Cross-border' Actions

i. Cross-border Preliminary Injunctions

In *Solvay v Honeywell*, the CJEU ruled[28] that a cross-border preliminary injunction is appropriate in circumstances where there is a 'risk of irreconcilable judgments'. In that case, the Dutch court accepted jurisdiction where each defendant (all members of the same corporate group) were allegedly infringing in their own country of domicile, and in the countries of their co-defendants. The alleged infringements concerned the same patent and the same facts of infringement were by supply of the same product by each defendant.

The relevant provision of the Brussels Regulation[29] and the reasoning that applies to *Solvay v Honeywell* may also be applied to preliminary injunction proceedings concerning

---

[26] Article 71c(1) of the amended Brussels I Regulation (recast).
[27] Article 71c(1) of the amended Brussels I Regulation (recast) is not limited to the transitional period in respect of the UPC and the non-contracting Member States.
[28] Under Article 6(1) of Council Regulation (EC) 44/2001 of 22 December 2000, now replaced by Article 8(1) of the Brussels I Regulation (recast).
[29] Article 8(1).

a non-contracting or non-ratifying Member State court and the UPC. Under the CJEU authority in *Solvay*, the UPC could potentially make a cross-border order for preliminary injunctive relief in respect of designations of a European patent in those countries on analogous facts. Conversely, it seems possible, in principle, for the national courts of these countries to make an order for a preliminary cross-border injunction that encompasses the UPC. The same principles apply to Unitary Patents in the UPC as well as European patents.

ii. 'Italian Torpedo' Actions

The 'Italian Torpedo' action has from time to time been a feature of the European patent system (see section I.B.iii above). Italy is a contracting Member State of the UPC Agreement and Articles 29 and 30 will apply as between Italy and the UPC for the duration of the transitional period. If, during the transitional period, Italy is first seised with a declaration of non-infringement of a patent that has not been opted out, there is potential for this to frustrate a later action lodged in the UPC concerning infringement of the same patent by the same parties (see also Chapter 8 in respect of UK cross-border declarations of non-infringement).

iii. The UPC 'Long-Arm' Jurisdiction

A 'long-arm' jurisdiction of the UPC has been introduced by amendment to the Brussels Regulation in Regulation 542/2014.[30] This gives the UPC jurisdiction over defendants domiciled outside the EU for acts of patent infringement committed within the territories covered by the court (see Chapter 9), amongst other tidying-up measures, but it also introduces the power, subject to limitations, for the UPC to award damages arising from infringement of a European patent in certain jurisdictions outside the EU,[31] including the UK.

Article 71(b) states as follows:

The jurisdiction of the UPC shall be determined as follows:

(1) a common court shall have jurisdiction where, under this Regulation, the courts of a Member State party to the instrument establishing the common court would have jurisdiction in a matter governed by that instrument;

(2) where the defendant is not domiciled in a Member State, and this Regulation does not otherwise confer jurisdiction over him, Chapter II shall apply as appropriate regardless of the defendant's domicile.

---

[30] ibid Article 71b(3), introduced by. Regulation 542/2014 of 15 May 2014 amending Regulation 1215/2012 as regards the rules to be applied with respect to the Unified Patent Court and the Benelux Court of Justice. For a detailed analysis, see Pierre Véron, 'Extent of the Long-Arm Jurisdiction conferred upon the Unified Patent Court by Art 71b(3) of the Brussels I Regulation as Amended by Regulation 542/2014 of 15 May 2014: Turkish Delight and a Bit of Swiss Chocolate for the Unified Patent Court' (2015) 37(9) *European Intellectual Property Review* 588.

[31] Not those EU Member States that are not contracting Member States or have not ratified the UPC Agreement.

Application may be made to a common court for provisional, including protective, measures even if the courts of a third State have jurisdiction as to the substance of the matter;

(3) where a common court has jurisdiction over a defendant under point 2 in a dispute relating to an infringement of a European patent giving rise to damage within the Union, that court may also exercise jurisdiction in relation to damage arising outside the Union from such an infringement.

Such jurisdiction may only be established if property belonging to the defendant is located in any Member State party to the instrument establishing the common court and the dispute has a sufficient connection with any such Member State.

a. Provisional Measures

Article 71(b)(1) establishes the common jurisdiction of the UPC to the ratified contracting states. Article 71(b)(2) establishes the jurisdiction of that court over non-EU domiciled defendants. However, it adds the perhaps surprising words: 'Application may be made to a common court for provisional, including protective, measures even if the courts of a third State have jurisdiction as to the substance of the matter.' As such, it purports to extend the reach of Article 35 of the Brussels Regulation ('Application may be made to the courts of a Member State for such provisional, including protective, measures as may be available under the law of that Member State, even if the courts of another Member State have jurisdiction as to the substance of the matter') to those non-EU countries of the EPC. In other words, the UPC may exercise its discretion to grant a preliminary injunction in respect of activity in, for example, the UK and Switzerland (subject to the application of the Lugano Convention in respect of Swiss defendants). The result is, in effect, a cross-border preliminary injunction; however, it is unclear whether the limitations in *Solvay v Honeywell*, developed under the Brussels Regulation (see section I.B.ii.b above), would apply to third states.

b. Damages Arising from Infringement

Article 71(b)(3) appears to provide that where the UPC has jurisdiction in relation to damages over a defendant in sub-paragraph (2), it 'may also exercise jurisdiction in relation to damage arising outside the Union from such an infringement'.[32] Apart from the limitations on the countries and defendants to which this provision applies, it is subject to the requirement that 'property belonging to the defendant is located in any Member State party to the instrument establishing the [UPC] and the dispute has a sufficient connection with any such Member State'.

It has been commented that although this jurisdiction is discretionary, the *travaux préparatoires* make it clear that the words in relation to damage arising outside the EU from such an infringement were intended to refer to the result of an infringement committed *outside* the territory of the EU,[33] which could be, for example, the UK or Switzerland. It is

---

[32] A jurisdiction which, within its limits, overrides the Court of Justice authority in *Shevill v Presse Alliance* (Case C-68/93) [1995] 2 AC 18 (7 March 1995).

[33] See Véron (n 30).

less clear what this means in practice. For example, it appears to imply that the UPC may need to decide on an infringement of a UK patent, under English law, in order to decide what damages flow from that infringement. Does this also imply that jurisdiction will be taken over validity in the UK or Switzerland?

The requirement for a 'connection' to a Member State in which the assets of a defendant are located is also unclear. Does this mean that the jurisdiction does not apply if the defendant has assets in, for example, Belgium, but the infringement takes place in Italy and that is where the defendant is sued?

8

Parallel Proceedings

The Courts of England and Wales and the UPC

For reasons that were explored in Chapter 1, the UK will not participate in the UPC. However, as the second largest economy in Europe and one of the three most designated countries for the grant of European patents, the UK – or, more accurately, the jurisdiction of the Patents Court of England and Wales – as well as the Intellectual Property and Enterprise Court (IPEC) will remain important for patent litigation in Europe and a partner to the UPC in European patent litigation. This chapter explores the likely relationship between patent proceedings in the English courts and UPC proceedings.

I. English National Actions

A. Extending General Persuasive Value

Patent proceedings in the English Patents Court and the IPEC have three particular characteristics:

(i) Speed – most final decisions on both infringement and validity come from the Court of Appeal[1] less than two and a half years after filing:[2] first instance decisions can be obtained in as little as 12 months, with expedition being possible in appropriate cases to shorten this time to just a few months (see below).

(ii) Evidential rigour – the procedures of the Patents Court are designed to elicit and scrutinise evidence in great detail: disclosure, party appointed experts and occasionally experiments. This rigour is reflected in the quantity and detail of the material typically placed before the Court, the cross-examination of experts, and the detailed reasoning and analysis of the evidence in judgments.

(iii) The reputation and integrity of the judges as highly experienced specialists in patent law and, often, with backgrounds in scientific disciplines.

Other European judges frequently take notice of English judgments (and vice versa). These judges are under no obligation to follow an English decision and, indeed, procedural and legal differences can present judges in the other national courts with different

---

[1] Appeals to the UK Supreme Court are rare in patent cases.
[2] See the Taylor Wessing Patent Map: https://united-kingdom.taylorwessing.com/patentmap.

evidence. However, it has been the practice for a number of years for judges to refer to and, where possible, be cognisant of and consistent with the decisions of other European judges. There is a procedural aspect to this, as Laddie J noted in *Research in Motion UK Ltd v Inpro Licensing SARL*:

> The existence of the German proceedings is a fact of life. It is no part of my function to interfere with German proceedings. I have to take account of the existence of the German proceedings as, no doubt, the German courts take account of the existence of English proceedings and their outcome. As I understand it from the evidence, Dr Klaus Grabinski, a well known judge in Germany, who is in the court which is seized with the German infringement action, has indicated, unsurprisingly, that he would take account of what the English courts do and the timetable imposed by the English courts. Just as a matter of courtesy, I would do the same for German actions or French or Dutch actions. Furthermore, we can no longer consider litigation in England in isolation when at least one of the parties is engaged in pan-European business, as RIM is here.[3]

There is also an element of recognising decisions and legal reasoning between the European courts. This was echoed by Henry Carr J in *Takeda v F Hoffmann-La Roche*[4] when he said:

> [A]ll courts deciding patent cases across Europe are interested to see judgments rendered by courts in other EPC contracting states on the equivalent EP.

An early success by a party in the English Patents Court therefore has a supranational value: the judgment may be a factor in the result of pending patent ligation concerning the same patent taking place, in parallel, in other European countries. In a UPC system in which most EU countries are served by the UPC, the influence of a quickly obtained and detailed English decision on the result of UPC litigation (whether concerning counterpart European patents or a Unitary Patent) may be more far-reaching.

i. A Factor in UPC Decisions

There are also specific preliminary stages in UPC actions for which a fast English decision may be an important factor. These are:

(i) a decision to stay a bifurcated infringement action; and
(ii) a decision to grant a preliminary injunction.

ii. A Factor in a Decision to Stay Bifurcated UPC Infringement Proceedings

Under the UPC Agreement, a revocation counterclaim may follow an infringement claim that has been lodged in a local or regional division[5] (see Chapter 9). The UPC Agreement then provides alternatives for the local or regional court seised with the action on how to proceed. This happens by way of a decision under Article 33(3) UPC Agreement.

---

[3] *Research in Motion UK Ltd v Inpro Licensing SARL* [2005] EWHC 1292 (Pat).
[4] *Takeda UK Ltd v F Hoffmann-La Roche AG* [2018] EWHC 2155 (Ch) (24 July 2018).
[5] Article 33(3). In these circumstances, if a central revocation action concerning the same patent and the same parties has already been lodged in the central division before the infringement action was started, it will be stayed (Rule 75.3 of the Rules of Procedure).

The Article 33(3) decision must be made as soon as practicable after the closure of the written procedure.[6] The alternatives for the local or regional panel are as follows:

(i) proceed with both the action for infringement and with the counterclaim for revocation;
(ii) refer the revocation counterclaim for a decision to the central division and suspend or proceed with the action for infringement; or
(iii) with the agreement of the parties, refer the case for decision to the central division.

Alternatively, infringement and revocation actions concerning the same patent and the same parties may be lodged in different divisions of the UPC from the beginning of the action (if the revocation is filed first), without a further revocation counterclaim. In this case, the local or regional division must decide, subject to the agreement of the parties, whether to refer the whole action to the central division or retain the infringement action only.[7]

If, by exercise of the above alternatives, the infringement and validity actions are bifurcated, or remain bifurcated, there are three further possibilities:

(i) the local or regional division proceeds with the infringement action in parallel to a revocation action in the central division (by original filing or by counterclaim). In this case, the central division must endeavour to accelerate the revocation proceedings;[8]
(ii) the panel, at its *discretion*, stays the infringement action pending a final decision in the revocation proceedings;[9] or
(iii) where there is a 'high likelihood' that the relevant claims of the patent being enforced are invalid, the panel *must* stay the infringement action until a decision has been made in the revocation action.[10]

Assuming the decision is obtained early enough, an invalidity decision of the Patents Court may be considered to be evidence of a high likelihood that the patent being enforced is invalid.

iii. Influencing a Decision on the Award of a Preliminary Injunction

The panels of the UPC divisions have a wide discretion to decide whether or not to grant a preliminary injunction (see Chapter 15). There is no mandatory requirement for the panels of the UPC to take into account decisions on an infringement or non-infringement of a foreign court when exercising their discretion in this regard. However, a panel hearing an application for a preliminary injunction *may* require the applicant to provide reasonable evidence that the patent is valid.[11] Specifically, the Rules of Procedure state that the Court should take into account whether the patent has been upheld in an opposition procedure

---

[6] The panel may take an earlier decision 'if appropriate' having given the parties an opportunity to be heard.
[7] Articles 33(5) and 33(3)(c) UPC Agreement.
[8] Rule 40(b) UPC Rules of Procedure.
[9] ibid Rule 37.4.
[10] ibid Rule 37.4. There is currently no guidance on the factors that the court would consider relevant to determining a 'high likelihood' for this purpose. These may include a finding that the patent is invalid by the EPO. It is also unclear in what level of detail a local or regional division will be prepared to consider this question.
[11] Rule 211.2 UPC Rules of Procedure.

114 *Parallel Proceedings*

before the EPO or has been the subject of proceedings 'in any other court'.[12] Hence, a decision of invalidity from the English court is relevant.

B. Expedition of English Proceedings

The challenge for a party seeking to use an English decision in both the ways described above will be timing. Any decision on whether to stay a bifurcated infringement action will come after the close of the UPC written procedure, approximately five to eight months after filing of the action. The timeframe for the hearing of a preliminary injunction can be expected to be much shorter.[13] This raises the role of pre-emptive action in the English court and expedition.

A first instance decision on the merits is normally obtained in the Patents Court in approximately one year. Filing an action in England and Wales before the UPC can therefore be expected to yield a highly reasoned decision on the merits before the UPC. Yet, in order to assist in the preliminary decisions described above, expedition may assist. The principles on expedition are set out by Lord Neuberger in *WL Gore & Associates GmbH v Geox SpA*:

> To my mind, when considering such an application there are four factors to take into account. The first is whether the applicants … have shown good reason for expedition; the second is whether expedition would interfere with the good administration of justice; the third is whether expedition would cause prejudice to the other party; and the fourth is whether there are any other special factors.[14]

The application of these factors has been illustrated in cases dealing with the relationship between English validity proceedings and infringement proceedings in Germany. These explore the circumstances in which English proceedings can be expedited to assist in obtaining a stay of infringement proceedings in Germany, pending a decision on validity by the Bundespatentgericht. The attitude of the English court to this is touched on in broad terms by Laddie J:

> It is not in any sense intended to be taken as a criticism or, indeed, a comment on German procedures, but I think that the fact that issues of infringement will be determined in Germany speedily is itself a reason why the issue of validity in this country for essentially the same patent should also be dealt with speedily. This is not a matter of trying to trump the German courts, but it seems to me that in all senses it would be fairer if RIM's ability to sell BlackBerrys and, in particular, the risk of it being held to have infringed a valid patent should be determined rapidly rather than slowly. The German courts happen to have in place a means by which infringement, at least in that country, will be determined rapidly. I see every reason for saying that the issue of validity should also be considered rapidly in this country. Even if on a normal timescale this trial would come into the lists next year, I think it is suitable for expedition to come on towards the end of November of this year and I will so direct.[15]

---

[12] ibid Rule 209.2.
[13] No specific timeframe is suggested in the UPC Rules of Procedure.
[14] *WL Gore & Associates GmbH v Geox SpA* [2008] EWCA Civ 622. See also *Evalve and Others v Edwards Lifesciences Ltd* (unreported, 27 March 2019).
[15] *Research in Motion UK Ltd v Inpro Licensing SARL* [2005] EWHC 1292 (Pat).

More recently, the specific issue of employing an expedited English decision on validity was raised in *HTC Europe Co Ltd v Apple Inc*.[16] The authorities are nuanced, as can be seen from the summary given by Arnold J:

> It seems to me that the position is as follows. To date, the English courts have accepted that a factor which may be relied upon by a party applying for expedition is that the finding of this court in relation to the validity of the European patent (UK), the German counterpart of which is being litigated in infringement proceedings in Germany, will be of assistance to that party with regard to the question of whether there should be a stay of [the German] proceedings. It is not, however, a factor which has been treated in any of the cases as being a particularly strong or important factor. Thus, by way of example, in RIM v Visto,[17] I said it was a factor to which I attached 'less weight', but one which provided 'some further support' to the request for expedition.

In the *HTC* case, HTC had wanted to get a validity decision on the UK counterpart of a patent being litigated in Mannheim. This was sought to persuade the Mannheim court to stay infringement proceedings. Although Arnold J was prepared in principle to take the German proceedings into account, the application failed, at least in part due to a lack of certainty about the actual dates of the relevant hearing in Germany.

However, in *HTC*, the judge did expedite the proceedings concerning two other patents, the counterparts of which were subject to infringement proceedings in Munich. Whilst the existence of the parallel proceedings in Munich appears to have been a factor in this decision, more important for the court was the commercial imperative for HTC and its customers to know whether it infringed certain patents, in the context of a precarious, fast-moving and expanding market, in which it had already gained a significant market share. As the same judge noted in a case heard a short time later, *ZTE (UK) Ltd v Ericsson*,[18] the existence of German proceedings so far as he was aware had never provided a ground for ordering expedition on its own; it was a factor, even though it was not a strong one.

This approach was reinforced in *Abbott v Dexcom*,[19] in which expedition sought in aid of German proceedings was refused by Mellor J. However, less than a month later, the same judge granted expedition in *Advanced Bionics*,[20] so that there would be a UK decision on validity before a German court reached a decision on infringement of the German equivalent patent. Yet, there was nothing of the asymmetry between the parties in *Bionics* that concerned the judge in *Abbott*, and the relevant product had the unusual characteristics that it had to be surgically inserted into patients for long-term use and so brand loyalty was key. The principal basis for seeking expedition was, consequently, to avoid Bionics suffering long-term and severe irreparable damage in the UK market caused by those in the market learning that a German court had injuncted its cochlear implant device. Mellor J put it like this:

> I am satisfied that word would go round the industry very quickly indeed. Many would then speculate whether the same was going to happen in the UK. This would lead both audiologists

---

[16] *HTC Europe Co Ltd v Apple Inc* [2011] EWHC 2396 (Pat).
[17] *Research in Motion UK Ltd v Visto Corp* [2008] EWHC 3025 (Pat). See also *Research in Motion UK Ltd v Inpro Licensing SARL* [2005] EWHC 1292 (Pat).
[18] *ZTE (UK) Ltd v Ericsson* [2011] EWHC 2709 (Pat).
[19] *Abbott Laboratories Ltd v Dexcom Incorporated* [2021] EWHC 2246 (Pat) (6 August 2021).
[20] *Advanced Bionics AG and Another v MED-El Elektromedizinische Gerate GmbH* [2021] EWHC 2415 (Pat) (31 August 2021).

and patients to doubt whether it was advisable to have a 3D device implanted and to discussions to that effect on the blogs. In the unusual circumstances of this product market, I conclude that the grant of an injunction in Germany around the end of February 2022 is highly likely to cause significant damage to AB and to the prospects of its 3D device recovering the market share AB had before the pandemic.

As a more general point, the judge emphasised that although avoiding the German injunction gap was a matter for the German courts, expedition depended on the effect this would have on the UK market:

> Once again, the circumstances which give rise to this application stem from the ability of a patentee to obtain a swift decision from a German court on infringement and before any court has examined the validity of the patent. As I indicated in a recent judgment (Abbott Laboratories) the position which the so-called 'injunction gap' creates in Germany is a matter for the German courts. The task for an English Court on an application of this type is to examine the effects that an early injunction in Germany may have on the UK market to the disadvantage of a party who believes the EP is invalid and/or not infringed, and to decide whether those effects justify expedition of a trial in this country.
>
> There may be many cases where the effect of a German injunction on the UK market is slight or even non-existent. Equally, a case may reveal a real risk that a party in the position of AB will suffer real damage in the UK market caused by knowledge that a German court has granted an injunction over their flagship product and the fact that it may be difficult if not impossible to overcome concerns in the UK market as to whether it is safe or prudent to take that party's product for fear that an injunction in the UK may well follow, even if in time that party secures a finding from the English court that the EP(UK) is invalid (and/or not infringed). If such damage is suffered, there is no redress against the patentee, it is truly irreparable damage.

The touchstone for granting expedition in Bionics was therefore irreparable damage, although the judge did not say that irreparable damage would need to be shown in every case. However, some kind of commercial and practical imperatives would be needed in the UK market if expedition of English proceedings is sought for the purpose of assisting a stay of infringement proceedings, or to defeat a preliminary injunction, in the UPC.

II. English Cross-border Declarations of Non-infringement

A. Overview of Powers under English Law

In *Actavis Group HF v Eli Lilly and Company*,[21] Arnold J had to decide whether the English Patents Court has jurisdiction to hear an action for declarations of non-infringement in respect of the UK, French, German, Italian and Spanish counterparts of a European patent.

As regards subject matter jurisdiction, Actavis accepted that jurisdiction could not be founded under Article 4(1) or 7(2) of the Brussels Regulation (recast) because Eli Lilly was domiciled in the State of Indiana in the US, with only a subsidiary registered in the UK. Jurisdiction was instead a matter of English law.[22] In this respect, in circumstances where

---

[21] Joined with *Medef EHF v Eli Lilly and Company* [2012] EWHC 3316 (Pat). The Court of Appeal later upheld Arnold J's decision that the English court has jurisdiction to hear the actions in [2013] EWCA Civ 517.
[22] Article 6(1) of the Brussels Regulation (recast).

Actavis had undertaken not to challenge validity, Eli Lilly did not dispute that the claims of the non-UK designations were justiciable before the English court. The substance of Eli Lilly's case was instead that service had not been validly effected in the UK and/or that Eli Lilly had not consented to it. Having found that service was validly effected, the court went on to consider whether the Patents Court was nonetheless a *forum non conveniens* – whether there was some other available forum, having competent jurisdiction, which was the appropriate forum for the trial of the action.[23] The judge held that the national courts of the respective European counterpart patents were not clearly and distinctly more appropriate than the Patents Court and declined to order a stay.

Subsequently, however, the UK left the Brussels Regulation (recast) and it is not currently a member of the Lugano Convention, which is drafted in similar terms in the relevant respects. As a consequence, *Actavis v Eli Lilly* jurisdiction will apply to EU domiciled defendants as well as non-EU domiciled defendants. What then is the potential impact on UPC proceedings if such a declaration of non-infringement is obtained in the English Patents Court?

B. Stay or Dismissal of a UPC Action

The award of a cross-border declaration of non-infringement in the English Patents Court raises the possibility of duplicative actions with the UPC, provided all the relevant proprietors and licensees likely to take part in a UPC infringement action are parties to the English action.[24] The risk of duplicative actions between the UPC and the national courts of the contracting Member States of the UPC Agreement during the transitional period is addressed in amendments to the Brussels Regulation.[25] The UK is not a contracting Member State and so it is the international *lis pendens* provisions in Article 33 of the Brussels Regulation[26] that apply:

Article 33 states as follows:

1. Where jurisdiction is based on Article 4 or on Articles 7, 8 or 9 and proceedings are pending before a court of a third State at the time when a court in a Member State is seised of an action involving the same cause of action and between the same parties as the proceedings in the court of the third State, the court of the Member State may stay the proceedings if:

    (a) it is expected that the court of the third State will give a judgment capable of recognition and, where applicable, of enforcement in that Member State; and

    (b) the court of the Member State is satisfied that a stay is necessary for the proper administration of justice.

---

[23] *Spiliada Maritime Corp v Cansulex Ltd* [1987] AC 460.
[24] To avoid a situation such as that in the pemetrexed litigation, in which the German regional court did not recognise the jurisdiction of the English court due to the different parties before them both.
[25] Article 71c of the Brussels Regulation (recast), as amended by Regulation (EU) 542 / 2014.
[26] Article 33 does not refer to the UPC, but only to the courts of the Member States. However, the UPC Agreement makes clear that the UPC is a court common to the contracting Member States and thus subject to the same obligations under EU law as any national court of the contracting Member States (Article 1(2) UPC Agreement).

2. The court of the Member State may continue the proceedings at any time if:
   (a) the proceedings in the court of the third State are themselves stayed or discontinued;
   (b) it appears to the court of the Member State that the proceedings in the court of the third State are unlikely to be concluded within a reasonable time; or
   (c) the continuation of the proceedings is required for the proper administration of justice.
3. The court of the Member State shall dismiss the proceedings if the proceedings in the court of the third State are concluded and have resulted in a judgment capable of recognition and, where applicable, of enforcement in that Member State.
4. The court of the Member State shall apply this Article on the application of one of the parties or, where possible under national law, of its own motion.

Further to Article 33.2, if the UPC is seised by an action concerning the same parties and the same cause of action as a court of a third state (eg, the English Patents Court), it has the discretion to stay its proceedings. If the action in the third state has resulted in a decision that is capable of recognition, the UPC must stay (Article 33.3).

A declaration of non-infringement of a patent is the same cause of action as a claim for infringement of that patent.[27] Therefore, a cross-border declaration of non-infringement from the Patents Court, concerning one or more European patents or a Unitary Patent and recognised in their countries of registration,[28] has the potential to trigger Article 33 in respect of an infringement action in the UPC. In respect of European patents, this raises the question of whether the UPC would be barred by the application of the international *lis pendens* provisions from proceeding with the infringement action with which it is seised in respect of all designations in the European bundle or some of them (see Chapter 7).

C. Accepting Cross-border Jurisdiction in the Context of the UPC

Would the English Patents Court accept jurisdiction for a cross-border declaration of non-infringement, in the context of parallel proceedings in the UPC? As described above, in *Eli Lilly*, Arnold J accepted jurisdiction for an action seeking a declaration of non-infringement for Italy, Spain, Germany, France and the UK. It was held that all of these actions are justiciable and that Eli Lilly had consented to them on accepting service of the action. However, the Patents Court went on to consider whether, had there been no consent, the principles of *forum non conveniens* would require the Court to stay the action.

The principles of this doctrine are set out by Lord Goff of Chieveley in *Spiliada Maritime Corp v Cansulex Ltd*.[29] As summarised in *Actavis v Eli Lilly*, these are as follows:

(a) The basic principle is that a stay will only be granted on the ground of forum non conveniens where the court is satisfied that there is some other available forum, having competent jurisdiction, which is the appropriate forum for the trial of the action, i.e. in which the case may be tried more suitably for the interests of all the parties and the ends of justice.
   …

---

[27] *Owners of Cargo Lately Laden on Board the Ship Tatry v Owners of the Ship Maciej Rataj* (Case C-406/92) [1999] QB 515.
[28] Or the relevant countries protected by the Unitary Patent.
[29] *Spiliada Maritime Corp v Cansulex Ltd* [1987] AC 460, 476–78.

(d) Since the question is whether there exists some other forum which is clearly more appropriate for the trial of the action, the court will look first to see what factors there are which point in the direction of another forum. These are the factors which Lord Diplock described, in MacShannon's case [1978] AC 795, 812, as indicating that justice can be done in the other forum at 'substantially less inconvenience or expense' ... Lord Keith of Kinkel, in The Abidin Daver [1984] AC 398, 415 ... referred to the 'natural forum' as being 'that with which the action had the most real and substantial connection.' So it is for connecting factors in this sense that the court must first look; and these will include not only factors affecting convenience or expense (such as availability of witnesses), but also other factors such as the law governing the relevant transaction ... and the places where the parties respectively reside or carry on business.

(e) If the court concludes at that stage that there is no other available forum which is clearly more appropriate for the trial of the action, it will ordinarily refuse a stay ...

(f) If however the court concludes at that stage that there is some other available forum which prima facie is clearly more appropriate for the trial of the action, it will ordinarily grant a stay unless there are circumstances by reason of which justice requires that a stay should nevertheless not be granted. In this inquiry, the court will consider all the circumstances of the case, including circumstances which go beyond those taken into account when considering connecting factors with other jurisdictions. One such factor can be the fact, if established objectively by cogent evidence, that the plaintiff will not obtain justice in the foreign jurisdiction ...

In *Eli Lilly*, the judge did not consider that the courts of Italy, Spain, France and Germany were clearly or distinctly more appropriate than the English courts. An influential factor in that decision was the approach taken by the Supreme Court in *Lucasfilm Ltd and Others v Ainsworth and Another*, a copyright case, as summarised by the following statement:

> There is no doubt that the modern trend is in favour of the enforcement of foreign intellectual property rights. First, article 22(4) of the Brussels I Regulation only assigns exclusive jurisdiction to the country where the right originates in cases which are concerned with registration or validity of rights which are 'required to be deposited or registered' and does not apply to infringement actions in which there is no issue as to validity ... Second, the Rome II Regulation also plainly envisages the litigation of foreign intellectual property rights and, third, the professional and academic bodies which have considered the issue, the American Law Institute and the Max Planck Institute, clearly favour them, at any rate where issues of validity are not engaged.[30]

In *Eli Lilly*, the judge was also impressed by the argument that even if different laws were applied for each patent (which the court decided they should be), it would mean that one court (and one court on appeal) would determine all five claims, helping to eliminate the prospect of inconsistent decisions.[31] The judge did not consider relevant the fact that the English courts (first instance and appeal) would be likely to arrive at a final decision in the action quicker than the foreign courts in question:

> [A] decision whether to grant or refuse a stay on forum non conveniens grounds, while technically an exercise of discretion, is not an exercise in determining what course appears most convenient. The question to be determined is the appropriate forum for trial.

In a UPC system that does not include the UK, similar questions would arise as to whether the balance of arguments in favour of the English courts as the appropriate jurisdiction.

---

[30] *Lucasfilm Ltd and Others v Ainsworth and Another* [2011] UKSC 39, paragraph 108.
[31] Subject to the different national approaches taken in relation to Article 69 of the European Patent Convention.

In particular, there is the fact that the UPC itself is designed to hear questions concerning multiple designations of European patents in a single set of proceedings. Would the English court be willing to provide effectively a rival centre of litigation to the UPC on such matters? The English court could, in theory, decide for the UK European patent designation and those for all EU Member States (including a Unitary Patent) – a jurisdiction broader than the UPC itself.

III. Cross-border *Arrow* Declarations?

What other forms of cross-border declaratory relief may be available in the English court? Is it possible to obtain a cross-border form of the declaration obtained in *Fujifilm Kyowa Biologics Company Ltd (FKB) v AbbVie Biotechnology Ltd*[32] and *Arrow Generics Ltd and Another v Merck & Co Inc*[33] (an '*Arrow* Declaration')?

In the *Fujifilm* proceedings, FKB sought a declaration that its *own product* is anticipated or obvious at the priority dates of two patents that had earlier been granted to AbbVie. The purpose of seeking the declaration was to ensure that FKB could market its own product, a biosimilar of adalimumab, in circumstances where divisionals sharing the same priority date as those patents and also concerning injections made subcutaneously every other week, in a single dose, were being prosecuted. As applications, the divisionals could not be challenged for invalidity in the English Patents Court. The purpose of the declaration was therefore to provide a '*Gillette* defence': that any claim asserted to cover the FKB product must also be novel or obvious. The Court of Appeal[34] confirmed at an interim stage that in principle, if the circumstances justify it, the courts have the jurisdiction to grant such a declaration.[35]

Significantly, in *FKB*,[36] by the time of trial AbbVie had abandoned all its relevant patent protection and applications in the UK and had provided undertakings to the court that neither it nor its affiliates would obtain UK patent protection covering the dosing regimens in suit. However, AbbVie was unwilling to consent to the declarations in the form sought.[37] The late Henry Carr J in *FKB* granted the declaration and provided guidance on the justifying circumstances.[38] In particular, he held that whatever the factual background, in order to be justified, the declarations must serve a useful purpose in the UK. Seeking a declaration for solely persuasive value in another jurisdiction would not be sufficient for this purpose. Yet, in the judge's view, the declaration would serve the useful purpose of providing more commercial certainty than the complex undertakings given by AbbVie, which would not have been readily understood by commercial people. The declaration would also help to

---

[32] *Fujifilm Kyowa Biologics Company Ltd (FKB) v AbbVie Biotechnology Ltd* [2016] EWHC 425 (Pat).
[33] *Arrow Generics Ltd and Another v Merck & Co Inc* [2007] EWHC 1900 (Pat).
[34] *Fujifilm Kyowa Kirin Biologics Co Ltd v Abbvie Biotechnology Ltd & Anor* [2017] EWCA Civ 1 (12 January 2017).
[35] It would be the role of the court at first instance to determine those circumstances on the facts.
[36] January and February 2017.
[37] Para 386, *Fujifilm Kyowa Kirin Biologics Company Ltd v Abbvie Biotechnology Ltd* (Rev 1) [2017] EWHC 395 (Pat) (03 March 2017).
[38] Para 394ff, *Fujifilm Kyowa Kirin Biologics Company Ltd v Abbvie Biotechnology Ltd* (Rev 1) [2017] EWHC 395 (Pat) (03 March 2017).

protect the claimants' European supply chains by reducing the risk of injunctive relief in other jurisdictions, and would serve to promote wider settlement by changing the parties' relative positions in any negotiations. The judge added that the facts of the case were highly unusual and that there were special reasons in favour of granting the declarations. In particular, these included the fact that AbbVie had threatened infringement proceedings whilst abandoning its patent portfolio in the UK in order to shield it from scrutiny.[39]

More recently, in *Pfizer Ltd v F Hoffmann-La Roche*,[40] an *Arrow* declaration was refused. Here, there were once again multiple second medical use patent applications being prosecuted, this time relating to combinations of bevacizumab with other known cancer drugs for use in treating various types of cancer. The UK applications were de-designated and the parties agreed that no UK patents existed (or could exist). The 'useful purpose' identified by Pfizer for the declaration was to support a decision to launch its own biosimilar product on a full or a skinny label across Europe, securing its supply chain and promoting wider settlement. It also argued that there was a compelling prima facie case for lack of novelty and/or obviousness of the patents and that a patentee with faith in their patents would be unlikely to need to shield them.

Unlike in *AbbVie*, where unclear undertakings were given and the patent rights in question were abandoned at the last moment, Roche abandoned its patent rights early and its position was clear. The judge said that had there been any pending applications in any of the families, this would be a plain case for an *Arrow* declaration. In the complete absence of this possibility, the reality was that the commercial value of an *Arrow* declaration to Pfizer would be its utility (along with a reasoned judgment) in helping Pfizer defend itself against suits brought by Roche in other European countries – in particular in Belgium, to influence a Belgian court against granting a preliminary injunction in that country, where the product is manufactured. This, as *FKB v AbbVie* had already held, was not a sufficient reason to grant one.

Therefore, it is clear that the court requires an *Arrow* declaration to serve a useful purpose domestically and not merely be used to influence foreign proceedings. If, as in the *AbbVie* case, there is a useful purpose domestically, then an *Arrow* declaration may have collateral influence in parallel UPC proceedings by indicating the invalidity of later granted patents.

---

[39] For a full discussion of the cases, see Paul England and Andrew Payne, 'Declaratory Relief in the English Patents Court' (2016) 15(3) *Bio-Science Law Review* 123.
[40] *Pfizer Ltd v F Hoffmann-La Roche AG and* Another [2019] EWHC 1520 (Pat) (20 June 2019).

9

UPC Jurisdiction

Where to Bring the Claim

The aim of the UPC is to provide a simplified system of pan-European patent litigation for all contracting Member States. However, the geographical spread of the UPC across up to 22 Member States and the continuing existence of national courts mean that jurisdictional rules are necessary to govern the location in which cases are lodged. There are two aspects to these rules: the Brussels Regulation, which governs the national and cross-border jurisdiction of disputes in the EU (see Chapter 7); and the jurisdictional rules governing the allocation of cases between the divisions of the UPC itself. The former are external rules of jurisdiction which govern the UPC as a court common to the Member States. The latter are internal jurisdictional rules that govern how actions are allocated between the divisions of the UPC. In particular, when the European patent package was negotiated, agreement could not be reached on whether the 'bifurcated system' or the 'principle of unity', which are seen in the national patent infringement systems of the contracting Member States,[1] should be applied in UPC proceedings. As a compromise, Article 33(3) UPC Agreement leaves some discretion to the UPC panels as to which system should be applied to the case at hand. This chapter considers these internal rules.

I. Forum by Agreement

Parties may agree with each other on the forum in which they would like the action to proceed. Evidence of such an agreement must be provided in the statement of claim.[2] There is no general rule enabling the parties to agree to a change of forum subsequent to the lodging of proceedings. However, a party may object to forum within a month of service of the statement of claim using a preliminary objection (see Chapter 10). Such an objection must be based on grounds that the division seised lacks competence. It is open to the parties to agree with the court that an infringement action lodged in a local or regional division (with or without a revocation counterclaim) should be consolidated with a revocation action lodged in the central division.[3]

---

[1] The national courts of Germany, Austria and Hungary follow the 'bifurcated system'. The national courts of all other contracting Member States apply the 'principle of unity'.
[2] Further to Article 33(7) UPC Agreement and with the exception of actions relating to decisions of the EPO under Article 32(1)(i) UPC Agreement.
[3] Further to Article 33(3)(c) UPC Agreement.

II. Forum by Operation of Article 33

In the absence of an agreement by the parties, Article 33 UPC Agreement governs the division of the Court of First Instance of the UPC in which an action, and counterclaims to that action, must be lodged.[4]

A. 'Domicile'

A number of the jurisdictional rules provided in Article 33 are based on the defendant's residence or principal place of business – or, in the absence of residence or principal place of business, its place of business. For the sake of convenience, in the discussion below, these are collectively referred to as the defendant's 'Domicile'.

B. Bringing Infringement and Related Actions

The jurisdictional rules that apply to these actions are based on the Contracting Member State where the defendant has its Domicile, and the contracting Member State where the infringing act occurs.[5]

i. Infringing Acts where there is a Division and the Defendant is Domiciled where there is a Division

In cases where an actual or threatened infringement occurs in or may occur in a contracting Member State that hosts a local division or participates in a regional division, and the defendant's Domicile is in a contracting Member State that hosts a local division or participates in a regional division, the action may be brought in either:

(a) the local division or regional division of the contracting Member State of the defendant's Domicile; or
(b) the local division or regional division of the contracting Member State where the actual or threatened infringement has or may occur (see Figure 9.1).

The claimant has a choice of forum in which to lodge the action, subject to the rules on consolidation (see Figure 9.1).

---

[4] In this book, the Rules are dealt with broadly according to the main causes of action and counterclaim for which the UPC has competence: bringing an infringement action; revocation actions and declarations of non-infringement; subsequent infringement and revocation claims (following an earlier claim concerning the same patent and between the same parties); infringement actions following a declaration of non-infringement; and actions for compensation for licences of right.

[5] See Article 33(1)(a) and (b). For the sake of convenience, in these scenarios, places of actual or threatened infringement concerning a local division or a regional division are treated together. Reference is made to actions based on actual or threatened infringement only.

124   UPC Jurisdiction

Figure 9.1 The claimant's choice of forum between Domicile and place of infringement

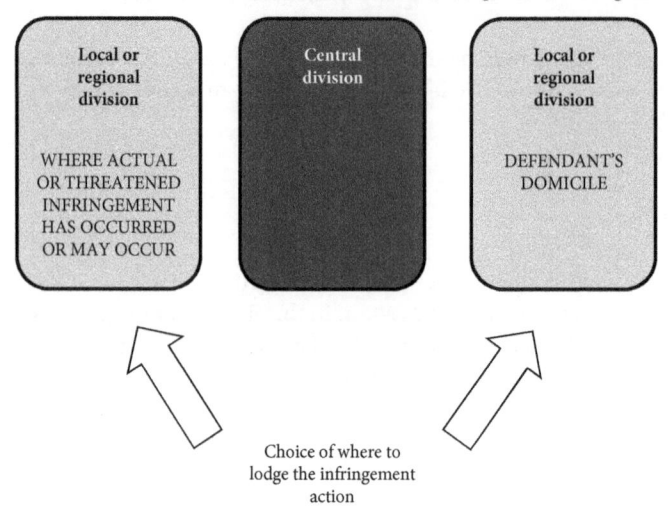

Local or regional division	Central division	Local or regional division
WHERE ACTUAL OR THREATENED INFRINGEMENT HAS OCCURRED OR MAY OCCUR		DEFENDANT'S DOMICILE

Choice of where to lodge the infringement action

ii. Infringing Acts in a Territory where there is a Division and the Defendant is Domiciled Outside the Contracting Member States

When an actual or threatened infringement occurs in or may occur in a contracting Member State that hosts a local division or participates in a regional division, but the defendant is Domiciled outside the territory of the Contracting Member States, the defendant's Domicile is no longer a factor in choosing forum. In such cases, the action may be brought in the local or regional division of the actual or threatened infringement, or in the central division[6] (Figure 9.2).

Figure 9.2 The claimant's choice when the defendant's Domicile is outside the contracting Member States

Local or regional division	Central division	Local or regional division
WHERE ACTUAL OR THREATENED INFRINGEMENT HAS OCCURRED OR MAY OCCUR		DEFENDANT DOMICILED OUTSIDE CONTRACTING MEMBER STATES

Choice of where to lodge the infringement action

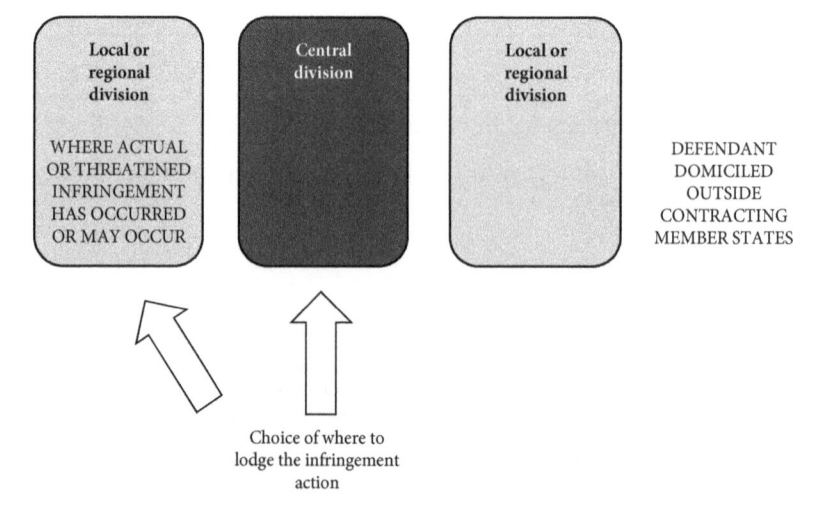

[6] Article 33(1) UPC Agreement.

iii. *Infringement where there is no Division and the Defendant is Domiciled Outside the Contracting Member States*

When a defendant's Domicile is outside the contracting Member States and the contracting Member State where the actual or threatened infringement occurs does not have a division, the action must be started in the central division (Figure 9.3). In these circumstances, the claimant does not have a choice of forum.

Figure 9.3 The claimant's choice when the defendant is domiciled outside the contracting Member States and the place of infringement has no local or regional division

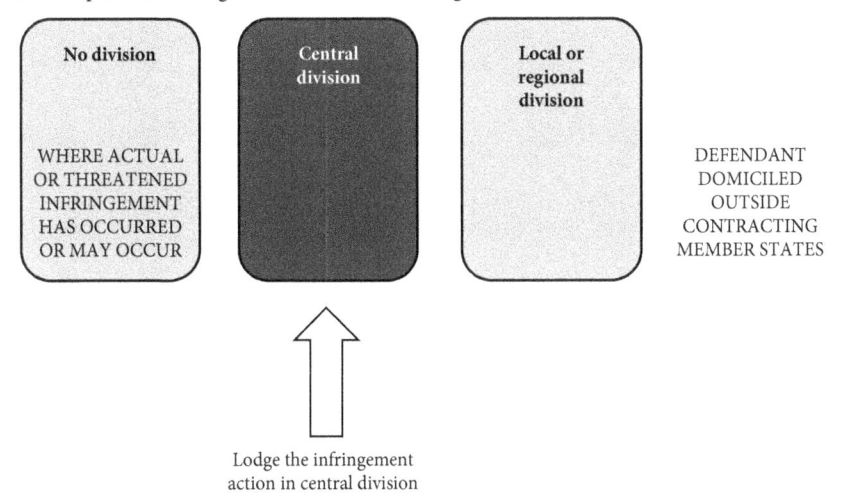

C. Infringement where there is no Division and the Defendant is Domiciled in a Contracting Member State

A party may wish to lodge an action for an act or threatened act of infringement (or other action to which the same rules apply) that has taken place in a country without a local or regional division. If the defendant is Domiciled in a Member State that does have a division, it is unclear from Article 33(1) whether the claimant can lodge in the central division or the division of the defendant, or whether they can only lodge in the division of the defendant's Domicile (see bottom row in Table 9.1).

Table 9.1 Examples of how Article 33(1) might be applied

Place of infringement	Domicile	Forum	
The Netherlands	France	Dutch local	French local
Germany	US	German local	Central
Malta	UK	Central	
Estonia	The Netherlands	Nordic-Baltic regional	Dutch
Luxembourg	Italy	Central?	Italian local

i. Provisional and Protective Measures, Injunctions, Damages or Compensation Derived from Provisional Protection etc

The jurisdictional rules that apply to infringement actions (see section II.B above) also apply to: actions for provisional and protective measures;[7] actions for damages and compensation derived from the provisional protection conferred by a published European patent application;[8] and actions relating to the use of the invention prior to the granting of the patent, or to the right based on prior use of the invention.[9] They do not apply to the lodging of revocation actions and declarations of non-infringement (see section II.F below).

When an infringement action on the merits has already been lodged, an application for provisional measures must immediately be forwarded by the Registry to the panel to which the action on the merits has been assigned or the single judge concerned (see also Chapter 15).[10]

D. Multiple Actions

i. Bringing a Second Action Concerning the Same Patent between the Same Parties

If an action is lodged in a division of the Court of First Instance for:

(a) infringement of a patent and/or SPC;[11]
(b) provisional and protective measures;[12]
(c) damages and compensation derived from the provisional protection conferred by a published classical European patent application;[13]
(d) use of the invention prior to the granting of the patent or to the right based on prior use of the invention;[14] or
(e) compensation for licences,[15]

the subsequent lodging of another one of these causes of action, between the same parties and concerning the same patent, must be brought before the same division as the first pending action.[16]

For example, a party that has brought an action for infringement of Patent A in contracting Member State X (on the basis that this is where the defendant has its place of Domicile) cannot later seek an injunction against the same defendant on the same patent in another Member State Y (where the infringement is alleged to occur).

If an action between the same parties on the same patent is brought before several different divisions, it is the division first seised that is competent to hear the whole case and the

---

[7] ibid Article 32(1)(c).
[8] ibid Article 32(1)(f).
[9] ibid Article 32(1)(g). It is unclear whether such an action should be lodged in the local or regional division of a contracting Member State according to where the activities of prior use take place, as acts of 'actual or threatened infringement'.
[10] Rule 208.3 of the Rules of Procedure.
[11] ibid Article 32(1)(a).
[12] ibid Article 32(1)(c).
[13] ibid Article 32(1)(f).
[14] ibid Article 32(1)(g).
[15] Article 8 UP Regulation.
[16] Article 33(2) UPC Agreement.

other divisions must declare it inadmissible.[17] For actions that concern the same patent, in which there is not identity of the parties, actions may proceed in different divisions.

ii. Consolidation of Infringement Actions against Commercially Related Defendants

If there is more than one potential defendant domiciled in more than one Contracting Member State and they have 'a "commercial relationship"[18] and the action relates to the same alleged infringement', the action may be brought against all the defendants in the place of Domicile of one of them.[19]

The consolidation provision applies only to infringement actions, actions for provisional and protective measures and injunctions, and actions for damages or compensation derived from the provisional protection conferred by a published European application.[20]

iii. General Joinder of Actions, whether or not between the Same Parties

Where it is for the 'proper administration of justice' and 'avoiding inconsistent decisions', Rule 340 of the Rules of Procedure provides that actions concerning the same patent, whether or not between the same parties, may by agreement between the parties 'on account of the connection between them' be heard together.[21]

Drafted in broader terms than the multiple defendants rule (see section II.D.ii above), Rule 340 allows revocation actions concerning the same patent to be heard together, whether or not the claimants in those actions are commercially related, providing they agree. It would also appear possible for Rule 340 to be applied in cases where the multiple defendants rule fails, because they do not have a sufficiently close commercial relationship for the purpose of that rule. However, it should be noted that the effect is different. The multiple defendants rule allows defendants to be joined in a single action. Rule 340 merely provides for actions to be heard together.

The court has the discretion to order revocation or infringement proceedings to be heard together if they concern the same patent or patents, but only if they are already before the same local or regional division, or the central division, and where it is in the interests of justice to do so. No agreement is necessary between the parties in these circumstances.[22] Actions that are commenced with a plurality of patents may also be split into separate proceedings at the discretion of the court.[23]

---

[17] Article 33(2) UPC Agreement.
[18] The meaning of 'commercial relationship' requires interpretation. On a broad view, group companies per se are commercially related regardless of whether their commercial activities are unconnected. More narrowly, control of a single entity within the group may be necessary. Alternatively, a common purpose may be required. The further requirement of Article 33(1)(b) that the action relates to the 'same alleged infringement' narrows the application of this provision.
[19] Article 33(1)(b) UPC Agreement. It is not relevant whether one or more of the defendants is domiciled outside the contracting Member States, but because reference is made to Article 33(1)(a), the action may only be brought in a local or regional division and not the central division.
[20] ibid Article 33(1(b). Article 32(1)(g) refers to actions based on prior use of the invention. So far as these are against the patentee as defendant, the question of multiple defendants would not arise.
[21] Where the Registry notes that two or more actions concerning the same patent are initiated before several divisions, it must inform the divisions concerned as soon as possible whether or not the actions are between the same parties (Rule 260.2 of the Rules of Procedure).
[22] ibid Rule 302.3.
[23] ibid Rule 302.1.

E. Centralisation of Infringement Action Concerning Multiple Territories

Where allegedly infringing activity affects territories represented by three or more regional divisions, a defendant can request that the action is transferred to the central division.[24] A similar transfer is not possible for alleged infringements affecting multiple local divisions. It is not open to the claimant to request the transfer.[25] On the basis that the Nordic-Regional division is the only regional division of the court, this rule is now defunct.

F. Bringing Revocation Claims and Declarations of Non-infringement

i. When No Infringement Action is Already Lodged

In the absence of an existing infringement claim on the merits concerning the same parties and the same patent, an initiating revocation claim[26] and/or declaration of non-infringement is lodged at the central division (see Figure 9.4). This is regardless of whether a claim for an action other than infringement on the merits – preliminary injunction, other provisional measure or any other action listed within the exclusive competence of the UPC – has been lodged in a local or regional division.[27] Actions lodged at the central division are allocated by the Registry to the London, Paris or Munich sections, according to the subject matter of the invention claimed (see Chapter 11).

Figure 9.4 Initiating revocation claims lodged in the central division

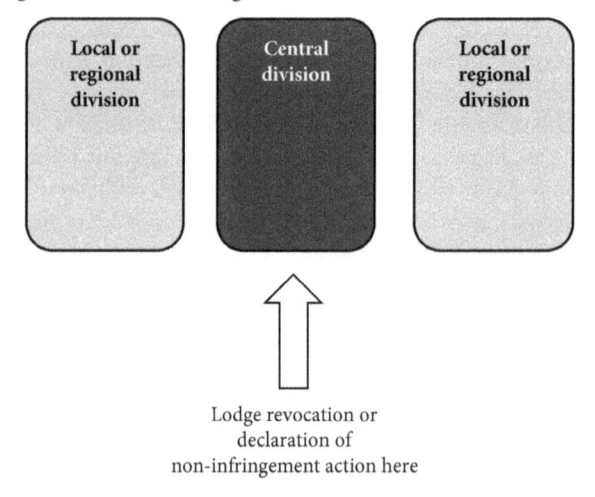

---

[24] Article 33(2) UPC Agreement.
[25] ibid.
[26] Initiating claims in contrast to counterclaims.
[27] Article 32 UPC Agreement.

ii. *When Related Infringement Action is Already Lodged*

If an infringement action on the merits has been lodged, a revocation action,[28] a revocation counterclaim[29] and/or a declaration of non-infringement between the same parties and relating to the same patent must be lodged in the same local or regional division as the earlier infringement action[30] (Figure 9.5).

Figure 9.5 Lodging a revocation, revocation counterclaim or declaration of non-infringement when an infringement action has already been lodged

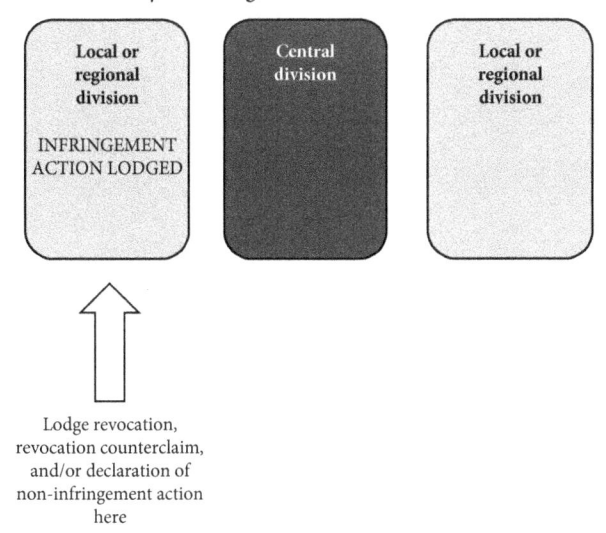

G. Subsequent Infringement and Revocation Claims

i. *A Subsequent Infringement Claim Lodged in the Central Division*

There is a choice of division in which to lodge an infringement action[31] if it follows the lodging of a revocation action between the same parties and concerning the same patent: the infringement action may be lodged in the central division together with the revocation

---

[28] ibid Article 33(4).
[29] ibid Article 33(3).
[30] Note that ibid Article 33(4) deals expressly with actions referred to in Article 32(1)(b) (declarations of non-infringement) and Article 32(1)(d) (revocations). Counterclaims under Article 32(1)(e) are not referred to. However, Article 33(4) makes no reference to bifurcation or transfer under Article 33(3) of either action when a revocation claim (as opposed to a counterclaim) is lodged in a local or regional court following a related infringement action. Consequently, a party that responds to an infringement action by way of an initiating claim apparently has no options to later remove themselves from the local or regional division in question under Article 33(3).
[31] Note that Article 33 does not refer to infringement 'counterclaims' as such, but merely infringement 'actions'. A party therefore has a choice to respond to a revocation action with a claim or counterclaim. The former provides the option to lodge in a local or regional division, whereas the latter apparently does not.

claim (see Figure 9.6)[32] or in a local or regional division (see Figure 9.7).[33] The revocation claim cannot be later transferred under Article 33(3), but the infringement action may be (see section II.H.ii below).

Figure 9.6 A subsequent infringement action lodged in the central division

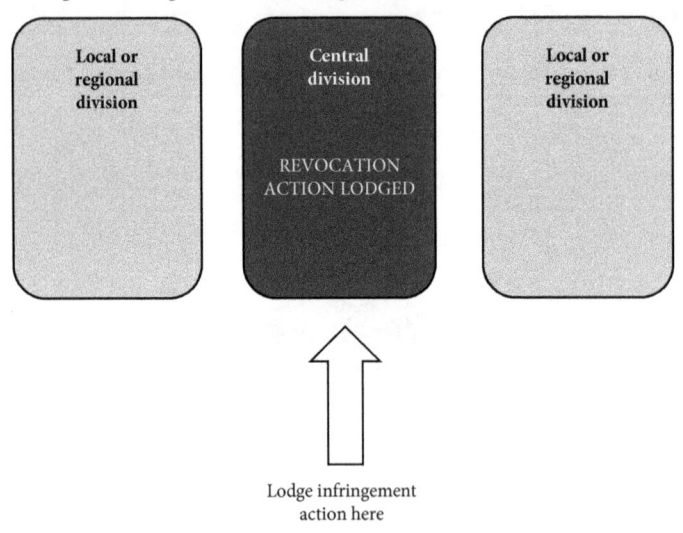

Figure 9.7 A subsequent infringement action lodged in local or regional division

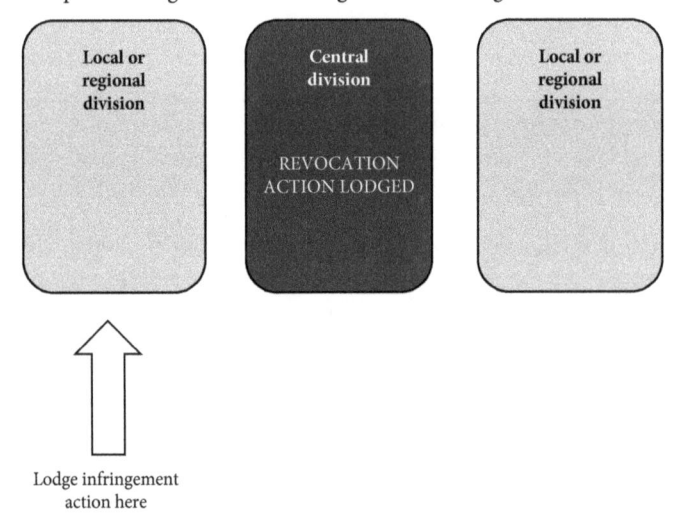

---

[32] In this case, the transfer or bifurcation decision under Article 33(3) does not follow. This is because both the revocation and infringement actions are lodged in the central division and there is no 'local or regional division concerned' (see ibid Article 33(5), final sentence).

[33] ibid Article 33(5).

ii. An Infringement Claim Lodged in the Regional/Local Division after Revocation has been Lodged in the Central Division

If the infringement action is lodged in a local or regional division, there is now a split forum between actions which concern the same parties and the same patent (see Figure 9.7). This scenario is therefore subject to a transfer decision by the local or regional division under Article 33(3).[34] The Article 33(3) decision may result in the infringement action being moved to the central division (see section II.H.ii below).[35]

If an action for a preliminary injunction or other provisional or protective measure has already been lodged in the local or regional division, the infringement action must be lodged in the same division.[36]

iii. A Revocation Counterclaim to Infringement

A revocation counterclaim (as distinct from a subsequent revocation claim)[37] may be lodged in response to an infringement action. This counterclaim must be filed in the same local or regional division as that seised with the infringement action.[38] The registry must then, as soon as practicable, notify the President of the Court of First Instance of the central revocation action, the infringement action and the counterclaim for revocation to the infringement claim.[39]

iv. Avoiding Duplicate Revocation Claims

If a revocation claim has already been filed in the central division before an infringement claim concerning the same patent and the same parties is lodged in the local or regional division, a counterclaim may subsequently be lodged against the infringement claim. In these circumstances, the panel assigned to hear the central revocation action must stay it (see Figure 9.8).[40] The action is stayed pending a decision of the local or regional panel seised with the infringement action under Article 33(3) (see section II.H.ii below).[41]

---

[34] ibid Article 33(5), final sentence.

[35] It is uncertain whether the UPC Agreement allows the revocation claim to be moved from the central division to the local or regional division. This is because it is not a 'counterclaim for revocation' as referred to in Article 33(3)(a).

[36] ibid Article 33(2).

[37] ibid Article 33(3). Article 33(3) deals expressly with counterclaims to an infringement action. These are to be contrasted with revocation claims that follow an infringement action, which are governed separately by Article 33(4). Article 33(3) in respect of counterclaims has potential bifurcation and transfer consequences; Article 33(4) does not.

[38] ibid Article 33(4).

[39] Rule 75.2 of the Rules of Procedure.

[40] The stay of the central division action was agreed by the drafting committee following public consultation in 2014 and is intended to give some protection to the defendant who initiated the counterclaim for revocation.

[41] Rule 75.3 of the Rules of Procedure.

Figure 9.8 A revocation counterclaim in the local or regional division and the stay of a central division revocation action

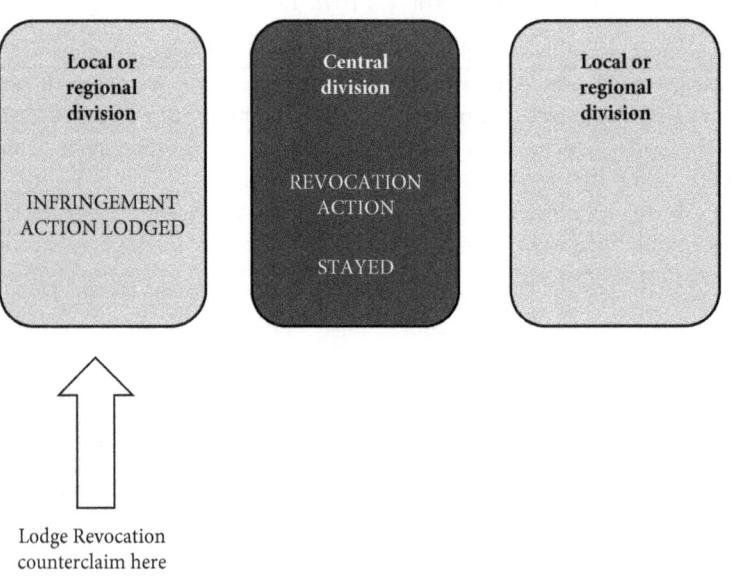

Local or regional division	Central division	Local or regional division
INFRINGEMENT ACTION LODGED	REVOCATION ACTION STAYED	

⬆ Lodge Revocation counterclaim here

H. Consolidation or Bifurcation of Actions (Article 33(3))

i. Bifurcation and the 'Injunction Gap'

Considerable attention has been given by commentators to the potential for bifurcation of infringement and revocation actions in the UPC to put patentees at a strategic advantage over alleged infringers. These concerns are based to a large extent on the experience of the German bifurcated system in which infringement and revocation actions are separate: infringement in the Gerichte der Länder (regional courts) and patent revocation in the Bundespatentgericht (Federal Patent Court) in Munich. In Germany, infringement proceedings are on average about one year faster than proceedings on validity. Injunctions can therefore be granted a considerable time before the defendant is able to test the validity of the patent on which the injunction was granted – the so-called 'injunction gap'. The regional courts have a discretion to stay proceedings until the outcome of proceedings on validity, but they rarely do so.

The split system described places the patentee at an advantage. In the UPC, the concern is that the possibility for bifurcated infringement and revocation actions (of the type shown in Figures 9.7 and 9.8) will similarly unduly lend itself to patentees. Forum shopping for regional and local courts that are inclined to allow bifurcation could be expected. This view presumes that a decision on infringement, as in Germany, is likely to be reached before a decision on revocation. However, there are a number of safeguards in the UPC, which are designed to limit this possibility: stay of the infringement action at the court's discretion or the acceleration of the revocation decision. In addition, it is not all actions that can be bifurcated. This is discussed further below.

ii. The Decision under Article 33(3) UPC Agreement

a. Article 33(3) Applied to a Local Revocation Counterclaim

If a revocation counterclaim follows an infringement claim in a local or regional division, and there is a central revocation action concerning the same patent and the same parties, the central revocation action is stayed (see Figure 9.8). However, whether or not there is an initiating central revocation action, in circumstances where a revocation counterclaim follows a locally or regionally lodged infringement claim, the UPC Agreement provides three alternatives for the local or regional court seised with the infringement action on how to proceed with both actions. This happens by way of a decision under Article 33(3) UPC Agreement. The Article 33(3) decision must be made as soon as practicable after the closure of the written procedure.[42] The three alternatives are as follows:

(a) proceed with both the action for infringement and with the counterclaim for revocation, and request the President of the Court of First Instance to allocate from the Pool of Judges in accordance with Article 18(3) a technically qualified judge with qualifications and experience in the field of technology concerned;
(b) refer the counterclaim for revocation for decision to the central division and suspend or proceed with the action for infringement; or
(c) with the agreement of the parties, refer the case for decision to the central division.

The local or regional division must choose between referring the whole action to the central division, retaining the infringement proceedings only (but transferring the revocation action such that the actions are bifurcated) or having the whole matter heard in the local or regional division. As Figure 9.9 shows, of the three alternatives open to the court, only one results in the permanent bifurcation of the action.[43]

b. Article 33(3) Applied to a Local Infringement Action with a Centrally Lodged Initiating Revocation Action

If an initiating revocation action has been lodged in the central division and is followed by an infringement claim between the same parties and concerning the same patent in a local or regional division, without a revocation counterclaim, the revocation claim apparently cannot be moved from the central division. This is because the first two options presented under Article 33(3) to move a revocation action apply only to counterclaims.[44] The only option available to the local or regional division making the Article 33(3) decision is to keep the status quo, or refer the infringement action to the central division, with the agreement of the parties. The latter option brings both actions to the central division (see Figure 9.9).

---

[42] The panel may take an earlier decision 'if appropriate', having given the parties an opportunity to be heard.
[43] Article 33(b) UPC Agreement.
[44] ibid Article 33(3)(a) and (b).

iii. Factors at Issue in the Decision to Bifurcate or Consolidate

When a panel has made a decision under Article 33(3), it is required to give 'brief reasons' for that decision in its order.[45] The factual context within which Article 33(3) decisions will be made by panels of the UPC can be expected to differ widely. Decisions under Article 33(3) are also discretionary. However, over time, guidance may be expected to emerge on the application of the alternatives available to a panel. The following considerations may be relevant.

a. Consistency

Hearing infringement and validity cases together has the benefit of ensuring that the patent claims at issue are construed consistently for both actions – preventing a broad construction of the patent for infringement purposes and a narrow construction for validity purposes, or vice versa. This supports a general principle that infringement and revocation should be heard together, either in a local/regional division or the central division.

b. Case Management

Consideration must be given to general principles of case management – in particular, the likelihood that taking a particular step justifies the cost of taking it and giving directions to ensure that the hearing of the case proceeds quickly and efficiently.[46] Specifically, in cases where a revocation counterclaim in a local or regional division follows an earlier revocation action in the central division, the panel is required to take into consideration how far the central revocation action in the central division had advanced before it was stayed.[47] If the central revocation case has advanced significantly – in particular, if it has already entered the interim procedure – maintaining the stay of the central revocation action may be difficult to justify. This tends to indicate that the infringement and revocation counterclaim should be transferred to the central division. Alternatively, if an infringement claim concerning the same patent and the same parties is lodged much later than the central revocation action, hearing both matters together might significantly delay the revocation.

iv. What Approach is Likely to be Taken?

The most influential group of judges who might be thought to favour bifurcation are the German judges sitting in the local divisions, but whilst the UPC *allows* bifurcation, it is not expected that these judges will encourage it, given the mitigating factors outlined above. Consequently, bifurcation, in the sense of splitting up validity and infringement issues between the same parties, is expected to be rare. The same arguments also ought to favour joining already bifurcated cases, but inertia, and the stage which the various cases have reached, may result in some continued bifurcation. However, in general, it is expected that the judges of the UPC will find ways to ensure that infringement and validity are decided together wherever this makes sense from a case management point of view (which will be the majority of the time).

---

[45] Rule 37.1 of the Rules of Procedure.
[46] ibid Rule 332(h) and (l), respectively.
[47] ibid Rule 75.4.

I. Stay of Infringement Action Following an Article 33(3) Decision

If the Article 33(3) decision is made in favour of bifurcation,[48] there are three further possibilities:

(a) the local or regional division proceeds with the infringement action in parallel to a revocation action in the central division (by original filing or by counterclaim). The central division must endeavour to accelerate the revocation proceedings (see below);[49]
(b) the panel, at its discretion, stays the *infringement* action pending a final decision in the revocation proceedings;[50] or
(c) where there is a 'high likelihood' that the relevant claims of the patent being enforced are invalid, the panel *must* stay the infringement action until a decision has been made in the revocation action.[51]

Figure 9.9 The options under Article 33(3) to bifurcate or consolidate[52]

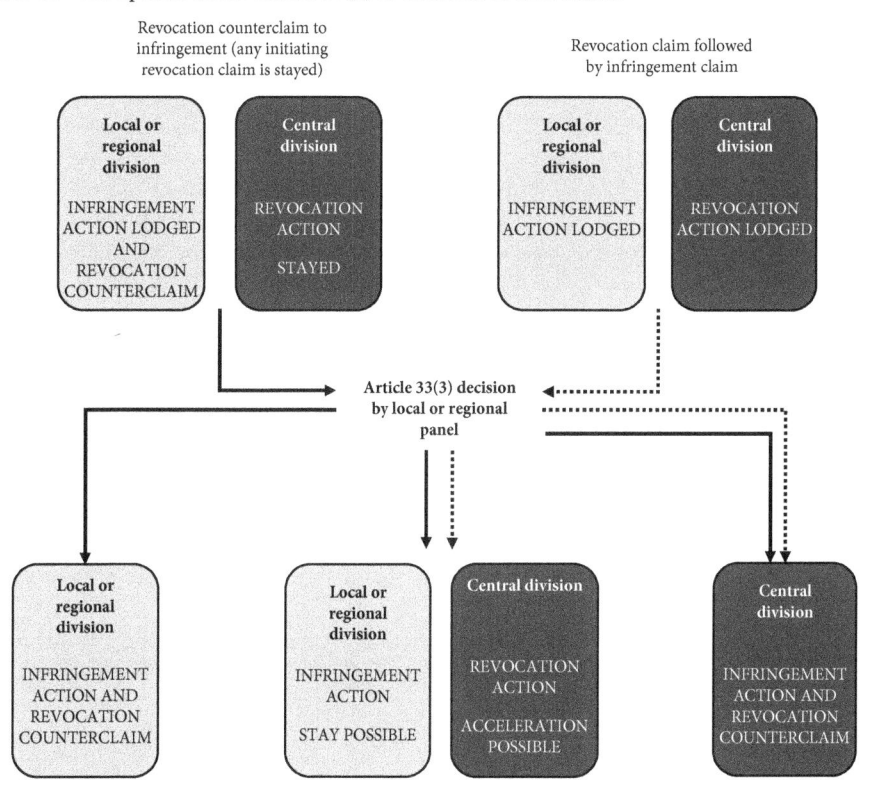

---

[48] Article 33(3)(b) UPC Agreement.
[49] Rule 40(b) of the Rules of Procedure.
[50] ibid Rule 37.4.
[51] ibid Rule 37.4. There is currently no guidance on the factors that the court would consider relevant to determining a 'high likelihood' for this purpose. These may include a finding that the patent is invalid by the Opposition Division of the EPO. It is also unclear in what level of detail a local or regional division will be prepared to consider this question, but it is unlikely to be more than necessary to make a provisional assessment.
[52] This figure presumes that proceedings, regarding the same patent and the same parties, begin with a central revocation action.

If there is a stay of the infringement action as a result of (b) or (c) above, bifurcation may have the consequence for a patentee that the patent in dispute is held invalid at first instance before a decision on infringement. This potential disadvantage to the patentee is a balancing factor with the injunction gap risk to the alleged infringer.

If the infringement action is not stayed, the judge-rapporteur of the local or regional division must communicate with the central division the dates of the interim and oral proceedings of the infringement action.[53] The judge-rapporteur of the central division must then endeavour to fix the oral hearing of the revocation action before that of the infringement action.[54]

J. Acceleration in the Central Division

i. Acceleration when Provisional Measures are Ordered

The judge-rapporteur is required to accelerate proceedings before the central division if an action for provisional measures has been lodged.[55] The purpose of this provision is to limit any potential prejudice to the party or parties against whom the provisional relief has been awarded if the decision on the merits demonstrates that the provisional measures should not have been awarded.

Provisional measures must be lodged in the same division as an infringement action between the same parties and concerning the same patent. Conversely, if provisional measures have been lodged before an infringement action on the merits, the action on the merits must be lodged in the same division as the claim for provisional measures. The requirement to accelerate proceedings applies in either case.

ii. Acceleration when Actions are Bifurcated

A revocation action must be accelerated by the judge-rapporteur in the central division if it has been transferred from a local or regional division. Furthermore, in these circumstances, the judge-rapporteur must endeavour to set a date for the oral hearing of the revocation actions that is before that of the infringement action.[56] This measure is intended to avoid an injunction gap in which a final injunction is obtained before the validity of the patent at issue can be tested.

The appropriate time for the judge-rapporteur to accelerate proceedings is during the scheduling of the further progress of proceedings at the interim conference.[57]

---

[53] Rule 37.5 of the Rules of Procedure. As stated by the explanatory notes to the changes made by the Legal Group of the Preparatory Committee in the 17th draft Rules of Procedure, this provision is intended to synchronise the calendars of the divisions dealing with parallel cases concerning the same parties and the same patents.

[54] ibid Rule 40(b).

[55] ibid Rule 40(a).

[56] ibid Rule 40(b). The explanatory notes to the changes made by the Legal Group of the Preparatory Committee in the 17th draft Rules of Procedure state that Rule 40(b) will not lead to an acceleration in all cases in which counterclaims for revocation are referred to the central division; it is only cases in which the parallel infringement action is not stayed that will be accelerated. The synchronisation of the calendars between parallel cases concerning the same patent and the same parties remains a matter of the judge-rapporteur's discretion.

[57] See ibid Rule 104(c) and (h).

K. The Effect of the Transfer of Revocation Counterclaim on Language

The language of proceedings before the regional or local division that has referred a counterclaim for revocation might not be the same as the language of the central division (the language of the patent) (see Chapter 5). The judge-rapporteur may order the written pleadings and other documents lodged during the written procedure to be translated (or excerpts of those documents) into the language of grant of the patent. This must take place within one month.[58]

L. Actions Following a Declaration of Non-infringement in the Central Division

An infringement action may be lodged in a local or regional division after a declaration for non-infringement has been lodged in the central division, in which the infringement action:

(a) relates to the same patent; and
(b) is between the same parties, or between the holder of an exclusive licence and the party requesting a declaration of non-infringement relating to the same patent.

This has two potential consequences, depending on whether or not the infringement claim is filed within three months of the non-infringement declaration (see also Chapter 12).

i. An Infringement Action Lodged within Three Months of a Non-infringement Action

The infringement action is lodged within three months of the non-infringement action. In these circumstances, the Registry proceeds to examine the formalities of the statement of claim and records the action in the register.[59] The Registry then notifies the President of the Court of First Instance and the presiding judges of the other panel seised of the existence of the co-pending actions as soon as possible, together with the relevant dates of the actions. If the date of receipt of the statement of claim for the infringement action is within three months of the date of the lodging of the declaration of non-infringement in the central division, the President of the Court of First Instance will require the non-infringement action to be stayed.[60]

---

[58] ibid Rule 39.1.
[59] ibid Rules 16 and 17.
[60] Article 33(6) UPC Agreement and Rule 76 of the Rules of Procedure. It is unclear from the Rules whether the legal interest in the non-infringement action is lost at this stage, allowing it to be dismissed (for example, see the Bundesgerichtshof, 21 December 2005, GRUR 2006, 217).

ii. An Infringement Action not Lodged within Three Months of a Non-infringement Action

If the infringement action is not filed within three months of the earlier non-infringement action, the earlier action is not stayed. Instead, the presiding judges of the central division in which the non-infringement action is lodged and the local or regional division in which the infringement action is lodged must consult in order to agree on the 'future progress of proceedings'.[61] The future progress of proceedings may be the stay of one of the actions, but the Rules of Procedure do not provide guidance on the circumstances in which this may happen. One factor determining the progress of the action is likely to be the period of time between the lodging of the actions. If the central division action is advanced, it may be appropriate to stay the infringement action.

iii. Actions for Revocation and Declaration of Non-infringement

An action for revocation may be lodged in the central division together with an action for a declaration of non-infringement if it relates to the same patent and is between the same parties.[62] In these circumstances, if an infringement action is lodged within three months of the lodging of the declaration of non-infringement action, the non-infringement action is stayed. The revocation action and infringement action are left pending and the rules discussed in section II.H.ii above for the consolidation or bifurcation of the actions under Article 33(3) apply.

If the infringement action is lodged after three months from the lodging of the non-infringement action, the applicable rules are less clear. The consolidation and bifurcation rules in Article 33(3) do not apply to a declaration of non-infringement and hence this action cannot be referred to the local or regional division of the infringement action. However, Article 33(3) provisions may apply, as between the infringement and revocation actions. This is in parallel to the obligation of the presiding judges of the central division and the local or regional division to consult in order to agree on the future progress of the proceedings. In the former case, the parties are heard and the central division is not involved; in the latter case, the parties are not consulted but the central division is. The possible outcomes of this process are: the transfer of all the actions to the central division; the stay of either the infringement action or the non-infringement action; or, to the extent that principles of good case management permit, allowing all the actions to continue.

M. Actions for Compensation for Licences of Right

The proprietor of a Unitary Patent may file a statement with the EPO to record their willingness to grant licences to any person in exchange for appropriate compensation.[63] The UPC Agreement expressly lists actions for compensation within its exclusive competence.[64]

---

[61] Rule 76.3 of the Rules of Procedure.
[62] ibid Rule 77.
[63] Article 8 UP Regulation.
[64] Article 32(1)(h) UPC Agreement.

The action must be lodged with the local division of the Contracting Member State in which the defendant has its Domicile. If the defendant's Domicile is outside the territory of the contracting Member States, the action must be brought before the local or regional division for the Member State in which the activity under the licence takes place or the central division.[65] If that contracting Member State does not have a local division and does not participate in a regional division, the action must be lodged in the central division (see Figures 9.10–9.12).

Figure 9.10 Lodging a compensation action under a licence of right in the division of defendant's Domicile

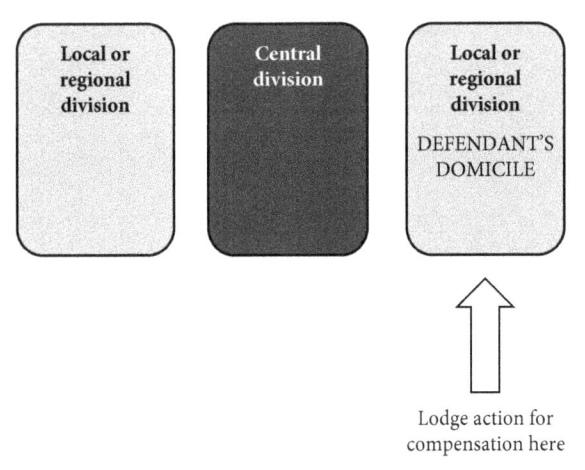

Figure 9.11 Lodging a compensation action under a licence of right when the defendant's Domicile is outside the contracting Member States

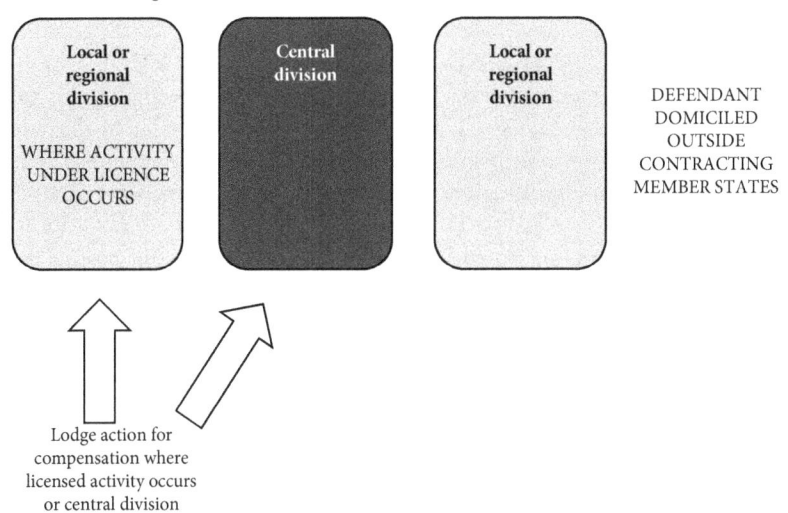

---

[65] ibid Article 33(1)(a).

140   *UPC Jurisdiction*

Figure 9.12 Lodging a compensation action under a licence of right in the central division

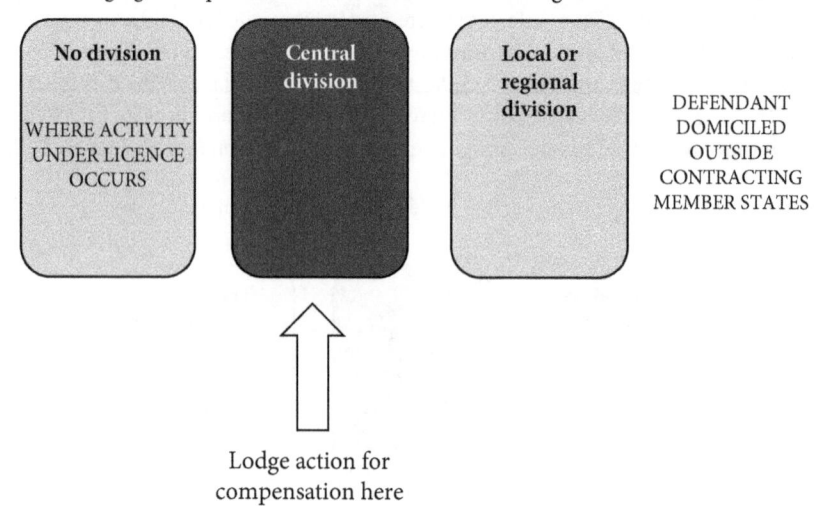

```
┌─────────────┐   ┌─────────────┐   ┌─────────────┐
│ No division │   │   Central   │   │  Local or   │
│             │   │  division   │   │  regional   │   DEFENDANT
│WHERE ACTIVITY│  │             │   │  division   │   DOMICILED
│UNDER LICENCE│   │             │   │             │   OUTSIDE
│   OCCURS    │   │             │   │             │   CONTRACTING
│             │   │             │   │             │   MEMBER STATES
└─────────────┘   └─────────────┘   └─────────────┘
                         ⇧
                  Lodge action for
                  compensation here
```

N. Actions Concerning Decisions of the EPO

Actions concerning decisions made by the EPO when carrying out its responsibilities for the Unitary Patent[66] must be lodged in the central division[67] (see Chapter 12).

III. Formalities Relating to Choice of Forum

When the division has been chosen in accordance with Article 33 UPC Agreement, this must be indicated in the statement of claim lodged, together with an explanation of why that division has competence.[68] Alternatively, if the division has been agreed by the parties,[69] the statement of claim must be accompanied by evidence of this agreement.[70] The Statement of Claim must also contain information about any prior or pending proceedings in a UPC division that relate to the same patent(s).[71] This includes any action for revocation or declaration of non-infringement that is pending before the central division, and the date of that action, and any other forum such as the EPO or a national court.

Among the other formalities of the statement of claim (see Chapters 10 and 11), the Registry will check that it has been lodged in the correct forum.[72] Provided the formal requirements have been complied with, action will be assigned to a panel or, where requested

---

[66] Article 9 UP Regulation.
[67] Article 33(9) UPC Agreement.
[68] Rule 13(1)(i) of the Rules of Procedure.
[69] Article 33(7) UPC Agreement.
[70] Rule 13(1)(i) of the Rules of Procedure.
[71] ibid Rule 13(1)(h).
[72] ibid Rule 16.2.

by the parties, to a single judge.[73] In cases filed in the central division, actions are distributed by the Registry according to the subject matter of the patent(s) in dispute in the action (see Chapter 11).[74] The action will be regarded as having commenced before the relevant panel of the UPC as from the date of receipt attributed to the statement of claim.[75]

IV. Preliminary Objections to Forum

Within one month of the service of the statement of claim, in any divisions, for any cause of action, the defendant may object to the competence of the division chosen by the claimant, the language of the statement of claim or an objection that the patent has been opted out. Such objections are made by 'preliminary objection'.[76]

A defendant may have an infringement action transferred from a regional division to the central division[77] by way of preliminary objection,[78] in cases where the alleged infringement occurs in territories collectively hosting three or more regional divisions.[79] In such a case, the preliminary objection should contain all the facts and evidence necessary to support the existence of the same infringement in the other regional divisions.

As soon as practicable after the filing of the preliminary objection, the Registry must invite the claimant to comment. The claimant then has the opportunity to correct the deficiency within 14 days of service of notification of the preliminary objection or they may submit written comments, also within 14 days. The judge-rapporteur is then informed of either activity. Then, if the claimant has corrected the deficiency and has indicated an alternative division that is competent, the judge-rapporteur will refer the action to this division. Otherwise, after expiry of the 14-day period, the judge-rapporteur will decide on the preliminary objection having given the parties the opportunity to be heard.[80] A decision by the judge-rapporteur to allow the preliminary objection may be appealed with leave of the Court of First Instance within 15 days of service of the court's decision to that effect. If the Court of First Instance refuses to grant leave within this period, a request for a discretionary review may be made to the Court of Appeal within a further 15 days.[81]

If there is no preliminary objection on the grounds that the claim was lodged in the incorrect forum, the defendant is presumed to submit to the competence of the division in which the claim is lodged[82] (see also Chapter 10).

---

[73] ibid Rule 17.2.
[74] ibid Rule 17.3.
[75] ibid Rule 17.4.
[76] ibid Rule 19.1(b).
[77] Article 33(2) UPC Agreement.
[78] Rule 19.4 of the Rules of Procedure.
[79] Under Article 33(1)(a) UPC Agreement.
[80] Rule 20.1 of the Rules of Procedure.
[81] ibid Rule 220.2.
[82] ibid Rule 19.7.

PART II

Proceedings in the Unified Patent Court

10

Written Procedure

Infringement Actions

I. Timeline of an Infringement Action

Figure 10.1 below gives an overview of the timeline of an infringement action on the merits from lodging the statement of claim to the oral hearing. Assuming that a full sequence of pleadings is served, up to and including rejoinder, the written procedure for an infringement action with revocation counterclaim will be eight months. The interim procedure is three months (see Chapter 13). The figure illustrates an oral hearing at 12 months, in keeping with the aim set out in the Preamble to the Rules of Procedure,[1] although the oral hearing may be earlier or later than this. This chapter explains the details of the written procedure in an infringement action.

Figure 10.1 An overview of the timeline of an infringement action on the merits

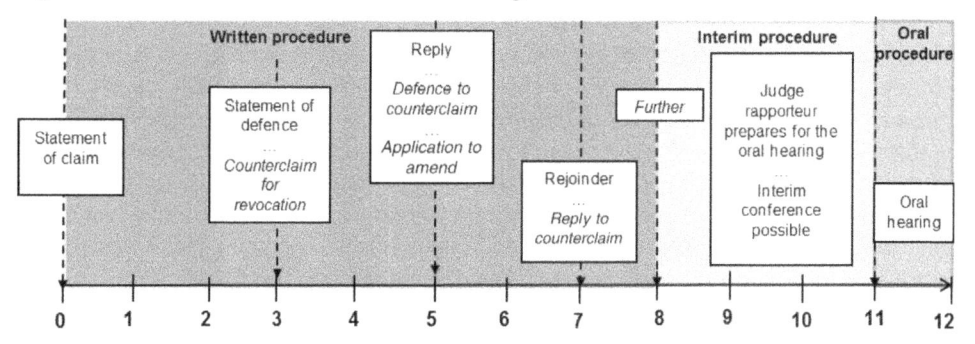

II. Initial Considerations

A. The Right to Bring an Action

i. A Patentee and Exclusive Licensee

The UPC Agreement stipulates that any natural or legal person, or any body equivalent to a legal person entitled to initiate proceedings in accordance with its national law, has the capacity to be a party to proceedings before the court. Under Article 47(1) UPC Agreement, the

---
[1] Recital 7.

patentee has the right to bring an action. Article 47(2) extends this right to the exclusive licensee, provided that the patentee has been informed about the action prior to its initiation.

ii. A Non-exclusive Licensee

A non-exclusive licensee, in contrast, does not generally have the right to bring an action. Such an entitlement is assumed only if the licence agreement expressly provides for it.[2] In addition, the non-exclusive licensee has to inform the patentee prior to bringing the action.

B. Response to an Assertion of Infringement

Article 47(6) UPC Agreement stipulates that any natural or legal person, or any body entitled to bring actions in accordance with national law, 'who is concerned' by a patent may also bring an action before the UPC. This provision is to be read in connection with Article 32(1)(b) UPC Agreement, which grants the UPC the authority to decide actions regarding the non-infringement of patents and supplementary protection certificates. There are three further prerequisites under which an action for non-infringement can be lodged.[3] In particular, such an action can be brought if the patent proprietor or the licensee has asserted to the claimant that a specific act is an infringement.[4] Declarations of non-infringement will be discussed in Chapter 12.

C. Parties to the Action

The parties to the complaint are the claimant patentee and/or licensee,[5] and the defendant alleged infringer(s). The number of claimants in an infringement action will usually be limited;[6] if the proceedings are started against a multitude of defendants, a panel can hear all of them if it has the respective competence with regard to all defendants.[7] The panel also has the power in this scenario to separate the proceedings.[8] If multiple patents are in dispute in an action, the court has the power to order separate proceedings.[9] It may also order that parallel infringement proceedings and/or revocation proceedings concerning parallel patents be heard together where it is in the interests of justice to do so[10] (see also Chapter 19).

The Rules of Procedure also provide for the possibility of intervention.[11] Any (third) party that can show a legal interest in the result of the action can lodge a request to intervene.[12] The request to intervene must be made in support of a claim, order or remedy sought by the intervener. On its own motion or after a reasoned request from a party, the judge-rapporteur

---

[2] Article 47(3) UPC Agreement.
[3] Rule 61 of the Rules of Procedure.
[4] ibid Rule 61(1). In the absence of such an assertion, an action for non-infringement can be lodged only if certain other criteria are fulfilled.
[5] As to whether this is an exclusive licensee or a non-exclusive licensee, see Article 47 UPC Agreement.
[6] It is possible that multiple licensee claimants may bring an action in respect of infringements in several contracting Member State territories if the licensees in those territories are different, in which case, Rule 302.1 of the Rules of Procedure may be relevant.
[7] ibid Rule 303.1.
[8] ibid Rule 303.2.
[9] ibid Rule 302.1.
[10] ibid Rule 302.3.
[11] ibid Rules 313–17.
[12] ibid Rule 313.1.

or the presiding judge may invite any person concerned by the outcome of the proceeding to intervene.[13] The parties to the proceedings also have the possibility to force an intervener to be bound by the decision in the action[14] (see Chapter 19 for more on this).

D. Service

The service of statements of claim, orders, decisions and pleadings documents is carried out by the Registry of the UPC. The Rules of Procedure set out the provisions concerning the service performed by the court in Part 5, Chapter 2. In addition, as regards statements of claim,[15] the provisions of Regulation (EC) 1393/2007 of the European Parliament and of the Council of 13 November 2007 on the service in the Member States of judicial and extrajudicial documents in civil or commercial matters[16] (hereinafter the 'Service Regulation') also apply[17] (see Chapter 19 for more on this).

III. The Written Procedure

A. The Structure of Proceedings

The UPC Agreement and the Rules and Procedure divide the proceedings before the Court of First Instance into three stages:[18] (i) written procedure; (ii) interim procedure; and (iii) oral procedure.[19] Article 52(1) UPC Agreement sets out that all of these procedures are to be organised in a flexible and balanced manner.[20]

B. Overview of the Infringement Procedure

The Rules of Procedure set out the four stages of the written procedure regarding the infringement action:[21]

(a) lodging of the statement of claim;
(b) lodging of the statement of defence;
(c) lodging of a reply to the statement of defence;
(d) lodging of a rejoinder to the reply.

---

[13] ibid Rule 316.
[14] ibid Rule 316A and 316.3.
[15] Meaning all originating pleadings in actions referred to in Article 32(1) UPC Agreement.
[16] Regulation (EC) 1393/2007 of the European Parliament and of the Council of 13 November 2007 on the service in the Member States of judicial and extrajudicial documents in civil or commercial matters [2007] OJ L324, 10 December, 79–120.
[17] Further to Rule 270.1 of the Rules of Procedure.
[18] See Articles 52, 68 and 69 UPC Agreement and Rule 10 of the Rules of Procedure. Rule 10 speaks of 'five stages' additionally comprising the 'procedure for the award of damages' and the 'procedure for cost damages'. However, the focus of the present chapter is on the infringement action and therefore adopts the scheme of Article 52 UPC Agreement.
[19] For details concerning revocation actions and declarations for non-infringement, see ch 12. For the interim procedure and the oral procedure, see chs 13 and 14, respectively.
[20] An apparent reference to the case management powers of the court to, amongst other matters, extend or shorten time periods referred to in the Rules (see Rule 9 of the Rules of Procedure). See also Rules 331–40 of the Rules of Procedure and ch 13 of this book.
[21] Rule 12.1 of the Rules of Procedure.

148 Written Procedure

The defendant's statement of defence may include a counterclaim for revocation, and the claimant's reply to the statement of defence may include an application to amend the patent.[22] If the defendant and/or the claimant lodges such a counterclaim and/or application, respectively, the Rules foresee further stages as described below. Figure 10.2 provides an overview of this process.

Figure 10.2 Order of pleadings in the written procedure of an infringement action

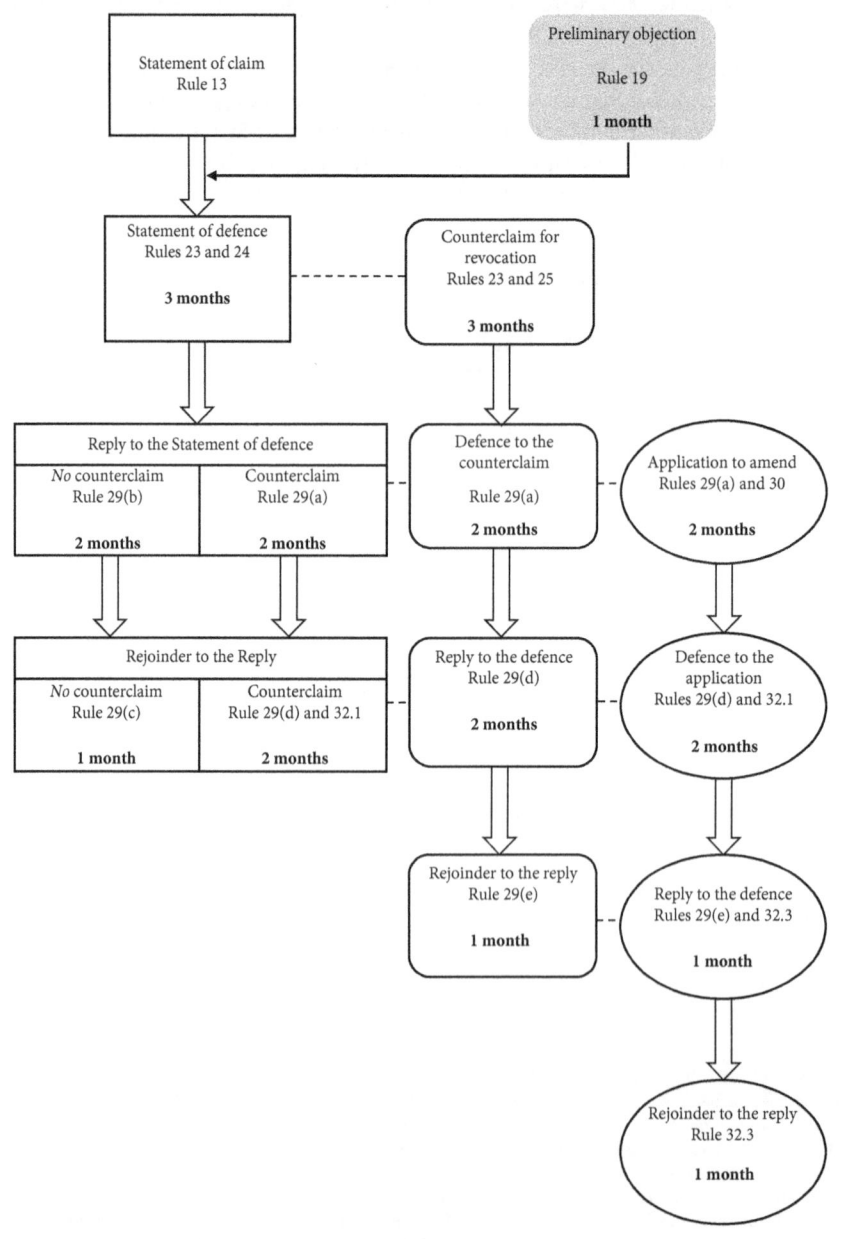

```
                Statement of claim                    Preliminary objection
                    Rule 13                                  Rule 19
                                                            1 month

                        ↓ ←──────────────────────────────────┘
                Statement of defence          Counterclaim for
                 Rules 23 and 24       ──── ─   revocation
                     3 months                 Rules 23 and 25
                                                  3 months
         ┌──────────────┴──────────────┐              ↓
         Reply to the Statement of defence     Defence to the
         ┌──────────────┬──────────────┐       counterclaim      Application to amend
         No counterclaim   Counterclaim  ─ ─ ─   Rule 29(a)  ─ ─ ─ Rules 29(a) and 30
           Rule 29(b)      Rule 29(a)           2 months            2 months
           2 months        2 months
                ↓              ↓                    ↓                   ↓
            Rejoinder to the Reply          Reply to the defence   Defence to the
         ┌──────────────┬──────────────┐       Rule 29(d)           application
         No counterclaim   Counterclaim   ─ ─ ─  2 months   ─ ─ ─ Rules 29(d) and 32.1
           Rule 29(c)   Rule 29(d) and 32.1                         2 months
            1 month         2 months
                                                    ↓                   ↓
                                           Rejoinder to the reply
                                                Rule 29(e)         Reply to the defence
                                                                 ─ ─ Rules 29(e) and 32.3
                                                 1 month              1 month
                                                                        ↓
                                                                 Rejoinder to the reply
                                                                     Rule 32.3
                                                                      1 month
```

---

[22] ibid Rule 12.2 and 12.4.

C. Appointment of the Judge-Rapporteur

Pursuant to Article 19 of the Statute of the UPC, one of the judges of the panel must act as the judge-rapporteur. Accordingly, the presiding judge of the panel to which the action has been assigned must designate one legally qualified judge of the panel as the judge-rapporteur.[23] The presiding judge is also entitled to appoint themself as the judge-rapporteur. The parties to the proceedings will as soon as practicable be notified about the identity of the judge-rapporteur. The judge-rapporteur is mainly responsible for the handling of the case, in particular the written procedure (see also Chapter 3).

D. The Statement of Claim

The Rules of Procedure set out a comprehensive and mandatory ('shall contain') list of information that the statement of claim has to exhibit.[24] Rule 13 is a clear expression of the UPC's intention to conduct so-called 'front-loaded' patent litigation – all information necessary for the determination of the alleged patent infringement must be included in the statement of claim when the claim is lodged. The statement of claim must include the following information:[25]

(a) the name of the claimant and, where the claimant is a corporate entity, the location of its registered office and of the claimant's representative;
(b) the name of the party against whom the statement is made (the defendant) and, where the defendant is a corporate entity, the location of its registered office;
(c) the postal and electronic addresses for service on the claimant and the names of the persons authorised to accept service;
(d) the postal and, where available, electronic addresses for service on the defendant and the names of the persons authorised to accept service, if known;
(e) where the claimant is not the proprietor or not, the only proprietor of the patent concerned, the postal and, where available, electronic addresses for service on the proprietor, and the names and addresses of the persons authorised to accept service, if known;
(f) where the claimant is not the proprietor of the patent concerned or not the only proprietor, evidence to show the claimant is entitled to commence proceedings;[26]
(g) details of the patent concerned, including the number;
(h) where applicable, information about any prior or pending proceedings relating to a patent concerned before a division of the UPC, including any action for revocation or a declaration of non-infringement pending before the central division and the date of any such action, the EPO or any other court or authority;
(i) an indication of the division which should hear the action with an explanation of why that division has competence[27] – where the parties have agreed on a division,[28]

---

[23] ibid Rule 18.
[24] ibid Rule 13.1.
[25] ibid.
[26] This may be an exclusive licensee, or a non-exclusive licensee in circumstances where the proprietor has been given prior notice and the licence so provides; see Article 47(2) and (3) UPC Agreement.
[27] See ibid Article 33(1)–(6).
[28] In accordance with ibid Article 3(7).

the indication of the division which should hear the action must be accompanied by evidence of the defendant's agreement (see Chapter 9);
(j) where applicable, an indication that the action should be heard by a single judge,[29] accompanied by evidence of the defendant's agreement;
(k) the nature of the claim and the order or the remedies sort by the claimant (see Chapter 18);
(l) an indication of the facts relied on, in particular:
  (i) one or more instances of alleged infringement or threatened infringement specifying the date and place of each,
  (ii) the indication of the patent claims alleged to be infringed;
(m) the evidence relied on,[30] where available, and an indication of any further evidence which will be offered in support (see Chapter 16);
(n) the reasons why the facts relied on constitute an infringement of the patent claims, including arguments of law and, where appropriate, an explanation of the proposed claim interpretation;[31]
(o) an indication of any order the claimant will seek during the interim procedure[32] (see Chapter 13);
(p) where the claimant assesses that the value of the infringement action exceeds €500,000, an indication of the value[33] (see Chapter 20); and
(q) a list of the documents, including any witnesses statements, referred to in the statement of claim, together with a copy of each document,[34] any request that all or part of any such document need not be translated and/or any request regarding confidentiality of documents[35] (see Chapter 16).

Apart from the standard information in the statement of claim, such as the name and address of the claimant and the defendant,[36] the comprehensive list of requirements obviously intends to give the panel of the court an insight into the size, complexity and importance of the patent infringement case at hand right from the outset. The claimant is required to give detailed information about the patent in suit itself, such as any prior or pending proceedings relating to the patent.[37] Specifically, the requirement is to provide information about revocation or declaration of non-infringement actions pending before the central divison of the UPC, or any action relating to the patent before the EPO or 'any other court or authority'. This provides the court with the necessary information to take the appropriate steps to: manage bifurcated actions within the UPC (see Chapter 18); manage parallel actions

---

[29] In accordance with ibid Article 8(7).
[30] Rule 170.1 of the Rules of Procedure.
[31] The use of claim integer tables is not expressly mentioned, but it is submitted that this is the intention, in keeping with a number of nation jurisdictions – for example, the German regional courts, the Dutch courts and the courts of England and Wales.
[32] In particular, see those orders listed in Rule 104(e) of the Rules of Procedure.
[33] Section 1.II of the Administrative Committee Table of Court Fees AC/05/08072022_E.
[34] Rule 13.2 of the Rules of Procedure.
[35] Further to ibid Rule 262.2 and 262A.
[36] ibid Rule 13.1(a) and (b).
[37] See ibid Rule 13.1(h).

between the EPO and the UPC (see Chapter 2); and managing *lis pendens* issues arising between the national courts and the UPC (see Chapter 7).

E. Preliminary Objections

The preliminary objection procedure under Rule 19 of the Rules of Procedure provides a special means for the defendant to dispute the infringement action on the grounds of jurisdiction (see also Chapter 7 and, in respect of revocation, Chapter 11) and competence of the court and/or the chosen division and the language of the proceedings. The preliminary objection has to be raised within one month of service of the statement of claim. If the defendant fails to comply with the one-month deadline, the court has to treat the defendant as though they have submitted to the jurisdiction and competence of the court, and the competence of the division chosen by the claimant.[38]

If a preliminary objection is raised, the Registry will invite the claimant to comment on the preliminiary objection as soon as practicable. Within 14 days of service of this notification, the claimant is either able to correct any deficiency brought forward (eg, the designation of a different division) or may alternatively submit written comments on the preliminary objection raised.

The request to transfer the case from a regional division to the central division pursuant to Article 33(2) UPC Agreement (see Chapter 7) must also be made by way of the preliminary objection. Under this procedure, the defendant can claim that an action that has been lodged with a regional division must be transferred to the central division if the infringement has occurred in the territories of three or more regional divisions.[39]

F. The Statement of Defence

The statement of defence must be lodged by the defendant within three months of service of the statement of claim.[40] The Rules of Procedure set out a comprehensive and mandatory list of information that the statement of defence must exhibit:[41]

(a) the names of the defendant and of the defendant's representative;
(b) the postal and electronic adresses for service on the defendant, and the names and addresses of the persons authorised to accept service;
(c) the action number of the file;

---

[38] ibid Rule 19(7). Note that paragraph (7) only mentions submission to the competence and jurisdiction of the UPC and/or the chosen division. In consequence, since paragraph (7) leaves out submission to the 'chosen language', such a 'submission' cannot be assumed automatically.
[39] Article 33(2) UPC Agreement intends to protect the defendant from being sued in the 'periphery' of Europe when their offering of allegedly infringing products/services takes place at a 'pan-European level'. Whether the contracting Member States do in fact set up at least three regional divisions remains to be seen.
[40] Rule 23 of the Rules of Procedure.
[41] ibid Rule 24.

(d) an indication as to whether the defendant has lodged a preliminary objection (see section III.E above);
(e) an indication of the facts relied on, including any challenge to the facts relied on by the claimant;
(f) the evidence relied on,[42] where applicable, and an indication of any further evidence which will be offered in support;
(g) the reasons why the action should fail, arguments of law and any argument of rights based on prior use of the invention[43] and, where appropriate, any challenge to the claimant's proposed claim interpretation;
(h) an indication of any order the defendant will seek in respect of the infringement action during the interim procedure;[44]
(i) a statement whether the defendant disputes the claimant's assessment of the value of the infringement action and the grounds for such dispute; and
(j) a list of the documents, including any witness statements, referred to in the statement of defence,[45] together with any request that all or part of any such document need not be translated and/or any request for confidentiality.[46] Such a request will be decided by the judge-rapporteur as soon as practicable after their appointment.

G. The Counterclaim for Revocation

i. Formalities

The defendant may challenge the validity of the patent in suit to defend against the infringement action. This invaldity challenge must be included in the statement of defence using a counterclaim for revocation. The counterclaim for revocation must include:[47]

(a) an indication of the extent to which revocation of the patent is requested;[48]
(b) one or more grounds for revocation, which shall as far as possible be supported by arguments of law, and, where appropriate, an explanation of the defendant's proposed claim construction;
(c) an indication of the facts relied on;
(d) the evidence relied on, where available, and an indication of any further evidence which will be offered in support;
(e) an indication of any order the defendant will seek during the interim procedure;[49]
(f) a statement of the defendant's position, if any, on the options provided for under Article 33(3) UPC Agreement (see Chapter 9) and Rule 37.4 of the Rules of Procedure;

---

[42] ibid Rule 170.1.
[43] Article 28 UPC Agreement.
[44] Rule 104(e) of the Rules of Procedure.
[45] Rule 13.2 applies such that the defendant must supply a copy of each document referred to in the statement of defence.
[46] Pursuant to ibid Rule 262.2 and 262A.
[47] ibid Rule 25.1.
[48] Rule 25.1(a) apparently refers to those independent claims of the patent alleged to be invalid.
[49] ibid Rule 104(e).

(g) a list of the documents, including any witness statements, referred to in the counterclaim for revocation, together with any request that all or part of any such documents need not be translated;[50] and
(h) insofar as the proprietor of the patent is not the claimant in the infringement proceedings, the name and address for service of the proprietor and other information that would be required for a statement of claim.[51]

If the claimant is not the proprietor or not the only proprietor of the patent, the Registry will serve a copy of the counterclaim on the relevant proprietor as soon as practicable.[52] Rule 271 shall apply mutatis mutandis. The proprietor in question shall become a party to the revocation proceedings and shall be treated as the defendant in all subsequent proceedings. The proprietor shall provide details pursuant to Rule 13.1(e) if these have not already been provided by the claimant.

ii. An Article 33(3) Decision

If a counterclaim for revocation has been lodged, the panel of the court, after having heard the parties, must decide under Article 33(3) UPC Agreement[53] whether it wants to decide infringement together with the validity of the patent in suit (according to the so-called 'principle of unity') or whether it wants to transfer the validity action to the central division for decision (so-called 'bifurcation') (see Chapter 9). In the latter case, it must also decide whether to stay or proceed with the action for infringement. The relevant panel is required to hear the parties on this decision and the counterclaimant has the opportunity to state their position on this matter in their counterclaim.[54] The panel has to give its decision after closure of the written procedure.[55]

iii. 'Squeeze Arguments'

In the UPC, a defendant can use 'squeeze' arguments in its counterclaim for revocation. In other words, at least in cases where infringement and validity are heard together by the same court, claims must be construed consistently, potentially creating a tension between validity and infringement arguments. If, on the other hand, the court decides to bifurcate the case (see Chapter 9), it is possible that a differing claim construction of the local or regional division handling the infringement and the central division handling the central revocation can be applied. In certain circumstances, as explained in Chapter 9, the rules may assist the central division to decide the validity case as close as possible to the local or regional division decision on infringement. However, it remains to be seen what the degree of consistency will be between the divisions in these cases.

---

[50] Rule 13.2 and .3 apply mutatis mutandis. Rule 25.1(g) refers for confidentiality requests to Rule 262.2 and 262A.
[51] By ibid Rule 13.1(b) and (d). As for revocation actions, the claim must be directed against the proprietor of the patent for which the revocation is sought (Rule 42.1). See also ch 11.
[52] In accordance with ibid Rule 13.1(e).
[53] And see ibid Rule 37.
[54] ibid Rule 25.1(f).
[55] ibid Rule 37.1.

H. Reply to the Statement of Defence and Defence to the Counterclaim for Revocation

Two months after service of the statement of defence, the claimant must lodge a reply to the statement of defence if a counterclaim for revocation has been included.[56] A timeframe of two months also applies if the statement of defence does not contain a counterclaim for revocation.[57]

I. Rejoinder to a Reply to the Statement of Defence and a Reply to the Defence to the Counterclaim for Revocation

The Rules of Procedure draw a difference regarding the timeframe of the subsequent rejoinder to the reply in the event of a counterclaim for revocation. If a counterclaim for revocation has been lodged, the defendant has two months after service of the claimant's reply to lodge the rejoinder to the claimant's reply, together with a reply to the counterclaim for revocation.[58]

However, if no counterclaim for revocation has been lodged, the timeframe of the defendant's rejoinder is only one month after service of the reply.[59]

J. Rejoinder to the Reply to the Defence to the Counterclaim for Revocation

In the event of a counterclaim for revocation, the claimant is subsequently allowed to lodge a rejoinder to the reply to the defence to the counterclaim within one month after service.[60]

K. Application by the Proprietor to Amend the Patent

The proprietor of the patent in suit also has the possibility to defend the patent against the counterclaim for revocation by lodging an application to amend the patent in its defence to the counterclaim for revocation.[61] Any subsequent request of the proprietor to amend the patent is subject to the permission of the relevant panel.[62]

The application to amend the patent must contain, inter alia, the proposed amendments of the claims concerned, including auxiliary requests, in the language in which the patent was granted.[63] If the language of proceedings is different from the language of grant,

---

[56] ibid Rule 29(a).
[57] ibid Rule 29(b).
[58] ibid Rule 29(d).
[59] ibid Rule 29(c).
[60] ibid Rule 29(e).
[61] Pursuant to ibid Rule 30.1.
[62] ibid Rule 30.2.
[63] ibid Rule 30.1(a).

the proprietor must: lodge a translation of the proposed amendments to the claims in the language of the proceedings; and, if the patent is a Unitary Patent and the defendant requests it, lodge a translation in the language of the defendant's domicile in an EU Member State or of the place of the infringement, or threatened infringement, in a contracting Member State (see also Chapter 5).

In the event that an application to amend the patent is lodged by the proprietor, the timeline follows that of the infringement proceedings, as described above:[64] the defendant can lodge a defence to the application within two months of service of the application to amend the patent; subsequently, the proprietor may lodge a respective reply to the defence within one month; and, in turn, the defendant may lodge a rejoinder to this reply within one month after service.[65]

L. Closure of the Written Procedure

The written procedure will be closed following the exchange of written pleadings.[66] The judge-rapporteur will inform the parties of the date on which they intend to close the written procedure.[67] Following a reasoned request by a party, the judge-rapporteur may allow the exchange of further written pleadings within the time period specified.[68]

As discussed above, following the closure of the written procedure, the panel of the Court has to give a decision regarding the application of Article 33(3) UPC Agreement, that is, whether to follow the principle of unity or to apply bifurcation. If the Court decides to follow the principle of unity in the proceedings, the President of the Court of First Instance will, at the judge-rappoteur's request, allocate a technically qualified judge with qualifications and experience in the field of technology concerned.[69]

IV. Available Remedies

A. Preliminary Injunctions

Reference should be made to Chapter 15 for a detailed discussion of the substantive and procedural aspects of preliminary injunctions.

B. Final Injunctions

Article 63 provides for obtaining permanent injunctions in the UPC, reflecting the terms of Article 11 of Directive 2004/48/EC of the European Parliament and of the Council of

---

[64] ibid Rule 32.
[65] ibid Rule 32.3.
[66] ibid Rule 35.
[67] ibid Rule 35(a).
[68] ibid Rule 36.
[69] Article 33(3)(a), UPC Agreement and Rule 37.3 of the Rules of Procedure.

29 April 2004 on the enforcement of intellectual property rights (hereinafter the 'Enforcement Directive').[70] Article 11 states:

(1) Where a decision is taken finding an infringement of a patent, the Court may grant an injunction against the infringer aimed at prohibiting the continuation of the infringement. The Court may also grant such injunction against an intermediary whose services are being used by a third party to infringe a patent.
(2) Where appropriate, non-compliance with the injunction referred to in paragraph 1 shall be subject to a recurring penalty payment to the Court.

Final injunctions are a discretionary rather than an automatic remedy and the UPC Agreement's wording appears to follow the common law approach in this regard. The common law perceives an injunction, being equitable in nature, to be a discretionary remedy which is not granted automatically. The civil law approach, by contrast, as applied, for example, in Germany, grants injunctions on a regular basis once infringement has been found. The German jurisdiction emphasises that an injunction can only be negated in 'exceptional cases'[71] (see Chapter 18). Similarly, in the Netherlands, the starting point is that whenever an infringement has been found, the patentee has a right to an injunction.

Such guidance as the UPC has on the application of this discretion is to be found in the General Obligation in Article 3.2 of the Enforcement Directive:

1. Member States shall provide for the measures, procedures and remedies necessary to ensure the enforcement of the intellectual property rights covered by this Directive. Those measures, procedures and remedies shall be fair and equitable and shall not be unnecessarily complicated or costly, or entail unreasonable time-limits or unwarranted delays.
2. Those measures, procedures and remedies shall also be effective, proportionate and dissuasive and shall be applied in such a manner as to avoid the creation of barriers to legitimate trade and to provide for safeguards against their abuse.

The option to apply alternative measures in Article 12 of the Enforcement Directive is also relevant:

Member States may provide that, in appropriate cases and at the request of the person liable to be subject to the measures provided for in this section, the competent judicial authorities may order pecuniary compensation to be paid to the injured party instead of applying the measures provided for in this section if that person acted unintentionally and without negligence, if execution of the measures in question would cause him/her disproportionate harm and if pecuniary compensation to the injured party appears reasonably satisfactory.

The relationship between these articles in the Enforcement Directive has been the subject of a number of CJEU rulings,[72] in which it has been established that Article 3(2) requires

---

[70] Directive 2004/48/EC of the European Parliament and of the Council of 29 April 2004 on the enforcement of intellectual property rights [2004] OJ L195, 2 June, 16–25.
[71] Düsseldorf Court of Appeal, docket number I-15 U 135/14 from 2 February 2015; ibid, docket number I-15 U 65/15 from 13 January 2016; Mannheim Regional Court NJOZ 2009, 1458 – *Unterlassungsansprüche einer Patentverwertungsgesellschaft*.
[72] See *Productores de Música de España (Promusicae) v Telefónica de España SAU* (Case C-275/06) [2008] ECR I-271; *DHL Express France SAS v Chronopost SA* (Case C-235/09) [2011] ECR I-2801; *L'Oréal SA v eBay International AG* (Case C-324/09) [2011] ECR I-6011; *Scarlet Extended SA v Société Belge des Auteurs, Composituers et Editeurs (SABAM)* (Case C-70/10) [2011] ECR I-11959; *Belgische Vereniging van Auteurs, Componisten en Uitgevers CVBA (SABAM) v Netlog NV* (Case C-360/10) [2012] ECR I-0000; *UPC Telekabel Wien GmbH v Constantin Film GmbH* (Case C-314/12) (26 November 2013).

courts to consider the proportionality of injunctions to restrain infringements of intellectual property rights. Therefore, it cannot be expected that the court will fully follow the 'strict' German approach. Nonetheless, it has also been remarked by the English Patents Court that it must be very cautious before making an order which is tantamount to a compulsory licence, in circumstances where no compulsory licence would be available; where no such countervailing right is in play, the burden on the party seeking to show that the injunction would be disproportionate is thus a heavy one. However, it remains to be seen to what extent and under which circumstances the court will refrain from granting an injunction. This question might be expected to arise with regard to a claimant non-practising entity, in particular considering the (potentially) broad geographical coverage of the court's judgment.[73] The scope of application of final injunctions to prevent an infringer from benefiting from their infringement – in particular, in the form of 'springboard relief' after patent expiry[74] – will be a matter for the court to develop in case law.

When a decision holds infringement of a patent, the court may grant a permanent injunction against an intermediary whose services are being used to infringe the patent, which aims at prohibiting the continuation of the infringement.[75] The provision reflects Article 11(3) of the Enforcement Directive. Its application in the context of patent matters is not clear. On the one hand, it may, more narrowly, cover indirect infringers that either, according to Article 26 UPC Agreement: supply or offer to supply means relating to an essential element of the patented invention for putting it into effect; or supply staple commercial products with an inducement to the person supplied to infringe. On the other hand, it may more broadly catch a 'joint tortfeasor', which facilitates an infringement, but whose activities fall outside the scope of infringing acts themselves. Such assistance as there is from outside the patent context comes from the CJEU's understanding[76] of operators of online marketplaces as 'intermediaries'. Such online operators can be ordered to take measures that not only prevent actual infringement of intellectual property rights by users of the marketplace, but also to prevent further infringements of that kind.

C. Award of Damages

The UPC can award damages to the claimant under Article 68 UPC Agreement if the infringer knowingly or with reasonable grounds to know engaged in patent infringing activities. The award of damages is intended to put the patent holder in the position it would have been in if no infringement had taken place. Article 68(3)(a) and (b) UPC Agreement addresses the three ways of calculation already known from the Enforcement Directive:[77]

(i) negative economic consequences of the injured party (including lost profits);
(ii) award of infringer's profit; and,
(iii) licence analogy.

---

[73] Article 34 UPC Agreement.
[74] See, eg, *Smith & Nephew plc v Convatec Technologies Inc* [2013] EWHC 3955; and *Merck Canada v Sigma (No 2)* [2013] RPC 2.
[75] Article 63(1) UPC Agreement.
[76] *L'Oreal SA et al v eBay International AG*, 12 July 2011 (docket number C-324/09) EuZW 2011, 754 ff.
[77] Article 13(1)(a) and (b) of the Enforcement Directive.

158 Written Procedure

When calculating the amount of damages, the UPC is also allowed in appropriate cases to take into account elements other than economic factors, such as the moral prejudice caused to the injured party. Without knowledge or at least reasonable grounds for such knowledge, the calculation of damage is restricted to the recovery of profits or payment of compensation.[78] Recovery in these circumstances again reflects a provision of the Enforcement Directive[79] (for details of damages recovery in the UPC, see Chapter 18).

D. Recall, Removing from the Channels of Commerce and Destruction

In addition to a final injunction and damages, the UPC Agreement provides a number of other corrective measures in Article 64:

(1) Without prejudice to any damages due to the injured party by reason of the infringement, and without compensation of any sort, the Court may order, at the request of the applicant, that appropriate measures be taken with regard to products found to be infringing a patent and, in appropriate cases, with regard to materials and implements principally used in the creation or manufacture of those products.
(2) Such measures shall include:
    (a) a declaration of infringement;
    (b) recalling the products from the channels of commerce;
    (c) depriving the product of its infringing property;
    (d) definitively removing the products from the channels of commerce; or
    (e) the destruction of the products and/or of the materials and implements concerned.
(3) The Court shall order that those measures be carried out at the expense of the infringer, unless particular reasons are invoked for not doing so.
(4) In considering a request for corrective measures pursuant to this Article, the Court shall take into account the need for proportionality between the seriousness of the infringement and the remedies to be ordered, the willingness of the infringer to convert the materials into a non-infringing state, as well as the interests of third parties.

The UPC may order a recall of infringing products from the channels of commerce,[80] a definite removal from the channels of commerce,[81] and the destruction of the products and/or the materials and implements principally used in the creation or manufacture of those products.[82] The wording of Article 64 UPC Agreement reflects Article 10 of the Enforcement Directive.[83] Article 10 of the Enforcement Directive has been codified, for example in Germany, in a mulitude of laws related to intellectual property rights[84] and has acquired importance in practice since recall and destruction of infringing goods have turned out to be effective means against infringers. These measures are available in addition

---

[78] Article 68(4) UPC Agreement.
[79] Article 13(2) of the Enforcement Directive.
[80] Article 64(2)(b) in connection with Article 64(1) UPC Agreement.
[81] ibid Article 64(2)(d) in connection with Article 64(1).
[82] ibid Article 64(2)(2)(e) in connection with Article 64(1).
[83] Directive 2004/48/EC (n 70).
[84] See, eg, section 140a) of the German Patent Act; section 24a) of the German Utility Model Act; section 18 of the German Trademark Act; section 43 of the German Design Act.

to damages and may be ordered at the time the court makes its order regarding the merits of the action. The measures sought should be identified in the statement of claim[85]

Like the Enforcement Directive, Article 64(4) requires the court to exercise proportionality between the remedy ordered and the seriousness of the infringement. In addition, the court must take into account the willingness of the infringer to convert the infringing article(s) into a non-infringing state as well as the interests of third parties. These requirements are thus considerations in their own right rather than factors to take into account when deciding proportionality, which may suggest that they carry particular weight with the court when considering the definitive removal of the goods from the channels of commerce, or even destruction. For example, the removal of infringing goods from the channels of commerce may be inappropriate in cases where it deprives the public of goods on which they have in some manner become dependent. However, it is not clear that a willingness of the infringer to convert infringing goods would necessarily avoid an order of removal or destruction. German courts principally grant a claim to destruction if the relevant materials and implements are predominantly used to produce infringing products or even essential parts of it[86] and if the destruction as such is not out of proportion. The German Supreme Court has opined that disproportionality is only found in narrowly defined circumstances.[87] Therefore, it can be assumed that the UPC will consider destruction of infringing goods to be disproportionate only in exceptional circumstances.

E. Publication of the Judgment

In addition to the corrective measures provided in Article 64, the UPC Agreement also provides a right to publicity measures in Article 80:

> The Court may order, at the request of the applicant and at the expense of the infringer, appropriate measures for the dissemination of information concerning the Court's decision, including displaying the decision and publishing it in full or in part in public media.

Article 80 reflects the requirement of the Enforcement Directive that judicial authorities of Member States may order 'appropriate measures for the dissemination of the information concerning the decision, including displaying the decision and publishing it in full or in part'.[88] The German courts have so far been reluctant to grant the claimant permission to publication of the respective judgment.[89] German commentators suggest that the claim to publication does not serve the purpose to publicly criticise the infringer.[90] Therefore, for the application of Article 80 UPC Agreement, whether the publication as such may help to deter the defendant from further infringement will be decisive. This will likely only be affirmed in exceptional cases.[91]

---

[85] Rule 13.1(k) of the Rules of Procedure.
[86] German Supreme Court GRUR 1995, 338 – *Kleiderbügel*.
[87] German Supreme Court GRUR 1997, 899 – *Vernichtungsanspruch*.
[88] Article 15 of the Enforcement Directive.
[89] Munich Regional Court, 24 November 2011, docket number 7 O 22100/10.
[90] See section 140e, paragraph 4 of Benkard/Grabinski/Zülch, *Patentgesetz, Kommentar*, 11th edn (CH Beck, 2015).
[91] See *Samsung Electronics (UK) Ltd v Apple Inc* [2012] EWHC 2049 (Pat). Publication orders are also rare in the English courts. In a registered design case, Apple was ordered by the Intellectual Property Enterprise Court

F. An Order of the Communication of Information

Under Article 67(1) UPC Agreement, the court may order an infringer to inform the applicant of:

- the origin and distribution channels of the infringing products or processes;
- the quantities produced, manufactured, delivered, received or ordered, as well as the price obtained for the infringing products; and
- the identity of any third person involved in the production or distribution of the infringing products or in the use of the infringing process.

Using the claim to information under Article 67(1) (which to a great extent resembles the wording of Article 8 of the Enforcement Directive), the claimant is able to acquire information from the infringer about the distribution channels and the quantity of infringing products. This information can be used to identify third parties that have taken part in the infringing activities and to possibly hold them to account in subsequent litigation before the court: for example, if the claimant wants to file an action against the producer or a retailer. The information obtained in this way may also be used to assist in a damages calculation.[92]

The claim to information can also be directed against a third party that was involved in the infringing activities 'on a commercial scale' – in particular: (i) that was found in the possession of the infringing products or to be using an infringing process;[93] (ii) that was found to be providing services used in infringing activities;[94] or (iii) that was indicated to be involved in the production, manufacture or distribution of the infringing products or processes or in the provision of the services.[95]

The wording of Article 67(1) UPC Agreement acknowledges the infringer's interest by stating that the request for information must be 'justified and proportionate'. This principle is also reflected in Rule 191 of the Rules of Procedure, which states that any information sought must be reasonably necessary for the purpose of advancing the claimant's case.[96] Moreover, the infringer may, for example, put forward the need to protect confidential information. Therefore, the court may order that certain information, if it is not necessary for pursuing the patent infringement claim against a third party or for calculation of damages, but is mixed with information that is, may be redacted.

---

to publicise an adverse decision. However, the parties had accepted that the Enforcement Directive was limited to publicity where a right holder is successful. The Court of Appeal has stated that such orders should normally only be made in the case of a successful intellectual property owner where they serve one of the two purposes set out in Article 27 of the Enforcement Directive and, in the case of a successful non-infringer, where there is a real need to dispel commercial uncertainty in the marketplace (either with the non-infringer's customers or the public in general).

[92] In particular, in this respect, the information obtained may corroborate that obtained from a 'Request to lay open books' under Rule 191 of the Rules of Procedure. See ch 16.

[93] Article 67(2)(a) UPC Agreement.

[94] ibid Article 67(2)(b).

[95] ibid Article 67(2)(c).

[96] Note that it is unclear from Article 67 UPC Agreement and Rule 191 of the Rules of Procedure whether an order to communicate information may be final or provisional, or both. Article 67 is situated amongst provisions dealing with other final measures in the UPC Agreement and refers to the 'infringer' rather than the 'alleged infringer' (for which cf Article 62). However, Article 74 refers to the 'main proceedings' continuing when an order under Article 67 is appealed.

11

Written Procedure

Revocation Actions

I. Timeline of a Revocation Action

The principal action available to a third party against a patent owner in the UPC is a revocation action. This can be by counterclaim, as was described in Chapter 10, or as a standalone claim, as explained in this chapter. Figure 11.1 shows the timeline of a revocation action in overview. Assuming that a full sequence of pleadings is served, up to and including rejoinder, the written procedure for a revocation action with an infringement counterclaim will be six months. The interim period is three months (see Chapter 13). Figure 11.1 illustrates an oral hearing at 10 months, although the oral hearing may be earlier or later than this. This chapter explains the details of the written procedure in a revocation action.

Figure 11.1 Overview of revocation and declaration of non-infringement actions

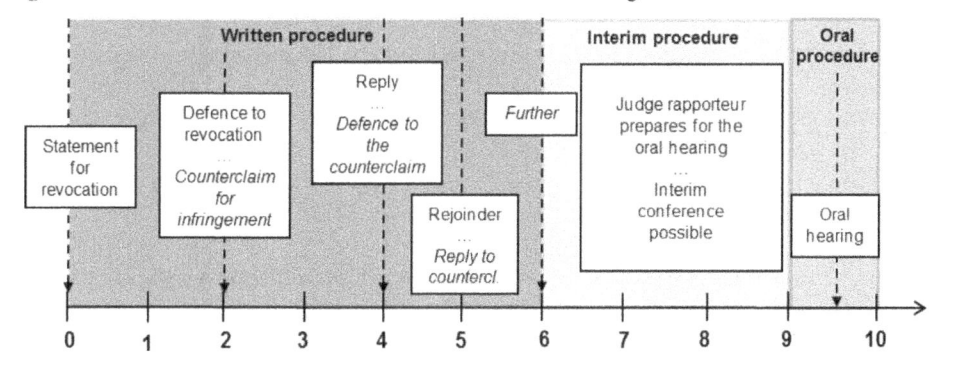

II. Revocation Actions

A. Parties

Actions for the revocation of a patent must be directed against the proprietor of the patent for which revocation is sought.[1] A patent therefore cannot be contested in an action for

---

[1] Rule 42.1 of the Rules of Procedure. Situations may arise in which the case is brought against the registered proprietor (under Rule 8.6), but another person whose name does not appear in the relevant patent register is entitled to proprietorship (under Rule 8.5(a) or (b)). In such cases, the registered proprietor must as soon as practicable after service of the statement of revocation apply to the UPC under Rule 305.1(c) for the substitution of the person so entitled (see Rule 42).

infringement brought by the holder of a licence alone,[2] but must be lodged as an action against the patentee.

B. Where to Start the Action

If an infringement action concerning the same patent and the same parties is not already lodged, Article 33(4) UPC Agreement states that a revocation claim must be lodged at the central division (see Chapter 9).[3] In this way, the central division is distinguished from the local and regional courts as the priority (but not exclusive) court for the hearing of revocation actions. The priority of the central division under Article 33(4) operates regardless of whether a claim for a preliminary injunction, or other provisional measures, concerning the same patent and the same parties has been filed in a regional or local court. Different rules apply when an infringement action on the merits has already been lodged, which is between the same parties and relates to the same patent as the revocation action. In this situation, Article 33(4) requires that the revocation claim is filed in the same local or regional division as the earlier infringement action (see also Chapter 9).

C. Allocation in the Central Division According to Subject Matter

Actions lodged at the central division are allocated by the Registry to the appropriate section in London, Paris or Munich according to the subject matter of the invention claimed. The Rules provide the following mechanism for achieving this:[4]

(a) If there is only one patent in the action, the action will be allocated by the Registry to the seat or the section of the central division responsible for the subject matter classification of that patent.[5]
(b) If there is more than one patent at issue in the action and a majority of the patents have a single subject-matter classification appropriate to the seat or other section of the central division, the action will be allocated by the Registry to the seat or the section responsible for that classification.[6]
(c) In other cases, particularly where the action involves a single patent having more than one classification, or where the action involves several patents with no majority having a single classification, the action will be referred by the Registry to the presiding judge of the seat or section responsible for the subject matter of the first classification of either the single patent or, where there is more than one patent, the patent first listed in the statement of claim. If the presiding judge considers that the reference of the action is appropriate, they

---

[2] Article 47(5) of the UPC Agreement.

[3] Written pleadings and other documents must be lodged at the Registry or Sub-registry in electronic form and parties must use the electronic forms available online. The lodging of documents is acknowledged by the automatic issue of an electronic receipt giving the date and local time of receipt (Rule 4.1 of the Rules of Procedure). Note that documents and pleadings may be lodged not only at the Registry, but also at the Sub-registry of the division responsible for the case (explanatory note to the changes made by the Legal Group of the Preparatory Committee in the 17th draft of the Rules of Procedure). See also Rule 3 of the Rules of Procedure.

[4] The action is regarded as having commenced before the court from the date of receipt of the statement of claim recorded by the Registry (see ibid Rule 17(4) and (1)(a)).

[5] ibid Rule 17(3)(a).

[6] ibid Rule 17(3)(b).

will assign a panel. If the judge considers that it would be more appropriate for the seat or other section of the central division to hear the action, they must refer the action to the relevant presiding judge. If that judge disagrees, they must refer the action to the President of the Court of First Instance to make the allocation that they consider appropriate.[7]

The Rules on the distribution of actions according to subject matter of the patents concerned govern all actions, including infringement. Hence, the correct section to hear an infringement action filed in the central division[8] will be determined according to the above scheme.

D. Language of the Statement of Revocation

i. *The Central Division*

At first instance, the language of proceedings in the central division is the language of grant of the patent.[9] This is the language in which the pleadings, written evidence and other documents are to be lodged.[10]

ii. *The Regional and Local Divisions*

A revocation action may be lodged in a local or regional court by way of a counterclaim to an infringement action or as a standalone claim following an infringement action concerning the same parties and the same patent. In these circumstances, the local or regional division has two options regarding the language to be used in that division and the statement of revocation. The division can adopt:[11]

(a) the official European language or one of the official European languages of the contracting Member State hosting the local division, or designated by the contracting Member States sharing the regional division;[12] or
(b) one or more of the official languages of the EPO.[13]

Contracting Member States may designate one or more languages of proceedings for use in the local or regional division for which they are responsible. The consequences of more than one language being chosen are discussed in Chapter 4.

E. Written Procedure in a Revocation Action

The written procedure in a revocation action, like that in an infringement action, consists largely of the exchange of pleadings: the lodging of a statement for revocation against the

---

[7] ibid Rule 17(c).
[8] Under Article 33(1) UPC Agreement.
[9] ibid Article 49(6).
[10] Rule 7.1 of the Rules of Procedure. Rule 45 provides separately that statements of revocation must be in the language of grant of the patent, except where the parties have agreed to bring the action in the division of their choice, further to Article 33(7) UPC Agreement.
[11] These are the languages used by a division *ab initio*. The language of proceedings may subsequently be changed (see Article 49(3), (4) and (5) of the UPC Agreement).
[12] ibid Article 49(1).
[13] ibid Article 49(2).

164   Written Procedure

proprietor of the patent[14] and the lodging of a defence within two months of the statement of revocation. These pleading may then be followed within two months by the lodging of a reply to the defence, and a rejoinder to the reply to the defence, within one month (see Figure 11.2). The defendant patent proprietor may include in the defence a request to amend the patent. The request to amend may itself be followed by a defence within two months, and a reply (within one month) and then a rejoinder may follow. The defence may include a counterclaim for infringement, in which case the claimant must lodge a defence to the counterclaim within two months.[15] The defendant may lodge a reply to the defence to the counterclaim for infringement within one month, and the claimant may lodge a rejoinder to the reply, also within one month.

Figure 11.2 Written procedure: revocation action

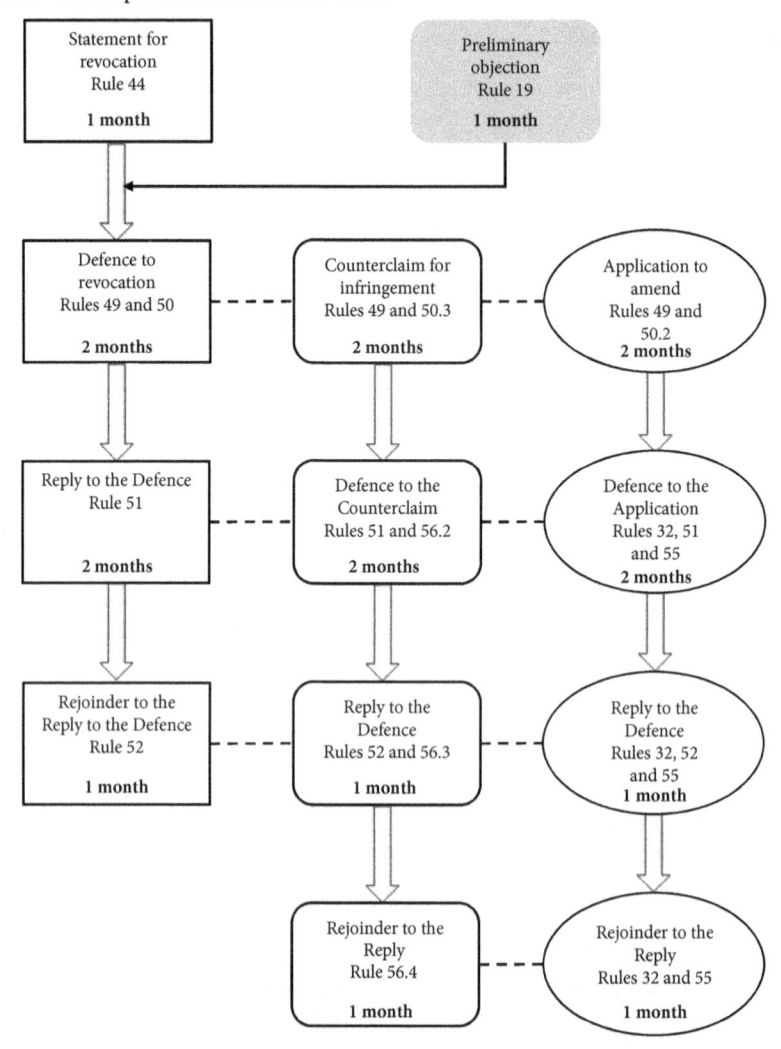

```
Statement for              Preliminary
revocation                 objection
Rule 44                    Rule 19
1 month                    1 month

        ↓                      ↓
Defence to         Counterclaim for      Application to
revocation         infringement          amend
Rules 49 and 50    Rules 49 and 50.3     Rules 49 and 50.2
2 months           2 months              2 months

        ↓                  ↓                  ↓
Reply to the Defence   Defence to the      Defence to the
Rule 51                Counterclaim        Application
                       Rules 51 and 56.2   Rules 32, 51 and 55
2 months               2 months            2 months

        ↓                  ↓                  ↓
Rejoinder to the       Reply to the        Reply to the
Reply to the Defence   Defence             Defence
Rule 52                Rules 52 and 56.3   Rules 32, 52 and 55
1 month                1 month             1 month

                           ↓                  ↓
                       Rejoinder to the    Rejoinder to the
                       Reply               Reply
                       Rule 56.4           Rules 32 and 55
                       1 month             1 month
```

---

[14] See ibid Article 47(5).
[15] As regards the lodging of an initiating infringement action in a local or regional division, as an alternative to the counterclaim, see ch 9.

i. Statement for Revocation

The case brought by the parties must be set out in detail in the pleadings. In particular, the statement for revocation must contain:[16]

(a) a number of the same particulars required for an infringement claim:[17] the name and address of the claimant, the defendant and any person authorised to accept service; details of the patent(s) concerned; and details of any other actions relating to the patent in the UPC, the EPO, the national courts or other national authority;
(b) evidence of any agreement by the parties to bring the action before a local or regional division; and, the identity of the division in question;[18]
(c) evidence of any agreement by the parties to have the action heard by a single judge;[19]
(d) an indication of the extent to which revocation of the patent(s) is requested;
(e) the claimant's grounds of revocation, including, so far as possible, legal arguments and the claimant's construction of the claims, where appropriate;
(f) the facts upon which the claimant relies;
(g) the available evidence and an indication of further evidence on which the claimant intends to rely;
(h) orders that will be sought during the interim procedure. These may include orders for: the production of documents; experts (including court experts); experiments; inspections; further written evidence; matters on which oral evidence is to be given; the scope of questions to be put to the witnesses (see Chapter 16);[20]
(i) a list of the documents referred to in the statement for revocation, including any witness statements, together with any request that all or part of those documents need *not* be translated and/or an application that material should be made available to the applicant and not subject to confidentiality protection (see Chapter 16).[21] The claimant must supply copies of the documents referred to in the list.[22]

ii. Preliminary Objections

Within one month of the service of the statement for revocation, the defendant may lodge a preliminary objection[23] concerning:

(a) the jurisdiction and competence of the court, including any objection that the patent concerned has been opted out;
(b) the competence of the division in which the claimant has indicated the action should be heard in its statement of revocation;
(c) the language of the statement of claim.

The filing of a preliminary objection does not affect the period for the filing of a defence unless the judge-rapporteur decides that this period may be extended.[24] The preliminary

---

[16] Rule 44 of the Rules of Procedure.
[17] The particulars are those in ibid Rule 13(1)(a)–(d), (g) and (h).
[18] Further to Article 33(7) UPC Agreement.
[19] Further to ibid Article 8(7).
[20] See Rule 104(e) of the Rules of Procedure.
[21] Further to ibid Rule 262.2 and 262A.
[22] See also ibid Rule 13.2 and 13.3.
[23] ibid Rule 19.1(b).
[24] ibid Rule 19.6.

objection may also be lodged as part of the defence, providing this is lodged within the one month period. If a preliminary objection is not filed, this will be treated as a submission to the jurisdiction and competence of the court and the competence of the division chosen by the claimant.[25] The preliminary objection must include,[26] in the language of proceedings:[27]

(a) the following particulars:[28] the names of the defendant and of the defendant's representative; the postal and electronic addresses for service on the defendant and the names and addresses of the persons authorised to accept service; and the action number of the file;
(b) the decision or order sought by the defendant;
(c) the grounds upon which the preliminary objection is based; and
(d) where appropriate, the facts and evidence relied on.

As soon as practicable after the filing of the preliminary objection, the Registry must invite the claimant to comment. The claimant then has the opportunity to correct the deficiency within 14 days of service of notification of the preliminary objection. Alternatively, the claimant may submit written comments, also within 14 days. The judge-rapporteur is then informed of either activity. If the claimant has corrected the deficiency, the judge-rapporteur will refer the action to this division. Otherwise, after expiry of the 14 day period, the judge-rapporteur will decide the preliminary objection having given the parties the opportunity to be heard.[29] A preliminary objection may be heard as part of the main proceedings, in which case the judge-rapporteur must inform the parties.[30']

A decision by the judge-rapporteur to allow the preliminary objection may be appealed with leave of the Court of First Instance within 15 days of service of the court's decision to that effect. If the Court of First Instance refuses to grant leave within this period, a request for a discretionary review may be made to the Court of Appeal within a further 15 days.[31] If an appeal is lodged, proceedings at first instance may be stayed by the judge-rapporteur or the Court of Appeal on a reasoned request by a party.[32']

iii. Response to a Revocation Claim

a. Defence to Revocation

The defence to revocation must include: the name of the defendant and its representative; the postal and electronic addresses for service on the defendant and any person authorised to accept service; and the number of the file.[33] The defence must also include: an indication of the facts relied on, including any challenge to the facts relied on by the claimant; the evidence relied on and an indication of any further evidence to be offered in support; the reasons why the revocation claim must fail, including arguments of law and why any

---

[25] ibid Rule 19.7.
[26] ibid Rule 19.2.
[27] ibid Rule 14 (see ch 14).
[28] ibid Rule 24(a)–(c).
[29] ibid Rule 20.1.
[30] ibid Rule 20.2.
[31] ibid Rule 220.2.
[32] ibid Rule 21.2.
[33] ibid Rules 50.1 and 24 (a)–(c).

dependent claim is independently valid; an indication of any order the proprietor will seek at the interim conference; and a list of documents, including any witness statements, referred to in the defence, together with any request that such documents should *not* be translated and/or an application that material should be made available to the applicant and not subject to confidentiality protection.[34] The defence may include a counterclaim for infringement[35] and an application to amend the patent.[36]

b. Counterclaim for Infringement

A counterclaim for infringement must address the following matters:[37]

(a) the nature of the claim and the order or remedy sought;
(b) the facts relied on – these must identify the patent claims that it is alleged are infringed and details of one or more examples of the alleged infringements, together with the date and place of the infringements;
(c) the available evidence that is relied on and an indication of further evidence that will be relied on;[38]
(d) an explanation, including legal argument, of why the facts that are relied upon constitute an infringement of the patent – this should include the claim construction relied on;
(e) orders sought;[39]
(f) an indication of the value of the infringement counterclaim, where this exceeds €500,000;
(g) a list of the documents referred to in the defence, together with any request that all or part of those documents need not be translated and/or an application that material should be made available to the applicant and not subject to confidentiality protection (see Chapter 16).[40] The claimant must supply copies of the documents referred to in the list.[41]

iv. *The Application to Amend the Patent*

a. Contents of the Application to Amend

The application to amend the patent must include:[42]

(a) the proposed amendments of the claims and/or specification of the patent concerned – where applicable and appropriate, one or more auxiliary requests should be included in the appropriate language;

---

[34] ibid Rule 29A(a)–(d) and (f).
[35] ibid Rule 49.2(b).
[36] ibid Rule 49.2(a).
[37] An initiating infringement action may be lodged in a local or regional division (see ch 9) and these are matters identical to those set out in Rules 13.1(k)–(q) of the Rules of Procedure for infringement claims.
[38] See also ibid Rule 170.1.
[39] See ibid Rule 104(e).
[40] ibid Rule 262.2 and 262A.
[41] ibid Rule 13.2 and 13.3.
[42] ibid Rules 50.2 and 30.1(a) and (c).

168   Written Procedure

(b) an explanation of why the auxiliary request(s) fulfil the requirements of the EPC;[43]
(c) an indication of whether the auxiliary requests are conditional or unconditional.[44]

Conditional auxiliary requests must be 'reasonable in number in the circumstances of the case'.[45] Requests to amend the patent that are made subsequent to the defence require the permission of the court.[46] A question arises as to how late in proceedings it is permissible to request the amendment of a patent (if not done at the counterclaim stage) and whether it is possible after the oral hearing. The central amendment procedure in the EPO[47] also provides a means of amendment of a European or Unitary Patent that may potentially be used after a decision on the merits regarding validity and infringement.

b. The Language of Auxiliary Requests

Auxiliary requests must be provided in the language of grant of the patent. If the language of the proceedings is other than the language of grant, the proprietor must lodge a translation of the auxiliary requests in the language of proceedings.[48]

v. Reply to the Defence to the Statement of Revocation and Rejoinder

A reply to the defence to a statement of revocation may be lodged within two months of service of the defence to the statement of revocation.[49] A rejoinder to the reply may be lodged within one month of service of the reply[50] (see Figure 11.2).

vi. Defence to the Counterclaim for Infringement

Within one month of service of a counterclaim for infringement, the claimant must lodge its defence to the counterclaim for infringement[51] (see Figure 11.2). The defence must include the following:[52]

(a) the facts relied on and any challenge to the facts relied on in the counterclaim;[53]
(b) the available evidence relied on and any further evidence that the claimant expects to be able to rely on;[54]

---

[43] Articles 84, 123(2) and (3) EPC.
[44] ibid Rule 30.1(c).
[45] ibid.
[46] ibid Rule 30.2.
[47] Introduced by Article 105a EPC 2000.
[48] Rule 30.1(a) of the Rules of Procedure.
[49] ibid Rule 51.
[50] ibid Rule 52.
[51] ibid Rule 51.
[52] ibid Rule 56.2. These are from amongst those matters required in a defence to infringement (those stipulated by Rule 24(e)–(h) and (j)).
[53] ibid Rule 24(e).
[54] ibid Rule 24(f).

(c) an explanation of why the counterclaim should fail, including legal argument and any challenge to the defendant's claim construction;[55]
(d) an indication of any order that will be sought at the interim conference;[56]
(e) a list of the documents referred to in the defence, together with any request that all or part of those documents need *not* be translated[57] and/or an application that material should be made available to the applicant and not subject to confidentiality protection (see Chapter 16).[58] The claimant must supply copies of the documents referred to in the list.[59]

The defence to counterclaim must also state whether the claimant disputes the defendant's assessment of the value of the counterclaim, with their reasons for doing so.[60]

vii. Reply to the Defence to the Counterclaim for Infringement and Rejoinder

A Reply to the defence to counterclaim may be lodged by the defendant within one month of service of the defence to counterclaim.[61] A Rejoinder to the Reply may be lodged within one month of service of the Reply,[62] together with any Rejoinder to the Reply to the defence to the Application to amend the patent,[63] but must be limited to the issues that were raised in the Reply.

F. Acceleration in the Central Division

The judge-rapporteur is required to accelerate proceedings before the central division if an action for provisional measures has been lodged[64] (see Chapter 9). A revocation action must also be accelerated by the judge-rapporteur in the central division if it is bifurcated from an infringement action in a local or regional division, which concerns the same parties and the same patent, following an Article 33(3) decision (see Chapter 9). Furthermore, in these circumstances, the judge-rapporteur must endeavour to set a date for the oral hearing of the revocation action that is before that of the infringement action.[65] The appropriate time for the judge-rapporteur to accelerate proceedings is during the scheduling of the further progress of proceedings at the interim conference.[66']

---

[55] ibid Rule 24(g).
[56] ibid Rule 24(h).
[57] ibid Rule 24(j).
[58] Further to ibid Rule 262.2 and 262A.
[59] ibid Rule 13.2.
[60] ibid Rule 56.2.
[61] ibid Rules 52 and 56.3.
[62] ibid Rule 56.4.
[63] ibid Rules 55 and 32.
[64] ibid Rule 40(a). The purpose of this provision is to bring a decision on the merits forward in circumstances where preliminary relief may be ordered in order to limit any potential prejudice to the party or parties against whom that relief was awarded, should the decision on the merits go in that party's favour.
[65] ibid Rule 40(b).
[66] See ibid Rule 104(c) and (h).

G. Stay of a Central Revocation Action Pending an Article 33(3) Decision

A revocation counterclaim may be lodged in response to an infringement action. Such a counterclaim must be filed in the same local or regional division as the infringement action.[67] The Rules of Procedure foresee situations in which there is identity of the parties between this revocation counterclaim in a local or regional division and an earlier lodged central division revocation action. In these circumstances, the central division action must be stayed, pending a decision of the local or regional panel seised with the infringement action under Article 33(3).[68] If there is no revocation counterclaim or the parties are not the same, the central revocation continues in parallel to the infringement action and counterclaim (see Chapter 9).

H. The Revocation Decision

An action for revocation or a counterclaim for revocation results in a decision by the court on the validity of the patent in suit.[69] The court may revoke the patent, either entirely or partly, only on the grounds referred to in Articles 138(1) and 139(2) EPC. If the grounds for revocation affect the patent only in part, the patent must be amended accordingly and revoked in part.[70] A decision to revoke a patent, either entirely or partly, must be sent to the EPO and, with regard to a European patent, to the national patent office of any contracting Member State of validation. The effect of a revocation in the UPC, like that in the EPC, is that the patent is deemed never to have existed from the outset.[71]

---

[67] Article 33(4) UPC Agreement.
[68] Rule 75.3 of the Rules of Procedure.
[69] Article 65(1) UPC Agreement.
[70] ibid Article 65(3).
[71] ibid Article 65(4); see also Articles 64 and 67 EPC.

12

Written Procedure

Declarations of Non-infringement and Actions against the EPO

I. Declaration of a Non-infringement Timeline

In addition to revocation, a further action that may be brought against a patent owner (and, in this case, a licensee) is a declaration or non-infringement. Figure 12.1 gives an overview of the timeline of a declaration of non-infringement. Assuming that a full sequence of pleadings is served, up to and including rejoinder, the written procedure for a declaration of infringement action will be four months, although a claim to infringement of the same patent by the counterparty may disrupt this timeline (see section II.D below and Chapter 9). Figure 12.1 assumes an interim period of three months (see Chapter 13) and illustrates an oral hearing at eight months, although the oral hearing may be earlier or later than this. This chapter explains the details of the written procedure in a declaration of non-infringement.

Figure 12.1 Overview of revocation and declaration of non-infringement actions

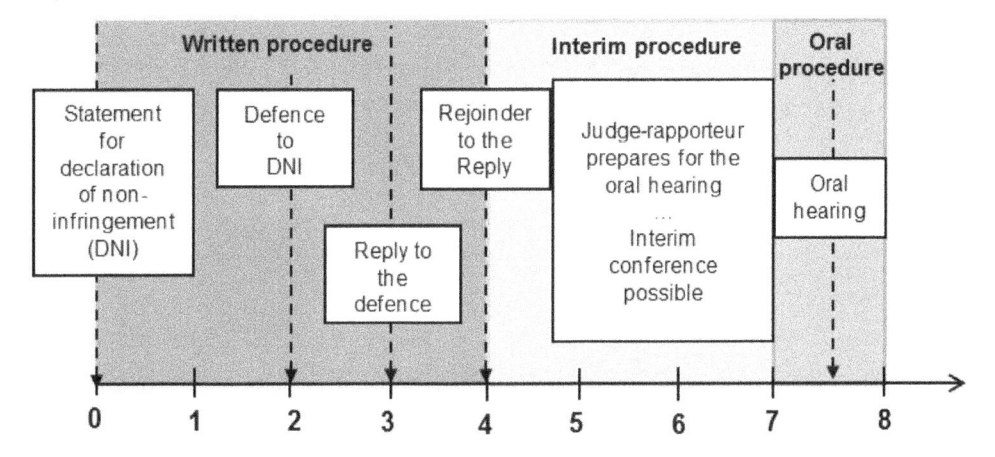

II. Declaration of Non-infringement

A. Parties

A declaration that a specific act does not, or would not, infringe a patent should be brought by the party proposing to do that act,[1] against the proprietor[2] of the patent or the licensee who has asserted infringement or refused to give an acknowledgement of non-infringement within one month.[3]

B. Prior Assertion

Prior to lodging a statement for a declaration of non-infringement against a patent proprietor or licensee entitled to bring an infringement action, in respect of an act or proposed act, either:[4]

- the proprietor or licensee must first have asserted that the act is an infringement; or
- the party seeking the declaration must have applied in writing to the proprietor or licensee for a written acknowledgement to the effect of the declaration sought, together with full particulars of the act concerned, and the proprietor or licensee must have refused or failed to give the acknowledgement within one month.

It is submitted that the full particulars submitted by an applicant must be sufficient for the patentee or licensee to determine whether each integer of the patent claims concerned is present in the product or process to which the act relates.

C. Where to Start the Action

An action for a declaration of non-infringement must be lodged in the central division, either alone or together with a revocation action. In cases where an action for non-infringement between the same parties and relating to the same patent has been lodged in a local or regional division, the declaration of non-infringement must be lodged in the same division as that action.[5]

---

[1] Rule 61.1 of the Rules of Procedure. The parties should consider whether all those who are potentially liable to infringement should participate in the proceedings.
[2] Situations may arise in which the case is brought against the registered proprietor (under ibid Rule 8.6), but another person whose name does not appear in the relevant patent register is entitled to proprietorship (under Rule 8.5(a) or (b)). In such cases, the registered proprietor must as soon as practicable after service of the statement of revocation apply to the UPC under Rule 305.1(c) for the substitution of the person so entitled.
[3] ibid Rule 61.2.
[4] ibid Rule 61.1.
[5] Article 33(4) UPC Agreement.

D. The Effect of Lodging a Later Infringement Action

An infringement action may be lodged in a local or regional division after a declaration for non-infringement has been lodged in the central division in which the infringement action relates to the same patent and is between the same parties, or between the holder of an exclusive licence and the party requesting the declaration of non-infringement. This has two potential consequences, depending on whether or not the infringement claim is filed within three months of the non-infringement declaration (also see Chapter 9):

(i) the infringement action is lodged within three months of the non-infringement action: the non-infringement action must be stayed;[6] or
(ii) the infringement action is not lodged within three months of the non-infringement action: the central division in which the non-infringement action is lodged and the local or regional division in which the infringement action is lodged must consult to agree on the 'future progress of proceedings'.[7]

E. A Non-infringement Claim Following an Infringement Claim

There is no provision in the UPC Agreement or the Rules of Procedure for a declaration of non-infringement to be brought by way of a counterclaim to an action for infringement. However, an action for a declaration of non-infringement concerning the same patent and the same parties as an earlier infringement action may be lodged. This must be in the same division as the infringement action.[8]

F. The Structure of Proceedings

The written procedure in a declaration for non-infringement action, like that in an infringement action, consists largely of the exchange of pleadings: the lodging of a statement for a declaration of non-infringement against the proprietor of the patent and the lodging of a defence to the statement for declaration of non-infringement. These pleadings may then be followed by the lodging of a Reply to the Defence and a Rejoinder to the Reply (see Figure 12.2). Further pleadings may follow at the discretion of the judge-rapporteur upon a reasoned request.[9] Unlike a revocation action, a Statement for a declaration of non-infringement may be directed against the licensee who has asserted infringement of

---

[6] ibid Article 33(6) and Rule 76 of the Rules of Procedure.
[7] Rule 76.3 of the Rules of Procedure. The Rule is silent on the right of the parties to be heard in these circumstances, but consistency with Rule 340(1) would suggest that the parties should be heard.
[8] There is no provision in the UPC Agreement or the Rules of Procedure as to how the division must then treat these actions, but it is submitted that Rule 340(1) would apply to allow such actions to be heard together, having heard the parties, in particular to avoid inconsistent decisions.
[9] Rule 36 of the Rules of Procedure.

the patent, or has refused or failed to given an acknowledgement in writing, as discussed above.[10] Within one month of the service of the statement for declaration of non-infringement, the defendant may lodge a preliminary objection,[11] the procedure for which is the same as for a revocation action.

Figure 12.2 Action for a declaration of non-infringement

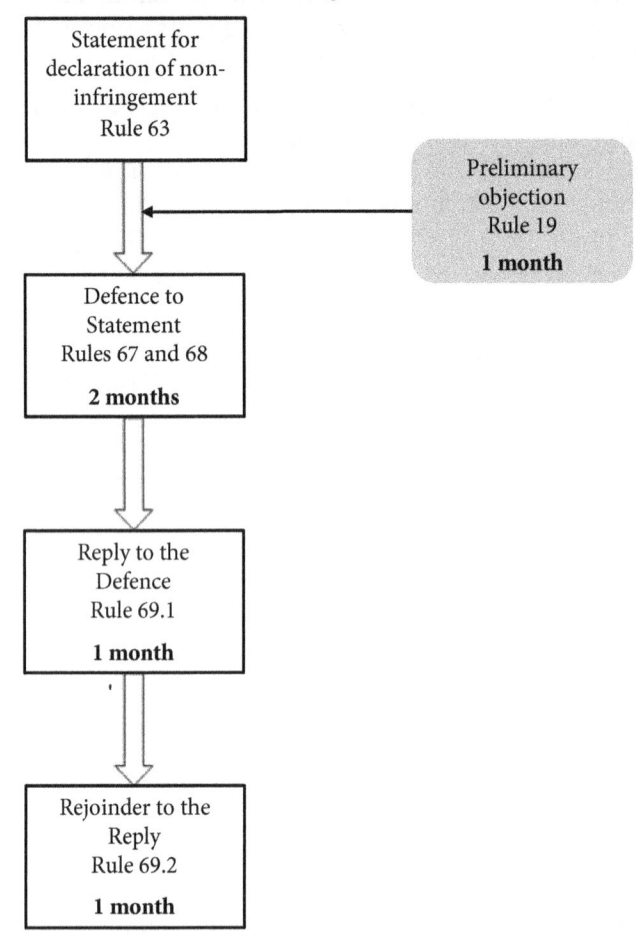

```
┌─────────────────────┐
│   Statement for     │
│ declaration of non- │          ┌──────────────┐
│   infringement      │◄─────────│  Preliminary │
│      Rule 63        │          │   objection  │
└──────────┬──────────┘          │    Rule 19   │
           │                     │   1 month    │
           ▼                     └──────────────┘
┌─────────────────────┐
│    Defence to       │
│    Statement        │
│  Rules 67 and 68    │
│     2 months        │
└──────────┬──────────┘
           │
           ▼
┌─────────────────────┐
│   Reply to the      │
│     Defence         │
│     Rule 69.1       │
│     1 month         │
└──────────┬──────────┘
           │
           ▼
┌─────────────────────┐
│  Rejoinder to the   │
│      Reply          │
│     Rule 69.2       │
│     1 month         │
└─────────────────────┘
```

G. The Language of a Statement for a Declaration of Non-infringement

A Statement for a declaration of non-infringement is lodged in the central division and the same language rules apply as to a Statement of revocation. In other words, the language must

---

[10] ibid Rule 61.2.
[11] ibid Rule 19.1(b).

be that of the patent concerned.[12] In those cases where the declaration of non-infringement has been lodged in a local or regional division, the language is determined by the division in question as for a Statement of revocation.[13]

H. The Contents of Pleadings

i. Statement for a Declaration of Non-infringement

The statement for a declaration of non-infringement must contain a number of the same particulars as an infringement action:[14]

(a) the name of the claimant (and, where the claimant is a corporate entity, the location of its registered office) and of the claimant's representative;
(b) the name of the party against whom the statement is made (the defendant – and, where the defendant is a corporate entity, the location of its registered office);
(c) the postal and electronic addresses for service on the claimant and the names of the persons authorised to accept service;
(d) the postal and, where available, electronic addresses for service on the defendant and the names of the persons authorised to accept service (if known);
(e) where the claimant is not the proprietor or not the only proprietor of the patent (or patents) concerned, postal and, where available, electronic addresses for service on the proprietor and the names and addresses of the persons authorised to accept service (if known);
(f) where the claimant is not the proprietor of the patent (or patents) concerned, or not the only proprietor, evidence to show that the claimant is entitled to commence proceedings;[15]
(g) details of the patent (or patents) concerned, including the number (or numbers);
(h) where applicable, information about any prior or pending proceedings relating to the patent (or patents) concerned before the UPC, including any action for revocation or a declaration of non-infringement pending before the central division and the date of any such action, the EPO or any other court or authority.

In addition, there are a number of other particulars that must be included in the Statement for a declaration of non-infringement:[16]

(a) confirmation that the prior assertion requirements of Rule 61 have been met;
(b) where the parties have agreed to bring the action in a local or regional division,[17] the division in question and evidence of the agreement;
(c) if applicable, that the action will be heard by a single judge[18] and evidence to that effect;

---

[12] ibid Rules 64 and 45.1.
[13] ibid Rules 64 and 45.2.
[14] ibid Rule 63. The requirements are those listed in Rule 13.1(a)-(h).
[15] It is not clear what evidence is required in the context of a statement for a declaration of non-infringement. In particular, evidence of prior assertion is stipulated separately in Rule 63(a).
[16] Rule 63(a)-(j) of the Rules of Procedure.
[17] As permitted by Article 33(7) UPC Agreement.
[18] Further to ibid Article 8(7).

176   Written Procedure

(d) the declaration sought by the claimant;
(e) the reasons why the performance of a specific act does not or a proposed act would not constitute an infringement of the patent(s) concerned – this should include arguments of law and, where appropriate, an explanation of the claimant's proposed claim construction;
(f) an indication of the facts relied on;
(g) the evidence relied on, where available, and an indication of any further evidence which will be offered in support;
(h) an indication of any orders that the claimant will seek at the interim conference;
(i) if the claimant assesses the claim to be worth more than €500,000, an indication of the value of the claim;
(j) a list of the documents referred to in the Statement for a declaration, including any witness statements. This should include any request that all or part of those documents need *not* be translated and/or an application that material should be made available to the applicant and not subject to confidentiality protection (see Chapter 16).[19]

In addition to the above, the claimant should provide a copy of each of the documents referred to in the statement for a declaration of non-infringement.

ii. Statement of Defence, and Counterclaim

The defence to a statement for a declaration of non-infringement must be lodged within two months of service of the statement.[20] The contents of the defence reflect in large part those in a defence to an infringement claim:[21]

(a) the names of the defendant and the defendant's representative;
(b) the postal and electronic addresses for service on the defendant, and the names and addresses of the persons authorised to accept service;
(c) the action number of the file;
(d) an indication as to whether the defendant has lodged a preliminary objection;[22]
(e) an indication of the facts relied on, including any challenge to the facts relied on by the claimant;
(f) the evidence relied on,[23] if it is available, and an indication of any further evidence which will be offered in support;
(g) the reasons why the action must fail, including arguments of law, any challenge to the claimant's proposed claim construction and any argument relating to rights based on prior use of the invention;[24]
(h) an indication of any order that the defendant will seek in respect of the declaration of non-infringement action during the interim procedure;[25]

---

[19] Further to Rule 262.2 and 262A of the Rules of Procedure.
[20] ibid Rule 67.
[21] ibid Rule 68. The contents set out in Rule 24(a)-(j).
[22] Further to ibid Rule 19.
[23] See ibid Rule 170.1.
[24] Further to Article 28 UPC Agreement.
[25] See Rule 104(e) of the Rules of Procedure.

(i) a statement of whether the defendant disputes the claimant's assessment of the value of the declaration of non-infringement action and the grounds for that dispute.

I. Reply to the Defence to the Statement for a Declaration of Non-infringement and a Rejoinder to the Reply

The claimant may lodge a Reply to the Defence to the Statement for a declaration of non-infringement. This must be lodged within one month of service of the Defence.[26] The defendant may lodge a Rejoinder to the Reply within one month of service of the Reply. The Rejoinder must be limited to the matters raised in the Reply.[27]

J. 'Torpedo' Non-infringement Actions

The 'Torpedo' action, which is a feature of the European patent system (see Chapter 7 for more on this), may remain a possibility in the new system in certain circumstances. Article 29 of the Brussels Regulation requires a court not first seised to stay its proceedings pending a decision on jurisdiction by the court that is first seised. During the transitional period, a national court first seised with a declaration of non-infringement of a non-opted-out patent may potentially frustrate a counterparty that wants to proceed with an infringement action in the UPC[28] (see also Chapter 8).

K. Actions for the Revocation and Declaration of Non-infringement

An action for revocation may be lodged in the central division together with an action for a declaration of non-infringement if it relates to the same patent and is between the same parties.[29] The consequences for the forum in which these actions are heard if an infringement action is lodged within three months or after three months of the lodging of the declaration of non-infringement action are discussed in Chapter 9.

III. Actions against Decisions of the EPO

There are two kinds of actions that may be brought in the UPC seeking to challenge a decision of the EPO. The first category of action is available to any party that can demonstrate that it has been adversely affected by a decision of the EPO made when carrying out its tasks

---

[26] ibid Rule 69.1.
[27] ibid Rule 69.2.
[28] It remains to be resolved whether such a national action prevents all designations of the European Patent being determined for infringement or non-infringement between the same parties, or whether the UPC may proceed with such an action for all designations of the European patent except that seised in the national action (see ch 7).
[29] Rule 77 of the Rules of Procedure.

under Article 9 UP Regulation. The second category is actions brought by a proprietor of a patent for which the EPO has refused unitary effect.

A. Further to an Article 9 Decision (Article 9 Actions)

Actions may be brought *ex parte* in the UPC to annul or alter decisions made by the EPO when carrying its tasks under Article 9 UP Regulation on the grounds that:[30]

(a) it has infringed the UP Regulation and/or the Translation Regulation, or a rule of law relating to their application;
(b) it has infringed any of the implementing rules of the EPO for carrying out the tasks referred to in Article 9(1) UP Regulation;
(c) it has infringed an essential procedural requirement; or
(d) it has misused its power.[31]

Subject to the possibility of an expedited action against the EPO, an Article 9 action comprises a written procedure, during which the EPO may conduct an interlocutory review, an interim procedure and an oral procedure.[32] An Article 9 action will have the effect of suspending the EPO action concerned.[33]

i. The Content of the Application

Applications for Article 9 actions must be made at the Registry within two months of service of the EPO decision disputed. They must be in the language in which the patent concerned was granted[34] and must contain:[35]

(a) the names of the claimant and, where applicable, their representative;
(b) in cases in which the applicant is not the proprietor or applicant for the Unitary Patent concerned, evidence that they have been adversely affected by the EPO decision being disputed and are entitled to start proceedings;[36]
(c) the postal and electronic addresses for service on the claimant, and the names and addresses of the persons authorised to accept service on their behalf;
(d) reference to the decision of the EPO that is disputed;

---

[30] ibid Rule 87.
[31] Although the grounds for an action under (a), (c) and (d) are broader than those under (b), it appears that they are limited to matters concerning decisions taken under Article 9(1). The preceding Rule 85 and the heading to Chapter 1, Section 6 of the Rules of Procedure suggest the grounds are so limited, rather than providing a general power of judicial review for actions taken by the EPO.
[32] Rule 85.1 of the Rules of Procedure.
[33] ibid Rule 86.
[34] ibid Rule 88.1.
[35] ibid Rule 88.2.
[36] See Article 47(7) UPC Agreement. An explanatory note to the changes made by the Legal Group of the Preparatory Committee in the 17th draft Rules of Procedure, states that it is only in these cases that the claimant has to give an additional explanation and evidence that they are adversely affected by the decision of the EPO and are entitled to start proceedings.

Actions against Decisions of the EPO 179

(e) the details of any other action relating to the patent that is pending before the UPC, the EPO or any other court or authority;
(f) an indication of whether the dispute may be heard by a single judge;
(g) the order or remedy sought;
(h) one or more of the grounds relied on for the alteration or nullity of the EPO decision;
(i) the facts, evidence and arguments that are relied on; and
(j) a list of the documents referred to in the application, including witness statements – requests that a document or part of it need not be translated should be included, together with any request that information recorded at the Registry is excluded from the public.[37]

A minimum fee of €11,000 is payable (see Chapter 20).

ii. Checking by the Registry

As soon as practicable after it has been lodged, the Registry will check that the application contains the matters above, that the fee has been paid, that the parties are entitled to make the application as persons affected by the EPO decision at issue[38] and that it is in the language of grant of the patent concerned.[39] If any of these requirements have not been complied with, the claimant must rectify them within 14 days of notification to the deficiencies, including, where relevant, payment of the fee. If the deficiencies or the payment are not made in this time, a decision may be entered in default (see Chapter 14).[40]

If the requirements of the application for an Article 9 action are satisfied, the Registry will, as soon as practicable, record the date on which the application was received and assign it an action number, and will inform the claimant of these. The application will then be sent to the EPO as admissible.[41]

iii. Interlocutory Revision by the EPO

Having received the application, the EPO may decide that the application to annul or alter the relevant decision is well founded. If this is the case, the EPO will rectify the decision in accordance with the order or remedy sought by the claimant and will inform the UPC.[42] The Court will inform the claimant that the matter is closed and may order full or partial reimbursement of the fee paid for the application.[43]

---

[37] Rule 262.2 and 262A of the Rules of Procedure. The judge-rapporteur must decide in any of these requests as soon as practicable after they have been designated.
[38] Article 47(7) UPC Agreement.
[39] ibid Article 49(6).
[40] Rule 89.3 of the Rules of Procedure. Rule 89.4 adds that any default decision will be made by the President of the Court of First Instance and that the claimant may have the opportunity of being heard. The claimant has the opportunity to apply to set aside the default decision further to Rule 356.
[41] ibid Rule 90.
[42] ibid Rule 91.1.
[43] ibid Rule 91.2.

iv. The Procedure if No Revision by the EPO

a. Written Procedure

After the expiry of the one-month period from receipt of the application, if the Article 9 action is not closed, it will be assigned to a panel of the central division, or a single judge if requested by the claimant in the application.[44] A judge-rapporteur will then examine the application and may invite the claimant to file further proceedings according to a specified time limit.[45]

b. Interim Procedure

The judge-rapporteur may consult with the claimant regarding the date and time of an interim conference.[46] The President of the EPO may, at their own request or the initiative of the judge-rapporteur, provide comments on any question arising in the Article 9 action and any appeal,[47] and the claimant will be entitled to submit their observations on the President's comments.[48] The judge-rapporteur will ask the claimant if they wish to have an oral hearing or may convene a hearing on their own initiative.[49]

c. Oral Procedure

After the closure of the interim proceedings, the presiding judge takes over the management of the action, having consulted with the judge-rapporteur.[50] If there is an oral hearing, it will be open to the public,[51] and the panel will endeavour to give its decision within six weeks of the oral hearing, giving reasons for doing so.[52] Where there is no oral hearing, the panel will make its decision based on the written pleadings and any evidence.[53]

Parties to an Article 9 action must bear their own costs.[54]

IV. Actions against the EPO for a Refusal of Unitary Effect (Actions to Annul)

Applications to annul a decision by the EPO to reject a request for unitary effect must be lodged at the Registry[55] by the proprietor of the patent concerned. The application must be in the language of grant and lodged within three weeks of service of the EPO's decision. It

---

[44] ibid Rule 92.
[45] ibid Rule 93.1.
[46] ibid Rule 93.2.
[47] Under ibid Rule 220.
[48] ibid Rule 94.
[49] Rule 95.
[50] ibid Rules 110.3 and 111.
[51] ibid Rule 115.
[52] ibid Rule 118.6.
[53] ibid Rules 96.2 and 117.
[54] ibid Rule 98.
[55] Rule 97.1.

must contain the same information as for an Article 9 action except that evidence that the proprietor has been adversely affected, and details of any other actions relating to the patent, are not required. Likewise, a list of the documents referred to in the application, including witness statements and requests that a document or part of a document need not be translated, together with any request that information recorded at the Registry as excluded from the public should be accessible, are not required.[56] The action to annul will be allocated to the central division branch responsible for the subject matter of the patent.[57] A fee of €1,000 is payable (see Chapter 20).

Provided that the above requirements have been complied with, the Registry will, as soon as practicable, record the date on which the application was received and will assign it an action number and inform the claimant of these. The application will then be sent to the EPO as admissible.[58] It will also be sent to the standing judge, who will invite the President of the EPO to comment on it, but in any event, the application will be decided within three weeks of the date of its receipt.

The decision of the standing judge may be appealed by the proprietor of the patent or the President of the EPO by lodging of a statement of appeal within three weeks of the service of the decision. The Statement of appeal must contain the particulars lodged with the application together with the reasons for setting aside the decision. A fee is payable. If the requirements of the Statement of appeal are complied with, the Registry will record the appeal and assign it to the standing judge of the Court of Appeal. The standing judge may invite the other party to comment on the appeal, but in any event will decide it within three weeks of receipt by the Registry of the statement of appeal.[59] The Registry will as soon as practicable notify the EPO of decisions made on the above application or appeal.[60]

Parties to an action to annul must bear their own costs.[61]

---

[56] Rule 97.2.
[57] According to Article 7(2) and Annex II UPC Agreement.
[58] Rule 90 of the Rules of Procedure applies.
[59] ibid Rule 97.5.
[60] ibid Rule 97.6.
[61] ibid Rule 98.

13

The Interim Procedure and Case Management

The second procedural stage in the UPC, following the closure of the written procedure, is the interim procedure. The focus of the interim procedure is the interim hearing, which allows the judge-rapporteur to establish the direction and scope of the proceedings ready for the oral hearing. It is also the period in which any decision under Article 33(3) is made (see Chapter 9). In addition to decisions made during the interim procedure, the Court has a number of specific case management powers, which it is entitled to exercise at the interim conference or at any other time. The interim procedure and case management powers are discussed in this chapter.

I. The Interim Procedure

A. Closure of the Written Procedure

After the exchange of written pleadings, the judge-rapporteur must inform the parties of the date on which the written procedure will be closed[1] and must either confirm the date and time for the interim conference or inform the parties that an interim conference will not be held.[2] However, further written pleadings may be permitted upon a reasoned request and within a specified time limit if the request is made before the date for closing the written procedure.[3] In these circumstances, the written procedure will close at the end of the specified time period.

B. Transfer of Actions Further to Article 33(3)

As soon as practicable after the closure of the written procedure, and in appropriate cases (see Chapter 9), the panel decides, having heard the parties, whether infringement and revocation actions will be bifurcated or heard together, setting out brief reasons in an order.[4] However, this decision is made by the panel of the division where the infringement action is lodged and not by the judge-rapporteur. As such, it is apparently separate from any interim conference.

---

[1] Rule 35(a) of the Rules of Procedure.
[2] ibid Rule 35(b).
[3] ibid Rule 36.
[4] ibid Rule 37.1. The panel may make an earlier decision if appropriate on the basis of the pleadings and having heard the parties (Rule 37.2).

i. A Stay of Infringement Further to an Article 33(3)(b) Decision

The panel of the division where the infringement action is lodged will decide, in circumstances where it decides to proceed in accordance with Article 33(3)(b), whether the action should be stayed.[5] The panel may decide at its discretion to stay the proceedings, and must stay the proceedings where there is a high likelihood that the relevant claims of the patent in dispute will be held invalid in revocation proceedings or by the EPO (where the EPO may be expected to do so rapidly) (see Chapter 2).[6]

ii. The Procedure Further to an Article 33(3)(a) and (b) Decision

If a revocation action remains in the regional or local division further to a decision under Article 33(3)(a), a technical judge is appointed.[7] In cases where a revocation counterclaim is referred to the central division further to Article 33(3)(b), it is designated to a panel (or a single judge at the parties' request)[8] at the appropriate seat (Paris, Munich or the city that will replace London in respect of human necessities subject matter),[9] one member of which will be designated the judge-rapporteur.[10] At this stage, the language may be changed to the language of grant,[11] and times are set for the interim conference and oral hearing.[12] If the infringement action is not stayed, the judge-rapporteur of the local or regional division concerned communicates the dates set for the interim conference and oral hearing to the central division.[13] The judge-rapporteur of the central division concerned gives any necessary directions for the future conduct of the written procedure before the central division[14] and must endeavour to accelerate proceedings so that the oral hearing of the revocation action is prior to the date of the infringement action.[15] The judge-rapporteur must also accelerate proceedings before the central division if an application for provisional measures has been lodged.[16]

iii. The Procedure Further to an Article 33(c) Decision

In cases where an infringement claim and a revocation counterclaim are both referred to the central division further to Article 33(3)(c), the case is designated to a panel (or a single judge at the parties' request)[17] at the appropriate seat (Paris, Munich or the city that will

---

[5] ibid Rule 37.4.
[6] ibid Rule 118.2(b).
[7] ibid Rule 37.3.
[8] ibid Rule 38(a), by reference to Rules 17.2.
[9] ibid Rule 38(a), by reference to Rules 17.3.
[10] ibid Rule 38(b).
[11] As directed by the judge-rapporteur, by lodging within one month a translation of any written pleading and other documents, or excerpts of them (ibid Rule 39.2), lodged during the written procedure (Rule 39.1).
[12] ibid Rule 13(d).
[13] ibid Rule 37.5.
[14] ibid Rule 38(c).
[15] ibid Rule 40(b).
[16] ibid Rule 40(a).
[17] ibid Rule 38(a), by reference to Rules 17.2.

184 *The Interim Procedure and Case Management*

replace London in respect of human necessities subject matter),[18] one member of which will be designated the judge-rapporteur.[19] Any dates already set by the judge-rapporteur of the local or regional division from which the action has been transferred must be confirmed wherever possible[20] and the judge-rapporteur of the central division will give any further directions necessary for the future conduct of the action.[21] The language of proceedings may be changed to the language of grant.[22]

C. The Purpose of the Interim Procedure

The purpose of the interim procedure is for the judge-rapporteur to make all the necessary preparations for the oral hearing. The judge-rapporteur has, where appropriate, the discretion to hold one or more interim conferences during this period; such discretion is 'subject to the mandate of the panel'.[23] The interim procedure should be completed within three months of closure of the written procedure, but this is subject to the principal of proportionality,[24] suggesting that in large and complex cases, longer periods may be appropriate.

D. Preparation for the Interim Conference

In preparation for an interim conference, the judge-rapporteur may also order the parties to provide further clarification on specific points, answer specific questions, produce evidence and lodge specific documents, including each party's summary of the orders they seek at the interim conference.[25]

E. The Interim Conference

The interim conference is intended to establish the following matters or make the following orders that are necessary for the oral hearing.[26] Whilst an interim conference will not always be ordered, it is presumed that if any of the following matters are relevant to a case, but not already agreed by the parties, an interim hearing will be necessary:

(a) the main issues and which relevant facts are in dispute;
(b) where appropriate, the position of the parties as regards those issues and facts;

---

[18] ibid Rule 38(a), by reference to Rules 17.3.
[19] ibid Rule 41(b).
[20] ibid Rule 41(c).
[21] ibid Rule 41(e).
[22] ibid Rule 41(d); lodging within one month a translation of any written pleading and other documents, or excerpts of them (Rule 39.2), lodged during the written procedure (Rule 39.1).
[23] ibid Rule 101.1. The meaning of this is unclear, but it may simply indicate that there may be circumstances in which the panel assigned to an action has decided otherwise.
[24] ibid Rule 101.3.
[25] ibid Rule 103.1. The words 'in particular' in Rule 103 are intended to make it clear that (a)–(d) is a non-exhaustive list of case management powers (see also the powers listed in Rule 9).
[26] ibid Rule 104 of the Rules of Procedure.

(c) deciding a schedule for the further progress of the proceedings;
(d) exploring the possibility of settling the dispute or using the facilities of the Patent Mediation and Arbitration Centre;[27]
(e) making the appropriate orders regarding the production of further pleadings, documents, experts (including court experts), experiments, inspections, further written evidence, the matters to be the subject of oral evidence and the scope of questions to be put to the witnesses;
(f) in the presence of the parties, holding preparatory discussions with witnesses and experts with a view to properly preparing for the oral hearing;
(g) making any other decision or order as deemed necessary for the preparation of the oral hearing, including, after consultation with the presiding judge, an order for a separate hearing of witnesses and experts before the panel;
(h) setting a date for any separate hearing pursuant to (g) above, confirm the date for the oral hearing and order, where appropriate, after consultation with the presiding judge and the parties that the oral hearing or a separate hearing of witnesses and experts be wholly or partly by video conference in accordance with Rule 112.3 (see Chapter 14);
(i) deciding the value of the particular dispute;
(j) ordering the parties to submit a preliminary estimate of the legal costs that they will seek to recover.[28]

Where practicable, it is to be held by telephone conference or video conference[29] and in any language agreed by the parties, where that differs from the language of proceedings (see Chapter 14).[30] The matters to be established in the interim procedure, by interim hearing or otherwise, are wide-ranging. They are aimed at educating the judge-rapporteur about the issues in dispute so that the necessary orders can be made for the timetable of proceedings, including the oral hearing. Importantly, the judge-rapporteur is able to order a separate hearing of expert and factual witnesses. Other important dates prior to the oral hearing are the service of expert opinion and other evidence, including (where relevant) inspections and experiments, and the matters they will cover. However, in addition to scheduling a

---

[27] Further to the second meeting of the Administrative Committee of the Unified Patent Court on 8 July 2022, the Organisational Rules of this Centre, to be set up with seats in Ljubljana and Lisbon, were agreed: https://www.unified-patent-court.org/sites/default/files/ac_06_08072022_rules_of_operation_mediation_arbitration_centre_en_final_for_publication.pdf.

[28] An explanatory note to the changes made by the Legal Group of the Preparatory Committee in the 17th draft of the Rules of Procedure states that in connection with Rule 118.6, 2nd sentence, which provides that parties should submit (in advance of the Court's decision on the merits) a preliminary estimate of the legal costs that they intend to seek to recover, the new Rule 104(j) clarifies at what stage of the proceedings parties may be ordered by the judge-rapporteur to submit such a preliminary estimate.

[29] Rule 105.1 of the Rules of Procedure. The interim conference may be held in court on the request of a party, in which case it will be open to the public unless the Court decides otherwise (Rule 105.2). An explanatory note to the changes made by the Legal Group of the Preparatory Committee in the 17th draft of the Rules of Procedure states that Rule 105.1 is intended to reinforce that the interim conference should, where practicable, be held by telephone conference or by video conference, saving time and means especially for those parties who would need to travel long distance to attend. It is a matter for the judge-rapporteur to assess whether the use of these means of electronic communications are practicable in the particular case. Rule 105.2 then clarifies that holding the interim conference in court is the exception to this general rule. The Rule is consistent with Article 44 UPC Agreement, which provides that the Court shall make 'best use of electronic procedures … such as video conferencing'.

[30] Rule 105.3 of the Rules of Procedure.

timetable, the Rules of Procedure also envisage that preparatory discussions with witnesses and experts will take place. The purpose of such discussions is unclear, but may be intended to clarify on which technical matters there is actually a material difference of opinion (see Chapter 16).

The directions and other decisions made by the judge-rapporteur will be set out in an order following the interim hearing.[31] If a party fails to comply with such an order, the judge-rapporteur may give a decision in default.[32]

F. Acceleration of Proceedings

It is the responsibility of the judge-rapporteur during the interim procedure to accelerate revocation proceedings before the central division if an application for provisional measures has been lodged, or where a counterclaim for revocation has been referred to the central division under Article 33(3)(b) and the infringement action has not been stayed.[33] In the latter case, the judge-rapporteur must endeavour to set a date for the oral hearing that is prior to the oral hearing of the infringement action.

G. The Closure of the Interim Procedure

The interim procedure ends when the judge-rapporteur is satisfied that the case is adequately prepared for the oral hearing and has informed the parties and the presiding judge of this fact.[34] It is deemed closed on the last date directed for an action to take place in the interim procedure.[35] The oral procedure then commences immediately and the presiding judge, in consultation with the judge-rapporteur, takes over the management of the case.[36]

II. Case Management Powers

A. General Case Management Powers

At the outset of the Rules of Procedure, a number of general powers of the court are set out in Rule 9. These include the power of the court, at any stage of the proceedings of its own motion or at a reasoned request of a party, to order any party to take a step, answer any question or provide any clarification or evidence, within time limits specified by the court;[37] to

---

[31] ibid Rule 105.5.
[32] ibid Rule 103.2. The Rule clarifies that a decision in default may be given in response to the failure of a party to comply with an order of the judge-rapporteur during the interim procedure.
[33] ibid Rule 40(b).
[34] ibid Rule 110.1.
[35] ibid Rule 110.2.
[36] ibid Rule 110.3.
[37] ibid Rule 9.1.

disregard any step, fact, evidence or argument which a party has not taken or submitted in accordance with a time limit set by the court or the Rules;[38] and, with certain exceptions,[39] to extend (including retrospectively) or shorten time periods.[40]

In particular, the judge-rapporteur is vested with a number of specific case management powers, which they are entitled to exercise at the interim conference or at any other time,[41] either on their own initiative or on the application of a party:[42]

(a) extend or shorten the period for compliance with any rule, practice direction or order;[43]
(b) adjourn or bring forward the interim conference or the oral hearing;
(c) communicate with the parties to instruct them about the wishes or requirements of the Court;
(d) direct a separate hearing of any issue;
(e) decide the order in which issues are to be decided;
(f) exclude an issue from consideration;
(g) dismiss or decide on a claim after a decision on a preliminary issue makes a decision on further issues that are irrelevant to the outcome of the action;
(h) dismiss a claim summarily if it has no prospect of succeeding;
(i) consolidate any matter or issue or order them to be heard together.

In addition to these general powers, during the interim procedure, the judge-rapporteur may order the parties to do the following, whether or not in preparation for an interim conference: provide further clarification on specific points; answer specific questions; produce evidence; and lodge specific documents including each party's summary of the orders to be sought at the interim conference.[44]

Cases may be heard together where more than one action concerning the same patent (whether or not between the same parties) is pending before different panels (in the same or different divisions or in the Court of Appeal), and where it is in the interests of the proper administration of justice and of avoiding conflicting decisions to do so. Such hearing of actions together must be by agreement of the relevant panels, after hearing the parties, and at any time, on account of the connection between them.[45] Such cases may be subsequently disjoined. See also Chapter 9 concerning multiple parties.

Case management decisions or orders made by the judge-rapporteur or the presiding judge of the panel, including those made during the interim procedure,[46] must be reviewed on a reasoned application by a party.[47] The application for review must be lodged within

---

[38] ibid Rule 9.2.
[39] ibid Rule 9.4. The exceptions are in respect of: revocation of an order to preserve evidence (Rule 198.1); revocation of provisional measures (Rule 213.1); and filing a Statement of Appeal (Rule 224.1).
[40] ibid Rule 9.3.
[41] The case management powers are set out in ibid Rule 334.
[42] ibid Rule 336. The court must hear the parties before making a decision on its own initiative (see Rule 337).
[43] See also ibid Rule 9.3.
[44] ibid Rules 103–09.
[45] ibid Rule 340. Note that although the Rule refers to 'joinder', it provides for cases to be heard together rather than the formal joining of the parties together in a single action.
[46] ibid Rule 102.
[47] ibid Rule 333.1.

15 days of service of the order, together with the fee, and must set out the grounds for review and the evidence (if any) in support of the grounds. The other party must be given the opportunity to be heard on the application.[48] The application must be decided as soon as practicable by the panel and, if necessary, any revised case management order must be made.[49] The decision of the panel may be appealed.[50] The court also has the power to vary or revoke its own case management orders.[51]

B. Leave to Change a Claim or Amend a Case

A party may apply to the Court for leave to change its claim or to amend its case, including adding a counterclaim, during the interim procedure or at any stage of the proceedings, provided that the applicant can satisfy the court that the amendment in question could not have been made with reasonable diligence at an earlier stage and that it will not unreasonably hinder the other party in the conduct of its action.[52] However, leave to limit a claim in a dispute unconditionally will always be granted.[53] The court may also reconsider any fees already paid in the light of an amendment.[54]

C. Preliminary Reference to the CJEU

During the interim procedure or at any other stage of the proceedings, if the relevant judge-rapporteur or panel considers that a question raised should be ruled upon by the CJEU, the Court of First Instance may, and the Court of Appeal must, refer the question to the CJEU, following the Rules of the CJEU.[55] The Court may also request the CJEU to use its expedited procedure, in which case the request must set out the matters of fact and law which establish the urgency of the reference and the reasons why an expedited ruling is appropriate.[56] The Registrar must as soon as practicable forward the request and any request for the expedited procedure to the Registrar of the CJEU.[57] The Court may stay the proceedings pending a ruling, but must not give a judgment until the CJEU has given a ruling on the question referred.[58]

---

[48] ibid Rule 333.2.
[49] ibid Rule 333.4.
[50] Further to ibid Rule 220.2.
[51] ibid Rule 335.
[52] ibid Rule 263.1 and 263.2. It is also implicit in paragraph 2 of the Preamble to the Rules of Procedure that the principles of fairness and equity should prevent any such amendment being made so late that the opposing party is unfairly prejudiced by it.
[53] ibid Rule 263.3.
[54] ibid Rule 263.4.
[55] ibid Rule 266.1 and 266.2.
[56] ibid Rule 266.3.
[57] ibid Rule 266.4.
[58] ibid Rule 266.5.

14

Oral Procedure, Final Decision and Early Termination

The oral procedure is primarily concerned with the conduct of the oral hearing or hearings[1] that will decide the case on its merits. Preparations for the oral hearing will have been made by the judge-rapporteur in the interim proceedings and it is essentially concerned with the hearing of the parties' oral submissions. If ordered, witnesses and experts may also be heard,[2] unless a separate hearing for these has been scheduled during the interim procedure (see Chapter 13). This chapter outlines the oral procedure and the decision on the merits that would normally follow. The possibility of the early termination of an action is also discussed.

I. Oral Procedure

A. Timing of the Oral Hearing

The judge-rapporteur summons the parties with at least two months' notice, unless an earlier time period is agreed by the parties,[3] of the date set for the oral hearing. The date for the oral hearing will have been set as soon as practicable after service of the statement of defence[4] and confirmed after the interim hearing.[5] The presiding judge will endeavour to complete the oral hearing within one day and time limits may be imposed on the parties' oral submissions in order to achieve this.[6] The oral hearing and any separate hearing of oral evidence will be open to the public unless it has been ordered otherwise in the interest of one or both parties, a third party or the general interests of justice and public order.[7] Oral hearings are also audio-recorded.

---

[1] If an oral hearing of evidence is heard separately.
[2] Note that a witness may give evidence in a language other than that of the proceedings with the consent of the court (Rule 112.6 of the Rules of Procedure).
[3] ibid Rule 108.
[4] ibid Rule 28.
[5] ibid Rule 104(h) – and, in cases where Article 33(3)(c) UPC Agreement applies, after the action has been transferred to the central division.
[6] Rule 113.1 of the Rules of Procedure. Oral submissions may be further limited if the presiding judge, having consulted with the panel, has been sufficiently informed of the party's case (Rule 113.3).
[7] ibid Rule 115.

B. The Presence of the Parties and Representatives

The absence of a party from the oral hearing does not oblige the court to delay any step in the procedure or its decision on the merits.[8] Instead, a party that is not represented will be treated as relying only on its written case.[9] However, the oral hearing may be adjourned upon a reasoned request by a party that is prevented from being represented at the oral hearing due to an 'exceptional occurrence'.[10] If both parties have informed the Registry that they do not wish to be represented at the oral hearing, the court will make its decision on the merits on the basis of the written documents submitted by the parties and any court-appointed expert.[11]

C. Questioning

The presiding judge and the panel may provide a preliminary introduction to the case and put their own questions to the parties, including their representatives, and to any witness of fact and expert.[12] Under the control of the presiding judge, the parties may themselves put questions to the witnesses and/or experts, but these must be designed to elicit admissible evidence.[13] They are also limited to the issues that were identified by the judge-rapporteur or presiding judge as requiring oral evidence.[14] In 'exceptional cases', the court may order an adjournment and call for further evidence.[15]

D. Simultaneous Interpretation

With the consent of the court, a witness may give evidence in a language other than the language of proceedings.[16] Consequently, a request may be made for the use of simultaneous

---

[8] ibid Rule 116.2. A party that does not wish to be represented at the oral hearing must inform the Registry in 'good time' (Rule 116.1).

[9] ibid Rule 116.3. An explanatory note to the changes made by the Legal Group of the Preparatory Committee in the 17th draft of the Rules of Procedure states that a balance is sought between, on the one hand, the need to protect a (duly summoned) party absent from an oral hearing against new submissions made by the other party during the oral hearing and, on the other hand, the need of the panel to bring proceedings to an end and reach a decision on the merits despite the absence of the party. Rule 116.3 intends to ensure that a (duly summoned but absent) party is treated as relying only on its written case, but it is not implied that the absent party will not wish to contest a new submission made by the other party at the oral hearing. It is within the discretion of the court whether to admit new submissions in the proceedings and – if they are admitted – whether they are of such relevance for the decision that the oral hearing should be adjourned so that the party absent from the oral hearing shall be given an opportunity to be heard. However, in line with Rule 355.1(b), Rule 116.5 clarifies that Rule 116 does not prevent the court from giving a decision by default against a party which has been duly summoned to the oral hearing, but has failed to appear.

[10] ibid Rule 116.4.
[11] ibid Rule 117.
[12] ibid Rule 112.4.
[13] ibid Rule 112.5.
[14] ibid Rule 113.2. There is no stipulation as to whether this questioning must be open or whether it may be leading. Consequently, cross-examination is possible, but the constraints on time and the fact that the scope of questions to be put to witnesses and experts is agreed during the interim procedure mean that cross-examination of witnesses is limited in scope compared to common law jurisdictions.
[15] ibid Rule 114.
[16] ibid Rule 112.6.

interpretation during proceedings. This must be lodged at the latest one month before the hearing of oral submissions and oral evidence[17] and must contain an indication of the language to or from which the simultaneous interpretation is required, the reasons it is requested, the field of technology that the evidence concerns and any other information of relevance.[18]

If the judge-rapporteur considers simultaneous interpretation to be appropriate, the Registry will be instructed to make arrangements. If the judge-rapporteur refuses to order simultaneous translation, the parties may request arrangements to be made at their own cost, or they can engage their own interpreter at their own cost.[19] Alternatively, the judge-rapporteur may order simultaneous translation on their own initiative.[20]

E. The Panel Sitting on an Oral Hearing

i. The Regional, Local and Central Divisions

An oral hearing is held before a panel of three judges, under the direction of the presiding judge (see Chapter 3).

ii. Allocating a Technically Qualified Judge to the Panel

Any party may apply for a technically qualified judge to be added to the panel, and this application should be made as early as possible during the written procedure.[21] The President of the Court of First Instance must then allocate the technically qualified judge after consulting the judge-rapporteur. The judge-rapporteur may themselves also request a technically qualified judge to be allocated after consulting with the presiding judge and the parties.[22]

F. Video Conferencing

Further to Rule 112.3 of the Rules of Procedure, the relevant panel of the UPC hearing an action may decide to:

(a) allow a party, representative or accompanying person to attend the oral hearing by video conference;
(b) hear a party, witnesses or expert through electronic means, such as video conference; or
(c) hold the oral hearing by video conference if all parties agree or the UPC considers it appropriate to do so due to exceptional circumstances.

---

[17] ibid Rule 109.1.
[18] ibid.
[19] ibid Rule 109.1–109.4. An explanatory note to the changes made by the Legal Group of the Preparatory Committee in the 17th draft of the Rules of Procedure states that Rule 109.5 clarifies that costs for simultaneous interpretation at an oral hearing are, as a general rule, considered as costs of the proceedings which shall be borne by the parties. Rule 109.5 also clarifies that where a party brings an interpreter (as provided for in Rule 109.4), the costs shall be borne by that party.
[20] ibid Rule 109.3.
[21] ibid Rule 33.
[22] ibid Rule 34.

In all cases, oral hearings will be transmitted simultaneously in picture and sound to the court room.[23]

II. The Decision Following an Oral Hearing

A. The Timing of the Decision

The presiding judge will make a decision on the merits as soon as possible after the oral hearing and in writing within six weeks, giving their reasons for doing do.[24] Alternatively, the court may give its decision immediately and provide reasons on a subsequent date.[25]

B. Orders Resulting from the Decision

The court may make the following orders as a result of its decision on the merits (see also Chapters 10, 11 and 18): full or partial revocation of a patent;[26] a permanent injunction;[27] corrective measures;[28] the communication of information;[29] and the publication of its decision.[30]

---

[23] As explained in the Amendments to the text of the UPC draft Rules of Procedure approved by the Preparatory Committee on March 2017 AC/04/08072022_E – ANNEX 1, the use of video-conferencing technology has gained importance during the COVID-19 pandemic and its associated restrictions. This addition to the Rules of Procedure also enables the panels of the UPC to conduct the whole oral hearing by video conference if all parties agree or the relevant panel considers it appropriate to do so in exceptional cases. Such exceptional circumstances could be, for example, travel restrictions or disproportionality (long journeys for short and simple oral proceedings).

[24] ibid Rule 118.6.

[25] ibid Rule 118.7. Following public consultation in 2014, the drafting committee considered the extent to which reasons should be given by the Court of First Instance. The committee was of the view that, particularly where the Court of First Instance hears evidence from witnesses, it should address its findings of fact. To fail to do so, in the committee's view, would make it hard for the Court of Appeal to deal with any appeal. However, it was noted by the committee that it might be more economical for the Court of First Instance to give only short decisions and that requiring reasons on all issues of principle might be insufficiently clear.
Further, at the drafting committee meeting on 14 December 2014, it was agreed that the EPO's practice of very limited decisions requiring referral back should not be emulated by the court. It was considered that where the Court of First Instance is in a position to decide issues and matters of fact (other than those strictly necessary for its decision) that might otherwise be raised on appeal, it should consider the desirability of doing so in the interests of efficiency. To reflect this, the committee agreed to add the words (to what became Rule 118.6) 'The Court shall give reasons for its decision' and to add at (what became) Rule 242.2(b) that: 'It shall not normally be an exceptional circumstance justifying a referral back that the Court of First Instance failed to decide an issue which it is necessary for the Court of Appeal to decide on appeal.'

[26] Rule 118.3 of the Rules of Procedure and Article 65 UPC Agreement.

[27] Further to Article 63 UPC Agreement. An explanatory note to the changes made by the Legal Group of the Preparatory Committee in the 17th draft of the Rules of Procedure states that where the Court finds an infringement of a patent, it will under Article 63 of the Agreement give order of injunctive relief. It is only under very exceptional circumstances that the Court will use its discretion not to give such an order. This follows from Article 25 of the Agreement, which recognises the right to prevent the use of the invention without the consent of the patent proprietor as the core right of the patentee. When exercising the discretion to award an injunction, the Court can also consider the use of alternative measures.

[28] Article 64 UPC Agreement.

[29] ibid Article 67.

[30] ibid Article 80.

C. Subsequent Conditions

An infringement action is pending before a local or regional division in respect of the same parties and the same patent as either a revocation action that is before the central division or an opposition before the EPO. In such a case, the local or regional division may render any decision or order on the merits of the infringement proceedings conditional subsequent to the patent not being held partially or wholly invalid, or under any other terms or conditions.[31] A party held to infringe may therefore provide for the repayment of damages and costs, and damages further to a final injunction, if the patent concerned is later revoked by a decision of the central division or the EPO.[32] A party applying for an order following a final decision of the central division, the Court of Appeal or the EPO must do so within two months of the final decision.[33]

D. Enforcement and Security

Any order following a decision on the merits, including damages and compensation, is only enforceable on the defendant after the claimant has notified the Court which part of the order has been relied on. A certified translation of the order, where applicable, into the language of the contracting Member State of enforcement is also required from the party seeking to rely on it. Both the notice and any certified translation must be served on the defendant by the Registry.[34] The order is then 'directly enforceable'[35] from the date of service in each of the contracting Member States concerned.[36]

A decision or order of the Court may require the payment of a periodic penalty, determined by the Court, by a party that fails to comply with the terms of that order or an earlier order.[37] In cases where such a failure is alleged to have taken place, the court may decide on its own motion or on the application by the other party that the penalty provided for in the order should be paid. It will hear both parties and the order on the penalty payment may be appealed.[38]

---

[31] Rule 118.4 of the Rules of Procedure. A party may also request that an order pursuant to a finding of infringement ceases to be enforceable if the patent is subsequently amended or revoked (Rule 354.2).

[32] See also ch 2 for a discussion of this problem.

[33] Rule 118.4 of the Rules of Procedure. Alternatively, in the appropriate circumstances, the defendant may seek a stay of the infringement action pending the outcome of the revocation or opposition (see Rule 118.2(b)). Decisions and orders may also be subject to the rendering of a security or to an award of damages on application, in circumstances where damage is likely to be incurred if they are subsequently revoked (see Rules 352 and 354.2).

[34] ibid Rule 118.8. In order to enforce a decision, the claimant must provide a certified translation of the decision in the official language of the contracting Member State in which the enforcement is to take place. This is an exception to the general rule that translations do not need to be certified (see Rule 7.2).

[35] ibid Rule 353: 'Enforcement shall take place in accordance with the enforcement procedures and conditions governed by the law if the particular Contracting Member State where enforcement takes place.' The apparent intention is that the decision takes effect as a national decision immediately upon service, but that national procedures must then be followed as they would for a national decision.

[36] The Rules of Procedure do not govern the enforcement of decisions in countries which are not contracting Member States to the UPC Agreement.

[37] Rule 354.3 of the Rules of Procedure.

[38] ibid Rule 354.4. The procedure followed is that provided in Rule 264.

The successful party may be required to give a security (by deposit, bank guarantee or otherwise) to the unsuccessful party for legal costs and other expenses and compensation for any damage likely to be incurred by the other party if the enforced decision is later subsequently revoked.[39] However, a party may also request compensation for any injury caused by the enforcement of an order that has been enforced and subsequently varied or revoked. A party may also request that an order pursuant to a finding of infringement ceases to be enforceable if the patent is subsequently amended or revoked.[40]

E. Damages and Costs in the Decision on the Merits

If requested, the Court may order the payment of damages or compensation (see Chapter 18).[41] The amount of the damages or compensation may be stated in the order or decided in separate proceedings (see Chapter 18). The court may make an interim award of damages in favour of the successful party in the decision on the merits,[42] which should cover at least the expected costs of the procedure for the award of damages. The court must also decide in principle on the obligation to bear costs (see Chapter 18).[43] For this purpose, the parties may be requested to submit a preliminary estimate of the costs that they intend to seek to recover.[44]

III. The Early Termination of Actions

A. Withdrawal

A claimant is at liberty to withdraw an action at any time provided that there has been no final decision.[45] If withdrawal is permitted, the Court must give a decision declaring that the proceedings are closed and order the decision to be entered into the register.[46] However, the withdrawal will have no effect on any counterclaim in the action, but the court may refer a counterclaim for revocation lodged in a local or regional division to be heard in the central division. The court must issue a decision with regard to the costs procedure (see Chapter 15).[47]

---

[39] ibid Rule 352.2. An example of where this may be necessary is in cases where a final injunction is awarded in a bifurcated action, which precedes the decision on revocation of the patent being enforced, or an appeal of the infringement decision. It would follow that local advice on enforcement is required in respect of each country in which enforcement is desired.
[40] ibid Rule 354.2.
[41] ibid Rule 118.1. Damages or compensation will be awarded according to Articles 68 and 32(1)(f) UPC Agreement.
[42] Rule 119 of the Rules of Procedure.
[43] In accordance with Article 69 UPC Agreement.
[44] Rule 118.5 of the Rules of Procedure. A preliminary estimate does not need to be submitted in all cases. See also Rule 104(j), which provides that the judge-rapporteur can order the parties at the interim conference to submit a preliminary estimate during the interim procedure.
[45] ibid Rule 265.1.
[46] ibid Rule 265.2(a) and (b).
[47] ibid Rule 265.2(c).

B. Decision by Default

A decision by default may be given against a defendant to a claim or counterclaim if the time limit for service of the defence to those claims has expired and so it is established that the service of the claim or counterclaim was effected in sufficient time to enable the defendant to enter a defence.[48] However, the remedy sought must be justified by the facts put forward by the claimant in the claim or counterclaim and the procedural conduct of the defendant does not preclude such a decision.[49] A decision by default may be given against other parties if they fail to take a step within the time limit set by the Rules of Procedure or the court,[50] or they have been summoned to an oral hearing but have failed to appear.[51]

An application to set aside a default decision may be made by the party in default against the decision. This must be lodged within one month of service of the decision.[52] The application must be made by reference to the date and number of the default decision, together with payment of the relevant fee, and must explain the default and, if it resulted from the failure to take a certain step, should be accompanied by the taking of that step.[53] An application to set aside a default decision must be allowed[54] unless the party concerned has been put on notice in an earlier decision that a subsequent decision by default will be final.[55]

C. Actions Bound to Fail or Manifestly Inadmissible

There are three categories of action specified by the Rules of Procedure in which a panel may dispose of an action:

(a) on the application of a party or at the court's own motion, at any time, if it decides the action has become devoid of purpose and there is no longer any need to decide it;[56]
(b) the court decides it has no jurisdiction for the action or certain of its claims, it is manifestly inadmissible or it is manifestly lacking any legal basis;[57]
(c) on the application of a party or at the court's own motion, if it decides there is an absolute bar to proceeding with the action.[58]

Orders on the above grounds must be made by the panel responsible for the action on the recommendation of the judge-rapporteur, having given the parties the opportunity to be

---

[48] ibid Rule 355.3.
[49] ibid Rule 355.2.
[50] ibid Rule 355.1(a). The previous draft of the Rules in which the UPC had the power to grant a decision by default whenever a party failed to take a step within the time limit set has been limited by Rule 355.1 to conform with Article 37(1) UPC Statute by specifying the situations where a decision by default may be given against a party.
[51] ibid Rule 355.1(b), subject to Rules 116 and 117.
[52] ibid Rule 356.1.
[53] ibid Rule 356.
[54] In which case a note of allowance will be included in any publication of the decision by default (ibid Rule 356.3).
[55] ibid Rule 356.3.
[56] ibid Rule 360.
[57] ibid Rule 361.
[58] ibid Rule 362. The example is given of the application of the principle of *res judicata*.

heard.[59] Such orders from the Court of First Instance are considered final decisions for the purpose of appeal (see Chapter 17).[60]

D. Settlement

The parties to a dispute are free at any time during the course of proceedings to settle the dispute between them.[61] Indeed, if the Court is of the view that it would be suitable, at any stage of proceedings, it may propose that the parties use the Patent Mediation and Arbitration Centre in order to settle or explore settlement of the dispute.[62] In particular, during the interim procedure and in particular at an interim conference, the judge-rapporteur must explore this possibility or settlement in general. If mediation is explored, limitation periods and other prescribed time limits are suspended.[63]

After a settlement has been reached, the parties must inform the judge-rapporteur and the settlement must be confirmed by a decision of the Court, and may be enforced as such.[64] A settlement may include a term that obliges the patent proprietor to limit surrender or agree to the revocation of the patent, or otherwise not assert it against certain parties.[65] Subject to any order that the details of the settlement are to be kept confidential, the decision of the court on the settlement will be entered into the register.[66] The judge-rapporteur will make a decision about costs in accordance with the terms of the settlement or, if there is no agreement on costs, at their discretion or under the costs procedure.[67]

Except for the purpose of enforcing a settlement agreement, discussions during settlement are without prejudice to proceedings before the court. As such, the opinions expressed, suggestions made, proposals put forward, concessions made or documents drawn up for the purpose of the settlement may not be relied on as evidence by the Court or the parties in proceedings before the Court or any other court.[68]

---

[59] ibid Rule 363.
[60] See ibid Rule 220.
[61] Article 79 UPC Agreement.
[62] The Patent Mediation and Arbitration Centre has yet to be established.
[63] Rule 11.1 of the Rules of Procedure. An explanatory note to the changes made by the Legal Group of the Preparatory Committee in the 17th draft of the Rules of Procedure explains that Rule 11.1 is drafted to recognise that an attempt to settle proceedings must have no negative impact on any rights under rules on limitation or prescription periods under Article 8 of Directive 2008/52/EC.
[64] Rule 365.1 of the Rules of Procedure. Article 82 UPC Agreement on enforcement applies to any settlement reached through the Patent Mediation and Arbitration Centre.
[65] Rule 11.2 of the Rules of Procedure. An explanatory note to the changes made by the Legal Group of the Preparatory Committee in the 17th draft of the Rules of Procedure explains that Rule 11.2 clarifies the type of award that can be enforced as settlement under Article 82 UPC Agreement by specifying that the parties must have consented to the arbitral award. Other arbitral awards are enforced by way of the New York Convention 1958. Following public consultation in 2014, the drafting committee was also of the view that Article 79 UPC Agreement prohibits revocation or limitation by way of settlement, but it is within the court's power to order such limitation or revocation if agreed as part of a settlement.
[66] Rules 365.2 and 365.3 of the Rules of Procedure.
[67] It is not clear whether the judge-rapporteur may use their discretion to decide costs or whether the determination of costs must be submitted to the costs procedure; cf ibid Rules 11.2 and 365.4.
[68] Parties that wish to protect settlement discussions must avoid any expression that these materials are made on an open basis and, for the avoidance of doubt, should be marked 'without prejudice' or 'without prejudice save as to costs', as appropriate.

15

Preliminary Injunctions and Other Provisional Measures

Assessing patent infringement and the validity of a patent involves extensive fact-finding and thorough legal analysis, which requires sufficient time, in particular when relevant documents have to be examined or to be translated into the language of the proceedings. Patentees and licensees may therefore have an interest in the grant of a provisional measure – particularly a preliminary injunction – if they would otherwise suffer significant damages waiting for the outcome of a decision on the merits. A provisional decision can be taken on a summary basis. However, a provisional measure – particularly a preliminary injunction – will have a substantial effect on the business of the defendant. Consequently, the basic legal right to be heard must be respected and there must be effective compensation in the event that a preliminary injunction turns out to have been granted without justified reason, whether because it is overturned upon appeal or because the patent is revoked later on. The procedures of the UPC aim to find a compromise between these two positions in order to ensure efficient protection and sufficient safeguards at the same time. This chapter discusses these procedures.

I. Obtaining a Provisional Measure

A. Competence of the Court

According to Article 32(1)(c) UPC Agreement, the UPC has exclusive competence in respect of, amongst other matters, actions for provisional and protective measures and injunctions. Article 62 explains in more detail which kind of provisional and protective measures the Court can order:[1]

(a) injunctions against a defendant;
(b) the seizure or delivery up of the products suspected of infringing a patent so as to prevent their entry into or movement within the channels of commerce;
(c) if the applicant demonstrates circumstances likely to endanger the recovery of damages, a precautionary seizure of the movable and immovable property of the defendant, including the blocking of their bank accounts or other assets;
(d) an interim award of costs for the above.

---

[1] See also Rule 211.1 of the Rules of Procedure.

The Court has the discretion to order the applicant to provide adequate security for appropriate compensation for any injury likely to be caused to the defendant which the applicant may be liable to bear in the event that the Court revokes the order for provisional measures.[2] The Court is obliged to order an adequate security when provisional measures are granted *ex parte*. The security is to be paid by deposit or bank guarantee. Where a security is ordered, the provisional measure only takes effect after the security has been given to the defendant.[3]

If proceedings on the merits are already pending, only the panel to which the action has been assigned, or the respective single judge, is competent.[4] In urgent cases, where the action has not been assigned to a single judge, it is also possible for the presiding judge or the judge-rapporteur, acting as single judge, to decide on the application.

Insofar as proceedings on the merits are not yet pending, the applicant is free to choose the forum according to the general rules (see Chapter 9). In such cases, a judge-rapporteur is designated or, in urgent cases, the presiding judge may decide that they or an experienced judge, acting as a single judge, may decide the case with a reduced timetable.[5]

B. Proceedings for Obtaining a Provisional Measure

Generally, provisional measures are treated by way of summary proceedings, which consist of a written procedure and an oral procedure.[6] 'Summary proceedings' are a special type of proceedings, both at first and second instance, which do not contain an interim procedure.

i. Application

Provisional measures may be applied for either in parallel to proceedings on the merits or before.[7] The application must contain the following:[8]

(a) the usual mandatory information required for a statement of claim;[9]
(b) an indication of the provisional measures which are being requested;[10]
(c) the reasons why provisional measures are necessary in order to prevent a threatened infringement, to forbid the continuation of an alleged infringement or to make such continuation subject to the lodging of guarantees;

---

[2] Articles 62.5 and 60.7 UPC Agreement and Rule 211.5 of the Rules of Procedure. An explanatory note by the Legal Group of the Preparatory Committee states that despite the general rule that the court must order adequate security when it orders preliminary measures without having heard the opposing party, this need not be provided in special circumstances (the note envisages circumstances where no damage can occur or only a sample of an inexpensive mass product is sought).
[3] Rule 211.5 of the Rules of Procedure.
[4] ibid Rule 208.3.
[5] ibid Rule 208.2.
[6] ibid Rule 205.
[7] ibid Rule 206.1.
[8] ibid Rule 206.2.
[9] ibid Rules 13.1(a)–(i). See ch 10.
[10] ibid Rule 211.1.

(d) the facts and evidence on which the application relies, including evidence for the necessity of provisional measures, such as:
   (i) the applicant's entitlement to commence proceedings,[11]
   (ii) the validity of the patent,[12]
   (iii) the infringement or the fact that infringement is imminent,[13]
   (iv) the interests of both parties that are to be weighed up, in particular the potential harm for either of the parties;[14]
(e) a concise description of the action which will be started before the court, including an indication of the facts and evidence which will be relied on in support of the proceedings on the merits.

If the applicant requests the grant of a provisional measure *ex parte* – that is, without hearing the defendant – the application must also contain the following:[15]

(a) the reasons for not hearing the defendant – in particular, that any delay is likely to cause irreparable harm to the applicant or where there is a demonstrable risk of evidence being destroyed or otherwise ceasing to be available;[16] and
(b) information about any prior correspondence between the parties concerning the alleged infringement.

Such prior correspondence may give important insight to the court, such as the defendant's view of the alleged infringement and potential counter-arguments on infringement or claim construction. In particular, in very urgent cases, the court might be persuaded to hear proceedings *ex parte* if the defendant had the possibility to be heard and to bring forward its arguments, even if this had been done out of court.[17] It is important to note that the applicant has the duty to disclose any material fact known to it which might influence the court in its decision.[18] This especially includes the information about any pending proceedings, whether these are infringement proceedings or proceedings for the declaration of non-infringement, revocation proceedings, opposition proceedings and the like with regard to the same patent(s). It also includes the duty to inform the court about any unsuccessful attempt in the past to obtain provisional measures.

The applicant must also pay the fixed fee for the application.[19] Otherwise, the application is considered as not having been lodged. According to the present fee proposal, the fixed

---

[11] ibid Rules 211.2 and 4.
[12] ibid Rule 211.2.
[13] ibid Rule 211.2.
[14] ibid Rule 211.3.
[15] ibid Rule 206.3.
[16] See also ibid Rule 197.1.
[17] In particular, for example, if the defendant did not respond to correspondence. Hence, defendants receiving any correspondence from rights holders out of court with regard to alleged patent infringement should very carefully consider their answer and be aware of the possibility that such correspondence might favour the granting of a provisional measure to the applicant.
[18] Rule 206.4 of the Rules of Procedure.
[19] ibid Rules 206.5 and 15.

fee will be €11,000 (see Chapter 20). The application has to be written in the language of the main proceedings (see Chapter 5).[20]

ii. Further Proceedings

a. Examination of Formalities

Once an application for provisional measures is lodged, the Registry will examine it for formal requirements[21] and whether a protective brief is recorded in the register. Where main proceedings have not yet been started, the Registry will record the case and assign it to a panel, and the presiding judge will assign the judge-rapporteur.[22] However, in urgent cases, the presiding judge may decide that they or an experienced judge of the panel, acting as single judge, may decide with all the necessary powers of the Court.[23] Where main proceedings are already pending, the application for provisional measures will be forwarded to the panel to which the main action has been assigned[24] (see Chapter 9).

b. The Decision Whether to Hear *Ex Parte*

The court has discretion – including where the application is made *ex parte*[25] – to decide whether:

(a) to inform the defendant about the application and to invite them to lodge an objection within a specified period of time;[26]
(b) to only summon the parties to an oral hearing;[27] or
(c) to summon the applicant to an oral hearing without the presence of the defendant.[28]

Where the defendant is invited to lodge an objection to the application, this must contain:[29] the reasons why the application should fail, the facts and evidence relied on and, in particular, any challenge to the facts and evidence relied on by the applicant. Where proceedings on the merits have not yet been started, reasons should be given why the action to be started will fail, and the facts and evidence for supporting this.[30]

In exercising its discretion as to whether to hear the defendant and whether to summon oral hearings, the Court must in particular 'take into account' whether: the patent has been upheld in an opposition procedure before the EPO or has been the subject of proceedings in

---

[20] ibid Rule 14.
[21] ibid Rules 208.1 and 16.
[22] ibid Rules 17, 18 and Rule 208.2.
[23] ibid Rule 208.2-4.
[24] ibid Rule 208.3.
[25] According to ibid Rule 206.3.
[26] ibid Rule 209.1(a) – and, it is inferred, to summon the parties to an oral hearing.
[27] ibid Rule 209.1(b) – without, it is inferred, prior written objections of the defendant.
[28] ibid Rule 209.1(c).
[29] ibid Rule 209.1(a).
[30] Regarding the defendant's right to be heard in court under Article 56(2), the most reasonable way to proceed – if an *ex parte* injunction is not granted – will be to give the defendant the possibility of an appropriate preparation of their defence by inviting them to file written objections to the application prior to the oral hearing. This in the same way allows the UPC to consider both parties' arguments in preparation of the oral hearing and to further elucidate the factual and legal questions during the oral hearing.

any other court; the urgency of the action; the applicant has requested provisional measures without hearing the defendant; whether the reasons for not hearing the defendant appear well founded; and any protective letter has been filed by the defendant.[31] By way of exception, the court may decide on the application immediately – that is, without scheduling any oral hearing and without hearing the defendant – in cases of extreme urgency.[32]

However, where provisional measures are heard without the defendant present, the court may summon the applicant to an oral hearing and order it to provide further information, documents and other evidence.[33]

If the applicant had applied for provisional measures without hearing the defendant, but the court refuses to exclude the defendant, the applicant may withdraw the application and may request that the court orders that the application and its contents remain confidential.[34] The application may also be withdrawn if it is the subject of a protective letter (see section III below).[35]

c. Oral Hearing

If an oral hearing is scheduled, the date should be set as soon as possible.[36] The court may order the parties to provide further information, documents or other evidence before or during the oral hearing.[37] The general rules on the oral procedure in the case of proceedings on the merits apply.[38] The court must reject the application if the applicant is absent from the oral hearing without reasonable excuse.[39] The decision of the court shall be given in writing as soon as possible. However, if the court deems it appropriate, it may also be given orally first at the end of the oral hearing, followed by the written decision as soon as possible.[40]

C. Grant of Provisional Measures *Ex Parte*

Provisional measures can be granted *inter partes* or *ex parte*. An oral procedure may include an oral hearing of the parties or one of the parties.[41] Similarly, the court has discretion if it wants to hear the defendant[42] (see section I.B.ii.b above).

---

[31] Rules 209.2(a)–(d) of the Rules of Procedure.
[32] ibid Rule 209.3. The term 'extreme urgency' is not defined in the Rules. From the context of Rules 212.1 and 209, it could be argued that extreme urgency is given where any delay is likely to cause irreparable harm to the applicant or where there is a demonstrable risk of evidence being destroyed (see also Articles 62.5 and 60.5 UPC Agreement). However, Rule 209.2 does not explicitly refer to Rule 212.1 or Rule 197.1, which leaves it unclear whether and to what extent cases of extreme urgency indeed overlap with the requirements for granting provisional measures *ex parte* according to Rule 212.1.
[33] Rules 212.2 and 210.
[34] ibid Rule 209.4.
[35] ibid Rule 209.5.
[36] ibid Rule 210.1.
[37] ibid Rule 210.2.
[38] ibid Rules 111–16 (see Rule 210.3).
[39] ibid Rules 210.3.
[40] ibid Rule 210.4.
[41] ibid Rule 205(b).
[42] ibid Rule 209.1.

i. Requirements

Provisional measures may be ordered without the defendant being heard, in particular where any delay is likely to cause irreparable harm to the applicant or where there is a demonstrable risk of evidence being destroyed.[43] The requirements of either 'any delay is likely to cause irreparable harm' or 'where there is a demonstrable risk of evidence being destroyed' correspond to those for an order to preserve evidence without hearing the defendant[44] (see Chapter 16). However, these two conditions do not appear to be mandatory for deciding not to hear the defendant (as opposed to deciding on the order) – the court has the discretion to decide not to hear the defendant even if there is neither irreparable harm nor the risk of evidence being destroyed[45] (see section I.B.ii.b above). However, given the interference with the defendant's procedural rights when they are not heard before the grant of a provisional measure, a similar level of severity in the applicant's case should be required. If ordered *ex parte*, the defendant must be given notice of the provisional measures without delay and at the latest immediately at the time of execution of the measures.[46]

ii. National Perspectives

Currently, German courts generally grant a preliminary measure – in particular, a preliminary injunction – in principle only after oral proceedings. A grant *ex parte* is usually only done in cases of particular urgency. This is, for example, the case when the patent will soon expire or when the infringement only lasts for a short period of time – for example, the defendant offers an infringing product at a fair or is sold. Furthermore, the courts consider any prior comments by the defendants, such as by means of an answer out of court on a warning letter or a protective brief. If the defendant has already commented on the infringement allegation, but the court does not find the arguments to be sufficient, it can grant a preliminary measure without hearing the defendant again in the preliminary proceedings.[47]

In the Netherlands, granting an injunction without hearing the defendant is the exception to the rule that relief is to be obtained in *inter partes* proceedings (called 'kort geding' when it regards provisional measures). The relevant statute provides that the judge is authorised to grant *ex parte* injunctive relief if, in particular, delay would cause irreparable harm to the applicant.[48] The party against which the injunction was issued may use an *inter partes kort geding*, reviewed by the same judge who granted *ex parte* relief, to claim that the injunction be lifted.[49] Decisions refusing applications for *ex parte* relief are normally not

---

[43] ibid Rule 212.1 and Article 60(5) UPC Agreement.
[44] Rule 197.1 of the Rules of Procedure. The requirements in Rules 197.1 and 212.1 should therefore be construed similarly.
[45] It should be noted that the word 'only' in the draft Rule 212.1 as provided by the 17th draft of the Rules of Procedure was deleted in the 18th version. Furthermore, it is not in the wording of Article 60(5) UPC Agreement. Furthermore, these requirements are not amongst the factors the court must consider when exercising its discretion to hear the defendant in Rule 209.2 of the Rules of Procedure.
[46] Rule 212.2 of the Rules of Procedure.
[47] T Kühnen, *Handbuch der Patentverletzung*, n° 2131, 7th edn (Carl Heymanns Verlag KG, 2014).
[48] Article 1019e (1) of the Dutch Code of Civil Procedure (DCCP).
[49] ibid Article 1019e (3) DCCP.

published; only granting decisions are. The latter contains no extensive reasoning regarding infringement and validity. However, it can be inferred from these decisions (of which there have only been a dozen in recent years) that relief is granted only in the case of prima facie infringement of a valid right. This may be the reason why although ex parte injunctive relief is granted regularly based on trade marks, typically in the case of clear counterfeit products, *ex parte* injunctions based on patents are relatively rare. In connection to this, it should be noted that the Dutch courts will not regard a European patent valid on its face just because it has survived opposition proceedings, let alone because of the mere fact it has been granted by the EPO.[50]

For comparison, in English proceedings an application for a preliminary injunction without notice is only to be made in circumstances of exceptional urgency or where secrecy is required. Such relief will be granted on a temporary basis of a few days, to be followed by a hearing of both parties. See, for example, *Warner-Lambert v Teva*,[51] which concerned the launch of generic atorvastatin 'at risk', in which an *ex parte* (as regards the second and third defendants) restraining order was obtained on the same day, until the full injunction application could be heard.

iii. Review upon the Defendant's Request

In cases involving the grant of a provisional measure without hearing the defendant, the defendant may request a review within 30 days after the execution of the measures.[52] Such a request must set out the reasons why the order must be revoked or modified and the facts and evidence relied on. Following the request for review, the UPC must order an oral hearing to review the order without delay.[53] The decision of the Court must be given in writing as soon as possible. However, if the Court deems it appropriate, it may also be given orally first at the end of the oral hearing, followed by the written decision as soon as possible.[54] The order may be modified, revoked or confirmed by the Court.[55]

iv. Refusal of an Application for Provisional Measures Ex Parte

If the applicant has applied for provisional measures without the defendant being heard, but the Court decides not to exclude the defendant, the applicant may withdraw the application and may request the Court to order that the application and the contents are to remain confidential.[56] In such a case, the defendant will not be informed about the application and will not get any notice of it. The applicant remains obliged to pay the necessary court fee.

---

[50] See section I.D.iii below.
[51] *Warner-Lambert Company LLC v Teva UK Ltd and Others* [2011] EWHC 1691 (Pat).
[52] Rules 212.3 and 197.3 of the Rules of Procedure.
[53] ibid Rules 212.3, 197.4 and 195.
[54] ibid Rule 195.3.
[55] ibid Rule 197.4.
[56] ibid Rule 209.4.

D. Substantive Requirements for Provisional Measures: Factors Relevant to the Court's Discretion

With regard to the requirements necessary for the grant of preliminary measures, the agreement only states that they are intended 'to prevent any imminent infringement'.[57] In taking its decision, the court:

- *may* require the applicant to provide reasonable evidence to satisfy the court with a sufficient degree of certainty;
    - (i) that the applicant is entitled to commence proceedings,[58]
    - (ii) that the patent is valid, and
    - (iii) that the patent is being infringed or such infringement is imminent;[59]
- *must* weigh up the interests of the parties – in particular, considering the potential harm for either of the parties resulting from the granting or the refusal of an injunction;[60]
- *must* also have regard to any unreasonable delay in seeking provisional measures.[61]

Hence, the court has a wide discretion to decide whether or not to grant provisional measures, and these factors are considered in more detail below.

The Court may require the applicant to provide reasonable evidence to satisfy it with a sufficient degree of certainty that the applicant is entitled to commence proceedings, that the patent in question is valid and that it is being infringed, or that such infringement is imminent. The application should also contain an indication of the facts and evidence which will be relied on in support of the main proceedings on the merits of the case.[62] Furthermore, the court may order the parties to provide further information, documents and other evidence before or during the oral hearing,[63] to the extent determined by the court[64] (see Chapter 16).

i. Infringement

a. The UPC Approach

The Court *may* require the applicant to provide reasonable evidence that there is an infringement or imminent infringement. This is not obligatory. Already with the request for provisional measures, the applicant has to give a concise description of the action which will be started before the court, including an indication of the facts and evidence which will

---

[57] Article 62 (1) UPC Agreement.
[58] ibid Article 47.
[59] Rule 211.2 of the Rules of Procedure.
[60] Article 62(2) UPC Agreement and Rule 211.3 of the Rules of Procedure. 'Potential harm for either of the parties' is a criterion only given in respect of preliminary injunction rather than the other preliminary measures available. This may not have been intended.
[61] Rule 211.4 of the Rules of Procedure.
[62] ibid Rule 206.2(e).
[63] ibid Rule 210.2.
[64] ibid Rule 210.2 states that: 'Part 2 of these Rules of Evidence shall be applicable only to the extent determined by the court.' It is apparently a reference to 'PART 2 – EVIDENCE' of the Rules of Procedure generally. See also Rule 211.2.

be relied on in support of the main proceedings.[65] The applicant is free to use any of the evidence allowed under the Rules of Procedure.[66] This includes in particular:

(a) any written evidence, whether printed, handwritten or drawn, in particular documents, written witness statements, plans, drawings or photographs;
(b) expert reports and reports on experiments carried out for the purpose of these proceedings;
(c) physical objects – in particular, devices, products, embodiments, exhibits and models;
(d) electronic files and audio/video recordings.

Given the nature of proceedings for the grant of provisional measures, any means of obtaining evidence[67] – in particular, those that imply the hearing of persons, be it the parties, witnesses or experts – is only allowed insofar as the court explicitly orders it.

b. National Perspectives

Comparison with national practice suggests that there is a spectrum of approaches the court can take to the infringement element when considering preliminary measures. At one end of the spectrum, it is possible to have a mini-trial in which it must be shown that the integers of the patent claim relied on are met and that the prospect of the patent being held not invalid at the trial on the merits is negligible, as is the practice in the Netherlands. At the other end of the spectrum is the practice of the English courts, in which there must be shown to be an infringement on the face of the evidence, but this need not be proved.

ii. Urgency

a. The UPC Approach

The court *must* have regard to any 'unreasonable delay in seeking provisional measures'.[68] This requirement is obligatory. On first sight, one might think that a provisional measure could only be granted if it is urgent. However, the avoidance of unreasonable delay may not necessarily correspond to a clear 'urgency' of the case. Even if it does, it is questionable from the wording of the Rules of Procedure whether the party seeking preliminary measures has the burden of explaining that there is no 'unreasonable delay' or whether an unreasonable delay is an exceptional factor that needs to be considered by the court where the facts of the case suggest it or it is substantiated by the defendant, if it is heard at all. The fact that an application for provisional measures does not necessarily need to contain information about the timewise urgency of the case[69] seems to support the latter view.

It is interesting to note that the 'urgency' of the matter as such is not mentioned as a factor in taking the decision.[70] From the wording of the Rules of Procedure, the impression is that the urgency of the measure is a more important factor of consideration when

---

[65] ibid Rule 206.2(e).
[66] As set out in ibid Rule 170.1.
[67] As listed in ibid Rule 170.2.
[68] ibid Rule 211.4.
[69] ibid Rule 206.2(d) only refers to Rule 211.2 and 211.3, but not to Rule 211.4.
[70] It is not one of the factors in ibid Rule 211.2 and 211.3.

deciding whether to inform the defendant about the application and whether or not to summon an oral hearing.[71]

Nonetheless, even if urgency is not mentioned as a positive requirement for the grant of a provisional measure as such,[72] it follows from the weighing of the parties' interests that the Court has to undertake[73] that the applicant has no interest in getting a provisional measure granted if they could wait for the outcome of the proceedings on the merits without suffering a harm that would outweigh the defendant's harm if the provisional measure was granted. It follows from the nature of provisional measures that a request must be urgent because otherwise the defendant's interest to have the possibility to defend in proper proceedings on the merits will always prevail.

b. National Perspectives

In Germany, an applicant has forfeited urgency when having waited too long after knowledge about the infringing act and the infringer. This creates the impression that the applicant is not interested in a rapid enforcement of its claims.[74] Thus, a request for a preliminary injunction is considered urgent if it is filed no later than four weeks to one month after the knowledge.[75] Within Germany, court practices vary, so there are courts, which grant a preliminary injunction even after a longer period than four weeks.[76] The OLG Düsseldorf recently held that 'if the preliminary injunction proceedings are part of a comprehensive, cross-border action against a large number of infringers and if various legal status proceedings are pending with regard to the patent for injunction and/or with regard to parallel IP rights, it must be taken into account in favour of the applicant that such an action regularly requires a coherent enforcement and legal status strategy that also takes into account the differences between individual jurisdictions'.[77]

Knowledge means positive knowledge to an extent that the applicant is able to show the credibility of its claim.[78] Knowledge of an executive employee is sufficient when it is to be expected that they would notify their management.[79] In the same way, the knowledge of a parent company about a patent infringement committed by a third party is attributed to the subsidiary company if the parent company actively exploits the patents while the subsidiary company merely acts as a patent holding company.[80] The applicant is generally not obliged to observe the market on potential infringements.[81] Nevertheless, the applicant has to acknowledge concrete evidence – when an infringement is obvious – and in this case has to further explore the facts. As a general rule, the applicant is allowed to gather all necessary

---

[71] cf ibid Rule 209.2(a)–(d).
[72] In ibid Rule 211.
[73] ibid Rule 211.3 and Article 62(2) UPC Agreement.
[74] OLG Hamburg, GRUR-RR 2008, 366, 367 – *Simplify Your Production*.
[75] Kühnen (n 47) n° 2114.
[76] OLG Frankfurt/ Main, GRUR 2002, 236, 237 – *Eilbedürfnis in Patentsachen*.
[77] OLG Düsseldorf, PharmR 2021, 270 – *Cinacalcet*.
[78] LG München I, decision of 27 August 2003, AZ. 7 O 14788/03.
[79] OLG Frankfurt/Main, NJW 2000, 1961 – *Pfändung einer Domain*; OLG Köln, GRUR-RR 2010, 493 – *Ausgelagerte Rechtsabteulung*; OLG Köln, GRUR-RR 2014, 127 – *Inhalator*.
[80] LG Hamburg, GRUR-RR 2014, 137, 138 – *Koronarstent*.
[81] OLG Köln, GRUR-RR 2014, 82 – *Qualitätssprung*.

facts and means of evidence before initiating preliminary proceedings. In particular, the applicant has a certain discretion to choose the means for exploring the facts – for example, to instruct an external laboratory for checking the internal analysis and even to combine the analysis of different defendants by one laboratory.[82] Even if it should turn out later on that this would not have been necessary, the urgency remains if such analysis seemed useful in an *ex ante* perspective.[83] Once the applicant has all the facts necessary to show the credibility of their claim, the preliminary injunction must be filed within four weeks.

The application may still be urgent when the applicant had longer knowledge, but can only pursue their claims at present due to a change in case law. Nevertheless, urgency is forfeited when preliminary relief is not sought within four weeks after knowledge of the change.[84] The general rule in English proceedings, by comparison, is that a person who asks for a preliminary injunction in order to protect a right until trial should do so promptly. Delay by the claimant after learning of an infringement will therefore be a bar to this form of relief, although the amount of delay will vary according to the nature and circumstances of the case, and the prejudice caused to the defendant.[85]

The applicant may also wait for a final judgment in the nullity proceedings without forfeiting urgency when a preliminary injunction would most likely not have been granted due to a dispute about the patent's validity.[86]

Settlement negotiations will in general not conflict with urgency if the applicant files a preliminary injunction soon after their failure.

Urgency is also required for preliminary relief in the Netherlands. It is standing case law of the Supreme Court of the Netherlands (Hoge Raad) that in the event of a systematic ('stelselmatige') infringement of a subjective right, like an intellectual property right, where damage is incurred continuously, an urgent interest in relief is likely to exist.[87] Whether the applicant in a given case has an urgent interest is a factual question, the answer to which depends on the circumstances of the case. The urgency of the applicant's case is to be determined as of the date of the decision, and also in relation to the defendant's interests.[88] One of the circumstances that may contribute to depriving the applicant's case of urgency is a period of idleness on their side, although this may not on its own be decisive.[89] Whether such circumstances exist and to what extent they touch upon the urgency of the applicant's case is up to the judge dealing with the facts. Particularly relevant in this regard is the extent to which the applicant has waited after becoming aware of the alleged infringement. In some cases, failure to act for six months after knowledge of the defendant's actions may lead to loss of urgency, in particular where the applicant offers no explanation for the delay. At the other extreme, six years may not lead to a loss of urgency in the event of a satisfying explanation. The policy of the court in this respect

---

[82] OLG Düsseldorf, PharmR 2021, 270 – *Cinacalcet*.
[83] OLG Düsseldorf, GRUR-RR 2013, 236 – *Flupirtin-Maleat*.
[84] LG Hamburg, NJOZ 2009, 1456 – *Laccio-Möbel*.
[85] See, for example, *Monsanto Co v Stauffer Chemical Co (NZ)* [1984] FSR 559.
[86] OLG Düsseldorf, InstGE 10, 124 – *Inhalator*.
[87] Supreme Court of the Netherlands, 23 January 1998, *Lancôme*, ECLI:NL:HR:1998:ZC2553, at 3.3, confirmed in subsequent Supreme Court decisions.
[88] Supreme Court of the Netherlands, 29 November 2002, ECLI:NL:HR:2002:AE4553.
[89] ibid 3.4.

seems to be that any delay period longer than six months requires some form of explanation. An open question is whether actual knowledge of the defendant's acts is required or whether the urgency window is opened once the applicant was supposed to know about these acts. For the UPC, the relevant territory is all of the contracting Member States. Hence, if infringement only takes place in one or a few contracting Member States and the patent owner has knowledge about this, they need to act in this Member State if preliminary relief is intended. The patent owner will lose urgency to act on a preliminary basis against the infringement if they wait until the infringement also take places in other Member States, for example, with the aim of choosing a particular local or regional division for filing the request for the preliminary measure.

iii. Validity

a. The UPC Approach

With regard to the validity of the patent on which preliminary measures are sought, the court *may* require the applicant to provide reasonable evidence that the patent is valid.[90] This is not an obligatory requirement (it is only obligatory for the Court to take into account whether the patent has been upheld in an opposition procedure before the EPO or has been the subject of proceedings in any other court for the purpose of deciding whether to hear the application *ex parte*).[91]

It is not specified in the Rules of Procedure whether such 'reasonable evidence that the patent is valid' could only be a simple extract of the Patent Register confirming that the patent is granted or whether there are stricter requirements. Given the risks involved for the defendant in granting provisional measures in patent cases and the general risk of patent revocation, it is arguable that in order to get a provisional measure granted, the patent should fulfil higher standards when it comes to validity. This means that the mere fact that the patent has been issued by the Patent Office as such may not suffice. At the other end of the spectrum, even if the patent has been upheld by the Opposition Division or any other court in contradictory proceedings, but this decision is found to be evidently wrong and there is a high likelihood that it will be overturned, a provisional measure is not per se excluded.[92] Hence, particularly when the defendant – for example, in its protective letter – brings forward relevant new prior art that has not yet been considered either in prosecution or any later validity proceedings, the court must assess the validity of the patent before granting a provisional measure and cannot simply rely on the fact that the patent was granted or even upheld in opposition or any other invalidity proceedings.[93]

---

[90] Rule 211.2 of the Rules of Procedure.
[91] ibid Rule 209.2. There is no contradiction between the UPC procedures and the decision of the CJEU in Contact GmbH & Co KG v Harting Deutschland GmbH & Co KG, Harting Electric GmbH & Co KG (Case C-44/21) (28 April 2022), but the case emphasises that the court will not be permitted to require a patent to be upheld in opposition or revocation proceedings before a preliminary injunction can be granted.
[92] *cf* OLG Düsseldorf, GRUR 2008, 1077 – *Olanzapin*.
[93] It is currently unclear whether the decision of the CJEU in *Phoenix Contact GmbH & Co KG v Harting Deutschland GmbH & Co KG, Harting Electric GmbH & Co KG* (Case C-44/21), which precludes *absolute* requirements for a patent to survive prior invalidity proceedings, requires any change in German legal practice. Further case law in this respect is needed.

b. National Perspectives

In Germany, there is currently a referral to the CJEU pending as regards the requirements of the validity of the patent for granting a preliminary injunction. In particular, the question has been raised as to whether the patent must have indeed survived first instance nullity or opposition proceedings, as required by the District Court of Düsseldorf and the Düsseldorf Appeals Court, called 'secured validity'.[94] This means that the pure grant of the patent by the patent office (despite the examination by the patent offices) is not sufficient, but the patent must have survived contradictory proceedings: either revocation proceedings or opposition proceedings where a third party has undertaken additional prior art searches and attacked the patent.[95] Exceptionally, when third-party observations have been filed during patent prosecution, this fact might be considered equivalent to contradictory proceedings.[96] In contrast, the Munich District Court raised concerns that this rather strict approach would not be in accordance with the EU Enforcement Directive. This leaded into the referral decision of the 21st chamber of the Munich District Court asking the CJEU whether it is 'compatible with Article 9(1) of Directive 2004/48/EC for the higher regional courts having jurisdiction at final instance in proceedings for interim relief to refuse in principle to grant interim measures for infringement of patents if the patent in dispute has not survived opposition or revocation proceedings at first instance'.[97] The outcome of this referral to the CJEU will also be of great importance for the grant of provisional measures under the UPC. Nevertheless, regardless of the dogmatic differences, the decisions rendered by the German courts in practice mirror a wide range of forms of pragmatism. In particular, if the defendant – usually by means of a protective brief – casts doubts on the validity of the patent, the courts will have to look into validity in the summary proceedings. Such doubt might in particular be founded on new prior art that has not been considered during the patent prosecution. On the other hand, particularly in the case of generic launches, all courts apply a rather strict standard and require the defendant basically to have cleared the way before the launch of the product, that is, to have obtained a positive first instance decision in opposition/revocation proceedings. The reasons for this exception given by the Düsseldorf courts are the high level of damages that the patentee will suffer once generic products enter the market due to the significant decrease of the prices for the pharmaceuticals which are considered to be irreparable even if the patent should be declared valid in parallel revocation proceedings later on.[98]

---

[94] The leading case is: OLG Düsseldorf, GRUR-RS 2010, 15862 – *Harnkatheterset*; there is a less strict standard in OLG Düsseldorf GRUR-RS 2018, 1291 – *Flupirtin Maleat*. For the relevance of provisional opinions issued by the Federal Patent Court or the Patent Office in opposition proceedings, *cf* OLG Düsseldorf, GRUR-RR 2021, 249 – *Cinacalcet II*; District Court Munich, PharmR 2017, 512 – *Truvada*; and GRUR-RS 2021, 37988 – *Sorafenib*.
[95] OLG Düsseldorf, InstGE 9, 140, 146 – *Olanzapin*; InstGE 12, 114 – *Harnkatheterset*. *cf* Italy, where European patents are generally assumed to be valid, due to the process of substantive examination undertaken in the EPO, although a summary report of an expert on validity is normally expected.
[96] Kühnen (n 47) n° 2039.
[97] LG München, GRUR 2021, 466 – *Rechtsbestand im Verfügungsverfahren*.
[98] OLG Düsseldorf, GRUR-RR 2013, 236 – *Flupirtin-Maleat*. Again, as has already been pointed out, 'irreparable' is applied rather widely, not considering that most of the damages such as a price drop can be calculated and recovered on the basis of damages claims in the event that the decision not to grant a provisional measure should turn out to be wrong.

In the Netherlands, a preliminary patent infringement injunction is denied if the patent runs 'a serious, not to be neglected chance' ('serieuze, niet te verwaarlozen kans')[99] to be revoked in opposition proceedings or court proceedings on the merits. Whether such a chance exists in a given case is a matter for the facts and circumstances of that case. As was stated earlier, in the Dutch *kort geding* in patent matters, although the outcome is a provisional decision, validity and infringement are pleaded and assessed in some depth, often with the aid of party experts. This implies an independent assessment of validity and infringement by the *kort geding* judge – that is, independent of the EPO. The mere fact that a patent has survived proceedings before the national patent office[100] or opposition proceedings at the EPO[101] has proven not to be decisive in this respect. A finding of validity or invalidity by a Technical Board of Appeal of the EPO or a foreign court, although not decisive on its own, may contribute to a similar finding by the Dutch court.[102] Whether a foreign or EPO decision carries weight will depend on whether the facts (for example, prior art or infringement evidence) and arguments put forward by the parties are the same as those before the Dutch court.

For comparison, in English cases, the courts require on the face of the evidence that there may be an infringement and that there is a valid patent, but these do not need to be proved. As such, the fact that the validity of a patent has been tested in the EPO is irrelevant. Indeed, the Court of Appeal has held that a preliminary injunction can be maintained on the appeal of the merits where the patent was held invalid at first instance by the Patents Court.[103]

iv. The Balance of Convenience

a. The UPC Approach

The potential harm of granting or refusing an injunction is specifically addressed in the Rules of Procedure by the requirement that the court *must* weigh up the interests of the parties – in particular, considering the potential harm for either of the parties resulting from the granting or the refusal of an injunction.[104] However, this is not an express requirement in the context of other preliminary measures. If this were intended, it might be due to the fact that the grant or refusal of a preliminary injunction is likely to have the biggest impact commercially. Although the consideration of potential harm is only explicitly addressed in the context of injunctions, the court should in any case weigh up the interests of the parties

---

[99] In *Solvay SA v Honeywell Fluorine Products Europe BV and Others* (Case C-616/10) (12 July 2012, ECLI:EU:C:2012:445) this criterion is referred to at paragraphs 16, 31 and 49 as 'reasonable, non-negligible possibility', which seems at first sight less stringent for the third party contesting the patent's validity. However, the decision provides no indication that any such difference was intended.

[100] *Matador v Bick*, District Court of The Hague (provisional measures judge), 22 April 2015, ECLI:NL:RBDHA:2015:8869.

[101] *Coloplast v Medical4you*, District Court of The Hague (provisional measures judge), 14 August 2015 ECLI:NL:RBDHA:2015:9655.

[102] *Apple v Samsung*, Court of Appeal of The Hague, 20 May 2014, ECLI:NL:GHDHA:2014:1727, at 24; *Applera v Stratagene*, District Court of The Hague (provisional measures judge), 13 July 2003, ECLI:NL:RBSGR:2007:BB6737.

[103] *Novartis AG v Hospira UK Ltd* [2013] EWCA Civ 583.

[104] Rule 211.3 of the Rules of Procedure, mirroring Article 62(2) UPC Agreement.

and the potential harm caused by the grant or the refusal of the provisional measure. This already results from the nature of the provisional measures as summary proceedings. It also corresponds to Recital 22 of the Enforcement Directive 2004/48/EC, which states that while it is essential to provide for provisional measures for the immediate termination of infringements, without awaiting a decision on the substance of the case, the rights of the defence must be observed, ensuring the proportionality of the provisional measures as appropriate to the characteristics of the specific case in question. This is also reflected in Article 3(2) of the Enforcement Directive, which requires that the measures applied are not only effective, but also proportionate.

When weighing up the parties' interests, the court has to balance the legal and economic disadvantages and damages that might be caused to the right holder if the provisional measure – in particular, a preliminary injunction – is denied if a decision on the merits would later come to the conclusion that there is an infringement and the provisional measure would have been well founded, with the legal and economic disadvantages that the defendant will suffer if the provisional measure is granted, but if this later turns out to be unfounded – for example, if the patent is revoked later on or if the court on the merits finds the patent not to be infringed. In this regard, the court might take into account whether and to what extent it is possible for the parties to enforce damages claims for either continued infringement or for the enforcement of an unfounded provisional measure. In particular, in the context of pharmaceutical cases, the specific circumstances of the pharmaceutical market as addressed in the EU sector inquiry of 2009,[105] and patent filing strategies contributing to generic delay also need to be taken into consideration when weighing up the parties' interests.[106] Furthermore, it needs to be borne in mind that most harms, like a price drop in case of generic launches, are reparable on the basis of subsequent damages claims should the decision to refuse the grant of a provisional measure turn out to be unfounded in the end. With regard to the likelihood of enforcing damages claims, the CJEU decision in *Bayer v Gedeon* with regard to Hungary[107] needs to be reflected in the UPC as the decision seems to say that there should not be an automatic claim for damages in cases of an unfounded preliminary injunction, but rather that the conduct of the parties should be taken into consideration, particularly whether the claimant abused the measure and whether the defendant mitigated risks (such as clearing the way). If the decision is to be taken into consideration in weighing up the parties' interests in the UPC – that is, lowering the standard for a defendant to claim damages if the provisional measure turns out to be wrong – the standards for granting a provisional measure must reciprocally be raised, especially with regard to the validity of the patent and the determination of the kind of damages that are indeed irreparable and those that are reparable. In general, balancing the interests very much depends on the individual facts of the case to be presented by the parties in the request for the grant of provisional measures and the protective brief or statement of defence.

---

[105] https://ec.europa.eu/competition/sectors/pharmaceuticals/inquiry/communication_en.pdf.
[106] Section 3.2, in particular section 3.2.1 of the EU Sector Inquiry. For more detail, see the White Paper of Medicines for Europe of 4 November 2020, https://www.medicinesforeurope.com/docs/2020.11.04-Medicines-for-Europe-Whitepaper.pdf.
[107] *Bayer v Gedeon Richter* (Case C-688/17) ECLI:EU:C:2019:722 (12 September 2019).

b. National Perspectives

In Germany, in addition to the validity discussion and the requirements applied there that are part of the general assessment of the balance of convenience,[108] the claimant's interest in the grant of the preliminary injunction must outweigh the defendant's interest – that is, the claimant's damage if a preliminary injunction would be refused must outweigh the defendant's damage if the preliminary injunction is granted, but turns out to be unfounded later on – for example, by the revocation of the patent. If the patent is clearly infringed and the validity is secured, the interests of the claimant generally outweigh the defendant's interests and a separate balancing of interests is no longer necessary.[109]

Dutch statute provides that upon request, a court will order a party to provide, do or refrain from doing something if such an obligation rests upon that party.[110] This is commonly regarded as binding on the court ruling on a case on its merits. Once infringement of a valid right (eg, an IP right) is established, the court must, unless there are exceptional circumstances, grant an injunction upon the claimant's request. In *kort geding* the situation is different, in that a judge may balance the parties' respective interests in granting or denying the relief requested – for example, on the one hand, the provisional character of a *kort geding* decision in connection with the grave consequences of an injunction for the defendant and, on the other hand, the potential damage for the applicant, especially when further infringement is imminent – when an injunction is denied.[111] However, in practice, only in exceptional cases is an injunction denied as a result of a balancing of interests in *kort geding*. That such balancing is less ubiquitous than in, for example, UK preliminary proceedings may have to do with the fact that the *kort geding*, especially when relating to patents, is more of a mini-trial.

Some guidance may be found in the English cases, where the balance of convenience is an important factor in deciding certain forms of relief, including preliminary injunctions. When considering whether to grant a preliminary injunction, the English court must be satisfied that there is a serious question in issue (meaning that on the face of the evidence, there may be an infringement rather than proof) and that damages are not an adequate remedy for the patentee such that, without the injunction, irreparable harm will be caused. If there is doubt as to the adequacy of damages, the court will take all the circumstances into account in order to establish whether the balance of convenience lies in favour of granting the preliminary injunction.[112] Meeting all of these criteria is difficult and in most cases the balance of convenience will favour preserving the status quo. However, pharmaceutical patent cases involving branded originator patents and generic competitors are arguably a special case. This is because the Patents Court has previously stated that alleged infringers in the pharmaceutical sector should 'clear the way' of any blocking patents before attempting to enter the market. Furthermore, the entry into the market of an infringing generic product

---

[108] *cf* above, D.iv.a.
[109] OLG Düsseldorf, GRUR-RS 2019, 33226.
[110] Article 3:296(1) of the Dutch Civil Code (DCC).
[111] *Procter & Gamble v Mölnlycke*, Supreme Court of the Netherlands, 15 December 1995, ECLI:NL:HR:1995:ZC1919, at 3.4.
[112] *American Cyanamid v Ethicon Ltd* [1975] RPC 513.

is usually (but not always) considered to risk causing irreparable damage to the branded market by forcing down the price.[113]

In *Neurim v Generics*,[114] Neurim and its exclusive licensee Flynn applied for a preliminary injunction to stop what they claimed were a threat and an intention by Mylan to infringe Neurim's patent for a prolonged release formulation of melatonin for treating insomnia (brand name Circadin). At the time of the preliminary injunction application, Mylan had obtained a marketing authorisation for a generic version of Circadin, although it had given undertakings not to launch whilst the interim injunction proceedings were pending. The Opposition Division of the EPO had also held the patent to be invalid, but that decision was suspended subject to appeal. Furthermore, by the time the preliminary action was decided, an expedited trial of the substantive proceedings had been ordered, meaning that the preliminary injunction, if granted, would cover a period of just over four months. Having first established that there was a serious issue to be tried, Mr Justice Marcus Smith went on to the second step of the *American Cyanamid* approach in order to determine whether damages would provide an adequate remedy instead of an injunction.[115]

The judge examined the likely damage in two periods:

(i) the period between the preliminary injunction hearing and the hypothetical point at which Mylan could be excluded from the market by obtaining a permanent injunction after trial (Period 1); and
(ii) the period between that point and the expiry of the patent (Period 2).

In Period 1, Neurim and Flynn argued that they would be challenged by generic competition; in Period 2, they argued that they would continue to suffer harm from the downward pressure on prices encountered in Period 1. Mylan responded that, nonetheless, in the approximately 20 months between the trial and the expiry of the patent, Neurim (and its partner Flynn) would be able to restore their position. And the judge agreed: 'Periods 1 and 2 together amount to just over two years – and, as I have noted, there will be considerable market data in the hands of Neurim, Flynn and Mylan to enable the losses in Periods 1 and 2 to be quantified.' Therefore, given that damages would be an adequate remedy, the claim for a preliminary injunction failed the second step of the *American Cyanamid* test.

On appeal,[116] Neurim and Flynn criticised the decision for failing to take account of their evidence on consequential loss – in particular, the result that Flynn Pharma would need to reduce or entirely cease investment in a number of key areas because of the substantially reduced returns it expected from Circadin sales if the injunction were not granted. However, as the Court of Appeal pointed out, the evidence on this issue had been prepared on the basis that there would be no expedited trial and that Neurim and Flynn would therefore be exposed to competition during a much longer Period 1 than actually proved to

---

[113] See *Cephalon, Inc and Others v Orchid Europe Ltd and Another* [2010] EWHC 2945 (Pat); and *Neurim Pharmaceuticals (1991) Ltd and Another v Teva UK Ltd* [2022] EWHC 954 (Pat) (26 April 2022).

[114] *Neurim Pharmaceuticals (1991) Ltd and Another v Generics UK Ltd (t/a Mylan) and Another* [2020] EWHC 1362 (Pat) (3 June 2020).

[115] For further discussion on these issues, see P England, *A Practitioner's Guide to European Patent Law*, 2nd edn (Hart Publishing, 2022).

[116] *Neurim Pharmaceuticals (1991) Ltd and Another v Generics UK Ltd (t/a Mylan) and Another* [2020] EWCA Civ 793 (24 June 2020).

be the case. The court also rejected the argument that consequential loss was nevertheless realistic because once a product had become generic, there would no longer be any point in investing in the type of activities which Neurim and Flynn supported – in other words, the court meant that competition from one company could not be regarded as making the drug 'generic' and it was not a rationale for not continuing to fund research into new products, or even Circadin, given that the patent still had two years left to run. In fact, in the court's view, the evidence fell a long way short of establishing that competition from other generic companies was likely during Period 1, and so there was no likelihood of multiple generic entries creating a real downward price spiral. The court also took account of evidence that changes to the Drug Tariff Category of Circadin would be slow, with the result that Flynn could maintain its list price for some time, and up to and including trial.

II. Enforcement of a Provisional Measure

The application for a provisional measure may be lodged by the applicant before or after the initiation of proceedings on the merits.[117] If it is lodged before the initiation of proceedings on the merits, the defendant may request that the injunction is revoked or otherwise ceases to have effect if the applicant does not bring, within a period not exceeding 31 calendar days or 20 working days (whichever is the longer), an action leading to a decision on the merits of the case before the court.[118] The court must ensure that such a request is granted.[119]

There is a difference between the Rules of Procedure and the UPC Agreement: whereas Rule 213.1 only requires that the applicant initiates proceedings on the merits, Articles 62.5 and 60.8 require that an action *leading to a decision on the merits* is filed. The wording of the Agreement 'action leading to a decision on the merits of the case before the Court' implies two requirements: first, the action must be initiated within the deadline. In addition, the action must lead to a decision on the merits.[120] Hence, the question arises as to whether the preliminary measure will be revoked, or cease to have effect, respectively, if an action is filed, but if, for whatever reason, there will not be a decision. While the UPC Agreement from its pure language is very strict from the applicant's point of view, Rule 213.1 is surprisingly generous for the applicant. This leads to a couple of questions that need to be answered by the UPC case law: what happens if the applicant initiates proceedings on the merits, but withdraws the complaint afterwards? Should this be considered similar to the case as if proceedings on the merits would never have been initiated at all? If the complaint is dismissed for lack of admissibility, it is clear that this is not a 'decision on the merits', but still, 'proceedings on the merits' were initiated.[121]

---

[117] Rule 206.1 of the Rules of Procedure.
[118] ibid Rule 213.1.
[119] Articles 62.5 and 60.8 UPC Agreement.
[120] This is different from German law, where Section 926, paragraph 1 of the German Code of Civil Procedure only requires that an action for proceedings on the merits is filed (if requested by the defendant).
[121] Unlike the present German law, it is not necessary for the applicant to formally serve the preliminary injunction to the defendant. Instead, the preliminary injunction will be served automatically by the registry upon the defendant.

III. Protective Letters

The main purpose of a protective letter is to prevent the grant of a preliminary measure *ex parte*, that is, without the defendant being heard. For this reason, a protective letter should include any argument with regard to non-infringement, invalidity, lack of urgency or any legal argument such as lack of the right to commence proceedings. Nevertheless, the potential defendant should be very careful about how they present their arguments: as they do not know yet how the patent right holder will argue in its request for a preliminary measure, they can only guess which arguments might be relevant. There is always the risk for the defendant that they give too much information in the protective brief which might only help the right holder to substantiate its request with any missing facts. For this reason, it is common in national practices that use protective letters to concentrate on a few, very convincing arguments only and to leave further arguments for a potential oral hearing. This is something to be carefully decided based on the facts of the particular case.

The protective letter is to be filed with the Registry of the UPC in Luxembourg in the language of the patent.[122] The documents are to be lodged in electronic form, using the official forms available online. Where it is not possible to lodge a document electronically for any reason, a party may lodge the document in hard-copy form. An electronic copy of the document must be lodged as soon as practicable thereafter.[123] According to the current fee proposal, the filing fee for a protective letter is set at €200 (see Chapter 20). Apart from the filing fee, there are no further fees at this stage. Court costs and the risk of reimbursement of the other party's attorneys only arise once proceedings on preliminary measures are initiated by the right holder. The protective letter remains valid for a period of six months.[124] It can be renewed afterwards or filed anew – both require the payment of an additional filing fee of €200.

From a strategic point of view with regard to European patents, as the right holder could at any time opt out, or in the case of an opt-out withdraw the opt-out if no bars apply, potential defendants may file protective letters not only with the UPC, but also nationally insofar as this is possible in the relevant jurisdiction.[125]

A protective letter must contain the following information:[126]

(a) the statement that it is a protective letter;
(b) the name of the defendant(s) filing the protective letter and of their representatives;
(c) the name of the presumed applicant(s);
(d) the postal and electronic addresses for service on the defendant and the names of the persons authorised to accept service;
(e) the postal and, where available, electronic addresses for service on the presumed applicant(s) and the names of the persons authorised to accept service if known – however, this is information that the defendant usually does not have at this stage of the proceedings;

---

[122] Rule 207.2 of the Rules of Procedure.
[123] ibid Rule 4.
[124] ibid Rule 207.8.
[125] For example, in Germany or the Netherlands. There is no system of protective letters, as such, in the English courts.
[126] Rule 207.2 of the Rules of Procedure.

(f) the number of the patent(s) concerned and, where applicable, information about any prior or pending proceedings, including any action for revocation or a declaration of non-infringement pending before the central division, the EPO or any other court or authority.[127]

Furthermore – and this is the substance of a protective letter – it may contain:[128]

(a) an indication of the facts relied on which may include a challenge to the facts expected to be relied on by the presumed applicant(s) and/or the assertion that the patent is invalid and the grounds for such assertion;
(b) any available written evidence relied on;
(c) the arguments of law, including the reasons why any application of a preliminary measure should be rejected.

It is fully at the discretion of the defendant which arguments to include. Nonetheless, it follows from the purpose of a protective letter itself that it should contain information concerning non-infringement, invalidity, lack of urgency or any further argument why a preliminary measure should not be granted, or a combination of such arguments.

The usual structure of a protective letter is that of a statement of defence, whereas it is recommended to focus only on one or a few strong arguments. The defendant is free to comment on any factual or legal situation that might be of relevance for the Court in its assessment as to whether or not to grant the preliminary measure. However, as the protective letter will be forwarded to the Court and to the applicant(s) once an application for preliminary measure is lodged,[129] the defendant should carefully consider which information to include in the protective letter without knowing the contents of the application and the applicant's way of argument. As the proceedings continue after the service of the protective letter and the application for a preliminary measure to the respective other party, each party might comment on the other party's allegations. If the defendant gives too much information – for example, on the way in which the attacked embodiment is designed or the method of working of the attacked process – this might only help the applicant to give sufficient reasons for its application. The defendant may rely on any means of evidence listed in the Rules of Procedure[130] reciprocally to the means of evidence allowed for the application of a provisional measure.

IV. Appeal Proceedings

Provisional measures ordered by the UPC are subject to appeal[131] (see Chapter 17). The appeal is to be lodged by the affected party.[132] The order on provisional measures must indicate that an appeal may be brought.[133] The deadline for filing an appeal amounts to

---

[127] cf ibid Rule 13.1(h).
[128] ibid Rule 207.3.
[129] ibid Rule 207.8.
[130] ibid Rule 170.1.
[131] ibid Rule 220.1(c).
[132] ibid Rule 220.1.
[133] ibid Rule 211.6, in accordance with Article 73 UPC Agreement and Rule 220.1 of the Rules of Procedure.

15 calendar days of the notification of the order to the applicant.[134] This deadline runs from the service of the order.[135] Court fees for the appeal proceedings relating to an application for provisional measures amount to an additional €11,000 (see Chapter 20), the same as the first instance proceedings.

With regard to the effect of appeal on proceedings on the merits, an appeal against an order for a provisional measure must not prevent the continuation of the main proceedings.[136] However, the Court of First Instance must not give a decision in the main proceedings before the decision of the Court of Appeal concerning the appeal order has been given.

V. Revocation of Provisional Measures

The defendant may request that the injunction is revoked or otherwise ceases to have effect if the applicant does not bring, within a period not exceeding 31 calendar days or 20 working days (whichever is the longer), an action leading to a decision on the merits of the case before the Court.[137]

The defendant has the right to request appropriate compensation for damage caused by the measures where the provisional measures are revoked or where they lapse due to any act or omission of the applicant, or where it is subsequently found that there has been no infringement or threat of infringement of the patent.[138]

It is interesting to note that Rule 213.1 of the Rules of Procedure speaks of 'revoked or otherwise ceases to have effect' when proceedings on the merits are not initiated in due time, while Rule 213.2 only grants a compensation claim to the defendant if the provisional measures were 'revoked'. The latter is inconsistent with Articles 62.5 and 60.9 UPC Agreement, which clearly grant a compensation claim not only in the event that the provisional measure is revoked, but also when it 'otherwise ceases to have effect'. As the UPC Agreement overrides the Rules of Procedure, Article 60.9 should be read into Rule 213.2 – that is, that there should not be a difference whether the provisional measure is revoked or otherwise ceases to have effect.

This raises the question of whether the defendant should also have a claim for compensation for the time where the provisional measure was in force, as 'cease to have effect' implies that the effect terminates for the future only, but not retroactively for the past (contrary to 'revoked'), or if such a claim for compensation should only be given for the time after it ceased to have effect, provided that the damage suffered continues to have effect, as the provisional measure is considered to have been legally in place for the time in between. It is also unclear whether this wording actually refers to a difference in the kind of the provisional measure, given that, for example, a delivery up that has already taken place cannot be revoked, but should still give the defendant a claim for compensation if it later transpires that the order was not justified.

---

[134] Article 73(2)(a) UPC Agreement.
[135] Rule 224.1(b) of the Rules of Procedure.
[136] Article 74(3) UPC Agreement.
[137] Rule 213.1 of the Rules of Procedure.
[138] ibid Rule 213.2.

There is no express reference in the Rules of Procedure to revocation of provisional measures and consequent compensation if the patent on which the measure was awarded is later revoked. However, it seems clear that in such a case, it would be 'found that there has been no infringement or threat of infringement of the patent' in the sense that an invalid patent cannot be infringed. Therefore, it should be possible to revoke provisional measures in such a case and for compensation to be available if the defendant has suffered loss.[139] In this context, given the clear statement of the damages obligation for an unjustified preliminary injunction, there should be no room for the application of the holdings of the CJEU decision in *Bayer v Gedeon Richter*,[140] which was only rendered with regard to Hungarian law and which did not have any provision on the applicant's obligation to pay damages in the case of an unjustified preliminary measure (see also the discussion in section I.D.iv above with regard to the balance of convenience).

The UPC will also be bound by Article 9(7) of the Enforcement Directive, which states that Member States can order the applicant, at the request of the defendant, to provide appropriate compensation for any injury caused by provisional measures that have been revoked, that have lapsed or where it is subsequently found that there is no infringement. In *Bayer v Richter*,[141] the CJEU provided guidance on the compensation that parties can receive when a patent holder has enforced a preliminary injunction against them that is later revoked. According to the CJEU, compensation should be awarded when a request for provisional measures is deemed to be unjustified at the time when the request is made. The fact that a preliminary injunction is later overturned does not automatically mean that the preliminary injunction was unjustified and compensation should be awarded.

Appropriate compensation for any injury caused may be awarded to a party against whom a provisional measure has been enforced. This is if the measure is subsequently varied or revoked such that the injury would not have occurred if the measure had been awarded in its varied form or not at all.[142]

VI. Preliminary Injunctions of Opted-out Patents in the UPC?

The Brussels Regulation[143] states that the UPC is a 'common court' of the contracting Member States and is therefore 'a court of a Member State' (see Chapter 2). A court of a Member State may grant preliminary injunctions, as well as other provisional measures, even when it does not have the jurisdiction to hear the action on the merits:

> Application may be made to the courts of a Member State for such provisional, including protective, measures as may be available under the law of that Member State, even if the courts of another Member State have jurisdiction as to the substance of the matter.[144]

---

[139] See the wording of Article 60.9 UPC Agreement and Rule 213.2 of the Rules of Procedure.
[140] *Bayer v Gedeon Richter* (Case C-688/17). For more detail, find a summary from the viewpoint of different national perspectives here: https://www.taylorwessing.com/synapse/february-20.html.
[141] *Bayer v Richter* (Case C-688/17) ECLI:EU:C:2019:722 (12 September 2019).
[142] Rule 354.2 of the Rules of Procedure.
[143] Articles 71a(1) and (2) of Regulation (EU) 542/2014 amending Regulation (EU) 1215/2012 on Jurisdiction and the Recognition and Enforcement of Judgments in Civil and Commercial Matters.
[144] Article 35 of the Brussels I Regulation (recast).

Does this raise the question of whether preliminary injunctions and other provisional protective measures[145] may be obtained in the UPC on an opted-out patent?

The Brussels Regulation determines jurisdiction for patent actions between Member States. This means that, to the extent that the Regulation appears to provide the UPC with competence for provisional measures, it is actually only providing the contracting Member States with the right to decide under the UPC Agreement whether the UPC can grant the preliminary relief in question. In the case of an opted-out patent, the UPC Agreement should already direct the contracting Member States that the UPC has no competence for provisional (or any other) measures.

---

[145] Under Article 62 UPC Agreement.

16

Obtaining and Using Evidence

Any allegation of infringement in the UPC must be proved to a sufficient standard with evidence. Similarly, evidence must support a claim that a patent is invalid before it may be revoked. The civil standard of proof – on the balance of probabilities – is common to most European jurisdictions in civil actions, but the measures available to obtain evidence vary. The need to harmonise these measures was recognised with the introduction of EU Directive 2004/48/EU on the Enforcement of Intellectual Property Rights Act (hereinafter the 'Enforcement Directive'),[1] which came into force in 2004. According to the recitals of the Enforcement Directive, its objective was to 'approximate legislative systems so as to ensure a high, equivalent and homogeneous level of protection in the internal market'. However, despite the harmonising aim of the Directive, differences remain. The UPC is also subject to the Enforcement Directive, which is reflected in the measures for obtaining evidence in the UPC Agreement and the Rules of Procedure, and aims to provide a consistent approach to the application of rules of evidence across the contracting Member States. Common law traditions are also apparent. For example, the role of party-appointed technical experts and the duties that are placed on them will be familiar to practitioners in England and Wales. Furthermore, legal advice privilege and litigation privilege, which have an express role in UPC proceedings, are areas of detailed and mature rules in common law countries. This chapter discusses the rules relating to these and related issues in the UPC.

I. Sources of Evidence

The forms of evidence that may be used to prove a party's case in a UPC action are expressly listed in the Rules of Procedure.[2] They include, but are not limited to: written evidence, whether printed, handwritten or drawn – in particular, documents, written witness statements, plans, drawings and photographs; expert reports and reports on experiments carried out for the purpose of the proceedings; physical objects – in particular, devices, products, embodiments, exhibits and models; and electronic files and audio/video recordings.

This evidence may be obtained using a number of measures, which are separately listed in the Rules.[3] These include, but are not limited to: hearing of the parties; requests for information; production of documents; summoning, hearing and questioning of witnesses;

---
[1] Directive 2004/48/EU on the Enforcement of Intellectual Property Rights Act [2004] OJ L157, 30 April.
[2] Rule 170.1 of the Rules of Procedure.
[3] Rule 170.2 of the Rules of Procedure.

appointing, receiving opinions from, summoning, hearing and questioning experts; ordering inspection of a place or a physical object; conducting comparative tests and experiments; sworn statements in writing; and certain measures to preserve evidence.[4]

These measures will be discussed in more detail below.

II. General Rules on Evidence

A. The Burden of Proof

The general rule is that the burden of proving facts is on the party wishing to rely on those facts.[5] The burden of proof is reversed in cases concerning patented processes for new products. In those cases, the patented process is deemed by the Court to have been used where[6] either:

(a) the identical product is obtained without consent, unless there is proof that the patented process was not used; or
(b) there is a 'substantial likelihood' that the product is made by the patented process and the patentee cannot, despite reasonable efforts, establish an alternative process by which it could have been made.[7]

In circumstances where the defendant has to provide evidence of its manufacturing process to show that the patented process has not been used, the court must take into consideration the defendant's need to protect its trade secrets and appropriate confidentiality protection may be ordered[8] (see section XIV below).

B. The Obligation to Produce Documents

i. The Extent of the Obligation to Produce Documents

A further general rule of evidence in the UPC is that a statement of fact that is not specifically contested by any party must be taken to be true as between them.[9] A party that wishes to rely on a statement of fact, which is contested or likely to be contested, must indicate the means of evidence that it claims prove that fact.[10] Furthermore, the party concerned must

---

[4] ibid Rule 170.3.
[5] Article 54 UPC Agreement.
[6] ibid Article 55(1).
[7] The second limb of Article 55(1) will require interpretation by the court, particularly on the meaning of a 'substantial likelihood'. The onus would also appear to be on the patentee to show substantial likelihood and to demonstrate that it cannot, despite reasonable efforts, establish an alternative process. Only then would it appear that the burden of proof moves to the defendant.
[8] ibid Article 55(3).
[9] Rule 171.2 of the Rules of Procedure.
[10] ibid Rule 171.1.

produce such evidence 'available' to it 'regarding' that statement of fact.[11] These obligations raise the following issues of interpretation:

(a) The evidence in question must be 'available' to the parties. On a narrow and subjective interpretation, this may mean documents of which the parties are aware. This is likely to be a limited number of documents. The preferred view is that 'available' requires a broader and objective interpretation, and covers documents that are accessible by a party without them knowing that fact – close to the notion of documents which are in the possession, custody or control of a party. A party does not have an obligation to try to obtain documents to which it does not have a right to possession or control, but conversely documents which are covered by such a right are available to it. This is potentially a larger number of documents, since it implies the need for the parties to search through company systems and archives for relevant documents that they possess, whether or not they are aware of their existence at the outset.

(b) The evidence produced must be 'regarding' the statement of fact. This word is chosen instead of narrower terms that could have been used such as 'proving' or 'supporting', and appears broad enough to include evidence that tends to *disprove* a fact as well as prove it.

The interpretation of these words will obviously have a significant effect on the scope and nature of the disclosure being given. It is submitted that this disclosure falls some way short of the English disclosure obligation, on its face, because the duty to disclose only falls on the party wishing to rely on a statement of fact. But the effect may be similar, because a defendant that does not provide a substantive defence risks failing to specifically contest the allegation and will need to substantiate its own statements of fact. This obligation may also extend to requiring a party to disclose documents that are detrimental to its own case.

However, there may be a significant difference compared to common law procedures. Disclosure in such procedures is governed by the issues, so that a document which tends to show that the invention was or was not obvious will be regarded as disclosable. There may be debate before the UPC as to whether such a broad-based approach to disclosure is justified, given that disclosure is tied specifically to disputed questions of fact. English judges would regard obviousness as a question of fact or a mixed question of law and fact, whereas some continental judges might say that obviousness is a question of law, or at least largely so. In any case, the Rules of Procedure and the UPC Agreement appear to be intended to safeguard a form of 'cards on the table' approach to litigation and one in which the parties are not able to confront their opponents with new evidence late in proceedings or at trial.

In Germany, further to the German Civil Procedure Code, the parties are under an obligation to support the proceedings[12] and should, as a rule of thumb, provide any evidence required to comply with their burden of proof as soon as possible. If evidence is brought too late or outside a court-set framework, the party runs the risks of it being disregarded as being filed too late.[13] This obligation to produce available evidence as soon as possible is

---

[11] ibid Rule 172.1.
[12] Section 282 of the German Civil Procedure Code.
[13] ibid section 296.

also needed with a view to any appeal, where generally the introduction of new facts is not permitted.[14]

A party may also be compelled by a court order to produce evidence that lies within its control relating to a statement of fact upon which it relies.[15] The failure by a party to produce evidence that has been ordered must be taken into consideration by the court when deciding on the issue concerned.[16]

ii. Indicating and Producing Documents

There are separate obligations on the parties to indicate the documents on which they will rely to prove their case and to produce evidence regarding the statements of fact that are relied on.

a. Indicating Documents

The indication of documents requires a statement describing the existence and nature of the material relied on. The place to do this is in the parties' respective pleadings during the written procedure. The requirement to 'indicate' the evidence (rather than 'specify' it) suggests that the description of the material may be in relatively broad terms.[17]

b. Producing Documents

The obligation to produce evidence is to make it physically available to the other party and the court so that it may be reviewed. This resembles the obligation in the English Civil Procedure Rules, which requires documents to be made available for inspection by an opponent, except where the document is no longer in the control of the disclosing party or it has a right to withhold inspection of it (see section XV below). It is the responsibility of the judge-rapporteur to make directions on the production of documents, during the interim procedure, with or without[18] an interim hearing. However, this does not prejudice the general power of the court at any time during proceedings (including the oral hearing) to order a party to produce evidence.[19] Again, a failure to produce documents when ordered to do so will be taken into account by the court when deciding on the issue the document relates to.[20]

---

[14] Rule 222.2 of the Rules of Procedure suggests that a similar regime will be followed before the UPC Court of Appeal, so that filing available evidence as soon as possible is advisable.
[15] ibid Rule 172.2.
[16] ibid.
[17] See ibid Rule 13.1(m) in respect of statements of claim generally, which must include 'the evidence relied on, where available, and an indication of any further evidence which will be offered in support'.
[18] Rule 103.1(c) of the Rules of Procedure. It will fall to the judge-rapporteur to establish the issues and facts in dispute, before making a production order. Relevant documents should, it is submitted, be produced at a time which is sufficiently early in proceedings to allow them to assist in the preparation of expert and, if necessary, witness evidence in appropriate cases.
[19] ibid Rule 172.2.
[20] ibid Rules 172.2.

German proceedings are, much like proceedings in the UPC,[21] 'front-loaded' requiring that a fully reasoned complaint is filed when initiating proceedings and evidence is typically gathered before an action is started; orders requiring the defendant to produce evidence to help the claimant to fulfil its burden of proof are only available in very narrow circumstances (see section IV.B below). These are typically brought before German patent infringement proceedings are started in order to determine if patent infringement has occurred and can be evidenced. Accordingly, in German patent infringement proceedings, the plaintiff is much less able to rely on the court ordering production of evidence or giving specific guidance on this. German courts do get involved where specific orders are required to keep information to be submitted confidential.[22] If it is apparent that such an order is required for confidentiality reasons, the party wishing to provide the document should request such a confidentiality order so as to be able to provide the relevant document within the set deadline for written submissions.

III. Specific Procedures for Obtaining Evidence from Opponents

The basic obligation on parties to produce all documents 'regarding' a statement of fact relied on appears to be intended to ensure a 'cards on the table' approach to litigation in the UPC – relevant material in the possession of one party is not to be kept from the other or produced at a late stage in proceedings. However, the general obligation is supplemented by a number of further specific measures to obtain evidence from opponents or third parties in more limited circumstances. These are of two types: those that permit a party to actively pursue evidence (an order to preserve evidence and order for inspection); and those that compel other parties, including third parties, to produce specific evidence (an order to produce evidence and an order to communicate information).

To obtain orders for these measures, the parties must lodge specific applications for each of them. Whilst there are common features between these applications, those for orders that allow searching for evidence and those that compel parties to give evidence all have specific requirements of their own. These are given below.

A. Common Points of the Applications

i. *The Competent Division to Decide on the Order*

The applicant must address its application for an order to the competent division. The competent division is the one where the applicant has begun the proceedings on the merits or where they intend to begin those proceedings.[23] The division competent to hear the

---

[21] ibid Rule 13, particularly at (l)(i) and (ii), (m) and (n).
[22] Section 142 of the German Civil Procedure Code and sections 16 and 19 of the Law of Business Secrets.
[23] Applications for preservation and inspection orders may be made before the proceedings on the merits of the case are lodged, subject to the time limits in Rule 198 of the Rules of Procedure.

proceedings on the merits is the local or regional division hosted by a contracting Member State where the alleged infringement is occurring or may occur, where the defendant has its residence or principal place of business or, in the event that the defendant has no such residence, the central division (see Chapter 9).

ii. Language

The language of the application is that of the proceedings of the merits or, if proceedings on the merits have not yet begun, one of the designated official languages of the division or the EPO under Article 49 UPC Agreement and subject to Rules 14.1 and 14.2 of the Rules of Procedure (see Chapter 5).

iii. 'Reasonably Available Evidence'

A party seeking an order from the court must support it with reasons based on reasonably available evidence.[24] This requirement to support the reasons with 'reasonably available evidence' is a transcription from the Enforcement Directive. However, it may be criticised on the ground that the very aim of the orders are to obtain such evidence. This requirement could be seen as stripping the measures of their main purpose. However, the requirement is one of the safeguards against abuse (see section IV.E below) and it is for the judges to adopt a practice on the issue that strikes the correct balance.

It should be noted that in Germany, where there is no discovery as such, abstract requests for potentially relevant evidence ('Ausforschungsbeweis') are not admissible.[25] A production of documents can only be requested if the individual piece of evidence can be identified (for example, a specific document), it has a relevance for establishing patent infringement, it is in possession of the other party or a third party, and its production is not considered disproportionate in the context of the facts at issue (for instance, if other sources of evidence may be available).[26]

iv. Confidentiality

The main issue arising from preservation and inspection orders, as well as orders to communicate and to produce evidence, is confidentiality (see also section XIV below). The need to respect the defendant's confidential information has to be balanced with the right of the applicant to obtain evidence of infringing procedures or products. In order to do so, the UPC Agreement's articles provide that measures seeking evidence are 'subject to the protection of confidential information'. In particular, for preservation orders and inspection orders, a means to that end is the prohibition on the applicant to be present during the

---

[24] In respect of orders to preserve evidence and inspect premises, this is stated in Article 60 UPC Agreement, although it is not expressly repeated in the relevant Rules of Procedure (Rules 192–99). As regards requests for an order to produce evidence and communicate information, the party must present 'reasonably available and plausible evidence', although the addition of the word 'plausible' would not seem to add any requirement that is not already implied.
[25] BGH, NJW 1974, 1710; BGH, GRUR 1975, 254, 256 – Ladewagen.
[26] Sections 142 German Civil Procedure Code or 485 ff of the German Civil Procedure Code.

inspection of the defendant's premises.[27] Likewise, orders to produce evidence are subject to the protection of confidential information.[28]

IV. Orders to Preserve Evidence and Order for Inspection

A. Orders to Preserve Evidence

i. The UPC Approach

The orders to preserve evidence in the UPC include, but are not limited to:[29] detailed description with or without the taking of samples; physical seizure of allegedly infringing goods; physical seizure of the materials and implements used in the production or distribution of these goods and any related documents; and preservation and disclosure of digital media and data, and the disclosure of any passwords necessary to access them. As a means to obtaining evidence, the preservation order should not be employed to stop the use of the allegedly infringing goods or processes; instead, its use must be proportionate. This means that only the amount of goods strictly necessary for the probative purpose of the order should be seized. The seizing of an entire stock may instead be achieved under the powers granted to the court by Article 62 UPC Agreement and Rule 211 of the Rules of Procedure (see Chapter 15). Furthermore, the evidence which has to be preserved through this type of order may not be used for the purpose of other proceedings, except when otherwise ordered by the court.[30] The order is enforceable immediately, unless otherwise ordered by the court, and may specify:[31] (a) who may represent the applicant when executing the order and under what conditions; and (b) any security that must be provided by the applicant. Penalties applicable to the applicant may be set by the court in the event that these conditions are not met. The order must also indicate that it can be appealed.[32]

ii. National Perspectives

The 'Order to preserve evidence' draws a number of its characteristics from the French *saisies-contrefaçons*, which are divided between *saisie descriptive* and *saisie réelle*. The distinction between the two is that the former is a detailed description of the alleged infringing matter either with or without seizing any sample and the latter consists in the sole material seizing of the matter without an accompanying detailed description.[33] The principle is that the measures are granted at the request of the applicant, without notice to the defendant.[34]

---

[27] Article 60(1) and (4) UPC Agreement.
[28] Rule 190.1 of the Rules of Procedure.
[29] Article 60(2) UPC Agreement; Rule 196.1 of the Rules of Procedure.
[30] Rule 196.2 of the Rules of Procedure.
[31] ibid Rule 196.3.
[32] Under ibid Rule 220.1.
[33] Article L615-5 of the French Intellectual Property Code.
[34] ibid.

Under German law, orders to preserve evidence ('Beweissicherungsanordnungen') are also available in the context of pending infringement proceedings, or before they are launched.[35] These are issued by way of a preliminary injunction, typically *ex parte* – for example, in cases where evidence of patent infringement may be destroyed or brought outside of the country. In this regard, the applicant has to demonstrate a certain indication that evidence that has a relevance for patent infringement will be lost; courts are critical regarding mere general assumptions that evidence could be destroyed by an alleged infringer.[36] The practice of 'seizure of evidence'(*bewijsbeslag*) also exists in the Netherlands. To obtain relief for such a seizure, the claimant must file a request with the court, demonstrating plausibility of infringement and necessity of the seizure for obtaining evidence and determining its legal position.

B. Orders for Inspection

i. The UPC Approach

The order for inspection appears quite similar to the order to preserve evidence in terms of its aims. Yet, as the name suggests, this measure does not include the seizing of samples or documentation. Instead, it allows the inspection of products, devices, methods, premises or what are referred to as 'local situations',[37] in situ, that may be deemed useful to resolve the case. Clearly, such an order may need to be combined with a preservation order, and the requirements of the Rules of Procedure are the same.[38] Like orders to preserve evidence, the evidence obtained by an inspection order may not be used for the purpose of other proceedings.[39] The order is enforceable immediately, unless ordered otherwise by the court, and may specify:[40] (a) who may represent the applicant when executing the order and under what conditions (see below); and (b) any security that must be provided by the applicant. Penalties applicable to the applicant may be set by the Court in the event that these conditions are not met. The order must also indicate that it can be appealed.[41]

ii. National Perspectives

The order has some similarities to the French notion of *saisie-description*[42] (although see IV.D.), which can be defined as a *saisie-contrefaçon* where there is no seizing of any

---

[35] Section 485 I of the German Civil Procedure Code.
[36] Düsseldorf Appeals Court, Order of 21 July 2011, I-2 W 23/11.
[37] Rule 199 of the Rules of Procedure.
[38] Set out in ibid Rules 192–98.
[39] ibid Rule 196.2.
[40] ibid Rule 196.3.
[41] Under ibid Rule 220.1.
[42] Article L332-4 of the French Intellectual Property Code. Comparison may also be made with the Spanish *ex parte* procedure for the inspection of premises called *diligencias* (Articles 129 ff of the Spanish Patents Act).

sample. It is therefore a detailed description of the alleged infringing matter. This must be distinguished from the *saisie réelle*, which consists solely of the seizing of evidence without an accompanying detailed description.[43]

In the Dutch system of seizure of evidence (*bewijsbeslag*), contrary to the French *saisie*, one does not automatically get access to the evidence seized. After the seizure, the applicant must request the Court for a relief of inspection of the seized material in preliminary proceedings (*kort geding*) unless the respondent party voluntarily grants access to it (which rarely happens). In order to obtain access, the applicant (patentee) must demonstrate the plausibility of (a threat of) a patent infringement.[44] This takes place in *inter partes* preliminary proceedings, in which the validity of the patent is also assessed if put forward by the respondent. Under German law, inspection orders ('Besichtigungsanordnungen') are also available[45] and are typically dealt with in *ex parte* preliminary injunction proceedings. The threshold for a court to issue such an order is that the object to be inspected is in the possession of the other party, the inspection has a relevance to determine patent infringement, and the inspection is proportionate with a view to the circumstances of the individual case. Such orders are usually sought before actual patent infringement proceedings on the merits are started in order to determine if there is patent infringement.

C. Procedure

i. The Contents of the Application

An application for an order to preserve evidence or for inspection[46] may be made by a party[47] to the appropriate division (see section III.A.i above). The application must contain those particulars stipulated for a statement of claim in an infringement action[48] (see Chapter 10), as well as a clear indication of the measures being requested.[49] These are:[50]

(a) preserving evidence by detailed description, with or without the taking of samples;
(b) physical seizure of allegedly infringing goods;
(c) physical seizure of the materials and implements used in the production and/or distribution of these goods and any related document;
(d) the preservation and disclosure of digital media and data and the disclosure of any passwords necessary to access them.

---

[43] Article 129 of the French Intellectual Property Code. For comparison, see also the judicial description order available in Italy, which may be used to inspect allegedly infringing goods or processes and also to the means of manufacturing the infringing goods and related evidence.

[44] Dutch Supreme Court, *AIB/Novisem*, ECLI:NL:HR:2015:3304, ro 4.1.5 (13 November 2015).

[45] Sections 809 and 810 of the German Civil Law; BGH, GRUR 2002 – *Faxkarte*; and section 140c of the German Patent Law.

[46] The Rules applicable to obtaining an orders to preserve evidence – Rules 192–98 of the Rules of Procedure – also apply to orders for inspection (Rule 199.2).

[47] According to Article 47 UPC Agreement.

[48] Rule 13.1(a)–(i) of the Rules of Procedure.

[49] ibid Rule 192.2(b).

[50] ibid Rule 196.1.

Orders to Preserve Evidence and Order for Inspection 229

If the application is being made before proceedings on the merits have been lodged in the court, it must contain a concise description of the action on the merits that will be lodged, including an indication of the facts and evidence that will be relied on.[51]

If the application is being made *ex parte*, it must set out the reasons why the defendant should not be heard and, in particular, whether delay is likely to cause irreparable harm to the applicant, or that there is a demonstrable risk of evidence being destroyed or otherwise ceasing to be available.[52] The applicant is also under a duty to disclose any material fact known to it which might influence the court in deciding whether to make an order without hearing the defendant.[53] The application will not be entered on the Register until notice has been given to the defendant.[54]

A fee of €350 is payable upon the application.

ii. Formalities

If proceedings on the merits have not yet been lodged,[55] the formalities of the application will be examined by the Registry,[56] its date of receipt will be recorded in the register, an action number will be assigned and it will be assigned to a panel or a judge-rapporteur.[57] If the main proceedings on the merits have already commenced,[58] the application will be examined by the Registry immediately and will be forwarded to the panel or the judge to whom the action on the merits is assigned.[59] In cases of extreme urgency, the standing judge[60] may decide immediately on an application to preserve evidence and the procedure to be followed on the application.[61]

iii. Examination of the Application

a. Exercise of Discretion

In common with applications for provisional measures, the court examining an application for an order to preserve evidence and/or inspection has the discretion to choose between a number of options with regard to whether it hears the application *ex parte* or *inter partes*, and whether the defendant may lodge an objection. It has the discretion to:[62]

(a) inform the defendant about the application and invite it to lodge, within a specified time period, an objection to the application for preserving evidence;

---

[51] ibid Rule 192.2.
[52] ibid Rule 197.1.
[53] ibid Rule 197.3.
[54] Immediately at the time of execution; see ibid Rule 197.2.
[55] See ibid Rule 193.1.
[56] ibid Rule 16.
[57] ibid Rules 17.1(a)–(c), 17.2 and 18. Further to Rule 194.3, the presiding judge may consequently decide that they, or the judge-rapporteur, or other single judge or the standing judge, may decide the application.
[58] See ibid Rule 193.2.
[59] ibid Rules 16, 17.2, 194.3 and 194.4.
[60] See ibid Rule 345.5.
[61] ibid Rule 194.4.
[62] ibid Rule 194.1.

230 *Obtaining and Using Evidence*

(b) summon both parties to an oral hearing;
(c) summon the applicant to an oral hearing without the presence of the defendant;
(d) decide the application without having heard the defendant (that is, by way of the objection or otherwise).

In exercising its discretion, the Court must take into account the urgency of the action and also whether the reasons for not hearing the defendant put forward by the applicant are well founded.[63] It must also consider the risk that the evidence may be destroyed or otherwise cease to be available.[64] If the Court decides to inform the defendant about the application, or the patent at issue is the subject of a protective letter,[65] the applicant will first be given the opportunity to withdraw the application. If this happens, the applicant can request that the application and its contents are kept confidential.[66]

b. The Defendant's Objection

If the court decides to invite the defendant to lodge an objection, it must contain the reasons why the application must fail, the facts and evidence relied on – in particular, any challenge to the facts and evidence relied on by the applicant – and, where the main action on the merits has not yet been lodged, the reasons why the action on the merits must fail and an indication of the facts and evidence relied on.[67]

iv. *The Oral Hearing*

The oral hearing of an application for an order to preserve evidence or order for inspection will then be set as soon as possible after the date of receiving the application. The oral hearing is conducted as for an action on the merits[68] (see Chapter 14), and the application may be rejected by the court if the applicant is absent without a reasonable excuse.[69] The decision of the court must be given in writing as soon as possible after the close of the oral hearing and may be given orally at the end of the hearing, followed as soon as practicable in writing.[70]

v. *Review of* Ex Parte *Decision*

If the hearing resulting in the order took place *ex parte* within 30 days after the execution of the measures, the defendant may request a review of an order to preserve evidence or inspection. Such a request must set out the reasons why the order must be revoked or modified, and the facts and evidence relied on.[71] The court must order an oral hearing to

---

[63] ibid Rule 194.2 (a) and (b). The Rules do not expressly mention the risk of irreparable harm, but see Rule 197.1.
[64] ibid Rule 194.2(c).
[65] Under ibid Rule 207.
[66] ibid Rule 194.5.
[67] ibid Rule 194.1(a)(i)–(iii).
[68] That is, Rules 111–16.
[69] ibid Rule 195.2.
[70] ibid Rule 195.3.
[71] ibid Rule 197.3.

review the order without delay,[72] following which the order may be revoked, modified or confirmed.

D. *Inter Partes* and *Ex Parte* Preservation and Inspection Orders

The order to preserve evidence and the order for inspection have the same aim: finding evidence that the opposing party or a third party may be inclined to destroy or change in the event it may go against its claim. Thus, both orders rely heavily on the effect of surprise: giving notice to the author of an alleged infringement would allow time to destroy or hide evidence of any product or process that would effectively be infringing the patentee's rights. Therefore, the possibility of requesting an order without the defendant being notified of the existence of the request – and consequently not being permitted to argue against such an order prior to its granting – is crucial to the success of the system. This is why the Rules of Procedure provide for an exception to the *inter partes* hearing usually required – in order to ensure the effectiveness of the order, the applicant may ask the judge for an *ex parte* measure.[73] This request must be substantiated either by showing that any delay is likely to cause irreparable harm[74] or that there is a (demonstrable) risk of evidence being destroyed or ceasing to be available.[75] However, because any action made without the defendant being heard is a breach of the adversarial principle – a core principle for a fair trial – any order to preserve evidence may be *ex parte* only if necessary.[76] It should be noted that the choice to make the procedures for obtaining evidence from opponents *inter partes* in principle and *ex parte* only as the exception is a clear distinction from the majority of the European systems. It may therefore initially be slightly confusing for those used to these systems, since it appears to limit the utility of an *ex parte* preservation and/or inspection order to exceptional circumstances[77] (see also section IV.E below). A *saisie* without the defendant being heard is also *ex parte* only insofar as notice is only given at the time of the execution of the measures.[78] Whilst the affected party cannot oppose the measure beforehand, it also benefits from a 30-day delay during which a review of the order to preserve evidence in order to have it revoked or modified can be requested.

E. Safeguards for the Defendant

There are a number of safeguards to avoid an *ex parte* preservation order and/or inspection order being used against a defendant or to remedy improper use.[79] Even before the orders

---

[72] ibid Rule 197.4.
[73] ibid Rule 192.3.
[74] ibid Rule 197.1. Note that irreparable harm is not an express requirement at the stage of examination of the application in Rule 194, but it is submitted that this is a factor that the court would take into account at that stage.
[75] Article 60(5) UPC Agreement; Rule 197.1 of the Rules of Procedure.
[76] In accordance with Article 60(5) UPC Agreement.
[77] In this respect, the UPC system may more closely resemble the application of comparable measures in England and Wales.
[78] Rule 197.2 of the Rules of Procedure.
[79] The Rules cited here are primarily concerned with orders to preserve evidence, but Rule 199.2 of the Rules of Procedure provides that they also apply to orders for inspection.

are granted, the court has the discretionary power to inform the defendant about the application and to ask them to lodge an objection.[80] Therefore, the Rules of Procedure open a way for the court or the judge-rapporteur to defeat the aim of the *ex parte* measure to take the defendant by surprise, which is the intention of an *ex parte* order. However, before informing the defendant, the applicant is offered the possibility to withdraw the application and to request a confidentiality order on this application and its content.[81]

At the time that an *ex parte* order to preserve evidence or for inspection is executed, the defendant must also be given notice immediately.[82] In the 30 days following the execution of the measure, the defendant may lodge a request for review of the order, which parallels the application as it must contain the reasons, supported by facts and evidence, why the order should be revoked.[83] Moreover, this objection to the preliminary order can double as an objection to the action on the merits under the same conditions.

In the event of the order being revoked or lapsing because of the action or lack thereof of the applicant, or when the proceedings on the merits end by finding there was no infringement or threat of infringement, the defendant may receive compensation.[84] The extension to the finding of no threat of infringement seems to prevent these orders being used as a means to further harm competitors. Like the French court in similar matters, the court may decide to subject the granting of the order to the payment of a security in order to cover the potential damages due in the event that the *saisie* is unfounded or abusive.[85]

For comparison, the Dutch system also provides safeguards:

(1) The fact that the applicant does not get immediate access, but the court must grant inspection after *inter partes* proceedings have taken place (including an oral hearing, which is again a mini-trial) in which the applicant must prove plausibility of (a threat of) infringement and validity (when put forward by the defendant).
(2) Requirements for the seizure, such as that the request must very specifically point out what the applicant wants to be seized and why this is necessary ('bepaalde bescheiden'), so as to prevent the seizure from being a fishing expedition. In addition, the applicant must prove that a juridical relationship between the parties exists, which comes down to explaining why the applicant is of the opinion that a (threat of) infringement exists. The applicant must also demonstrate that the seizure it asks for meets the requirements of proportionality and subsidiarity. And last but not least, confidential information must be safeguarded. In practice, this means that an independent expert is appointed to fulfil the inspection.

---

[80] ibid Rule 194.1.
[81] ibid Rule 194.5.
[82] ibid Rule 197.2. Further to Rule 192.3, the application for the preservation or inspection cannot be entered on the Register until this is done. However it is not clear from Rule 192.3 what the consequences for the applicant is of a failure to enter on the Register in these circumstances, although this might be expected to provide a basis for revocation under Rule 197.4.
[83] ibid Rule 197.3.
[84] ibid Rule 198.2.
[85] ibid Rule 196.3(b). An explanatory note by the Legal Group of the Preparatory Committee states that despite the general rule that the court must order adequate security when it orders measures to preserve evidence, this need not be provided in special circumstances (the note envisages circumstances where no damage can occur or only a sample of an inexpensive mass product is sought).

F. The Parties Present

The applicant is not allowed to be present during the execution of the measures in order to preserve confidentiality and avoid suspicions of industrial spying. However, the applicant may be represented, in accordance with Article 48 UPC Agreement as long as the representative is not an employee or a director of the applicant.[86] The person carrying out the measure must be a professional person or expert designated by the court with regard to their expertise, independence and impartiality.[87]

This suggested UPC approach is in line with German practice; the applicant must appoint a person who will carry out the inspection and has to define in the request exactly what this person will be able to do. The inspection is then carried out by a court bailiff alongside the person appointed to carry out the inspection and the attorneys of the applicant. The persons present at the inspection are not allowed to communicate findings to the applicant; rather, following the inspection, a report on the findings is written and the probability of infringement is assessed. The party being inspected is then heard as to confidentiality interests and the extent to which the report can be made available to the applicant. As a general principle, if the findings support patent infringement, the potential confidentiality interests will (unless these can be dealt with by redactions that still allow an understanding of the findings) be overruled by the interests of the patentee to use the evidence in assertion of its patent.[88]

G. The Timing of the Application

i. Urgency

The orders to preserve evidence may be requested by a party either before the proceedings on the merits have started or during these proceedings.[89] Although the Enforcement Directive does not mention urgency as a criterion for the granting of preserving evidence measures, the Rules of Procedure state that the court 'shall take into account the urgency of the action'.[90] However, the phrase 'take into account' does not mean that urgency is always mandatory for the granting of such measures, therefore allowing for measures without urgency to be granted, which lets the court create its own rules on the subject.

The question of urgency is subject to debate among German courts: some seem to require it with a view to the wording in the Enforcement Directive and proportionality

---

[86] Article 60(4) UPC Agreement; Rule 196.3(a) and 196.5 of the Rules of Procedure.
[87] Rule 196.4 of the Rules of Procedure. The Rules of Procedure refer only to the applicable national law regarding the assistance of the person executing the act. In practice, it should often be either an expert or a bailiff. The French *saisie* states that the applicant may choose any locally competent bailiff. While the French Code of Intellectual Property (Article L615-5) does explicitly state that the bailiff carrying out the measure may be assisted by a skilled person – usually another expert – it appears that he may be assisted by any number of persons as long as they are authorised by the judge's Ordonnance.
[88] T Kühnen, *Handbuch der Patentverletzung*, 14th edn, B. II.3. at Nr. 155 (Carl Heymanns, 2022).
[89] Article 60(1) UPC Agreement; Rule 192.1 of the Rules of Procedure.
[90] Rule 194.2(a),of the Rules of Procedure.

considerations,[91] while others (for example, the Düsseldorf Appeals Court) consider this dispensable with a view to the aim of an inspection to gain certainty over patent infringement.[92] This aim should be treated differently from aims of 'regular' preliminary injunctions, where it is important to get a quick enforceable injunction against an infringer.

ii. Starting Proceedings on the Merits

The timing of the application is particularly important if it is made before the beginning of the proceedings on the merits, as it determines the date by which these proceedings must be started: pursuant to Rule 198 of the Rules of Procedure, they must begin within 31 calendar days or 20 working days of the date (whichever is the longer) contained in the order. Working days do not include the official holidays of the contracting Member State in which the concerned division, the seat of the central division or the branch of the central division is located (see Chapter 19).

H. Security

The Court has the discretion to order an applicant for a preservation order or inspection order to provide an adequate security, by deposit or bank guarantee, for the legal costs and other expenses and compensation for any injury incurred or likely to be incurred by the defendant. The Court must order the applicant to provide such a security if the order was made without hearing the defendant, other than in special circumstances.[93]

V. Orders to Produce Evidence and Orders to Communicate Information

A. General Considerations

Orders to produce evidence and to communicate information supplement the general obligation to produce documents regarding statements of fact relied on (see section II.B above) and reflect the practice adopted by most civil law systems, where, in the absence of a general duty of disclosure, the only means for a party to access documentation relating to the matter which is in possession or control of its opponent is to specifically ask the Court for the document(s) in question.[94]

---

[91] Karlsruhe Appeals Court, Beck RS 2011, 18386.
[92] Düsseldorf Appeals Court, GRUR-RR 2011, 289 – *späte Besichtigung*.
[93] Rule 196.6 of the Rules of Procedure.
[94] For example, the Articles 59 (order to produce evidence) and 67 (order to communicate information) UPC Agreement' – detailed in Rules 190 and 191 – roughly reflect the measures available in France under the 'right to information' (Article L615-5-2 of the French Intellectual Property Code).

B. Orders to Produce Evidence

i. The UPC Approach

Orders to produce evidence may be requested by a party during the interim or the written procedures.[95] The granting of this order is subject to a particular prerequisite: that the applicant's claim is supported by 'reasonably available and plausible evidence'.[96] One must infer from this prerequisite that in order to ask the court to order the opposing party or a third party to disclose supplementary evidence, one must have knowledge of the evidence. In other words, the object of the order must be evidence known to the applicant as opposed to assumed evidence. To obtain the order, the applicant must list the reasons why the order ought to be granted by the court and support these reasons with reasonably available facts and evidence. This might, like the preservation and inspection orders, be criticised on the ground that the aim of the order is to obtain such evidence. It will therefore be up to the judges to adopt an approach to the scope and nature of the circumstantial evidence required to justify such an order.

ii. National Perspectives

The order to produce evidence appears to be similar to a provision in the French Code of Intellectual Property, according to which the order to produce evidence aims at determining the matter that could be subject to a *saisie*.[97] It divides the material subject to the order into two categories: on the one hand, banking, financial, accounting or commercial documentation, which should be *communicated*; and, on the other hand, *relevant* information, which can only be *accessed*. The French equivalent[98] may be ordered without the need for a previous *saisie-contrefaçon*, but it usually is ordered as a follow-up. The French version defines quite strictly what information may be communicated through this order.

Under German law, in restrictive circumstances, production orders ('Vorlageanordnungen') are also available. If the party from which the identified evidence is sought does not agree to its production, the court will make a decision on necessity and proportionality, and will also consider any potential third-party interests (for example, in a licence contract to be submitted). Such orders may be more important for the defendant in proceedings; a claimant would generally try to secure evidence before commencing proceedings – for example, by inspection proceedings. This approach is more common given that German proceedings require that – as is the case before the UPC – a fully reasoned complaint is already filed with evidence when commencing proceedings.

---

[95] Rule 190(1) of the Rules of Procedure. This order results from the transposition of Article 6 of the Enforcement Directive 2004/48.
[96] Article 59(1) UPC Agreement and Rule 190.1 of the Rules of Procedure.
[97] Article L521-6 §2, last sentence of the French Intellectual Property Code.
[98] ibid L615-5-2.

C. Orders to Communicate Information

Under Article 67(1) UPC Agreement, the UPC may order an infringer to inform the applicant of:

(a) the origin and distribution channels of the infringing products or processes;
(b) the quantities produced, manufactured, delivered, received or ordered, as well as the price obtained for the infringing products; and
(c) the identity of any third person involved in the production or distribution of the infringing products or in the use of the infringing process.

Orders to communicate information are restricted in the Rules of Procedure to information that is deemed 'reasonably necessary for the purpose of advancing that party's case'.[99] This appears to extend beyond the information envisaged by Article 67 UPC Agreement, which concerns the infringing products' origin, distribution channels, quantities and price, as well as the identity of third parties involved in the production or distribution of these products.[100]

Such orders to communicate information on origin and supply channels are available in Germany.[101] They are typically asserted as an ancillary requests to a preliminary injunction to gain information on the supply channels in order to effectively stop further infringement. Such requests are awarded in preliminary injunction proceedings if there is a clear case of infringement.

VI. Party Experts and Witnesses

A. Overview of the Approach

Decisions and orders on how and when expert evidence is to be used in proceedings are made by the judge-rapporteur at the interim conference. At this stage, the judge-rapporteur can issue orders on, among other matters: experts (party-appointed and court-appointed), the matters to be the subject of oral evidence; the scope of questions to be put to witnesses and experts;[102] and the separate hearing of witnesses and/or experts before the panel.[103] Preparatory discussions with witnesses and experts to properly prepare for the oral hearing may also happen at the interim stage (see Chapter 13).[104]

The evidence of an expert or witness will be heard in person during the oral proceedings if this has been ordered by the court of its own motion or because the statement concerned has been challenged by the other party. Furthermore, if a party seeking evidence

---

[99] Rule 191 of the Rules of Procedure. Comparison may be made with the Danish rules on preservation of evidence, in which the court uses the principle of proportionality to balance the claimant's interest in securing evidence and the right of privacy, protection of trade secrets and other considerations.
[100] Article 6 UPC Agreement.
[101] Section 140b I of the German Patent Law.
[102] Rule 104(e) of the Rules of Procedure.
[103] ibid Rule 104(g).
[104] ibid Rule 104(f).

cannot obtain a written statement, they may apply with reasons to have the witness heard in person.[105] Questions may also be put to the witness or expert (see Chapters 13 and 14).

B. Duties of Experts and Witnesses

i. General Duties

Witnesses and experts must obey a summons to attend the oral hearing.[106] Failure to appear, refusal to give evidence or refusal to make the declaration of truth may be result in a pecuniary fine not exceeding €50,000 and a further summons may follow at the witness' expense.[107] However, no witness is obliged to give oral evidence or sign a statement if they are a spouse, partner equal to a spouse under the applicable national law, descendant, sibling or parent of a party.

A witness or expert may also refuse to answer questions that would violate a professional privilege or other duty of confidentiality in the applicable national law, or expose that person, their spouse, partner equal to a spouse, descendant, sibling or parent to criminal prosecution under applicable national law. A witness or expert may also refuse to give evidence protected by litigation privilege, which means that a party-appointed expert, for example, is not required to reveal the instructions and drafts behind their served report. The giving of false evidence by a witness or expert may be reported to the authorities of the contracting Member State whose courts have criminal jurisdiction for the country in which the false evidence was given.[108]

ii. The Overriding Duty of the Expert to the Court

In the UPC, experts may be instructed by one of the parties to the dispute, as well as by the court. However, such a party-appointed expert must give evidence independently and impartially[109] – they must not be partisan. To ensure this and to protect experts, the Rules of Procedure put in place duties designed to make the process of preparing evidence transparent. In the case of party-appointed experts, it is expressly stipulated that this duty overrides any duty to the party instructing them. This means that the expert must be independent and objective, and must not act as an advocate for any party to the proceedings[110] whether or not they are paid by them (see section VII below).

---

[105] Rule 176 of the 17th draft Rules of Procedure.
[106] ibid Rule 179.1.
[107] ibid Rule 179.2.
[108] ibid Rule 179.4.
[109] Article 57(3) UPC Agreement.
[110] Rule 181.2(a) and (b) of the Rules of Procedure. These duties will be set out in the order of the court summoning the expert. Reference may be had to EuroExpert, the organisation for European expert associations, which provides a code of practice and general requirements for expert reports, designed to provide a common, minimum standard for the transparency and quality of expert evidence in the EU; see https://euroexpert.org/standards/code-of-practice. Guidance may also be derived from the Civil Procedure Rules of England and Wales, Practice Direction 25B, paras 3.1, 4.1 and 9.1.

C. Statements of Truth and Conflicts of Interest

Witness and expert evidence must be lodged by a written statement or written summary of the evidence to be given.[111] The statement must be signed and include a statement by the witness that they are aware of their obligation to tell the truth.[112] The witness must also state that they are aware of their liability under the applicable national law in the event that this obligation is breached.[113]

The witness statement or summary must also state any current or past relationship between the witness and the party submitting the statement, and any actual or potential conflict of interest that may affect the witness' impartiality.[114] If necessary, the statement or summary should also state the language in which the witness will give oral evidence.[115]

D. Application and Summons to an Oral Hearing

Subject to any order already made at the interim conference (see Chapter 13), a party must make an application to have expert and witness evidence heard orally.[116] The application must state:

(a) the reasons why the witness should be heard in person;
(b) the facts which the party expects the witness to confirm; and
(c) the language in which the witness shall give evidence.

In addition to ordering that a witness or expert is heard in person, in response to an application by the party submitting the evidence, the court may make such an order of its own motion or where the written statement of the witness or expert is being challenged by another party.[117] In addition to the personal details of the witness, the date and place of the oral hearing, and information about the reimbursement of the witness' expenses, the order summoning a witness to an oral hearing will also state that the witness is to be questioned by the court and the parties. The order will also give an indication of the facts of the action about which the witness will be examined.[118] It will also state the language of proceedings and provide the opportunity to arrange simultaneous interpretation of the language of the witness or expert.[119]

---

[111] Rule 175.1 of the Rules of Procedure.
[112] ibid Rule 175.2.
[113] ibid Rule 175.2. The UPC has no supranational rules of perjury or contempt. The obligation is that of the national law of the country in which the relevant division is situated. These may carry criminal penalties. The division in question may report a witness who has given false evidence to the relevant criminal authorities of the contracting Member State concerned (Rule 179.4).
[114] ibid Rule 175.3.
[115] ibid Rule 175.2.
[116] ibid Rule 176.
[117] ibid Rule 177.
[118] ibid Rule 177.2.
[119] ibid Rule 177.2(f); see also Rule 109.

E. Hearing Experts and Witnesses

i. During the Interim Procedure

Among other matters to be decided at the interim conference, the Rules of Procedure envisage that the Court will 'in the presence of the parties, hold preparatory discussions with witnesses and experts with a view to properly preparing for the oral hearing'.[120] The extent of such preparatory discussions with witnesses and experts that is intended at this stage is unclear. It would seem that the court is to be given the opportunity to at least establish on which issues there is agreement between experts and on which there is disagreement. To this extent, the discussions may be intended to assist the court to establish those matters to be the subject of oral evidence and the scope of questions to be put to the witnesses, which are also an important aspect of the interim conference.[121]

ii. The Oral Hearing

Oral testimony will begin with identification of the witness or expert. The witness or expert will then be asked by the presiding judge to make the following declaration:

> I solemnly, sincerely and truly declare and affirm that the evidence I shall give shall be the truth, the whole truth and nothing but the truth.[122]

The witness or expert, if they have made a written statement, must confirm the evidence in their statement, although they may elaborate on it. There are then two sources of possible questioning of the witness or expert:

(a) questions from the judges of the panel; and
(b) questions from the parties.

The Rules of Procedure state that the questioning by the parties is 'under the control of the presiding judge'. In particular, the presiding judge may prohibit any question 'which is not designed to adduce admissible evidence'.[123] The scope of matters outside the 'admissible evidence' referred to is unclear, but appears intended to include matters protected by litigation privilege (see section XV.B below), matters on which the witness may refuse to give evidence under the Rules of Procedure and issues that have not been identified by the judge-rapporteur or the presiding judge for attention.

With the consent of the court, the witness or expert may be heard in a language other than that of the proceedings[124] and simultaneous interpretation into the language of proceedings can be provided in these circumstances.

Much of the procedure relating to the appointment of experts by the parties is derived from English proceedings where it is the mainstay of evidence in patent proceedings.

---

[120] ibid Rule 104(f).
[121] ibid Rule 104(e).
[122] ibid Rule 178.1.
[123] ibid Rule 178.5.
[124] ibid Rule 178.6.

Provided that the expert duties and formalities are complied with in the English court, the court will treat such evidence as prima facie objective and impartial, although it will be tested in cross-examination and can be the subject of judicial criticism in appropriate cases. However, due to the protection of litigation privilege, opponents and the court are not normally entitled to 'look behind' the expert reports served to see preparatory drafts.

In Germany, parties can appoint experts and provide their findings, for example, by way of an expert report. However, such party experts are not considered as neutral experts (contrary to court-appointed experts); accordingly, their pleading is considered as party pleading. The approach of the UPC differs from this, as Rule 181 II(a) and (b) of the Rules of Procedure requires that party experts must be independent and objective and not act as an advocate for any party in the proceedings. Parties may also independently submit one or more expert opinions in the Netherlands. These opinions will be taken into account and seriously discussed by the Court. Nevertheless, they are never decisive and, in practice, once a party has submitted an expert opinion, the other party will find another expert and file an expert opinion stating the opposite. It is up to the Court to then assess the independence and quality of such expert opinions.

VII. Court-Appointed Experts

A. The Role of the Court-Appointed Expert

The court, at its discretion, may at any time appoint one or more court experts in order to provide expertise for specific technical or other aspects of the case.[125] The expert must prepare a report and attend the oral hearing if requested to by the Court, and must answer questions from the Court and the parties.[126] The UPC Agreement states that the appointment of a court expert is without prejudice to the possibility for the parties to produce expert evidence.[127] Consideration will therefore need to be given by the Court and the parties as to when an issue is covered by a court-appointed expert, when it is subject to the evidence of party-appointed experts only, or when it is addressed by both.[128] It remains to be seen when the court will consider it appropriate to take evidence from a court-appointed expert as opposed to, or in addition to, party experts. National approaches differ widely in this respect: for example, court-appointed experts are the norm in the German courts, but a rarity in the English Patents Court. However, it is clear that the Rules of Procedure specifically envisage the use of court-appointed experts for the conduct of experiments that are ordered by the court on the application by a party (see below).

---

[125] ibid Rule 185.1. For this purpose, the court is to draw up an indicative list of experts from which court-appointed experts can be drawn. This list is to be kept by the Registrar (Article 57.2 UPC Agreement).
[126] Rule 186.6 of the Rules of Procedure.
[127] Article 57(1) UPC Agreement.
[128] Indeed, Rule 185.4(c) of the Rules of Procedure implies that the court-appointed expert may be giving evidence on matters that are already addressed by party-appointed experts.

B. Duties

The court-appointed expert has an overriding duty to the court and must be independent and impartial.[129] This approach reflects the strict duties under the English Civil Procedure Rules[130] and it is submitted that many aspects of the English approach would be appropriate in the UPC, such as including a statement at the end of the expert's report that the expert understands and has complied with their duty to the court[131] and taking great care to avoid any suggestion that the expert has been led or placed under undue pressure to come to a particular view, or that their views are unsubstantiated, in conflict with their duties (see also section VI.B above). In inventive step cases, in particular, the expert should be instructed in such a way that the use of hindsight is avoided.[132]

In the UPC, the parties may also be heard on the expertise, independence and impartiality of the court expert.[133] The rules governing conflicts of interest that are applicable to the judges, set out in Article 7 of the Statute to the UPC Agreement, also apply by analogy to court experts.[134] Specifically, the court-appointed expert must inform the court of their progress in writing their report and present the report in writing within the time period specified by the court order.[135] If the report is not prepared within the time specified, or any agreed extension of time, the Court may appoint another expert.[136] The report must cover only those matters that have been put to the expert.[137] The court-appointed expert is also under a duty not to communicate with one of the parties without the other party being present, or without their consent to such communications, and all such communications must be documented in the expert's report.[138] The expert must not communicate the contents of their report to third parties.[139]

C. Appointment

The parties may make suggestions about the identity of the court expert, their technical or other background, and the questions that should be put to the court expert.[140] It is the

---

[129] Rule 186.7 of the Rules of Procedure.
[130] CPR 35.3. An expert's report must comply with the requirements set out in Practice Direction 35.
[131] CPR 35.10(2).
[132] For guidance, see *Medimmune Ltd v Novartis Pharmaceuticals* [2011] EWHC 1669; *FibroGen v Akebia* [2020] EWHC 866 (Pat); *MSD v Wyeth* [2020] EWHC 2636 (Pat); *Fisher & Paykel v Flexicare* [2020] EWHC 3282 (Pat); and *Neurim v Mylan* [2020] EWHC 3270 (Pat).
[133] Rule 185.3 of the Rules of Procedure.
[134] The expert may not take part in proceedings in which they: have taken part as an adviser; have been a party or have acted for one of the parties; have been called upon to pronounce as a member of a court, tribunal, board of appeal, arbitration or mediation panel, a commission of inquiry or in any other capacity; have a personal or financial interest in the case or in relation to one of the parties; or are related to one of the parties or the representatives of the parties by family ties.
[135] Rules 186.1 and 186.2 of the Rules of Procedure.
[136] ibid Rule 185.8.
[137] ibid Rules 186.3.
[138] ibid Rules 186.4.
[139] ibid Rule 186.5.
[140] ibid Rule 185.2.

242 *Obtaining and Using Evidence*

court's responsibility to then provide the expert with all the information necessary for them to provide their advice,[141] further to appointment by an order specifying the following:[142]

(a) the name and address of the expert;
(b) a short description of the facts of the action;
(c) the evidence submitted by the parties in respect of the technical or other question that the court-appointed expert is to address;
(d) the questions put to the experts, with the appropriate level of detail, including suggestions as to any experiments that it may be appropriate to carry out;
(e) when and under what conditions the expert may receive other relevant information;
(f) the time period in which the expert report must be presented;
(g) information about the reimbursement of the expert's expenses;
(h) information about the sanctions that may be imposed on a defaulting expert;
(i) the expert's duties (see section VII.B above).

The expert must receive a copy of the order and confirm in writing that they will present their report in the time specified by the Court.[143] The court must agree a fee with the expert for the preparation of the report and attendance at the oral hearing.[144] Any expert advice given to the court by court experts will be made available to the parties, giving them the opportunity to comment on it.[145]

In German patent infringement litigation, the appointment of an impartial court-appointed expert is typically reserved to rare cases, in which the technical questions or facts underlying the determination of patent infringement are particularly complex. Against the background that appointing an expert (both parties can make suggestions as to a neutral expert) and having the expert provide their report can be a lengthy process, German courts rely on this only in a few complex cases, as it will considerably delay litigation and also require a further oral hearing to hear the expert on their findings. The Dutch courts may also appoint an independent technical expert to answer specific questions set by the Court (or as formulated by the parties together). Such an independent technical expert appointed by the Court will have more value than a party-appointed expert, but might be more of a risk as well.

VIII. Court-Appointed or Party-Appointed Experts?

In the negotiations that led up to the UPC Agreement and beyond, the UK (and some other countries) fought hard to preserve the possibility of calling party-appointed experts. This was on the basis of the experience in the UK, where the oral evidence of an expert subjected to cross-examination was regarded as very helpful by national judges in reaching a conclusion on questions such as obviousness and insufficiency. The value of such evidence was

---

[141] Article 57(1) UPC Agreement.
[142] Rule 185.4 of the Rules of Procedure.
[143] ibid Rule 185.5 and 185.6.
[144] This fee may be reduced if the report is prepared late and/or it is not of the quality to be expected (ibid Rule 185.7).
[145] Article 57(4) UPC Agreement.

seen primarily in filling in the background as to how the skilled person was thinking at the priority date of the patent, and the *reasons* why the skilled person would or would not take a particular step.

Those from jurisdictions where the courts rely on court-appointed experts were unconvinced of the value of the party-appointed expert, believing that an expert can ultimately be found to represent any point of view and that experts favour helping the party who instructs them rather than doing their duty to the court. The UPC and the Rules of Procedure therefore represented a compromise under which both ways of obtaining expert evidence remain available. With the lack of continued involvement of the UK judges, the practice is likely to favour court-appointed experts where expert evidence is deemed necessary.

The choice made in any individual case as to whether to use court-appointed or party-appointed experts may still depend in part on the nationality of the parties and the national background of the judge-rapporteur. One factor which may be relevant is the constraint on the length of hearing under the UPC, which will not allow for the style of cross-examination of party-appointed experts permitted in the English courts. If party-appointed expert witnesses are to be provided for within the procedure, one may expect there to be quite strict limits on cross-examination. In this respect, the practice in the Intellectual Property Enterprise Court of severe limits on cross-examination may serve as a model for what may be permitted in the UPC. However, there is the view that if party-appointed experts know that they are not going be cross-examined or if they are going to be cross-examined under severe time pressure, the value of their evidence overall will be reduced.

IX. The Relationship between the Advice of Technical Judges and Experts

In the UPC, there may be as many as three sources of technical advice to the court: the technical judge; court expert; and experts appointed by the parties. What is the relationship between the advice given by a technical judge, where one is appointed, and that of the experts? In the context of a panel of legal judges who do not have technical backgrounds, the technical judge can be expected to assist the panel to resolve conflicts between the evidence of the party-appointed experts. However, the extent to which the court may in certain cases reject the need for an expert opinion if it considers the expertise of its own technical judge as sufficient to assess a technical question remains to be seen.[146] There may be such cases, and there is precedent in the Boards of Appeal of the EPO, which undoubtedly take this view of themselves.[147] Yet, it is submitted that this approach would be regrettable. Such a process of deciding a case lacks the transparency which either form of taking expert evidence provides. The parties do not have the same means of testing the technical views of a member of the UPC Panel as they will have of testing the views of an expert.

---

[146] A possibility raised by the EPLIT Mock UPC Trial, 22 January 2016, Munich.
[147] Opinions from technically trained judges in the German validity courts also carry some weight and are considered in much the same way as expert opinions are by the non-technically staffed infringement courts.

X. The Expert and the Skilled Person

The expert is normally asked to address at least the claims of a disputed patent, pieces of prior art and the common general knowledge. Having been called to give their opinion, the expert must do so as if they are standing in the shoes of the objective and notional figure known as the 'man skilled in the art' (the 'skilled person' or, where there is more than one such person, the 'skilled team'). Similarly, when assessing this evidence and making its decision, the court must 'don the mantle of the skilled man'. Having adopted the role of the skilled person, there is a question regarding whether an expert may be permitted to give their opinion on the ultimate questions in an action that are mixed matters of law and fact, such as whether a patent is obvious.[148]

A recurring difficulty for experts and those instructing them is also how closely the expert's knowledge and skill must match that of the skilled person. If an expert is found whose skills in reality are a close match for those of the skilled person, it follows that they will probably be someone with less professional impact and credibility than a leading academic. On the other hand, leading academics and experts of similar standing are open to the accusation that they are naturally inventive and too far removed from the skilled person; the latter will be inventive and so more liable to regard a disputed invention to be obvious. The UPC judges will need to decide where they think this balance is to be struck. For comparison, in England and Wales, the court has said that it will take into account over-qualification.[149] It does not matter whether the expert only approximates to the skilled person, provided that they are good at explaining things. Nonetheless, it is ideal that an expert should have personal experience of the particular technology in dispute and at the relevant period of the patent's priority date.[150]

In German proceedings, the question to which degree an expert qualifies as the person skilled in the art plays a lesser role as in infringement proceedings, experts are not appointed by default, but rather only in cases when the court requires it. As the person skilled in the art is a legal concept that can oftentimes consist of a team of people, the discussion on the (one) expert qualifying as the person skilled in the art plays a lesser role.

XI. Court-Ordered Experiments

A. The Procedure for Proving Facts by Experiment

Having heard the parties, the judge-rapporteur may of its own motion or on a reasoned request by a party order an experiment to prove a statement of fact.[151] A party making

---

[148] In English law, the expert may give their opinion on such ultimate questions, but the court is not obliged to follow it; see *Routestone Ltd v Minories Finance Ltd* [1997] BCC 180.
[149] *Generics (UK) Ltd v Yeda Research & Development Co Ltd* [2012] EWHC 1848 (Pat).
[150] For guidance, see *Generics (UK) Ltd v Daiichi Pharmaceutical Co Ltd, Daiichi Sankyo Co Ltd* [2008] EWHC 2413 (Pat)).
[151] Rule 201.1 of the Rules of Procedure. Note that the court cannot of its own motion order an experiment to be carried out.

the request must lodge it as soon as practicable in the written or interim procedures. The request must:[152]

(a) give the reasons for carrying out the proposed experiments, including identifying the facts that it is intended the experiments will establish;
(b) describe the proposed experiments in detail;
(c) propose an expert to carry out the proposed experiment; and
(d) disclose any previous attempts to carry out similar experiments.

Further to the request, the other parties to the proceedings will be invited to state whether they dispute the facts that the experiment is intended to prove. The other parties will also be invited to comment on the request, including the identity of the expert proposed and the description of the experiments.[153]

An order allowing the experiment will: specify the detail of the experiment; give the name and address of the expert (or experts) who will carry out the experiments as the court's expert and draw up the report on the experiments; give the time period for carrying out the experiment and, where appropriate, the exact time and place where it is to be carried out; and give the time period for producing the report and, where appropriate, directions relating to the contents of the report.[154] Other conditions for carrying out the experiment may be specified, as necessary. Where appropriate, the Court may order that the experiment is carried out in the presence of the parties and their experts.[155] Once the report on the experiments is produced to the court, the parties will be invited to comment on it either in writing or during the oral hearing. The expert or experts who conducted the experiment may be summoned to the oral hearing.[156] Unless ordered by the Court on its own motion, the costs of an experiment must be borne by the party requesting it.[157]

B. Experiments not Sanctioned by the Court

A request that the court order an experiment to prove a statement of fact does not prevent a party or its expert carrying out experiments of its own. However, the inference of the Rules of Procedure is that such experiments are not admissible without the sanction of the court. Furthermore, the request for an order must disclose any experiment that the party has already conducted on its own account. Such experiments would otherwise be protected from production by litigation privilege (see section XV.B below). Therefore, a party may not secretly rehearse an experiment or series of experiments prior to using it to prove a statement of fact in proceedings ('litigation chemistry'),[158] without waiving privilege in the earlier attempts. This obligation extends to 'similar' experiments.

---

[152] ibid Rule 201.2.
[153] ibid Rule 201.3.
[154] ibid Rule 201.5.
[155] ibid Rule 201.6.
[156] ibid Rule 201.7.
[157] ibid Rule 201.4.
[158] See Jacob LJ in *Smithkline Beecham and Another v Apotex Europe Ltd and Others* [2004] EWCA Civ 1568.

In German litigation, experiments are typically carried out by court-appointed experts, if ordered by the court. The infringement court will then, once the expert report containing the result of the experiments is available, evaluate the results. In the Dutch system, it is very rare for the Court to order an experiment of its own, or even on request. However, parties do perform their own experiments (with or without an independent expert) and submit a report of that experiment as evidence.

XII. Judicial Cooperation in the Taking of Evidence

Rule 173 of the Rules of Procedure provides that as regards judicial cooperation in the taking of evidence ('letters rogatory'), the relevant panel of the UPC must apply any method provided by EU Regulation 2020/1783[159] (in relation to taking evidence within the EU) or The Hague Convention of 18 March 1970 on the Taking of Evidence Abroad in Civil or Commercial Matters, where it applies or any other applicable bilateral or multilateral convention or agreement that applies (as regards taking evidence from outside the EU).[160] Where no such instruments apply, the national law of the state where the requesting court is located must be followed.[161]

XIII. Border Seizures under the Customs Regulation

The procedure for the seizure of infringing goods at the EU border is provided by Regulation (EU) 608/2013[162] (hereinafter the 'Customs Regulation') and is an important adjunct to the procedures for obtaining evidence in the UPC. This is because the Customs Regulation provides a means to monitor, through the customs authorities of EU Member States, the passage of infringing products through customs, either at the request of a right holder or on discovery by the customs authorities through routine inspections.

---

[159] Regulation 2020/1783 repealed and replaced Regulation 1206/2001 on 1 July 2022. As Amendments to the text of the UPC draft Rules of Procedure approved by the Preparatory Committee on 15 March 2017 AC/04/08072022_E – ANNEX 1, explain: 'Regulation (EU) 2020/1783 aims to improve and simplify judicial cooperation within the European Union. Articles 5 to 22 of the new EU regulation contain the provisions for the transmission and execution of requests. Article 19 regulates the direct taking of evidence in another EU Member State. Article 20 provides for taking of evidence by videoconferencing or other distance communications technology. The model forms for requests for the taking of evidence under the applicable EU regulation on the taking of evidence are available on the European e-Justice Portal (https://e-justice.europa.eu/76/EN/taking_of_evidence).'

[160] To which there are 64 contracting parties, including Australia, China, the UK and the US (https://www.hcch.net/en/instruments/conventions/status-table/?cid=82). Model forms for letters of request under The Hague Evidence Convention are available for download in different languages on the website of The Hague Conference on Private International Law (https://www.hcch.net/en/publications-and- studies/details4/?pid=6557&dtid=65).

[161] National law must be applied by a UPC division in cases of judicial cooperation with a national court of the same country where the UPC division is located or where the requested court is a court of a third country not bound by any agreement or convention.

[162] Regulation (EU) 608/2013 of the European Parliament and of the Council of 12 June 2013 concerning customs enforcement of intellectual property rights and repealing Council Regulation (EC) No 1383/2003.

A. The Application for Customs Seizure

The Customs Regulation provides for two types of application: either a national application requesting the customs authorities of a Member State to take action in that Member State; or a single EU application, designating one or more other Member States. Assuming that the customs authorities grant the application, the application takes effect for a period of one year, which can be extended.[163]

Under the Customs Regulation, the patentee (or any person formally authorised by the patentee to initiate legal proceedings) must make an application to the relevant customs authority giving information, including technical data on the authentic goods and information relevant to the customs authorities' analysis and assessment of the risk of infringement of the relevant patent. The provision of detailed information in the application is important to reduce the risk that genuine goods will be detained, exposing the patentee to liability for damages to the owner of the goods in question.[164]

B. Notification of Infringing Goods

Where the customs authorities identify goods suspected of infringing a patent, or other right, covered by the application, they must suspend the release of the goods or detain them. Once goods have been suspended or detained, the procedure under the Customs Regulation is for the customs authority to notify the owner of the goods within one working day of that suspension or detention. The right holder must then be informed of the suspension or detention on the same day. The customs authority is required to inform both the owner and the patentee of the actual or estimated quantity and nature of the goods, and inform the patentee of the owner's name and address. Both parties are then given the opportunity to inspect the goods and, importantly for evidential purposes, at the patentee's request, the customs authority may take samples and send them to the patentee for analysis (subject to various strict conditions).

C. Matters Outside the Customs Regulation

The Customs Regulation does not apply to parallel imports or to overruns (ie, goods which are manufactured as genuine goods, but are beyond the quantity authorised by the right holder). It also does not apply to goods simply transiting through the EU. The position for the latter remains as determined in the *Nokia v HMRC*[165] CJEU judgment, namely that even if the goods infringe rights in the country where they are detained, they cannot be seized unless there is a 'substantial likelihood' that they will be diverted from their transit into the EU market.

---

[163] The European Commission, in conjunction with the Member States, has developed a database, currently known as COPIS, for registering and disseminating companies' applications for action among customs authorities.
[164] The application form requires the applicant to give an undertaking assuming liability, including liability to the owner for damage suffered where the goods seized are subsequently found not to infringe.
[165] *Nokia v HMRC* (Joined Cases C-446/09 and C-495/09) (1 December 2011).

XIV. Confidentiality Protection

A. General Considerations

Article 58 is concerned with the 'protection of confidential information'. It begins by defining this notion as 'trade secrets, personal data or other confidential information of a party or of a third party'. Thus, confidential information is not restricted to trade secrets and personal data, but also extends to other documentation. Some of the Rules of Procedure explicitly address this: professional privilege,[166] attorney-client privilege,[167] any communication between a party, its legal representatives and a third party aimed at obtaining documentation for use in proceedings[168] (litigation privilege), and, more generally, any documentation from a representative benefiting from immunity.[169]

The UPC Agreement states that the collection and use of evidence in proceedings may be 'restricted or prohibited or [its access] be restricted to specific persons',[170] who could be either impartial experts or the parties' legal representative; the Rules of Procedure also provide that confidential information may be subject to additional terms of non-disclosure.[171] Additionally, Article 45 of the Agreement allows the possibility for the court to issue 'confidentiality orders' closing the proceedings to the public. Such a solution may be used when the confidential information is harmful only if revealed to the wider public (as opposed to revealed to the other party).

It is difficult to imagine that the court would not have the power to sanction the violation of its orders regarding the protection of confidentiality. For instance, the effectiveness of the order to produce evidence is guaranteed by a provision making mandatory (the indicative 'shall' is an imperative) the specification of 'any sanction which may be imposed if the evidence is not produced according to the order';[172] however, such a provision is neither repeated nor referred to in Rule 191 with regard to orders to communicate information contrary to provisions regarding the protection of confidentiality.[173] Applying the mere letter of the Rule would result in leaving the violation of this order to communicate information unsanctioned and ineffective.

B. Public Access to the Register

i. The Status of Hearings, Orders, Pleadings and Evidence

The UPC broadly operates according to the principle of 'open justice' in which proceedings are, by default, open to the public. This principle is explicit in the Rules of Procedure

---

[166] Rule 179 of the Rules of Procedure.
[167] ibid Rule 287.
[168] ibid Rule 288.
[169] ibid Rule 289.
[170] Article 58 UPC Agreement.
[171] Rule 190(1) of the Rules of Procedure.
[172] ibid Rule 190(4)(b).
[173] ibid Rule 190(1) second sentence, (5) and (6).

for the interim conference[174] and the oral hearing.[175] Originally, written pleadings, written evidence, decisions and orders lodged at or made by the court and recorded by the Registry were all, by default, available to the public. This still applies to decisions and orders, which are to be published automatically on a website.[176] However, under final amendments of the Rules of Procedure agreed on 1 September 2022,[177] where applicable, personal data within the meaning of EU Regulation 2016/679 and confidential according to paragraph of Rule 262.2 will be redacted. Furthermore, according to the same amendments, written pleadings and evidence are carved out from the general default and can only be obtained by a reasoned request to the Registry.[178] Even if such a request is successful, the party lodging the documents may request, providing specific reasons, that certain information in those written pleadings or evidence is kept confidential[179] (see also sections XIV.B.ii and XIV.C below).

ii. An Application to Exclude Documents from Public Access

A party may request that certain information be kept confidential, provided there are specific reasons for that confidentiality.[180] Where the request is to keep confidential parts of written pleadings or written evidence, copies of the documents concerned must be provided in the request with the relevant parts redacted. If such a request has been made, the Registrar is required to ensure that the information concerned is not made available, pending an application[181] to provide access to that material to the applicant.

iii. An Application to Access Restricted Material

Any member of the public may lodge an application with the Court[182] for an order that any information that has been excluded from public access[183] be made available to them, as applicant. Such an application must contain:

(a) details of the information alleged to be confidential, so far as possible;
(b) the grounds upon which the applicant believes the reasons for confidentiality should not be accepted; and
(c) the purpose for which the information is needed.

---

[174] ibid Rule 105.
[175] ibid Rule 115.
[176] To be established.
[177] Amendments to the text of the UPC draft Rules of Procedure approved by the Preparatory Committee on 15 March 2017, AC/04/08072022_E – ANNEX 1.
[178] Rule 262.1(b) of the Rules of Procedure. The explanatory note to the amendments explains that the case management system is configured in such a way that the public can take note of the existence of documents and orders, but not their contents. In order to see the contents of such documents, an application will be necessary. The requested information will be provided after a data check and, where applicable, the redaction of personal information.
[179] ibid Rule 262.2.
[180] ibid. Questions may arise as to whether a document is confidential if it is regarded as such under the laws of one contracting Member State or other country, but not others. For the purpose of an application to exclude access, legal tests may be less important than commercial factors and the general balancing of the interests of justice (Rule 262.6 of the Rules of Procedure suggests that the test may be whether the confidentiality of the information outweighs the interest of the public in having access to that information).
[181] Under ibid Rule 262.3.
[182] Under ibid Rule 262.3.
[183] Under ibid Rule 262.2.

250 *Obtaining and Using Evidence*

The court must then invite written comments from the parties before it makes any order. The application must be allowed unless there are legitimate reasons given for maintaining confidentiality that clearly outweigh the interests of the applicant in gaining access to it.[184] The Registrar must then take all such steps to give effect to an order granting access to the register as soon as practicable.[185]

This should be compared to German proceedings, where parties can rely on the Law on Business Secrets (Geschäftsgeheimnisgesetz GeschGehG) in the context of patent infringement proceedings.[186] In accordance with the Law on Business Secrets, any production of documents can be accompanied by a court order on confidentiality, restricting access to counsel in the proceedings and – if required – a limitation on party representatives that can have access to a document. Further, it is possible to exclude the public or even party individuals from hearings in which confidential information is discussed. Likewise, briefs filed by the parties and covered by a respective confidentiality order can only be subject to a third-party file inspection if the confidential passages are redacted. Further, the court can exclude any confidential information when pronouncing a decision. Judgments are not generally published by German courts; if they are published, the court generally ensures that confidential information has, in agreement with the parties, been redacted.

C. Restricting the Availability of Information to Other Parties

i. General Measures

In order to protect trade secrets, personal data or other confidential information of a party to proceedings in the UPC, or of a third party,[187] the UPC Agreement provides that the court may order that the collection and use of evidence in proceedings is restricted or prohibited, or that access to this evidence is restricted to specific persons.[188] As explained by the Amendments to the text of the UPC draft Rules of Procedure approved by the Preparatory Committee on 15 March 2017,[189] this is now elaborated by Rule 262, which lays down the general principle of availability of written pleadings, evidence, decisions and orders to the public, and the conditions for restriction of certain information from public knowledge. The amendments also introduced a new Rule 262A, by which a party may make an application to the relevant panel of the UPC for an order that certain information contained in its pleadings or the collection and use of evidence in proceedings may be restricted or prohibited, or that access to such information or evidence be restricted to specific persons.[190]

---

[184] ibid Rules 262.5 and 262.6.
[185] ibid Rule 262.7.
[186] Section 145 of the German Patent Law.
[187] Witnesses may themselves refuse to answer questions if to do so would breach a professional privilege or a duty of confidentiality imposed by the national law applicable to them (Rule 179.3 of the Rules of Procedure).
[188] Article 58 UPC Agreement. For orders to produce evidence, see Article 59 and also Rule 190 of the Rules of Procedure; for orders to preserve evidence and inspect premises, see Article 60 and also Rules 194.5, 196.1 and 197.4; for orders for inspection, see Rule 199.1; for applications for provisional measures, see Rules 207.7 and 209.4; for statements of intervention, see Rule 315.2; and for settlements, see Rule 365.2.
[189] AC/04/08072022_E – ANNEX 1.
[190] Rule 262A.1 of the Rules of Procedure. See also Article 58 UPC Agreement.

ii. Confidentiality Clubs

As a result of the power of the court to restrict information to specific persons, it appears that 'confidentiality clubs' agreed by the parties on their own terms may be endorsed by the court or, in circumstances where there is no agreement, the court may impose confidentiality obligations of non-disclosure by a party or the Registry. These measures reflect the text of the Directive of the European Parliament and of the Council on the protection of undisclosed know-how and business information (trade secrets) against their unlawful acquisition, use and disclosure (hereinafter the 'Trade Secrets Directive').[191] The Trade Secrets Directive provides for judicial authorities to take the specific measures necessary to preserve the confidentiality of any trade secret in the course of legal proceedings.[192] In particular, the text of the Trade Secrets Directive provides that the measures that Member States must make available to competent judicial authorities must at least include the possibility of restricting access to documents and hearings containing trade secrets, or alleged trade secrets, to a limited number of persons. There is a condition that this limited number of persons must include at least one natural person from each party and the respective lawyers or other representatives of those parties to the proceedings.

For comparison, confidentiality clubs are already an established feature of English patent proceedings.[193] These are typically limited to lawyers and certain individuals of a party who need to see them in order to give instructions.[194] The exclusion of a party and the public altogether from certain material in the case raises fundamental principles of natural justice. However, there is an exception to this rule:[195]

> [W]here the whole object of the proceedings is to protect a commercial interest, full disclosure may not be possible if it would render the proceedings futile. This problem occurs in intellectual property proceedings. It is commonplace to deal with the issue of disclosure by establishing 'confidentiality rings' of persons who may see certain confidential material which is withheld from one or more of the parties to the litigation at least in its initial stages. Such claims by their very nature raise special problems which require exceptional solutions. I am not aware of a case in which a court has approved a trial of such a case proceeding in circumstances where one party was denied access to evidence which was being relied on at the trial by the other party.

In the English court, a balance is therefore sought between these countervailing principles. In *Oneplus Technology v Mitsubishi*,[196] the Court of Appeal drew together from the authorities[197] the following factors that may be relevant to striking this balance, which it is submitted are also relevant to practice in the UPC:

(i) In managing the disclosure of highly confidential information in intellectual property litigation, the court must balance the interests of the receiving party in having the

---

[191] Agreed by the European Council on 27 May 2016.
[192] Article 9(2).
[193] CPR Part 31.22(2).
[194] As agreed by the court: PD 51U, para 15; see in particular *TQ Delta LLC v Zyxel Communications UK Ltd* [2018] EWHC 1515 (Ch).
[195] *Al Rawi and Others v Security Service and Others* [2011] UKSC 34 (13 July 2011).
[196] *Oneplus Technology (Shenzhen) Co Ltd and Others v Mitsubishi Electric Corporation and Another* [2020] EWCA Civ 1562 (19 November 2020).
[197] *IPCom GmbH & Co KG v HTC Europe Co Ltd and Others* [2013] EWHC 52 (Pat); *IPCom GmbH & Co KG v HTC Europe Co Ltd and Others* [2013] EWHC 2880 (Ch); *TQ Delta LLC v Zyxel Communications UK Ltd and Another* [2018] EWHC 1515 (Ch); *Anan Kasei Co Ltd and Another v Neo Chemicals & Oxides (Europe) Ltd* [2020] EWHC 2503 (Pat).

fullest possible access to relevant documents against the interests of the disclosing party, or third parties, in the preservation of their confidential commercial and technical information.

(ii) An arrangement under which an officer or employee of the receiving party gains no access at all to documents of importance at trial will be exceptionally rare, if indeed it can happen at all.

(iii) There is no universal form of order suitable for use in every case, or even at every stage of the same case.

(iv) The court must be alert to the fact that restricting disclosure to external eyes only at any stage is exceptional.

(v) If an external eyes-only tier is created for initial disclosure, the court should remember that the *onus* remains on the disclosing party throughout to justify that designation for the documents so designated.

(vi) Different types of information may require different degrees of protection, according to their value and potential for misuse. The protection to be afforded to a secret process may be greater than the protection to be afforded to commercial licences where the potential for misuse is less obvious.

(vii) Difficulties of policing misuse are also relevant.

(viii) The extent to which a party may be expected to contribute to the case based on a document is relevant.

(ix) The role which the documents will play in the action is also a material consideration.

(x) The structure and organisation of the receiving party is a factor which feeds into the way in which the confidential information has to be handled.

The Court of Appeal added that, in all cases, the court must be alert to the misuse of the opportunity to designate documents as confidential.

iii. *The Application for Restrictions*

An application under Rule 262A must contain the grounds upon which the applicant believes the information or evidence in question should be restricted, in accordance with Article 58 of the UPC Agreement.[198] The application must be made at the same time as the document containing the information or evidence in question is lodged, and must provide a copy of the unredacted and redacted document.[199]

The relevant panel must then invite written comments from the representatives of the other parties[200] and may then allow the application, having considered in particular whether the grounds relied upon by the applicant for the order significantly outweigh the interest of the other party to have full access to the information and evidence in question.[201] The number of persons to whom access is granted must be no greater than necessary in order to ensure compliance with the right of the parties to the legal proceedings to an effective

---

[198] Rule 262A.2 of the Rules of Procedure.
[199] ibid Rules 262A.3.
[200] ibid Rules 262A.4.
[201] ibid Rules 262A.5.

remedy and to a fair trial. It must also include at least one natural person from each party and the respective lawyers or other representatives of those parties to the legal proceedings.[202]

iv. Confidential Hearings

The relevant panel of the UPC may also decide to hear a matter confidentially, including the interim conference and oral hearing. It will do so to the extent necessary, in the interests of one of the parties or other affected persons, or in the general interests of justice or public order.[203] The determination of these interests will be a matter for the judges to develop in case law. The publication of decisions of the court may also be subject to the protection of confidential information.[204]

XV. Privilege

Privilege or 'legal professional privilege' is a general expression, familiar from English law, which covers two concepts: (1) attorney-client privilege; and (2) litigation privilege. These two concepts, in outline, have been implemented in the Rules of Procedure.

A. Attorney-Client Privilege

Attorney-client privilege is the right to protect advice[205] sought by a client from their lawyer, or patent attorney, from disclosure in UPC proceedings or in arbitration or mediation proceedings before the Patent Mediation and Arbitration Centre of the UPC (hereinafter 'the Centre').[206] The privilege also prevents a lawyer, or patent attorney, and their client from being questioned or examined about the privileged material.[207]

The advice does not have to be sought in connection with proceedings, but must remain confidential in order for privilege to be preserved and may be waived by the client.[208]

Attorney-client privilege extends to:

(a) communications between the client and a lawyer, or patent attorney, who is employed by them for the purpose of providing advice;[209]

---

[202] Rules 262A.6.
[203] Article 45 UPC Agreement.
[204] Article 23(2)(d) of the Statute of the UPC Agreement.
[205] Questions may arise about the breadth of meaning of 'advice'. In the UK, where privilege is a well-developed doctrine, this is broader than advice on the state of the law as such, and includes advice as to what should be done in the relevant legal context. See *Three Rivers (No 6)* [2004] 3 WLR 1274, in which the House of Lords said the existence of legal advice privilege depended on whether there is a 'relevant legal context'. Authorisation to give information to lawyers is not enough; authorisation is needed to seek and receive legal advice on behalf of the client (see *Re RBS (Rights Issue Litigation)* [2016] EWHC 3161 (Ch) (8 December 2016).
[206] Rule 287.1 of the Rules of Procedure.
[207] ibid Rule 287.4.
[208] ibid Rule 287.5.
[209] ibid Rule 287.2.

(b) the work product of the lawyer, or patent attorney, in connection with the advice and to any record of a privileged communication;[210] and
(c) communications between lawyers and/or patent attorneys employed in the same firm or entity or between lawyers and/or patent attorneys employed by the same client, in connection with the advice.[211]

The Rules do not state expressly whether client-attorney privilege extends to communications with 'agents' employed by the client to seek and receive advice and to their work product. However, it is submitted that it would be out of keeping with the provisions on client-attorney privilege if agents were not protected in these circumstances. Questions may arise about the breadth of meaning of 'advice'. In the English courts, this question has been at issue in a series of cases, in which advice was held to be broader than advice on the state of the law, as such, and includes advice as to what should be done in the relevant legal context.[212] In this case, the House of Lords said that the existence of legal advice privilege depended on whether there is a 'relevant legal context'. Authorisation to give information to lawyers is not enough; authorisation is needed to seek and receive legal advice on behalf of the client.[213] Questions may also arise as to the scope of the client in these circumstances. In the English courts, this is construed narrowly and great care needs to be exercised in determining who the client is.[214]

B. Litigation Privilege

Litigation privilege protects communications between a client, or a lawyer or patent attorney instructed by a client in their professional capacity, and a third party. The communications must be to obtain information or evidence of any nature for the purpose of or for use in proceedings. Documents protected by litigation privilege are exempt from production in proceedings and the client, or their lawyer of patent attorney, may not be questioned on them.

There are two key differences between litigation privilege and client-attorney privilege:

(a) litigation privilege protects communications between the client, lawyer or patent attorney and *third parties*; and
(b) the privilege only extends to communications made *for the purpose of or for use in proceedings*.

Unlike client-attorney privilege, litigation privilege extends generally to the preparatory work of experts when producing evidence for UPC proceedings and is crucial in guarding the preparation of such evidence against the general duty of disclosure (a relationship that is now mirrored in the disclosure rules of the UPC and the use of party-appointed experts). However, as with client-attorney privilege, parties must be careful to maintain the

---

[210] ibid Rule 287.3.
[211] ibid.
[212] *Three Rivers (No 6)* (n 197).
[213] *Re RBS (Rights Issue Litigation)* (n 197).
[214] *Three Rivers (No 5)* [2003] QB 1556 (not to be confused with *Three Rivers (No 6)* (n 197)).

confidentiality of privileged documents and communications. Even a partial disclosure of information may be deemed to have waived privilege in a document or a wider group of materials more generally. The panels of the UPC will, in due course, need to clarify questions on the application of the privilege in a number of respects, including the following:

(a) Must litigation be in progress or merely in contemplation before the privilege applies?[215]
(b) Must the communications be made for the sole or dominant purpose of conducting that litigation?[216]
(c) Do the words 'any proceedings' include mediation or arbitration before the Centre?[217]
(d) What effect does the exchange of expert reports to the other parties in proceedings have on privilege?
(e) Are documents referred to by the expert and the instructions given to them privileged?

C. Lawyers and Patent Attorneys

The expressions lawyer and the patent attorney are specifically defined for the purpose of the privilege rules.[218] A 'lawyer' is not limited to a representative authorised to practice before the UPC,[219] but includes any person who is qualified to practise as a lawyer and to give legal advice under the law of the state where they practise.[220] A 'patent attorney' is a person who is recognised as eligible to give advice under the law of the state where they practise concerning the protection of inventions or to the prosecution or litigation of patents or patent applications.[221] This includes a professional representative before the EPO.[222]

D. The Relationship with Confidentiality

Privilege is not to be confused with confidentiality – a document can be confidential without being privileged. However, the right to withhold production of a document on the grounds of privilege is lost in a document once it ceases to be confidential. Hence, a client may without restrictions consent to privileged documents being produced to another party, but in

---

[215] Guidance is provided in English law, where a party must be aware of circumstances rendering litigation between itself and a person or class of persons a reasonable prospect; see *USA v Philip Morris Inc and British American Tobacco (Investments) Ltd* [2001] 1 CLC 811.
[216] In the English law example, litigation privilege protects communications with third parties providing that they come into existence with the dominant purpose of gathering evidence in circumstances where legal proceedings are in existence or in reasonable prospect; see *Waugh v British Railways Board* [1980] AC 521.
[217] Rule 288 of the Rules of Procedure are clear that proceedings in this context include proceedings before the EPO. The omission of any reference to arbitration and mediation also contrasts with the express reference to the application of client-attorney privilege in the Centre in Rule 287.
[218] Compare to the separate definition of lawyer in ibid Rule 286.1.
[219] See ibid Rule 286.
[220] ibid Rule 287.6(a). Questions may arise regarding whether trainee lawyers, apprentice lawyers, legal executives and paralegals qualify for protection.
[221] ibid Rule 287.6(b) of the Rules of Procedure.
[222] Pursuant to Article 134(1) of the European Patent Convention.

this case the right to withhold production of the documents is lost.[223] Questions may arise regarding whether a client can agree to produce privileged documents for a limited purpose only – can the client assert the right not to produce the same documents for any purpose outside the limited purpose for which it was agreed to produce them? Furthermore, if documents are produced to a party on the express basis that privilege is not to be waived, can that party then retain those documents when consent is withdrawn?[224]

An important issue will be how to ensure that documents which are accidentally produced to another party remain confidential and privileged. The proper approach, it is submitted, ought to be that such documents must be returned without being read. Determining whether production is accidental would be a matter of examining the relevant acts of production and putting them in their context.[225]

E. Common Interest Privilege

The concept of 'common interest privilege', though not a substantive form of privilege of its own, describes in English practice the principle under which documents already protected by privilege may be shared by parties with a common interest without losing the right to protection from production.[226] The essential notion behind common interest privilege is that the parties have a common interest in the confidentiality of the advice at issue. The fact that differences may arise between parties does not necessarily mean that they cannot be parties with a common interest for the purpose of this concept.[227]

There is no such privilege expressly provided by the UPC Agreement or the Rules of Procedure and it remains to be seen whether the court will recognise a shared privilege in matters of common interest.

F. Without Prejudice Communications

Without prejudice privilege is different in kind from legal advice privilege and litigation privilege as it does not protect communications between the lawyer and the client. Instead, it protects communications between parties to a dispute from being generally admissible in evidence if they are made for the purpose of a genuine attempt to resolve that dispute. As such, it is founded on the public policy of encouraging the settlement of disputes, even though this may conflict with the policy of providing the court with the best evidence.[228] Public policy also requires those negotiations to be protected from disclosure to third

---

[223] Rule 287.5 of the Rules of Procedure.
[224] Under English law, the answer to both questions appears to be yes; see *B v Auckland District Law Society* [2003] 2 AC 736 (Privy Council, New Zealand); see also *British Coal Corporation v Dennis Rye Ltd (No 2)* [1988] 1 WLR 1113.
[225] From English law, see *Susan Yvonne Dore v Leicestershire County Council* [2010] EWHC 34 (Ch).
[226] See *Buttes Gas & Oil Company v Hammer (No 3)* [1981] 1 QB 223.
[227] See *Formica Ltd v ECGD* [1995] 1 Lloyd's Rep 692.
[228] *Oceanbulk Shipping & Trading SA v TMT Asia Ltd* [2010] EWCA Civ 79.

parties.[229] Without prejudice protection is provided in the case of attempted settlement in the UPC.[230]

Similarly, in the Netherlands, all attorney-attorney communication is non-privileged, unless a communication expressly bears a remark of 'privileged communication'. It is up to a party to mark their communication as 'privileged'.

---

[229] See *Rush & Tompkins Ltd v Greater London Council* [1989] AC 1280.
[230] Rule 11.3 of the Rules of Procedure.

17

Appeal

The system of appeals against decisions and orders of the Court of First Instance is regulated by Article 73 UPC Agreement.[1] Appeal may be brought to the Court of Appeal by any party which has been unsuccessful in its submissions, in whole or in part.[2] Remedies both against decisions as well as against orders are referred to as 'appeals' by the UPC Agreement and the Rules of Procedure. However, there is an important difference between the appeal of final decisions and certain 'privileged orders' compared to all other orders as regards the need to obtain leave to appeal. This is designed as a safeguard against the UPC becoming clogged up with appeals, particularly in the early stages of its development. These issues, the procedure on appeal and cross-appeal, and rehearings are discussed in this chapter. For more on the structure of the Court of Appeal and an overview of its decision-making powers, see Chapter 3.

I. The Scope and Effect of Appeal

A. Appealable Decisions and Time Periods

Appeal may be brought by a party adversely affected by a final decision of the Court of First Instance[3] and decisions terminating proceedings as regards one of the parties[4] within two months of the decision being appealed. Decisions of the standing judge concerning an application to annul a decision of the EPO must be brought within three weeks of the decision.[5] Orders that proceedings are heard in the language of grant of the patent,[6] orders to produce evidence,[7] orders to preserve evidence and to inspect premises,[8] freezing orders,[9] provisional and protective measures[10] or orders relating to the communication of information[11] (sometimes referred to as 'privileged orders') may also be appealed within 15 days of service of the decision.[12]

---

[1] There is no possibility of filing an appeal or any other kind of remedy; see Peter Meier-Beck, 'Quo vadis, iudicium unitarium?' (2014) 9(3) *Journal of Intellectual Property Law & Practice* 241.
[2] Article 73(1) and (2) UPC Agreement.
[3] Rule 220.1(a) of the Rules of Procedure.
[4] ibid Rule 220.1(b).
[5] ibid Rule 97.5.
[6] Article 49(5) UPC Agreement.
[7] ibid Article 59.
[8] ibid Article 60.
[9] ibid Article 61.
[10] ibid Article 62.
[11] ibid Article 67; Rule 220.1(c) of the Rules of Procedure.
[12] Rule 224.1(b) of the Rules of Procedure; Article 73(2)(a) UPC Agreement.

Decisions and orders other than those mentioned in the preceding paragraph may be either:

(a) the subject of an appeal together with the appeal against the final decision of the Court of First Instance; or
(b) appealed with the leave of the Court of First Instance within 15 days of service of the Court's decision to that effect.[13]

The route to obtaining leave to appeal is addressed below.

B. Leave to Appeal

An extensive explanatory note by the Legal Group of the Preparatory Committee[14] made at the time the substance of the present Rule was drafted states that Rule 220 concerning leave to appeal is designed to give the Court of Appeal means to effectively control procedural orders of the Court of First Instance, but at the same time to allow the Court of Appeal to limit its intervention to cases of particular importance and thus avoid systematic appeals that paralyse proceedings.[15]

For those decisions and orders concerned, where the Court of First Instance has not given leave to appeal within 15 days of its order,[16] a party adversely affected by the order may request a discretionary review by the Court of Appeal within a period of a further 15 days.[17] In the request for discretionary review, the party must set out the reasons for the request and the necessary facts, evidence and arguments relied on.[18] As the review is discretionary, the standing judge of the Court of Appeal may or may not admit the review having heard the other party,[19] allowing the Court of Appeal to step in only in those cases of importance that merit a decision by the Court of Appeal on pending procedural issues before the Court of First Instance. If the review is admitted by the standing judge, that judge will order any further steps the parties must take and within what time limits. The President of the Court of Appeal will then assign the review of the decision on leave to appeal to a panel of the Court of Appeal. The panel of the Court of Appeal then decides on the review and may

---

[13] Rule 220.2 of the Rules of Procedure.
[14] See Oral Hearing on the 17th draft of the Rules of Procedure of the Unified Patent Court, 3 November 2014, https://www.unified-patent-court.org/news/oral-hearing-17th-draft-rules-procedure-unified-patent-court.
[15] The note explains that most of the procedural orders which have not been privileged under Article 73(2)(a) UPC Agreement do not touch upon the basic interests of the parties. In the interests of a speedy and efficient procedure, their control should in principle be dealt with together with the appeal against the final decision. However, some of the orders which have not been privileged may in certain cases touch basic interests of parties, and a consistent application and interpretation of the Rules of Procedure governing such orders is desirable. To achieve this, these orders may be appealed where the 'Court grants leave'. The issue is whether the leave procedure is: (i) a means for the independent Court of First Instance to seek guidance from the Court of Appeal on certain procedural questions; or (ii) a mechanism of control of proceedings pending before the Court of First Instance by the Court of Appeal. On the one hand, the possibility to appeal against each procedural decision of the Court of First Instance might, where systematically done, have a negative impact on serenity of proceedings. On the other hand, not allowing the parties to address themselves to the Court of Appeal, where leave has been refused by the Court of First Instance, might mean that an important way to guarantee uniform procedures would be missing.
[16] Rule 220.3 of the Rules of Procedure.
[17] ibid Rule 220.3.
[18] ibid Rule 221.2.
[19] ibid Rule 220.4.

consult the panel in the Court of First Instance (its presiding judge or its judge-rapporteur) which has given the order.[20]

As a separate matter, a party adversely affected by a cost decision[21] may lodge an application for leave to appeal to the Court of Appeal within 15 days of service of the decision of the Court.[22] In these cases, the decision to grant leave to appeal is made by the standing judge.

C. Suspensive Effect

i. Final Decisions

An appeal of a final decision has in principle *no* suspensive effect unless the court exceptionally grants suspensive effect upon request of one of the parties.[23] A major exception to the principle of no suspensive effect applies to decisions on actions or counterclaims for revocation and – much less common in practice – on actions concerning decisions of the EPO in carrying out the tasks referred to in Article 9 of UP Regulation.[24] An appeal against these decisions always has suspensive effect.[25]

ii. Privileged and Other Orders

An appeal against the privileged orders – a decision to use the language of the patent in proceedings, orders to produce evidence, orders to preserve evidence and to inspect premises, freezing orders, provisional and protective measures and orders on the communication of information[26] – does not prevent the continuation of the main proceedings.[27] However, it should be noted that a first instance decision in proceedings on the merits must not be rendered as long as proceedings on provisional measures are still pending under appeal. There is no suspensive effect for appeals of non-privileged orders.[28]

iii. An Application for Suspensive Effect

Suspensive effect may be granted by the court following an application for suspensive effect to be filed by the appellant,[29] except for non-privileged orders.[30] Usually, it will be the alleged

---

[20] Where the first instance procedural order is given by the judge-rapporteur, the party adversely affected must first request an early review by the panel of the Court of First Instance (ibid Rules 102.2 and 333.1). An application for a discretionary review by the Court of Appeal therefore applies to orders given or upheld by the first instance panel.
[21] ibid Rule 157.
[22] Under ibid Rule 221.1.
[23] Article 74(1) UPC Agreement; Rule 223 of the Rules of Procedure. There is no suspensive effect for an appeal pursuant to Rule 220.2 (procedural appeal with the leave of the Court of First Instance), 220.3 (discretionary review) or 221.3 (costs appeal).
[24] Under Article 32(1)(i) UPC Agreement.
[25] ibid Article 74(2).
[26] ibid Articles 49(5), 59–62 and 67 Agreement, respectively.
[27] According to ibid Article 74(3).
[28] Rule 223.5 of the Rules of Procedure. The Rule is silent as to whether a final decision may be made by the Court of First Instance in these circumstances.
[29] Under ibid Rule 223.
[30] ibid Rule 223.5.

infringer who lost the first instance proceedings who will have an interest in postponing the injunctive relief ordered at the first instance.

The application must set out the reasons why lodging the appeal should have suspensive effect, and the facts, evidence and arguments relied on.[31] The Court of Appeal must decide the application without delay.[32] However, in cases of 'extreme urgency', the applicant may apply at any time for suspensive effect without formalities.[33]

The effect of the suspensive effect is the interruption of the enforceability of the first instance decision. The UPC will have to develop case law on the requirements under which conditions to grant suspensive effect and to interrupt the enforcement of the first instance decision. In this regard, the fact that the Court of First Instance already has the possibility and to some extent the obligation to apply proportionality considerations should be taken into consideration. Hence, the reasons why the lodging of the appeal should have suspensive effect must go beyond the general considerations that are already applied by the court when granting the order in first instance.[34]

II. Written Procedure

Appeal proceedings are divided into three major parts: written procedure, interim procedure and oral hearing. The appeal proceedings as such and the written procedure start with the filing of the statement of appeal.

A. The Statement of Appeal

i. Contents

The contents of the statement of appeal must contain:[35]

(a) the names of the appellant and of the appellant's representative;
(b) the names of the respondent and of the respondent's representative;
(c) postal and electronic addresses for service on the appellant and on the respondent, as well as the names of the persons authorised to accept service;
(d) the date of the decision or order appealed against and the action number attributed to the file in proceedings before the Court of First Instance; and
(e) the order or remedy sought by the appellant, including any order for expedition of the appeal pursuant to Rule 9.3(b) and the reasons justifying such an order for expedition.

---

[31] ibid Rule 223.2.
[32] ibid Rule 223.3.
[33] ibid Rule 223.4.
[34] From a German law perspective, the requirements for interrupting the enforceability of a first instance decision are very high, even though equity considerations are not even considered by the first instance courts when, for example, granting injunctive relief. It is required that the defendant suffers an irreparable harm that goes beyond the effect of the enforcement of the decision itself (cf in detail the comments in Moritz Cepl, Ulrike Voß and Anje Lunze (eds), *Der Prozess im Gewerblichen Rechtsschutz*, 2nd edn (CH Beck, 2018) section 707). Furthermore, bringing sufficient reliable evidence for the damage that might be suffered due to the enforcement is in practice hardly possible for the defendant.
[35] Rule 225 of the Rules of Procedure.

ii. Language

The statement of appeal and the statement of grounds of appeal must be drawn up either in the language of the proceedings before the Court of First Instance or, where the parties have agreed, in the language in which the patent was granted.[36] In exceptional cases and to the extent deemed appropriate, the Court of Appeal may decide on another official language of a contracting Member State as the language of proceedings[37] (see Chapter 5 for more on this).

iii. Fees

The appellant must pay a fixed fee for the appeal of €11,000[38] as well as – in cases of infringement actions, counterclaims for infringement and declarations for non-infringement – an additional value-based fee calculated on the same scale as the first instance action. In the case of an appeal in a revocation action, there is only a fixed fee of €20,000 to be paid by the appellant. For an appeal regarding an application for provisional measures, only a fixed fee of €11,000 applies (see Chapter 20).

iv. Examination as to Formal Requirements

The Registry must, as soon as practicable after the lodging of the statement of appeal, examine whether the above requirements[39] have been complied with.[40]

Should the appellant not yet have complied with the requirements, the Registry will invite the appellant to correct the deficiencies within 14 days of service of such notification. This deadline of 14 days also applies in the event that the appeal fee has not yet been paid when the statement of appeal was filed.[41] At the same time, the Registry must inform the appellant that if the appellant fails to correct the deficiencies or to pay the fee within the time stated, a decision by default may be given.[42]

If the appellant fails to correct the deficiencies or pay the fee, the Registry will inform the President of the Court of Appeal, who will reject the appeal as inadmissible by a decision by default. They may give the appellant an opportunity to be heard beforehand.

v. Recording in the Register and Further Handling of the Appeal

If the statement of appeal complies with the above requirements,[43] the Registry must record the date of receipt to the statement of appeal and an action number to the appeal file, record the appeal file in the register, inform the appellant of the action number and the date of receipt, and serve the statement of appeal on all parties to the proceedings at first instance.[44]

---

[36] See Article 50(2) UPC Agreement; Rule 227 of the Rules of Procedure.
[37] Article 50(3) UPC Agreement; Rule 227.1(a) of the Rules of Procedure.
[38] Rule 228 of the Rules of Procedure.
[39] As set out in Rules 224.1, 225, 227 and 228 of the Rules of Procedure.
[40] ibid Rule 229.1.
[41] ibid Rule 229.2.
[42] ibid Rules 229.3 and Rule 357.
[43] Referred to in ibid Rule 229.1.
[44] ibid Rule 230.1.

The action must be assigned to a panel[45] and the panel must as soon as practicable decide whether to grant any order for expedition,[46] having given the parties an opportunity to be heard.

The presiding judge of the panel to which the action has been assigned must designate one legal judge of the panel as judge-rapporteur.[47] The Registry will as soon as practicable notify the appellant and respondent of the identity of the judge-rapporteur.

B. The Statement of Grounds of Appeal

The statement of appeal is to be followed by the statement of the grounds of appeal, which is the heart of the appeal proceedings[48] as it defines and delimits the scope of the appeal proceedings. It must be lodged within four months of service of a final decision of first instance and decisions terminating proceedings as regards one of the parties[49] or 15 days of service of an order concerning a privileged order (see above) and any other order.[50]

i. The Content of the Statement of Grounds of Appeal

The statement of grounds of appeal must contain:[51]

(a) an indication of which parts of the decision or order are contested;
(b) the reasons for setting aside the contested decision or order; and
(c) an indication of the facts and evidence on which the appeal is based.[52]

The appeal against a decision or an order of the Court of First Instance may be based on points of law and matters of fact.[53] However, there are important limitations as to the subject matter of the appeal proceedings. Requests, facts and evidence which have not been submitted during first instance proceedings may be disregarded by the Court of Appeal.[54] In order to expedite proceedings and to avoid delaying tactics and late lodging, new facts and new evidence may only be introduced in accordance with the Rules of Procedure and where the submission by the party concerned could not reasonably have been expected during proceedings before the Court of First Instance.[55] When exercising its discretion in this regard, the Court shall in particular take into account:

(a) whether new submissions could not reasonably have been made during first instance proceedings;

---

[45] ibid Rules 230.1, 230.2, 345.3 and 345.8.
[46] Further to ibid Rule 225(e).
[47] ibid Rule 231.
[48] Note that, further to Rule 97.5, appeals concerning an application to annul a decision of the EPO follow their own procedure.
[49] ibid Rule 224.2(a).
[50] ibid Rule 224.2(b).
[51] ibid Rule 226.
[52] ibid Rules 222.2.
[53] Article 73(3) UPC Agreement.
[54] Rule 222.2 of the Rules of Procedure.
[55] Article 73(4) UPC Agreement.

(b) the relevance of new submissions for the decision on the appeal; and
(c) the position of the other party regarding the lodging of new submissions.

The appellant has to apply care when working out the statement of grounds of appeal. In practice, the parties have in fact to be very careful to present all facts and submissions already in the Court of First Instance as far as possible. This in particular applies to the patent owner insofar as they defend the patent in a revocation action with an amended claim set or with auxiliary requests on amended claims: these must in principle all already be filed at first instance. The extent to which the Court of Appeal will accept the submission of newly amended claims[56] or new auxiliary requests in particular where it is a reaction to the specific reasoning given in the first instance decision – and to which extent these new submissions must have already been, at least implicitly, part of the submissions of the first instance – will depend on the future UPC practice.

ii. Preliminary Examination of the Statement of Grounds of Appeal

The judge-rapporteur must examine whether the statement of grounds of appeal satisfies the above requirements.[57] If the statement of grounds of appeal does not comply with these requirements, the judge-rapporteur must give the appellant leave to amend the statement of grounds of appeal within such period as they may decide. If the appellant fails to amend the statement within such period the judge-rapporteur may reject the appeal as inadmissible. The judge-rapporteur must give the appellant an opportunity to be heard beforehand. Grounds of appeal which are not raised within the period specified for the statement of grounds of appeal will not be admissible.[58]

C. Challenge to the Decision to Reject an Appeal as Inadmissible

The appellant may challenge a decision to reject the appeal as inadmissible[59] within one month of service of the decision, without providing new grounds of appeal. The challenge will be assigned to a panel to be heard[60] and if the decision to reject is set aside, the appeal will continue.[61]

D. The Statement of Response

The other party, which is referred to as the 'respondent' by the Rules of Procedure, must respond by submitting a statement of response, or the Court of Appeal may give a

---

[56] For example, through the central amendment procedure of the EPO under Article 105a EPC (see ch 3).
[57] Rule 233 of the Rules of Procedure.
[58] ibid Rule 233.3.
[59] ibid Rule 234.1 (under the time limits in Rules 224.2 or, where there is a failure to comply with the requirements of Rule 226, under Rule 233.2).
[60] ibid Rule 234.2.
[61] ibid Rule 234.3.

reasoned decision.[62] The deadline for the response is three months from the service of the statement of grounds of appeal in the case of an appeal against a decision of the Court of First Instance and decisions terminating proceedings as regards one of the parties.[63] In the case of an appeal against orders of the Court of First Instance, including costs orders and privileged orders (see section I.C.ii above), the deadline is 15 days of the service of the grounds of appeal.[64]

The statement of response must contain:[65]

(a) the names of the respondent and the respondent's representative;
(b) postal and electronic addresses for service on the respondent, and the names and addresses of the persons authorised to accept service;
(c) the action number of the appeal file; and
(d) a response to the grounds of appeal.

The respondent may also support the decision of the Court of First Instance on grounds other than those given in the decision.[66]

i. Cross-appeal

Despite the fact that a party has not lodged a statement of appeal within the required period,[67] it may still bring an appeal by way of a statement of cross-appeal in response to one of the other parties lodging a statement of appeal.[68] The statement of cross-appeal must be included in the statement of response according to the same time periods and must contain the same content as a statement of appeal and grounds of appeal, and is subject to the same examination of formal requirements and preliminary examination, respectively, as these documents.[69]

A cross-appeal may not generally be used by the cross-appellant to make new arguments or submit new facts or evidence in addition to those of the first instance, and thus attempt to extend the scope of the litigation.[70]

It is important to note that the cross-appeal is only a dependent remedy – dependent on the statement of appeal. This means that it is deemed to be withdrawn if the statement of appeal is withdrawn.[71] Should a party have partially lost at first instance, it will therefore

---

[62] ibid Rule 235.3.
[63] ibid Rule 224.2(a).
[64] ibid Rule 224.2(b).
[65] ibid Rule 236.1.
[66] ibid Rule 236.2.
[67] ibid Rule 224.1.
[68] ibid Rule 237.1.
[69] ibid Rule 237.2.
[70] ibid Rule 222. In the current court practice in Germany, cross-appeals are not uncommon due to the requirement to bring any action against the defendant on account of the same or a similar act on the basis of another patent with the first lawsuit (section 145 of the German Patent Act). If a further patent (eg, a divisional patent) is granted while litigation based on the first patent is still pending, the second patent cannot be separately enforced, but must be included in the first litigation. Under the UPC, there is no such rule and the practical importance of cross-appeals will be comparatively limited under the UPC compared to the current situation in Germany.
[71] Rule 237.5 of the Rules of Procedure.

need to consider whether to lodge an independent statement of appeal within the deadline[72] in order to maintain its own independent appeal. Should a party win at first instance, it has no legal interest in filing an independent statement of appeal.

Cross-appeal might in particular play a role in the event of bifurcated infringement and invalidity proceedings (see Chapter 9) or when parallel opposition proceedings are still pending with the EPO, and if the scope of the patent in the infringement proceedings and hence the scope of the injunctive relief requested by the claimant needs to be adjusted to any limitation of the patent in the parallel invalidity or opposition proceedings.

For the cross-appeal, the same fee is due as for a statement of appeal (see Chapter 20).[73]

E. Reply to a Statement of Cross-appeal

The appellant may, in proceedings concerning a final decision of the Court of First Instance or a decision terminating proceedings as regards one of the parties, within two months of service of a statement of cross-appeal[74] lodge a reply to the statement of cross-appeal which must contain a response to the grounds of appeal raised in the statement of cross-appeal.[75] In the case of appeal proceedings against orders of the Court of First Instance, including costs orders and privileged orders (see section I.C.ii above), the reply to the statement of cross-appeal must be lodged within 15 days of service of the statement of cross-appeal.

F. Decision to Refer

The panel to which the action has been assigned may refer it to the full Court of Appeal if the panel considers, on a proposal from the presiding judge, the case to be of exceptional importance and, in particular, where the decision in the action may affect the consistency and unity of the case law of the Court[76] (See Chapter 3).

III. Interim Procedure

The written procedure is closed and the interim procedure starts with the expiry of the periods for filing the statement of response to appeal and/or the statement of response to cross-appeal. It is then the judge-rapporteur's responsibility to start preparing the oral hearing. In this regard, the judge-rapporteur has the same powers and may exercise the same duties as in the interim procedure of the first instance (see Chapter 13).[77] As soon as the

---

[72] Set out in ibid Rule 224.1.
[73] ibid Rule 237.4.
[74] Under ibid Rules 237 and 235.1.
[75] ibid Rule 238.
[76] ibid Rule 238A.
[77] ibid Rules 101–10 apply mutatis mutandis (see Rule 239.1).

judge-rapporteur considers that the appeal is ready for oral hearing, they must summon the parties to the oral hearing.[78]

IV. Oral Procedure

The oral hearing must in principle be held before the panel and must be directed by the presiding judge. The rules on the oral hearing in first instance[79] apply mutatis mutandis.[80] Only in the case of an appeal against a cost decision is an oral hearing heard by the standing judge, who has all the powers of the Court of Appeal.[81] The Court of Appeal may hear appeals against separate decisions on the merits in infringement proceedings and in validity proceedings together.[82]

V. The Decision of the Court of Appeal

The Court of Appeal must either reject the appeal or set the decision or order aside totally or in part substitute its own decision or order, including an order for costs both in respect of the proceedings at first instance and on appeal.[83] In this regard, the Court of Appeal may exercise any power within the competence of the Court of First Instance.[84]

In exceptional circumstances, the Court of Appeal may refer the action back to the Court of First Instance for decision or for retrial.[85] A failure of the Court of First Instance to decide an issue which it is necessary for the Court of Appeal to decide on appeal is not considered as an exceptional circumstance and hence is not a matter to be referred back[86] (see Chapter 3).

A. Referral Back

The decision referring an action back to the Court of First Instance must specify whether the same panel whose earlier decision or order is revoked must deal further with the action or whether another panel will be appointed by the presiding judge of the division concerned.[87] Where an action is referred back to the Court of First Instance, the Court is bound by the decision of the Court of Appeal on points of law.[88]

---

[78] ibid Rule 239.2.
[79] ibid Rules 111, 112, 115, 116 and 117.
[80] According to ibid Rule 240, subject to Rule 222.
[81] ibid Rule 241.
[82] ibid Rule 220.5.
[83] Following ibid Rule 242.1.
[84] ibid Rule 242.2(a).
[85] Article 75(1) UPC Agreement.
[86] ibid Rule 242.2(b).
[87] ibid Rule 243.1.
[88] Article 75(2) UPC Agreement; Rule 243.2 of the Rules of Procedure.

VI. Rehearing

A. Overview

A right for a rehearing after a final decision of the UPC may exceptionally be granted by the Court of Appeal either:[89] on discovery of a fact by the party requesting the rehearing, which is of such a nature as to be a decisive factor and which, when the decision was given, was unknown to the party requesting the rehearing; or, in the event of a fundamental procedural defect (see section VI.B.i below) – in particular, when a defendant who did not appear before the Court was not served with the document initiating the proceedings or an equivalent document in sufficient time and in such a way as to enable them to arrange for the defence.

The ultimate deadline for filing a request for a rehearing is 10 years from the date of the decision, but not later than two months from the date of the discovery of the new fact or of the procedural defect.[90] The request for rehearing must not have suspensive effect unless the Court of Appeal decides otherwise.[91] If the request for a rehearing is well founded, the Court of Appeal must set aside, in whole or in part, the decision under review and re-open the proceedings for a new trial and decision.[92] Furthermore, persons using patents which are the subject matter of a decision under review and who act in good faith should be allowed to continue using such patents.[93]

B. Timeline and Content of the Application

An application for a rehearing may be lodged by any party (a 'petitioner') adversely affected by a final decision of the Court of First Instance, for which the time for lodging an appeal has expired, or of the Court of Appeal.[94] The petitioner must pay the fee of €2,500 for the rehearing.[95]

The application for rehearing must be lodged at the Court of Appeal. If the application is based on the ground of a fundamental procedural defect, this must be within two months of the discovery of the fundamental defect or of service of the final decision, whichever is the later. If the application is based on an act which has been held by a final court decision to constitute a criminal offence, this must be within two months of the date on which the criminal offence has been so held or service of the final decision, whichever is the later. In any event, it cannot be lodged later than 10 years of service of the final decision.[96]

---

[89] Article 81(1) UPC Agreement.
[90] ibid Article 81(2), first sentence. The procedural details for the request of a rehearing are set out in Rules 245 ff of the Rules of Procedure.
[91] Article 81(2), 2nd sentence UPC Agreement; and Rule 251 of the Rules of Procedure.
[92] Article 81(3) UPC Agreement.
[93] ibid Article 81(4).
[94] Rule 245.1 of the Rules of Procedure.
[95] ibid Rule 250.
[96] ibid Rule 245.2(1); and Article 81(2), first sentence UPC Agreement.

The application for rehearing must contain the names of the petitioner and of the petitioner's representative, the postal and electronic addresses for service on the petitioner, the names and addresses of the persons authorised to accept service, and an indication of the decision to be reviewed.[97] Furthermore, the application shall indicate the reasons for setting aside the final decision, as well as the facts and evidence on which the application is based.

i. Fundamental Procedural Defects

Examples of fundamental procedural defects include:[98]

(a) a judge of the Court took part in the decision in breach of judicial independence and impartiality;[99]
(b) a person not appointed as a judge of the Court sat on the panel which took the final decision;
(c) a fundamental violation of the basis of decision making and the right to be heard occurred in the proceedings which have led to the final decision;[100]
(d) the decision was made without deciding on a request relevant to that decision; or
(e) a breach of Article 6 of the Convention for the Protection of Human Rights and Fundamental Freedoms has occurred.

Admissibility of the application for rehearing requires that the objection in respect of the procedural defect was raised during the proceedings before the Court of First Instance or the Court of Appeal and was dismissed, except where such an objection could not have been raised during the proceedings before the Court of First Instance or the Court of Appeal.[101] An application for rehearing based upon the ground of a fundamental procedural defect is not admissible where the party could have brought an appeal in respect of the defect, but failed to do so.

A criminal offence must only be considered to have occurred if it is finally held to be such an offence by a competent court or authority. A conviction is not necessary.[102]

ii. Examination as to Formal Requirements of the Application for Rehearing and Handling of the Application

The Registry must examine compliance with the formal requirements.[103] If this is not the case, it must invite the petitioner to correct the deficiencies within 14 days and, where applicable, pay the fee for the rehearing within 14 days. If the petitioner fails to correct the deficiencies or pay the fee, the case must be assigned to the standing judge who may reject the application for rehearing as inadmissible. They must give the petitioner an opportunity to be heard beforehand.

---

[97] Rule 246 of the Rules of Procedure.
[98] ibid Rule 247.
[99] Article 17 UPC Agreement; and Article 7 of the Statute of the UPC Agreement.
[100] Article 76 UPC Agreement.
[101] Rule 248 of the Rules of Procedure.
[102] ibid Rule 249.
[103] ibid Rules 245, 246 and 250 (see Rule 252).

270   *Appeal*

The application will then be recorded in the register and served to all other parties by the Registry.[104] It must be assigned to a panel consisting of three legally qualified judges. The President of the Court of Appeal may order that judges of the Court who participated in taking the decision to be reviewed must not sit on the panel.[105]

iii. Decision on the Application for Rehearing

The Court should hear the parties and afterwards either decide to reject the application as not allowable or to allow it. The decision to reject must be by a majority vote of the judges on the panel.[106] If the application for rehearing is allowed, it must set aside or suspend the decision under review, in whole or in part, and re-open the proceedings for a new hearing and decisions. Where proceedings are re-opened, the panel must give directions for the future proceedings.

iv. Fees

For an application for rehearing, a fee of €2,500 is due (see Chapter 20).

---

[104] ibid Rule 253.1.
[105] ibid Rule 253.2.
[106] ibid Rule 255(a). In keeping, with Article 77 UPC Agreement, like other decisions and orders, the decision on the rehearing must be reasoned. The court has the discretion to add reasons (for example, to deter frivolous applications).

18

Final Remedies and Costs

In keeping with the requirements of Directive 2004/48/EC of the European Parliament and of the Council of 29 April 2004 on the Enforcement of Intellectual Property Rights (hereinafter the 'Enforcement Directive'), the UPC must provide for a successful party in a decision on the merits to obtain damages and other remedies for the harm suffered due to a past or ongoing infringement of their patent. The UPC Agreement deals with damages in Article 68 UPC Agreement and it follows that the court must have a procedure by which the successful party in a decision on the merits may recover damages. This includes the possibility of requesting the laying open of books of the infringer for the purpose of gaining evidence of sales and profits made from their infringement. Other corrective measures are provided in Article 64 UPC Agreement.

The Enforcement Directive, as reflected in the UPC Agreement, also allows the reasonable and proportionate legal costs and expenses of the successful party in bringing proceedings to also be recovered in a costs procedure, subject to certain ceilings and safeguards. The court also allows the possibility of obtaining interim costs and security for the costs of a party.

The scope of these remedies and the procedures for obtaining them are explained in this chapter (reference should also be made to Chapter 10).

I. Damages

A. Overview

The award of damages in the UPC is provided by Article 68:

> The court shall, at the request of the injured party, order the infringer who knowingly, or with reasonable grounds to know, engaged in a patent infringing activity, to pay the injured party damages appropriate to the harm actually suffered by that party as a result of the infringement.
>
> (1) The injured party shall, to the extent possible, be placed in the position it would have been in if no infringement had taken place. The infringer shall not benefit from the infringement. However, damages shall not be punitive.
> (2) When the Court sets the damages:
>   (a) it shall take into account all appropriate aspects, such as the negative economic consequences, including lost profits, which the injured party has suffered, any unfair profits made by the infringer and, in appropriate cases, elements other than economic factors, such as the moral prejudice caused to the injured party by the infringement; or

(b) as an alternative to point (a), it may, in appropriate cases, set the damages as a lump sum on the basis of elements such as at least the amount of the royalties or fees which would have been due if the infringer had requested authorization to use the patent in question.

(3) Where the infringer did not knowingly, or with reasonable grounds to know, engage in the infringing activity, the Court may order the recovery of profits or the payment of compensation.

Damages must take into account all appropriate aspects to the harm actually suffered by the injured party. The appropriate aspects relevant to the calculation of damages are thus the negative economic consequences suffered by the patentee, including:

(a) lost profits;
(b) unfair profits of the infringer;
(c) non-economic considerations such as moral prejudice caused to the injured party.

Alternatively, and where it is appropriate, the damages may be awarded as a lump sum on the basis of royalties or fees that would have been due if the infringer had requested and been given a licence to use the invention. So far as national cases are a guide, the circumstances in which compensation may be awarded on the basis of a royalty may include those in which a licence would have been granted, or where it cannot be proved that a loss of a sale would have occurred due to the infringement, or where the patentee is not working the invention.[1]

Article 68 is closely based on the wording of the Enforcement Directive.[2] In the Directive, like Article 68, compensation for lost profits and unfair profits of the infringer are not explicitly described as alternative factors to be considered in the calculation of damages. However, that they are intended to be alternatives is supported by the wording of the Recitals of the Enforcement Directive.[3] This interpretation also prevents double recovery of damages (as both profits lost to the innocent party and profits gained by the infringer on the same items), a result that is consistent with the requirement that damages should be appropriate to the harm actually suffered.[4]

In circumstances in which the infringer did not knowingly, or with reasonable grounds to know, engage in the infringing activity ('innocent infringement'), the awarding of the

---

[1] The Düsseldorf Court of Appeals referred to the CJEU questions concerning the proper calculation of a reasonable royalty, in particular the issue of whether an infringer's surcharge is required: I-15 U 21/14 16 October 2014. However, the decision of the CJEU did not provide guidance on the interpretation of the Enforcement Directive in this regard (see *Jørn Hansson v Jungpflanzen Grunewald GmbH* (Case C-481/14) (9 June 2016).

[2] Article 13; and see also *Jørn Hansson v Jungpflanzen Grunewald GmbH* (n 1). However, note *Stowarzyszenie 'Olawska Telewizja Kablowa' v Stowarzyszenie Filmowców Polskich* (Case C-367/15) (25 January 2017), which holds that Article 13 of the Enforcement Directive does not preclude national legislation under which the holder of an intellectual property right may demand from the infringer payment of a sum corresponding to twice the appropriate licence fee.

[3] Recital (26): 'damages awarded to the rightsholder should take account of all appropriate aspects, such as loss of earnings incurred by the rightholder, or unfair profits made by the infringer'. However, the distinction is not clear in all contracting Member States. While the UK, Germany and the Netherlands offer a choice between recovery based on the infringer's profits or the injured party's loss, in France the former is only a factor to be considered in calculating damages.

[4] Not all EU countries provide the right to recovery unfair profits of the infringer as an alternative to compensation for lost profits. In Italy, the recovery of profits may be made in addition to compensation although this may be inconsistent with the Enforcement Directive (see G Dragotti, The Implementation of the Enforcement Directive in Italy [2006] *Italian Intellectual Property* 105).

infringer's profits or damages becomes a matter at the court's discretion rather than being mandatory. The practices of the European national courts vary with regard to innocent infringement and there is therefore no clear model for the UPC to follow on the issue, in particular with regard to the circumstances in which an infringement is 'innocent'.[5]

Punitive damages are not available in the UPC.[6] However, damages for moral prejudice may be awarded. There is no common practice with regard to moral prejudice from which the UPC may draw. Instead, in the national courts, damages may be justified under this heading to compensate for mental distress or other emotional harm[7] damage to the reputation of the inventor or to round up the damages for infringement per se; alternatively, they may not be available at all.[8]

The general basis for the assessment of damages is that, to the extent possible, the award should place the injured party in the position in which it would have been had the infringement not taken place. In simple cases, this will be the profits lost by the injured party to sales of the infringing product if it can be shown that the loss is caused by the infringement.[9] Potentially more problematic will be how the court approaches the calculation of damages in cases in which the infringing article is a small part of a larger item.[10] In the national cases, damages may also be awarded on the 'springboard' basis that the infringer has obtained the advantage of an increased market share that would not have been possible without the infringement,[11] or the loss caused by permanent price erosion.[12]

B. Procedure for the Determination of Damages and Compensation

When making a decision on the merits following the oral procedure, the court may make an interim award of damages to the successful party, at least covering the anticipated costs of the procedure for the award for damages and compensation.[13] Alternatively, it may make a final order awarding damages or compensation to be paid to the successful party.[14] If a final award of damages is not made in the order on the decision on the merits, the damages awarded to the successful party may be determined in separate proceedings.[15] The damages awarded may include an amount based on the provisional protection conferred by a published patent application,[16] and damages payable for the harm caused by a provisional

---

[5] If existing practice on innocence in the leading European national courts is carried through to the UPC cases (a lack of knowledge or negligence in Germany and the Netherlands, and a lack of awareness or reasonable grounds for supposing in the UK), innocence is likely to be established only rarely. There is no innocent infringer defence in France.

[6] Article 68 UPC Agreement.

[7] As regards English practice, see *Henderson v All Around the World Recordings Ltd* [2014] EWHC 3087 (IPEC). Although possible, the awarding of damages for moral prejudice is rare in the UK and the Netherlands.

[8] As is the practice, respectively, in France and Germany.

[9] In some jurisdictions, it is also possible to claim loss of 'convoyed goods', that is, products or services that would have followed the sale but for the infringement, such as spare parts; see *Gerber Garment Technology Inc v Lectra Systems Ltd* (1997) RPC 443.

[10] Discussed in *Coflexip v Stolt* [2003] FSR 41 and *Fabio Perini v LPC/PCMC* [2012] EWHC 1393 (Pat).

[11] See TGI Paris, *Agilent / Waters*, 97/10725 (14 January 2009).

[12] *Alexander & Co v Henry & Co* (1895) 12 RPC, 360.

[13] Rule 119 of the Rules of Procedure.

[14] ibid Rule 118.1.

[15] ibid Rule 125.

[16] Under Article 32(1)(f) UPC Agreement.

measure, preservation or inspection order that has been revoked[17] (see Chapters 15 and 16), as well as damages due to liability established in the decision on the merits and any interest thereon.

i. Application for the Determination of Damages

A successful party wishing to have damages determined must lodge an application no later than one year from service of the final decision on the merits on validity and infringement (including any final appeal decision). If the damages to be determined concern provisional protection of a published patent application or the harm caused by a provisional measure, the application must be made no later than a year after the relevant order. The application may include an order to lay open books.[18]

The application for the determination of damages must contain the following details[19] and the appropriate fee;[20]

(a) the particulars of name and address for the party claiming the damages, as would be required for a statement of claim (see Chapter 10);[21]
(b) the date of the decision on the merits and the number of the action;
(c) where required, a request for an order to lay open books.

If there is no laying open of books, or the procedure for the laying open of books is completed, the applicant must state:[22]

(a) the requested redress (damages, licence fees or profits) and the interest thereon;
(b) an indication of the facts relied on – in particular, calculations concerning lost profits or profits made by the unsuccessful party;
(c) the evidence relied on;
(d) whether the decision on the merits is being appealed; and
(e) an assessment of the damages claimed.

As soon as practicable after the lodging of the application, the Registry must examine whether the above requirements have been complied with.[23] A failure by the applicant to comply must be corrected within a time period to be specified by the Registry.[24] If the application is compliant, then the Registry will as soon as practicable record the date of receipt of the application and enter it into the register, as well as informing the applicant of the date of receipt and serving the application on the unsuccessful party.[25] The Registry must also inform the panel that gave the decision on the merits about the lodging of the application.

---

[17] See Rules 198.2 and 213.2 of the Rules of Procedure.
[18] ibid Rule 126.
[19] ibid Rule 131.1.
[20] This is a fixed fee plus any additional fee based on the value of the applicant's damages claim that exceeds €500,000 (ibid Rule 370) (see ch 20).
[21] ibid Rule 13.1(a)–(d).
[22] ibid Rule 131.2.
[23] Specifically, ibid Rules 126, 131.1 and 131.2(d) and (e) and 132 (see Rule 134.1).
[24] ibid Rule 134.2. Failure to correct the deficiencies or pay the fee may result in a decision that the application is inadmissible by a decision by default (by the application of Rule 16.4 and 16.5).
[25] ibid Rule 135.1.

This same panel must also decide the determination of damages, unless for any reason this is not possible or practical, in which case the presiding judge of the relevant division will appoint a new panel.[26]

ii. Stay of Application

The unsuccessful party may make a reasoned request that the application for a determination of damages is stayed, pending an appeal of the decision on the merits.[27] The court must give the applicant an opportunity to be heard, and if it is decided that there should be no stay, the court may order the applicant to render a security.[28]

iii. Defence and Further Pleadings

The unsuccessful party must inform the Registry whether it accepts the claim for damages made in the application within two months of service, in which case the judge-rapporteur must make the order for damages in accordance with the application. If the unsuccessful party opposes the claim, it must lodge a defence to the application within two months of receipt of service of the application[29] or, where there has been a laying open of books, within two months of the applicant's statement of the redress it is seeking.[30]

The defence to the application for the determination of damages must contain:[31]

(a) the names of the unsuccessful party and their representative;
(b) the postal and electronic addresses for service on the unsuccessful party, and the names and addresses of those authorised to accept service;
(c) the number attributed to the action;
(d) the reasons for contesting the application;
(e) an indication of the facts relied on; and
(f) the evidence relied on.

Within one month of receipt of the defence, the applicant may lodge a reply, which must be limited to the matters raised in the defence. The unsuccessful party may then lodge a rejoinder to the reply within one month of receipt of the reply, which must be limited to the matters raised in the reply.[32] The judge-rapporteur may order the exchange of further written pleadings and specify the relevant time periods.[33] The provisions of the Rules of Procedure applying to interim and oral procedures (see Chapters 13 and 14) then apply, but with shorter time periods as may be ordered by the judge-rapporteur. The judge-rapporteur will decide on which party is to bear the costs of the determination of damages.[34]

---

[26] ibid Rule 135.2.
[27] ibid Rule 136.
[28] Under ibid Rule 352.
[29] ibid Rule 137.2.
[30] Further to ibid Rule 131.2.
[31] ibid Rule 138.
[32] ibid Rule 139.
[33] ibid Rule 140.1.
[34] In accordance with Article 69 UPC Agreement.

C. A Request to Lay Open Books

A request to lay open books made in an application for the determination of damages must be examined as to formal requirements,[35] recorded in the Register and served.[36] The laying open of books may also be stayed pending appeal of the relevant decision on the merits.[37] The request must contain:[38]

(a) the particulars of name and address for the party claiming the damages, as would be required for a statement of claim (see Chapter 10);[39]
(b) the date of the decision on the merits and the number of the action;
(c) a description of the information held by the unsuccessful party for which access is sought, in particular documents relating to turnover and profits generated by the infringing product or process, and accounts and bank documents and related documents concerning the infringement;
(d) the reasons why access to this information is necessary;
(e) the facts relied on; and
(f) the supporting evidence.

Within two months of receipt of the request to lay open books, the unsuccessful party must either inform the Registry that it accepts the request, in which case the judge-rapporteur will make the appropriate order to lay open books,[40] or it must lodge a defence to the Request.[41] The applicant then has within 14 days of receipt of service of the defence to lodge a reply. The reply must be limited to the issues raised in the defence. The unsuccessful party may lodge a rejoinder to the reply within a further 14 days.[42]

The judge-rapporteur may order the exchange of further written pleadings and specify the relevant time periods.[43] The provisions of the Rules of Procedure applying to interim and oral procedures (see Chapters 13 and 14) then apply, but with shorter time periods as may be ordered by the judge-rapporteur. The judge-rapporteur will decide on which party is to bear the costs.[44]

The court may then order the unsuccessful party to open its books to the applicant within a specified time period and subject to any other terms that the court deems appropriate,[45] including the protection of confidential information.[46] In particular, it may order that the

---

[35] Under Rule 134 of the Rules of Procedure.
[36] Under ibid Rule 135.
[37] As for the application for the determination of damages under ibid Rule 136.
[38] ibid Rule 141.
[39] ibid Rule 13.1(a)–(d).
[40] ibid Rule 142.1.
[41] ibid Rule 142.2.
[42] ibid Rule 142.3.
[43] ibid Rule 140.1.
[44] In accordance with Article 69 UPC Agreement.
[45] In particular, in what form and within what time period the evidence must be produced, and any sanction which may be imposed if the evidence is not produced according to the order (see Rule 190.4 of the Rules of Procedure).
[46] Further to Article 58 UPC Agreement.

evidence is disclosed to certain named individuals and is subject to the appropriate terms of non-disclosure.[47] Whether or not the request is allowed, the court must specify a time period within which the procedure for the award of damages is to be resumed.[48]

i. National Perspectives

In Germany, like the UPC, establishing liability for damages and actual determination of the amount of damages are separate proceedings. Liability for damages is established if the defendant has intentionally or at least by negligence committed patent infringement.[49] Under German law, a company practising in a certain field is required to monitor for patents relevant in this field so that, as a practical matter, at least negligent behaviour is typically assumed giving rise to damages. When asserting a damage claim, German courts typically require a timeframe of one month following publication of the mention of grant of the patent; after this period has lapsed, it is assumed that the infringer had the opportunity to take note.[50]

When determining a liability for damages, the patentee does not have to choose which methodology it wishes to subsequently calculate damages. The patentee in Germany requests full accounting (laying open of books) and subsequently, once having received this information, decides by way of which calculation method it wishes to calculate damages. These may be calculated by either (i) infringer`s profits, (ii) lost profits or (iii) a reasonable royalty. Typically, calculating damages by way of lost profits is the least common, as the patentee will have to causally demonstrate that it would have made the lost profits (ie, in practice this may require a monopoly position on the product market) and also requires the disclose of its own profit calculation. Typically, this calculation model is confined to monopoly-type market situations, such as in a blockbuster pharma case, where a generics company enters a monopoly market protected by a patent of the originator. Once the patentee has calculated its damages by one of the three methods, it approaches the defendant. If payment is refused, the patentee would need to start separate proceedings in which a court determines damages the infringer has to pay. During such litigation, the patentee can still switch calculation methods. In the end, damages will be determined and the defendant has to pay. As a general principle, damages will not be punitive. Damages ordered are intended to compensate for actual damages suffered, that is, to put the claimant in the position it would have been in had no infringement occurred.

While the UPC also envisages a two-step system (determining liability and then determining the amount), a key difference is apparent: Under German law, a request to lay open books is already available in proceedings determining a liability for damages (if determined and requested, books have to be laid open). However, UPC Rule 126 sets out that a request to lay open books is only available in the context of separate proceedings for determining the amount of damages. From a practical perspective, this may have the consequence that

---

[47] Rule 190.1 of the Rules of Procedure.
[48] ibid Rule 144.1(b) and 144.2.
[49] Section 139 II of the Patentgesetz.
[50] BGH, GRUR 1986, 803 – *Formstein*.

separate proceedings to determine the amount of damages are regularly brought before the UPC (in order to be able to calculate damages), whereas in Germany, such determination proceedings may not be required, as the plaintiff can calculate its damages and if the defendant agrees or a settlement can be reached, no separate determination proceedings will be required. A similar approach is taken in England and Wales.

II. Damages Following the Revocation of a Preliminary Measure

A provisional measure must be revoked, or lapse due to an act or omission by the applicant, or it may be found that there has been no infringement or threat of infringement of the patent[51] (see Chapter 15). In these circumstances, the court may order the applicant, upon the request of the defendant, to provide the defendant with compensation for any injury caused by the measure revoked.[52] Any such compensation should be sought under the general procedure for determining damages described in this chapter.

Under German law, there is a strict liability provision of section 945 of the German Civil Procedure Code: in the event that a preliminary measure is lifted, the respective applicant is liable to compensate damages and only the amount needs to be determined.

III. Damage Caused Outside the EU

When assessing damages for an infringement of a European patent[53] in which the defendant is domiciled outside an EU Member State, the division of the UPC concerned may in certain circumstances take into account damage caused by the same infringement of designations of the European patent which are in force outside the EU (see Chapter 7).[54] The damage caused by the infringement in dispute must also occur within the EU, and the defendant must have property within a contracting Member State which has a 'sufficient connection' to the dispute.[55]

---

[51] Rules 213.2 and 354.2 of the Rules of Procedure.

[52] Given the clear provision in Rule 213.2, there should be no room for applying the evaluations raised by the CJEU in *Bayer/Gedeon Richter* (Case C-688/17) (12 September 2019), as this decision was rendered with regard to Hungarian law which had no provisions on damages in the event of an unjustified preliminary injunction (see Chapter 15).

[53] It would seem that the reference to 'European patent' in Article 71(b)(3) of Regulation (EU) 542/2014 is intended to include European patents that are equivalent to a European patent having unitary effect.

[54] See Table I.1 in the Introduction for a full list of EPC contracting countries that are not members of the EU. However, because Spain, Poland and Croatia are contracting Member States of the UPC Agreement, they are not subject to this jurisdiction.

[55] Article 71b(3) of Regulation (EU) 542/2014 of the European Parliament and of the Council of 15 May 2014, amending the Brussels I Regulation (recast). Article 71b(3) refers to damage inside and outside the EU rather than the contracting Member States. Therefore, it applies to damage caused outside the EU by a non-domiciled defendant when it also occurs in Spain or Poland.

IV. Other Corrective Measures

In addition to damages, the UPC Agreement provides a number of other corrective measures in Article 64:

(1) Without prejudice to any damages due to the injured party by reason of the infringement, and without compensation of any sort, the Court may order, at the request of the applicant, that appropriate measures be taken with regard to products found to be infringing a patent and, in appropriate cases, with regard to materials and implements principally used in the creation or manufacture of those products.

(2) Such measures shall include:

(a) a declaration of infringement;
(b) recalling the products from the channels of commerce;
(c) depriving the product of its infringing property;
(d) definitively removing the products from the channels of commerce; or
(e) the destruction of the products and/or of the materials and implements concerned.

(3) The Court shall order that those measures be carried out at the expense of the infringer, unless particular reasons are invoked for not doing so.

(4) In considering a request for corrective measures pursuant to this Article, the Court shall take into account the need for proportionality between the seriousness of the infringement and the remedies to be ordered, the willingness of the infringer to convert the materials into a non-infringing state, as well as the interests of third parties.

These measures are available in addition to damages and may be ordered at the time the Court makes an order regarding the merits of the action. The measures sought should be identified in the statement of claim.[56] The corrective measures provided in Article 64 broadly reflect those in the Enforcement Directive.[57]

There is also a right to publicity measures provided for in the UPC Agreement in Article 80:

The Court may order, at the request of the applicant and at the expense of the infringer, appropriate measures for the dissemination of information concerning the Court's decision, including displaying the decision and publishing it in full or in part in public media.

This reflects the requirement of the Enforcement Directive that judicial authorities of Member States may order 'appropriate measures for the dissemination of the information concerning the decision, including displaying the decision and publishing it in full or in part'.[58]

Like the Enforcement Directive, Article 64(4) requires the court to exercise proportionality between the remedy ordered and the seriousness of the infringement. An obvious example of where such proportionality should be considered, given in paragraph (4), is an order that an infringing article is deprived of its infringing property in cases where this is possible, instead of definitive removal of the goods from the channels of commerce or even

---

[56] Rule 13.1(k) of the Rules of Procedure.
[57] Article 10 of the Enforcement Directive.
[58] ibid Article 15.

destruction. Similarly, the removal of infringing goods from the channels of commerce may be inappropriate in cases where it deprives the public of goods on which they have in some manner become dependent.

Looking at practical application from a German perspective, claims for recall and definitive removal from the supply channels typically concern scenarios in which the infringer no longer has any legal title in the products (for example, has lost possession and ownership to distributors). Otherwise, destruction claims would apply if the infringer still had ownership or possession Against this background of having lost legal title, an actual return cannot be expected to be enforced. Compliance with a claim for recall and removal is thus confined to an obligation to approach the downstream supply channel in a clear and direct manner; referring to the infringement judgment; requesting return of delivered products; and offering to compensate associated costs. Typically, such correspondence is made in writing, in order to prove compliance with the request.

A. Final Injunction

Article 63 UPC Agreement provides for obtaining permanent injunctions in the UPC:

(1) Where a decision is taken finding an infringement of a patent, the Court may grant an injunction against the infringer aimed at prohibiting the continuation of the infringement. The Court may also grant such injunction against an intermediary whose services are being used by a third party to infringe a patent.

(2) Where appropriate, non-compliance with the injunction referred to in paragraph 1 shall be subject to a recurring penalty payment to the Court.

Article 63 again reflects the terms of the Enforcement Directive.[59] Most importantly, final injunctions are a discretionary rather than an automatic remedy. Such guidance as the court has on the application of this discretion is to be found in the general obligation in Article 3(2) of the Enforcement Directive:

1. Member States shall provide for the measures, procedures and remedies necessary to ensure the enforcement of the intellectual property rights covered by this Directive. Those measures, procedures and remedies shall be fair and equitable and shall not be unnecessarily complicated or costly, or entail unreasonable time-limits or unwarranted delays.
2. Those measures, procedures and remedies shall also be effective, proportionate and dissuasive and shall be applied in such a manner as to avoid the creation of barriers to legitimate trade and to provide for safeguards against their abuse.

There is also the option to apply alternative measures in Article 12 of the Enforcement Directive:

Member States may provide that, in appropriate cases and at the request of the person liable to be subject to the measures provided for in this section, the competent judicial authorities may order pecuniary compensation to be paid to the injured party instead of applying the measures provided for in this section if that person acted unintentionally and without negligence, if execution of the measures in question would cause him/her disproportionate harm and if pecuniary compensation to the injured party appears reasonably satisfactory.

---

[59] ibid Article 11.

The relationship between these articles in the Enforcement Directive has been the subject of a number of CJEU rulings,[60] in which it has been established that Article 3(2) requires courts to consider the proportionality of injunctions to restrain infringements of intellectual property rights.[61]

When a decision is taken that finds an infringement of a patent, the court may grant a permanent injunction against the infringer and against an intermediary whose services are being used to infringe the patent.[62] The meaning of the word 'intermediary', which is again taken from the Enforcement Directive, is unclear in the patents context. 'Intermediary' might cover indirect infringers, who either supply or offer to supply means relating to an essential element of the patented invention, suitable for putting it into effect, or supply staple commercial products with an inducement to the person supplied to infringe. Alternatively, it might catch anyone assisting with an infringing act. However, the latter would create more extensive acts of contributory infringement than those provided for indirect infringement in Article 26(1) and (2) UPC Agreement.

The scope of application of the final injunction – for example, to 'springboard relief'[63] – will be a matter for the court to develop in case law.

For comparison, German courts have adopted a very narrow interpretation of the proportionality requirement of the Enforcement Directive, basically providing an injunction as an automatic consequence of patent infringement. Recently, the German Patent Act has been amended to include proportionality requirements in a more direct context following a judgment of the Federal Court of Justice, in which a grace period with a view to an injunction was discussed.[64] The new section 139 of the Patent Act now includes the following limitation in relation to injunctions: 'The relief is denied insofar as the seeking of this relief with a view to the individual facts of the case and good faith presents a disproportionate hardship by way of the exclusive right for the infringer or third parties. In such a case, the infringed party is to be awarded a just compensation in money.' However, despite its codification, it remains to be seen what impact and practical application the new law will have on injunction claims: with a view to Standard Essential Patents (SEPs), the *Huawei v ZTE* case law[65] already sets out specific considerations on the application of an injunction claim; similarly, in pharma cases, compulsory licenses[66] can provide for exceptions to an injunction claim.

---

[60] See *Productores de Música de España (Promusicae) v Telefónica de España SAU* (Case C-275/06) [2008] ECR I-271; *DHL Express France SAS v Chronopost SA* (Case C-235/09) [2011] ECR I-2801; *L'Oréal SA v eBay International AG* (Case C-324/09) [2011] ECR I-6011; *Scarlet Extended SA v Société Belge des Auteurs, Compositeurs et Editeurs (SABAM)* (Case C-70/10) [2011] ECR I-11959; *Belgische Vereniging van Auteurs, Componisten en Uitgevers CVBA (SABAM) v Netlog NV* (Case C-360/10) [2012] ECR I-0000; *UPC Telekabel Wien GmbH v Constantin Film GmbH* (Case C-314/12) (26 November 2013).

[61] However, where the right sought to be enforced by the injunction is a patent, it has been remarked that the court must be very cautious before making an order which is tantamount to a compulsory licence in circumstances where no compulsory licence would be available – where no other countervailing right is in play, the burden on the party seeking to show that the injunction would be disproportionate is thus a heavy one (see *HTC Corporation v Nokia Corporation* [2013] EWHC 3778 (Pat)).

[62] Article 63 UPC Agreement.

[63] See *Smith & Nephew plc v Convatec Technologies Inc* [2013] EWHC 3955; and *Merck Canada v Sigma (No 2)* [2013] RPC 2.

[64] BGH, GRUR 2016, 1031 – Wärmetauscher.

[65] European Court of Justice, decision of 15 July 2015, C-170/17; GRUR 2015, 764.

[66] BGH, GRUR 2017, 1017 – Raltegravir.

282 Final Remedies and Costs

The English court will similarly consider whether a final injunction should be granted according to the benchmark of whether it would be 'grossly disproportionate' to award the injunction,[67] and may apply principles including consideration of the public interest.[68] Refusal, or even carve out, of a final injunction is nonetheless very rare outside the SEP cases.

B. Enforcement

The powers of the UPC will be 'directly enforceable … in each Contracting Member State'[69] on the same terms as if the order had been made by a national court of that country.[70] UPC decisions are therefore effectively those of a national court of each and every contracting Member State, which are enforceable according to national procedures.

V. Costs

Article 69 UPC Agreement provides for the recovery of costs by a successful party to an action in the UPC:

(1) Reasonable and proportionate legal costs and other expenses incurred by the successful party shall, as a general rule, be borne by the unsuccessful party, unless equity requires otherwise, up to a ceiling set in accordance with the Rules of Procedure.
(2) Where a party succeeds only in part or in exceptional circumstances, the Court may order that costs be apportioned equitably or that the parties bear their own costs.
(3) A party should bear unnecessary costs it has caused the Court or another party.
(4) At the request of the defendant, the Court may order the applicant to provide adequate security for the legal costs and other expenses incurred by the defendant which the applicant may be liable to bear, in particular in the cases referred to in Articles 59–62.

Article 69 is derived from the provisions of the Enforcement Directive.[71] However, in paragraphs (2)–(4), Article 69 is more specific than the Enforcement Directive; it expressly allows the court to apportion costs between the parties 'equitably' in 'exceptional circumstances'[72] or where a party has succeeded 'only in part'. The latter suggests that costs will not be determined by the outcome of the case as a whole, but issue by issue; the court will examine the issues pleaded by each party and will award costs according to who won on each of

---

[67] *Evalve Inc and Others v Edwards Lifesciences Ltd* [2020] EWHC 513 (Pat) (12 March 2020).
[68] *Chiron v Organon (No 10)* [1995] FSR 325.
[69] Rule 354 of the Rules of Procedure.
[70] Article 82(3) UPC Agreement.
[71] Article 14.
[72] Exceptional circumstances may include those where the conduct of the successful party has been particularly unreasonable in choosing to raise and pursue certain allegations or issues and the manner in which they do so (for guidance, see Rule 44.3(5) of the Civil Procedure Rules of England & Wales).

those issues.[73] This may mean, for example, that if the patent is valid but not infringed, the patentee will be awarded the costs of the invalidity part of the case, but the defendant will be awarded the costs of the infringement part of the case. The costs award could be further apportioned on the basis of those grounds on which the validity case was successful, but not those for which it was not successful, or if the patent is found partially valid.[74]

The Rules on Court Fees and Recoverable Costs also emphasise that the general rule on costs recovery by the successful party is subject to safeguards. These include the ceiling on recoverable representation costs as well as the requirement that such costs be reasonable and proportionate, but also that 'equity may also serve as a self-standing ground for rendering the general rule inapplicable. Furthermore, in cases of partial success or in exceptional circumstances, the Court may order the parties to bear their own costs, or apply a different apportionment of cost, based on equity'. The Rules on Court Fees and Recoverable Costs also envisage that unnecessary costs that are incurred by a party should be borne by that party and that there is also a 'large margin of appreciation' for the Court when applying these safeguarding principles before making a costs decision, in the context of which the recovery ceiling is only a 'safety net'.

A. Costs of Provisional Measures

When ordering provisional measures (see Chapter 15), the court may also make an interim award of costs according to the party that has been successful in either obtaining the measure or defending it.[75]

B. Costs of a Decision on the Merits

i. *The Scope of Recoverable Costs*

When giving its decision on the merits, the Court must decide in principle which party is to bear the legal costs in accordance with Article 69 UPC Agreement. In advance of its decision, the Court may also order that the parties submit a preliminary estimate of the legal costs that they will seek to recover.[76] The Court may also award interim costs to the successful party in the decision on the merits and in a decision for the determination of damages.[77]

---

[73] In case of partial success, the applicable ceiling in the cases must correspond to the proportion of success of the party seeking costs recovery; see Rules on Court Fees and Recoverable Costs, 25 February 2016: https://www.unified-patent-court.org/sites/default/files/agreed_and_final_r370_subject_to_legal_scrubbing_to_secretariat.pdf.

[74] Whether it was reasonable for the parties to raise a particular issue may be an influencing factor on apportionment. Apportionment of costs is well established in English practice. See, for example, *SmithKline Beecham Plc v Apotex Europe Ltd (No 2)* [2004] EWCA Civ 1703. In France, the amount of costs awarded to the successful party is at the discretion of the court and may include attorney's fees and the costs of bailiffs. In the Netherlands, the full costs borne by the successful party are, in principle, recoverable unless they are manifestly unreasonable (Article 1019h DCCP). However, by contrast, in Germany there is no requirement for the successful party's costs to be reimbursed by the unsuccessful party in German patent litigation (see section 142a of the Patentgesetz).

[75] Rule 211.1(d).
[76] ibid Rule 118.5.
[77] ibid Rule 150.2.

A full decision on costs is the subject of separate proceedings following a decision on the merits and, where applicable, a decision determining damages. The costs decision must include:[78]

(a) costs incurred by the court during proceedings, such as the costs of: simultaneous interpretation, of reimbursement of witness expenses,[79] of fees and expenses of any court expert,[80] and costs incurred pursuant to experiments;[81]
(b) the costs of the successful party (subject to the considerations above), including their court fees.

The costs of interpretation and translation, which are necessary for the judges to conduct the case in the language of proceedings, are borne by the court.[82]

ii. Recoverable Attorney Fees

Further to the Rules on Court Fees and Recoverable Costs of the Preparatory Committee,[83] ceilings on recoverable 'costs of representation per instance and party' are based on the case value.[84] This is one of a number of measures intended to ensure that recoverable costs are 'reasonable and proportionate'. As shown in Table 18.1, the scale of the recoverable costs ranges from a ceiling of €38,000 for an action valued up to and including €250,000, to a ceiling of €2 million for actions valued at over €50 million.

The Rules on Court Fees and Recoverable Costs allow for the ceiling on recovery of costs of representation to be modified in certain circumstances:

(1) The ceiling may be raised 'to a certain extent' if, for example, the case is of particular complexity, or multiple languages are used such that there is an impact on the costs of representation, upon the request of one party and having regard to the financial capabilities of the other party to meet the costs.[85]
(2) The ceiling may be lowered upon the application of the unsuccessful party if its economic existence is threatened by the amount of costs of representation payable to the successful party – in particular, if the unsuccessful party is a micro-enterprise, SME or non-profit organisation, university, public research organisation or natural person.[86] There is no limit by which the ceiling may be lowered.

---

[78] ibid Rule 150.1.
[79] Further to ibid Rule 180.1.
[80] Further to ibid Rule 185.7.
[81] ibid Rule 201.
[82] ibid Rule 150.1. An explanatory note to the changes made by the Legal Group of the Preparatory Committee in the 17th draft of the Rules of Procedure states that this Rule applies to 'exceptional' cases in which interpretation and translation is necessary for the judges of the Court to conduct the case in the language of proceedings. In these cases, the costs of such interpretation and translation are not to be the subject of the cost decision, but are considered as overheads of the court to be covered by the Court's budget.
[83] See also Article 69 and Rule 152.2 of the Rules of Procedure.
[84] The ceiling is applied to each instance of the Court regardless of the number of parties, claims or patents concerned (Article 1(3) of the Rules on Court Fees and Recoverable Costs).
[85] Article 2(1): (a) by up to 50% of the applicable level in the scale corresponding to a value of the proceeding up to and including €1 million; (b) by up to 25% of the applicable level in the scale corresponding to a value of the proceeding of more than €1 million and up to and including €50 million; (c) up to €5 million in cases with a value of the proceeding of more than €50 million.
[86] Article 2(2) of the Rules on Court Fees and Recoverable Costs.

As regards lowering the ceiling, the Court must take into consideration all available information on the parties, including, where possible, their procedural behaviour, the applicable level of the ceiling for recoverable costs in comparison with the annual turnover of both parties, the type of economic activity that those parties conduct and the impact of lowering the ceiling on the other party.[87]

Any request to raise or lower the recoverable costs ceiling must be made as soon as possible and practicable in the proceedings. This should ideally be with the statement of claim (claimant) and the statement of defence (defendant) so that the Court can make a decision on the issue before the close of the interim procedure.[88] The request should include all reasonably available evidence.

Table 18.1 Scale of recoverable 'costs of representation per instance and party'

Value of action (€)	Costs ceiling (€)[89]
Up to and including 250,000	Up to 38,000
Up to and including 500,000	Up to 56,000
Up to an including 1,000,000	Up to 112,000
Up to and including 2,000,000	Up to 200,000
Up to and including 4,000,000	Up to 400,000
Up to and including 8,000,000	Up to 600,000
Up to and including 16,000,000	Up to 800,000
Up to and including 30,000,000	Up to 1,200,000
Up to and including 50,000,000	Up to 1,500,000
More than 50,000,000	Up to 2,000,000

iii. Procedure

The applicant for costs must lodge an application for costs within one month of receipt of service of the decision on the merits.[90] This must include:

(a) the name and address for the party claiming the damages, as would be required for a statement of claim (see Chapter 10);[91]
(b) the date of the decision on the merits and the number of the action;
(c) a statement as to whether the decision on the merits is the subject of an appeal, if known at the date of the application;
(d) an indication of the costs for which compensation is requested;
(e) any preliminary legal costs estimate submitted by the party prior to the decision on the merits.

---

[87] ibid Article 2(3).
[88] ibid Article 2(4).
[89] An early review of the ceilings for recoverable costs will be undertaken in the light of the practice of how judges apply the cost recovery rules; see the Rules on Court Fees and Recoverable Costs.
[90] Rule 151 of the Rules of Procedure.
[91] ibid Rule 13.1(a)–(d).

The judge-rapporteur may request written evidence from the applicant of all costs requested and must allow the unsuccessful party an opportunity to comment in writing on the costs requested. In particular, the unsuccessful party may identify any item of costs that it says should be apportioned or borne by each party in accordance with Article 69(1)–(3) UPC Agreement.[92] The judge-rapporteur will decide in writing on the costs to be awarded or apportioned and the time period within which they must be paid.[93]

C. Security for Costs

On a reasoned request by a party, the court may order that the other party pays the requesting party adequate security for the legal costs and other expenses being incurred and/or that will be incurred, which the other party may be liable to bear.[94] The order can be made by the court at any time during proceedings, having given both parties the opportunity to be heard[95] and it may be appealed.[96] The court will decide whether the security should be made by deposit or bank guarantee and the period within which it must be provided. If the security is not provided within the time period specified, the court may make a decision in default.[97]

The court may order that one or both parties provides adequate security to cover costs incurred and/or that will be incurred in the proceedings by the court, pending a costs decision covering the court's costs.[98]

German law also provides for security for costs;[99] however, the potential obligation only arises for a claimant that is domiciled in a country where German cost decisions cannot be enforced. The procedure suggested by the UPC Rules of Procedure seems to envision a much broader scope that would basically provide protection against insolvency for either party.

---

[92] ibid Rule 156.1.
[93] ibid Rule 156.2 and 156.3.
[94] ibid Rule 158.1.
[95] ibid Rule 158.2.
[96] ibid Rules 158.3 and 220.2. The order must indicate that an appeal may be lodged.
[97] Pursuant to ibid Rule 355. The court must inform the party concerned that this may be the consequence of a failure to provide the security ordered (Rule 158.4).
[98] ibid Rule 159, except where a party has made a deposit to reimburse the expenses of a witness on which that party relies, further to Rule 180.2 of the Rules of Procedure.
[99] Section 110 of the German Civil Procedure Code.

19

Service and Miscellaneous Matters

The Rules of Procedure setting out the provisions concerning the service performed by the court are discussed in this chapter. Parties to the proceedings, intervention, representation and the interpretation of time limits are also described here. This chapter also covers the legal aid scheme which is available on application in certain circumstances in the UPC.

I. Service

A. Rules Applicable to Service by the Court

The service of statements of claim, orders, decisions and pleadings is carried out by the Registry of the court according to the Rules of Procedure.[1] In addition, as regards statements of claim,[2] the provisions of Regulation (EU) 2020/1784 of the European Parliament and of the Council of 25 November 2020 on the service in the Member States of judicial and extrajudicial documents in civil or commercial matters (service of documents) (recast) applies[3] (hereinafter the 'Service Regulation') also apply.[4]

B. Service within the Contracting Member States

i. Address for Service

Electronic service of the statement of claim is the preferred way of service under the Rules of Procedure. The statement of claim must be served by the Registry at an electronic address where the conditions referred to in Article 19 of the Service Regulation are met on the defendant at the electronic address provided for this purpose by the defendant[5] – or, alternatively,

---

[1] Part 5, Chapter 2 of the Rules of Procedure.
[2] Meaning all originating pleadings in actions referred to in Article 32(1) UPC Agreement.
[3] Regulation (EU) 2020/1784 of the European Parliament and of the Council of 25 November 2020 on the service in the Member States of judicial and extrajudicial documents in civil or commercial matters (service of documents) (recast) [2020] OJ L405, 2 December 2020, 40–78.
[4] Further to Rule 270.1 of the Rules of Procedure. The Service Regulation replaced Regulation (EC) 1393/2007, which was the point of reference for all but the final draft of the Rules of Procedure. Several changes to the Rules were made as a consequence, which have been adopted in this chapter. For further explanation, see Amendments to the text of the UPC draft Rules of Procedure approved by the Preparatory Committee on 15 March 2017 AC/04/08072022_E – ANNEX 1.
[5] ibid Rule 271.1(a).

on a representative of the defendant[6] if the defendant has provided an electronic address of the representative as an address for service.[7] Furthermore, the representative itself can notify either the Registry or the claimant that they accept service of the statement of claim on behalf of the defendant at a respective electronic address.[8] If the electronic address for service of a party changes, that party must give notice of the change to the Registry and every other party in the proceedings as soon as it has taken place and in writing.[9]

The Registry must advise the defendant of the right to refuse to accept a statement of claim if it is not written or not accompanied by a translation into a language that the defendant understands or is an official language of the place where service is to be effected.[10]

ii. Additional Requirements for a Revocation or Declaration of an Infringement Claim

If the statement of claim relates to a revocation action[11] or a declaration of non-infringement[12] a nomination of a representative according to the above must also include professional representatives or legal practitioners who are entitled to representation before the EPO[13] and who are recorded as the representative for the patent that is the subject of the proceedings either in the Register for unitary patent protection[14] or in the respective national patent register.[15]

iii. Non-electronic Service

In the absence of an electronic address for service, the Registry must use any other method set out in the Service Regulation,[16] which is inter alia transmission by consular or diplomatic channels,[17] service by diplomatic or consular agents,[18] and in particular service by registered letter with acknowledgement of receipt or the equivalent.[19] Service under the Service Regulation is effected at the following places:[20]

(a) where the defendant is a company or other legal entities: the statutory seat, central administration or principal place of business within the contracting Member States or

---

[6] Pursuant to ibid Rule 8.1. Where a representative accepts service on behalf of a party, service may be effected within the closed electronic system of the UPC Case Management System.
[7] ibid Rule 271.1(b).
[8] ibid Rule 271.1(c).
[9] ibid Rule 279.
[10] By enclosing with the document to be served form L in Annex I of the Service Regulation. See Rule 271.7 and 271.8 of the Rules of Procedure.
[11] Under Rule 44 of the Rules of Procedure.
[12] Under ibid Rule 63.
[13] According to Article 134 EPC.
[14] According to Article 2(e) UP Regulation.
[15] Rule 271.3 of the Rules of Procedure. The person entitled to be registered as the proprietor under the law of the contracting Member State concerned, whether or not they are in fact registered as such (see Rule 8.5 of the Rules of Procedure).
[16] ibid Rule 271.4(a) and (b).
[17] Article 16 of the Service Regulation.
[18] ibid Article 17.
[19] ibid Article 18. See also Rule 271.6(b) of the Rules of Procedure.
[20] ibid Rule 271.5.

at any place within the contracting Member States where the company or other legal person has a permanent or temporary place of business;
(b) where the defendant is an individual: at the individual's usual or last known residence within the contracting Member States; or
(c) for a statement of revocation or a statement for a declaration of non-infringement: at the place of business of a professional representative or legal practitioner who is entitled to representation before the EPO[21] and who is recorded as the appointed representative for the patent in dispute in the Register of Unitary Patents[22] or of the patent office of a contracting Member State.

If all possibilities of non-electronic service fail, the Registry may use any method of service available according to the national law of the respective EU Member State where the service is to be effected.[23] Alternatively, the court can make an order allowing an alternative method of service (see section I.D below).[24]

iv. Deemed Date of Service

A statement of claim is deemed to be served by electronic communication on the day when the relevant electronic message was sent.[25] The Registry will inform the claimant of the deemed date of service.[26]

In the event that the statement of claim is served by way of registered letter with acknowledgement of receipt or equivalent, such a letter is deemed to be served on the tenth day following posting unless it has failed to reach the addressee, has in fact reached the addressee on a later date or the acknowledgement of receipt or equivalent has not been returned. Service will be deemed effective even if acceptance of the letter is refused, unless the defendant was entitled to refuse service.[27]

C. Service Outside the Contracting Member States

Where a statement of claim is to be served outside the contracting Member States it must be served by the Registry.[28] There are three alternative methods for conducting service outside the contracting Member States. If the service takes place in an EU Member State that is not a contracting Member State, the Service Regulation is still applicable.[29] If the service has to be effected outside the EU Member States, the Registry either has the possibility of conducting service through diplomatic or consular channels of the contracting Member State in which the sub-registry conducting the service is situated,[30] or the service

---

[21] According to Article 134 EPC.
[22] Article 2(e) UP Regulation.
[23] Rule 271.4(c) and Rule 275 of the Rules of Procedure.
[24] Under ibid Rule 275.
[25] ibid Rule 271.6(a).
[26] See ibid Rule 272.1–272.3.
[27] ibid Rule 271.6(b).
[28] Rule 274.1.
[29] ibid Rule 274.1(a)(i).
[30] ibid Rule 274.1(a)(iii).

can be conducted by way of The Hague Convention, if applicable.[31] If none of these methods is possible, then any method permitted by the law of the state where service is to be effected may be used, or a method ordered by the court (see section I.D below).[32] In order for the service to be effective, it must not be contrary to the law of the state where the service is to be effected.[33]

D. Alternative Method or Place of Service of the Statement of Claim

The court may order service of a statement of claim by a method or at a place not otherwise permitted under the Rules of Procedure and the Service Regulation.[34] Such an order is made upon application by the claimant where there is 'a good reason'.[35] The order has to specify:[36] (a) the method or place of service; (b) the date on which the statement of claim is deemed served; and (c) the period for filing the statement of defence. It is also possible for the court, upon a reasonable request by the claimant, to order that steps already taken to bring the statement of claim to the attention of the defendant by an alternative method, or at an alternative place, are good service.[37] However, the order must not be contrary to the law of the state where service is to be effected.[38]

E. Service of Orders, Decisions and Written Pleadings

i. Orders and Decisions (Including Decisions by Default)

The same principles as set out above apply to the service of orders and decisions.[39]

Decisions by default (for which see Chapter 14) resulting from a failure of the defendant to lodge a defence to a statement of revocation or a statement for a declaration of non-infringement within the time limits set out in the Rules of Procedure may be served on the defendant at the place of business of a professional representative or legal practitioner who is entitled to representation before the EPO[40] and who is recorded as the appointed representative for the patent that is subject of the proceedings either in the Register for unitary patent protection[41] or in the respective national patent register.[42]

---

[31] ibid Rule 274.1(a)(ii).
[32] ibid Rule 274.1(b).
[33] ibid Rule 274.2.
[34] ibid Rule 274.1(b).
[35] For example, if none of the alternatives under ibid Rule 274.1(a) are possible.
[36] ibid Rule 275.3.
[37] ibid Rule 275.2.
[38] ibid Rule 275.4.
[39] ibid Rule 276.1.
[40] According to Article 134 EPC.
[41] According to Article 2(e) UP Regulation.
[42] The person entitled to be registered as the proprietor under the law of the contracting Member State concerned, whether or not they are in fact registered as such (see Rule 8.5 of the Rules of Procedure).

ii. Written Pleadings and Other Documents

Written pleadings exchanged in the course of proceedings and other documents concerning the proceedings pending before the court will be served on the other parties, unless the pleading contains a request for an *ex parte* proceeding, by the Registry as soon as practicable after receipt. The Registry will use electronic means to serve these documents.[43] If electronic service is not possible, the Registry must serve by registered letter with acknowledgement of receipt or the equivalent[44] or any other method authorised by the court (as detailed in section I.D above) and is deemed to be served according to the same rules that apply to the other documents.

II. Parties to Proceedings

A. A Plurality of Parties

Actions that are commenced with a plurality of claimants or which concern a plurality of patents may be split into separate proceedings as the discretion of the court.[45] In this situation, the court must decide on any additional court fee to be paid.

The court also has a discretion to order that separate and parallel infringement proceedings, or revocation proceedings, in which the same patent or patents is at issue, are heard together. However, the proceedings must both already be before the same local or regional division, or the central division.[46]

Provided the court has competence in respect of all of them, proceedings may be started against a plurality of defendants.[47] However, the court may also separate proceedings into two or more proceedings,[48] in which case the claimants in the new proceedings must pay the relevant fee,[49] unless the court orders otherwise.[50]

B. Change in Party

i. The Addition, Removal or Substitution of a Party

A party may apply to the court for an order that a person is added as a party, ceases to be a party or is substituted for a party.[51] As soon as is practicable after such an application has been served, the court will invite other parties to proceedings to comment on it.

---

[43] ibid Rule 278.1.
[44] ibid Rule 278.3(a) and (b).
[45] ibid Rule 302.1.
[46] ibid Rule 302.3.
[47] ibid Rule 303.1.
[48] ibid Rule 303.2.
[49] Parties who take the same position and who are jointly represented are treated as one party for the purpose of the payment of fees.
[50] Rule 303.3 of the Rules of Procedure.
[51] ibid Rule 305.1.

When adding or removing a party, the court may make appropriate orders about court fees and costs payable by that party.[52]

When a party is added, removed or substituted, the court must give any directions necessary for the purposes of case management. It must also determine the extent to which a new party is bound by the proceedings at the time of joining.[53]

ii. Death or Demise of a Party

Proceedings are stayed for a period specified by the court if a solitary claimant or solitary defendant dies or ceases to exist, until that party is replaced by a successor.[54] If there is more than one claimant or defendant and one of them dies or ceases to exist, the court may continue with proceedings between the remaining party separately and stay the proceedings concerning the party that no longer exists.[55]

Any party to the proceedings may apply to have the successor added or substituted to proceedings if the successor does not do so of their own motion within a time period specified by the court.[56]

iii. Insolvency of a Party

If a party is declared insolvent under their national insolvency law, the court must stay proceedings for up to three months until the authority or person dealing with the insolvency has decided whether to continue the proceedings in the court. A temporary administrator who has been appointed before insolvency is declared may also request the stay proceedings.[57] If it is decided that the proceedings will not be continued, the other party may nonetheless make a reasoned request that proceedings should continue in accordance with the relevant national insolvency law.[58] Alternatively, a claimant may withdraw an action against an insolvent defendant and a defendant may withdraw a counterclaim against an insolvent claimant.[59] The effect of a decision in proceedings that have been continued must be determined by the law applicable to the insolvency.[60]

III. Intervention

A. Intervention by Application

Any person establishing a legal interest in the outcome of an action of the Court of First Instance or the Court of Appeal and wishing to be bound by the decision of that action[61]

---

[52] ibid Rule 305.3.
[53] ibid Rule 306.
[54] ibid Rule 310.1.
[55] ibid Rule 310.2.
[56] ibid Rule 310.3.
[57] ibid Rule 311.2.
[58] ibid Rule 311.1.
[59] ibid Rule 311.3.
[60] ibid Rule 311.4.
[61] ibid Rule 316.3.

may apply to intervene in that action.[62] Such an application to intervene must be made in full or partial support of a claim, order or remedy sought by one of the parties to the action. The application must be made before the closure of the written procedure unless the relevant court orders otherwise.[63]

The application to intervene must contain:[64]

(a) a reference to the action number of the file;
(b) the names of the intervener and of the intervener's representative, as well as postal and electronic addresses for service and the names of the persons authorised to accept service;
(c) the claim, order or remedy in support of which intervention is sought by the intervener; and
(d) a statement of the facts establishing the right to intervene.

Having given the other parties the opportunity to be heard, the judge-rapporteur must decide on the admissibility of the application to intervene and make an order accordingly.[65]

If the judge-rapporteur decides that the application to intervene is admissible, they or the presiding judge must inform the parties to proceedings and specify a period within which the intervener may lodge a statement of intervention. The statement of intervention must contain:[66]

(a) a statement as to the issues involving the intervener and one or more of the parties, and their connection to the matters in dispute;
(b) the arguments of law; and
(c) the facts and evidence relied on.

The Registry must then serve on the intervener, as soon as practicable, any written pleading served by the existing parties to the proceedings. Such pleading may in whole or in part be subject to a confidential information order, further to a reasoned request, restricting its disclosure to certain persons. The intervener is then treated as a party, unless otherwise ordered by the court.[67]

B. Intervention by Invitation

The judge-rapporteur or the presiding judge may of their own motion, or on a reasoned request by a party, invite a person concerned by the outcome of the action to intervene.[68] If this is of the court's own motion, the parties must first be heard. The person invited must inform the court whether they wish to intervene within a period specified by the court. A person wishing to accept the invitation must make their application to intervene within one month of the service of invitation. Their statement of intervention must then follow within

---

[62] ibid Rule 313.1.
[63] ibid Rule 313.2. *cf* Rule 313.1, which states that the application may be made 'at any stage of the proceedings'.
[64] ibid Rule 313.4.
[65] ibid Rule 314. Note that there is no appeal against an order refusing an application to intervene (Rule 317).
[66] ibid Rule 315.3.
[67] ibid Rule 315.4.
[68] ibid Rule 316.1.

a further period to be specified by the court. The contents of the application and statement must be the same as those described above.

C. Forced Intervention

In the event that a person refuses to intervene, a party to proceedings may contend that the person should be bound by the decision in the action by making a reasoned request.[69] The person who does not wish to be bound by the decision must lodge a statement saying so within the one-month period from service of the application to intervene, as described above.[70]

i. Statement Lodged against Being Bound

If such a statement is lodged within the timeframe specified, the court must hear the parties to the action and the person invited to intervene, and then decide whether the person invited to intervene should be bound by the outcome of the proceedings. If they are to be bound, then the person may lodge their own application to intervene within one month of service of the court's decision. Failure to do so will result in the person being bound by the court's decision in the action.

ii. No Statement Lodged against Being Bound

If a statement is not lodged within a one-month time period from the filing of the application to intervene, then the person will be bound by the decision in the proceedings. The forced intervener will not be entitled to argue that the decision in the action is wrong or that the proceedings were not conducted properly by the parties.

D. Change of Patent Proprietor during Proceedings

The court may authorise the addition or substitution to proceedings[71] of a new proprietor of a patent if, after proceedings relating to the patent or patent application have started, that patent has been transferred for one or more contracting Member States to that new proprietor.[72] If the new proprietor declines to participate, the decision resulting from the proceedings, as recorded in the register, will be binding on them.[73] A new proprietor is not liable to pay a new court fee, even if they have a new representative.[74]

---

[69] ibid Rule 316A.1.
[70] ibid Rule 316A.2.
[71] Further to ibid Rule 305.
[72] ibid Rule 312.1.
[73] ibid Rule 312.3.
[74] ibid Rule 312.2.

IV. Representatives

The representation of parties before the UPC is based on Article 48 UPC Agreement:

(1) Parties shall be represented by lawyers authorised to practise before a court of a Contracting Member State.[75]
(2) Parties may alternatively be represented by European Patent Attorneys who are entitled to act as professional representatives before the European Patent Office pursuant to Article 134 of the EPC and who have appropriate qualifications such as a European Patent Litigation Certificate.
(3) The requirements for qualification pursuant to paragraph 2 shall be established by the Administrative Committee. A list of European Patent Attorneys entitled to represent parties before the Court shall be kept by the Registrar.
(4) Representatives of the parties may be assisted by patent attorneys, who shall be allowed to speak at hearings of the Court in accordance with the Rules of Procedure.
(5) Representatives of the parties shall enjoy the rights and immunities necessary for the independent exercise of their duties, including the privilege from disclosure in proceedings before the Court in respect of communications between a representative and the party or any other person, under the conditions laid down in the Rules of Procedure, unless privilege is expressly waived by the party concerned.
(6) Representatives of the parties shall be obliged not to misrepresent cases or facts before the Court either knowingly or with good reason to know.
(7) Representation in accordance with paragraphs 1 and 2 of this Article shall not be required in proceedings under Article 32(1)(i).

The starting point as regards representation before the UPC in Article 48 is that a party must be represented,[76] unless they are applying to annul or alter a decision of the EPO[77] (see Chapter 12) or applying for legal aid.[78] Representation must be by a lawyer who is authorised to practise before a court in a contracting Member State. Alternatively, appropriately qualified European Patent Attorneys (EPAs) may act as professional representatives before the court. Furthermore, while contracting Member States have their own codes of practice and ethics to which representatives must abide, the UPC sets certain standards and privileges of its own. These are set out further below.

A. Lawyers

In order to represent parties before the UPC, a lawyer, under Article 48(1) UPC Agreement,[79] must lodge at the Registry their practising certificate or equivalent authorisation to practise

---

[75] See ibid Rule 294 as to an application to remove a representative's name from the register of representatives.
[76] ibid Rule 8.1 and 8.2. There is no provision allowing for litigants in person before the UPC.
[77] ibid Rule 88.4.
[78] ibid Rule 378.
[79] Further to ibid Rule 286.1, a lawyer, for the purposes of Article 48(1) UPC Agreement, is a person who is authorised to pursue professional activities under a title referred to in Article 1 of Directive 98/5/EC. Article 1(2)(a) states that a 'lawyer' means any person who is a national of a Member State and seemingly restricts those lawyers entitled to represent a client in a UPC hearing by nationality as well as the country in which they are entitled to practise. However, 'by way of exception', this definition includes a person with equivalent legal professional

in a Member State court.[80] Once lodged, the lawyer may refer back to the certificate or equivalent authorisation in subsequent actions.

The EU UK Trade and Cooperation Agreement[81] guarantees the right of UK lawyers to advise on public international law matters within the EU.[82] This includes advising on strategy and case preparation in the UPC, which, based as it is on international treaty, is a matter of public international law. However, UK lawyers are not permitted to represent parties in UPC hearings either under the UPC Agreement or the EU Trade and Cooperation Agreement. Where UK lawyers are required to be registered as foreign lawyers in an EU country in order to undertake the above, that country is also obliged to permit registration on terms no less favourable than those applicable to a nationally qualified lawyer. Requalification must not be required.[83]

B. European Patent Attorneys

In order to practise before the UPC, an EPA, under Article 48(2) UPC Agreement, must lodge at the Registry a European Patent Litigation Certificate (EPLC) or otherwise justify that they have appropriate qualifications to represent a party before the court. Article 48(3) UPC Agreement states that the Administrative Committee must establish the requirements for such qualifications. Under Article 48(2), EPAs can therefore prove that they have appropriate qualifications by different means, of which the EPLC is just one. The significance of this is that the EPLC will not be available before the entry into force of the UPC Agreement. The recognition of other appropriate qualifications is therefore needed to ensure a sufficient number of qualified EPA representatives at the UPC start date.

For the purpose of the EPLC, the Administrative Committee issued a draft EPLC Decision[84] proposing a decentralised system, in which the UPC accredits courses leading to the EPLC, delivered by universities or other non-profit educational bodies of higher or professional education. The requirement for other appropriate qualifications under Article 48(2) UPC Agreement does not require that EPAs have the same qualification as lawyers to conduct litigation before the national courts, but nor does it mean a qualification

---

qualifications who, owing to national rules, is permitted to practise in patent infringement and invalidity litigation, but not under such a title. It is unclear whether this exception for 'equivalent legal professional qualifications' would extend to patent lawyers who are nationals of the UK or other non-EU country who are entitled to practise in a an EU Member State.

[80] Rule 286.1 of the Rules of Procedure. The reference in the Rule to the EU means that lawyers authorised to practise before courts of EU Member States which are not – or not yet – contracting Member States to the UPC Agreement may also lodge the certificate. The term 'lawyer' is defined by a reference to Directive 98/5/EC. However, an explanatory note of the Legal Group of the Preparatory Committee states that the language 'by way of exception a person with equivalent legal professional qualifications' also addresses a specific situation in Sweden and Finland by which national rules permit certain persons to practise in patent infringement and invalidity litigation, but not under the title governed by the Directive.

[81] Agreement between the European Union and the European Atomic Energy Community, of the one part, and the United Kingdom of Great Britain and Northern Ireland, of the other part [2021] OJ L149/10, 30 April.

[82] ibid Article 194(1).

[83] ibid Article 194(2)(a) and (b).

[84] At the time of writing, this is a draft Decision of the Administrative Committee, Rules of the European Patent Litigation Certificate and Other Appropriate Qualifications Pursuant to Article 48(2) of the Agreement on a Unified Patent Court, agreed 3 September 2015. However, it has been confirmed that EPAs with qualifications gained at the institutions listed in the UK will be able to represent parties before the UPC.

as a national patent attorney is sufficient per se in order to represent parties before the UPC. As a result, Rule 11 of the Draft Decision provides that EPAs who have a bachelor's or master's degree in law according to the relevant educational standards of an EU Member State or who have passed an equivalent state exam in law in an EU Member State will qualify to apply for registration on the list of entitled representatives. Although such diplomas do not generally give a right to act as an advocate before the national courts, they provide EPAs with the necessary knowledge of private and procedural law that is required to conduct patent litigation.[85] In addition, Rule 12 introduces a transitional measure recognising that specific courses (which are listed in the Rule) are already available to prepare EPAs for patent litigation and that in some Member States, patent attorneys are already authorised to represent parties before the national court of a contracting Member State in patent infringement cases. Alternatively, qualification extends to EPAs who have represented a party on their own without the assistance of a lawyer admitted to the relevant court, or having acted as a judge, in at least three patent infringement actions initiated before a national court of a contracting Member State within the five years preceding the application for registration.

C. Assisting Patent Attorneys

Aside from the qualifications for EPAs to represent a party in their own right in the UPC, patent attorneys are permitted to assist representatives in court.[86] Subject to the representative's responsibility to coordinate the presentation of the party's case and subject to the discretion of the court, such patent attorneys may also be heard.[87] A 'patent attorney' for this purpose is an EPA or otherwise a person who is recognised as eligible to give advice under the law of the state where they practise in relation to the protection of any invention or to prosecute or litigate any patent or patent application and is professionally consulted to give such advice.[88]

D. Conduct of Representatives

i. Duties

Representatives before the UPC must comply strictly with any code of conduct that the Administrative Committee adopts.[89] Specifically, a party's representative is under an obligation not to misrepresent either cases or facts before the court where they know or have good reason to know they are doing so.[90] There is no express duty for a representative to draw the court's attention to innocent errors or omissions made by an opponent of which the representative is aware. However, it is arguable that a failure to do so in certain circumstances that

---

[85] See Explanatory Memorandum to the Draft Decision of the Administrative Committee, Rules of the European Patent Litigation Certificate and Other Appropriate Qualifications.
[86] See also Rule 292.1 of the Rules of Procedure.
[87] ibid Rule 292.2.
[88] ibid Rule 287.6.
[89] ibid Rule 290.2.
[90] ibid Rule 284.

lead the court to proceed on an erroneous basis would amount to misrepresentation of the representative's own case.

A party, through their representative, must not communicate with the court without informing the other party. Any such communication that is made in writing should be copied to the other party unless otherwise provided for in the Rules of Procedure.[91]

ii. Exclusion

The court will inform a representative if it considers that their conduct towards the court, the judge or any member of staff of the Registry is incompatible with the dignity of the court or with the requirements of the proper administration of justice, that such representative uses their rights for purposes other than those for which they were granted, or that the representative is otherwise in breach of any code of conduct adopted by the Administrative Committee.[92] Having given the person concerned the opportunity to be heard, the court may make an order to exclude that person from the proceedings with immediate effect. In these circumstances, the court must stay the proceedings for a fixed period in order to allow the party concerned to appoint a new representative.[93]

E. Privileges and Immunities

In the interests of the proper conduct of proceedings, representatives have immunity in relation to words spoken or written by them concerning the relevant action or the parties to it before the court.[94]

F. Change of Representative

A change of representative takes effect from receipt by the Registry of notification that the new representative has been appointed. Until receipt of such notice, the former representative remains responsible for communications between the court and the party concerned.[95]

V. Time Periods

A. Calculating Time Periods

The basic rule for the calculation of time periods in the UPC is that the period begins the day after the event referred to occurs.[96] If the event is the service of a document, the time period begins the day after the document was received. For example, a defence to revocation

---

[91] ibid Rule 8.3.
[92] ibid Rule 291.1.
[93] ibid Rule 291.2.
[94] ibid Rule 289.1.
[95] ibid Rule 293.
[96] ibid Rule 300(a). Time periods are not suspended during judicial vacations.

must be lodged within two months of service of the statement for revocation, according to Rule 49 of the Rules of Procedure. The two-month period therefore runs from the day after receipt of the statement for revocation. The consequence of this rule for periods expressed in years, months and weeks is as follows.[97]

i. Years

A time period of one or more years expires in the relevant subsequent year in the month of the same name and on the day having the same number and the month and day on which the event occurred.

ii. Months

A time period of one or more months expires in the relevant subsequent month on the day that has the same number as the day on which the event occurred. If there is no day of the same number, the period expires on the last day of that month. Representatives are also entitled to travel in the course of their duties without hindrance.[98] The court may waive these immunities where it considers that a representative is guilty of conduct contrary to the proper conduct of proceedings.[99]

iii. Weeks

A time period of one or more weeks expires on the day having the same name as the day on which the event occurred.

iv. Days

Days are calendar days, unless it is expressly stated that they are working days.[100] Calendar days include official holidays and Saturdays and Sundays.[101] Working days do not include the official holidays of the contracting Member State of location of the concerned division, the seat of the central division, the branch of the central division or, where applicable, the Court of Appeal.[102] Working days also do not include Saturdays and Sundays.

B. Failure to Observe Time Limits

The Court may disregard any step, fact, evidence or argument which a party has not taken or submitted within a set time limit.[103] Therefore, if a party fails to observe a time limit set by the Rules of Procedure or the court for a reason that was outside that party's control, despite

---

[97] ibid Rule 300(b)–(d).
[98] ibid Rule 289.3.
[99] ibid Rule 289.5.
[100] ibid Rule 300(e).
[101] ibid Rule 300(f).
[102] ibid Rule 300(g).
[103] ibid Rule 9.2.

having taken all due care, the party may lose a right or means of redress as a consequence. In these circumstances, the relevant panel may re-establish that right or means of redress upon an application for re-establishment of rights.[104] The application must be lodged within one month of removing the cause of the failure to observe the time limit and, in any event, within six months of the time limit that was not observed.[105] At the same time that the application is made, the act for which the time limit was set must be performed or completed.[106]

The application for re-establishment of rights must state the grounds on which it is based and the facts on which it relies. It must also contain evidence in the form of affidavits from all those involved in the failure to observe the time limit, and those involved in establishing the precautionary measures of due care that were taken to avoid the possibility of non-compliance.[107] The panel will decide the application, having given the other parties an opportunity to be heard. The decision of the panel cannot be appealed.[108]

Except regarding revocation of an order to preserve evidence,[109] revocation of provisional measures[110] or lodging statements of appeal and grounds of appeal,[111] the Court may, on a reasoned request by a party, extend (including retrospectively) a time period referred to in the Rules of Procedure or imposed by the Court, or shorten any time period.[112]

VI. Legal Aid

A. The Scope of Legal Aid

The Rules of Procedure provide a legal aid scheme designed to ensure effective access to justice in the court in any of its proceedings.[113] The costs covered by the scheme are provided in Rule 375:[114]

(a) Court fees; and
(b) Costs of legal assistance and representation regarding:
   (i) Pre-litigation advice with a view to reaching a settlement prior to commencing legal proceedings;
   (ii) Commencing and maintaining proceedings before the court;
   (iii) All costs relating to proceedings including the application for legal aid;
   (iv) Enforcement of decisions;
   (v) Other necessary costs related to the proceedings to be borne by a party, including costs of witnesses, experts, interpreters and translators and necessary travel, accommodation and subsistence costs of the applicant and his representatives.

---

[104] ibid Rule 320.1.
[105] ibid Rule 320.2. A fee is payable for an application for re-establishment of rights (see Rule 370).
[106] ibid Rule 370.4. There is no re-establishment of rights available in respect of a failure to observe the time limits for this application or the performance or completion of the act set by the original time limit (Rule 370.5).
[107] ibid Rule 320.3.
[108] ibid Rule 320.7.
[109] ibid Rule 198.1.
[110] ibid Rule 213.1.
[111] ibid Rule 224.1.
[112] ibid Rule 9.3.
[113] ibid Rule 375.
[114] ibid Rule 376.1.

In the event that the applicant loses the action, legal aid will also cover the costs award payable to the successful party.[115]

The maximum legal aid that may be granted in respect of legal assistance and representation is set at the maximum amount of recoverable costs allowed by a successful party on the fixed scale.[116] However, this maximum may be lowered, having taken into account the necessary costs for legal representation in the contracting Member States and the need to ensure access to justice.

A legal aid order may provide for:[117] a full or partial exemption from legal fees; an interim amount to be paid to enable the applicant to meet a request by the judge-rapporteur or standing judge before they have made a final order on granting legal aid; a limit on the amount to be paid to the applicant's representative, or a limit that the representative's disbursements and fees may not exceed; a contribution to the costs related to the proceedings, including witnesses, experts, interpreters and translators, and the necessary travel, accommodation and subsistence costs.[118]

If the opponent is ordered to pay the costs of a legal aid applicant who is the successful party in the action, the sum must be paid to the court. The applicant may be required to meet any shortfall between the costs ordered and the legal aid awarded from a compensation award or sum received in settlement.[119]

B. Eligibility

Legal aid is available to any applicant, provided:

(a) they are wholly or partly unable to meet the costs legal aid can cover, owing to their economic situation;
(b) the action for which legal aid is sought has a reasonable prospect of success, considering the applicant's procedural position; and
(c) the claimant applying for legal aid is entitled to bring actions further to Article 47 UPC Agreement.

Although the Administrative Committee may define a threshold above which legal aid applicants are deemed wholly or partly able to bear the cost of proceedings, applicants whose economic situation places them above these thresholds may still be eligible for legal aid if they can prove that they are nonetheless unable to pay the costs of proceedings due to the cost of living in their contracting Member State of domicile or habitual residence.[120] In making its decision about legal aid, the court must also consider all the relevant circumstances, including the importance of the action to the applicant and the nature of the action when it concerns a claim arising directly out of the applicant's trade or self-employed profession.[121]

---

[115] Rule 376.2.
[116] Rule 152.1.
[117] Rule 379.6.
[118] See Rule 376.1(c).
[119] Rule 382.
[120] ibid Rule 377.2.
[121] ibid Rule 377.3.

An applicant's financial situation must be assessed on the basis of their disposable income[122] and assets.[123]

The Rules envisage the applicant making monthly instalments towards their legal aid cover, to be defined by the Administrative Council.[124]

C. The Application and Evidence

An application for legal aid may be lodged before or after the proceedings to which it relates have started. It must be drafted in the language of a contracting Member State and contain the following information:[125]

(a) the name of the applicant;
(b) the postal and electronic addresses for service on the applicant and the names of the persons authorised to accept service;
(c) the name of the other party, as well as the postal and electronic addresses for service on the other party where available and the names of the persons authorised to accept service (if known);
(d) the action number of the action in respect of which the applicant is made or, where the application is lodged before the action has been brought, a brief description of the action;
(e) an indication of the value of the action and the costs to be covered by legal aid;
(f) where legal aid is requested for costs of legal assistance and representation, the name of the proposed representative;
(g) an indication of the applicant's financial resources, such as income, assets and capital, and of the applicant's family situation including an assessment of the resources of persons who are financially dependent on the applicant;
(h) where appropriate, a reasoned request for suspension of a time limit which would otherwise need to be observed until the date of notification of the order deciding on legal aid.

The application must also contain a statement of the facts and legal situation of the applicant relating to the action, and specific mention of the evidence to be presented.[126]

The application must be supported by evidence in the form of a statement of the economic and financial situation of the applicant. In addition, the following documents must be attached:[127]

(a) the latest property and income declarations of the applicant;
(b) a document showing the personal monthly income for the previous year, or a declaration of unemployment delivered by the competent authorities, or a certificate proving that the applicant is receiving aid or financial support under a social welfare scheme;

---

[122] Earnings in money or equivalent value after deducting all reasonable living costs and costs of dependants (ibid Rule 377A.2). The Administrative Committee must define the deductions from income and assets to be taken into account when assessing the applicant's financial situation (Rule 377A.3).
[123] ibid Rule 377A.1.
[124] ibid Rule 377A.3.
[125] ibid Rule 378.2.
[126] ibid Rule 378A.1. Rule 378.3(b) appears to restrict the need to evidence supporting the action to applications made before the action for which aid is sought is started.
[127] ibid Rule 378.3(a).

(c) a certificate of composition of household;
(d) any other official document that can provide proof of the financial situation of the applicant.

The court may request further documentation from the applicant and an affidavit of the truthfulness of any statements made. Official documents should not be more than three months old. In appropriate cases, the application should also attach a certificate of the income of other members of the household of the applicant.[128]

If the economic circumstances of the applicant change, the court must be informed.[129]

D. The Decision to Award Legal Aid

The Registry examines the formal admissibility of the application for legal aid, specifically with regard to the financial situation of the applicant. The applicant must be invited to correct the application within 14 days if it does not meet the requirements that the applicant is: wholly or partly unable to meet the costs of the action; above the threshold for receiving legal aid defined by the Administrative Committee, having taken into account the relevant income and assets and the deductions defined by the Administrative Committee; missing the required contents of the application; and missing the required evidence.[130] If these requirements are met, or the applicant fails to correct a deficiency, an order will be made by the judge-rapporteur.[131] If the application is made before the relevant action is commenced, the standing judge will make the order.

Before making an order, and unless it is apparent from the application that the action in respect of which aid is sought does not have a reasonable prospect of success, the opponent must be invited to make written observations.[132] Documents relating to the financial situation of the applicant will not be shown to the opponent without the applicant's consent, unless that consent is unreasonably withheld or the court considers that the opponent has a right to the information.

If legal aid is refused, the order must state the reasons on which this decision was made.[133] If an order is made granting legal aid, the award must be limited to the period from receipt of the application,[134] and any legal representative or assistant of the applicant must be designated.[135] Any such representative may request that payment from the award is made in advance.[136] Time limits for a step in proceedings may be suspended until the payment of legal aid according to a request made in the application.[137]

---

[128] ibid Rule 378A.2.
[129] ibid Rule 379A.
[130] ibid Rule 379.2.
[131] ibid Rule 379.3.
[132] ibid Rule 379.4.
[133] ibid Rule 379.5.
[134] ibid Rule 379.7.
[135] ibid Rule 379.8.
[136] ibid Rule 379.9.
[137] ibid Rule 379.10.

E. Withdrawal and Appeal

The court may, of its own motion or following a reasoned request by the opponent, and having first heard the applicant, withdraw legal aid in part or in full if the financial situation of the applicant changes during proceedings.[138]

The court may also withdraw legal aid, giving reasons for doing so,[139] if the applicant has:

(a) given an inaccurate account of the circumstances of its case, misrepresenting its prospects of success, and this was determinative of the decision to make the award;
(b) grossly negligently made false statements as to their personal or economic circumstances;
(c) not immediately informed the court of a considerable improvement in their financial circumstances; or
(d) has been in arrears for longer than three months with the payment of a monthly instalment or with the payment of any other amount.

If legal aid is withdrawn, the applicant may be required to refund the court with any sums advanced.[140]

An order wholly or partly refusing or withdrawing legal aid may be appealed to the Court of Appeal within one month after receipt of the order. The President of the Court of Appeal must appoint a panel to decide on the appeal having heard the applicant.[141]

---

[138] ibid Rule 380.
[139] ibid Rule 380.3.
[140] ibid Rule 382.2.
[141] ibid Rule 381.1 and 381.2.

20

Court Fees

The court fees (both fixed and value-based) payable for lodging, actions, applications or appeals pursuant to Article 36(3) UPC Agreement were agreed by the Preparatory Committee in the Rules on Court fees and Recoverable costs of 25 February 2016 and were incorporated into the Rules of Procedure on 30 June 2016, followed by amendments agreed on 1 September 2022.[1] This chapter discusses the scope and application of these fees together with the issue of reimbursement and examines how the value of a case may be calculated for the purpose of applying the value-based fee.

I. Fixed and Value-Based Court Fees

Article 36(3) UPC Agreement states:

> Court fees shall be fixed by the Administrative Committee. They shall consist of a fixed fee, combined with a value-based fee above a pre-defined ceiling. The Court fees shall be fixed at such a level as to ensure a right balance between the principle of fair access to justice, in particular for small and medium-sized enterprises, micro-entities, natural persons, non-profit organisations, universities and public research organisations and an adequate contribution of the parties for the costs incurred by the Court, recognising the economic benefits to the parties involved, and the objective of a self-financing Court with balanced finances. The level of the Court fees shall be reviewed periodically by the Administrative Committee. Targeted support measures for small and medium-sized enterprises and micro entities may be considered.

Only one fixed fee is payable for each action or application lodged, regardless of the number of parties or patents concerned.[2] Further to Article 36(3), these are divided into two different groups:

(a) Actions attracting a fixed court fee and an additional value based fee for cases having an estimated value exceeding €500,000. Actions in this group are infringement actions, actions for declaration of non-infringement, counterclaims for infringement, actions for compensation for licences of right and applications to determine damages. The fixed fee for the first four of these is €11,000 and the fee for the latter is €3,000 (see Table 20.1).

(b) Actions subject only to a fixed fee. This category covers the following actions or applications: revocation (€20,000), counterclaim for revocation (a €20,000 ceiling),

---

[1] https://www.unified-patent-court.org/sites/default/files/ac_05_08072022_table_of_court_fees_en_final_for_publication.pdf.
[2] See section A.7 of the Rules on Court fees and Recoverable Costs.

preliminary injunction (€11,000), concerning a decision of the EPO (€1,000), to preserve evidence (€350), order for inspection (€350), order to freeze assets (€1,000), filing a protective letter (€200), prolonging the period that a protective letter is kept on the register (€100), reviewing a case management order (€300) and setting aside a decision by default (€1,000) (see Table 20.2).

Table 20.1 Court fees for actions: infringement, counterclaim for infringement, declaration of non-infringement, compensation for licence of right and application to determine damages[3]

Value of action (€)	Fee (fixed + value-based) (€)
Up to and including 500,000	11,000 (11,000 fixed fee + 0 value-based fee)
Up to and including 750,000	13,500 (11,000 fixed fee + 2,500 value-based fee)
Up to and including 1,000,000	15,000 (11,000 fixed fee + 4,000 value-based fee)
Up to and including 1,500,000	19,000 (11,000 fixed fee + 8,000 value-based fee)
Up to and including 2,000,000	24,000 (11,000 fixed fee + 13,000 value-based fee)
Up to and including 3,000,000	33,000 (11,000 fixed fee + 20,000 value-based fee)
Up to and including 4,000,000	37,000 (11,000 fixed fee + 26,000 value-based fee)
Up to and including 5,000,000	43,000 (11,000 fixed fee + 32,000 value-based fee)
Up to and including 6,000,000	50,000 (11,000 fixed fee + 39,000 value-based fee)
Up to and including 7,000,000	57,000 (11,000 fixed fee + 46,000 value-based fee)
Up to and including 8,000,000	63,000 (11,000 fixed fee + 52,000 value-based fee)
Up to and including 9,000,000	69,000 (11,000 fixed fee + 58,000 value-based fee)
Up to and including 10,000,000	76,000 (11,000 fixed fee + 65,000 value-based fee)

(continued)

---

[3] For applications to determine damages, the fixed fee of €11,000 should be replaced with €3,000 for each action value.

Table 20.1 *(Continued)*

Value of action (€)	Fee (fixed + value-based) (€)
Up to and including 15,000,000	86,000
	(11,000 fixed fee + 75,000 value-based fee)
Up to and including 20,000,000	111,000
	(11,000 fixed fee + 100,000 value-based fee)
Up to and including 25,000,000	136,000
	(11,000 fixed fee + 125,000 value-based fee)
Up to and including 30,000,000	161,000
	(11,000 fixed fee + 150,000 value-based fee)
Up to and including 50,000,000	261,000
	(11,000 fixed fee + 250,000 value-based fee)
More than 50,000,000	336,000
	(11,000 fixed fee + 325,000 value-based fee)

Table 20.2 Fixed fees

Value of action (€)	Fixed fee (€)
Revocation action	20,000
Counterclaim for revocation	The same fee as the infringement action subject to a 20,000 ceiling
Application for provisional measures	11,000
Action against a decision of the EPO	1,000
Application to preserve evidence	350
Application for an order for inspection	350
Application for an order to freeze assets	1,000
Filing a protective letter	200
Application to prolong the period that a protective letter is kept on the register	100
Application for re-establishment of rights	350
Application to review a case management order	300
Application to set aside decision by default	1,000

As Table 20.2 shows, for revocation actions, only a fixed fee of €20,000 is payable. However, if the revocation action is lodged by counterclaim, the fee will be calculated on the same basis as the infringement action, up to a ceiling of €20,000; for counterclaims to smaller value infringement actions, the fee for the revocation counterclaim may be less than €20,000.

Fees on the lodging of an appeal to a decision on the merits are the same as for the first instance action:[4] an appeal to a final decision on infringement, a counterclaim of

---

[4] Rule 228 and Part 6 of the Rules of Procedure.

infringement, an action for a declaration of non-infringement or an action for compensation for licence of right is the fixed fee of €11,000 plus the value-based fee; and an appeal to an action to determine damages is €3,000 plus the value-based fee. An appeal to an application for provisional measures is a fixed fee of €11,000.

Fees on the lodging of an appeal to those interlocutory decisions for which the right of appeal is automatic[5] are liable for a fixed fee of €3,000 (see Table 20.3). Appeals to costs decisions, matters that fall within the discretionary review procedure and the re-establishment of rights attract a fixed fee, as do reviews of case management orders and applications to set aside a decision by default (see Table 20.3).

Table 20.3 Fees on appeal

Type of appeal	Fee (€)
Appeal pursuant to a final decision of the Court of First Instance or a decision terminating proceedings as to an infringement action[6]	11,000 + additional value-based fee according to Table 20.1.
Appeal pursuant to a final decision of the Court of First Instance or a decision terminating proceedings as to a counterclaim for infringement[7]	11,000 + additional value-based fee according to Table 20.1
Appeal pursuant to a final decision of the Court of First Instance or a decision terminating proceedings as to a revocation action[8]	20,000
Appeal pursuant to a final decision of the Court of First Instance or a decision terminating proceedings as to a counterclaim for revocation[9]	Fee paid at first instance
Appeal pursuant to a final decision of the Court of First Instance or a decision terminating proceedings as to an action for declaration of non-infringement[10]	11,000 + additional value-based fee according to Table 20.1
Appeal pursuant to a final decision of the Court of First Instance or a decision terminating proceedings as to an action for compensation for licence of right[11]	11,000 + additional value-based fee according to Table 20.1
Appeal pursuant to a final decision of the Court of First Instance or a decision terminating proceedings as to an application to determine damages[12]	3,000 + additional value-based fee according to Table 20.1

(continued)

[5] Under ibid Rule 220.1.
[6] ibid Rule 15.
[7] ibid Rule 53.
[8] ibid Rule 46.
[9] ibid Rule 26.
[10] ibid Rule 70.
[11] ibid Rule 80.2.
[12] ibid Rule 132.

Fixed and Value-Based Court Fees 309

Table 20.3 *(Continued)*

Type of appeal	Fee (€)
Appeal as to an application for provisional measures[13]	11,000
Interlocutory appeals on matters for which automatic appeal is available under Rule 220.1(c) in relation to: the use of the language of the patent as the language of proceedings;[14] orders to produce evidence;[15] orders to preserve evidence and inspect premises;[16] freezing orders,[17] provisional and protecting measures;[18] and orders to communicate information[19]	3,000
Application for rehearing[20]	2,500
Appeal pursuant to a final decision of the Court of First Instance or a decision terminating proceedings as to an action against a decision of the EPO[21]	1,000
Appeal for which leave has been granted by the Court of First Instance or which has been allowed by the Court of Appeal.	1,500
Request for discretionary review to the Court of Appeal – the fee does not arise of the appeal is allowed.	350
Appeal against a cost decision[22]	3,000
Application for leave to appeal against a cost decision[23] – the fee does not arise if the appeal is allowed	1,500
Application for re-establishment of rights[24]	350
Application to review a case management order[25]	300
Application to set aside decision by default[26]	1,000

[13] Article 62 UPC Agreement and Rule 206.5 of the Rules of Procedure.
[14] Article 49(5) UPC Agreement.
[15] ibid Article 59.
[16] ibid Article 60.
[17] ibid Article 61.
[18] ibid Article 62.
[19] ibid Article 67.
[20] Rule 250 of the Rules of Procedure.
[21] ibid Rules 88.3 and 97.2.
[22] ibid Rule 228.
[23] ibid Rule 221.
[24] Further to ibid Rule 320.2.
[25] ibid Rule 333.3.
[26] ibid Rule 356.2.

II. Reduction and Reimbursement of Court Fees

A. Fee Reductions for Small Enterprises and Micro-enterprises

'Small enterprises' and 'micro-enterprises'[27] are entitled to pay only 60 per cent of the fixed and value-based fees shown in Tables 20.1 and 20.2, provided they comply with the following procedure:[28]

The applicant must lodge a notification affirming that it fulfils the criteria of a 'small enterprise' or 'micro-enterprise' in its statement of claim, counterclaim or other relevant application when it is lodged with the Registry. These requirements will be assessed by the Registry as part of the formal examination.[29]

The application will be dealt with by the Court without delay, but the Court may, of its own motion, order the applicant to supply further documentation, including any document linked to its financial resources.

However, the Court may, of its own motion and at any time, having first heard the applicant, order the payment of:

(a) the remaining 40 per cent of the fee, if the payment of just 60 per cent payment is manifestly disproportionate and unreasonable in respect of the financial capacity of the applicant; or
(b) the remaining 40 per cent of the fee plus an additional 50 per cent if the affirmation given by the applicant is found to be wholly or partially incorrect.

An order to pay the additional fee ordered by the Court may be appealed.[30] Failure to pay the additional fee within the time stipulated by the court will result in a decision in default against the applicant.[31]

B. Fee Reimbursements

A reimbursement of 25 per cent will be made to the party liable for the court fees if an action is heard by only a single judge.[32]

The Rules on Court Fees and Recoverable Costs also provide for reimbursement of a certain proportion of fees to reward early termination of an action by withdrawal or settlement. The amount of the reimbursement depends on the stage of the proceedings at which this event occurs, as shown in Table 20.4.

If both of the above reimbursements are triggered, only the larger of the two will be paid to the party liable for the fees.[33] In exceptional cases, having regard to the stage of

---

[27] As defined in Title I of Annex of the Recommendation of the European Commission No 2003/361 of 6 May 2003.
[28] See section A.8 of the Rules on Court fees and Recoverable Costs.
[29] Rule 16 of the Rules of Procedure.
[30] ibid Rule 220.2.
[31] ibid Rule 355.
[32] Further to ibid Rule 345.6.
[33] See section A.9(d) of the Rules on Court Fees and Recoverable Costs.

the proceedings and the 'procedural behaviour' of the parties, the Court may decrease the reimbursement or deny it entirely.[34]

Table 20.4 Fee reimbursements for withdrawal or settlement of an action

60%	If withdrawal or settlement occurs before the conclusion of the written procedure
40%	If withdrawal or settlement occurs before the conclusion of the interim procedure
20%	If withdrawal or settlement occurs before the conclusion of the oral proceedings

C. Threat to the Party's Economic Existence

If the court fee for which a party that is not a natural person is liable threatens its economic existence, the Court may upon request by that party wholly or partially reimburse the fixed and value-based fee. The party must present reasonably available and plausible evidence to support its request. The Court must deal with such a request without delay and in giving its decision must reflect on the circumstances of the case, including the procedural behaviour of the party. It may also give the other party the opportunity to be heard.[35]

III. Calculating the Case Value

The Rules on Court Fees and Recoverable Costs offer no practical guidance as to how the value-based fee must be calculated, other than stating that the assessment of the relevant action must reflect the objective interest pursued by the filing party at the time of filing the action, and in deciding on the value, the Court may in particular take into account the guidelines laid down in the decision of the Administrative Committee for this purpose.[36] Until the availability of this guideline, and given the clear references to the German experience in the explanatory notes to an earlier proposal on court fees, it is currently likely that the UPC will follow the German practice in assessing the value of an action.

In Germany, in an action for infringement of intellectual property rights, the claimant usually claims for injunctive relief, disclosure and account, award of damages, destruction and recall or removal from the channels of trade. Due to a lack of detailed knowledge of the extent of the claimant's loss, the damages are not quantified. The German courts determine an overall case value. The case value of the claim for an injunction is defined mainly by the

---

[34] See ibid section A.9(e).
[35] The adversely affected party may also appeal pursuant to Rule 220 of the Rules of Procedure.
[36] Section A.6 of the Rules on Court Fees and Recoverable Costs; and see also Rule 370.5 of the Rules of Procedure. An explanatory note to the Rules on Court Fees and Recoverable Costs also states that: 'The issue as to when to assess the case value and pay the value-based fee was also discussed in depth by the Expert Panel. The Panel recommended that claimants make their own value assessment and pay the fee based on that at the same time as the fixed fee; that is when lodging the relevant application. If there is any contention over the assessment this will be rectified at the interim conference.'

plaintiff's interest in having the infringing act stopped. The possible criteria to determine this interest include:

(a) the remaining term of the intellectual property right at the time of filing of the action;
(b) the sales figures, size and market position of the plaintiff;
(c) the nature, extent and detrimental effects of the infringing act;
(d) the intensity of the risk of commission and repetition.

In recent years, it has become common practice under German law to apply a hypothetical royalty regarding injunctive relief (the licence analogy) to determine the value of the action. Based on the information disclosed by the defendant, the applicable licensee fee can be estimated and thus quantified. In addition to the infringer's revenues, the calculation includes the estimated revenue for the complete term of the patents. Hence, the formula for the calculation of the value is usually:[37]

> value of the matter = sales protected by the patent per year
>
> x reasonable royalty for the patent
>
> x remaining lifetime of the patent (in years).

However, other factors, such as the scale and intensity of the infringement – that is, the nature, extent and detrimental effect of the infringing act and the level of risk of commission and repetition – must not be ignored as they act to objectify the claimant's interest: if, for example, only the offering of a product is alleged to be patent-infringing, the intensity of the infringement is significantly less than it would be if the product had already been widely introduced to the market.

For revocation actions, the German Federal Court of Justice has held[38] that a case value consistent with the value of the infringement action 'does not fully reflect the fair market value of the patent which normally exceeds the interest of the revocation plaintiff'. In other words, the value of the patent usually exceeds this individual interest and the patentee's own use of the patent has to be taken into account as well. 'Absent other evidence', a fixed 25 per cent uplift is added to the case value of the infringement action to obtain the value of the revocation action.[39]

Although there are many parameters that allow for a transparent calculation of the case value, which is the only relevant basis for assessing the court fees and recoverable legal costs, the UPC has a wide scope of discretion.[40] In particular, the relevant UPC territory in each case will have to be used as a basis to calculate the potential reasonable royalty.

---

[37] For this purpose, the Düsseldorf Court of Appeals (I-2 W 15/11, 10 May 2011) urges all parties to a litigation to disclose information about sales prices, sales volumes in Germany, market shares, customary royalty rates and average manufacturing costs.
[38] X ZR 28/09, 12 April 2011.
[39] See detailed discussion in Anja Lunze and Jan Phillip Rektorschek, 'Can You Afford to Litigate in the UPC?', September 2015, https://www.taylorwessing.com/-/media/taylor-wessing/files/germany/2015/mip-lunze_rektorschek-25-29-feature-upc.pdf; Sabine Rojahn and Anja Lunze, 'Die Streitwertfestsetzung im Patentrecht – Ein Mysterium?' [2011] *Mitteilungen der deutschen Patentanwälte* 533, 538.
[40] See the open definition in Rule 370.5 of the Rules of Procedure.

ANNEX A: STAY OF PROCEEDINGS

Table A below sets out the circumstances in which a division of the UPC may or must stay its proceedings. Any stay of proceedings must take effect on the date indicated in the order to stay or, in its absence, on the date of the order. The UPC must stipulate the effect that the stay has on any existing orders in the proceedings.[1] If the length of the stay is not fixed in the order, it must end on the date indicated in the order to resume proceedings. If there is no date indicated in the order to resume proceedings, the stay ends on the date of the order to resume.[2] An order for the resumption of proceedings before the end of the stay must be made by order of the judge-rapporteur, having heard the parties, and may be referred to the panel of the division concerned.[3]

A stay of proceedings has the effect that time will cease to run on procedural periods. Procedural periods will 'begin to run afresh' from the date on which the stay of proceedings comes to an end.[4]

Table A The circumstances in which a stay of proceedings may be ordered and the division concerned

Circumstances in which stay may be ordered	Division concerned	Rule/ reference
If the patent in dispute is also subject to opposition proceedings or limitation proceedings (including appeal) before the EPO[5] or a national authority where a decision may be expected rapidly	Any division	Rule 295(a) Rule 118.2[6] Article 33(10)
If infringement proceedings are before a local or regional division and concern the same parties and the same patent as a revocation in the central division, the local or regional division *may* stay the infringement proceedings Such a decision may, in particular, be taken after a decision resulting in bifurcation of proceedings further to Article 33(3)(b)	Local or regional division	Rule 295(g) Rule 118.2(a) See also Rule 295(e) and Rule 37.4

(continued)

---

[1] Rule 296.1 of the Rules of Procedure.
[2] ibid Rule 296.2.
[3] ibid Rule 297.
[4] ibid Rule 296.3. The wording is ambiguous, but the intention of the Rule appears to be that periods will restart at the point in time at which they were suspended rather than starting again from the beginning.
[5] Of its own motion, or at the request of the parties, the Court may request that opposition proceedings or limitation proceedings (including any subsequent appeal proceedings) before the EPO be accelerated. However, the result of the request does not prejudice the power of the Court to stay its proceedings; see ibid Rule 298.
[6] Note that Rule 295(a) provides the court with the discretion to stay proceedings when opposition or limitation proceedings are pending before a 'national authority'. By contrast, Rule 118.2 refers only to proceedings concerning the same patent in the EPO or a local or regional division.

Table A *(Continued)*

Circumstances in which stay may be ordered	Division concerned	Rule/ reference
If infringement proceedings are before a local or regional division and concern the same parties and the same patent as a revocation in the central division, the local or regional division *must* stay the infringement proceedings if it is of the view that the relevant claims of the patent will be held to be invalid on any ground in the final decision in the revocation proceedings Such a decision may, in particular, be taken after a decision resulting in bifurcation of proceedings further to Article 33(3)(b)	Local or regional division	Rule 295(g) Rule 118.2(a) See also Rule 295(e) and Rule 37.4
If infringement proceedings are before a local or regional division and concern the same parties and the same patent as an opposition in the EPO, the local or regional division *must* stay the infringement proceedings if it is of the view that the relevant claims of the patent will be held to be invalid on any ground in the final decision of the EPO and the decision of the EPO may be expected to be given rapidly	Local or regional division	Rule 295(g) Rule 118.2(a)
Where a counterclaim for revocation is brought against an infringement action in a local or regional division, and a revocation action concerning the same patent and the same parties has already been lodged in the central division – in these circumstances, the central division *must* stay the central division revocation action pending a decision of the local or regional division on where the actions are to proceed, further to Article 33(3)	Central division	Rule 295(f) Rule 75.3[7]
In respect of a declaration of non-infringement, where an action of infringement concerning the same patent and the same alleged infringement is filed by the defendant proprietor or licensee in the non-infringement action within three months of that action	Central division	Rule 295(f) Rule 76.3
When the court is seised with an action relating to a patent which is also the subject of opposition proceedings or limitation proceedings (including subsequent appeal proceedings) before the EPO or a national authority where a decision in such proceedings may be expected to be given rapidly	Any division	Rule 295(a)
Where the Court is seised with an action relating to a supplementary protection certificate which is also the subject of proceedings before a national court or authority	Any division	Rule 295(b)
Where an appeal is brought before the Court of Appeal against a decision or order of the Court of First Instance disposing of the substantive issues in part only	Any division	Rule 295(c)(i)

(continued)

---

[7] Reference to this Rule is omitted from the list of circumstances in Rule 295 of the Rules of Procedure.

Table A *(Continued)*

Circumstances in which stay may be ordered	Division concerned	Rule/ reference
Where an appeal is brought before the Court of Appeal against a decision or order of the Court of First Instance disposing of an admissibility issue or a preliminary objection	Any division	Rule 295(c)(ii)
At the joint request of the parties	Any division	Rule 295(d)
Where, pursuant to Article 33(3)(b) UPC Agreement, the panel may stay infringement proceedings pending a final decision in the revocation action, and must stay where there is a high likelihood that the relevant claims of the patent will be held to be invalid	Local or regional division	Rule 295(e) Rule 37(4)
Where a revocation action is pending before the same parties in the central division or an opposition is pending before the EPO, the infringement proceedings may be stayed. The infringement proceedings must be stayed if there is a high likelihood that the relevant claims of the patent will be held invalid. The decision of the EPO must be expected rapidly	Local or regional division	Rule 295(g)
An application for damages pending any appeal on the merits	Any division	Rule 295(h) Rule 136
Where the Court has requested that the CJEU gives a ruling	Any division	Rule 295(i) Rule 266
If a party dies or ceases to exist during the proceedings, the proceedings *must* be stayed until the party is replaced by their successor	Any division	Rule 295(j) Rule 310
If a party is declared insolvent, proceedings *must* be stayed for up to three months. They *may* be stayed pending a decision by the authority dealing with the insolvency whether or not to continue the proceedings	Any division	Rule 295(j) Rule 311.1
At the request of a temporary administrator who has been appointed before a party is declared insolvent	Any division	Rule 295(j) Rule 311.2
A party objects to a judge taking part in proceedings	The President of the Court of First Instance or the President of the Court of Appeal.	Rule 295(k) Rule 346 Article 7(4) of the Statute of the UPC Agreement
To give effect to EU law, in particular the provisions of the UP Regulation and the Lugano Convention	Any division	Rule 295(l)
In any other case where the proper administration of justice so requires	Any division	Rule 295(m)

ANNEX B:
APPLICATIONS AND HEARINGS

Table B below lists those matters for which a party may apply in UPC proceedings, the stage at which the application should be made and whether there is an associated hearing of other parties. Where these Rules provide that a party shall or may be given an opportunity to be heard before the Court makes an order or takes some action, the Court must or may (as the case may be) request the parties to provide written submissions within a specified period and/or must or may invite the parties to an oral hearing on a fixed date by the Court.[8] It may also order that a hearing takes place by telephone or video conference.

Table B Table of applications and hearings provided by the Rules of Procedure

Application	Rule	Stage of proceedings	Who is heard?
Application to opt out and withdrawal of an opt-out	Rule 5	Before proceedings are lodged	No hearing.
Application for substitution of new proprietor	Rules 8.4 and 305.1(c)	At any stage	Other parties to the proceedings are invited to comment.
Application to amend patent	Rules 12.3(a) and 30	Together with a counterclaim for revocation, or at other times with the permission of the court (Rule 30.2)	All parties to action, at the oral hearing.
Claimant heard regarding rejection of a statement of claim on the formalities	Rule 16.5	Upon examination of the formalities of a statement of claim	Claimant.
Defendant's preliminary objection to statement of claim	Rule 19	Within one month of service of a statement of claim	Both parties (Rule 20.1).
Defendant may be heard on the examination of formalities of defence	Rule 27	Upon examination of the statement of defence	Defendant

(continued)

[8] Rule 264 of the Rules of Procedure.

Table B *(Continued)*

Application	Rule	Stage of proceedings	Who is heard?
Application by any party for appointment of a technically qualified judge	Rule 33	As early as possible in the written procedure An application lodged after the close of the written procedure will only be granted if it is justified by a change in circumstances (Rule 33.2)	No hearing Judge-rapporteur is consulted
Application of Article 33(3)	Rule 37	As soon as practicable after the closure of the written procedure The Panel may by order take an earlier decision if appropriate	The parties are given an opportunity to be heard in both cases
Application for declaration of non-infringement	Rule 62	Written procedure.	All parties heard at oral hearing
Defendant's preliminary objection to a statement for a declaration of non-infringement	Rule 66	Within one month of service of a statement for a declaration of non-infringement (Rule 19.1)	Both parties (Rule 20.1).
Application for compensation for licence of right	Rule 80	Written procedure	All parties heard at oral hearing
Application to annul or alter a decision of the office	Rule 88	Within two months of the decision of the EPO	The EPO is given an opportunity to rectify the contested decision (Rule 91) If no rectification, the claimant may be invited to lodge further written pleadings (Rule 93) The President of the EPO may comment on issues arising in proceedings, including any appeal (Rule 94) There may be an oral hearing, which is *ex parte*

(continued)

318 Annex B

Table B *(Continued)*

Application	Rule	Stage of proceedings	Who is heard?
Claimant heard on rejection of the application to annul	Rule 89	Upon examination of the application	The claimant may be given an opportunity to be heard
Application to annul an EPO rejection of a unitary effect request	Rule 97	Within three weeks of service of the decision of the EPO	The President of the EPO may be invited to comment on the application (Rule 97.4). No hearing stated
Application for orders consequential to an invalidity decision	Rule 118.4	Within two months of a final decision of the central division, the Court of Appeal or the EPO	No hearing stated
Application for the determination of damages	Rule 131		All parties heard in oral procedure
Rejection of an application for the determination of damages	Rules 16.5 and 134.4	Upon examination of the formalities of an application for the determination of damages	Claimant
Application for a costs decision	Rule 151	Within one month of service of the decision	The unsuccessful party has the option to comment in writing on the costs requested (Rule 156.1)
Application for the hearing of a witness in person	Rule 176	During the interim procedure (Rule 112.2(b))	All parties heard in the interim procedure
Application for communication of information	Rule 191 and Article 67	The Rule is silent[9]	The Rule is silent[10]
Application for preserving evidence	Rules 192 and 197, and Article 60	Before proceedings, during written procedure or interim procedure	May be *ex parte* (Rule 197)

(continued)

[9] A comparison with Rule 190 suggests the application should be made during the written or interim procedures.
[10] A comparison with Rule 190 suggests that the parties should have the opportunity to be heard.

Table B *(Continued)*

Application	Rule	Stage of proceedings	Who is heard?
Application for provisional measures	Rules 206 and Rule 212, and Article 62(2) and (4)	Before proceedings, during the written procedure or the interim procedure	May be *ex parte* (Rule 212)
Discretionary review of refusal of leave to appeal	Rule 220.3	Within 15 days of the decision of the Court refusing leave to appeal	The other party is heard (Rule 220.4)
Application for leave to appeal a cost decision	Rule 221	Within 15 days of service of the decision of the Court	The Rule is silent[11]
Application for suspensive effect of appeal	Rule 223 and Article 74	Further to the lodging of an appeal	The Rule is silent
Application for a rehearing	Rule 245	Pursuant to a final decision of the Court of First Instance for which the time for lodging an appeal has expired. Pursuant to a decision of the Court of Appeal	The petitioner will be heard before an application can be rejected as deficient on the formalities (Rule 253.2) The parties will be heard as to whether the application should succeed (Rule 255)
Application for access to excluded information	Rule 262	At any time further to the confidentiality of a document lodged at the Registry being requested (Rule 262.1).	Written comments are invited from the parties (Rule 262.4)
Application for leave to amend case	Rule 263	At any stage	The Rule is silent
Application to withdraw action	Rule 265	Prior to a final decision	The other party will be heard as to whether the action should be decided
Application for service by an alternative method	Rule 275	At the time of service	Not applicable

(continued)

---

[11] A comparison with Rule 220 suggests that the parties should have the opportunity to be heard.

Table B (Continued)

Application	Rule	Stage of proceedings	Who is heard?
Application for a change in parties	Rule 305	At any stage	The other parties are invited to comment
Application to have successors added	Rule 310	At any stage	Another party may apply to have a successor added or substituted if the successor fails to do so
Application to intervene	Rule 313	At any stage	The other parties must be given the opportunity to be heard
Application for the re-establishment of rights	Rule 320	Further to the loss of a right or means to redress, when a time limit has not been met	The other parties must be given the opportunity to be heard
Application to use language of a grant of patent (with the agreement of the parties)	Rules 321 and 322	During the written procedure	The application must be made by both parties (Rule 321) in agreement or by request of one party (Rule 322), following which it is proposed by the judge-rapporteur and the parties agree
Application (by one party) to use language of a grant of patent	Rule 323	During the written procedure	The other party is invited by the President to indicate its position within 10 days
Application for a review of case management orders	Rule 333	Subsequent to a case management decision or an order by the judge-rapporteur	The other party must be given the opportunity to be heard
Application to use case management powers	Rule 336	At any stage	The Rule is silent[12]
Application to release a security	Rule 352	Further to the ordering of a security	The Rule is silent

(continued)

---

[12] If case management powers are exercised at the Court's own motion, under Rule 337, the parties must be heard. There is therefore no apparent reason why the parties should not be heard under Rule 336.

Table B *(Continued)*

Application	Rule	Stage of proceedings	Who is heard?
Application to rectify mistakes in decisions and orders	Rule 353	Within one month of service of the decision or order to be rectified	The parties must be heard
Application to set aside decision by default	Rule 356	Further to a decision by default	The Rule is silent
Application for the disposal of an action	Rule 360	At any stage prior to a decision	The parties must be given an opportunity to be heard
Application to bar proceeding with an action	Rule 362	At any time	The parties must be given an opportunity to be heard
Application for legal aid	Rule 377	Before or after proceedings have been started	The other party may be invited to make written observations. If the other party later makes an application for withdrawal of legal aid (Rule 380.1) the applicant must be heard.

ANNEX C: REGULATION (EU) 1257/2012 OF 17 DECEMBER 2012

(UP Regulation)

REGULATION (EU) No 1257/2012 OF THE EUROPEAN PARLIAMENT AND OF THE COUNCIL

of 17 December 2012

implementing enhanced cooperation in the area of the creation of unitary patent protection

THE EUROPEAN PARLIAMENT AND THE COUNCIL OF THE EUROPEAN UNION,

Having regard to the Treaty on the Functioning of the European Union and in particular the first paragraph of Article 118 thereof,

Having regard to Council Decision 2011/167/EU of 10 March 2011 authorising enhanced cooperation in the area of the creation of unitary patent protection[1],

Having regard to the proposal from the European Commission,

After transmission of the draft legislative act to the national parliaments,

Acting in accordance with the ordinary legislative procedure[2],

Whereas:

(1) The creation of the legal conditions enabling undertakings to adapt their activities in manufacturing and distributing products across national borders and providing them with greater choice and more opportunities contributes to the attainment of the objectives of the Union set out in Article 3(3) of the Treaty on European Union. Uniform patent protection within the internal market, or at least a significant part thereof, should feature amongst the legal instruments which undertakings have at their disposal.

(2) Pursuant to the first paragraph of Article 118 of the Treaty on the Functioning of the European Union (TFEU), measures to be taken in the context of the establishment and functioning of the internal market include the creation of uniform patent protection throughout the Union and the establishment of centralised Union-wide authorisation, coordination and supervision arrangements.

(3) On 10 March 2011, the Council adopted Decision 2011/167/EU authorising enhanced cooperation between Belgium, Bulgaria, the Czech Republic, Denmark, Germany, Estonia, Ireland, Greece, France, Cyprus, Latvia, Lithuania, Luxembourg, Hungary, Malta, the Netherlands, Austria, Poland, Portugal, Romania, Slovenia, Slovakia,

Finland, Sweden and the United Kingdom (hereinafter 'participating Member States') in the area of the creation of unitary patent protection.

(4) Unitary patent protection will foster scientific and technological advances and the functioning of the internal market by making access to the patent system easier, less costly and legally secure. It will also improve the level of patent protection by making it possible to obtain uniform patent protection in the participating Member States and eliminate costs and complexity for undertakings throughout the Union. It should be available to proprietors of a European patent from both the participating Member States and from other States, regardless of their nationality, residence or place of establishment.

(5) The Convention on the Grant of European Patents of 5 October 1973, as revised on 17 December 1991 and on 29 November 2000 (hereinafter 'EPC'), established the European Patent Organisation and entrusted it with the task of granting European patents. This task is carried out by the European Patent Office (hereinafter 'EPO'). A European patent granted by the EPO should, at the request of the patent proprietor, benefit from unitary effect by virtue of this Regulation in the participating Member States. Such a patent is hereinafter referred to as a 'European patent with unitary effect'.

(6) In accordance with Part IX of the EPC a group of Contracting States to the EPC may provide that European patents granted for those States have a unitary character. This Regulation constitutes a special agreement within the meaning of Article 142 of the EPC, a regional patent treaty within the meaning of Article 45(1) of the Patent Cooperation Treaty of 19 June 1970 as last modified on 3 February 2001 and a special agreement within the meaning of Article 19 of the Convention for the Protection of Industrial Property, signed in Paris on 20 March 1883 and last amended on 28 September 1979.

(7) Unitary patent protection should be achieved by attributing unitary effect to European patents in the post-grant phase by virtue of this Regulation and in respect of all the participating Member States. The main feature of a European patent with unitary effect should be its unitary character, i.e. providing uniform protection and having equal effect in all the participating Member States. Consequently, a European patent with unitary effect should only be limited, transferred or revoked, or lapse, in respect of all the participating Member States. It should be possible for a European patent with unitary effect to be licensed in respect of the whole or part of the territories of the participating Member States. To ensure the uniform substantive scope of protection conferred by unitary patent protection, only European patents that have been granted for all the participating Member States with the same set of claims should benefit from unitary effect. Finally, the unitary effect attributed to a European patent should have an accessory nature and should be deemed not to have arisen to the extent that the basic European patent has been revoked or limited.

(8) In accordance with the general principles of patent law and Article 64(1) of the EPC, unitary patent protection should take effect retroactively in the participating Member States as from the date of publication of the mention of the grant of the European patent in the European Patent Bulletin. Where unitary patent protection takes effect, the participating Member States should ensure that the European patent is deemed not to have taken effect on their territory as a national patent, so as to avoid any duplication of patent protection.

(9) The European patent with unitary effect should confer on its proprietor the right to prevent any third party from committing acts against which the patent provides protection. This should be ensured through the establishment of a Unified Patent Court. In matters not covered by this Regulation or by Council Regulation (EU) No 1260/2012 of 17 December 2012 implementing enhanced cooperation in the area of unitary patent protection with regard to the applicable translation arrangements[3], the provisions of the EPC, the Agreement on a Unified Patent Court, including its provisions defining the scope of that right and its limitations, and national law, including rules of private international law, should apply.

(10) Compulsory licences for European patents with unitary effect should be governed by the laws of the participating Member States as regards their respective territories.

(11) In its report on the operation of this Regulation, the Commission should evaluate the functioning of the applicable limitations and, where necessary, make appropriate proposals, taking account of the contribution of the patent system to innovation and technological progress, the legitimate interests of third parties and overriding interests of society. The Agreement on a Unified Patent Court does not preclude the European Union from exercising its powers in this field.

(12) In accordance with the case-law of the Court of Justice of the European Union, the principle of the exhaustion of rights should also be applied to European patents with unitary effect. Therefore, rights conferred by a European patent with unitary effect should not extend to acts concerning the product covered by that patent which are carried out within the participating Member States after that product has been placed on the market in the Union by the patent proprietor.

(13) The regime applicable to damages should be governed by the laws of the participating Member States, in particular the provisions implementing Article 13 of Directive 2004/48/EC of the European Parliament and of the Council of 29 April 2004 on the enforcement of intellectual property rights[4].

(14) As an object of property, a European patent with unitary effect should be dealt with in its entirety, and in all the participating Member States, as a national patent of the participating Member State determined in accordance with specific criteria such as the applicant's residence, principal place of business or place of business.

(15) In order to promote and facilitate the economic exploitation of an invention protected by a European patent with unitary effect, the proprietor of that patent should be able to offer it to be licensed in return for appropriate consideration. To that end, the patent proprietor should be able to file a statement with the EPO that he is prepared to grant a licence in return for appropriate consideration. In that case, the patent proprietor should benefit from a reduction of the renewal fees as from the EPO's receipt of such statement.

(16) The group of Member States making use of the provisions of Part IX of the EPC may give tasks to the EPO and set up a select committee of the Administrative Council of the European Patent Organisation (hereinafter 'Select Committee').

(17) The participating Member States should give certain administrative tasks relating to European patents with unitary effect to the EPO, in particular as regards the administration of requests for unitary effect, the registration of unitary effect and of any limitation, licence, transfer, revocation or lapse of European patents with unitary effect, the collection and distribution of renewal fees, the publication of translations for information purposes during a transitional period and the administration of a

compensation scheme for the reimbursement of translation costs incurred by applicants filing European patent applications in a language other than one of the official languages of the EPO.

(18) In the framework of the Select Committee, the participating Member States should ensure the governance and supervision of the activities related to the tasks entrusted to the EPO by the participating Member States, ensure that requests for unitary effect are filed with the EPO within one month of the date of publication of the mention of the grant in the European Patent Bulletin and ensure that such requests are submitted in the language of the proceedings before the EPO together with the translation prescribed, during a transitional period, by Regulation (EU) No 1260/2012. The participating Member States should also ensure the setting, in accordance with the voting rules laid down in Article 35(2) of the EPC, of the level of the renewal fees and the share of the distribution of the renewal fees in accordance with the criteria set out in this Regulation.

(19) Patent proprietors should pay a single annual renewal fee for a European patent with unitary effect. Renewal fees should be progressive throughout the term of the patent protection and, together with the fees to be paid to the European Patent Organisation during the pre-grant stage, should cover all costs associated with the grant of the European patent and the administration of the unitary patent protection. The level of the renewal fees should be set with the aim of facilitating innovation and fostering the competitiveness of European businesses, taking into account the situation of specific entities such as small and medium-sized enterprises, for example in the form of lower fees. It should also reflect the size of the market covered by the patent and be similar to the level of the national renewal fees for an average European patent taking effect in the participating Member States at the time when the level of the renewal fees is first set.

(20) The appropriate level and distribution of renewal fees should be determined in order to ensure that, in relation to the unitary patent protection, all costs of the tasks entrusted to the EPO are fully covered by the resources generated by the European patents with unitary effect and that, together with the fees to be paid to the European Patent Organisation during the pre-grant stage, the revenues from the renewal fees ensure a balanced budget of the European Patent Organisation.

(21) Renewal fees should be paid to the European Patent Organisation. The EPO should retain an amount to cover the expenses generated at the EPO in carrying out tasks in relation to the unitary patent protection in accordance with Article 146 of the EPC. The remaining amount should be distributed among the participating Member States and should be used for patent-related purposes. The share of distribution should be set on the basis of fair, equitable and relevant criteria, namely the level of patent activity and the size of the market, and should guarantee a minimum amount to be distributed to each participating Member State in order to maintain a balanced and sustainable functioning of the system. The distribution should provide compensation for having an official language other than one of the official languages of the EPO, having a disproportionately low level of patenting activity established on the basis of the European Innovation Scoreboard, and/or having acquired membership of the European Patent Organisation relatively recently.

(22) An enhanced partnership between the EPO and central industrial property offices of the Member States should enable the EPO to make regular use, where appropriate, of

the result of any search carried out by central industrial property offices on a national patent application the priority of which is claimed in a subsequent European patent application. All central industrial property offices, including those which do not perform searches in the course of a national patent-granting procedure, can play an essential role under the enhanced partnership, inter alia, by giving advice and support to potential patent applicants, in particular small and medium-sized enterprises, by receiving applications, by forwarding applications to the EPO and by disseminating patent information.

(23) This Regulation is complemented by Regulation (EU) No 1260/2012, adopted by the Council in accordance with the second paragraph of Article 118 of the TFEU.

(24) Jurisdiction in respect of European patents with unitary effect should be established and governed by an instrument setting up a unified patent litigation system for European patents and European patents with unitary effect.

(25) Establishing a Unified Patent Court to hear cases concerning the European patent with unitary effect is essential in order to ensure the proper functioning of that patent, consistency of case-law and hence legal certainty, and cost-effectiveness for patent proprietors. It is therefore of paramount importance that the participating Member States ratify the Agreement on a Unified Patent Court in accordance with their national constitutional and parliamentary procedures and take the necessary steps for that Court to become operational as soon as possible.

(26) This Regulation should be without prejudice to the right of the participating Member States to grant national patents and should not replace the participating Member States' laws on patents. Patent applicants should remain free to obtain either a national patent, a European patent with unitary effect, a European patent taking effect in one or more of the Contracting States to the EPC or a European patent with unitary effect validated in addition in one or more other Contracting States to the EPC which are not among the participating Member States.

(27) Since the objective of this Regulation, namely the creation of unitary patent protection, cannot be sufficiently achieved by the Member States and can therefore, by reason of the scale and effects of this Regulation, be better achieved at Union level, the Union may adopt measures, where appropriate by means of enhanced cooperation, in accordance with the principle of subsidiarity as set out in Article 5 of the Treaty on European Union. In accordance with the principle of proportionality, as set out in that Article, this Regulation does not go beyond what is necessary in order to achieve that objective,

HAVE ADOPTED THIS REGULATION:

CHAPTER I
GENERAL PROVISIONS

Article 1
Subject matter

1. This Regulation implements enhanced cooperation in the area of the creation of unitary patent protection, authorised by Decision 2011/167/EU.

2. This Regulation constitutes a special agreement within the meaning of Article 142 of the Convention on the Grant of European Patents of 5 October 1973, as revised on 17 December 1991 and on 29 November 2000 (hereinafter 'EPC').

Article 2
Definitions

For the purposes of this Regulation, the following definitions shall apply:

(a) 'Participating Member State' means a Member State which participates in enhanced cooperation in the area of the creation of unitary patent protection by virtue of Decision 2011/167/EU, or by virtue of a decision adopted in accordance with the second or third subparagraph of Article 331(1) of the TFEU, at the time the request for unitary effect as referred to in Article 9 is made;

(b) 'European patent' means a patent granted by the European Patent Office (hereinafter 'EPO') under the rules and procedures laid down in the EPC;

(c) 'European patent with unitary effect' means a European patent which benefits from unitary effect in the participating Member States by virtue of this Regulation;

(d) 'European Patent Register' means the register kept by the EPO under Article 127 of the EPC;

(e) 'Register for unitary patent protection' means the register constituting part of the European Patent Register in which the unitary effect and any limitation, licence, transfer, revocation or lapse of a European patent with unitary effect are registered;

(f) 'European Patent Bulletin' means the periodical publication provided for in Article 129 of the EPC.

Article 3
European patent with unitary effect

1. A European patent granted with the same set of claims in respect of all the participating Member States shall benefit from unitary effect in the participating Member States provided that its unitary effect has been registered in the Register for unitary patent protection.

A European patent granted with different sets of claims for different participating Member States shall not benefit from unitary effect.

2. A European patent with unitary effect shall have a unitary character. It shall provide uniform protection and shall have equal effect in all the participating Member States.

It may only be limited, transferred or revoked, or lapse, in respect of all the participating Member States.

It may be licensed in respect of the whole or part of the territories of the participating Member States.

3. The unitary effect of a European patent shall be deemed not to have arisen to the extent that the European patent has been revoked or limited.

Article 4
Date of effect

1. A European patent with unitary effect shall take effect in the participating Member States on the date of publication by the EPO of the mention of the grant of the European patent in the European Patent Bulletin.

2. The participating Member States shall take the necessary measures to ensure that, where the unitary effect of a European patent has been registered and extends to their territory, that European patent is deemed not to have taken effect as a national patent in their territory on the date of publication of the mention of the grant in the European Patent Bulletin.

CHAPTER II
EFFECTS OF A EUROPEAN PATENT WITH UNITARY EFFECT

Article 5
Uniform protection

1. The European patent with unitary effect shall confer on its proprietor the right to prevent any third party from committing acts against which that patent provides protection throughout the territories of the participating Member States in which it has unitary effect, subject to applicable limitations.

2. The scope of that right and its limitations shall be uniform in all participating Member States in which the patent has unitary effect.

3. The acts against which the patent provides protection referred to in paragraph 1 and the applicable limitations shall be those defined by the law applied to European patents with unitary effect in the participating Member State whose national law is applicable to the European patent with unitary effect as an object of property in accordance with Article 7.

4. In its report referred to in Article 16(1), the Commission shall evaluate the functioning of the applicable limitations and shall, where necessary, make appropriate proposals.

Article 6
Exhaustion of the rights conferred by a European patent with unitary effect

The rights conferred by a European patent with unitary effect shall not extend to acts concerning a product covered by that patent which are carried out within the participating Member States in which that patent has unitary effect after that product has been placed on the market in the Union by, or with the consent of, the patent proprietor, unless there are legitimate grounds for the patent proprietor to oppose further commercialisation of the product.

CHAPTER III
A EUROPEAN PATENT WITH UNITARY EFFECT AS AN OBJECT OF PROPERTY

Article 7
Treating a European patent with unitary effect as a national patent

1. A European patent with unitary effect as an object of property shall be treated in its entirety and in all the participating Member States as a national patent of the participating Member State in which that patent has unitary effect and in which, according to the European Patent Register:

(a) the applicant had his residence or principal place of business on the date of filing of the application for the European patent; or
(b) where point (a) does not apply, the applicant had a place of business on the date of filing of the application for the European patent.

2. Where two or more persons are entered in the European Patent Register as joint applicants, point (a) of paragraph 1 shall apply to the joint applicant indicated first. Where this is not possible, point (a) of paragraph 1 shall apply to the next joint applicant indicated in the order of entry. Where point (a) of paragraph 1 does not apply to any of the joint applicants, point (b) of paragraph 1 shall apply accordingly.

3. Where no applicant had his residence, principal place of business or place of business in a participating Member State in which that patent has unitary effect for the purposes of paragraphs 1 or 2, the European patent with unitary effect as an object of property shall be treated in its entirety and in all the participating Member States as a national patent of the State where the European Patent Organisation has its headquarters in accordance with Article 6(1) of the EPC.

4. The acquisition of a right may not be dependent on any entry in a national patent register.

Article 8
Licences of right

1. The proprietor of a European patent with unitary effect may file a statement with the EPO to the effect that the proprietor is prepared to allow any person to use the invention as a licensee in return for appropriate consideration.

2. A licence obtained under this Regulation shall be treated as a contractual licence.

CHAPTER IV
INSTITUTIONAL PROVISIONS

Article 9
Administrative tasks in the framework of the European Patent Organisation

1. The participating Member States shall, within the meaning of Article 143 of the EPC, give the EPO the following tasks, to be carried out in accordance with the internal rules of the EPO:

(a) to administer requests for unitary effect by proprietors of European patents;

(b) to include the Register for unitary patent protection within the European Patent Register and to administer the Register for unitary patent protection;
(c) to receive and register statements on licensing referred to in Article 8, their withdrawal and licensing commitments undertaken by the proprietor of the European patent with unitary effect in international standardisation bodies;
(d) to publish the translations referred to in Article 6 of Regulation (EU) No 1260/2012 during the transitional period referred to in that Article;
(e) to collect and administer renewal fees for European patents with unitary effect, in respect of the years following the year in which the mention of the grant is published in the European Patent Bulletin; to collect and administer additional fees for late payment of renewal fees where such late payment is made within six months of the due date, as well as to distribute part of the collected renewal fees to the participating Member States;
(f) to administer the compensation scheme for the reimbursement of translation costs referred to in Article 5 of Regulation (EU) No 1260/2012;
(g) to ensure that a request for unitary effect by a proprietor of a European patent is submitted in the language of the proceedings as defined in Article 14(3) of the EPC no later than one month after the mention of the grant is published in the European Patent Bulletin; and
(h) to ensure that the unitary effect is indicated in the Register for unitary patent protection, where a request for unitary effect has been filed and, during the transitional period provided for in Article 6 of Regulation (EU) No 1260/2012, has been submitted together with the translations referred to in that Article, and that the EPO is informed of any limitations, licences, transfers or revocations of European patents with unitary effect.

2. The participating Member States shall ensure compliance with this Regulation in fulfilling their international obligations undertaken in the EPC and shall cooperate to that end. In their capacity as Contracting States to the EPC, the participating Member States shall ensure the governance and supervision of the activities related to the tasks referred to in paragraph 1 of this Article and shall ensure the setting of the level of renewal fees in accordance with Article 12 of this Regulation and the setting of the share of distribution of the renewal fees in accordance with Article 13 of this Regulation.

To that end they shall set up a select committee of the Administrative Council of the European Patent Organisation (hereinafter 'Select Committee') within the meaning of Article 145 of the EPC.

The Select Committee shall consist of the representatives of the participating Member States and a representative of the Commission as an observer, as well as alternates who will represent them in their absence. The members of the Select Committee may be assisted by advisers or experts.

Decisions of the Select Committee shall be taken with due regard for the position of the Commission and in accordance with the rules laid down in Article 35(2) of the EPC.

3. The participating Member States shall ensure effective legal protection before a competent court of one or several participating Member States against the decisions of the EPO in carrying out the tasks referred to in paragraph 1.

CHAPTER V
FINANCIAL PROVISIONS

Article 10
Principle on expenses

The expenses incurred by the EPO in carrying out the additional tasks given to it, within the meaning of Article 143 of the EPC, by the participating Member States shall be covered by the fees generated by the European patents with unitary effect.

Article 11
Renewal fees

1. Renewal fees for European patents with unitary effect and additional fees for their late payment shall be paid to the European Patent Organisation by the patent proprietor. Those fees shall be due in respect of the years following the year in which the mention of the grant of the European patent which benefits from unitary effect is published in the European Patent Bulletin.

2. A European patent with unitary effect shall lapse if a renewal fee and, where applicable, any additional fee have not been paid in due time.

3. Renewal fees which fall due after receipt of the statement referred to in Article 8(1) shall be reduced.

Article 12
Level of renewal fees

1. Renewal fees for European patents with unitary effect shall be:

(a) progressive throughout the term of the unitary patent protection;
(b) sufficient to cover all costs associated with the grant of the European patent and the administration of the unitary patent protection; and
(c) sufficient, together with the fees to be paid to the European Patent Organisation during the pre-grant stage, to ensure a balanced budget of the European Patent Organisation.

2. The level of the renewal fees shall be set, taking into account, among others, the situation of specific entities such as small and medium-sized enterprises, with the aim of:

(a) facilitating innovation and fostering the competitiveness of European businesses;
(b) reflecting the size of the market covered by the patent; and
(c) being similar to the level of the national renewal fees for an average European patent taking effect in the participating Member States at the time the level of the renewal fees is first set.

3. In order to attain the objectives set out in this Chapter, the level of renewal fees shall be set at a level that:

(a) is equivalent to the level of the renewal fee to be paid for the average geographical coverage of current European patents;

(b) reflects the renewal rate of current European patents; and
(c) reflects the number of requests for unitary effect.

Article 13
Distribution

1. The EPO shall retain 50 per cent of the renewal fees referred to in Article 11 paid for European patents with unitary effect. The remaining amount shall be distributed to the participating Member States in accordance with the share of distribution of the renewal fees set pursuant to Article 9(2).

2. In order to attain the objectives set out in this Chapter, the share of distribution of renewal fees among the participating Member States shall be based on the following fair, equitable and relevant criteria:

(a) the number of patent applications;
(b) the size of the market, while ensuring a minimum amount to be distributed to each participating Member State;
(c) compensation to the participating Member States which have:
    (i) an official language other than one of the official languages of the EPO;
    (ii) a disproportionately low level of patenting activity; and/or
    (iii) acquired membership of the European Patent Organisation relatively recently.

CHAPTER VI
FINAL PROVISIONS

Article 14
Cooperation between the Commission and the EPO

The Commission shall establish a close cooperation through a working agreement with the EPO in the fields covered by this Regulation. This cooperation shall include regular exchanges of views on the functioning of the working agreement and, in particular, on the issue of renewal fees and their impact on the budget of the European Patent Organisation.

Article 15
Application of competition law and the law relating to unfair competition

This Regulation shall be without prejudice to the application of competition law and the law relating to unfair competition.

Article 16
Report on the operation of this Regulation

1. Not later than three years from the date on which the first European patent with unitary effect takes effect, and every five years thereafter, the Commission shall present to the European Parliament and the Council a report on the operation of this Regulation and, where necessary, make appropriate proposals for amending it.

2. The Commission shall regularly submit to the European Parliament and the Council reports on the functioning of the renewal fees referred to in Article 11, with particular emphasis on compliance with Article 12.

Article 17
Notification by the participating Member States

1. The participating Member States shall notify the Commission of the measures adopted in accordance with Article 9 by the date of application of this Regulation.

2. Each participating Member State shall notify the Commission of the measures adopted in accordance with Article 4(2) by the date of application of this Regulation or, in the case of a participating Member State in which the Unified Patent Court does not have exclusive jurisdiction with regard to European patents with unitary effect on the date of application of this Regulation, by the date from which the Unified Patent Court has such exclusive jurisdiction in that participating Member State.

Article 18
Entry into force and application

1. This Regulation shall enter into force on the twentieth day following that of its publication in the *Official Journal of the European Union*.

2. It shall apply from 1 January 2014 or the date of entry into force of the Agreement on a Unified Patent Court (the 'Agreement'), whichever is the later.

By way of derogation from Articles 3(1), 3(2) and 4(1), a European patent for which unitary effect is registered in the Register for unitary patent protection shall have unitary effect only in those participating Member States in which the Unified Patent Court has exclusive jurisdiction with regard to European patents with unitary effect at the date of registration.

3. Each participating Member State shall notify the Commission of its ratification of the Agreement at the time of deposit of its ratification instrument. The Commission shall publish in the *Official Journal of the European Union* the date of entry into force of the Agreement and a list of the Member States who have ratified the Agreement at the date of entry into force. The Commission shall thereafter regularly update the list of the participating Member States which have ratified the Agreement and shall publish such updated list in the *Official Journal of the European Union*.

4. The participating Member States shall ensure that the measures referred to in Article 9 are in place by the date of application of this Regulation.

5. Each participating Member State shall ensure that the measures referred to in Article 4(2) are in place by the date of application of this Regulation or, in the case of a participating Member State in which the Unified Patent Court does not have exclusive jurisdiction with regard to European patents with unitary effect on the date of application of this Regulation, by the date from which the Unified Patent Court has such exclusive jurisdiction in that participating Member State.

6. Unitary patent protection may be requested for any European patent granted on or after the date of application of this Regulation.

This Regulation shall be binding in its entirety and directly applicable in the participating Member States in accordance with the Treaties.

Done at Brussels, 17 December 2012.

For the European Parliament
The President
M. SCHULZ
For the Council
The President
A. D. MAVROYIANNIS

[1] OJ L 76, 22.3.2011, p. 53.
[2] Position of the European Parliament of 11 December 2012 (not yet published in the Official Journal) and decision of the Council of 17 December 2012.
[3] See page 89 of this Official Journal.
[4] OJ L 157, 30.4.2004, p. 45.

ANNEX D: REGULATION (EU) 1260/2012 OF 17 DECEMBER 2012

(Translation Regulation)

COUNCIL REGULATION (EU) No 1260/2012

of 17 December 2012

implementing enhanced cooperation in the area of the creation of unitary patent protection with regard to the applicable translation arrangements

THE COUNCIL OF THE EUROPEAN UNION,

Having regard to the Treaty on the Functioning of the European Union, and in particular the second paragraph of Article 118 thereof,

Having regard to Council Decision 2011/167/EU of 10 March 2011 authorising enhanced cooperation in the area of the creation of unitary patent protection[1],

Having regard to the proposal from the European Commission,

After transmission of the draft legislative act to the national parliaments,

Having regard to the opinion of the European Parliament,

Acting in accordance with a special legislative procedure,

Whereas:

(1) Pursuant to Decision 2011/167/EU, Belgium, Bulgaria, the Czech Republic, Denmark, Germany, Estonia, Ireland, Greece, France, Cyprus, Latvia, Lithuania, Luxembourg, Hungary, Malta, the Netherlands, Austria, Poland, Portugal, Romania, Slovenia, Slovakia, Finland, Sweden and the United Kingdom (hereinafter 'participating Member States') were authorised to establish enhanced cooperation between themselves in the area of the creation of unitary patent protection.

(2) Under Regulation (EU) No 1257/2012 of the European Parliament and of the Council of 17 December 2012 implementing enhanced cooperation in the area of the creation of unitary patent protection[2], certain European patents granted by the European Patent Office (hereinafter 'EPO') under the rules and procedures of the Convention on the Grant of European Patents of 5 October 1973, as revised on 17 December 1991 and on 29 November 2000 (hereinafter 'EPC') should, at the request of the patent proprietor, benefit from unitary effect in the participating Member States.

(3) Translation arrangements for European patents benefiting from unitary effect in the participating Member States (hereinafter 'European patent with unitary effect') should be established by means of a separate Regulation, in accordance with the second paragraph of Article 118 of the Treaty on the Functioning of the European Union (TFEU).

(4) In accordance with Decision 2011/167/EU the translation arrangements for European patents with unitary effect should be simple and cost-effective. They should correspond to those provided for in the proposal for a Council Regulation on the translation arrangements for the European Union patent, presented by the Commission on 30 June 2010, combined with the elements of compromise proposed by the Presidency in November 2010 that had wide support in the Council.

(5) Such translation arrangements should ensure legal certainty and stimulate innovation and should, in particular, benefit small and medium-sized enterprises (SMEs). They should make access to the European patent with unitary effect and to the patent system as a whole easier, less costly and legally secure.

(6) Since the EPO is responsible for the grant of European patents, the translation arrangements for the European patent with unitary effect should be built on the current procedure in the EPO. Those arrangements should aim to achieve the necessary balance between the interests of economic operators and the public interest, in terms of the cost of proceedings and the availability of technical information.

(7) Without prejudice to the transitional arrangements, where the specification of a European patent with unitary effect has been published in accordance with Article 14(6) of the EPC, no further translations should be required. Article 14(6) of the EPC provides that the specification of a European patent is published in the language of the proceedings before the EPO and includes a translation of the claims into the other two official languages of the EPO.

(8) In the event of a dispute concerning a European patent with unitary effect, it is a legitimate requirement that the patent proprietor at the request of the alleged infringer should provide a full translation of the patent into an official language of either the participating Member State in which the alleged infringement took place or the Member State in which the alleged infringer is domiciled. The patent proprietor should also be required to provide, at the request of a court competent in the participating Member States for disputes concerning the European patent with unitary effect, a full translation of the patent into the language used in the proceedings of that court. Such translations should not be carried out by automated means and should be provided at the expense of the patent proprietor.

(9) In the event of a dispute concerning a claim for damages, the court hearing the dispute should take into consideration the fact that, before having been provided with a translation in his own language, the alleged infringer may have acted in good faith and may have not known or had reasonable grounds to know that he was infringing the patent. The competent court should assess the circumstances of the individual case and, inter alia, should take into account whether the alleged infringer is a SME operating only at local level, the language of the proceedings before the EPO and, during the transitional period, the translation submitted together with the request for unitary effect.

(10) In order to facilitate access to European patents with unitary effect, in particular for SMEs, applicants should be able to file their patent applications at the EPO in any official language of the Union. As a complementary measure, certain applicants obtaining European patents with unitary effect, having filed a European patent application in one of the official languages of the Union, which is not an official language of the EPO, and having their residence or principal place of business within a Member State, should receive additional reimbursements of the costs of translating from the language of the patent application into the language of the proceedings of the EPO, beyond what is currently in place at the EPO. Such reimbursements should be administered by the EPO in accordance with Article 9 of Regulation (EU) No 1257/2012.

(11) In order to promote the availability of patent information and the dissemination of technological knowledge, machine translations of patent applications and specifications into all official languages of the Union should be available as soon as possible. Machine translations are being developed by the EPO and are a very important tool in seeking to improve access to patent information and to widely disseminate technological knowledge. The timely availability of high quality machine translations of European patent applications and specifications into all official languages of the Union would benefit all users of the European patent system. Machine translations are a key feature of European Union policy. Such machine translations should serve for information purposes only and should not have any legal effect.

(12) During the transitional period, before a system of high quality machine translations into all official languages of the Union becomes available, a request for unitary effect as referred to in Article 9 of Regulation (EU) No 1257/2012 should be accompanied by a full translation of the specification of the patent into English where the language of the proceedings before the EPO is French or German, or into any official language of the Member States that is an official language of the Union where the language of the proceedings before the EPO is English. Those arrangements would ensure that during a transitional period all European patents with unitary effect are made available in English which is the language customarily used in the field of international technological research and publications. Furthermore, such arrangements would ensure that with respect to European patents with unitary effect, translations would be published in other official languages of the participating Member States. Such translations should not be carried out by automated means and their high quality should contribute to the training of translation engines by the EPO. They would also enhance the dissemination of patent information.

(13) The transitional period should terminate as soon as high quality machine translations into all official languages of the Union are available, subject to a regular and objective evaluation of the quality by an independent expert committee established by the participating Member States in the framework of the European Patent Organisation and composed of the representatives of the EPO and the users of the European patent system. Given the state of technological development, the maximum period for the development of high quality machine translations cannot be considered to exceed 12 years. Consequently, the transitional period should lapse 12 years from the date of application of this Regulation, unless it has been decided to terminate that period earlier.

(14) Since the substantive provisions applicable to a European patent with unitary effect are governed by Regulation (EU) No 1257/2012 and are completed by the translation arrangements provided for in this Regulation, this Regulation should apply from the same date as Regulation (EU) No 1257/2012.

(15) This Regulation is without prejudice to the rules governing the languages of the Institutions of the Union established in accordance with Article 342 of the TFEU and to Council Regulation No 1 of 15 April 1958 determining the languages to be used by the European Economic Community[3]. This Regulation is based on the linguistic regime of the EPO and should not be considered as creating a specific linguistic regime for the Union, or as creating a precedent for a limited language regime in any future legal instrument of the Union.

(16) Since the objective of this Regulation, namely the creation of a uniform and simple translation regime for European patents with unitary effect, cannot be sufficiently achieved by the Member States and can therefore, by reasons of the scale and effects of this Regulation, be better achieved at Union level, the Union may adopt measures, where appropriate by means of enhanced cooperation, in accordance with the principle of subsidiarity as set out in Article 5 of the Treaty on European Union. In accordance with the principle of proportionality, as set out in that Article, this Regulation does not go beyond what is necessary in order to achieve that objective,

HAS ADOPTED THIS REGULATION:

Article 1
Subject matter

This Regulation implements enhanced cooperation in the area of the creation of unitary patent protection authorised by Decision No 2011/167/EU with regard to the applicable translation arrangements.

Article 2
Definitions

For the purposes of this Regulation, the following definitions shall apply:

(a) 'European patent with unitary effect' means a European patent which benefits from unitary effect in the participating Member States by virtue of Regulation (EU) No 1257/2012;

(b) 'Language of the proceedings' means the language used in the proceedings before the EPO as defined in Article 14(3) of the Convention on the Grant of European Patents of 5 October 1973, as revised on 17 December 1991 and on 29 November 2000 (hereinafter 'EPC').

Article 3
Translation arrangements for the European patent with unitary effect

1. Without prejudice to Articles 4 and 6 of this Regulation, where the specification of a European patent, which benefits from unitary effect has been published in accordance with Article 14(6) of the EPC, no further translations shall be required.

2. A request for unitary effect as referred to in Article 9 of Regulation (EU) No 1257/2012 shall be submitted in the language of the proceedings.

Article 4
Translation in the event of a dispute

1. In the event of a dispute relating to an alleged infringement of a European patent with unitary effect, the patent proprietor shall provide at the request and the choice of an alleged infringer, a full translation of the European patent with unitary effect into an official language of either the participating Member State in which the alleged infringement took place or the Member State in which the alleged infringer is domiciled.

2. In the event of a dispute relating to a European patent with unitary effect, the patent proprietor shall provide in the course of legal proceedings, at the request of a court competent in the participating Member States for disputes concerning European patents with unitary effect, a full translation of the patent into the language used in the proceedings of that court.

3. The cost of the translations referred to in paragraphs 1 and 2 shall be borne by the patent proprietor.

4. In the event of a dispute concerning a claim for damages, the court hearing the dispute shall assess and take into consideration, in particular where the alleged infringer is a SME, a natural person or a non-profit organisation, a university or a public research organisation, whether the alleged infringer acted without knowing or without reasonable grounds for knowing, that he was infringing the European patent with unitary effect before having been provided with the translation referred to in paragraph 1.

Article 5
Administration of a compensation scheme

1. Given the fact that European patent applications may be filed in any language under Article 14(2) of the EPC, the participating Member States shall in accordance with Article 9 of Regulation (EU) No 1257/2012, give, within the meaning of Article 143 of the EPC, the EPO the task of administering a compensation scheme for the reimbursement of all translation costs up to a ceiling, for applicants filing patent applications at the EPO in one of the official languages of the Union that is not an official language of the EPO.

2. The compensation scheme referred to in paragraph 1 shall be funded through the fees referred to in Article 11 of Regulation (EU) No 1257/2012 and shall be available only for SMEs, natural persons, non-profit organisations, universities and public research organisations having their residence or principal place of business within a Member State.

Article 6
Transitional measures

1. During a transitional period starting on the date of application of this Regulation a request for unitary effect as referred to in Article 9 of Regulation (EU) No 1257/2012 shall be submitted together with the following:

(a) where the language of the proceedings is French or German, a full translation of the specification of the European patent into English; or
(b) where the language of the proceedings is English, a full translation of the specification of the European patent into any other official language of the Union.

2. In accordance with Article 9 of Regulation (EU) No 1257/2012, the participating Member States shall give, within the meaning of Article 143 of the EPC, the EPO the task of publishing the translations referred to in paragraph 1 of this Article as soon as possible after the date of the submission of a request for unitary effect as referred to in Article 9 of Regulation (EU) No 1257/2012. The text of such translations shall have no legal effect and shall be for information purposes only.

3. Six years after the date of application of this Regulation and every two years thereafter, an independent expert committee shall carry out an objective evaluation of the availability of high quality machine translations of patent applications and specifications into all the official languages of the Union as developed by the EPO. This expert committee shall be established by the participating Member States in the framework of the European Patent Organisation and shall be composed of representatives of the EPO and of the non-governmental organisations representing users of the European patent system invited by the Administrative Council of the European Patent Organisation as observers in accordance with Article 30(3) of the EPC.

4. On the basis of the first of the evaluations referred to in paragraph 3 of this Article and every two years thereafter on the basis of the subsequent evaluations, the Commission shall present a report to the Council and, if appropriate, make proposals for terminating the transitional period.

5. If the transitional period is not terminated on the basis of a proposal of the Commission, it shall lapse 12 years from the date of application of this Regulation.

Article 7
Entry into force

1. This Regulation shall enter into force on the twentieth day following that of its publication in the *Official Journal of the European Union*.

2. It shall apply from 1 January 2014 or the date of entry into force of the Agreement on a Unified Patent Court, whichever is the later.

This Regulation shall be binding in its entirety and directly applicable in the participating Member States in accordance with the Treaties.

Done at Brussels, 17 December 2012.

For the Council
The President
S. ALETRARIS

[1] OJ L 76, 22.3.2011, p. 53.
[2] See page 1 of this Official Journal.
[3] OJ 17, 6.10.1958, p. 385/58.

ANNEX E: AGREEMENT ON A UNIFIED PATENT COURT OF 19 FEBRUARY 2013

(UPC Agreement)

AGREEMENT ON A UNIFIED PATENT COURT (UPC)

THE CONTRACTING MEMBER STATES,

CONSIDERING that cooperation amongst the Member States of the European Union in the field of patents contributes significantly to the integration process in Europe, in particular to the establishment of an internal market within the European Union characterised by the free movement of goods and services and the creation of a system ensuring that competition in the internal market is not distorted;

CONSIDERING that the fragmented market for patents and the significant variations between national court systems are detrimental for innovation, in particular for small and medium sized enterprises which have difficulties to enforce their patents and to defend themselves against unfounded claims and claims relating to patents which should be revoked;

CONSIDERING that the European Patent Convention ('EPC') which has been ratified by all Member States of the European Union provides for a single procedure for granting European patents by the European Patent Office;

CONSIDERING that by virtue of Regulation (EU) No 1257/2012[1], patent proprietors can request unitary effect of their European patents so as to obtain unitary patent protection in the Member States of the European Union participating in the enhanced cooperation;

WISHING to improve the enforcement of patents and the defence against unfounded claims and patents which should be revoked and to enhance legal certainty by setting up a Unified Patent Court for litigation relating to the infringement and validity of patents;

CONSIDERING that the Unified Patent Court should be devised to ensure expeditious and high quality decisions, striking a fair balance between the interests of right holders and other parties and taking into account the need for proportionality and flexibility;

CONSIDERING that the Unified Patent Court should be a court common to the Contracting Member States and thus part of their judicial system, with exclusive competence in respect of European patents with unitary effect and European patents granted under the provisions of the EPC;

---

[1] Regulation (EU) No 1257/2012 of the European Parliament and of the Council of 17 December 2012 implementing enhanced cooperation in the area of the creation of unitary patent protection (OJEU L 361, 31.12.2012, p. 1) including any subsequent amendments.

CONSIDERING that the Court of Justice of the European Union is to ensure the uniformity of the Union legal order and the primacy of European Union law;

RECALLING the obligations of the Contracting Member States under the Treaty on European Union (TEU) and the Treaty on the Functioning of the European Union (TFEU), including the obligation of sincere cooperation as set out in Article 4(3) TEU and the obligation to ensure through the Unified Patent Court the full application of, and respect for, Union law in their respective territories and the judicial protection of an individual's rights under that law;

CONSIDERING that, as any national court, the Unified Patent Court must respect and apply Union law and, in collaboration with the Court of Justice of the European Union as guardian of Union law, ensure its correct application and uniform interpretation; the Unified Patent Court must in particular cooperate with the Court of Justice of the European Union in properly interpreting Union law by relying on the latter's case law and by requesting preliminary rulings in accordance with Article 267 TFEU;

CONSIDERING that the Contracting Member States should, in line with the case law of the Court of Justice of the European Union on non-contractual liability, be liable for damages caused by infringements of Union law by the Unified Patent Court, including the failure to request preliminary rulings from the Court of Justice of the European Union;

CONSIDERING that infringements of Union law by the Unified Patent Court, including the failure to request preliminary rulings from the Court of Justice of the European Union, are directly attributable to the Contracting Member States and infringement proceedings can therefore be brought under Article 258, 259 and 260 TFEU against any Contracting Member State to ensure the respect of the primacy and proper application of Union law;

RECALLING the primacy of Union law, which includes the TEU, the TFEU, the Charter of Fundamental Rights of the European Union, the general principles of Union law as developed by the Court of Justice of the European Union, and in particular the right to an effective remedy before a tribunal and a fair and public hearing within a reasonable time by an independent and impartial tribunal, the case law of the Court of Justice of the European Union and secondary Union law;

CONSIDERING that this Agreement should be open to accession by any Member State of the European Union; Member States which have decided not to participate in the enhanced cooperation in the area of the creation of unitary patent protection may participate in this Agreement in respect of European patents granted for their respective territory;

CONSIDERING that this Agreement should enter into force on 1 January 2014 or on the first day of the fourth month after the 13th deposit, provided that the Contracting Member States that will have deposited their instruments of ratification or accession include the three States in which the highest number of European patents was in force in the year preceding the year in which the signature of the Agreement takes place, or on the first day of the fourth month after the date of entry into force of the amendments to Regulation (EU) No 1215/2012[2] concerning its relationship with this Agreement, whichever is the latest,

---

[2] Regulation (EU) No 1215/2012 of the European Parliament and of the Council of 12 December 2012 on jurisdiction and the recognition and enforcement of judgments in civil and commercial matters (OJEU L 351, 20.12.2012, p. 1) including any subsequent amendments.

HAVE AGREED AS FOLLOWS:

PART I – GENERAL AND INSTITUTIONAL PROVISIONS

CHAPTER I – GENERAL PROVISIONS

ARTICLE 1
Unified Patent Court

A Unified Patent Court for the settlement of disputes relating to European patents and European patents with unitary effect is hereby established.

The Unified Patent Court shall be a court common to the Contracting Member States and thus subject to the same obligations under Union law as any national court of the Contracting Member States.

ARTICLE 2
Definitions

For the purposes of this Agreement:

(a) 'Court' means the Unified Patent Court created by this Agreement.
(b) 'Member State' means a Member State of the European Union.
(c) 'Contracting Member State' means a Member State party to this Agreement.
(d) 'EPC' means the Convention on the Grant of European Patents of 5 October 1973, including any subsequent amendments.
(e) 'European patent' means a patent granted under the provisions of the EPC, which does not benefit from unitary effect by virtue of Regulation (EU) No 1257/2012.
(f) 'European patent with unitary effect' means a patent granted under the provisions of the EPC which benefits from unitary effect by virtue of Regulation (EU) No 1257/2012.
(g) 'Patent' means a European patent and/or a European patent with unitary effect.
(h) 'Supplementary protection certificate' means a supplementary protection certificate granted under Regulation (EC) No 469/2009[1] or under Regulation (EC) No 1610/96[2].
(i) 'Statute' means the Statute of the Court as set out in Annex I, which shall be an integral part of this Agreement.
(j) 'Rules of Procedure' means the Rules of Procedure of the Court, as established in accordance with Article 41.

---

[1] Regulation (EC) No 469/2009 of the European Parliament and of the Council of 6 May 2009 concerning the supplementary protection certificate for medicinal products, (OJEU L 152, 16.6.2009, p. 1) including any subsequent amendments.
[2] Regulation (EC) No 1610/96 of the European Parliament and of the Council of 23 July 1996 concerning the creation of a supplementary certificate for plant protection products, (OJEC L 198, 8.8.1996, p. 30) including any subsequent amendments.

ARTICLE 3
Scope of application

This Agreement shall apply to any:

(a) European patent with unitary effect;
(b) supplementary protection certificate issued for a product protected by a patent;
(c) European patent which has not yet lapsed at the date of entry into force of this Agreement or was granted after that date, without prejudice to Article 83; and
(d) European patent application which is pending at the date of entry into force of this Agreement or which is filed after that date, without prejudice to Article 83.

ARTICLE 4
Legal status

(1) The Court shall have legal personality in each Contracting Member State and shall enjoy the most extensive legal capacity accorded to legal persons under the national law of that State.

(2) The Court shall be represented by the President of the Court of Appeal who shall be elected in accordance with the Statute.

ARTICLE 5
Liability

(1) The contractual liability of the Court shall be governed by the law applicable to the contract in question in accordance with Regulation (EC) No. 593/2008[1] (Rome I), where applicable, or failing that in accordance with the law of the Member State of the court seized.

(2) The non-contractual liability of the Court in respect of any damage caused by it or its staff in the performance of their duties, to the extent that it is not a civil and commercial matter within the meaning of Regulation (EC) No. 864/2007[2] (Rome II), shall be governed by the law of the Contracting Member State in which the damage occurred. This provision is without prejudice to the application of Article 22.

(3) The court with jurisdiction to settle disputes under paragraph 2 shall be a court of the Contracting Member State in which the damage occurred.

---

[1] Regulation (EC) No 593/2008 of the European Parliament and of the Council of 17 June 2008 on the law applicable to contractual obligations (Rome I) (OJEU L 177, 4.7.2008, p. 6) including any subsequent amendments.
[2] Regulation (EC) No 864/2007 of the European Parliament and of the Council of 11 July 2007 on the law applicable to non-contractual obligations (Rome II) (OJEU L 199, 31.7.2007, p. 40) including any subsequent amendments.

CHAPTER II – INSTITUTIONAL PROVISIONS

ARTICLE 6
The Court

(1) The Court shall comprise a Court of First Instance, a Court of Appeal and a Registry.

(2) The Court shall perform the functions assigned to it by this Agreement.

ARTICLE 7
The Court of First Instance

(1) The Court of First Instance shall comprise a central division as well as local and regional divisions.

(2) The central division shall have its seat in Paris, with sections in London and Munich. The cases before the central division shall be distributed in accordance with Annex II, which shall form an integral part of this Agreement.

(3) A local division shall be set up in a Contracting Member State upon its request in accordance with the Statute. A Contracting Member State hosting a local division shall designate its seat.

(4) An additional local division shall be set up in a Contracting Member State upon its request for every one hundred patent cases per calendar year that have been commenced in that Contracting Member State during three successive years prior to or subsequent to the date of entry into force of this Agreement. The number of local divisions in one Contracting Member State shall not exceed four.

(5) A regional division shall be set up for two or more Contracting Member States, upon their request in accordance with the Statute. Such Contracting Member States shall designate the seat of the division concerned. The regional division may hear cases in multiple locations.

ARTICLE 8
Composition of the panels of the Court of First Instance

(1) Any panel of the Court of First Instance shall have a multinational composition. Without prejudice to paragraph 5 of this Article and to Article 33(3)(a), it shall sit in a composition of three judges.

(2) Any panel of a local division in a Contracting Member State where, during a period of three successive years prior or subsequent to the entry into force of this Agreement, less than fifty patent cases per calendar year on average have been commenced shall sit in a composition of one legally qualified judge who is a national of the Contracting Member State hosting the local division concerned and two legally qualified judges who are not nationals of the Contracting Member State concerned and are allocated from the Pool of Judges in accordance with Article 18(3) on a case by case basis.

(3) Notwithstanding paragraph 2, any panel of a local division in a Contracting Member State where, during a period of three successive years prior or subsequent to the entry into

force of this Agreement, fifty or more patent cases per calendar year on average have been commenced, shall sit in a composition of two legally qualified judges who are nationals of the Contracting Member State hosting the local division concerned and one legally qualified judge who is not a national of the Contracting Member State concerned and is allocated from the Pool of Judges in accordance with Article 18(3). Such third judge shall serve at the local division on a long term basis, where this is necessary for the efficient functioning of divisions with a high work load.

(4) Any panel of a regional division shall sit in a composition of two legally qualified judges chosen from a regional list of judges, who shall be nationals of the Contracting Member States concerned, and one legally qualified judge who shall not be a national of the Contracting Member States concerned and who shall be allocated from the Pool of Judges in accordance with Article 18(3).

(5) Upon request by one of the parties, any panel of a local or regional division shall request the President of the Court of First Instance to allocate from the Pool of Judges in accordance with Article 18(3) an additional technically qualified judge with qualifications and experience in the field of technology concerned. Moreover, any panel of a local or regional division may, after having heard the parties, submit such request on its own initiative, where it deems this appropriate.

In cases where such a technically qualified judge is allocated, no further technically qualified judge may be allocated under Article 33(3)(a).

(6) Any panel of the central division shall sit in a composition of two legally qualified judges who are nationals of different Contracting Member States and one technically qualified judge allocated from the Pool of Judges in accordance with Article 18(3) with qualifications and experience in the field of technology concerned. However, any panel of the central division dealing with actions under Article 32(1)(i) shall sit in a composition of three legally qualified judges who are nationals of different Contracting Member States.

(7) Notwithstanding paragraphs 1 to 6 and in accordance with the Rules of Procedure, parties may agree to have their case heard by a single legally qualified judge.

(8) Any panel of the Court of First Instance shall be chaired by a legally qualified judge.

ARTICLE 9
The Court of Appeal

(1) Any panel of the Court of Appeal shall sit in a multinational composition of five judges. It shall sit in a composition of three legally qualified judges who are nationals of different Contracting Member States and two technically qualified judges with qualifications and experience in the field of technology concerned. Those technically qualified judges shall be assigned to the panel by the President of the Court of Appeal from the pool of judges in accordance with Article 18.

(2) Notwithstanding paragraph 1, a panel dealing with actions under Article 32(1)(i) shall sit in a composition of three legally qualified judges who are nationals of different Contracting Member States.

(3) Any panel of the Court of Appeal shall be chaired by a legally qualified judge.

(4) The panels of the Court of Appeal shall be set up in accordance with the Statute.

(5) The Court of Appeal shall have its seat in Luxembourg.

ARTICLE 10
The Registry

(1) A Registry shall be set up at the seat of the Court of Appeal. It shall be managed by the Registrar and perform the functions assigned to it in accordance with the Statute. Subject to conditions set out in this Agreement and the Rules of Procedure, the register kept by the Registry shall be public.

(2) Sub-registries shall be set up at all divisions of the Court of First Instance.

(3) The Registry shall keep records of all cases before the Court. Upon filing, the sub-registry concerned shall notify every case to the Registry.

(4) The Court shall appoint the Registrar in accordance with Article 22 of the Statute and lay down the rules governing the Registrar's service.

ARTICLE 11
Committees

An Administrative Committee, a Budget Committee and an Advisory Committee shall be set up in order to ensure the effective implementation and operation of this Agreement. They shall in particular exercise the duties foreseen by this Agreement and the Statute.

ARTICLE 12
The Administrative Committee

(1) The Administrative Committee shall be composed of one representative of each Contracting Member State. The European Commission shall be represented at the meetings of the Administrative Committee as observer.

(2) Each Contracting Member State shall have one vote.

(3) The Administrative Committee shall adopt its decisions by a majority of three quarters of the Contracting Member States represented and voting, except where this Agreement or the Statute provides otherwise.

(4) The Administrative Committee shall adopt its rules of procedure.

(5) The Administrative Committee shall elect a chairperson from among its members for a term of three years. That term shall be renewable.

ARTICLE 13
The Budget Committee

(1) The Budget Committee shall be composed of one representative of each Contracting Member State.

(2) Each Contracting Member State shall have one vote.

(3) The Budget Committee shall take its decisions by a simple majority of the representatives of the Contracting Member States. However, a majority of three-quarters of the representatives of Contracting Member States shall be required for the adoption of the budget.

(4) The Budget Committee shall adopt its rules of procedure.

(5) The Budget Committee shall elect a chairperson from among its members for a term of three years. That term shall be renewable.

ARTICLE 14
The Advisory Committee

(1) The Advisory Committee shall:

(a) assist the Administrative Committee in the preparation of the appointment of judges of the Court;
(b) make proposals to the Presidium referred to in Article 15 of the Statute on the guidelines for the training framework for judges referred to in Article 19; and
(c) deliver opinions to the Administrative Committee concerning the requirements for qualifications referred to in Article 48(2).

(2) The Advisory Committee shall comprise patent judges and practitioners in patent law and patent litigation with the highest recognised competence. They shall be appointed, in accordance with the procedure laid down in the Statute, for a term of six years. That term shall be renewable.

(3) The composition of the Advisory Committee shall ensure a broad range of relevant expertise and the representation of each of the Contracting Member States. The members of the Advisory Committee shall be completely independent in the performance of their duties and shall not be bound by any instructions.

(4) The Advisory Committee shall adopt its rules of procedure.

(5) The Advisory Committee shall elect a chairperson from among its members for a term of three years. That term shall be renewable.

CHAPTER III – JUDGES OF THE COURT

ARTICLE 15
Eligibility criteria for the appointment of judges

(1) The Court shall comprise both legally qualified judges and technically qualified judges. Judges shall ensure the highest standards of competence and shall have proven experience in the field of patent litigation.

(2) Legally qualified judges shall possess the qualifications required for appointment to judicial offices in a Contracting Member State.

(3) Technically qualified judges shall have a university degree and proven expertise in a field of technology. They shall also have proven knowledge of civil law and procedure relevant in patent litigation.

ARTICLE 16
Appointment procedure

(1) The Advisory Committee shall establish a list of the most suitable candidates to be appointed as judges of the Court, in accordance with the Statute.

(2) On the basis of that list, the Administrative Committee shall appoint the judges of the Court acting by common accord.

(3) The implementing provisions for the appointment of judges are set out in the Statute.

ARTICLE 17
Judicial independence and impartiality

(1) The Court, its judges and the Registrar shall enjoy judicial independence. In the performance of their duties, the judges shall not be bound by any instructions.

(2) Legally qualified judges, as well as technically qualified judges who are full-time judges of the Court, may not engage in any other occupation, whether gainful or not, unless an exception is granted by the Administrative Committee.

(3) Notwithstanding paragraph 2, the exercise of the office of judges shall not exclude the exercise of other judicial functions at national level.

(4) The exercise of the office of technically qualified judges who are part-time judges of the Court shall not exclude the exercise of other functions provided there is no conflict of interest.

(5) In case of a conflict of interest, the judge concerned shall not take part in proceedings. Rules governing conflicts of interest are set out in the Statute.

ARTICLE 18
Pool of Judges

(1) A Pool of Judges shall be established in accordance with the Statute.

(2) The Pool of Judges shall be composed of all legally qualified judges and technically qualified judges from the Court of First Instance who are full-time or part-time judges of the Court. The Pool of Judges shall include at least one technically qualified judge per field of technology with the relevant qualifications and experience. The technically qualified judges from the Pool of Judges shall also be available to the Court of Appeal.

(3) Where so provided by this Agreement or the Statute, the judges from the Pool of Judges shall be allocated to the division concerned by the President of the Court of First Instance. The allocation of judges shall be based on their legal or technical expertise, linguistic skills and relevant experience. The allocation of judges shall guarantee the same high quality of work and the same high level of legal and technical expertise in all panels of the Court of First Instance.

ARTICLE 19
Training framework

(1) A training framework for judges, the details of which are set out in the Statute, shall be set up in order to improve and increase available patent litigation expertise and to ensure a broad geographic distribution of such specific knowledge and experience. The facilities for that framework shall be situated in Budapest.

(2) The training framework shall in particular focus on:

(a) internships in national patent courts or divisions of the Court of First Instance hearing a substantial number of patent litigation cases;
(b) improvement of linguistic skills;
(c) technical aspects of patent law;
(d) the dissemination of knowledge and experience in civil procedure for technically qualified judges;
(e) the preparation of candidate-judges.

(3) The training framework shall provide for continuous training. Regular meetings shall be organised between all judges of the Court in order to discuss developments in patent law and to ensure the consistency of the Court's case law.

CHAPTER IV – THE PRIMACY OF UNION LAW, LIABILITY AND RESPONSIBILITY OF THE CONTRACTING MEMBER STATES

ARTICLE 20
Primacy of and respect for Union law

The Court shall apply Union law in its entirety and shall respect its primacy.

ARTICLE 21
Requests for preliminary rulings

As a court common to the Contracting Member States and as part of their judicial system, the Court shall cooperate with the Court of Justice of the European Union to ensure the correct application and uniform interpretation of Union law, as any national court, in accordance with Article 267 TFEU in particular. Decisions of the Court of Justice of the European Union shall be binding on the Court.

ARTICLE 22
Liability for damage caused by infringements of Union law

(1) The Contracting Member States are jointly and severally liable for damage resulting from an infringement of Union law by the Court of Appeal, in accordance with Union law concerning non-contractual liability of Member States for damage caused by their national courts breaching Union law.

(2) An action for such damages shall be brought against the Contracting Member State where the claimant has its residence or principal place of business or, in the absence of

residence or principal place of business, place of business, before the competent authority of that Contracting Member State. Where the claimant does not have its residence, or principal place of business or, in the absence of residence or principal place of business, place of business in a Contracting Member State, the claimant may bring such an action against the Contracting Member State where the Court of Appeal has its seat, before the competent authority of that Contracting Member State.

The competent authority shall apply the *lex fori*, with the exception of its private international law, to all questions not regulated by Union law or by this Agreement. The claimant shall be entitled to obtain the entire amount of damages awarded by the competent authority from the Contracting Member State against which the action was brought.

(3) The Contracting Member State that has paid damages is entitled to obtain proportional contribution, established in accordance with the method laid down in Article 37(3) and (4), from the other Contracting Member States. The detailed rules governing the Contracting Member States' contribution under this paragraph shall be determined by the Administrative Committee.

ARTICLE 23
Responsibility of the Contracting Member States

Actions of the Court are directly attributable to each Contracting Member State individually, including for the purposes of Articles 258, 259 and 260 TFEU, and to all Contracting Member States collectively.

CHAPTER V – SOURCES OF LAW AND SUBSTANTIVE LAW

ARTICLE 24
Sources of law

(1) In full compliance with Article 20, when hearing a case brought before it under this Agreement, the Court shall base its decisions on:

(a) Union law, including Regulation (EU) No 1257/2012 and Regulation (EU) No 1260/2012[1];
(b) this Agreement;
(c) the EPC;
(d) other international agreements applicable to patents and binding on all the Contracting Member States; and
(e) national law.

(2) To the extent that the Court shall base its decisions on national law, including where relevant the law of non-contracting States, the applicable law shall be determined:

(a) by directly applicable provisions of Union law containing private international law rules, or

---

[1] Council Regulation (EU) No 1260/2012 of 17 December 2012 implementing enhanced cooperation in the area of the creation of unitary patent protection with regard to the applicable translation arrangements (OJEU L 361, 31.12.2012, p. 89) including any subsequent amendments.

(b) in the absence of directly applicable provisions of Union law or where the latter do not apply, by international instruments containing private international law rules; or
(c) in the absence of provisions referred to in points (a) and (b), by national provisions on private international law as determined by the Court.

(3) The law of non-contracting States shall apply when designated by application of the rules referred to in paragraph 2, in particular in relation to Articles 25 to 28, 54, 55, 64, 68 and 72.

ARTICLE 25
Right to prevent the direct use of the invention

A patent shall confer on its proprietor the right to prevent any third party not having the proprietor's consent from the following:

(a) making, offering, placing on the market or using a product which is the subject matter of the patent, or importing or storing the product for those purposes;
(b) using a process which is the subject matter of the patent or, where the third party knows, or should have known, that the use of the process is prohibited without the consent of the patent proprietor, offering the process for use within the territory of the Contracting Member States in which that patent has effect;
(c) offering, placing on the market, using, or importing or storing for those purposes a product obtained directly by a process which is the subject matter of the patent.

ARTICLE 26
Right to prevent the indirect use of the invention

(1) A patent shall confer on its proprietor the right to prevent any third party not having the proprietor's consent from supplying or offering to supply, within the territory of the Contracting Member States in which that patent has effect, any person other than a party entitled to exploit the patented invention, with means, relating to an essential element of that invention, for putting it into effect therein, when the third party knows, or should have known, that those means are suitable and intended for putting that invention into effect.

(2) Paragraph 1 shall not apply when the means are staple commercial products, except where the third party induces the person supplied to perform any of the acts prohibited by Article 25.

(3) Persons performing the acts referred to in Article 27(a) to (e) shall not be considered to be parties entitled to exploit the invention within the meaning of paragraph 1.

ARTICLE 27
Limitations of the effects of a patent

The rights conferred by a patent shall not extend to any of the following:

(a) acts done privately and for non-commercial purposes;
(b) acts done for experimental purposes relating to the subject matter of the patented invention;
(c) the use of biological material for the purpose of breeding, or discovering and developing other plant varieties;

(d) the acts allowed pursuant to Article 13(6) of Directive 2001/82/EC[1] or Article 10(6) of Directive 2001/83/EC[2] in respect of any patent covering the product within the meaning of either of those Directives;
(e) the extemporaneous preparation by a pharmacy, for individual cases, of a medicine in accordance with a medical prescription or acts concerning the medicine so prepared;
(f) the use of the patented invention on board vessels of countries of the International Union for the Protection of Industrial Property (Paris Union) or members of the World Trade Organisation, other than those Contracting Member States in which that patent has effect, in the body of such vessel, in the machinery, tackle, gear and other accessories, when such vessels temporarily or accidentally enter the waters of a Contracting Member State in which that patent has effect, provided that the invention is used there exclusively for the needs of the vessel;
(g) the use of the patented invention in the construction or operation of aircraft or land vehicles or other means of transport of countries of the International Union for the Protection of Industrial Property (Paris Union) or members of the World Trade Organisation, other than those Contracting Member States in which that patent has effect, or of accessories to such aircraft or land vehicles, when these temporarily or accidentally enter the territory of a Contracting Member State in which that patent has effect;
(h) the acts specified in Article 27 of the Convention on International Civil Aviation of 7 December 1944[3], where these acts concern the aircraft of a country party to that Convention other than a Contracting Member State in which that patent has effect;
(i) the use by a farmer of the product of his harvest for propagation or multiplication by him on his own holding, provided that the plant propagating material was sold or otherwise commercialised to the farmer by or with the consent of the patent proprietor for agricultural use. The extent and the conditions for this use correspond to those under Article 14 of Regulation (EC) No. 2100/94[4];
(j) the use by a farmer of protected livestock for an agricultural purpose, provided that the breeding stock or other animal reproductive material were sold or otherwise commercialised to the farmer by or with the consent of the patent proprietor. Such use includes making the animal or other animal reproductive material available for the purposes of pursuing the farmer's agricultural activity, but not the sale thereof within the framework of, or for the purpose of, a commercial reproductive activity;
(k) the acts and the use of the obtained information as allowed under Articles 5 and 6 of Directive 2009/24/EC[5], in particular, by its provisions on decompilation and interoperability; and
(l) the acts allowed pursuant to Article 10 of Directive 98/44/EC[6].

---

[1] Directive 2001/82/EC of the European Parliament and of the Council of 6 November 2001 on the Community code relating to veterinary medicinal products (OJEC L 311, 28.11.2001, p. 1) including any subsequent amendments.
[2] Directive 2001/83/EC of the European Parliament and of the Council of 6 November 2001 on the Community code relating to medicinal products for human use (OJEC L 311, 28.11.2001, p. 67) including any subsequent amendments.
[3] International Civil Aviation Organization (ICAO), 'Chicago Convention', Document 7300/9 (9th edition, 2006).
[4] Council Regulation (EC) No 2100/94 of 27 July 1994 on Community plant variety rights (OJEC L 227, 1.9.1994, p. 1) including any subsequent amendments.
[5] Directive 2009/24/EC of the European Parliament and of the Council of 23 April 2009 on the legal protection of computer programs (OJEU L 111, 05/05/2009, p. 16) including any subsequent amendments.
[6] Directive 98/44/EC of the European Parliament and of the Council of 6 July 1998 on the legal protection of biotechnological inventions (OJEC L 213, 30.7.1998, p. 13) including any subsequent amendments.

ARTICLE 28
Right based on prior use of the invention

Any person, who, if a national patent had been granted in respect of an invention, would have had, in a Contracting Member State, a right based on prior use of that invention or a right of personal possession of that invention, shall enjoy, in that Contracting Member State, the same rights in respect of a patent for the same invention.

ARTICLE 29
Exhaustion of the rights conferred by a European patent

The rights conferred by a European patent shall not extend to acts concerning a product covered by that patent after that product has been placed on the market in the European Union by, or with the consent of, the patent proprietor, unless there are legitimate grounds for the patent proprietor to oppose further commercialisation of the product.

ARTICLE 30
Effects of supplementary protection certificates

A supplementary protection certificate shall confer the same rights as conferred by the patent and shall be subject to the same limitations and the same obligations.

CHAPTER VI – INTERNATIONAL JURISDICTION AND COMPETENCE

ARTICLE 31
International jurisdiction

The international jurisdiction of the Court shall be established in accordance with Regulation (EU) No 1215/2012 or, where applicable, on the basis of the Convention on jurisdiction and the recognition and enforcement of judgments in civil and commercial matters (Lugano Convention)[1].

ARTICLE 32
Competence of the Court

(1) The Court shall have exclusive competence in respect of:

(a) actions for actual or threatened infringements of patents and supplementary protection certificates and related defences, including counterclaims concerning licences;
(b) actions for declarations of non-infringement of patents and supplementary protection certificates;
(c) actions for provisional and protective measures and injunctions;
(d) actions for revocation of patents and for declaration of invalidity of supplementary protection certificates;
(e) counterclaims for revocation of patents and for declaration of invalidity of supplementary protection certificates;

---

[1] Convention on jurisdiction and the recognition and enforcement of judgments in civil and commercial matters, done at Lugano on 30 October 2007, including any subsequent amendments.

(f) actions for damages or compensation derived from the provisional protection conferred by a published European patent application;
(g) actions relating to the use of the invention prior to the granting of the patent or to the right based on prior use of the invention;
(h) actions for compensation for licences on the basis of Article 8 of Regulation (EU) No 1257/2012; and
(i) actions concerning decisions of the European Patent Office in carrying out the tasks referred to in Article 9 of Regulation (EU) No 1257/2012.

(2) The national courts of the Contracting Member States shall remain competent for actions relating to patents and supplementary protection certificates which do not come within the exclusive competence of the Court.

ARTICLE 33
Competence of the divisions of the Court of First Instance

(1) Without prejudice to paragraph 7 of this Article, actions referred to in Article 32(1)(a), (c), (f) and (g) shall be brought before:

(a) the local division hosted by the Contracting Member State where the actual or threatened infringement has occurred or may occur, or the regional division in which that Contracting Member State participates; or

(b) the local division hosted by the Contracting Member State where the defendant or, in the case of multiple defendants, one of the defendants has its residence, or principal place of business, or in the absence of residence or principal place of business, its place of business, or the regional division in which that Contracting Member State participates. An action may be brought against multiple defendants only where the defendants have a commercial relationship and where the action relates to the same alleged infringement.

Actions referred to in Article 32(1)(h) shall be brought before the local or regional division in accordance with point (b) of the first subparagraph.

Actions against defendants having their residence, or principal place of business or, in the absence of residence or principal place of business, their place of business, outside the territory of the Contracting Member States shall be brought before the local or regional division in accordance with point (a) of the first subparagraph or before the central division.

If the Contracting Member State concerned does not host a local division and does not participate in a regional division, actions shall be brought before the central division.

(2) If an action referred to in Article 32(1)(a), (c), (f), (g) or (h) is pending before a division of the Court of First Instance, any action referred to in Article 32(1)(a), (c), (f), (g) or (h) between the same parties on the same patent may not be brought before any other division.

If an action referred to in Article 32(1)(a) is pending before a regional division and the infringement has occurred in the territories of three or more regional divisions, the regional division concerned shall, at the request of the defendant, refer the case to the central division.

In case an action between the same parties on the same patent is brought before several different divisions, the division first seized shall be competent for the whole case and any division seized later shall declare the action inadmissible in accordance with the Rules of Procedure.

(3) A counterclaim for revocation as referred to in Article 32(1)(e) may be brought in the case of an action for infringement as referred to in Article 32(1)(a). The local or regional division concerned shall, after having heard the parties, have the discretion either to:

(a) proceed with both the action for infringement and with the counterclaim for revocation and request the President of the Court of First Instance to allocate from the Pool of Judges in accordance with Article 18(3) a technically qualified judge with qualifications and experience in the field of technology concerned.
(b) refer the counterclaim for revocation for decision to the central division and suspend or proceed with the action for infringement; or
(c) with the agreement of the parties, refer the case for decision to the central division.

(4) Actions referred to in Article 32(1)(b) and (d) shall be brought before the central division. If, however, an action for infringement as referred to in Article 32(1)(a) between the same parties relating to the same patent has been brought before a local or a regional division, these actions may only be brought before the same local or regional division.

(5) If an action for revocation as referred to in Article 32(1)(d) is pending before the central division, an action for infringement as referred to in Article 32(1)(a) between the same parties relating to the same patent may be brought before any division in accordance with paragraph 1 of this Article or before the central division. The local or regional division concerned shall have the discretion to proceed in accordance with paragraph 3 of this Article.

(6) An action for declaration of non-infringement as referred to in Article 32(1)(b) pending before the central division shall be stayed once an infringement action as referred to in Article 32(1)(a) between the same parties or between the holder of an exclusive licence and the party requesting a declaration of non-infringement relating to the same patent is brought before a local or regional division within three months of the date on which the action was initiated before the central division.

(7) Parties may agree to bring actions referred to in Article 32(1)(a) to (h) before the division of their choice, including the central division.

(8) Actions referred to in Article 32(1)(d) and (e) can be brought without the applicant having to file notice of opposition with the European Patent Office.

(9) Actions referred to in Article 32(1)(i) shall be brought before the central division.

(10) A party shall inform the Court of any pending revocation, limitation or opposition proceedings before the European Patent Office, and of any request for accelerated processing before the European Patent Office. The Court may stay its proceedings when a rapid decision may be expected from the European Patent Office.

ARTICLE 34
Territorial scope of decisions

Decisions of the Court shall cover, in the case of a European patent, the territory of those Contracting Member States for which the European patent has effect.

CHAPTER VII – PATENT MEDIATION AND ARBITRATION

ARTICLE 35
Patent mediation and arbitration centre

(1) A patent mediation and arbitration centre ('the Centre') is hereby established. It shall have its seats in Ljubljana and Lisbon.

(2) The Centre shall provide facilities for mediation and arbitration of patent disputes falling within the scope of this Agreement. Article 82 shall apply mutatis mutandis to any settlement reached through the use of the facilities of the Centre, including through mediation. However, a patent may not be revoked or limited in mediation or arbitration proceedings.

(3) The Centre shall establish Mediation and Arbitration Rules.

(4) The Centre shall draw up a list of mediators and arbitrators to assist the parties in the settlement of their dispute.

PART II – FINANCIAL PROVISIONS

ARTICLE 36
Budget of the Court

(1) The budget of the Court shall be financed by the Court's own financial revenues and, at least in the transitional period referred to in Article 83 as necessary, by contributions from the Contracting Member States. The budget shall be balanced.

(2) The Court's own financial revenues shall comprise court fees and other revenues.

(3) Court fees shall be fixed by the Administrative Committee. They shall consist of a fixed fee, combined with a value-based fee above a pre-defined ceiling. The Court fees shall be fixed at such a level as to ensure a right balance between the principle of fair access to justice, in particular for small and medium-sized enterprises, micro-entities, natural persons, non-profit organisations, universities and public research organisations and an adequate contribution of the parties for the costs incurred by the Court, recognising the economic benefits to the parties involved, and the objective of a self-financing Court with balanced finances. The level of the Court fees shall be reviewed periodically by the Administrative Committee. Targeted support measures for small and medium-sized enterprises and micro entities may be considered.

(4) If the Court is unable to balance its budget out of its own resources, the Contracting Member States shall remit to it special financial contributions.

ARTICLE 37
Financing of the Court

(1) The operating costs of the Court shall be covered by the budget of the Court, in accordance with the Statute.

Contracting Member States setting up a local division shall provide the facilities necessary for that purpose. Contracting Member States sharing a regional division shall provide jointly the facilities necessary for that purpose. Contracting Member States hosting the central division, its sections or the Court of Appeal shall provide the facilities necessary for that purpose. During an initial transitional period of seven years starting from the date of the entry into force of this Agreement, the Contracting Member States concerned shall also provide administrative support staff, without prejudice to the Statute of that staff.

(2) On the date of entry into force of this Agreement, the Contracting Member States shall provide the initial financial contributions necessary for the setting up of the Court.

(3) During the initial transitional period of seven years, starting from the date of the entry into force of this Agreement, the contribution by each Contracting Member State having ratified or acceded to the Agreement before the entry into force thereof shall be calculated on the basis of the number of European patents having effect in the territory of that State on the date of entry into force of this Agreement and the number of European patents with respect to which actions for infringement or for revocation have been brought before the national courts of that State in the three years preceding entry into force of this Agreement.

During the same initial transitional period of seven years, for Member States which ratify, or accede to, this Agreement after the entry into force thereof, the contributions shall be calculated on the basis of the number of European patents having effect in the territory of the ratifying or acceding Member State on the date of the ratification or accession and the number of European patents with respect to which actions for infringement or for revocation have been brought before the national courts of the ratifying or acceding Member State in the three years preceding the ratification or accession.

(4) After the end of the initial transitional period of seven years, by which the Court is expected to have become self-financing, should contributions by the Contracting Member States become necessary, they shall be determined in accordance with the scale for the distribution of annual renewal fees for European patents with unitary effect applicable at the time the contribution becomes necessary.

ARTICLE 38
Financing of the training framework for judges

The training framework for judges shall be financed by the budget of the Court.

ARTICLE 39
Financing of the Centre

The operating costs of the Centre shall be financed by the budget of the Court.

PART III – ORGANISATION AND PROCEDURAL PROVISIONS

CHAPTER I – GENERAL PROVISIONS

ARTICLE 40
Statute

(1) The Statute shall lay down the details of the organisation and functioning of the Court.

(2) The Statute is annexed to this Agreement. The Statute may be amended by decision of the Administrative Committee, on the basis of a proposal of the Court or a proposal of a Contracting Member State after consultation with the Court. However, such amendments shall not contradict or alter this Agreement.

(3) The Statute shall guarantee that the functioning of the Court is organised in the most efficient and cost-effective manner and shall ensure equitable access to justice.

ARTICLE 41
Rules of Procedure

(1) The Rules of Procedure shall lay down the details of the proceedings before the Court. They shall comply with this Agreement and the Statute.

(2) The Rules of Procedure shall be adopted by the Administrative Committee on the basis of broad consultations with stakeholders. The prior opinion of the European Commission on the compatibility of the Rules of Procedure with Union law shall be requested. The Rules of Procedure may be amended by a decision of the Administrative Committee, on the basis of a proposal from the Court and after consultation with the European Commission. However, such amendments shall not contradict or alter this Agreement or the Statute.

(3) The Rules of Procedure shall guarantee that the decisions of the Court are of the highest quality and that proceedings are organised in the most efficient and cost effective manner. They shall ensure a fair balance between the legitimate interests of all parties. They shall provide for the required level of discretion of judges without impairing the predictability of proceedings for the parties.

ARTICLE 42
Proportionality and fairness

(1) The Court shall deal with litigation in ways which are proportionate to the importance and complexity thereof.

(2) The Court shall ensure that the rules, procedures and remedies provided for in this Agreement and in the Statute are used in a fair and equitable manner and do not distort competition.

ARTICLE 43
Case management

The Court shall actively manage the cases before it in accordance with the Rules of Procedure without impairing the freedom of the parties to determine the subject-matter of, and the supporting evidence for, their case.

ARTICLE 44
Electronic procedures

The Court shall make best use of electronic procedures, such as the electronic filing of submissions of the parties and stating of evidence in electronic form, as well as video conferencing, in accordance with the Rules of Procedure.

ARTICLE 45
Public proceedings

The proceedings shall be open to the public unless the Court decides to make them confidential, to the extent necessary, in the interest of one of the parties or other affected persons, or in the general interest of justice or public order.

ARTICLE 46
Legal capacity

Any natural or legal person, or any body equivalent to a legal person entitled to initiate proceedings in accordance with its national law, shall have the capacity to be a party to the proceedings before the Court.

ARTICLE 47
Parties

(1) The patent proprietor shall be entitled to bring actions before the Court.

(2) Unless the licensing agreement provides otherwise, the holder of an exclusive licence in respect of a patent shall be entitled to bring actions before the Court under the same circumstances as the patent proprietor, provided that the patent proprietor is given prior notice.

(3) The holder of a non-exclusive licence shall not be entitled to bring actions before the Court, unless the patent proprietor is given prior notice and in so far as expressly permitted by the licence agreement.

(4) In actions brought by a licence holder, the patent proprietor shall be entitled to join the action before the Court.

(5) The validity of a patent cannot be contested in an action for infringement brought by the holder of a licence where the patent proprietor does not take part in the proceedings. The party in an action for infringement wanting to contest the validity of a patent shall have to bring actions against the patent proprietor.

(6) Any other natural or legal person, or any body entitled to bring actions in accordance with its national law, who is concerned by a patent, may bring actions in accordance with the Rules of Procedure.

(7) Any natural or legal person, or any body entitled to bring actions in accordance with its national law and who is affected by a decision of the European Patent Office in carrying out the tasks referred to in Article 9 of Regulation (EU) No 1257/2012 is entitled to bring actions under Article 32(1)(i).

ARTICLE 48
Representation

(1) Parties shall be represented by lawyers authorised to practise before a court of a Contracting Member State.

(2) Parties may alternatively be represented by European Patent Attorneys who are entitled to act as professional representatives before the European Patent Office pursuant to Article 134 of the EPC and who have appropriate qualifications such as a European Patent Litigation Certificate.

(3) The requirements for qualifications pursuant to paragraph 2 shall be established by the Administrative Committee. A list of European Patent Attorneys entitled to represent parties before the Court shall be kept by the Registrar.

(4) Representatives of the parties may be assisted by patent attorneys, who shall be allowed to speak at hearings of the Court in accordance with the Rules of Procedure.

(5) Representatives of the parties shall enjoy the rights and immunities necessary for the independent exercise of their duties, including the privilege from disclosure in proceedings before the Court in respect of communications between a representative and the party or any other person, under the conditions laid down in the Rules of Procedure, unless such privilege is expressly waived by the party concerned.

(6) Representatives of the parties shall be obliged not to misrepresent cases or facts before the Court either knowingly or with good reasons to know.

(7) Representation in accordance with paragraphs 1 and 2 of this Article shall not be required in proceedings under Article 32(1)(i).

CHAPTER II – LANGUAGE OF PROCEEDINGS

ARTICLE 49
Language of proceedings at the Court of First Instance

(1) The language of proceedings before any local or regional division shall be an official European Union language which is the official language or one of the official languages of the Contracting Member State hosting the relevant division, or the official language(s) designated by Contracting Member States sharing a regional division.

(2) Notwithstanding paragraph 1, Contracting Member States may designate one or more of the official languages of the European Patent Office as the language of proceedings of their local or regional division.

(3) The parties may agree on the use of the language in which the patent was granted as the language of proceedings, subject to approval by the competent panel. If the panel does not approve their choice, the parties may request that the case be referred to the central division.

(4) With the agreement of the parties the competent panel may, on grounds of convenience and fairness, decide on the use of the language in which the patent was granted as the language of proceedings.

(5) At the request of one of the parties and after having heard the other parties and the competent panel, the President of the Court of First Instance may, on grounds of fairness and taking into account all relevant circumstances, including the position of parties, in particular the position of the defendant, decide on the use of the language in which the patent was granted as language of proceedings. In this case the President of the Court of First Instance shall assess the need for specific translation and interpretation arrangements.

(6) The language of proceedings at the central division shall be the language in which the patent concerned was granted.

ARTICLE 50
Language of proceedings at the Court of Appeal

(1) The language of proceedings before the Court of Appeal shall be the language of proceedings before the Court of First Instance.

(2) Notwithstanding paragraph 1 the parties may agree on the use of the language in which the patent was granted as the language of proceedings.

(3) In exceptional cases and to the extent deemed appropriate, the Court of Appeal may decide on another official language of a Contracting Member State as the language of proceedings for the whole or part of the proceedings, subject to agreement by the parties.

ARTICLE 51
Other language arrangements

(1) Any panel of the Court of First Instance and the Court of Appeal may, to the extent deemed appropriate, dispense with translation requirements.

(2) At the request of one of the parties, and to the extent deemed appropriate, any division of the Court of First Instance and the Court of Appeal shall provide interpretation facilities to assist the parties concerned at oral proceedings.

(3) Notwithstanding Article 49(6), in cases where an action for infringement is brought before the central division, a defendant having its residence, principal place of business or place of business in a Member State shall have the right to obtain, upon request, translations of relevant documents in the language of the Member State of residence, principal place of business or, in the absence of residence or principal place of business, place of business, in the following circumstances:

(a) jurisdiction is entrusted to the central division in accordance with Article 33(1) third or fourth subparagraph, and
(b) the language of proceedings at the central division is a language which is not an official language of the Member State where the defendant has its residence, principal place of business or, in the absence of residence or principal place of business, place of business, and
(c) the defendant does not have proper knowledge of the language of the proceedings.

CHAPTER III – PROCEEDINGS BEFORE THE COURT

ARTICLE 52
Written, interim and oral procedures

(1) The proceedings before the Court shall consist of a written, an interim and an oral procedure, in accordance with the Rules of Procedure. All procedures shall be organized in a flexible and balanced manner.

(2) In the interim procedure, after the written procedure and if appropriate, the judge acting as Rapporteur, subject to a mandate of the full panel, shall be responsible for convening an interim hearing. That judge shall in particular explore with the parties the possibility for a settlement, including through mediation, and/or arbitration, by using the facilities of the Centre referred to in Article 35.

(3) The oral procedure shall give parties the opportunity to explain properly their arguments. The Court may, with the agreement of the parties, dispense with the oral hearing.

ARTICLE 53
Means of evidence

(1) In proceedings before the Court, the means of giving or obtaining evidence shall include in particular the following:

(a) hearing the parties;
(b) requests for information;
(c) production of documents;
(d) hearing witnesses;
(e) opinions by experts;
(f) inspection;
(g) comparative tests or experiments;
(h) sworn statements in writing (affidavits).

(2) The Rules of Procedure shall govern the procedure for taking such evidence. Questioning of witnesses and experts shall be under the control of the Court and be limited to what is necessary.

ARTICLE 54
Burden of proof

Without prejudice to Article 24(2) and (3), the burden of the proof of facts shall be on the party relying on those facts.

ARTICLE 55
Reversal of burden of proof

(1) Without prejudice to Article 24(2) and (3), if the subject-matter of a patent is a process for obtaining a new product, the identical product when produced without the consent of

the patent proprietor shall, in the absence of proof to the contrary, be deemed to have been obtained by the patented process.

(2) The principle set out in paragraph 1 shall also apply where there is a substantial likelihood that the identical product was made by the patented process and the patent proprietor has been unable, despite reasonable efforts, to determine the process actually used for such identical product.

(3) In the adduction of proof to the contrary, the legitimate interests of the defendant in protecting its manufacturing and trade secrets shall be taken into account.

CHAPTER IV – POWERS OF THE COURT

ARTICLE 56
The general powers of the Court

(1) The Court may impose such measures, procedures and remedies as are laid down in this Agreement and may make its orders subject to conditions, in accordance with the Rules of Procedure.

(2) The Court shall take due account of the interest of the parties and shall, before making an order, give any party the opportunity to be heard, unless this is incompatible with the effective enforcement of such order.

ARTICLE 57
Court experts

(1) Without prejudice to the possibility for the parties to produce expert evidence, the Court may at any time appoint court experts in order to provide expertise for specific aspects of the case. The Court shall provide such expert with all information necessary for the provision of the expert advice.

(2) To this end, an indicative list of experts shall be drawn up by the Court in accordance with the Rules of Procedure. That list shall be kept by the Registrar.

(3) The court experts shall guarantee independence and impartiality. Rules governing conflicts of interest applicable to judges set out in Article 7 of the Statute shall by analogy apply to court experts.

(4) Expert advice given to the Court by court experts shall be made available to the parties which shall have the possibility to comment on it.

ARTICLE 58
Protection of confidential information

To protect the trade secrets, personal data or other confidential information of a party to the proceedings or of a third party, or to prevent an abuse of evidence, the Court may order that the collection and use of evidence in proceedings before it be restricted or prohibited or that access to such evidence be restricted to specific persons.

ARTICLE 59
Order to produce evidence

(1) At the request of a party which has presented reasonably available evidence sufficient to support its claims and has, in substantiating those claims, specified evidence which lies in the control of the opposing party or a third party, the Court may order the opposing party or a third party to present such evidence, subject to the protection of confidential information. Such order shall not result in an obligation of self-incrimination.

(2) At the request of a party the Court may order, under the same conditions as specified in paragraph 1, the communication of banking, financial or commercial documents under the control of the opposing party, subject to the protection of confidential information.

ARTICLE 60
Order to preserve evidence and to inspect premises

(1) At the request of the applicant which has presented reasonably available evidence to support the claim that the patent has been infringed or is about to be infringed the Court may, even before the commencement of proceedings on the merits of the case, order prompt and effective provisional measures to preserve relevant evidence in respect of the alleged infringement, subject to the protection of confidential information.

(2) Such measures may include the detailed description, with or without the taking of samples, or the physical seizure of the infringing products, and, in appropriate cases, the materials and implements used in the production and/or distribution of those products and the documents relating thereto.

(3) The Court may, even before the commencement of proceedings on the merits of the case, at the request of the applicant who has presented evidence to support the claim that the patent has been infringed or is about to be infringed, order the inspection of premises. Such inspection of premises shall be conducted by a person appointed by the Court in accordance with the Rules of Procedure.

(4) At the inspection of the premises the applicant shall not be present itself but may be represented by an independent professional practitioner whose name has to be specified in the Court's order.

(5) Measures shall be ordered, if necessary without the other party having been heard, in particular where any delay is likely to cause irreparable harm to the proprietor of the patent, or where there is a demonstrable risk of evidence being destroyed.

(6) Where measures to preserve evidence or inspect premises are ordered without the other party in the case having been heard, the parties affected shall be given notice, without delay and at the latest immediately after the execution of the measures. A review, including a right to be heard, shall take place upon request of the parties affected with a view to deciding, within a reasonable period after the notification of the measures, whether the measures are to be modified, revoked or confirmed.

(7) The measures to preserve evidence may be subject to the lodging by the applicant of adequate security or an equivalent assurance intended to ensure compensation for any prejudice suffered by the defendant as provided for in paragraph 9.

(8) The Court shall ensure that the measures to preserve evidence are revoked or otherwise cease to have effect, at the defendant's request, without prejudice to the damages which may be claimed, if the applicant does not bring, within a period not exceeding 31 calendar days or 20 working days, whichever is the longer, action leading to a decision on the merits of the case before the Court.

(9) Where the measures to preserve evidence are revoked, or where they lapse due to any act or omission by the applicant, or where it is subsequently found that there has been no infringement or threat of infringement of the patent, the Court may order the applicant, at the defendant's request, to provide the defendant with appropriate compensation for any damage suffered as a result of those measures.

ARTICLE 61
Freezing orders

(1) At the request of the applicant which has presented reasonably available evidence to support the claim that the patent has been infringed or is about to be infringed the Court may, even before the commencement of proceedings on the merits of the case, order a party not to remove from its jurisdiction any assets located therein, or not to deal in any assets, whether located within its jurisdiction or not.

(2) Article 60(5) to (9) shall apply by analogy to the measures referred to in this Article.

ARTICLE 62
Provisional and protective measures

(1) The Court may, by way of order, grant injunctions against an alleged infringer or against an intermediary whose services are used by the alleged infringer, intended to prevent any imminent infringement, to prohibit, on a provisional basis and subject, where appropriate, to a recurring penalty payment, the continuation of the alleged infringement or to make such continuation subject to the lodging of guarantees intended to ensure the compensation of the right holder.

(2) The Court shall have the discretion to weigh up the interests of the parties and in particular to take into account the potential harm for either of the parties resulting from the granting or the refusal of the injunction.

(3) The Court may also order the seizure or delivery up of the products suspected of infringing a patent so as to prevent their entry into, or movement, within the channels of commerce. If the applicant demonstrates circumstances likely to endanger the recovery of damages, the Court may order the precautionary seizure of the movable and immovable property of the alleged infringer, including the blocking of the bank accounts and of other assets of the alleged infringer.

(4) The Court may, in respect of the measures referred to in paragraphs 1 and 3, require the applicant to provide any reasonable evidence in order to satisfy itself with a sufficient degree of certainty that the applicant is the right holder and that the applicant's right is being infringed, or that such infringement is imminent.

(5) Article 60(5) to (9) shall apply by analogy to the measures referred to in this Article.

ARTICLE 63
Permanent injunctions

(1) Where a decision is taken finding an infringement of a patent, the Court may grant an injunction against the infringer aimed at prohibiting the continuation of the infringement. The Court may also grant such injunction against an intermediary whose services are being used by a third party to infringe a patent.

(2) Where appropriate, non-compliance with the injunction referred to in paragraph 1 shall be subject to a recurring penalty payment payable to the Court.

ARTICLE 64
Corrective measures in infringement proceedings

(1) Without prejudice to any damages due to the injured party by reason of the infringement, and without compensation of any sort, the Court may order, at the request of the applicant, that appropriate measures be taken with regard to products found to be infringing a patent and, in appropriate cases, with regard to materials and implements principally used in the creation or manufacture of those products.

(2) Such measures shall include:

(a) a declaration of infringement;
(b) recalling the products from the channels of commerce;
(c) depriving the product of its infringing property;
(d) definitively removing the products from the channels of commerce; or
(e) the destruction of the products and/or of the materials and implements concerned.

(3) The Court shall order that those measures be carried out at the expense of the infringer, unless particular reasons are invoked for not doing so.

(4) In considering a request for corrective measures pursuant to this Article, the Court shall take into account the need for proportionality between the seriousness of the infringement and the remedies to be ordered, the willingness of the infringer to convert the materials into a non-infringing state, as well as the interests of third parties.

ARTICLE 65
Decision on the validity of a patent

(1) The Court shall decide on the validity of a patent on the basis of an action for revocation or a counterclaim for revocation.

(2) The Court may revoke a patent, either entirely or partly, only on the grounds referred to in Articles 138(1) and 139(2) of the EPC.

(3) Without prejudice to Article 138(3) of the EPC, if the grounds for revocation affect the patent only in part, the patent shall be limited by a corresponding amendment of the claims and revoked in part.

(4) To the extent that a patent has been revoked it shall be deemed not to have had, from the outset, the effects specified in Articles 64 and 67 of the EPC.

(5) Where the Court, in a final decision, revokes a patent, either entirely or partly, it shall send a copy of the decision to the European Patent Office and, with respect to a European patent, to the national patent office of any Contracting Member State concerned.

ARTICLE 66
Powers of the Court concerning decisions of the European Patent Office

(1) In actions brought under Article 32(1)(i), the Court may exercise any power entrusted on the European Patent Office in accordance with Article 9 of Regulation (EU) No 1257/2012, including the rectification of the Register for unitary patent protection.

(2) In actions brought under Article 32(1)(i) the parties shall, by way of derogation from Article 69, bear their own costs.

ARTICLE 67
Power to order the communication of information

(1) The Court may, in response to a justified and proportionate request of the applicant and in accordance with the Rules of Procedure, order an infringer to inform the applicant of:

(a) the origin and distribution channels of the infringing products or processes;
(b) the quantities produced, manufactured, delivered, received or ordered, as well as the price obtained for the infringing products; and
(c) the identity of any third person involved in the production or distribution of the infringing products or in the use of the infringing process.

(2) The Court may, in accordance with the Rules of Procedure, also order any third party who:

(a) was found in the possession of the infringing products on a commercial scale or to be using an infringing process on a commercial scale;
(b) was found to be providing on a commercial scale services used in infringing activities; or
(c) was indicated by the person referred to in points (a) or (b) as being involved in the production, manufacture or distribution of the infringing products or processes or in the provision of the services, to provide the applicant with the information referred to in paragraph 1.

ARTICLE 68
Award of damages

(1) The Court shall, at the request of the injured party, order the infringer who knowingly, or with reasonable grounds to know, engaged in a patent infringing activity, to pay the injured party damages appropriate to the harm actually suffered by that party as a result of the infringement.

(2) The injured party shall, to the extent possible, be placed in the position it would have been in if no infringement had taken place. The infringer shall not benefit from the infringement. However, damages shall not be punitive.

(3) When the Court sets the damages:

(a) it shall take into account all appropriate aspects, such as the negative economic consequences, including lost profits, which the injured party has suffered, any unfair profits made by the infringer and, in appropriate cases, elements other than economic factors, such as the moral prejudice caused to the injured party by the infringement; or

(b) as an alternative to point (a), it may, in appropriate cases, set the damages as a lump sum on the basis of elements such as at least the amount of the royalties or fees which would have been due if the infringer had requested authorisation to use the patent in question.

(4) Where the infringer did not knowingly, or with reasonable grounds to know, engage in the infringing activity, the Court may order the recovery of profits or the payment of compensation.

ARTICLE 69
Legal costs

(1) Reasonable and proportionate legal costs and other expenses incurred by the successful party shall, as a general rule, be borne by the unsuccessful party, unless equity requires otherwise, up to a ceiling set in accordance with the Rules of Procedure.

(2) Where a party succeeds only in part or in exceptional circumstances, the Court may order that costs be apportioned equitably or that the parties bear their own costs.

(3) A party should bear any unnecessary costs it has caused the Court or another party.

(4) At the request of the defendant, the Court may order the applicant to provide adequate security for the legal costs and other expenses incurred by the defendant which the applicant may be liable to bear, in particular in the cases referred to in Articles 59 to 62.

ARTICLE 70
Court fees

(1) Parties to proceedings before the Court shall pay court fees.

(2) Court fees shall be paid in advance, unless the Rules of Procedure provide otherwise. Any party which has not paid a prescribed court fee may be excluded from further participation in the proceedings.

ARTICLE 71
Legal aid

(1) A party who is a natural person and who is unable to meet the costs of the proceedings, either wholly or in part, may at any time apply for legal aid. The conditions for granting of legal aid shall be laid down in the Rules of Procedure.

(2) The Court shall decide whether legal aid should be granted in full or in part, or whether it should be refused, in accordance with the Rules of Procedure.

(3) On a proposal from the Court, the Administrative Committee shall set the level of legal aid and the rules on bearing the costs thereof.

ARTICLE 72
Period of limitation

Without prejudice to Article 24(2) and (3), actions relating to all forms of financial compensation may not be brought more than five years after the date on which the applicant became aware, or had reasonable grounds to become aware, of the last fact justifying the action.

CHAPTER V – APPEALS

ARTICLE 73
Appeal

(1) An appeal against a decision of the Court of First Instance may be brought before the Court of Appeal by any party which has been unsuccessful, in whole or in part, in its submissions, within two months of the date of the notification of the decision.

(2) An appeal against an order of the Court of First Instance may be brought before the Court of Appeal by any party which has been unsuccessful, in whole or in part, in its submissions:

(a) for the orders referred to in Articles 49(5), 59 to 62 and 67 within 15 calendar days of the notification of the order to the applicant;
(b) for other orders than the orders referred to in point (a):
   (i) together with the appeal against the decision, or
   (ii) where the Court grants leave to appeal, within 15 days of the notification of the Court's decision to that effect.

(3) The appeal against a decision or an order of the Court of First Instance may be based on points of law and matters of fact.

(4) New facts and new evidence may only be introduced in accordance with the Rules of Procedure and where the submission thereof by the party concerned could not reasonably have been expected during proceedings before the Court of First Instance.

ARTICLE 74
Effects of an appeal

(1) An appeal shall not have suspensive effect unless the Court of Appeal decides otherwise at the motivated request of one of the parties. The Rules of Procedure shall guarantee that such a decision is taken without delay.

(2) Notwithstanding paragraph 1, an appeal against a decision on actions or counterclaims for revocation and on actions based on Article 32(1)(i) shall always have suspensive effect.

(3) An appeal against an order referred to in Articles 49(5), 59 to 62 or 67 shall not prevent the continuation of the main proceedings. However, the Court of First Instance shall not give a decision in the main proceedings before the decision of the Court of Appeal concerning an appealed order has been given.

ARTICLE 75
Decision on appeal and referral back

(1) If an appeal pursuant to Article 73 is well-founded, the Court of Appeal shall revoke the decision of the Court of First Instance and give a final decision. The Court of Appeal may in exceptional cases and in accordance with the Rules of Procedure refer the case back to the Court of First Instance for decision.

(2) Where a case is referred back to the Court of First Instance pursuant to paragraph 1, the Court of First Instance shall be bound by the decision of the Court of Appeal on points of law.

CHAPTER VI – DECISIONS

ARTICLE 76
Basis for decisions and right to be heard

(1) The Court shall decide in accordance with the requests submitted by the parties and shall not award more than is requested.

(2) Decisions on the merits may only be based on grounds, facts and evidence, which were submitted by the parties or introduced into the procedure by an order of the Court and on which the parties have had an opportunity to present their comments.

(3) The Court shall evaluate evidence freely and independently.

ARTICLE 77
Formal requirements

(1) Decisions and orders of the Court shall be reasoned and shall be given in writing in accordance with the Rules of Procedure.

(2) Decisions and orders of the Court shall be delivered in the language of proceedings.

ARTICLE 78
Decisions of the Court and dissenting opinions

(1) Decisions and orders of the Court shall be taken by a majority of the panel, in accordance with the Statute. In case of equal votes, the vote of the presiding judge shall prevail.

(2) In exceptional circumstances, any judge of the panel may express a dissenting opinion separately from the decision of the Court.

ARTICLE 79
Settlement

The parties may, at any time in the course of proceedings, conclude their case by way of settlement, which shall be confirmed by a decision of the Court. A patent may not be revoked or limited by way of settlement.

ARTICLE 80
Publication of decisions

The Court may order, at the request of the applicant and at the expense of the infringer, appropriate measures for the dissemination of information concerning the Court's decision, including displaying the decision and publishing it in full or in part in public media.

ARTICLE 81
Rehearing

(1) A request for rehearing after a final decision of the Court may exceptionally be granted by the Court of Appeal in the following circumstances:

(a) on discovery of a fact by the party requesting the rehearing, which is of such a nature as to be a decisive factor and which, when the decision was given, was unknown to the party requesting the rehearing; such request may only be granted on the basis of an act which was held, by a final decision of a national court, to constitute a criminal offence; or

(b) in the event of a fundamental procedural defect, in particular when a defendant who did not appear before the Court was not served with the document initiating the proceedings or an equivalent document in sufficient time and in such a way as to enable him to arrange for the defence.

(2) A request for a rehearing shall be filed within 10 years of the date of the decision but not later than two months from the date of the discovery of the new fact or of the procedural defect. Such request shall not have suspensive effect unless the Court of Appeal decides otherwise.

(3) If the request for a rehearing is well-founded, the Court of Appeal shall set aside, in whole or in part, the decision under review and re-open the proceedings for a new trial and decision, in accordance with the Rules of Procedure.

(4) Persons using patents which are the subject-matter of a decision under review and who act in good faith should be allowed to continue using such patents.

ARTICLE 82
Enforcement of decisions and orders

(1) Decisions and orders of the Court shall be enforceable in any Contracting Member State. An order for the enforcement of a decision shall be appended to the decision by the Court.

(2) Where appropriate, the enforcement of a decision may be subject to the provision of security or an equivalent assurance to ensure compensation for any damage suffered, in particular in the case of injunctions.

(3) Without prejudice to this Agreement and the Statute, enforcement procedures shall be governed by the law of the Contracting Member State where the enforcement takes place. Any decision of the Court shall be enforced under the same conditions as a decision given in the Contracting Member State where the enforcement takes place.

(4) If a party does not comply with the terms of an order of the Court, that party may be sanctioned with a recurring penalty payment payable to the Court. The individual penalty

shall be proportionate to the importance of the order to be enforced and shall be without prejudice to the party's right to claim damages or security.

PART IV – TRANSITIONAL PROVISIONS

ARTICLE 83
Transitional regime

(1) During a transitional period of seven years after the date of entry into force of this Agreement, an action for infringement or for revocation of a European patent or an action for infringement or for declaration of invalidity of a supplementary protection certificate issued for a product protected by a European patent may still be brought before national courts or other competent national authorities.

(2) An action pending before a national court at the end of the transitional period shall not be affected by the expiry of this period.

(3) Unless an action has already been brought before the Court, a proprietor of or an applicant for a European patent granted or applied for prior to the end of the transitional period under paragraph 1 and, where applicable, paragraph 5, as well as a holder of a supplementary protection certificate issued for a product protected by a European patent, shall have the possibility to opt out from the exclusive competence of the Court. To this end they shall notify their opt-out to the Registry by the latest one month before expiry of the transitional period. The opt-out shall take effect upon its entry into the register.

(4) Unless an action has already been brought before a national court, proprietors of or applicants for European patents or holders of supplementary protection certificates issued for a product protected by a European patent who made use of the opt-out in accordance with paragraph 3 shall be entitled to withdraw their opt-out at any moment. In this event they shall notify the Registry accordingly. The withdrawal of the opt-out shall take effect upon its entry into the register.

(5) Five years after the entry into force of this Agreement, the Administrative Committee shall carry out a broad consultation with the users of the patent system and a survey on the number of European patents and supplementary protection certificates issued for products protected by European patents with respect to which actions for infringement or for revocation or declaration of invalidity are still brought before the national courts pursuant to paragraph 1, the reasons for this and the implications thereof. On the basis of this consultation and an opinion of the Court, the Administrative Committee may decide to prolong the transitional period by up to seven years.

PART V – FINAL PROVISIONS

ARTICLE 84
Signature, ratification and accession

(1) This Agreement shall be open for signature by any Member State on 19 February 2013.

(2) This Agreement shall be subject to ratification in accordance with the respective constitutional requirements of the Member States. Instruments of ratification shall be deposited with the General Secretariat of the Council of the European Union (hereinafter referred to as 'the depositary').

(3) Each Member State having signed this Agreement shall notify the European Commission of its ratification of the Agreement at the time of the deposit of its ratification instrument pursuant to Article 18(3) of Regulation (EU) No 1257/2012.

(4) This Agreement shall be open to accession by any Member State. Instruments of accession shall be deposited with the depositary.

ARTICLE 85
Functions of the depositary

(1) The depositary shall draw up certified true copies of this Agreement and shall transmit them to the governments of all signatory or acceding Member States.

(2) The depositary shall notify the governments of the signatory or acceding Member States of:

(a) any signature;
(b) the deposit of any instrument of ratification or accession;
(c) the date of entry into force of this Agreement.

(3) The depositary shall register this Agreement with the Secretariat of the United Nations.

ARTICLE 86
Duration of the Agreement

This Agreement shall be of unlimited duration.

ARTICLE 87
Revision

(1) Either seven years after the entry into force of this Agreement or once 2000 infringement cases have been decided by the Court, whichever is the later point in time, and if necessary at regular intervals thereafter, a broad consultation with the users of the patent system shall be carried out by the Administrative Committee on the functioning, efficiency and cost-effectiveness of the Court and on the trust and confidence of users of the patent system in the quality of the Court's decisions. On the basis of this consultation and an opinion of the Court, the Administrative Committee may decide to revise this Agreement with a view to improving the functioning of the Court.

(2) The Administrative Committee may amend this Agreement to bring it into line with an international treaty relating to patents or Union law.

(3) A decision of the Administrative Committee taken on the basis of paragraphs 1 and 2 shall not take effect if a Contracting Member State declares within twelve months of the date

of the decision, on the basis of its relevant internal decision-making procedures, that it does not wish to be bound by the decision. In this case, a Review Conference of the Contracting Member States shall be convened.

ARTICLE 88
Languages of the Agreement

(1) This Agreement is drawn up in a single original in the English, French and German languages, each text being equally authentic.

(2) The texts of this Agreement drawn up in official languages of Contracting Member States other than those specified in paragraph 1 shall, if they have been approved by the Administrative Committee, be considered as official texts. In the event of divergences between the various texts, the texts referred to in paragraph 1 shall prevail.

ARTICLE 89
Entry into force

(1) This Agreement shall enter into force on 1 January 2014 or on the first day of the fourth month after the deposit of the thirteenth instrument of ratification or accession in accordance with Article 84, including the three Member States in which the highest number of European patents had effect in the year preceding the year in which the signature of the Agreement takes place or on the first day of the fourth month after the date of entry into force of the amendments to Regulation (EU) No 1215/2012 concerning its relationship with this Agreement, whichever is the latest.

(2) Any ratification or accession after the entry into force of this Agreement shall take effect on the first day of the fourth month after the deposit of the instrument of ratification or accession.

In witness whereof the undersigned, being duly authorised thereto, have signed this Agreement,

Done at Brussels on 19 February 2013 in English, French and German, all three texts being equally authentic, in a single copy which shall be deposited in the archives of the General Secretariat of the Council of the European Union.

ANNEX I

STATUTE OF THE UNIFIED PATENT COURT

ARTICLE 1
Scope of the Statute

This Statute contains institutional and financial arrangements for the Unified Patent Court as established under Article 1 of the Agreement.

CHAPTER I – JUDGES

ARTICLE 2
Eligibility of judges

(1) Any person who is a national of a Contracting Member State and fulfils the conditions set out in Article 15 of the Agreement and in this Statute may be appointed as a judge.

(2) Judges shall have a good command of at least one official language of the European Patent Office.

(3) Experience with patent litigation which has to be proven for the appointment pursuant to Article 15(1) of the Agreement may be acquired by training under Article 11(4)(a) of this Statute.

ARTICLE 3
Appointment of judges

(1) Judges shall be appointed pursuant to the procedure set out in Article 16 of the Agreement.

(2) Vacancies shall be publicly advertised and shall indicate the relevant eligibility criteria as set out in Article 2. The Advisory Committee shall give an opinion on candidates' suitability to perform the duties of a judge of the Court. The opinion shall comprise a list of most suitable candidates. The list shall contain at least twice as many candidates as there are vacancies. Where necessary, the Advisory Committee may recommend that, prior to the decision on the appointment, a candidate judge receive training in patent litigation pursuant to Article 11(4)(a).

(3) When appointing judges, the Administrative Committee shall ensure the best legal and technical expertise and a balanced composition of the Court on as broad a geographical basis as possible among nationals of the Contracting Member States.

(4) The Administrative Committee shall appoint as many judges as are needed for the proper functioning of the Court. The Administrative Committee shall initially appoint the necessary number of judges for setting up at least one panel in each of the divisions of the Court of First Instance and at least two panels in the Court of Appeal.

(5) The decision of the Administrative Committee appointing full-time or part-time legally qualified judges and full-time technically qualified judges shall state the instance of the Court and/or the division of the Court of First Instance for which each judge is appointed and the field(s) of technology for which a technically qualified judge is appointed.

(6) Part-time technically qualified judges shall be appointed as judges of the Court and shall be included in the Pool of Judges on the basis of their specific qualifications and experience. The appointment of these judges to the Court shall ensure that all fields of technology are covered.

ARTICLE 4
Judges' term of office

(1) Judges shall be appointed for a term of six years, beginning on the date laid down in the instrument of appointment. They may be re-appointed.

(2) In the absence of any provision regarding the date, the term shall begin on the date of the instrument of appointment.

ARTICLE 5
Appointment of the members of the Advisory Committee

(1) Each Contracting Member State shall propose a member of the Advisory Committee who fulfils the requirements set out in Article 14(2) of the Agreement.

(2) The members of the Advisory Committee shall be appointed by the Administrative Committee acting by common accord.

ARTICLE 6
Oath

Before taking up their duties judges shall, in open court, take an oath to perform their duties impartially and conscientiously and to preserve the secrecy of the deliberations of the Court.

ARTICLE 7
Impartiality

(1) Immediately after taking their oath, judges shall sign a declaration by which they solemnly undertake that, both during and after their term of office, they shall respect the obligations arising therefrom, in particular the duty to behave with integrity and discretion as regards the acceptance, after they have ceased to hold office, of certain appointments or benefits.

(2) Judges may not take part in the proceedings of a case in which they:

(a) have taken part as adviser;
(b) have been a party or have acted for one of the parties;
(c) have been called upon to pronounce as a member of a court, tribunal, board of appeal, arbitration or mediation panel, a commission of inquiry or in any other capacity;
(d) have a personal or financial interest in the case or in relation to one of the parties; or
(e) are related to one of the parties or the representatives of the parties by family ties.

(3) If, for some special reason, a judge considers that he or she should not take part in the judgement or examination of a particular case, that judge shall so inform the President of the Court of Appeal accordingly or, in the case of judges of the Court of First Instance, the President of the Court of First Instance. If, for some special reason, the President of the Court of Appeal or, in the case of judges of the Court of First Instance, the President of the Court of First Instance considers that a judge should not sit or make submissions in a particular case, the President of the Court of Appeal or the President of the Court of First Instance shall justify this in writing and notify the judge concerned accordingly.

(4) Any party to an action may object to a judge taking part in the proceedings on any of the grounds listed in paragraph 2 or where the judge is suspected, with good reason, of partiality.

(5) Any difficulty arising as to the application of this Article shall be settled by decision of the Presidium, in accordance with the Rules of Procedure. The judge concerned shall be heard but shall not take part in the deliberations.

ARTICLE 8
Immunity of judges

(1) The judges shall be immune from legal proceedings. After they have ceased to hold office, they shall continue to enjoy immunity in respect of acts performed by them in relation to their official capacity.

(2) The Presidium may waive the immunity.

(3) Where immunity has been waived and criminal proceedings are instituted against a judge, that judge shall be tried, in any of the Contracting Member States, only by the court competent to judge the members of the highest national judiciary.

(4) The Protocol on the privileges and immunities of the European Union shall apply to the judges of the Court, without prejudice to the provisions relating to immunity from legal proceedings of judges which are set out in this Statute.

ARTICLE 9
End of duties

(1) Apart from replacement after expiry of a judge's term pursuant to Article 4, or death, the duties of a judge shall end when that judge resigns.

(2) Where a judge resigns, the letter of resignation shall be addressed to the President of the Court of Appeal or, in the case of judges of the Court of First Instance, the President of the Court of First Instance for transmission to the Chairman of the Administrative Committee.

(3) Save where Article 10 applies, a judge shall continue to hold office until that judge's successor takes up his or her duties.

(4) Any vacancy shall by filled by the appointment of a new judge for the remainder of his or her predecessor's term.

ARTICLE 10
Removal from office

(1) A judge may be deprived of his or her office or of other benefits only if the Presidium decides that that judge no longer fulfils the requisite conditions or meets the obligations arising from his or her office. The judge concerned shall be heard but shall not take part in the deliberations.

(2) The Registrar of the Court shall communicate this decision to the Chairman of the Administrative Committee.

(3) In the case of a decision depriving a judge of his or her office, a vacancy shall arise upon that notification.

ARTICLE 11
Training

(1) Appropriate and regular training of judges shall be provided for within the training framework set up under Article 19 of the Agreement. The Presidium shall adopt Training Regulations ensuring the implementation and overall coherence of the training framework.

(2) The training framework shall provide a platform for the exchange of expertise and a forum for discussion, in particular by:

(a) organising courses, conferences, seminars, workshops and symposia;
(b) cooperating with international organisations and education institutes in the field of intellectual property; and
(c) promoting and supporting further vocational training.

(3) An annual work programme and training guidelines shall be drawn up, which shall include for each judge an annual training plan identifying that judge's main training needs in accordance with the Training Regulations.

(4) The training framework shall in addition:

(a) ensure appropriate training for candidate-judges and newly appointed judges of the Court;
(b) support projects aimed at facilitating cooperation between representatives, patent attorneys and the Court.

ARTICLE 12
Remuneration

The Administrative Committee shall set the remuneration of the President of the Court of Appeal, the President of the Court of First Instance, the judges, the Registrar, the Deputy-Registrar and the staff.

CHAPTER II – ORGANISATIONAL PROVISIONS

SECTION 1 – COMMON PROVISIONS

ARTICLE 13
President of the Court of Appeal

(1) The President of the Court of Appeal shall be elected by all judges of the Court of Appeal for a term of three years, from among their number. The President of the Court of Appeal may be re-elected twice.

(2) The elections of the President of the Court of Appeal shall be by secret ballot. A judge obtaining an absolute majority shall be elected. If no judge obtains an absolute majority, a second ballot shall be held and the judge obtaining the most votes shall be elected.

(3) The President of the Court of Appeal shall direct the judicial activities and the administration of the Court of Appeal and chair the Court of Appeal sitting as a full Court.

(4) If the office of the President of the Court of Appeal falls vacant before the date of expiry of his or her term, a successor shall be elected for the remainder thereof.

ARTICLE 14
President of the Court of First Instance

(1) The President of the Court of First Instance shall be elected by all judges of the Court of First Instance who are full-time judges, for a term of three years, from among their number. The President of the Court of First Instance may be re-elected twice.

(2) The first President of the Court of First Instance shall be a national of the Contracting Member State hosting the seat of the central division.

(3) The President of the Court of First Instance shall direct the judicial activities and the administration of the Court of First Instance.

(4) Article 13(2) and (4), shall by analogy apply to the President of the Court of First Instance.

ARTICLE 15
Presidium

(1) The Presidium shall be composed of the President of the Court of Appeal, who shall act as chairperson, the President of the Court of First Instance, two judges of the Court of Appeal elected from among their number, three judges of the Court of First Instance who are full-time judges of the Court elected from among their number, and the Registrar as a non-voting member.

(2) The Presidium shall exercise its duties in accordance with this Statute. It may, without prejudice to its own responsibility, delegate certain tasks to one of its members.

(3) The Presidium shall be responsible for the management of the Court and shall in particular:

(a) draw up proposals for the amendment of the Rules of Procedure in accordance with Article 41 of the Agreement and proposals regarding the Financial Regulations of the Court;
(b) prepare the annual budget, the annual accounts and the annual report of the Court and submit them to the Budget Committee;
(c) establish the guidelines for the training programme for judges and supervise the implementation thereof;
(d) take decisions on the appointment and removal of the Registrar and the Deputy-Registrar;
(e) lay down the rules governing the Registry including the sub-registries;
(f) give an opinion in accordance with Article 83(5) of the Agreement.

(4) Decisions of the Presidium referred to in Articles 7, 8, 10 and 22 shall be taken without the participation of the Registrar.

(5) The Presidium can take valid decisions only when all members are present or duly represented. Decisions shall be taken by a majority of the votes.

ARTICLE 16
Staff

(1) The officials and other servants of the Court shall have the task of assisting the President of the Court of Appeal, the President of the Court of First Instance, the judges and the Registrar. They shall be responsible to the Registrar, under the authority of the President of the Court of Appeal and the President of the Court of First Instance.

(2) The Administrative Committee shall establish the Staff Regulations of officials and other servants of the Court.

ARTICLE 17
Judicial vacations

(1) After consulting the Presidium, the President of the Court of Appeal shall establish the duration of judicial vacations and the rules on observing official holidays.

(2) During the period of judicial vacations, the functions of the President of the Court of Appeal and of the President of the Court of First Instance may be exercised by any judge invited by the respective President to that effect. In cases of urgency, the President of the Court of Appeal may convene the judges.

(3) The President of the Court of Appeal or the President of the Court of First Instance may, in proper circumstances, grant leave of absence to respectively judges of the Court of Appeal or judges of the Court of First Instance.

SECTION 2 – THE COURT OF FIRST INSTANCE

ARTICLE 18
Setting up and discontinuance of a local or regional division

(1) A request from one or more Contracting Member States for the setting up of a local or regional division shall be addressed to the Chairman of the Administrative Committee. It shall indicate the seat of the local or regional division.

(2) The decision of the Administrative Committee setting up a local or regional division shall indicate the number of judges for the division concerned and shall be public.

(3) The Administrative Committee shall decide to discontinue a local or regional division at the request of the Contracting Member State hosting the local division or the Contracting Member States participating in the regional division. The decision to discontinue a local or regional division shall state the date after which no new cases may be brought before the division and the date on which the division will cease to exist.

(4) As from the date on which a local or regional division ceases to exist, the judges assigned to that local or regional division shall be assigned to the central division, and cases still pending before that local or regional division together with the sub-registry and all of its documentation shall be transferred to the central division.

ARTICLE 19
Panels

(1) The allocation of judges and the assignment of cases within a division to its panels shall be governed by the Rules of Procedure. One judge of the panel shall be designated as the presiding judge, in accordance with the Rules of Procedure.

(2) The panel may delegate, in accordance with the Rules of Procedure, certain functions to one or more of its judges.

(3) A standing judge for each division to hear urgent cases may be designated in accordance with the Rules of Procedure.

(4) In cases where a single judge in accordance with Article 8(7) of the Agreement, or a standing judge, in accordance with paragraph 3 of this Article, hears a case that judge shall carry out all functions of a panel.

(5) One judge of the panel shall act as Rapporteur, in accordance with the Rules of Procedure.

ARTICLE 20
Pool of Judges

(1) A list with the names of the judges included in the Pool of Judges shall be drawn up by the Registrar. In relation to each judge, the list shall at least indicate the linguistic skills, the field of technology and experience of, as well as the cases previously handled by, that judge.

(2) A request addressed to the President of the Court of First Instance to assign a judge from the Pool of Judges shall indicate, in particular, the subject matter of the case, the official language of the European Patent Office used by the judges of the panel, the language of the proceedings and the field of technology required.

SECTION 3 – THE COURT OF APPEAL

ARTICLE 21
Panels

(1) The allocation of judges and the assignment of cases to panels shall be governed by the Rules of Procedure. One judge of the panel shall be appointed as the presiding judge, in accordance with the Rules of Procedure.

(2) When a case is of exceptional importance, and in particular when the decision may affect the unity and consistency of the case law of the Court, the Court of Appeal may decide, on the basis of a proposal from the presiding judge, to refer the case to the full Court.

(3) The panel may delegate, in accordance with the Rules of Procedure, certain functions to one or more of its judges.

(4) One judge of the panel shall act as Rapporteur, in accordance with the Rules of Procedure.

SECTION 4 – THE REGISTRY

ARTICLE 22
Appointment and removal from office of the Registrar

(1) The Presidium shall appoint the Registrar of the Court for a term of six years. The Registrar may be re-appointed.

(2) Two weeks before the date fixed for appointing the Registrar, the President of the Court of Appeal shall inform the Presidium of the applications which have been submitted for the post.

(3) Before taking up his or her duties, the Registrar shall take oath before the Presidium to perform the duties of the Registrar impartially and conscientiously.

(4) The Registrar may be removed from office only if the Registrar no longer meets the obligations arising from his or her office. The Presidium shall take its decision after having heard the Registrar.

(5) If the office of the Registrar falls vacant before the date of expiry of the term thereof, the Presidium shall appoint a new Registrar for a term of six years.

(6) If the Registrar is absent or prevented from attending or where such post is vacant, the President of the Court of Appeal after having consulted the Presidium shall designate a member of the staff of the Court to carry out the duties of the Registrar.

ARTICLE 23
Duties of the Registrar

(1) The Registrar shall assist the Court, the President of the Court of Appeal, the President of the Court of First Instance and the judges in the performance of their functions. The Registrar shall be responsible for the organisation and activities of the Registry under the authority of the President of the Court of Appeal.

(2) The Registrar shall in particular be responsible for:
(a) keeping the register which shall include records of all cases before the Court;
(b) keeping and administering lists drawn up in accordance with Articles 18, 48(3) and 57(2) of the Agreement;
(c) keeping and publishing a list of notifications and withdrawals of opt-outs in accordance with Article 83 of the Agreement;
(d) publishing the decisions of the Court, subject to the protection of confidential information;
(e) publishing annual reports with statistical data; and
(f) ensuring that the information on opt-outs in accordance with Article 83 of the Agreement is notified to the European Patent Office.

ARTICLE 24
Keeping of the register

(1) Detailed rules for keeping the register of the Court shall be prescribed in the Rules governing the Registry, adopted by the Presidium.

(2) The rules on access to documents of the Registry shall be provided for in the Rules of Procedure.

ARTICLE 25
Sub-registries and Deputy-Registrar

(1) A Deputy-Registrar shall be appointed for a term of six years by the Presidium. The Deputy-Registrar may be re-appointed.

(2) Article 22(2) to (6) shall apply by analogy.

(3) The Deputy-Registrar shall be responsible for the organisation and activities of sub-registries under the authority of the Registrar and the President of the Court of First Instance. The duties of the Deputy-Registrar shall in particular include:

(a) keeping records of all cases before the Court of First Instance;
(b) notifying every case before the Court of First Instance to the Registry.

(4) The Deputy-Registrar shall also provide administrative and secretarial assistance to the divisions of the Court of First Instance.

CHAPTER III – FINANCIAL PROVISIONS

ARTICLE 26
Budget

(1) The budget shall be adopted by the Budget Committee on a proposal from the Presidium. It shall be drawn up in accordance with the generally accepted accounting principles laid down in the Financial Regulations, established in accordance with Article 33.

(2) Within the budget, the Presidium may, in accordance with the Financial Regulations, transfer funds between the various headings or subheadings.

(3) The Registrar shall be responsible for the implementation of the budget in accordance with the Financial Regulations.

(4) The Registrar shall annually make a statement on the accounts of the preceding financial year relating to the implementation of the budget which shall be approved by the Presidium.

ARTICLE 27
Authorisation for expenditure

(1) The expenditure entered in the budget shall be authorised for the duration of one accounting period unless the Financial Regulations provide otherwise.

(2) In accordance with the Financial Regulations, any appropriations, other than those relating to staff costs, which are unexpended at the end of the accounting period may be carried forward, but not beyond the end of the following accounting period.

(3) Appropriations shall be set out under different headings according to type and purpose of the expenditure, and subdivided, to the extent necessary, in accordance with the Financial Regulations.

ARTICLE 28
Appropriations for unforeseeable expenditure

(1) The budget of the Court may include appropriations for unforeseeable expenditure.

(2) The employment of these appropriations by the Court shall be subject to the prior approval of the Budget Committee.

ARTICLE 29
Accounting period

The accounting period shall commence on 1 January and end on 31 December.

ARTICLE 30
Preparation of the budget

The Presidium shall submit the draft budget of the Court to the Budget Committee no later than the date prescribed in the Financial Regulations.

ARTICLE 31
Provisional budget

(1) If, at the beginning of the accounting period, the budget has not been adopted by the Budget Committee, expenditure may be effected on a monthly basis per heading or other division of the budget, in accordance with the Financial Regulations, up to one-twelfth of the budget appropriations for the preceding accounting period, provided that the appropriations thus made available to the Presidium do not exceed one-twelfth of those provided for in the draft budget.

(2) The Budget Committee may, subject to the observance of the other provisions laid down in paragraph 1, authorise expenditure in excess of one-twelfth of the budget appropriations for the preceding accounting period.

ARTICLE 32
Auditing of accounts

(1) The annual financial statements of the Court shall be examined by independent auditors. The auditors shall be appointed and if necessary dismissed by the Budget Committee.

(2) The audit, which shall be based on professional auditing standards and shall take place, if necessary, in situ, shall ascertain that the budget has been implemented in a lawful and proper manner and that the financial administration of the Court has been conducted in accordance with the principles of economy and sound financial management. The auditors shall draw up a report after the end of each accounting period containing a signed audit opinion.

(3) The Presidium shall submit to the Budget Committee the annual financial statements of the Court and the annual budget implementation statement for the preceding accounting period, together with the auditors' report.

(4) The Budget Committee shall approve the annual accounts together with the auditors' report and shall discharge the Presidium in respect of the implementation of the budget.

ARTICLE 33
Financial Regulations

(1) The Financial Regulations shall be adopted by the Administrative Committee. They shall be amended by the Administrative Committee on a proposal from the Court.

(2) The Financial Regulations shall lay down in particular:

(a) arrangements relating to the establishment and implementation of the budget and for the rendering and auditing of accounts;
(b) the method and procedure whereby the payments and contributions, including the initial financial contributions provided for in Article 37 of the Agreement are to be made available to the Court;
(c) the rules concerning the responsibilities of authorising and accounting officers and the arrangements for their supervision; and
(d) the generally accepted accounting principles on which the budget and the annual financial statements are to be based.

CHAPTER IV – PROCEDURAL PROVISIONS

ARTICLE 34
Secrecy of deliberations

The deliberations of the Court shall be and shall remain secret.

ARTICLE 35
Decisions

(1) When a panel sits in composition of an even number of judges, decisions of the Court shall be taken by a majority of the panel. In case of equal vote, the vote of the presiding judge shall prevail.

(2) In the event of one of the judges of a panel being prevented from attending, a judge from another panel may be called upon to sit in accordance with the Rules of Procedure.

(3) In cases where this Statute provides that the Court of Appeal shall take a decision sitting as a full court, such decision shall be valid only if it is taken by at least 3/4 of the judges comprising the full court.

(4) Decisions of the Court shall contain the names of the judges deciding the case.

(5) Decisions shall be signed by the judges deciding the case, by the Registrar for decisions of the Court of Appeal, and by the Deputy-Registrar for decisions of the Court of First Instance. They shall be read in open court.

ARTICLE 36
Dissenting opinions

A dissenting opinion expressed separately by a judge of a panel in accordance with Article 78 of the Agreement shall be reasoned, given in writing and shall be signed by the judge expressing this opinion.

ARTICLE 37
Decision by default

(1) At the request of a party to an action, a decision by default may be given in accordance with the Rules of Procedure, where the other party, after having been served with a document instituting proceedings or with an equivalent document, fails to file written submissions in defence or fails to appear at the oral hearing. An objection may be lodged against that decision within one month of it being notified to the party against which the default decision has been given.

(2) The objection shall not have the effect of staying enforcement of the decision by default unless the Court decides otherwise.

ARTICLE 38
Questions referred to the Court of Justice of the European Union

(1) The procedures established by the Court of Justice of the European Union for referrals for preliminary rulings within the European Union shall apply.

(2) Whenever the Court of First Instance or the Court of Appeal has decided to refer to the Court of Justice of the European Union a question of interpretation of the Treaty on European Union or of the Treaty on the Functioning of the European Union or a question on the validity or interpretation of acts of the institutions of the European Union, it shall stay its proceedings.

ANNEX II

Distribution of cases within the central division[1]

LONDON Section	PARIS Seat	MUNICH Section
President's Office		
(A) Human necessities	(B) Performing operations, transporting	(F) Mechanical engineering, lighting, heating, weapons, blasting
(C) Chemistry, metallurgy	(D) Textiles, paper	
(E) Fixed constructions		
(G) Physics		
(H) Electricity		

[1] The classification into 8 sections (A to H) is based on the International Patent Classification of the World Intellectual Property Organisation (http://www.wipo.int/classifications/ipc/en).

INDEX

Agreement on a Unified Patent Court 19 February 2013 *see* **UPC Agreement**
appeals
  cross-appeals, replies to statements   266
  decisions   267
  grounds, statement of   263–4
  interim procedure   266–7
  leave to appeal   259–60
  oral procedure   267
  referral back   267
  referral decisions   266
  rehearings   268–70
  rejection, challenges to   264
  response, statement of   264–6
  scope and effect   55–6, 258–61
  statement of   261–3
  suspensive effect   260–1
  timing   258–9
  written procedures   261–7
applications   316–21
***Arrow* Declarations**   120–1
assignments, recordal of   69–70
attorney-client privilege   253–4

bifurcated infringement actions   112–13, 132–4
Brexit   8–9
Brussels I Regulation (recast)   30–2, 95–103, 218–19
burden of proof   221

case management   56–7, 186–8
CJEU *see* **European Union, Court of Justice**
common interest privilege   256
communication of information orders   234, 236
Community Patent (CP)   3–4
Community Patent Conventions (EU)   1–2
compulsory licences   39–40, 73
confidentiality and privilege   255–6
confidentiality protection   248–53
corrective measures   279–82 *see also* **damages**
costs   282–6
court fees   305–13
CP (Community Patent)   3–4
CPC (Community Patent Conventions)   1–2
cross-border patent actions
  under Brussels I Regulation (recast)   95–102
  infringement   98–101

  invalidity   97–8
  'Italian Torpedo' actions   108
  'long-arm' jurisdiction of UPC   108–10
  non-infringement declarations   101–2, 116–20
  preliminary injunctions   107–8
customs seizures   246–7

damages   109–10, 157–8, 271–8
default decisions   195
destruction of products   158–9
document production   221–4
double patenting   18–19

employee rights   38–9, 70, 71
England & Wales
  non-infringement declarations   116–20
  parallel proceedings   111–21
  patent proceedings
    Arrow Declarations   120–1
    cross-border jurisdiction   118–21
    expedition   114–16
    persuasive value of   111–14
    stay or dismissal of UPC actions   117–18
    and Unified Patent Court (UPC)   111–21
EPC (European Patent Convention)   1, 32–3, 68, 94
EPLA (European Patent Litigation Agreement)   4
EPO *see* **European Patent Office (EPO)**
EU *see* **European Union**
European Patent Convention (EPC)   1, 32–3, 68, 94
European Patent Litigation Agreement (EPLA)   4
European Patent Office (EPO)
  actions against   177–81
  administrative tasks of   23–4
  central amendment proceedings   47
  and national proceedings   43–5
  role of   2, 19–21
  and stays of proceedings   45–7
  Unitary Patents   47, 140
European patents   19–21
  assignments, recordal of   69–70
  damages   278
  exhaustion of rights   28–9
  infringement, law of   61–3
  language of   77
  licences, recordal of   69–70

as objects of property 70–1
opt-outs 84–93
scope of claims 65
and supplementary protection certificates 27–8
transitional period 84–93
European Union
Community Patent Conventions 1–2
Court of Justice
obligation to refer to 40–1
preliminary reference to 186–8
questions subject to referral 41–3
role of 40–3
unified patent litigation system (UPLS) 6
law, primacy of 11
regulations
469/2009 (supplementary protection certificate for medicinal products) 2
1215/2012 (Jurisdiction and the Recognition and Enforcement of Judgments in Civil and Commercial Matters (recast)) *see* Brussels I Regulation (recast)
1257/2012 (implementation of enhanced cooperation in the creation of unitary patent protection) *see* UP Regulation
1260/2012 (creation of unitary patent protection with regard to the applicable translation arrangements) 74–7
evidence
communication of information orders 234, 236
confidentiality protection 248–53
customs seizures 246–7
document production 221–4
experiments 244–6
experts 236–44
inspection orders
ex parte 231–2
inter partes 231–2
national perspectives 227–8
parties present 233
procedure 228–31
security 234
timing 233–4
UPC approach 227
judicial cooperation in taking 246
obtained from opponents 224–6
preservation orders
ex parte 231–2
inter partes 231–2
national perspectives 226–7
parties present 233
procedure 228–31
security 234
timing 233–4
UPC approach 226

privilege 253–7
production orders 234–5
rules on 221–4
sources of 220–1
witnesses 236–40
exhaustion of rights 28–9
experiments 244–6
experts
conflicts of interest 238
court appointed 240–3
duties of 237
oral hearings 238
and skilled persons 244
statements of truth 238
and technical judges 243

final injunctions 155–7, 280–2
forums for actions
by agreement 122
under Article 33 123–40
choice of 140–1
objections 141

GAT v LuK 97–8
Germany, challenges to UPC 10–12

harmonization of patent regimes 1–2
hearings 316–21

infringement, law of 61–8
infringement actions *see also* **non-infringement declarations**
acceleration 136
application to amend the patent 154–5
bifurcated 112–13, 132–4
claim statements 149–51
communication of information orders 160
cross-border 98–101
damages arising from 109–10, 157–8
defence statements 151–2, 154
jurisdiction 123–40
parties to 146–7
preliminary objections 151
procedure 147–55
publication of judgments 159
remedies 155–60
responses to assertions 146
revocation claims 128–32, 137–8, 152–4, 161–70
right to bring 145–6
service 147
stay of 135–6
timeline of 145
written procedure 147–55
inspection orders for evidence 227–34

Index

interim procedure of UPC   182–6
interpreters in proceedings   82
intervention   292–4
'Italian Torpedo' actions   108

judge-rapporteurs   49–50, 149
judges, roles of   48–51

language   74–83, 137
lawyers   255, 295–6
legal aid   300–4
licences, recordal of   69–70
licences of right   40, 72, 138–9
litigation privilege   254–5
'long-arm' jurisdiction of UPC   108–10

non-infringement declarations   101–2, 116–20, 128–9, 137–8, 171–7 *see also* **infringement**

objects of property   38, 68–71
oral procedure of UPC   189–94, 238–40

panels   51–5, 191
parallel proceedings
   UPC and England & Wales   111–21
   UPC and member state courts   102–10
   UPC and non-contracting Member States   107
patent agreements   39–40, 70, 71–2
patent attorneys   255, 296–7
personal possession defence   40, 67–8
preliminary injunctions   107–8, 113–14, 197–219
preservation orders for evidence   226–7, 228–34
presiding judges   49, 50
prior use rights   67–8
privilege   253–7
production of evidence orders   234–5
protective letters   215–16
provisional measures
   appeals   216–17
   costs   283
   enforcement   214
   and 'long-arm' jurisdiction of UPC   109
   obtaining   197–214
   protective letters   215–16
   revocation   217–18, 278

recall of products   158–9
regulations
   469/2009 (supplementary protection certificate for medicinal products)   2
   1215/2012 (Jurisdiction and the Recognition and Enforcement of Judgments in Civil and Commercial Matters (recast)) *see* **Brussels I Regulation (recast)**

   1257/2012 (creation of unitary patent protection) *see* **UP Regulation**
   1260/2012 (creation of unitary patent protection with regard to the applicable translation arrangements)   74–7
representatives   295–8
revocation actions   128–32, 137–8, 152–3, 161–70
Roche v Primus   98–9

service   287–91
settlements   196
skilled persons   244
Solvay v Honeywell   100
sources of law   60–73
SPC Regulation   2
SPCs (supplementary protection certificates)   27–8, 88
standing judges   49, 50–1
statements of truth   238
stays of proceedings   45–7, 117–18, 135–6, 313–16
supplementary protection certificates (SPCs)   27–8, 88

technical judges   48–9, 243
time periods in UPC   298–300
Translation Regulation   74–7, 335–40
translations of documents in proceedings   82

UK *see* **United Kingdom**
Unified Patent Court (UPC) *see also* **infringement actions; UPC Agreement**
   appeals   55–6, 258–70
   applications   316–21
   Brussels I Regulation (recast)   102–3
   case management   56–7, 186–8
   central division, subject matter jurisdiction   34–6
   challenges in Germany   10–12
   competence   36–40
   compulsory licences   39–40
   corrective measures   279–82 *see also* **damages**
   costs   282–6
   court fees   305–13
   Court of Appeal   267
   damages   271–8
   declaratory powers   37
   default decisions   195
   disposal of actions   195–6
   draft Agreement on   6–7
   employee rights   38–9
   EU Member States, restriction to   12
   evidence   220–57
   exclusive competence   36–7

forums for actions
  by agreement   122
  under Article   33 123–40
  choice of   140–1
  objections   141
hearings   316–21
history of   6–8
interim procedure   182–6
intervention   292–4
judges   3, 48–51, 57–8
jurisdiction   122–41
language of   77–81, 82, 137
legal aid   300–4
licences of right   40
'long-arm' jurisdiction   108–10
and member state courts   30–2, 102–10
non-exclusive competence   37–40
objectives of   2–3
oral procedure   189–94, 238–40
panels   51–4
parallel proceedings   107, 111–21
participants   12–13
parties to proceedings   291–2
patent agreements   39–40
personal possession defence   40, 67–8
preliminary injunctions *see* preliminary injunctions
prior use rights   67–8
provisional measures   109, 197–219, 278, 283
representatives   295–8
revocation actions   161–70
scope of claims   66
service   287–91
settlements   196
stays of proceedings   135–6, 313–16
structure of   33–4
subject matter classification   35–6
time periods   298–300
transitional period   84–93, 103–7
uniformity of approach   57–9
withdrawal of actions   194
unified patent litigation system (UPLS)   4–6
Unitary Patents *see also* **UP Regulation**
  co-ownership   70
  and double patenting   18–19
  entitlement   70
  and European Patent Office (EPO)   47, 140
  and European patents   19–21
  features of   21–3

infringement, law of   63–5
language of   74–6
licensing   22–3
limitations on   22
maintaining   25–6
and national patents   17–21
as objects of property   68–70
obtaining   24–5
participants   12–13
protection, uniformity of   21
revocation, uniformity of   21–2
scope of claims   65
and supplementary protection certificates   27–8, 88
transfers   22
United Kingdom   8–9 *see also* **England & Wales**
UP Regulation
  compulsory licences   73
  employee rights   70, 71
  exhaustion of rights   28–9
  infringement, law of   63–5
  licences of right   72
  objects of property   38
  patent agreements   70, 71–2
  text of   322–34
UPC *see* **Unified Patent Court**
UPC Agreement *see also* **Unified Patent Court**
  Article 33   123–40
  exhaustion of rights   28–9
  infringement, law of   61–3
  late ratification   93
  non-contracting member states   32
  opt-outs   84–93
  text of   341–87
  transitional period   73, 84–93
  validity, law of   68
UPLS (unified patent litigation system)   4–6

validity, law of   68
video conferencing   191–2

withdrawal of actions   194
without prejudice privilege   256–7
witnesses   236–40
written procedures
  appeals   261–7
  infringement actions   147–55
  non-infringement declarations   171–7
  revocation actions   163–70